MW01121561

The Future of Children's Rights

The Future of Children's Rights

Edited by

Michael Freeman

BRILL

NIJHOFF

LEIDEN · BOSTON
2014

Originally published as Volume 21, Nos. 2-3 (2013) of Brill's *International Journal Children's Rights*

Cover illustration: William Hogarth, Moses Brought Before Pharaoh's Daughter, 1746, oil on canvas © Coram in the care of the Foundling Museum. Image reproduced with the kind permission of The Foundling Museum, London.

Library of Congress Control Number: 2014953753

This publication has been typeset in the multilingual "Brill" typeface. With over 5,100 characters covering Latin, IPA, Greek, and Cyrillic, this typeface is especially suitable for use in the humanities. For more information, please see brill.com/brill-typeface.

ISBN 978-90-04-27176-0 (hardback)
ISBN 978-90-04-27177-7 (e-book)

Printed by Printforce, the Netherlands

CONTENTS

Preface

It is not so long ago that children were being described as "an endangered species", when we were told that it was strange to think of children as having rights, when a leading philosopher could tell us that the "main remedy" for children was "to grow up".

It is now 25 years since the world put together the landmark document that we know as the Convention on the Rights of the Child. And it is 23 years since the *International Journal of Children's Rights* first appeared. We mark this event by republishing a two- part "Special Issue" which was first published in the journal in 2013. We include two additional articles, by Philip Veerman and Ellen Desmet, respectively, which take the debate further.

The *International Journal of Children's Rights* has grown from small beginnings and is now established as the pre-eminent fount of scholarship in this very important area . Early next year we will publish our 500th article. It is difficult to think of a subject not thus far covered. Articles have been published from over 50 countries, and from a whole range of disciplines. Long may this continue .

The journal was the brainchild of Philip Veerman, and to him we all express our gratitude. Thanks are also offered to our publisher, Lindy Melman, for her encouragement and patience, and to the many who have assisted me over the years to produce the journal.

Professor Michael Freeman F.B.A
28 September 2014

Introduction
Children's Rights Past, Present, and Future: Some Introductory Comments

Michael Freeman

Children's rights have come a long way in a relatively short time. It is after all only 150 years since John Stuart Mill refused to extend his 'liberty' principle to children (Mill, 1859, Kleinig, 1976). He coupled them with 'backward nations'. The age of majority then was 21, not 18, as it is now. Though his contemporary in France, Jules Vallès (2005) was more sympathetic to the plight of children – he wrote after all in the aftermath of the Paris Commune – as was Karl Marx rather surprisingly, and the child-saving movement had some successes, (the establishment of compulsory education and of the juvenile court (Platt, 1969; Wood, 1968), there were very few authentic voices for children before World War One. In the USA there was Florence Kelley (1905), who as early as 1905 asserted a 'right to childhood'. And Kate Douglas Wiggin, the author of the best-selling novel *Rebecca of Sunnybrook Farm*, the story of a rambunctious, rule-breaking ten-year-old orphan, who wrote an article for Scribner's magazine entitled "Children's Rights" (1892). In it she drew a distinction between child protection – the child's right to special protection from extreme forms of abuse and neglect – and children's rights – which included an independent legal identity, a degree of autonomy from parents, and the right to a "free, serene, healthy, bread and butter childhood," unburdened by heavy labour. In answer to the question "Who owns the child?" Wiggin answered pointedly: no one. "The parent is simply a divinely appointed guardian." Wiggin's idea that children have a right to a proper childhood and that adults have a duty to serve as their stewards remain a challenge today.

There was also Ellen Key in Sweden, who looked to the 20th century as 'the century of the child', much as, it was claimed, the 19th century had been the 'century of the woman'! (Key, 1900, 1909). It became the century of the 'child professional' (Perhaps, the child sentry!) Like many social reformers of the period, she was a eugenicist. She argued for important reforms. She looked, for example, to child-centred education and the end of corporal punishment. More significantly, there was, of course, that icon of children's rights, Janusz Korczak in Poland (1920, 2007), who emphasised the need to love and respect children, and who wrote what is arguably the first children's charter. His work was hardly known about then, or frankly now (Eichsteller, 2009). He died (in Treblinka), as he lived, putting children first. He has rightly been named 'the King of children' (Lifton, 1986, see also A. Cohen, 1994). It is a pity that Korczak seems to have permeated the consciousness of so few contemporary writers on children – he does not get a mention in James and James (2004), Wyness (2011), Cockburn (2013), Oswell (2013), Cunningham's history (2006), or, for that matter in Freeman (1983, 1997), but see Philip Veerman (1992, 93-111), who first introduced me to his writings.

In the aftermath of the First World War, there was the Declaration of Geneva in 1924, spearheaded by Eglantyne Jebb (1929), who also founded Save The Children (and see Kerber-Ganse , 2015). The Declaration captured the mood of the time. It stressed society's obligations to children, rather than their rights. Its Preamble explains where it is coming from: 'Mankind owes to the Child the best it has to give'. It was another 35 years before children's rights received international attention again. The Declaration of 1959 was broader in coverage. The emphasis was still on protection and welfare and on what has been called 'the investment motive' (Meyer, 1973). There is no recognition of a child's agency, the importance of a child's views, nor any appreciation of the concept of empowerment. It is a case of two P's, most definitely not three, and certainly not four (Quennerstedt, 2010).

The 1970s saw the short-lived children's liberation movement (Gross and Gross, 1977, Holt, 1974, Farson, 1974, Cohen, 1980, Adams, 1972). It was self-determination that Farson saw as at the root of all other rights that children were entitled to claim. Responding to the anticipated criticism that such rights might not be 'good' for children, since children's rights hitherto had aimed at furthering 'the good' for children, Farson argued:

> asking what is good for children is beside the point. We will grant children rights for the same reason we grant rights to adults, not because we are sure that children will then become better people, but more for ideological reasons, because we believe that expanding freedom as a way of life is worthwhile in itself. And freedom, we have found, is a difficult burden for adults as well as for children (1974, 31).

The children's liberation movement was ridiculed at the time. Farson favoured the end of compulsory education, sexual freedom, the right to vote. Holt added to travel, drive and use drugs. As to drugs, adults use them 'excessively and unwisely' (1975, 194, 201): so how could we justify denying this 'pleasure' to children? This still strikes as a silly argument: is it not important to break the cycle? Men use violence against women 'excessively and unwisely': surely it is right to teach boys that this is unacceptable behaviour.

Did the liberation movement influence what happened next? Is there any link between the liberation movement and the proclamation of 1979 as the

International Year of the Child? And what influence did this 'year' have, if any, on the initiative to formulate a convention? Perhaps it was the catalyst for change. It would be nice to think that the child liberationist 'movement' of the 1970s had some influence on the decision, to proclaim the IYC, but this is doubtful. The movement was short-lived and at the time very much marginalised. The writing of Farson (1974), Holt (1975), Coigney (1975), Cohen (1989), Neill (1978) and see Cooper (2014) are significant, and they deserve a reassessment.

The Convention on the Rights of the Child was 10 years in the making. It was significant in the year of Tiananmen Square and in the month the Berlin Wall was torn down. It was the product of much negotiation and considerable compromise. On many issues there was only a veneer of consensus. The Convention lacks a coherent philosophy – this may be a reason why agreement on certain rights was reached. There were no childhood studies scholars in on the drafting, nor truly many scholars from any discipline. And there were no children able to offer an insight. Many have speculated whether the Convention would have looked any different had children had a say. But they were given no opportunity to participate much more recently when the Third Protocol was being debated and this, despite the fact that the Protocol was to establish a complaints procedure (Egan, 2014; Spronk, 2013; Lee, 2010).

In 1989, children were still regarded as 'becomings' rather than as 'beings'. The Convention in tandem with the children's studies movement has helped to turn this round.

Whatever its defects (Freeman, 2000, 2014, Reynaert *et al*, 201), the Convention is a magnificent achievement, and will remain for posterity a landmark in the history of childhood (Heywood, 2001; Stearns, 2011). Ratified by all nations except the USA (The Economist, 2013), Somalia and South Sudan, it has had a real impact on our thinking about children. We can now talk of 'childism', much as we have come to castigate racism and sexism (Young-Bruehl, 2012). It has influenced our language (Saunders and Goddard, 2001, Saunders, 2013). Courts in Norway (Sandberg, 2014), South Africa (Sloth-Nielsen, 2013), South America, India, England (Fortin, 2006) and elsewhere have been influenced by it. It assisted the U.S. Supreme Court to conclude that capital punishment was impermissible for children (*Roper v Simmons*), even though the U.S.A. has obstinately refused to ratify the Convention.

The Convention has influenced policy-makers (Woll, 2000), legislatures, think-tanks, researchers from many disciplines. The research project has come under its spell; this has proved to be both valuable and deleterious. Harmful when, as happens, the research fails to problematize the Convention and takes it as the 'last word' on the subject (Quennerstedt, 2013). The Convention has been the model for children's rights legislation in many countries. An example is the proliferation of anti-spanking laws (there are now 38 – there were only 6 in 1989). And this is despite the fact that the hitting of children is not explicitly proscribed by Article 19 of the Convention. Given the Convention is a 'living instrument', to interpret it to include spanking within 'violence' is perfectly acceptable.

The Convention has its critics (Reynaert *et al,* 2003, 2010, 2013), Archard and Macleod, 2002). Those who think it does not go far enough. Those who are opposed to children's rights generally. Those who dislike encoding children's rights within an international normative code. And those who think there are better routes to take to improve the lives of children (King, 1987).

The main criticisms of the Convention can be stated briefly and responded to with little difficulty. Thus it is said the children lack the capacity to have or exercise rights. There are two answers to this. First, it is not true that children lack capacity (Alderson, 2012). Secondly, this criticism presumes that the basis of children's rights is 'the exercise of will', but it is clear that the Convention is protecting children's interests (Thomas and O' Kane, 1998), and even the youngest baby has legitimate interests (Alderson, 2012). Indeed, so do foetuses. This, of course, raises the question of abortion and women's rights. The Convention neatly side-stepped this by defining a child as only from birth (Article 1 and see Morss, 2013). But one day we will have to grasp this nettle, however uncomfortable it makes us feel (Sheila McLean (1993) offers one way out of the dilemma).

Secondly, the Convention is said to be 'anti-family'. What the critics – Martin Guggenheim (2005) is a good example – really mean is that it undermines the interests of parents. Goldstein, Freud and Solnit (1980), it may be remembered, thought that the only right children had was the right to autonomous parents (see Freeman, 1996). There are two answers to this criticism as well.

The first confronts the criticism face on. The history of childhood makes it obvious that there is a need to curb parental rights. It is salutary that we now talk of parental responsibilities rather than parental rights (for example in the English Children Act 1989). It is not so long ago that children were seen as the property of their parents. Legacies of this remain. To take examples just from England, look at the *Williamson* case (and Baroness Hale's brave intervention), *Re T* (199) (the liver transplant decision), and *Re A* (2001) (the conjoined twins case). Secondly, the critics have clearly leapt to the conclusion they wanted to find without thoroughly examining the Convention. Guggenheim for example, seems to have a weak grasp of the Convention (Freeman, 2000). A careful examination of the Convention reveals, that, if anything, it is over-protective in parents. There are at least 8 articles of the Convention, starting with Article 5, which put parents first. I will not give the full list since Tobin in this volume does so. The conclusion is that the Convention is not guilty of this alleged offence. The Convention, incidentally, nowhere defines 'family', a point to bear in mind when addressing also the next criticism.

The third criticism is that the Convention is a form of neo-colonialism (Ncube, 1998), that it reflects the interests and values of the developed world, essentially that it endorses a model of childhood found in liberal Western democracies (Harris-Short, 2002). One answer to this is to plead guilty! Would you rather be a child in the U.K. or North Korea? – you would get the vote in North Korea at 17! Or in Sweden or the D.R. of Congo? But we are not allowed to pose such questions. Fools rush in where angels fear to tread! Particularly fools who are not P.C. enough! (*cf* Valentin and Meinert, 2009). However, the Convention was not drafted by the developed world exclusively and there is input, admittedly rather meagre from poor nations like Senegal.

There are references to 'culture' in the Convention. Again, interestingly, 'culture' is not defined. The Convention was no more drafted by anthropologists than it was by philosophers (or for that matter, children). The most obvious references to culture is Article 24(3) which targets traditional practices harmful to the health of children. No particular practice is cited, though it is well-known that those who drafted the Convention had female genital mutilation (FGM) (on which see Boyle, 2002) in their focus. This is a practice endemic in parts of the world where liberal western democratic values do not prevail. So, it could be interpreted as an assault on culture. But Article 24(3) equally indicts other traditional practices found in developed societies. But it does not, and in my opinion, should not extend to male circumcision which is a religious, not a traditional, practice, and is not 'harmful' (in the long-term) even if the boy is 'harmed by' it (he experiences momentary pain) in the short-term (Feinberg, 1984).

Of course, on the whole the Convention adopts monism (or universalism, Freeman, 1995). It is a convention about the rights of the child'. All children come within its remit. But it also accepts cultural pluralism, whilst rejecting cultural relativism(Freeman, 1995). Thus, for example, it does not prescribe a minimum age of marriage. Pluralism accepts that there are different views on this. But it is not a case of 'anything goes' – the relativist position – so unduly low ages would be rejected, for example marriage before puberty. In my opinion the Convention stipulates that there should be a minimum age for marriage, though I concede it is difficult to indicate what this should be. Similarly, there is no age prescribed for imposing criminal responsibility. This leaves the question to be solved by each country using its own discretion, and its understanding of child development etc. But again relativism must be rejected. To make a child liable to criminal sanctions at 4 and 6 would fail the test of acceptability. Arguably, so does the current English standard, which exposes children to the criminal law at 10 – hence the notorious *Bulger* trial in 1993.

There are other criticisms of the Convention. I made some of these as long ago as 2000 (Freeman, 2000), and Philip Veerman, in an excellent recent article did so too, and referred to the 'ageing' of the Convention (Veerman, 2010). In brief, there are gaps in the Convention. Certain groups of children were marginalised. Insufficient attention was given to girl children, to gay children, to children with disabilities, to refugees and asylum-seeking children, to indigenous children, to children of prisoners. Issues were not always addressed properly: the age of criminal responsibility, early and forced marriage, child soldiers. Citizenship questions (the right to vote?) were largely ignored. Socioeconomic rights not given sufficient attention (Nolan, 2012, 2013). Do children have the right to food? (Van Bueren, 2014). The enforcement machinery was weak. Thus, for example, there was initially no complaints procedure. The Committee itself is weak and not professional enough. It has some members with scant knowledge of the issues, and some with little interest in or concern for children. It is imperative that it is professionalised if confidence is to be restored in it.

Protocols have addressed two of these criticisms. There is now a complaints procedure, operative from 2014 (see Egan, 2013; Lee, 2010). The provision on child soldiers is now more realistic. Another convention (The UN Convention on the Rights of Persons with Disabilities) has effected improvements as far as children with disabilities are concerned (Sabatello). But other failings remain. The policing process remains weak. Reports are late or missing, criticisms are ignored. There are too many reservations (Hathaway, 2002). Should we be grateful for small mercies, or should we look to something better?

The world has changed since 1989. The end of Communism and the rise of a 'capitalist' China. How many draftsmen of the Convention anticipated this? The World Wide Web – this only dates from 1989, though this seems difficult to believe so 'ordinary' it has become. The sexual abuse of children – the "Cleveland Affair" (Butler-Sloss, 1981) had only just turned this into a recognisable social problem. Globalisation (Stiglitz, 2002; Darian-Smith, 2013) was not the force it is now. Only a few scientists spoke of global warming and climate change. Few, if any, spoke of biodiversity or sustainable development. The medically assisted revolution was still in its infancy. Human enhancement was science fiction as was neuro-enhancement and discussion of cloning belonged to the fantasy world (*The Boys From Brazil* and such like). Islamophobia, like Anti-Semitism (Hertz, 2014), was embedded deep in the cultural heritage of Western civilisation, but hadn't yet boiled over – this only happened in the wake of 9/11.

These changes affect the world's children more than any other section of society. It is they who will live with the impact of global warming, the I.T. revolution, the reproductive revolution, neuroscience. It is they who are being groomed – and 'Jim Won't Fix It' (Davies, 2014). They who are being trafficked (O' Connell Davidson, 2005).

Childhood has always been exploited: now there are new ways of exploiting children (Giroux and Pollock, 2010). Subjected to 'corporate capture' (Nairn, 2013), children are becoming more and more 'materialistic, overweight, stressed, depressed and self-destructive' (Beder, Varney and Gosden, 2009, 223).

Girls' bodies are more commercialised than ever (Orbach, 2013, Carey, 2011, Pilcher, 2011). *Vogue* can happily publish 17 pages of paedophile images of a 10-year-old model, and it takes *The Daily Mail* (2011) to expose this. The Internet has created a global market for child sexual abuse (Girling, 2013). Childhood is said to be 'toxic' (Palmer, 2006), 'under siege' (Bakan, 2011), to suffer from 'nature-deficit disorder' (Louv, 2005). There has been a 'criminalisation' of natural play, and the rise of ' play' (Louv, 2005; Hawes, 2013). The porn culture turns women (and therefore girls) into sexual objects (Mackinnon,1992); the 'music' culture encourages misogyny (Kistler and Moon, 2010; Warburton, 2012). It is not only boys who are affected by this. Adolescent women exposed to 'rap music' with lyrics about female subordination seem to accept date violence towards women more than those not so subjected (Johnson, Jackson and Gatto, 1995). Child abuse is barely recognisable as even related to what Henry Kempe wrote about 50 years ago. (Kempe, 197). As an example look at the following as reported by Joel Bakan.

> In the spring of 2008 the video game *Grand Theft Auto IV* was released, selling in its first week six million units for a half billion dollars and thus smashing every entertainment industry record. It was now clear that brutal and sometimes sexual violence was a top entertainment choice for kids (sic). Tween and teenage boys loved the video game (nearly half of all thirteen-year-old boys reported it as their favourite), which like many other popular video games allows players to choose among and create different, and usually violent, scenarios for a protagonist avatar.
>
> In one possible *GTA IV* scenario, inspired by a promotional trailer for the game and posted on YouTube, protagonist Nick Bellic, a grizzled Balkan Wars vet, has sex with a female prostitute in his car and then murders her. The murder is brutal. Bellic beats her with a baseball bat and then as she runs away, he throws a bomb at her. The bomb explodes, she catches fire, and falls to the ground, engulfed in flames, her body quivering. Bellic then sprays her with bullets from a machine gun. Once she stops moving, Bellic reaches into her pants pocket to retrieve the money he paid her for sex. He then saunters back to his car.
>
> Despite its "mature" rating (the industry's designation that a game is inappropriate for kids under the age of eighteen), *GTA IV*, like other mature-rated games, is often sold to underage kids who happily buy and play it. Nearly one half of all twelve-to sixteen-year-olds and a quarter of eight-to eleven-year-olds own mature-rated games (2011, 19).

So what of the future? Is it as good as it gets? Or can we still hope for a better deal for our children? Let's face it – the plight of children has got worse in the 25 years since the Convention. Laws can only achieve so much. I have said many times that rights require remedies, and remedies require the injection of resources. Much from which children suffer such as a degraded environment for example – can only be put right by a world committed to children and ultimately to humane world governance (Falk, 2014).

To this end, it is worth drawing attention to a parallel development to the Convention. I refer to the Millennium Development Goals. The agenda of these is due to be completed in 2015. But, as UNICEF explained, 'investment in children is a fundamental means to eradicate poverty, and enhance inter-gen-erational equity .... Sustainable development starts and ends with safe, healthy and well-educated children' (UNICEF, 2013). This is equally important, but it cannot be a substitution for children's rights. It is not a project which should allow us to bypass children's rights. As UNICEF admitted in 2004, 'A Child-Friendly City is a local system of good governance committed to fulfilling children's rights' (UNICEF, 2004).

The 2013 UNICEF report identified three principles behind the post-2015 agenda for children.

> Sustainable development starts with safe, healthy and well-educated children: Safe and sustainable societies are, in turn, essential for children; and children's voices and partici-pation are critical for the sustainable future we want. (UNICEF, 2013, 3).

This was emphasised too in UNICEF's *State of the World's Children Report* for 2012:

> Equity must be the guiding principle in efforts for all children in urban areas. The children of slums ... will require particular attention. But this must not come at the expense of chil-dren elsewhere. The larger goal must remain in focus: fairer, more nurturing cities and societies for all people – starting with children'. (UNICEF 2012, 75)

One way the Child Friendly Cities Initiative can, at the same time, advance children's rights is by engaging with children and recognising that they can play a role in the rehabilitation of their environments. The UN Resolution *The Future We Want* in 2012 made this clear.

> We stress the importance of the active participation of young people in decision-making processes, as the issues ... have a deep impact on present and future generations and as the contribution of children and youth is vital to the achievement of sustainable development.

There are already examples of this and there are positive results. In India, 'chil-dren's direct participation in local area planning and design for slum improve-ments ... [was] a good step forward in creating child-friendly cities' (Chatterjee, 2012, 23). Children's needs and rights are thus inter-dependent with sustaina-ble development (see also Bradshaw, 1993).

1989 and beyond has seen many new challenges. All affect children, some of them acutely. These range from financial instability to global warming, pan-demics such as HIV/AIDS, SARS and H1N1, widening disparities in wealth and well-being, cultural and religious conflicts (these are destined to surpass the notorious 'thirty years War' of the 17th century (Wedgewood, 1953), the repro-duction revolution, the Human Genome mapping, the possibility of human enhancement, even now neuro-enhancement, environmental degradation including food scarcity, increasing migratory problems (the European election of 2014 was driven by moral panics about the consequences of these), threats to cyber security (Livingstone, 2009).

The generation of adults now engaged in production are the first to have grown up global (Katz, 2004; Fass, 2007). Globalisation will have had – and continue to have – a profound impact on their lives, more than the Convention of 1989 will have had though, of course, the CRC is itself an example of the inexorable drive towards globalisation. (Nieuwenhuys, 2010). Nor does the Convention do much to protect children from the 'swings and arrows' of globalisation.

The effects of globalisation clone require many books. Perhaps this is what the writer of *Ecclessiastes* had in mind when he wisely observes that 'of the making of many books there is no end'! But he also thought there was nothing new under the sun, and there clearly is!

The Convention is, of course, an example of globalisation in action. So is the work of UNICEF and the World Bank and other international development agencies. UNICEF assumed a role to protect children worldwide (Burr, 2002). But the tendency is to impose a Western model of childhood on the developing world's children (Smith, 2012). Thus, Erica Burman argues that 'the concept of childhood on offer is a Western construction that is now being incorporated, as though it were universal, into aid and development policies' (Burman, 1999, 178). The measuring-rod of all societies is the Western standard. Lewis puts it thus:

> The problem with the globalisation of Western models of childhood ... is not a normative, but a political one. By setting this standard '*southern* childhood is not only effectively erased from international view, but the western model of childhood becomes the standard by which to judge *southern societies* .... The southern child ... becomes the object of Western intervention either in the form of aid or nurture, or as a constraint and moral condemnation of southern societies as a whole. (Lewis, 1998, 95)

And Jones explains:

> ... The notion of the "global child" as the holder of rights is a barely-obscure western-centric view of "normal" child - adult and child-society relations that condemns "other" styles of upbringing as "outside" childhood (Jones, 2005, 338, see also 2014).

It is difficult to know how best way to deal with this. One answer is to regionalise. But then there is already an African Charter, and it is remarkably close in content to the Convention. It is all very well having doubts about the application of Western norms to African children. But take a simple example. On the whole, the West condemns violence against children. In most Western societies corporal punishment in schools (at least) is a thing of the past. Caning remains endemic in African schools. Are we wrong to want to rid African schools of the cane? In the same way, are we not right to condemn FGM? Should it survive censure just because it is their cultural practice?

The work/education balance is more difficult. It is easy to condemn child labour and advocate schooling for all children (including girls), but take away the income from work (and it is pathetically small – children are exploited), and children can starve. Children without jobs do not necessarily end up in schools. They may end up as street children or in the informal economy (in prostitution, for example). The application of Western standards may actually harm children (Kaufman, 2002). Is it an answer that it will benefit future generations of such children? That today's children must suffer to foster a cultural revolution? Also, we know there is often resistance to imposed change.

There can be no real conclusion to this Introduction, partly because it is work -in- progress , but also because the thrust towards a better world for children is itself work - in - progress. And unquestionably progress has been made. It is a subject upon which we have worked for less than a century. Where will we be in 2039 when the Convention is 50 years old ? We can only speculate. I am to offer my predictions at a celebratory conference in Leiden in November 2014, and also in my Hamlyn Lectures "Even Lawyers were Children Once" in November 2015. I invite you to watch this space!

References

Adams, P., *Children's Rights* (London, Granada, 1972).

Alderson, P., *et al.*, 'The participation rights of premature babies,' *The International Journal of Children's Rights* 3 (2005): 31–50.

Alderson, P., *Young Children's Rights* (London: Jessica Kingsley, 2008).

Alderson, P., 'Young children's human rights: A sociological analysis,' *The International Journal of Children's Rights* 20 (2012): 177–198.

Archard, D. & Macleod, C., *The Political and Moral Status of Children* (Oxford: Oxford University Press, 2002).

Bakan, J., *Children under Siege* (London: Bodley Head, 2011).

Beder, S., *This Little Kiddy Went to Market* (London: Pluto Press, 2009).

Bee-Gates, D. *I Want It Now* (New York: Palgrave Macmillan, 2006).

Blank, R.K., *Intervention in the Brain* (Cambridge, MA: MIT Press, 2013).

Boyle, E.H., *Female Genital Cutting – Cultural Conflict in the Global Community* (Baltimore: Johns Hopkins Press, 2002).

Bradshaw, Y.W., 'New directions in International Development Research', *Childhood* 1 (1993): 134–142.

Burman, E., 'Morality and goals of developing'. In *Making Sense of Social Development*. eds. M. Woodhead, *et al.* (London: Routledge, 1999).

Burr, R., 'Report of global and local approaches to children's rights in Vietnam', *Childhood* 9 (2002): 49–61.

Butler-Sloss, E., *Inquiry into Child Abuse in Cleveland* (Cm 412. London: HMSO, 1988).

Chatterjee, S., 'Children growing up in London slums: Challenges and opportunities for new urban imaginations', *Early Childhood Matters* 118 (2012): 19–23.

Cohen, A., *The Gate of Light* (Cranbury, NJ: Associated University Press, 1994).

Cohen, H., *Equal Rights for Children* (Totowa, NJ: Adams, Littlefield, 1980).

Coigney, V., *Children Are People Too* (New York, William Murrow, 1975).

Cooper, D., *Everyday Utopias* (Durham, NC: Duke University Press, 2014).

Cordero, M. Luiz, 'Towards an emancipatory discourse of children's rights', *The International Journal of Children's Rights* 20: 365–421.

Cunningham, H., *The Invention of Childhood* (London: BBC Books, 2005).

Darian-Smith, E., *Laws and Societies in Global Contexts* (New York: CUP, 2013).

Davies, D., *In Plain Sight* (London: Quercus, 2014).

De Laet, D., 'Genital autonomy', *The International Journal of Children's Rights* 20 (2012): 554–583.

Desmet, E., 'Implementing the CRC for 'youth': Who and how?' *The International Journal of Children's Rights* 20 (2012): 3–25.

Economist, The 2013 (October).

Egan, S., 'The new complaints mechanism for the convention on the rights of the child: A mini step forward for children?' *The International Journal of Children's Rights* 21.

Eichsteller, G., 'Janusz Korczak – His legacy and relevance for children's rights today', *The International Journal of Children's Rights* 17 (2009): 377–391.

Falk, R., (Re) *Imagining Humane Global Governance* (Abingdon: Routledge, 2014).

Farson, R., *Birthrights* (Harmondsworth: Penguin Books, 1984).

Fass, P., *Children of A New World* (New York: New York U.P., 2009).

Federle, K.H., 'Rights, Not Wrongs', *The International Journal of Children's Rights* 17 (2009): 321–329.

Federle, K.H., 'On the road to preconceiving rights for children: A postfeminist analysis of the capacity principle', *DePaul Law Review* 983 (2009).

Feinberg, J., *Harm to Others* (New York: OUP, 1984).

Ferguson, L., 'Not merely rights for children but children's rights: The theory gap and the assumption of the importance of children's rights', *The International Journal of Children's Rights* 21 (2013): 177–208.

Fortin, J., 'Children's rights: Are the courts taking them more seriously?', *Kings College Law Journal* 15 (2004): 253.

Freeman, M., *The Rights and Wrongs of Children* (The Hague: Frances Pinter, 1983).

Freeman, M., *The Moral Status of Children* (Leiden: Martinus Nijhoff Publishers, 1989).

Freeman, M., 'The Morality of Pluralism', *The International Journal of Children's Rights*, 3 (1995): 1–17.

Freeman, M., 'Towards a Sociology of Children's Rights'. *Children and Society* (2000).

Freeman, M., 'Why it remains important to take children's rights seriously', *The International Journal of Children's Rights* 15 (2007): 5–23.

Freeman, M., 'Towards a Sociology of Children's Rights'. In *The Law and Michael Freeman*, eds. A. Diduck, N. Peleg & H. Reece (2014, forthcoming 2015: Brill Nijhoff).

Giroux, H. & Pollock, G. *The Mouse That Roared.* (Lanham: MD, Rowman & Littlefield).

Goldstein, J., Freud, A. & Solnit, A. *Before The Best Interests of the Child* (New York: Free Press, 1980).

Gross, B. & Gross, R., *The Children's Rights Movement* (Garden City, New York: Anchor Press, 1977).

Guggenheim, M., *What's Wrong with Children's Rights* (Cambridge, MA: Harvard University Press, 2005).

Harris-Short, S., International human rights law: Imperialist, ineffective and inept?' *Human Rights Quarterly* 24 (2003): 130–151.

Hathaway, O.A., Do human rights treaties make a difference', *Yale Law Journal* 111 (2002).

Hertz, N., *The Guardian*, June 20, 2014.

Heywood, C. *A History of Childhood* (Cambridge: Polity Press, 2001).

Hoyles, M., *Changing Childhood* (London: Writers and Readers Co-operative, 1979).

Holt, J. *Escape from Childhood – The Needs and Rights of Children* (New York: Dutton, 1974).

James, A. & James, A.L. *Constructing Childhood* (Basingstoke: Palgrave Macmillan, 2004).

Jebb, E., *Save The Child: A Posthumous Essay* (London: Weardale Press, 1929).

Jones, G. 'Children and development rights: Globalisation and poverty', *Progress in Development Studies* 5 (2008): 336–342.

Jones, G. & Thomas de Benitez, S. 'Lost opportunity. The Lydia Cacho Case and Civil Rights in Mexico', *The International Journal of Children's Rights* 22 (2014): 313–338.

Katz, C., *Growing Up Global* (Minneapolis: University of Minnesota Press, 2004).

Katz, M. 'Child-Saving', *History of Education* Ch. 26 (1986): 423–424.

Kaufman, N.H., 'The status of children in international law'. In *Globalisation and Children*, eds. N. Kaufman & I. Rizzini (Leiden: Kluwer, 2002).

Kempe, R.S. & Kempe, C.H., *Child Abuse* (London: Fontana, 1978).

Kerber-Ganse, W., 'Eglantyne Jebb – A pioneer of the CRC', *The International Journal of Children's Rights* 23 (forthcoming, 2015).

Key, E., *The Century of the Child* (New York: Putnam, 1909; originally published in Swedish as *Barnets Arhundrade* Stockholm, Albert Bonniers, 1900).

King, M., *A Better World for Children* (London: Routledge, 1997).

Kleinig, J., 'Mill, children and rights', *Educational Philosophy and Rights* 8 (1976): 8–16.

Korczak, J., 'How to love a child'. In *Selected Works of Janusz Korczak*. ed. M. Wolins (Warsaw, 1920).

Korczak, J., *Loving Every Child* (Algonquin Books of Chapel Hill, 2007).

Latonero, M., *The Rise of Mobile and the Diffusion of Technology – Facilitated Trafficking* (University of Southern California, 2012).

Lee, Y., 'Communications procedure under the convention on the rights of the child: 3rd optional protocol', *The International Journal of Children's Rights* 18 (2010).

Lewis, N., 'Human rights, law and democracy in an unfree world'. In *Human Rights Fifty Years On: A Reappraisal*, ed. T. Evans (Manchester: Manchester University Press, 1995).

Lifton, B.J. *The King of Children* (London: Chatto and Windus, 1988).

Livingstone, S., *Children and the Internet* (Cambridge: Polity Press, 2009).

Louv, R., *Last Child in the Woods* (London: Atlantic Books, 2010).

Lyness, M., *Childhood and Society* (Basingstoke: Palgrave Macmillan, 2011).

MacKinnon, C., *Only Words* (London: Harper Collins, 1994).

Mayall, B., 'Sociology can further children's rights', *Education Journal* 72 (2003): 7.

McLean, S., *Journal of Law and Society* 19 (1990): 106–123.

Meyer, P., 'The exploitation of the American growing class'. In *Children's Liberation*. ed. Gottlieb, D. (Englewood Cliffs, NJ: Prentice Hall, 1973), 35–52.

Mill, J.S., *On Liberty* (Cambridge: CUP, 1859).

Morrow, V., 'What's in a number? Unsettling the boundaries of age' *Childhood* 20 (2013): 151–155.

Neill, A., *Summerhill* (Harmondsworth: Penguin Books, 1968).

Nieuwenhuys, O., 'Keep asking: Why childhood? Why children? Why global? *Childhood* 17 (2010): 29–296.

Nolan, A., *Children's Socio-Economic Rights, Democracy and the Courts* (Oxford: Hart Publishing, 2011).

Nolan, A., 'Economic and social rights: Budgets and the CRC', *The International Journal of Children's Rights* 21 (2013): 248–277.

O'Connell Davidson, J., *Children in the Global Sex Trade* (Cambridge: Polity Press, 2005).

Oswell, D., *The Agency of Children* (Cambridge: CUP, 2013).

Palmer, S., *Toxic Childhood* (London: Orion Books, 2006).

Pilcher, J., 'No logo: Children's consumption of fashion', *Childhood* 18 (2011): 128–141.

Platt, A., *The Child Savers – The Invention of Delinquency* (Chicago: University of Chicago Press, 1969).

Purdy, L., *In Their Best Interest?* (Ithaca, NY: Cornell University Press, 1992).

Quennerstedt, A., 'Children, but not really humans? Critical Reflections on the Hampering effect of the 3 'Ps', *The International Journal of Children's Rights* 8 (2010): 619–635.

Quennerstedt, A., 'Children's rights research moving into the future – Challenges on the way forward', *The International Journal of Children's Rights* (2013): 233–247.

Reynaert, D., *et al.,* 'A review of children's rights literature since the adopting of the United Nations Convention on the Rights of the Child', *Childhood* 16(4) (2009): 518–534.

Reynaert, D., *et al.,* 'Children's rights education and social work: Contrasting models and understandings', *International Social Work* 53(4) (2010): 443–456.

Reynaert, D., *et al.,* 'Between "Believers" and "Opponents"', *The International Journal of Children's Rights* 20 (2012): 155–168.

Sabatello, M., 'Children with disabilities – A critical approach' (this volume).

Sandberg, K., 'The role of national courts in promoting children's rights – the case of Norway', *The International Journal of Children's Rights* 22 (2014): 1–20.

Saunders, B., 'Ending the physical punishment of children by parents in the English-speaking world: The impact of language, tradition and law', *The International Journal of Children's Rights* 21 (2013): 278–304.

Sloth-Nielsen, J. & Kruuse, H., 'A maturing manifesto: The constitutionalisation of children's rights in South Africa', *The International Journal of Children's Rights* 21 (2013): 646–678.

Smith, R., *A Universal Childhood?* (London: Palgrave Macmillan, 2012).

Spronk, S., 'Realizing children's right to health', *International Journal of Children's Rights* 22 (2014): 189–204.

Srivastava, A., *et al.,* Cyberbullying in Australia: Clarifying the problem, considering the solutions', *International Journal Children's Rights* 21 (2013): 25–45.

Stearns, P., *Childhood in World History* (Abingdon: Routledge, 2011).

Stiglitz, J., *Globalization and Its Discontents* (London: Penguin Books, 2002).

Thomas, N. & O'Kane, C., 'When children's wishes and feelings clash with their best interests', *The International Journal of Children's Rights* 7 (1999): 179–220.

Tiboris, M., 'Blaming the kids – Children's agency and diminished responsibility', *Journal of Applied Philosophy* 31 (2014): 77–90.

United Nations, *The Future We Want* (New York: UN Publications, 2012).

UNICEF, *Building Child Friendly Cities: A Framework for Action* (Florence: Innocenti Research Centre, 2004).

UNICEF, *State of the World of Children 2012* (New York: UNICEF, 2012).

UNICEF, *A Post-2015 World Fit for Children: Sustainable Development Starts and Ends with Safe, Healthy and Well-Educated Children* (New York: UNICEF, 2013).

Valentin, K. & Meinert, L., The adult North and the young South: Reflections on the civilizing mission of children's rights, 2009.

Vallès, J., *L'Enfant* [*The Child*] (New York: New York Book Reviews, 2007).

Van Bueren, G., *Letter to The Times,* June 9 (2014).

Veerman, P., *The Rights of the Child and the Changing Image of Childhood* (Dordrecht: Martinus Nijhoff, 1992).

Veerman, P., 'The ageing of the CRC', *International Journal of Children's Rights* 18 (2010): 585–618.

Warburton, W. & Braunstein, D., *Growing Up Fast and Furious* (Annandale, NSW: Federation Press, 2008).

Wedgwood, V., *The Thirty Years War* (London: Jonathan Cape, 1938).

Wiggin, K.D., *Children's Rights* (Boston: Houghton Mifflin, 1892).

Wild, J., 201 , *Exploiting Childhood.*

Woll, L., 'Reporting to the UN committee on the rights of the child: A catalyst for domestic debate and policy change?' *The International Journal of Children's Rights* 8 (2000): 71–81.

Wood, S., *Constitutional Politics in the Progressive Era: Child Labour and the Law* (Chicago: University of Chicago Press, 1968).

Young-Bruehl, E., *Childism* (New Haven: Yale University Press, 2012).

The Ageing of the UN Convention on the Rights of the Child

Philip E. Veerman

Psychologist with Bouman Mental Health Services (in Rotterdam) and independent expert of the juvenile courts, Den Bosch, the Netherlands[1]

Introduction

With the celebrations of the 20th anniversary of the adoption of the U.N. Convention on the Rights of the Child in Geneva and other places in the world behind us (which mostly focused on achievements), it is important to point out that the first signs of ageing of this Convention can be noticed. This is not surprising because the modern world is changing fast and the U.N. Convention on the Rights of the Child reflects the image of childhood and world views of the drafting period (between January 1978 and November 1989). On January 18 1978 the Ambassador of Poland (then still the People's Republic of Poland) presented for the first time (at the U.N. Commission of Human Rights in Geneva) "the question of the Convention on the Rights of the Child" (Ek, 2007) and on November 20 1979 the U.N. General Assembly adopted the text of the Convention. Between these two dates the Convention was shaped. Much of how we looked at children in this drafting period still stands. However, in the light of developments in modern science and society (and consequently how our children and adolescents are behaving) we cannot afford to treat the text of the U.N. Convention on the Rights of the Child as 'holy' any longer. To illustrate how the Convention is no longer 'up to date' I look especially at the articles 17 (access to appropriate information), 24 (the right to the enjoyment of the highest standard of health and health services) and 33 (protection from illicit narcotic drugs).

Paradoxically, young people are behaving as adults (by twittering, sending SMS-messages, being active on the internet with on-line-gambling and gaming, drinking alcoholic beverages, smoking nicotine and using drugs). The problem does not seem that there is no information available to children, but for them to know how to make the right choice. Some educators even now plead passionately for media education as a special subject in schools. Many cable radio or TV

---

stations cater especially to children or adolescents. A lot of children spend many hours a day in front of the TV screen, the computer screen or playing video games, and they have a cell phone with access to the internet. Where the drafters of the Convention had only just stopped working on their typewriter and had started to use a computer, had to pay for buying records, the new generation (the "dot com" generation) have already had computers available at kindergarten. Now many children play videogames, have a cell phone in the schoolbag and download free music from the internet. This is a total new reality where children are sometimes more up to data then their parents. At the time of the drafting of the Convention drinking among adolescents was probably less 'normal' then it is now and market-ing (special) alcoholic beverages for adolescents was not as extensive as it is now. But also then adolescents were already drinking alcohol. The drafters of the Convention did not take sufficiently into account the fact that adolescents can already become addicted to alcohol. Article 24 – the child's rights to health and health services – does not sufficiently address alcohol consumption or the misuse and addiction of youth to alcohol. Further, article 33 does not sufficiently address that children and adolescents themselves can become addicted to drugs. The focus of the drafters was on prevention (children were seen as one of the "vulner-able groups" on which prevention efforts should be focused). It was maybe hard for the drafters to imagine that children (like adults) could be addicted to alcohol or drugs.

Times are changing and even an uncontroversial article as article 1 (definition of the child) needs in my opinion to be reviewed in the light of new findings from modern neurobiological science and neuro-imaging (for instance MRI-scans). Thus, neuroscientists argue the case for expanding the period of special protection of childhood until 24 years of age (because the brain is growing until that age).

Adapting the Definition of the Child?

The U.N. Convention on the Rights of the Child considers "every human being below the age of 18 years" to be a child "unless, under the law applicable to the child, majority is attained earlier". On both sides of the continuum (on the side of the minus nine months before birth and on the other side 18 years of age and above) biological and medical science forces us to take a fresh look at article 1 (the definition of the child). With new technologies (neuro-imaging, for instance the CT-scan) came new insights from medical science. We now know much more about the influence of stress in pregnancy, drinking, smoking nicotine and drug use (Nulman, 2001)[2] during pregnancy and how this may have an influence on

---

[2] (Ernst, T., *et al*, 2000; Levitt, P. 1998).

the child's development, for instance on depression in later life and even antisocial behaviour (Varvarigiou, 2009).[3] For some decades we have not paid much
attention to the Preamble to the United Nations Declaration of the Rights of the
Child of 1959 in which was stated that the child needed "special safeguards and
care, including appropriate legal protection (...) by reason of his physical and
mental immaturity (...) before as well as after birth". But this paragraph is highly
relevant now.

In several places in the Netherlands for instance in Rotterdam (GGD-Rijnmond,
2007) the organizations caring for women who are addicted try to limit damage to
their unborn children as a result of the addiction of these mothers[4]. A network of
organizations with Bouman mental health care (an organisation of addiction psychiatry) as a key organization in this 'chain', advise the Child Protection Agency of
the Ministry of Justice which in turn advises the court. If the addicted pregnant
woman does not cooperate, it is feared that irreparable and permanent damage
will be done to the child. In Rotterdam for instance pregnant drug-addicted prostitutes were admitted to a psychiatric department under court order. Kievits and
Adriaanse (also from the Netherlands) have called in 2007 for admitting (even
against their will) women who expose their children to excessive alcohol and/or
drug use (and they call it "prenatal child abuse"). A court in the Netherlands has
already placed an embryo from 24 weeks under supervision of a guardian,
appointed by the court. Pregnant addicted prostitutes are a group of women
especially at risk (Schneider, 2004). The "right of the child to choose its parents
wisely", which was formulated in 1900 by Ellen Key,[5] comes to mind. Key actually
meant by this the right of the child to be born into a healthy condition or not to
be born at all.

On the other side of the continuum a child psychiatrist in the Netherlands
(Prof. Theo Doreleijers, 2009) has pleaded to extend the period of extra protection
of childhood until the age to 23 years of age. Doreleijers argues that: "from 1988
onwards persons in the Netherlands who are older than 18 years of age and are
accused of having broken the law, are no longer brought before an juvenile court.
But most of the accused are between 18 and 23 years of age and are clearly not
behaving like an adult. I believe that treatment in an institute for juveniles makes
much more sense". Dorleijers is of the opinion that all 18-23 year olds against
whom the prosecutor brings charges against should be tried as minors. In the
United States many years ago the concept of 'an emancipated minor' was discussed. Joseph Goldstein, Anna Freud and Albert Solnit (1970) were not for such

---

[3] (Lewinn, K., *et al.*, 2009; Dougherty, L. R. *et al.*, 2009).
[4] Recently the United Nations Assistance Mission to Afghanistan (UNAMA) noticed that
many young children (including babies) in Afghanistan are addicted to opium (Mojumdar,
2010) because their mothers are addicted.
[5] See the Chapter about Ellen Key in: Philip E. Veerman, 1992.

exceptions "in each and every case". They were in favour that *somewhere* a line had to be drawn and eighteen was for them the best choice. Medical research in the Netherlands confirms his views, says Doreleijers. He quotes in a newspaper article (Doreleijers, in the *NRC Handelsblad*, 2009) new brain research that not until 25 years of age "the prefrontal cortex develops fully (and only from then on can we as an *adult* plan and prioritize our impulses and have adequate inhibition of impulses)". Doreleijers quotes the psychologist Jeffrey Jensen Arnett of the University of Missouri (Arnett, 2004 and 2006), who speaks of the period up to 25 years of age as the phase of *emerging adulthood,* the period from the late teens to mid twenties (mainly ages 18-25) in which slowly the young adult learns to make independent decisions and can learn to take responsibility. In correspondence with me Dr. Arnett notes: "yes, there is certainly a movement in the U.S. to raise the age of majority in some respects. For young people in foster care, whose are not living with their original parents, usually due to parental abuse or neglect, they were once thrown out of the social welfare system at age 18, but now they are supported until age 21 in most States. Also, in the health care bill that is about to become law, insurance companies will be required to allow children to remain on their parents' health insurance policy through age 26. However, there has also been a counter-trend toward charging juveniles as adults in the justice system[6]".

In the Netherlands developmental psychologist Michiel Westenberg of the University of Leiden added his voice to this line of thinking by stating that adolescents of 16 years of age can often not yet make the right choices. He says that it is "craziness" to force adolescents to choose what they are going to study later. He says that even if the brain development is ready for it, the emotional development needs more time.[7] In many other fields experts are promoting extending youth law till after 18 years of age and with this extending the period of being a child.[8] In the Netherlands the government announced in May 2009 that they will invest 250 million euro's in keeping adolescents in school longer.[9]

It should be investigated if the global graying (Pilkington, 2009) of the world (where for the first time the proportion of the global population aged 65 and over is set to outnumber children under five) has influenced such thinking as described above. The magazine *The Economist* predicts that by 2050 a third of the population of rich countries will be aged over 60. "Once these people retire" *The Economist* claims "they can expect to live another 20 years or more".[10] It can be argued (as did

---

[6] Some States have recently also lowered or proposed lowering the age of criminal responsibility. They include Argentina, Brazil, Georgia, South Korea, the Philippines and Spain.

[7] Quoted by journalist Hagers, 2008.

[8] In the field of foster care in the Netherlands a debate started if the period in foster care should be extended. See: Kerbusch and Fetlzer, 2006.

[9] The Dutch government expressed on May 25, 2009 their plans to keep young people longer in school in an action plan against unemployment of youth. <www. *Nieuwsbrief regering.nl*>.

[10] *The Economist*, 2009.

Harry van Dalen and Ewald Engelen, 2008) that in a time when the number of children is 'shrinking' (at least in Europe) this is now compensated by extending the length of childhood. In a time that some countries finally are lowering the age of majority to 18 years of age (Argentina[11] for instance did so only recently), often on the advice of the U.N. Committee on the Rights of the Child, we see experts pleading again in the opposite direction.

In an interview with a Dutch newspaper Maurits van der Molen (professor of biological developmental psychology at the University of Amsterdam) was asked how he defines adulthood. "Is it when you are able to stand on your own two feet?" the interviewer asked.[12] "Well", van der Molen answered "one hundred and fifty years ago we had to stand on our own two feet when we were 13. At present some young people still live with their parents at the age of 25. Aren't we functioning as adults for longer than we used to do in the past? Maybe we are". Van der Molen draws his conclusion: "the more 'modern' the society, the later people will be ready to be seen as an adult for longer than previously". Childhood is a social construct, I argued (Veerman, 1992), but now research from cortical development[13] supports expanding the age of majority until the age of twenty four. And this is new.

Using the Internet, Watching TV, Having Cell Phones and the Explosion of Text Messages

The General Discussion Day on the Child and the Media (organized by the U.N. Committee on the Rights of the Child in October 1996) was for a large part dedicated to how the media could help the Committee and tried to make the point that "the press and other media had essential functions in promoting and protecting the fundamental rights of the child in helping to implement in practice the principles and standards of the Convention".[14] The Committee also expressed the view that the media could play a pivotal role in monitoring and the realisation of the rights of the child. Reference was made to protection by the media of the privacy of the child in reporting (for instance when reporting on criminal activities and sexual abuse). Reference was also made to the role of the media in offering the possibility for children to express themselves. One could imagine such a General Discussion Day of the U.N. Committee on the Rights of the Child taking place again. If one looks at the organisations that were represented on the 6th of October 1996, one can conclude that today many new and specialised organisations would

---

[11] CRIN (Child *Rights* Information Network) 2009.
[12] Beintema (2009).
[13] See also the research of Dr. Nitin Gogtay of the Child Psychiatry Branch of the National Institute of Mental Health in the United States.
[14] See document CRC/C15/ add.65 pp. 40-45 and Document CRC/C/57, paras 242-257. The rapporteur was Mr. Thomas Hammarberg.

be represented. Many special NGOs have been founded in the last decade to work on the protection of children in this very area. At the time only *Childnet International* and the *Centre International du Film pour l' Enfance et la Jeunesse* were NGOs that specialised in this issue. For the rest it was up to the usual organisations expected to attend such a meeting (UNICEF, UNHCHR, ILO, UNESCO, Save the Children Alliance, etc.). The number of specialised organisations trying to make the internet a safer place for children has since 1996 expanded enormously (such as the Internet Watch Foundation based in the United Kingdom, Just Think Org, which teaches young people to understand the media, Media Watch and so on) but at the same time child abuse networks of paedophiles have grown extensively as well. A *Virtual Global Taskforce* (VGT) made up of law enforcement agencies around the world is trying to help children in need and is trying to get predators arrested. The Dutch Minister of Justice, Mr. Ernst Hirsch Ballin, recently pleaded for "an international agency with authority, like the World Health Organization, that can fight cybercrime because on the internet there is no police".[15] In 1997 a follow up was given to the issue of the General Discussion Day of the Committee, when at UNESCO headquarters in Paris a Working Group convened. In May 1997 they produced their report to the Committee (Working Group on Children and the Media, 1997). Another follow up took place when on the occasion of the tenth anniversary of the U.N. Convention on the Rights of the Child the Norwegian government and UNICEF organized a meeting to identify challenges in relation to development of children's rights and the role of the media.[16] In 2009 a follow up was given to the issue of the child and the media by the Institute of Education of London University and the Open University. That Conference was on the subject of representations of children in the media.

In the Spring of 2008 *The Future of Children*[17] was dedicated to Children and Electronic media. In this issue Donald Roberts and Ulla Foehr noted that American youth "spend more time with the media than any single activity other than sleeping, with the average American eight to eighteen year old reporting more than six hours daily media use. The growing phenomenon of 'media multitasking' – using several media concurrently – multiplies that figure to eight and a half hours of media exposure daily" (Roberts and Foehr, 2008). They concluded that "the media give American youngsters almost instantaneous access to more than has ever been available to any previous generation. Access that by the teen years, is generally unsupervised". This suggests that the scrutiny should be intense.[18]

---

[15] Eijsvogel and Rijlaarsdam (2010).
[16] This led to the "Oslo Challenge". This Declaration which can be read at the website of MAGIC: www.unicef.org/magic. Organisations like ECPAT international (see: www.ecpat.net) monitor also the situation of how safe children are on the internet.
[17] See: <www.futureofchildren.org> at Spring 2008.
[18] See also: Amanda Lenhart *et al.*, 2001 and 2005.

There are enormous opportunities for children in developing countries (Zucker and Light, 2009). One such an example I found in the *One Laptop per Child* project initiated by Professor Nicholas Negroponte from MIT. He experienced first-hand how connected laptops transformed the lives of many children and families in a Cambodian village. The foundation he leads (*One Laptop per Child*) created also a special laptop (the XO), which is easy and cheap to produce and user-friendly. In Uruguay, the government ordered 100,000 laptops from *One laptop per Child* for children who do not have a computer at home". Rwanda is also one of the largest African customers of the *One Laptop per Child* movement (Warman, 2009). In some remote villages a bus arrives and after it has been hooked up to electricity, it becomes once a week a workplace for children to work on laptops. Not related to Mr. Negroponte's initiative are the Ethiopia's progressive IT programmes (they want to connect all the Ethiopian villages to the internet within a few years and they are building an IT infrastructure for it). According to Michael Cross (Cross, 2007), Ethiopia's plans are "an extreme example of the aspiration of several African countries to leap out of their quagmire of decaying public services by skipping an entire generation of infrastructure and going directly to internet technology".

In article 17 (child's access to appropriate information) paragraph (c) states that the States Parties shall "encourage the production and dissemination of children's books". But many children are reading not only children's books any more. The Library Concept Center (DOK) in the Netherlands (located in Delft) wants to become one of the world's most modern libraries. In Delft children cannot only borrow books, but also read comics, play games on the computer or the PlayStation or listen to music. There is also a collection of CD's, LP's, DVD's and books of sheet music. Children can borrow games for Sony Play station 2 and 3, Microsoft Xbox 360 or Nintendo Wii. In the centre there are also 360 computers. Children might watch in the future there on line videos maybe. This is something more and more young people do already in the United States.

Because of the growing number of cable-TV stations, audiences for each cable have become smaller. Sandra Calvert claims that this is one of the reasons why advertising and marketing among youngsters has become more important: "digital interactive technologies have simultaneously opened new routes to narrow cast to children, thereby creating a growing media space just for children and children's products" (Calvert, 2008). Calvert points out that children under eight lack the cognitive skills "to understand the persuasive intent of television or online advertisements".

In the Bouman mental health services outpatient clinic for young people I have been involved in overseeing the therapeutic work with adolescents who spend long days before the computer internetting or video gaming and some adolescents and young adults play games like 'warcraft'[19] almost the whole day. And

---

[19] The "World of Warcraft" claims that they have 11 million players online. Publishers of such games have in my opinion a responsibility for the many adolescents playing excessively games,

this led to enormous quarrels with the parents and siblings (who also want to use the computer). I have advised in several cases after this had led to violence between the family members. For some (who have difficulty with social interaction such as adolescents with an autistic spectrum disorder, like PDD-NOS) being on the internet is a less scary way to meet others because they then do not have immediately 'life' contact.

A recent report about teenagers in the United States and the use of mobile phones (Linhart, 2010) indicated that "cell-phone texting has become the preferred channel of basic communication between teens and their friends and cell calling is a close second". According to these research data 75% of the 12-17 year-olds in the United States now own cell-phones (up from 45% in 2004). "Those phones have become indispensable tools in teen communication patterns. Fully 72% of all teens – or 88% cell phone users – are sending text messages. Among all teens, the frequency of the use of texting has now overtaken the frequency of every other communication form. Fully two-third of teen-texters say they are more likely to use cell-phones to text their friends than to call them by cell-phone".[20] For parents phones can make their children's lives more safe and convenient. However, their children's attachment to their phones is often an area of conflict. According to Rich Ling[21] texting is happening *in addition* to other forms of social interaction. Ling argues that "teens have already more informal, casual contact because of the texting. (...) The research data might actually point in the direction of more social interaction, not less". It has been noted that young people have learned to speak not only with their tongues, but also with their thumbs. Castells sees here the emerging of a 'mobile youth culture' (Castells, 2007). I have sometimes the feeling that the cell phone to which adolescents get so passionately attached is like a 'transitional object' (Winnicott, 1953). It was the paediatrician and psychoanalyst Donald Woods Winnicott who introduced the concept. With 'transition' Winnicott meant the intermediate development phase between the psychic and external reality. A transitional object is something, which helps the child to make a step towards a next phase of development. Examples are dolls, teddy bears and blankets. Because it is impossible that the mother is always there to bring the world to the small child, he or she faces the world with the transitional object. Through fantasising about the object of his or her wishes, the child finds comfort and it helps him or her to enter the next phase of development. It seems to me that with a cell-phone some adolescents face the world more courageously, like small children with a blanket or doll.

---

just like the Tobacco industry is also for a part responsible for people getting addicted to nicotine. Games like 'Warcraft' are designed especially to keep adolescents on line as long as possible and as often as possible.

[20] Lenhart *et al.*, 2010.

[21] On the website of the Pew Internet and American Life project, May 12, 2010.

Internet "Addiction" Does Not Become a Mental Disorder (Yet)

A few years ago the term 'addiction' would have been reserved for addiction to alcohol or drugs. But according to Mark Griffiths "there is now a growing movement which views a number of behaviours as potentially addictive, including many behaviours which do not involve the ingestion of a psychoactive drug" (Griffiths, 2008). Now the definition of addiction has been extended by some psychologists and psychiatrists to addiction to computer game playing, internet use and so on. A lot of research has been done on Japanese adolescents doing video games. Fleeing the harsh reality from school and its strict discipline might be one of the reasons in Japan that young people turn to gaming. Doing something else in order not to think about problems (a 'palliative reaction' as psychologists call it) is probably also why many adolescents use excessively the internet. The working group of the American Psychiatric Association (APA) drafting the most used diagnostic classification system (the Diagnostic and Statistical Manual of Mental Disorders, the DSM-IV-TR),[22] did not foresee these new developments and syndromes related to them. The APA is at present finalising the updated DSM-5 classification system and is discussing if internet addiction merits inclusion in the DSM-5. Their question was: "if the 'Substance Use Disorders' and the co-called 'Non-Substance Addictions' (such as pathological gaming) are related and if so, what are the nature and strength of the relationships?".[23] The DSM-5 will probably become officially available in 2011 and psychiatrists and psychologists are eagerly awaiting if *internet addiction*, or *on-line-gambling addiction* and so on get a place as a mental disorder. As it stands now, *internet addiction* did not make it into the DSM-5 as a special classification, but *pathological gambling* stays in the DSM classification system (it is already included in the present DSM-IV classification system). The APA press release stated that "the work groups have been creating a new category 'behavioural addictions', in which gambling will be the sole disorder. Internet addiction was considered for this category, but work group members decided there was insufficient research data to do so, so they recommended it be included in the manual's appendix instead, with a goal of encouraging additional study". Excessive use of the internet and gaming, however, remain a field of great concern and adolescents will seek in the future help for these problems in the mental health field.

The first evidence based therapies in the field of addictions have in the meantime become available. In general, cognitive psychotherapy is the most promising approach. And an evidence-based therapy is in my opinion certainly *not* the

---

[22] (American Psychiatric Association, 2000). The APA has in the meantime put a draft of the DSM-5 on the internet. See also the report of the *DSM-5 Substance-Related Disorders Work Group* and the report by Charles O'Brien, MD from November 2008 on the APA website.
[23] See the APA Press release on the draft diagnostic criteria for DSM-5, (APA, 2010).

electro-shock therapy practiced in China with which a small group of "therapists" have tried "to treat internet-addiction". Also in South Korea excessive use of the internet and gaming became "a vast growing problem"[24] (Cao and Sue, 2007). It was reported that the average South Korean high school student spends 23 hours each week gaming (Kim, 2007). China has limited computer use and rules were adopted limiting computer use per day.[25] But in the case of China one should have an open eye for healthy political oppositional behaviour which gets there sometimes a psychiatric label.[26]

The Term 'Alcohol' Cannot Be Found in the CRC

It is interesting that in a Convention on the Rights of the Child which its the drafters believed it would be comprehensive, problems caused by alcohol were not included. One can argue that treatment for misuse or addiction of alcohol can be found in paragraph 1 of article 24 (the child's rights to health and health services). Elsewhere in article 24 one finds a general paragraph about the need to develop preventive health care and to give guidance to parents. Rachel Hodgkin and Peter Newell observed that alcohol use did not find a place in relation to young people in all international human rights treaties. "It is a blind spot of those who worked so hard to establish an international human rights treaty for children" (Hodgkin and Newell, 2002). In the first ten years of meetings drafting the CRC the word *alcohol* was only uttered once in relation to young people. In 1986 a representative from the United States, proposed when article 33 (children and drug abuse) was discussed during the drafting process of the Convention, to include under this article a reference to "other drugs, *such as alcohol*" (see Detrick, 1992: 427). A follow up to this proposal was never made.

Essau and Hutchinson (2008) state that "alcohol is one of the most commonly used substances in most Western societies, especially among adolescents. The use of alcohol is so common in this age group that it has become a 'normal' phenomenon, and socially acceptable". A number of studies have been done regarding the

---

[24] Cao and Sues state that "internet addiction is not rare among Chinese adolescents". The decision of Google to review their business opportunities in China (after they had been victim of cyber attacks and theft of intellectual property) shows that in China internet use is a more complex (and also a political) issue. Freedom of expression is limited in China (see the *press release* of Google of 12 January 2010). The author of this article (Ph. E. Veerman) wants to remark that the Chinese authorities have blocked access to many internet sites and a (healthy) political opposition can get a psychiatric stigma (although pathological internet use can certainly be a problem, also in China, which Cao and Sue refer to).
[25] (China Daily, 2007) <www.people.com.cn>.
[26] Quoted from *The Times,* on the website of the *Children's Rights Information Network* 2009 (June 9).

prevalence of alcohol, abuse and dependence among adolescents. Essau and Hutchinson claim however that studies are hard to compare, since there are so many methodological differences. They describe that the introduction of breezers or alcopops (soft drinks mixed with alcohol) and different kinds of mixed drinks make comparison even more difficult. Very active marketing of drinks with alcohol among young people (Hastings, 2005), catered especially for taste buds of adolescents,[27] have contributed greatly to the increase of alcohol consumption among 13-16 year old adolescents. Even if the epidemiological studies are hard to compare, some were alarming enough that even the Minister of Health in a traditionally wine drinking country like France was proposing that teenagers should be banned from buying alcohol. This French Health Minister Madam Roselyne Bachelot bravely announced on July 12 2008 in the newspaper *Journal du Dimanche* that she wanted "to impose a total prohibition of alcohol sales to minors and intended to ban the open bars during celebrations" (where people can drink unlimited amounts in exchange for a flat fee).[28] In Italy (Cortese, 2010) notions of alcohol use also have become part of the collective identity but seem more immune from change. In other places in Europe concern was also expressed about the "happy hours" of bars where drinks are offered with reduced prices, encouraging heavy drinking. One of the alarming studies (from Ontario in Canada) found that alcohol use at an early age (between 11-14 years of age) heightens the danger of developing later alcohol addiction disorders (de Wit *et al.*, 2000). In this respect it was recommended, as a strategy, to delay as long as possible the first consumption of alcohol. Alcohol intoxication among teenagers is everywhere a growing problem and is caused often by drinking many different alcoholic beverages at the same time.

There are certain vulnerable groups. If one parent is an alcoholic that child is part of a vulnerable group. Education of these children should aim at achieving abstinence. Another vulnerable group is 'the children in the making' of pregnant women who drink. This will damage the brain of the foetus, which might lead to many behavioural problems later in life. This is often referred to as the Foetal Alcohol Spectrum Disorder, FASD (Astley, 2004). In The Netherlands the University of Utrecht[29] recently started to work with adopted children from Poland. There is concern that many of these adopted children suffer from the consequences of having FASD. By drinking the pregnant woman takes an enormous risk. A lot is dependent, however, on the genetic makeup of the mother. In the

---

[27] See also: Center on Alcohol Marketing and Youth, 2006, Washington DC, Center on Alcohol Marketing and Youth).
[28] See also Crumley, (2008) and Adam (2008).
[29] From 1971 more than 480 Polish children were adopted in the Netherlands. The department of study of adoption of the University of Utrecht started a project to study if the children might have FASD (because of heavy drinking by the mothers during pregnancy). The project is headed by Prof. R. Hoksbergen (e mail: r.a.c.hoksbergen@uu.nl).

Netherlands the Health Council has advised for the past six years pregnant women: do not drink *at all.* Many family physicians of pregnant women in the Netherlands still say that it cannot hurt to take a drink once in a while. The Dutch Health Council wrote: "Should pregnant women and women who are breastfeeding drink no alcohol at all or can one glass not hurt? The advice that is given [by family physicians] differs. However, from scientific work we know that the only safe option is not to drink at all. Preceding the conception it is safe that both partners do not drink, to exclude potential damaging effects" (Health Council of the Netherlands, 2005). Nevertheless, it is estimated by the Health Council of the Netherlands that 35-50% of the pregnant women in the Netherlands continue to consume alcohol.

A researcher of youth and risk taking behaviour (Monshouwer, 2004) saw as one of the most important changes of youth behaviour the age by which they for the first time start to drink alcohol. It can be that entering the market of alcoholic beverages mixed with a sweet substance has made it easier for youngsters to start drinking, but most of the adolescents learn to drink at home though. One third of the Dutch teenagers (interviewed in 2003) said that their parents allow them to drink at home. In the United Kingdom recently the chief medical officer, Sir Liam Donaldson, was asked by the Minister of Health to advise him when parents should be allowed to give their children alcohol at home (Doward, 2008). In many places in the world alcohol can easily be obtained by teenagers in supermarkets or shops and although there are often official age limits, the cashiers do not ask an identification in most cases. In the Netherlands the shopkeepers or their employees has to tell a customer now (who wants to buy alcohol or tobacco) and who is not yet 16 years old, that he or she cannot buy the product. In the Netherlands the government promised Parliament (in a letter of March 24 2005) to supervise closer the implementation of the minimum age of sale of alcohol by supermarkets. This is certainly an improvement (although it is not hard to ask an older friend to buy it). The Dutch Institute for Mental Health (the Trimbos Institute)[30] recently asked Parliament to increase the age limit for drinking and they propose it will be 18 years old. They believe this is the *only* effective way to fight the rise of alcohol consumption among youngsters.

The influence of alcohol on the start of violent behaviour by adolescents should, in my opinion, be taken up by Marta Santos Pais, the Special Representative (of the U.N. Secretary-General) on Violence against Children. It is interesting to note that children and adolescents (quite often "under the influence") can be very violent to other children and adolescents, but also to adults. There are many examples of dance parties or soccer matches getting out of hand and becoming violent, where alcohol and/or cocaine play an important role.

---

[30] Trimbos Instituut, Utrecht, letter to the Second Chamber of the Dutch Parliament on May 12 2010.

It is important for adolescents to experiment. The temperament of a person is a variable of importance as well (some like risky behaviour, others not at all). Adolescents often experiment with alcohol or drugs at parties or in discotheques. Use of alcohol or drugs is attractive to youngsters and drinking or using drugs together with other adolescents makes it additionally attractive. In the Netherlands many adolescents start drinking a lot already at home (called "indrinken" in Dutch) with other friends *before* going to the discotheque (around midnight). By the time they get to the disco, they are already drunk. In the past adolescents got drunk, but recently it has become fashionable to drink until one of them ends up being in a coma. In the Netherlands several times a month this leads to hospital admissions of adolescents with alcohol intoxication. After having been in hospital and on a drip they often can go home the next day. This is, however, not necessarily a sign of addiction. One has to start worrying if the adolescents come to the discotheque solely to drink or to use drugs. One has to distinguish between misuse of alcohol and getting addicted. The first signs that there are problems are: being tired at school, academic results deteriorating, coming late to school, behavioural problems or getting in trouble with the police. When alcohol (or drugs as we will see later in this article) is getting a more central place in the life of the adolescent and there is strong *craving*, one can speak of addiction.[31]

New methods of treatment (such as CRA, the Community Reinforcement Approach, which helps adolescents to find other reinforcements) are promising for therapeutic work with adolescents. An important cause of mortality of adolescents and young adults is related to the alcohol consumption (Nordström, 2001). It is according to Nordström the most important cause of death among European adolescents and young adults (between 15 and 29 years of age).

It seems that the image of childhood of the drafters of the U.N. Convention on the Rights on the Child did not include that a child or adolescent can be addicted to alcohol. Does the image of the child here underestimates what a child is already able to do? "A child is a moral and rational human being – although in a different manner than an adult is – and he or she contributes (as he or she gets older) more and more to his or her own development" wrote Snik (1986). The Convention itself with its new participation rights of children sees the child not only as a passive object of rights who needs to be protected. But the lack of attention for alcohol and drug dependence of children depicts the child as a too passive human being (not capable of the bad habits which belong to adulthood) and this is still a residue of 'old thinking'.

Since the drafting of the Convention a lot has been changed in the field of alcohol addiction. At the time of the drafting of the Convention it was the paradigm

---

[31] Addiction does not come alone, because there are often other disorders (co-morbidity). Alcohol can be the trigger for a disturbance (for instance a depression or an anxiety disorder). But the presence of psychopathology increases also the chance that addiction will develop.

that addiction to alcohol or drugs was *learned behaviour* and it was often thought that one had to strengthen the will of the patients to do something to tackle their addiction. Many institutes for the treatment of addiction have started around the year 2000 to work on the basis of a new paradigm. Addiction was now considered to be not only learned behaviour[32], but more significantly a brain disease (van den Brink, 2006). This shift was based on new developments in neuroscience and genetic research. The developments in neurobiological science have been dazzling since 2000. In the field of addiction the work of George Koob, MD at the Scripps Research Institute in La Jolla has been very influential. In the nature-nurture debate, the pendulum has been swung back to the nature side, since the influence of biology and importance of inheritance and DNA became more prominent. Since the 1960's it was thought that the influence of the social environment were the roots of behaviour. In psychiatry there was considerable influence of the anti-psychiatry movement (Cooper, 1967; Laing, 1960 and 1964; Szasz, 1961) and the authors from this anti-psychiatry movement even had explanations for schizophrenia. In the social sciences it became a taboo to see biological origins of behaviour. This has totally changed. Also in the field of psychiatry and criminology the neurobiological situation became again prominent.

New Insights Show That the Convention Article on Children and Drug Abuse Is Outdated

It has become known that craving for drugs is often linked in the brain with a memory of a situation where the drugs once were used, even many years later. This means that if a person "kicked off" the drugs habit, he or she can suddenly (many years later) again get craving (when a memory triggers it) and this can cause a relapse. It should be stated that using drugs in a period of adolescence, when the brain is still developing, might give irreversible problems. The first research from the field of neuro-imaging point this out (Hardin and Ernst, 2009). Using drugs in adolescence might have for later in life more grave consequences than using them in adulthood. Koob states that if you use drugs you pay an enormous price (Koob and LeMoal, 2008). He looked at changes in the body when somebody takes a certain amount of drugs and he or she takes it more obsessively (Koob and Kreek, 2007). A negative emotional situation emerges, not so much when the drugs are taken, but in the period when the drugs are *not* taken. The reward system is compromised, Koob states. And this is a different point of view than the assumption that people use drugs 'because they like it' and because

---

[32] To see alcoholism as learned behaviour was already a step forward from the moralisation-approach of the temperance movement (see: van der Stel, 1990).

'it gives them pleasure', which is often assumed. Koob argues: "The neuro-chemical systems (which are affected when someone takes a drug to get high) become compromised during addiction. We have come to believe that the stress-systems in the brain and the pituitary hormone stress system become activated during drug addiction, as well as the reward system. (...) And we have come full circle and are beginning to realize that neuro-chemical systems affected by drugs are the ones that form the natural reward system. The immediate response to the drug is this release of rewarding neurotransmitters. But over the long term those pleasure neurotransmitters become compromised. Using chronically (...) you're exiting and activating a system of transmitters that exists to regulate – to minimize, in this case – pleasure. Once the change is established it's very hard to get out of the cycle. There is the pleasure that you got in the first place, but after a while the system has become so compromised that you are taking the drug to return yourself to a normal state. In my view the essence of drug addiction is that you have created an artificial but negative state. In effect, you spend lots of your time not trying to get some extra bliss. (...) You have bankrupted the system. There is no pleasure in your account...".[33] According to Koob the triggered brain *anti-reward system* creates an allostatic (stability through change) emotional adaptation which leads to pathology. The new DSM-5 classification system of the American Psychiatric Association (APA) is going to do away with the neutral term *dependence* and is 'pushing' again the term *addiction*. "It was found that the term dependence is misleading because people confuse it with addiction, when in fact the tolerance and the withdrawal patients experience, are also normal responses to prescribed medications that affect the central nervous system" stated Charles O'Brien.[34]

Drugs (or what the U.N. Convention on the Rights of the Child in article 33 calls illegal *narcotic drugs and psychotropic substances*) did (contrary to alcohol) receive a special article in the Convention, but the focus is on prevention, not on treatment if misuse of drugs takes place or if there is drug addiction. There is attention in article 33 to protection of minors who might be involved in the illegal production of drugs and trafficking[35] of "such substances". The trafficking issue is of serious concern and in some places like Rio de Janeiro[36] children are used as drug runners on a grand scale (Dowdney, 2003).

---

[33] Bill Moyers, (2009) see: www.close to home-science
[34] Charles O'Brien, MD (chair of the APA DSM Substance-related Disorders Working Group, in a news feature ("DSM-5 Draft includes Major Changes to Addictive Disease Classifications") on the website www.jointogether.org.
[35] Here also *ILO Convention on the Worst Forms of Child Labour* (ILO Convention no. 182) applies.
[36] The phenomenon of children in Rio de Janeiro in Brazil working as traffickers of drugs often gives associations with the use of child soldiers. Luke Dowdney: "They are armed, there is a command structure and the police often shoots fast". Elsewhere in the world children also

It is interesting though to see that the text of the article does pay more attention to children who can be abused as traffickers of drugs than children as active users of drugs and the youngsters who are addicted. In 1986 it was proposed in the Working Group [drafting the U.N. Convention on the Rights of the Child] that the text of the article on children and drug abuse would include that "the competent national authorities should investigate cases of drug abuse by a child and timely medical treatment should be proposed so that he or she may be assured prompt rehabilitation and healthy growth" (see: Detrick, 1992). Little is known why the drafters did not take up this issue further.

What treatment of young people concerns one can, according to the latest state of the art, distinguish between those youngsters with problematic use of drugs (the less serious cases) and those who are already addicted. New is to offer youngsters from the first group of 'problematic use' mainly participation in a life style training. With young people of the second group (those youngsters being addicted), more diagnostic work then has to start. More diagnostic work is needed in order to fine tune the treatment to the personality structure of the patient. With addiction there is often a double diagnosis (a mental disorder *and* an addiction). Possibilities for success in treatment often depends on what diagnosis the patient has. 'Roadmaps' have in the last years been described for psychiatric problems in combination with different kind of addictions (cocaine addiction, heroin addiction, etc.). Such 'roadmaps for treatment' are important in order to evaluate the results later. All organisations in the field of drug addiction try to work nowadays with evidence based therapies.

Even if an adolescent is not yet addicted, the use of drugs can have the effect that his or her school attendance is diminishing. He or she looks more and more tired and truanting starts to be noticed. But such adolescent often will not come to mental health organizations in order to get help. Having some motivational talks (Miller, 2002) with the adolescent at school can be important. The aim is motivating the adolescent for therapy. Several approaches in this respect are promising.[37] Also with the use of drugs there are vulnerable groups which are extra at risk. One such group is children of whom in the family schizophrenia is present. Use of drugs can trigger a (first) psychosis. Even after using the 'softdrug' cannabis a psychosis can be triggered when there is schizophrenia in the family. In general one can say also that children of drug users are more at risk, so are adolescents with ADHD and those adolescents who have intellectual borderline functioning. The problems of children of whom one of the parents is addicted or both are addicted

---

work as traffickers (often together with family members) to bring the drugs, which they have to swallow for instance on the flight from the Netherlands Antilles to the Netherlands), Source: Ramdharie, (2005).

[37] One of them came from the field of behavioral and cognitive psychotherapy. See: Miller (2002) and www.motivationalinterviewing.org.

to drugs can also not be ignored, since these children suffer a lot from the addiction of the parent(s). Their families are often unstable, chaotic and children often have to care for the parents (which is called parentification).

Cannabis, XTC, Cocaine, Crystal Meth, GHB and Glue

A change relating to cannabis use around 1978 (when the U.N. started to think about a Convention) and the present time is that often now the active ingredient THC (tetrahydrocannabinol) in cannabis is higher than 1978, so that the hallucinatory value of the cannabis on 'the market' is now higher. The sellers of cannabis have manufactured over the years a more "heavier stuff" and it is probably more addictive and is likely that it has more of a negative influence on memory. Some evidence based therapies such as MDFT (Multidimensional Family Therapy) including half a year of intensive family therapy for cannabis addiction of adolescents have some success (and is developed at the Centre for the Treatment of Drug Addiction and Adolescent Drug Abuse of the University of Miami). MDFT (Liddle, 2009) has spread to other places in the world. Hall *et al.* (2008) state that risks of developing cannabis dependence are around one in six of adolescents who ever use cannabis in Australia, New Zealand and the USA.

XTC is a synthetic drug which has a dose of MDMA (methylendioxy - methamfitamine) and is a very popular drug in discotheques and at parties. In the 80's it led in Europe to a lot of house parties for adolescents where the drugs were taken and one could dance to music all night.

There are many reports about cocaine addiction of adolescents[38]. But base coke (smoked with a pipe and therefore quicker taken in by the body) is popular and makes the physical situation of those adolescents particularly something to worry about (especially the lungs). Addiction to base coke often leads to antisocial behaviour (to get money for the addiction by stealing or doing robberies). Even in some rural communities in the Netherlands base coke from the nearby town is faster delivered by a dealer on a scooter than an order of a pizza from the same town. In many countries we see that cocaine use leads to financial debts and the adolescent being drawn into criminality.

Crystal meth was once called the "poor man's cocaine" but TV personalities like Oprah Winfrey claim that crystal meth has spread to "all corners of mainstream America". It is no doubt spreading rapidly. And it is destroying families and communities especially in the United States and Mexico. Winfrey: "it has seduced

---

[38] From my clinical experience at Bouman mental health services often young people with ADHD (Attention Deficit/Hyperactivity Disorder) get addicted to coke. This drug seems to make them calm and can be considered as a form of 'self medication'.

soccer moms, robbed children of their parents and parents of their children and destroyed families". The 'War on Drugs' in the United States has in the past tried to fight the supply side (by which prices went up). Nowadays getting as many patients as possible to treatment has become the aim. Meth is cheap and instantly addictive. Oprah Winfrey reported in her show of May 13, 2005 that in the State of Iowa officials of a town had banned children from bringing baked goods to school, because so many parents are cooking meth with the same utensils.

GHB (gamma-hydroxybutyrate) is taken by some adolescents to get in an euphoric state or to become sexually aroused. GHB is one of the newest drugs taken for recreational use, but if taken excessively the risk increases to pass out and end up in hospital. Misuse of GHB places adolescents at a significant risk (Nicholson and Balster, 2001).[39]

In many places in the world it are mostly street children who turn to dangerous glue sniffing. Several organisations try to help these children in the slums of big cities,[40] but it seems like a drop in the ocean.

In many places if special treatment for drug abuse of adolescents is given, it is often still provided in a centre where adult addicts come as well, and this is an inappropriate environment for minors.

Some people are a victim of drugs their whole life. Take this young woman who is a patient of Bouman mental health services, (but of whom because of reasons of privacy more details are of course not given). This young woman was born addicted, because both her parents were dependent on heroin. Soon after birth she was placed by the childcare authorities in a foster family and she has a long history of placements in foster care (where she was also abused). At age thirteen she decided she had enough and demanded to be able to live with her father (her mother had passed away due to her addiction). When her father was detained a short period, it appeared that she was also dependent on opiates (she had taken regular zips of the methadone of father). To cope with stress this patient often used cannabis and benzodiazepine, but recently (with the help of the new outpatient clinic for young people of Bouman mental health) reduced her use of drugs. It seems to me that such histories were not on the mind of the drafters of the Convention and its article 33.

A *Declaration on the Guiding Principles of Drug Demand Reduction* was adopted by the General Assembly of the United Nations ten years after the adoption of the United Nations Convention on the Rights of the Child.[41] The term, drug demand

---

[39] See also: Iten, P. X., and Oestreich, A. (2002).

[40] Also in the Kathmandu Valley in Nepal. See the reports by *Child Workers in Nepal Concerned Center (CWIN). See:* www.cwin.org.np. For Pakistan see: (UNODC Country Office for Pakistan, 2004).

[41] *Declaration on the Guiding Principles of Drug Demand Reduction*, A/RES/S-20/3 (1998). Three Conventions are also relevant in this respect respectively adopted in 1961, 1971 and 1998 (*The Single Convention on Narcotic Drugs, The Convention on Psychotropic Substances* and the *Convention against Illicit Traffic in Narcotic Drugs and Psychotropic Substances*).

reduction, was introduced by the UNODC in Vienna to describe policies and programmes "directed towards reducing the consumer demand of narcotic drugs
and psychotropic substances covered by international drug control conventions".
A "balanced approach" was adopted by the Declaration "between demand reduction and supply reduction, each reinforcing each other, in an integrated approach
to solving the drug problem". Paragraph 13 of the Declaration focused on special
needs of young people: "demand reduction programmes should be designed to
address the needs of the population in general, as well as those of specific population groups, special attention being paid to youth". Since the drafting of the U.N.
Convention on the Rights of the Child the 'drug scene' has changed a lot. The
then Secretary-General of the U.N. Kofi Annan said about the increased drug
abuse that "the proliferation of drugs over the past 30 years is an example of the
previously unimaginable becoming reality very quickly. A tragic reality".[42] In 1990
world leaders already recognized at their Summit in New York (in paragraph 6 of
the Word Declaration on the Survival, Protection and Development of Children)
that effects of the drug problem was part of their challenge. They pledged "we
will do our best to ensure that children are not drawn into becoming victims of
the sourge of illicit drugs". Drug abuse is of course already a long time an enormous problem and was first addressed on an international level by the
International Opium Convention of the Hague in 1912 (which dealt with opium,
cocaine and heroin).

     In many places in the world drugs dominate life. In Mexico the war with the
drug cartels escalated (Stolz, 2008 and de Waal, 2009) into warlike situations. In
Colombia the drug cartels have created a catastrophic situation and the FARC
seem to have expanded the coca fields[43] and the Taliban in Afghanistan have
become a drug mafia.[44] However, since the retreat of the Taliban from some areas
in Afghanistan, it is also claimed that these parts of Afghanistan are in the grip of
the drugs trade. For farmers planting alternatives to opium poppies or coca leaves
is often not attractive because then they earn less money. Drug traffickers and the
mafia have obtained an important base for trafficking of drugs (from Latin America
to Europe) in some West African countries and bring with them a lot of negative
influence on daily life. Whole societies are more and more in the grip of drugs,
making the life of children very hard. In Ciudad Juárez, the most violent city in
Latin America's war on drugs, 110 children were killed the past three years. More
and more children are in the line of fire.[45]

---

[42] Quoted by McArdle 2008.
[43] (Caro-Rojas, 2005).
[44] (Bolopion, 2008).
[45] See: http://globalgeopolitics.net/worldpress/2010/050/01/mexico-children-in-the-line-of
-fire

The CRC and Developments Worldwide: Globalisation

During the last decades, according to Axel Dreher (2008), human dynamics, institutional change, political relations and the natural environment has become more intertwined. The integration of national or regional economies into the international economy has been referred to as globalisation. Economists, according to Dreher,[46] usually speak of several waves of globalisation (the first wave covering migration prior to the first World War). Even years before the adoption of the U.N. Convention on the Rights of the Child, the University of Warwick started to publish in 1982 a *Globalisation Index* for the measurement of economic, social and political dimensions of globalisation. With the help of the index one can look now if a particular country has been more globalised in the last years. In the last years also *Foreign Policy* has published a globalisation index. The impact of globalisation on children was not a concern of the drafters of the Convention. The year after the Convention was adopted a project (the impact of globalisation on children) was started at the Evaluation and Policy Planning Division of UNICEF's Headquarters in New York. At the *UNICEF Innocenti Research Center* in Florence, to which the project was transferred, the project on the influence of globalisation on children continued. Giovanni Andrea Cornia (one of the key-researchers on this project) argued that children can gain substantially from globalisation (but only if domestic conditions are improved, if distortions of international markets are corrected and more representative institutions of local and global governance are created).

The economy had not so much prominence in the U.N. Convention on the Rights of the Child except in article 4 (implementation of rights in the Convention). There the drafters included a place for the budget of a country: "with regard to economic, social and cultural rights, States Parties shall undertake such measures to the maximum extent of their available resources...". The economy had also a place in article 32 (child labour) where "States Parties recognized the right of the child to be protected from economic exploitation". Edmonds (2002) explained that globalisation and child labour interact in two basic ways: "first globalisation may increase the employment and opportunities to earn money available to poor households in developing countries. Second, globalisation increases the influence of rich countries in the domestic policies of the developing world. Changes in local labor markets from globalisation may increase or decrease child labour". Globalisation also has led to unemployment in Western countries where workplaces were closed and moved to places in the world where wages are cheaper. In Ethiopia[47] it has led (Abebe, 2007) to migration of adult household members to

---

[46] E mail from Axel Dreher (Director of the Center or European, Governance and Economic Research at the University of Goettingen) to the author on 10 January 2010.
[47] See for instance: Abebe (2007).

secure employment and has according to Abebe led to the "participation in a deeply unequal and exploitative system of international trade". There are different interpretations of the data of globalisation and the impact on children (different economic schools and different political ideas seem to influence the interpretations). An expert in the field (Urban Jonsson)[48] wrote to me that "we all know that the 'economic globalisation' has been 'bad' for many children in communities with people who are poor. However, it is also clear that 'globalisation' has meant a dramatic improvement in 'connectivity', which may be used to improve the lives of children who are poor. Imagine: in a few years time almost everybody in the world will be able to talk to anybody in the world at no cost! Do we really know what that will mean? We do not!".

A traction from the integrated approach of globalisation can be seen and there is more focused attention on different global phenomena. Since the time of the drafting of the Convention, there has been, according to David Parker,[49] "clearly increased attention to the influence of social, economic and political factors on the situation and well-being of children – through the particular lens of realization of children's rights – by numerous stakeholders and analysts at the national and international levels. The process of globalisation became the focus of academic, political and public attention. It is arguable that globalisation, as an overall concept, has perhaps diminished in particular focus since the early 2000s, and much greater attention has been given individually to more specific dimensions of the phenomenon: global finance, trade, migration (and trafficking and the overall movement of children), cross-national elements of armed conflict and civil conflict, climate change, global information and the internet".

In a review of the Convention the influence of globalisation (which is now felt stronger than in 1989) and the vast disparities of economic conditions of children in the world should have a place.

Attention for the Environment and the Climate

The last years a lot of attention has been given to climate change. The influence of the environment on children did not get a place of importance in the Convention (only under the aims of education) even though the Chernobyl disaster took place in 1986. Hodgkin and Newell are of the opinion that the paragraph about the environment "reflects the growing urgency of concern about the environment".[50] And indeed if we look at paragraph (e) of article 29 (the aims of education) it looks

---

[48] Urban Jonsson, personal communication by e-mail (16.1.2010).
[49] David Parker, deputy director of the UNICEF Innocenti Research Center in an e-mail to the author on the 11th of January 2010.
[50] (Hodgkin, R. and Newell, P., 2002).

rather up to date when we read that States Parties to the U.N. Convention in the Rights of the Child have agreed that education shall be directed to "the development of respect for the natural environment". However, with the knowledge we have today we can conclude that the text could have been stronger. At the time of the drafting of the Convention the drafters seemed not so aware of how horrific the consequences of problems with the environment can be for children, even though in December 1984 a toxic cloud escaped from a factory in Bhopal in India and about 20.000 people died (and in that area of India still today many children are born handicapped). We are at present more aware that problems in the environment can damage the DNA and that children can be born handicapped as a result this. The long term effects on children born after the Chernobyl disaster for instance could not have been imagined at the time. Twenty years later children suffer, even though they are born after the disaster. UNICEF 's Deputy Executive Director observed that "one thing is absolutely clear. Increased incidence of childhood thyroid cancer caused by radioactive iodine fallout has been the most dramatic health impact of Chernobyl. There are 4,000 cases of thyroid cancer affecting the Chernobyl generation. But cancer is only the tip of the iceberg. Widespread iodine deficiency in the vicinity of Chernobyl and other parts of Belarus, the Russian Federation and Ukraine is leading to a whole generation of children growing up potentially brain-damaged".[51] Also – to give another example – spraying poison on fields effected the offspring of farmers, as was claimed that it has in Nicaragua. Many people in the banana plantations were exposed to DBCP, a key chemical in the pesticides Nemagon and Fumazone. Many mothers gave birth to handicapped children because of the exposure to the poison. It lead to the passage of Nicaraguan Law 364 and two court rulings where companies had to pay compensation to inhabitants. In Nigeria oil is polluting the waters (from which people drink and catch fish to eat). The list of hard consequences for the lives of children caused by problems in the environment is long. We all saw the consequences of oil spills on our TV screens. Deforestation (for instance in Brazil and Indonesia) is another important problem, which had less attention than it should.

In 1990 when the first climate report appeared it was not yet so widely recognized that humans had an important influence on the change of the climate. In 2001 the role of human beings in the warming of the earth was called "probable", but the 2007 report called it (Knip, 2007) now "very probable". Many children know now that glaciers are melting faster than in the last centuries and that this is an important indication for a warmer climate. A report by Save the Children UK (2007) described what the consequences of climate change mean for the lives up to 175 million children a year who are endangered by floods, drought, earthquakes

---

[51] Gautam, (20 April 2006) see: <www.cwin.org.np>.

and tsunamis over the next decade (according to Save the Children – UK a potential increase of 40 per cent on the previous decade). The report by Save the Children UK points out that "despite political rhetoric about children being our future, the scale of the threat faced by today's children is barely acknowledged". Authors like Conisbee and Simms (2003) predict a scenario of possibly millions of "environmental refugees" (fleeing for floods, storms or other natural disasters) in the years to come and plead for the redefining the refugee status under which people can be granted refugee status and get protection. It was advised that European countries should already prepare themselves for such flow of refugees (Taylor, 2008 and Solana, 2008).

It is likely that had the Convention been drafted now, concern with the environment would have been more reflected in the text of the Convention. To stimulate schools and the community to teach about the environment (as the U.N. Committee on the Rights of the Child proposes in its *General Comment 1*, 2001) "and actively involve children in local regional or global environmental projects" is a good idea. However, it seems to me, that promoting *child impact statement*s by local, regional and national governments would have more meaningful. With such statements (Corrigan, 2007) local authorities would have been compelled to think about the impact a decision (to build a road, develop a certain industry etc.) potentially can have on the lives of children.

In September 1990 world leaders committed themselves that they "will work for common measures for the protection of the environment, at all levels, so that all children can enjoy a safer and healthier future", as was formulated in the World Declaration on the Survival, Protection and Development of Children of 1990, paragraph 20 (9). One of the biggest changes since the adoption of the U.N. Convention on the Rights of the Child is that twenty years ago 6 percent of the world's population lived in cities of over 5 million people. According to data from the United Nations Population Bureau this is now 9 percent (up from 308 million to 520 million). With the growth of megacities, the slums are also growing. During the drafting process of the Convention the majority of the world population lived in rural areas, now the balance tipped and the majority of the world population lives in urban areas. The pace of the changes is scary and we are faced with enormous challenges.

HIV/AIDS

In 1981 the first article was published about to the symptoms of AIDS and in 1982 for the first time the term Acquired Immune Deficiency Syndrome was used. In the meantime AIDS has begun to cause a social and economic crisis and even threatened economic stability in many African countries. "HIV/AIDS has become a human security and governance issue, with the potential to undo decades of human, economic and national development and progress in Southern Africa" (Pharaoh and Schönteig, 2003). Many children or grandparents now care for their siblings because their parents have died from AIDS. Many teachers have died from AIDS as well. Fifteen million children under 15 years of age have lost one or both parents due to AIDS it was reported.[52] According to Linda Richter (Richter, 2008) 2 million children were living with HIV in 2007 and 90% of them in Sub-Saharan Africa (and only 10% received ARV's). The many orphans and children of "child-headed households" (Kesbey *et al.*, 2006) have confronted people in child protection and the rights of the child field with new challenges. Many adolescent girls are at risk to be infected. Antiretroviral drugs are still expensive and many governments cannot buy them at the scale that is needed and individuals for instance in Sub-Saharan Africa cannot afford them. And the same is the situation with many medicines for other illnesses. Article 24 (child's right to health and health services) does not address specifically the issue of HIV/AIDS. A year after the adoption of the U.N. Convention on the Rights of the Child world leaders meeting in New York included [the prevention of] children dying from AIDS as one of their challenges. However, in the paragraphs in the World Declaration on the Survival, Protection and Development of Children about their *Commitment* no further reference has been made to this enormous problem.

Progress in Medical Sciences

With the progress of medical science techniques like In Vitro Fertilization (IVF), fertilizing manually in the laboratory dish an egg and sperm, gave hope to women who could not conceive a child. But with progress in this field extreme situations also occur. Already (still a very small number of) women at an age in which others retire now become mothers.[53]

The fast progressing medical techniques create new ethical dilemmas. The right to know your background seems to be more relevant than ever. In some countries data of donors of sperm are better registered now. In the Netherlands for instance all sperm, egg and embryo donors are registered since 2004 by a special foundation (Stichting Donorgegevens Kunstmatige Bevruchting).[54] In the light of the new fast progressing medical science it can be noted that article 7 does not include the right to see the birth records of or the background of the donor. Article 7 of the CRC (the right to identity) was not drafted for "test tube" babies, but was more

---

[52] (UNAIDS/WHO, 2006).

[53] The Independent newspaper in an article by Maxine Frith reported about a woman who at 63 became the oldest mother in Britain, after fertility treatment in Italy. "Maxine Frith, mother of 63 defends decision to have a baby", in: *The Independent*, 5 May 2006.

[54] The address of this Foundation is: PO Box 16077, 2500 BB The Hague, the Netherlands.

drafted with the sad history of Argentinian disappeared children in mind who were given for adoption to people associated with the military junta.

In countries in Asia (India and Pakistan for instance) boys are valued more by many parents and ultrasound makes it in the early stages possible to see if the mother is expecting a boy or a girl. When a girl is expected often an abortion is carried out (Dagar, 2007). In many West European countries the alumin method makes gender selection possible, because the X (responsible for baby girls) or Y chromosome can be determined and separated. Some private clinics promote this as a method of "family balancing". In Europe more prenatal screening (not for gender selection) is taking place. Such screening on a large scale led in the Netherlands often to stopping of the pregnancy if a child with a handicap such as spina bifida was expected.[55] Certainly the large scale in which abortions are carried out in Asia (made possible by the new echoscope techniques) was not foreseen by the drafters of the Convention.

In the field of child and adolescent pharmacology (Deveaugh-Geiss *et al.*, 2006) it seems that the pharmaceutical industry and academia "have not shared an agenda for research in children and adolescents". Nevertheless more children are receiving drug treatment (Zito, 2000), especially related to a diagnosis of one of the types of Attention-Deficit/Hyperactivity Disorder (ADHD). In the past two decades after the adoption of the Convention, many children who were found to be very impulsive, hyperactive or inattentive, could stay in school with the help of methylphenidate. However, the use of this medication has also been advised by teachers or heads of schools, which is illegal. In the field of medical research of psychiatric syndromes and pharmacology the last decade of research saw advances in statistical methodologies and laboratory-based gene-hunting techniques. We can expect that we will see the next years more understanding of biological and environmental factors that contribute to mental illness. According to Matthew State *et al.* (2000) "researchers are on the verge of identifying and characterizing genetic vulnerabilities involved in common childhood psychiatric syndromes".

Conclusion: It Is Time to Review the CRC

The U.N. Convention on the Rights of the Child was adopted in a period of optimism, when the Cold War seemed to come to an end. On the day the Convention was adopted (20 November 1989) the Romanian Embassy in Berlin was sending a memorandum to the Ministry of Foreign Affairs in Bucharest regarding "the state of the internal political situation in the German Democratic Republic, the

---

[55] (Zuijderland in the *NRC Handelsblad*, 2010).

uncertainty of the future of the GDR, protests by citizens of the GDR in front of the Romanian Embassy and the need for change in the Romanian approaches to relations with the GDR".[56] Eleven days before the adoption of the Convention on the Rights of the Child the Berlin Wall fell. The German Socialist State came to an end on October 3, 1990. The Soviet Union collapsed in 1991. The above mentioned telegram was send to the government of the Rumanian President Gheorghe Ceauşecu, who was executed a month after the adoption of the U.N. Convention on the Rights of the Child (Ceauşescu was executed on December 25, 1989).

The cold war period was not an easy time for many children and adolescents. Sibylle Escalona (1965, 1982), Milton Schwebel (1982) and John Mack (1981) found that many young people in these Cold War years were deeply troubled and in real fear of a nuclear war (Sommers, 1986). The first studies on this issue dated from the time of the Berlin crisis of 1961 and the Cuban crisis in 1962. Some feeling of pessimism from the cold war years might have been related to worries of children, although Beardslee and Mack (1983) also thought that changing patterns of family structure and other issues could have influenced the results of the studies. When world leaders met in New York for the World Summit on Children in September 1990 and they formulated their joint commitment "to give every child a better future", a more optimistic atmosphere could be felt than in the height of the Cold War. There was, by the way, some backtracking in the text of the Declaration of the world leaders in 1990 as compared to the commitments in the U.N. Convention on the Rights of the Child (Brodie-Olles and Veerman, 1990).

The Dutch historian of childhood Dasberg (1975) has written that the child is not only socially, economically but also historically defined. Elsewhere[57] I have described how the ideas concerning the rights of the child are dependent upon the prevailing image of childhood and when that image changes, the ideas on the rights of the child also change.

In 1978, the year that Poland brought the idea of a Convention on the Rights of the Child to the U.N., Bill Gates presented the MS-DOS system for computers and in 1979 Texas Instruments introduced the personal computer (TI-99/4). In 1979 Mr. R. Frenkel (of Bell Labs) filed his patent for a cellular radiotelephone system. From the year the Convention on the Rights of the Child was debated in the United Nations the speed of the technological developments was enormous. Of course, many children and adolescents in the world still do not benefit from these developments, but for many mobile phones, a pc or a laptop, texting messages, e-mailing and being on the internet have become a part of life. The new developments

---

[56] Archives of the Ministry of Foreign Affair, Berlin. Available from the Cold War International History Project of the Woodrow Wilson International Center for Scholars in Washington D.C. <www.CWIHP.org>.

[57] See the Chapter "To What Extent Did the Image of Childhood Change?" (Veerman, 1992).

call for new ways of protecting children. At the same time new insights from medical science call for prolonging the period of special protection to emerging adulthood and in several countries protection measures for adolescents are being extended to this age group of young people of over 18 years of age. More studies on the issue of child development are needed and it seems too quick now to enter a track of drastic new legal 'borders' and extend childhood by a few years. However, one cannot close ones eyes for new relevant data from the medical sciences. At least people from the child rights community have to study the new research data concerned and debate its consequences for children's rights.

As we compare the research on young people who misuse alcohol and/or drugs or can (like adults) become addicted, with the text of the relevant articles of the Convention, we can conclude that the Convention often does not look relevant for the realities of our children and adolescents. Excessive use of the computer, on-line-gaming or addiction to on-line-gambling could not have been foreseen by the drafters of the U.N. Convention on the Rights of the Child, but make the Convention look 'old'.

Technology can be a positive force but, as discussed, it is also easy to use modern technology for bullying, seducing young people to undress in front of webcams or even to meet adults whose intentions are to bring children into prostitution. When most were celebrating the 20th anniversary of the U.N. Convention on the Rights of the Child by again talking about the drafting process and the achievements, it started to dawn on some that the Convention might not be up to date any more. A now former British Labour Member of Parliament, Mr. Derek Wyatt, circulated last year a petition[58] to the U.N. Committee on the Rights of the Child "on behalf of the children of the world" to "examine and assess whether the Convention on the Rights of the Child fully addresses the needs and expectations of children in a digital age". Will Gardner of Childnet International has written to me: "we do see that technology has become integral to educational and social lives of our children, and has become so relevant to many of the key children's rights – to privacy, access to mass medias and protection from sexual exploitation, freedom of expression, to mention some examples. The importance of technology is fundamental".[59] Basic principles from the Convention as the best interests of the child, the evolving capacities of the child and the rights to participation and be heard will, as it seems now, still in the years to come guide us. But we face new challenges. Were we in the past concerned that children would not have enough access to information, now they are swamped with information. Amy Jordan writes that "it is likely that in the decade to come, regulators will need to rethink the original premise of much of what has driven media policy" (Jordan,

[58] See : http://www.derekwyattmp.co.uk.
[59] Personal e-mail from Will Gardner, CEO of Childnet International. See also the work of this Group on their website: www.childnet.com.

2008). I believe we also have to rethink the content of the U.N. Convention in the Rights of the Child.

Some Proposals

Much of what is happening can be seen as a positive development for children's rights. Expressing an opinion and access to information has become a lot easier. Society has become less paternalistic. However, as discussed in this article, the chances that children cannot foresee if they put themselves in possible danger, have also increased. The chance that children will be abused increased. New challenges and new dangers make it therefore unavoidable to review the text of the Convention itself. Some (international) organizations have already started to formulate guidelines in new fields of concern. The International Telecommunications Union (ITU, 2009) is leading the way here with their Guidelines for Child On-Line Protection. Such Guidelines and reports from different fields can serve as a starting point of the new debate. Twenty years after the adoption of the U.N. Convention on the Rights of the Child most authors (with the exception of Freeman, 2000)[60] still stay uncritical of the Convention itself. It is time to tone down our euphoria and find remedies for where the U.N. Convention on the Rights of the Child does not give protection to children. The speed of the developments call for an evaluation how up to date the U.N. Convention on the Rights of the Child is.

Of course two Optional Protocols[61] have been adopted and a third is under consideration, but this should, in my opinion, mainly be seen as a 'correction mechanism' of mistakes during the drafting process rather than a reflection on a fast changing society.

To be more in line with modern ways of communication the Chair of the Committee on the Rights of the Child could already start writing a blog on the UNHCHR's website and the meetings of the Committee could be made available

---

[60] Michael Freeman wrote in 2000 that "the Convention on the Rights of the Child is an imperfect instrument and new Conventions or Protocols need to address many children whose rights are currently neglected".

[61] Optional Protocol to the Convention on the Rights of the Child on the sale of children, child prostitution and child pronography, *General Assembly of the United Nations Resolution 54/263* (New York, 25 May 2000) and the Optional Protocol to the Convention on the Rights of the Child on the involvement of children in armed conflict, *General Assembly of the United Nations, resolution 54/263* (New York, 25 May 2000). On March 24, 2010 the U.N. Human Rights Council in Geneva agreed to start drafting a new Optional Protocol to the Convention on the Rights of the Child to provide a Communications procedure (to receive and provide communications from children and their representatives alleging violations of their rights). See: Human Rights Council document A/HRC/13/L.5.

on the web. At the website of the International Criminal Court[62] one can for instance watch sessions of the court. That could also be possible with the Committee's constructive dialogues with the State Parties. The Chair of the U.N. Committee on the Rights of the Child could also Twitter what is happening in the Committee. Here the medium is the message. Using modern communication techniques will help to close the gap somewhat with young people. This is especially of importance now a Third Optional Protocol (on communications with the Committee) is under consideration. Until now it looked like the Committee did not understand the media many children use. Here the Committee does not stand alone and the members share this with many other adults. As Amy Jordan writes: "In all likelihood, the media will continue to evolve rapidly (...) leaving the generation gap as wide as ever".[63]

For the U.N. Committee on the Rights of the Child a good start would be the appointment of a Working Group, followed by a new General Discussion Day of the Committee to give the opportunity to representatives from the different professional fields to speak. The U.N. Convention on the Rights of the Child itself does not foresee a broad or systematic review after several years by for instance an Assembly of the States Parties. But it seems in the light of the above a relevant idea (although it should be proposed by a State Party and needs to be prepared meticulously).

References

Abebe, T., "Changing Livelihoods, Changing Childhoods: Patterns of Children's Work in Rural Southern Ethiopia", *Children's Geographies*, 2009, (5 (12)), 77-93.

Adam, S., "French Curb on Alcohol Sales as teenagers discover le Binge Drinking", *The Times*, 2008 (August 26).

American Psychiatric Association, *Diagnostic and Statistical Manual of Mental Disorders*, fourth edition, DSM-IV-TR, (Arlington, VA, APA, 2000).

American Psychiatric Association, "APA Announces Draft Diagnostic Criteria for DSM-5", *Press release*, (Arlington, VA, APA, 2010).

Arnett, J. J., *Emerging Adulthood: the Winding Road from Late Teens through the Twenties* (Oxford, Oxford University Press, 2004).

Arnett, J. J., "Emerging Adulthood: Understanding the New Way of Coming of Age", in: Arnett, J. J. and Tanner, J. L., *Emerging Adults in America: Coming of Age in the 21st Century*, (APA books, Arlington, VA, 2006) 3-19.

Astley, S., *Diagnostic Guide for Foetal Alcohol Spectrum Disorders: The 4-Digit Diagnostic Code* (University of Washington, Seattle, 2004).

Beardslee, W. R. and Mack, J., "Adolescents and the Threat of Nuclear War; the Evolution of a Perspective", *Yale Journal of Biology and Medicine*, 1983 (56), 79-91.

Beintema., N., "We zijn erg laat volwassen", *NRC Weekblad* (*Wetenschap*), 2009, (25-31 (July)).

---

[62] See: www.icc-cpi.int. The ICC is also on Twitter.
[63] Jordan, op. cit.

Bloch, A., Sigona, N. and Zetter, R., *No Right to dream; The Social and Economic Lives of Young Undocumented Migrants in Britain* (London, Paul Hamlyn Foundation, 2009).

Bolopion, Ph., "2007, nouvelle année-record pour la production d' ópium en Afghanistan", *Le Monde*, 2008 (June (27)).

Bongaarts, J., "Population Aging and the Rising Cost of Public Pensions", *Population and Development Review*, 2005 (30) 1-23.

Brodie-Olles, M. and Veerman, P. E., "A World Summit for Children", *The Jerusalem Post*, 1990, (September (23)).

Cao, F. and Sue, L., "Internet Addiction among Chinese Adolescents: Prevalence and Psychological Features", *Child Care, Health and Development*, 2007, (May) 275-271.

Calvert, S. L., "Children as Consumers: Advertising and Marketing", *The Future of Children*, 2008 (18 (1)), 205.

Caro-Rojas, F., *La Colombie et le Traffic de Cocaine 2004-2005*, (Capacite Interuniversitaire Parisienne d'Addictologie Clinique, 2005).

Castells, M. *et al.*, *Mobile Communication and Society: A Global Perspective* (Cambridge, MA, MIT Press, 2007).

Center on Alcohol Marketing and Youth, *Still Growing after all These Years: Youth Exposure to Alcohol Advertising on Television 2001-2005*, (Washington, D.C., CAMY, 2006).

China Daily, "The More they Play, the More they Lose", 2007 (April (10)).

Conisbee, M. and Simms, A., *Environmental Refugees: the Case for Recognition* (London, New Economics Foundation, 2003).

Cooper, D., *Psychiatry and Anti-Psychiatry*, (London, Penguin Books, 1967).

Cornia, G.A., editor, *Harnessing Globalisation for Children: A Report to UNICEF*, (Florence, UNICEF Innocenti Research Institute, 1991).

Corrigan, C., "Child Impact Statements: Protecting Children's Interests in Policy and Provision?", *Journal of Children's Services*, 2007, (2, 4)), 30-43.

Cortese, G., "Identities, Subjectivities and Language in Juvenile Alcohol Issues", *International Journal of Children's Rights*, 2010, (18 (2)) 233-252.

Cross., M., "Ethiopia's Digital Dream: After Years of Turmoil, a New Revolution is Sweeping the Land", *The Guardian Weekly*, 2007, (August (19-25)) 27.

Crumley, B., "French Combat Youth Binge-Drinking", *Time*, 2008 (July (17)).

Dagar, R., "Rethinking Female Foeticide; Perspectives and Issues", in: Putel, T. (editor), *Sex Selective Abortions in India: Gender, Society and New Reproductive Techniques*, (New Delhi, Sage Publications, 2007).

Dasberg, L., *Grootbrengen door Kleinhouden, als Historisch Verschijnsel*, (Meppel, Boom, 1975) [in Dutch].

Declas, M., "En Colombie, la chute de 'Don Mario', l'un des barons du trafic de drogue", *Le Monde*, 2009 (April 17).

De Waal, M., "Ook leger wijkt nu voor kartels", *NRC Handelsblad*, 2009 (23 April) [in Dutch].

De Wit, D. *et al.*, "Age of First Alcohol Use: A Risk Factor for the Development of Alcohol Disorders", in: *Am. J. Psychiatry*, 2000 (157), 745-755.

Detrick, S., (editor), *The United Nations Convention on the Rights of the Child, A Guide to the 'Travaux Préparatoires'*, (Dordrecht, Martinus Nijhoff Publishers, 1992).

Deveaugh-Geiss, J. *et al.*, "Child and Adolescent Psychopharmacology in the New Millennium: A Workshop for Academia, Industry and the Government", *J. Am. Acad. Child. Adolesc. Psychiatry*, 2006 45 (3)) 261-270.

Doreleijers, Th., *Te oud voor het servet, te jong voor het tafellaken*, (Leiden, Universiteit Leiden, 2009).

Doreleijers, Th., "Berecht adolescenten niet als volwassenen, verhoog de leeftijdsgrens van het volwassen strafrecht van 18 naar 23 jaar", *NRC Handelsblad*, 2009 (8 mei) [in Dutch].

Dougherty, L.R., *et al*, "Increased Waking Saliva, Cortisol and Depression Risk in Preschoolers; the Role of the History of Maternal Depression and early Childhood Depression", *J. of Child psychiatry and Psychology*, (2009) (50)12)), 1495-1503.

Doward, J., "Crackdown to tackle behavior of Britain's antisocial teenagers", *The Guardian Weekly* 2008 (June 6), 13.

Dowdney, L., *Children of the Drug Trade, a Case Study of Children and Organized Armed Violence in Rio*, (Rio de Janeiro, Viva Rio Association, 2003).

Dreher, A., Gaston, N. and Martens, P., *Measuring Globalisation, Gauging its Consequences*, (New York, N.Y., Springer, 2008).

Edmonds, E. V., "Reduciert die Globalisierung die Kinderarbeit?" *Neue Zurcher Zeitung*, 2002, (23/24 (February)).

End Child Prostitution Child Pornography and Trafficking of Children for Sexual Purposes, *Protecting Children Online: An ECPAT Guide*, (Bangkok, ECPAT International, 2000).

European Monitoring Centre for Drugs and Drug Addiction, *Children's Voices: Experiences and Perceptions of European Children on Drug and Alcohol Issues*, (Lisbon, EMCDDA, 2010).

Eijsvogel, J. and Rijlaarsdam, B. "We hebben een WHO voor het internet nodig; Eureopees initiatief Hirsch Ballin", NRC Handelsblad, 2010 (June 3).

Ek, S. (of Swedish Save the Children), editor , *Legislative History of the Convention on the Rights of the Child*, (New York and Geneva, United Nations, 2007), Vol. I., 310-35.

El Marroun, H., *Prenatal Cannabis Exposure and Infant Development*, (Rotterdam, Erasmus University, Faculty of Medicine, 2010).

Ernst, T., *et al*, "Evidence for Long-term Neurotoxicity Associated with Metamphitamine Abuse", *Neurology*, 2000 (51) 109-125.

Escalona, S., Children and the Threat of Nuclear War, in: Schwebel, M., editor, *Behavioural and Human Survival* (Palo Alto, A Science and Behavioral Book, 1965).

Escalona, S., "Growing up with the Fear of Nuclear War: Some Indirect Effects on Personality Development", *American Journal of Orthopsychiatry*, 1982, (52) 4)) 600-607.

Essau, C. A. and Hutchinson, D., "Alcohol Use, Abuse and Dependence", in: Essau, C. A., editor, *Adolescent Addiction: Epidemiology, Assessment and Treatment*, (London, Burlington MA and San Diego, CA, 2008), 61-116.

Freeman, M., The Future of Children's Rights, in: *Children and Society*, 2000, (14) 277-293.

GGZ-Rijnmond, *Zwangerschap en het gebruik van verslavende middelen*, [Pregnancy and the Use of Addictive Drugs], Rotterdam, Health Services in the Greater Rotterdam Area, 2007). [in Dutch].

Goggin, G., *Cell Phone Culture: Mobile Technology in Everyday Life* (London, Routledge, 2006).

Gogtay, N., Dynamic Mapping of Human Cortical Development During Childhood through Early Adulthood, in: *Proc. Nati. Acad. Sci. USA*, 2004, (101 (21)) 8184-8170.

Goldstein, J., Freud, A. and Solnit, A., *Before the Best Interests of the Child* (New York, Free Press, 1970).

Grifith, M., "Internet and Video-Game Addiction", in: Essau, C. A., editor , *Adolescent Addiction, Epidemiology, Assessment and Treatment*, (London, Burlington MA and San Diego, Academic Press, 2008), 231-265.

Hall, W., Degenhardt, L. and Patton, D., "Cannabis Abuse and Dependence", in: Essau, C. A., editor, *Adolescent Addiction: Epidemiology, Assessment and Treatment*, London, Burlington , MA and San Diego, CA, Academic Press, 2008), 139-145.

Health Council of the Netherlands (Gezondheidsraad), *Alcohol Consumption Related to Conception, Pregnancy and Breastfeeding*, (the Hague, Gezondheidsraad, 2005) [originally published in Dutch in 2004].

Hagers, M., "De waanzin van vroeg te kiezen", *NRC Handelsblad*, 2008 (9 and 10 February) [in Dutch].

Hardin, M. G. and Ernst, M., "Functional Brain Imaging and Development Related Risks and Vulnerability for Substance Abuse in Adolescents", *J. of Addiction Medicine*, 2009 (3 (2)) 47-54.

Hastings, G. *et al.*, "Alcohol Marketing and Young People's Drinking: A Review of the Research", *J. of Public Health* 2005 (26), 296-311.

Hodgkin, R. and Newell, P., *Implementation Handbook for the Convention of the Rights of the Child* (New York and Geneva, UNICEF, 2002).

International Telecommunication Union (ITU), *Guidelines for Child Online Protection* (Geneva, ITU, 2009).

Iten, P. X. and Oestreich, A., "Gamma-hydroxybutyrate (GHB): A New Generation of Drugs from the Chemical Shelf", *CHIMIA International Journal for Chemistry*, 2002 (56 (3)), 91-95.

Jordan, A. B., "Children's Media Policy", *The Future of Children*, 2008 (18 (1)), 2008, 235.

Kerbusch, M. and Feltzer, M. J. A., "Achttien Jaar, Hoera of Ojee", *Mobiel, Tijdschrift voor Pleegzorg*, 2006 (33) 5-7.

Kesbey, M. *et al.*, "Theorizing Other, 'Other Childhoods': Issues Emerging from Work on HIV in Urban and Rural Zimbabwe", *Children's Geographies*, 2006, (4 (2)) 185-202.

Key, E. , *The Century of the Child* (New York and London, G. P. Putnam and Sons, 1909), originally published in Swedish in 1900.

Kievits, F. and Adriaanse, M. T., "Prenatale Kindermishandeling", *Nederlands Tijdschrift voor Geneeskunde*, 2007 (151), 2231.

Kim, B. N., "From Internet to 'family-Net': Internet Addict vs. Digital Leader, in: *2007 International Symposium on the Counseling and Treatment of Youth Internet Addiction*, (Seoul, Korea, National Youth Commission, 2007), 196.

Knip, K., "Ja, de mens verandert het klimaat", *NRC Handelsblad*, 2007 (January 30).

Koob, G. and Kreek, M. J., "Dysregulation and Reward Pathways and the Transition to Drug Dependence", *Am. J. Psychiatry*, 2007, (184 (8), 1149-1159.

Koob, G. and LeMoal, M., "Addiction and the Brain Antireward System", *Ann. Rev. Psychol.*, 2008, (59), 29-53.

Koopman, E., "Cocathee ja, cocaine nee", *Trouw, de Verdieping*, 2008 (December 4).

Laing, R. D., *The Divided Self; An Existential Study in Society and Madness* (London, Penguin Books, 1960).

Laing, R. D. and Esterson, A., *Society, Madness and the Family*, (London, Penguin Books, 1964).

Lenhart, A., *et al*, *The Rise of the Instant-Messaging Generation and the Internet; Impact on Friendship and Family Relations* (Washington D.C., Pew Internet and American Life Project, 2010).

Lenhart, A. *et al.*, *Teens and Mobile Phones* (Washington D.C., Pew Internet and American Life Project, 2010).

Lenhart, A., *Cyberbullying 2010: What Research Tells Us*, (Washington D.C., Pew Internet and American Life Project, 2010).

Lenhart, A., *et al.*, *Teens and Technology: Youth Are Leading the Transition to a Fully Wired and Mobile Nation* (Washington D.C., Pew Internet and American Life Project, 2005).

Lenhart, A., Teens, *Teenage Life Online*, (Washington D.C., Pew Internet and American Life Project, 2001).

Lenhart, A., *The Internet and Education*, (Washington D.C., The American Life and Internet project, 2001).

Levitt, P. "Prenatal Effects of Drugs of Abuse on Brain Development", *Drug Alcohol Depen.*, 1998 (5) 109-125.

Lewinn, K., *et al*, "Elevated maternal Cortisol Levels During Pregnancy associated with Reduced Childhood IQ", *Int. J. Epidemiology*, 2009 (38 (6)), 1700-1710.

Liddle, H. A., *Multidimensional Family Therapy for Adolescents Drug Abuse: Clinician's Manual*, (Center City, MN, Hazelden Publishing Comp., 2009).

Mack, J. E., "Psychosocial Effects of the Nuclear Arms Race", *The Bulletin of the Atomic Scientists*, 1981, (37 (4)), 18-23.

Mayers, B., "An Interview with Gerge Koob" on: Close to Home-Science, Mayers on Addiction, Public Broadcasting organization: www.closetohome-science.

McArdle, P., "Social and Political Implications", in: Essau, C. A., editor, *Adolescent Addiction: Epidemiology, Assessment and Treatment* (London, Burlington, MA and San Diego, CA, Academic Press, 2008) 315-326.

Miller, W. R. and Rollninck, S., *Motivational Interviewing, preparing people for change*, (New York, Guilford Press, 2002).

Monshouwer, K. *et al.*, *Jeugd en Riskant Gedrag, Kerngegevens uit het Peilstation 2003* (Utrecht, Trimbos Instituut, 2004).

Mojumdar, A., "Verslaafde baby's in Afghanistan", *NRC Handelsblad*, 2010 (June 9).

Nicholson, K. L. and Balster, R. L., "GHB: a New and Novel Drug of Abuse", *Drug and Alcohol Dependence*, 2001 (63), 1-22.

Nordström, T., "Per Capita Alcohol Consumption and All-Cause Mortality in 14 European Countries", *Addiction*, 2001, (96) S. 113-128 (Supplement).

Nulman, I., *et al.*, "Neurodevelopment of Adopted Children Exposed in Utero to Cocaine: the Toronto Adoption Study", *Clin. Invest. Med.*, 2001 (24) 129-127.

Pharoah, R. and Schönteig, *AIDS, Security and Governance in Southern Africa, Exploring the Impact*, 2003 (Tshwane/Pretoria, Institute for Security Studies, ISS, South Africa), ISS paper 65.

Pilkington, E., "Global Graying Will Test Rich and Poor Nations", *The Guardian Weekly*, 2009 (27 July).

Ramdhanie, S., "Bolita's Sikken voor Mama", *De Volkskrant*, 2005 (August 11) [in Dutch].

Richter, L., *No Small Issue: Children and Families, Universal Action*, (Human Sciences Research Council, Tshwane/Pretoria, 2008).

Roberts, D. F. and Foehr, U. G., "Trends in Media Use", *The Future of Children*, 2008 (18 (1)) 11-37.

Rodgers, J. *et al.*, "Liquid Ecstasy: a New Kid on the Dance Floor", *British J. of Psychiatry* 2004 (184), 104-106.

Safer, D. J., *et al*, "Increased Methylphenidate Usage for Attention Deficit Disorder in the 1990s", *Pediatrics*, 1996 (98 (6)) 1084-1088.

Save the Children UK, *Legacy Of Disasters, The Impact Of Climate Change On Children* (London, Save the Children UK, 2007).

Schneider, A. J. *et al.*, "Zwangere verslaafde prostituées: soms gedwongen opname in het belang van het kind", *Nederlands Tijdschrift voor Geneeskunde*, 2004 (148 (October)), 1949-1952.

Sheridan, M., "China's Parents Try Shock Tactics to Cure Net Addicts", *The Sunday Times* 2009 (June 7).

Sommers, F. G. *et al.*, "Children In Fear of Nuclear War", *World Health Forum*, 1986, (7), 399.

State, M. W. *et al.*, "The Genetics of Childhood Psychiatric Disorders: A Decade of Progress", in: *J. Am. Acad. Child Adolesc. Psychiatry*, 2000 (39 (8)), 946-962.

Stolz, J., " 'Saint' des pauvres et des 'narcos'; Mexicains, Jésus Malverde ne cesse d'attirer des nouveaux fidèles", *Le Monde*, 2008 (Mardi 22 Jullet) 2008.

Szasz, T., *Myth and Mental Illness; Foundations of a Theory of Personal Conduct*, (New York, Harper & Row, 1961).

Snik, G., "Ontwikkeling en Opvoeding", in: Van Haaften, A. W. *et al.*, *Ontwikkelingsfilosofie*, (Muiderberg, Coutinho, 1986).

Schwebel, M., "Effects of the Nuclear War Threat on Children and Teenagers: Implications for Professionals, *American Journal of Orthopsychiatry*, 1982 (52 (4)) 608-618.

The Joint United Nations Program on HIV/AIDS, *2008 Report on the Global AIDS Epidemic*, (Geneva UNAIDS, 2008).

United Nations Children's Fund, *Enhanced Protection for Children Affected by AIDS*, (New York, N.Y., UNICEF, 2007).

United Nations Committee on the Rights of the Child, *The Aims of Education (article 29)*, *General Comments*, 17 April 2001, CRC/GC/2001/1.

United Nations Office on Drugs and Crime, *Solvent Abuse among Street Children in Pakistan*, (Islamabad, UNODC Country Office for Pakistan, 2004).

United Nations, *Declaration on the Guiding Principles of Drug Demand Reduction*, (New York, U.N. 2003), A/RES/S-20/3, General Assembly, 9th Plenary Meeting, (1998) (June 10).

Van Dalen, H. and Engelen, E., editors, "Krimp: zegen of vloek?" [introduction to the special issue of B&M], *B&M, Tijdschrift Beleid, Politiek en Maatschappij*, 2008, (35(4)).

Van Dalen, H., "De angst voor Bevolkingskrimp, vergrijzing en bevolkingspolitiek", *TB&M Tijdschrift Beleid, Politiek en Maatschappij*, 2008 (35 (4)), 257.

Van der Stel, J. C., *Drinken, Drank en Dronkenschap; Vijf Eeuwen Drankbestrijding en Alcoholhulpverlening in Nederland*, (Uitgeverij Verloren, Hilversum, 1995) [in Dutch].

Van den Brink, W., "Verslaving: een chronische recidiverende hersenziekte", *Justitiële Verkenningen*, 2006, (8 (6)) 59-75.

Varvarigou, A. *et al*, "Effects of Maternal Smoking on Cord Blood Estriol, Placental Lactogen, Chorionic Gonadotropin, FSH, CH and Cortisol", *J. of Perinatal Medicine*, 2009, (37 (4)), 364-369.

Veerman, P. E., *The Rights of the Child and the Changing Image of Childhood*, (Dordrecht, Boston and London, Martinus Nijhoff Publishers, 1992).

Warman, M., "One Laptop per Child; How Technology and the OLPC Movement Has Become Key Factors in Rwanda's Economic Growth", *The Telegraph*, 2009 (October 1).

Wikström, A-K *et al*, "Tobacco Use During Pregnancy and Preeclampsia Risk", *Hypertension*, 2010 (22) 1254.

Winnicott, D. W., "Transitional Objects and Transitional Phenomena - A Study of the First Not-Me Possession", *International Journal of Psycho-Analysis*, 1953, (34) 89-97.

Working Group on Children and the Media: *Report to the Committee on the Rights of the Child* (Geneva, Center for Human Rights/United Nations High Commissioner for Human Rights, May 1997).

Zito, J. M. *et al*, "Trends in the Prescribing of Psychotropic Medications in Preschoolers", *JAMA Journal of the American Medical Association*, 2000 (283) 1025-1030.

Zucker, A. A. and Light, D., "Laptops for Students", *Science*, 2009, (23 (5910)), 82-85.

Zuijderland, M. "Weghalen van Foetus met Afwijking is legitiem", *NRC Handelsblad*, 2010 (June 4).

Not Merely Rights for Children but Children's Rights: The theory Gap and the Assumption of the Importance of Children's Rights

Lucinda Ferguson
University Lecturer in Family Law, University of Oxford;
Tutorial Fellow in Law, Oriel College, Oxford
lucinda.ferguson@law.ox.ac.uk

1. Introduction

In a recent discussion of the difficulties that arise in legal practice through the use of 'children's rights'[1] arguments, Martin Guggenheim (2005) asks 'who would be comfortable being anti-children's rights?' (p. xiii).[2] I suggest that not many people would. Herein lies the essential difficulty. The theoretical debates that took place throughout the 1980s and 1990s over what it means to say that children have rights failed to reach a consensus on how best to understand the notion of children's rights. No proposed theoretical basis for children's rights was (and is) without its difficulties, including the most successful proposals advocated by Eekelaar (1992, 1994, 1998) and Freeman (1983, especially ch. 3).[3]

---

[1] For the purpose of my discussion, I understand a 'right' to be a relational claim, capable of being asserted against specific individuals or the community at large, giving rise to a duty in those specific individuals or in the population as a whole to render some performance vis-à-vis the rights-holder, and in some sense an imperative in legal reasoning. In terms of Hohfeld's analytical rights framework, this most strongly identifies with his notion of 'claim rights', though operates together with certain elements of the three other heads of rights Hohfeld identified.

Hohfeld identified four types of rights: (1) claim rights, (2) liberty rights or privileges, (3) powers or abilities, and (4) immunities. See discussion in Wesley Newcomb Hohfeld in W Cook, ed., *Fundamental Legal Conceptions* (New Haven: Yale University Press, 1919). Whilst these are four distinct types of rights, they are purely conceptual notions. As such, they can be seen to work conjunctively in relation to any single assertion of a legal right, such as a child's right to education, free speech, or free assembly. In addition, since Hohfeldian rights are intended as conceptual tools only, they are not subject to criticism on the grounds that they do not explain legal understandings of particular rights, or that they do not fit with our moral rights theories.

[2] Guggenheim himself argues against rights for children within the family. For critical discussion of his thesis, see Freeman (2006); Federle (2009).

[3] Federle's (1994; 1995) 'empowerment perspective' also adds an important dimension to this discussion. Both Eekelaar (1994; 1998) and Freeman (1983) adopt 'modified will theory'

Yet, rights language continues to be widely employed, and even relied upon, in many situations involving the legal treatment of children.

In this article, I understand 'children's rights' to refer to a class of rights that includes both rights targeted specifically at children and rights in relation to which the identity of the right-holder, who happens to be a child, is critical. The law proceeds with apparent lack of concern over the absence of any agreed-upon theoretical account of children's rights. Describing the larger theoretical debate over the nature of rights as 'somewhat esoteric', Dwyer (2006) notes that 'few people need [this theoretical debate] resolved before they are willing to attribute rights to children' (p. 291). This is at least in part because, of course, who amongst us would want to say that they were against giving children legal rights?

This desire to assign rights to children despite theoretical difficulties with children's rights is also a product of the confused conflation and disaggregation of different parts of the debate over rights for children. After outlining the distinction between rights for children and children's rights, I discuss why children's rights are important for children: what is at stake in the debate over the future of children's rights? Next, I consider how courts become confused in their application of children's rights principles to disputes involving children. I identify two sites of confusion: The first occurs at the content stage of the analysis, when the court is determining the content of a particular child's rights in a specific dispute. When deciding the content of a particular child's rights claims, the court's reasoning operates within the confines of one of the two conventional approaches to rights theory, the 'will theory' and the 'interest theory'. I argue that both of these theories, including attempts to modify one approach with insights from the other, fail as accounts of children's rights. The second site of confusion is at the 'framing' stage of the analysis, when the court is considering how to approach any particular dispute and how to evaluate competing interests, whether in respect of one or multiple individuals.

There is a sense in which a debate over the value of children's rights both begins and ends with the social construction of childhood. The modern conception of childhood sees children as distinctly set apart from adults, marked out by their dependency and vulnerability, yet at the same time inextricably

---

perspectives on the nature of children's rights. For further explanation, see section 4, below. Eekelaar (1994) is quite clear about the nature of his argument. He does not wish to demonstrate that children have rights, but rather to present a proper understanding of what we mean when we say that children have rights:

> [T]his is not an argument about what rights people, and children in particular, should have, nor even an argument that they should have *any* rights at all. It is merely an attempt to identify an essential element of decisions which recognize that people have rights (p. 49).

bound to adults by their inevitable process of becoming (themselves and adults).[4] In this way, our construction of childhood creates a situation in which contradictory impulses are inevitable. The very nature of the modern construction of childhood dictates a privileging of children's special interests at the same time as continuing to see children through the medium of adulthood to measure children's approach to that status. The law mediates this conception of childhood until the child enters legal adulthood. The notion of rights speaks directly to both the task of privileging particular interests and to that of regulating children as adults-in-becoming. The contradictory yet complementary nature of these tasks, however, suggests the inherent difficulty, perhaps impossibility, of developing a rights account that can reconcile the competing impulses whose irresolution defines the modern construction of childhood.

2. Rights for children and children's rights

The academic literature has continued to consider the scope and content of children's legal rights despite the uncertainty over the theoretical basis of children's rights. The theoretical dilemma has been avoided by the combination of two strategies in thinking about children and rights, disaggregating and conflating the legal practice and theoretical debates.

On the one hand, there has been a tendency to disaggregate the debate over the basis of children's rights as a matter of theory from the issue of children's rights in legal practice. There may be a sense in which some disaggregation is uncontroversial. Thus, Brighouse (2002) notes that there is a class of legal rights that '... do not reflect fundamental rights (at least in any straightforward way) but are none the worse for that: the right to drive an automobile, or to import sushi, for example' (p. 32). For such rights, we do not lose anything in terms of justifying the current scope, being able to predict or make reasoned argument as to its future application and development, by approaching the right without a clear view on its theoretical basis. The debate in this article is not focused on these bare legal rights, but on legal rights that do embody fundamental rights, both fundamental rights for all, including children, as well as specifically children's fundamental rights. It is in respect of this type of legal right that disaggregation is much more problematic.

In summarising the approach to children's rights taken by judges and practitioners Fortin (2009), for example, notes '... an unfortunate disjunction between theory and practice' (p. 29). This disaggregation is used to validate the

---

[4] For an excellent discussion of the modern conception of childhood, see Archard (2004, especially ch. 3).

assumption of the existence of children's rights in law, so that their interpretation and application can then become the focus of discussion, despite the irresolution of the larger, theoretical questions. O'Neill (1988) also disaggregates the two debates, but for an additional purpose: she aims to leave unchallenged children's positive legal rights, but to question the best theoretical account of children's rights. In particular, she contends

> ... that children's fundamental rights are best grounded by embedding them in a wider account of fundamental obligations, which can also be used to justify positive rights and obligations. We can perhaps go *further* to secure the ethical basis of children's positive rights if we do *not* try to base them on claims about fundamental rights (emphasis in original, pp. 445-46).

Yet, to the extent that this disaggregation relates to children's rights in particular, it is not clear that it is justifiable. If children's rights have a special nature because of the very identity of children as rights-holders,[5] then the failure to determine what this means in theoretical terms suggests critical difficulties for working with children's rights in the sphere of legal practice.

On the other hand, other participants in the legal context[6] have tended to conflate the theoretical and practical debates. Whilst the disaggregation engaged with children's rights as a separate class of rights, the conflation between the positive and theoretical status centres on a vision of the rights of children as either simply rights or as human rights. Both strategies have the laudable aim of enabling discussion of the children's legal rights whilst the theoretical debate remains unsettled. Hence, in critiquing one particular theory of rights, Dwyer (2006: 301) draws on the significance of legal practice and usage over time of the term 'rights' in respect of children.[7]

To the extent that children's rights are simply fundamental human rights for children, this conflation strategy is appealing. Herring (2011) comments that '... it is hard to resist the argument "children have human rights, because children are human"' (p. 434). Thus, we do not need to explore fully the theoretical basis

---

[5] Thus, for the purpose of this article, I understand 'children's rights' as encompassing rights where the fact that it is a child who is the rights-holder is critical to determining the scope and content of the right. This encompasses both additional rights given to (sometimes, some) children but not to adults, as well as fundamental human rights, the content of which is inextricably connected to the identity of the rights-holder.

[6] There is less evidence for such conflation in the theoretical literature. Griffin (2002), for example, begins his discussion of the rights of children as follows: 'Of course, children have legal rights. But do they also have human rights?' (p. 19). The clear distinction between the larger debate and legal practice makes sense here, of course, as there is no end-objective of underpinning the examination of children's rights in law.

[7] Dwyer himself employs this argument as part of the basis for his rejection of the 'will theory' of rights and endorsement of an 'interest theory' of rights for children.

for the right to life, for example, in respect of children in particular as that debate has already been settled to such an extent that we are happy to recognise Article 2, ECHR as containing a real right. Similarly, Article 3 has been successfully employed to enhance children's protection against physical punishment (*A v. UK* (1998), domestic reaction: s. 58, Children Act 2004). Even then, it does not help us determine the content of all fundamental human rights as they apply to children. So with the Article 9, ECHR right to freedom of religion, we cannot derive from the mere fact that the child is a human how she should be raised if her separated parents profess affiliations to different religious faiths.

The same difficulty arises in relation to this strategy as in relation to the first. Whilst both approaches appear to enable us to work around the theoretical difficulties and focus on children's legal rights in practice, the fact that the child is a rights-holder is critical to understanding the scope and content of the particular right in question. This means that, rather than enhancing children's status by conflating the theoretical and legal debates, we actually risk undermining much of what we hope to achieve.

Once we recognise that we cannot simply disaggregate or conflate various aspects of the theoretical and practice debate in order to focus on advancing children's legal rights, the significance of reinvigorating the theoretical debate becomes clear. Whilst it is intuitively appealing that children have rights, the critical difficulty is to determine whether we can say that they have *children's* rights – as opposed to the less interesting claim that they have certain fundamental human rights[8] – and what it means when we say that. In what follows, I argue that confusion over what it means to say that children have rights has led to judicial and legislative approaches that fail to realise fully the aspirations of rights for children.

My argument is not that children do not or should not have rights in the sense of any rights at all – to the extent that children possess at least some fundamental human rights, asking this question is an unnecessary distraction.[9] What I am concerned with are the difficulties that flow from the assertion that children have *children's* rights. Even then, I am not arguing that it is not *possible* that children do not or should not possess children's rights. For this reason, my argument is not to be aligned with Guggenheim's (2005), which

---

[8] Excepting, as above, that some fundamental human rights, such as the right to freedom of religion, may need to be seen as part of the debate over children's rights, rather than as human rights of children, because of the way in which their application to children is critically dependent on the fact that it is a child who is the rights-holder. In contrast to this characterization of certain fundamental human rights, Griffin (2002) presents a narrower personhood account, which excludes infants from possessing any human rights.

[9] Gardner (2008) presents an illuminating response to this type of basic objection to rights in respect of the status of human rights more generally.

is opposed to what he sees as the overemphasis on children's rights. I do not consider that the emphasis on children's rights *of itself* is problematic, but rather that it is *currently* problematic because we lack a sufficiently workable child-centred conception of children's rights.

As a consequence, I suggest that it is not advantageous, but actually disadvantageous to children to regulate their situation legally through the lens of rights when that perspective is grounded in any of the currently available theories of children's rights. In making this argument, I see the theoretical basis of children's rights as intimately connected to their legal implementation. Fortin (2009) rightly highlights that '[p]ractitioners are wrong to assume that such a voluminous body of theoretical inquiry should be confined to the realm of intellectual speculation' (p. 3). A fresh look at the theoretical arguments reveals why we are bound to struggle in practice in effecting children's rights.

3. Why and how children's rights matter for children

Both those who disaggregate and those who conflate the legal and theoretical debates assume the importance of rights to children. In this section, I address this assumption. I ask both why it matters that children have and are seen to have rights, as well as why it matters that children have and are seen to have *children's* rights. I suggest there are three types of reasons at stake here: expressive, procedural, and substantive. I explore each in turn, making clear how they relate to rights more generally and children's rights in particular. Considering the typology of the various arguments about why rights and children's rights matter for children enables us to get a clear view of the interconnection between individual arguments without getting lost in their detail. In relation to children's rights, I propose that the three types of reason are necessarily connected, so that the value of thinking that children have children's rights at least in part turns on outcomes for children.

Aspirations and expressive value

The first type of argument as to why children should be seen to have rights and/or children's rights centres on rights' signalling function. There can be a tendency to think of this type of argument as one of last resort, i.e. that if we fail to demonstrate that thinking of children in terms of rights or children's rights leads to improved outcomes, we should nevertheless move to a rights-based approach because of the value in seeing children as rights-holders. Yet, taking that approach both underplays the potential significance of this expressive argument and suggests a separation between outcomes and signalling that I would reject, at least in relation to children as rights-holders.

Rights have real expressive content (Sunstein, 1995-96) that should not be readily dismissed as mere semantics. The statement that a child has a particular right is both an expression of an existing social norm that recognises the importance of the content of that legal right to the child, as well as a means of changing social norms to be more reflective of that importance. This is evident in the speed and extent of the ratification of the United Nations Convention on the Rights of the Child. National governments were quick to demonstrate, in symbolic terms at least, that they value children's choices, needs, and interests.

Freeman (2007: 7) understands this expression of social value in terms of the dignity of the rights-holder: 'Rights are important because they recognise the respect the bearers are entitled to. To accord rights is to respect dignity: to deny rights is to cast doubt on humanity and integrity'. Gardner (2008) explores the nature of this relationship between dignity and human rights. He suggests that human dignity is both independent of and partly constituted by human rights; those independent features help justify at least some rights, and those constitutive elements only become clear after we have relied on other normative arguments to inform our list of human rights (Gardner, 2008: 21-22).

This is helpful in shaping how we might think about the expressive aspects of children as rights-holders. Insofar as children have rights generally, we might best understand seeing children as rights-holders as an expression of respect for children's dignity independent of the content of the rights claims; holding these rights signals that children deserve the same respect as others. Insofar as children have children's rights, we might best understand seeing children as rights-holders as showing respect for their dignity at least partly constituted by the content of the particular rights under discussion; this type of right signals particular ways in which we are concerned about children, such as by offering additional protection in response to their unique vulnerabilities.

However, this content-(in)dependent construction of the argument from dignity raises some difficult questions for the expressive value of rights and children's rights for children. In the content-independent sense of respecting children's dignity by thinking of them in terms of rights, we assume that they will be respected as rights-holders in the same sense that other rights-holders are. This is most evident in relation to rights-holders' claims of entitlement to particular processes or outcomes. As Feinberg (1992) argues,

> [t]he activity of claiming, finally, as much as any other thing, makes for self-respect and respect for others, gives a sense to the notion of personal dignity, and distinguishes this otherwise morally flawed world from the even worse world of Nowheresville [a world in which duties alone, and no rights, exist] (p. 155).

Dignity here is about equal respect for children, and thereby also an argument from non-discrimination.

We might also relate this equal respect argument to the suggestion that rights talk is beneficial because it empowers children through seeing them as deserving of equal respect. Whether that empowerment is of the same nature as that for women and other minorities has been much contested.[10] The empowerment argument can be understood in two ways: it could be seen as empowering children in the sense of ensuring their equal respect, or it could be seen as enfranchising them in the sense of enabling their unique narratives and perspectives to be shared. In either sense, the argument, if sustained, contributes to existing perspectives but, if rejected, does not invalidate those other, larger contentions. Though he accepts an argument from empowerment is mistaken, Brighouse (2002) rightly notes this does not invalidate thinking of children in terms of children's rights because '... the critique would have power only if children's rights talk systematically *misled* people into neglecting the facts of children's vulnerability, dependence, and inabilities' (emphasis in original, p. 35).

An equal respect account of rights as expressing respect for children's dignity, requires children to engage with their rights in the same manner and to the same extent as other rights-holders. But we cannot simply make such an assumption, and need to examine how children are treated when they seek to assert their rights contrary to an external assessment of their 'best interests.' In this sense, as it relates to children, the expressive value of rights is dependent on outcomes in practice.

In the content-dependent sense of respecting children's dignity by thinking of them in terms of children's rights, we assume that they will benefit from better outcomes – 'better' from a child-centred perspective – than if we took a welfare or duty-based approach. 'One can ... maintain ... that rights do not exhaust the moral domain. There are things we ought to do which do not correspond to the obligations we have as correlates of rights. As adults, we should protect and promote the welfare of children, but it need not follow that they have rights against us' (Archard, 2003: 16-17). So, of those various theoretical approaches to children, we would need good reason to prefer a rights-based approach. Arneil (2002) argues that children's rights theorists indeed have such good reason:

> Children's rights theorists have very good reason for advocating rights for children. Rights are ultimately moral trump cards (Dworkin, 1978). If you want to take children's needs and interests seriously, and make claims on their behalf that will compete with any other

---

[10] For: Freeman (2009: 379), Dwyer (2006: 14); against: O'Neill (1988: 461-62). This issue does not need to be resolved here.

moral claims, it is necessary to make such claims in the language of rights. It is clear that any non-rights moral claim simply does not carry the same weight in contemporary moral or political debate (p. 86).

Implicit in Arneil's argument is that the 'trump card' yields better results for children than otherwise. Similarly, Archard (2004) reasons that

> [p]erhaps it is a fundamental mistake legally to give children that to which they are not morally entitled. Nevertheless, giving children legal rights will make a huge difference to how we think about them (p. 56).

Both Arneil and Archard assume that thinking about children in terms of rights improves outcomes for children. This assumption may hold true in relation to the impact of human rights more generally, but needs to be challenged as regards children's rights in particular.

Imagine if we had evidence that in high-conflict residence and contact disputes, children benefitted from outcomes more in accordance with what was best for them where parents were asked to put their position in terms of what they owed to their child. Would it show more respect for children's dignity if we approached these disputes through the language of rights? Arguably, if respecting children's dignity means respecting a truly-child centred vision of their interests, then reasoning in terms of duty would have more expressive value in this hypothetical scenario. Yet, this does not support a rejection of the idea that children have rights or children's rights. Rather, this example highlights that, once properly understood, the expressive value of rights does not of itself provide a reason for thinking of children in those terms. The expressive value of thinking of children in terms of rights or children's rights is a contingent one.

Procedural protections and recognition

Alongside arguments about the signalling function, another type of reason advanced for thinking of children in terms of rights and children's rights relates to the impact on the process of regulation and legal decision-making. Contentions here can be understood to centre on three different aspects of the process of decision-making: the number and nature of factors taken into account in decision-making; the methodology of taking these various factors into account; and the wider consequences of that methodology. It is particularly important to separate out individual arguments as they relate to rights or children's rights in this context.

The first type of procedural argument raised focuses on the number and nature of factors that will be taken into account in the decision-making exercise. This is a necessarily comparative point insofar as it suggests that a rights-based approach can better accommodate the range of relevant factors than the current welfare-based approach. Choudhry and Fenwick (2005) explicitly contrast the two approaches, and argue that thinking in terms of rights makes it more likely that we consider all the relevant interests at stake because of the explicit articulation such an analysis requires (especially pp. 454, 468-69; cf. Bainham, 2002). Considering the issue in broader terms, Freeman (2007) argues that '[t]he language of rights can make visible what has for too long been suppressed. It can lead to different and new stories being heard in public' (p. 6). This argument could apply to both describing individual factors in rights-based terms, as well as to adopting a rights-based framework for thinking about children. The suggestion is that, even if outcomes remained unchanged, it would be better for children to be seen through the lens of rights (Freeman: 7).

However, this needs to be investigated. If taking into account all of the relevant interests and hearing these 'different and new stories' did not result in improved outcomes for children from a child-centred perspective, would there still be a good process-oriented reason for thinking of children in terms of rights? To the extent that this argument is focused on process, I would argue not. If we consider this more of an argument based in expressive value, it also encounters difficulties, and becomes dependent on outcomes for its persuasive force.

Could the process-oriented argument for thinking of children in terms of rights or children's rights be strengthened by shifting the emphasis from the impact on the factors taken into consideration to the methodology through which the analysis is conducted? A rights-based or children's rights-based approach might secure a greater role for competent children in the decision-making process. Of course, this would support thinking of children in term of rights or children's rights only if we believed that competent children should be more involved in the process. Some might value this only if children's views influenced outcomes, whereas others might value participation of itself. Freeman (2007), for example, suggests that one of the reasons why rights are important is because rights-holders 'can exercise agency. Agents are decision-makers... As agents, rights-bearers can participate' (p. 6).

Valuing rights because they understand children as decision-makers is more an argument about the importance of children's rights than rights more generally, and also assumes that we have a theory of children's rights that enables them to be seen as decision-makers. For this process argument to be sustained we need evidence, therefore, of both a viable theory of children's rights that determines when children should be seen as decision-makers, as well as improved outcomes for children in situations in which they have exercised their decision-making rights. As other individuals' interests are also recognised more clearly via independent rights, it is not clear whether this greater role for competent children would impact on outcomes and, if it did not, whether it would be beneficial to children to be more involved in the decision-making process in any event. If we were to value participation of itself, this would become part of the dignity argument in respect of the expressive value of rights, the force of which I suggested is itself contingent on improved outcomes.

Whilst these agency arguments centre on children's rights, there are also general arguments about benefits of the process of rights-thinking. Fortin (2009) contends that a rights-based approach should be more transparent and that it may be more child-centred (p. 297; cf. Choudhry and Herring, 2010: 113):

> [Convention rights-based reasoning] will avoid the rather loose discretion-based decision making produced by the welfare principle, and will perhaps lead, in turn, to less emphasis on adult issues. ... [T]he family judiciary will be required to concentrate far more on a legal analysis of the child's own position than on the extensive summaries of expert advice that have become a feature of their current decision-making (Fortin (2006): 314).

Choudhry and Herring (2010: 111) similarly argue that using rights should lead to greater clarity of reasoning, and that rights are less likely to be distorted to achieve other parties' ends than alternative processes of reasoning. Brighouse (2002) emphasises the importance of separating out children's interests as a way of '... draw[ing] the attention of governments, welfare agencies, and parents to the independent standing of the child...' (p. 36; cf. Choudhry and Herring, 2010: 427; Fortin, 2006: 297).

Yet, these are arguments in favour of thinking of children in terms of rights, not necessarily children's rights. More critically, these arguments are comparative, contrasting the likely benefits of a rights-based process to the current welfare-based inquiry. The current approach is not dictated by a proper reading of the 'welfare principle', and it would be quite simple to structure the application of the 'welfare principle' so that a number of matters on a checklist, such as that in s. 1(3) of the Children Act 1989, were required to be explicitly addressed. A welfare-oriented analysis is not inevitably more opaque, uncertain, or rooted in untested assumptions. If the overriding concern were clear and transparent reasoning, it could straightforwardly be attained within a welfare framework. Whilst the articulation of individual competing rights makes it more likely that all relevant factors and their interrelationship will be explicitly explored, this likelihood is significant only if decision-makers do not want to clearly and comprehensively articulate their process of reasoning.

In order for this reply to be inadequate, there must be some idea of a connection between process and outcome, that an explicit rights-based process has the potential to lead to different outcomes than articulated welfare-oriented reasoning. Thus, we need to ask two questions. First, how likely is it that decision-makers will adopt clearer reasoning when thinking in terms of rights rather than welfare? Second, even if there are a slim number of situations in which the *likelihood* of an improved *process* is secured by rights-based reasoning, is that of itself a significant reason in favour of thinking of children in terms of rights, or is it necessary that this clearer process improves outcomes for children?

In the sense that a more transparent process underpins the legitimacy and justifiability of any outcome reached, this process argument has weight independent of its impact on the content of outcomes reached. But, to the extent that it applies to the basis of the decision-making process more generally, it is a reason in favour of resolving all disputes in rights-based terms, and not specifically concerned with why children in particular should be seen as rights-holders. It is thus an argument for greater clarity and transparency in reasoning, but not necessarily for thinking of children in terms of rights or children's rights.

These process-centred arguments relate to broader contentions about the impact of a rights-based approach. Some have suggested that the type of clarity of reasoning and separate consideration of individuals' positions that is more likely within a rights-based framework will improve outcomes. Dwyer (2006) reasons that '... to the extent one believes significant change in treatment of children is morally requisite, one will find rights-talk useful, even necessary, in a practical sense' (p. 14). Rights matter to children, therefore, because they improve the treatment of children. This remains to be tested, particularly because, as I explained above, the argument for improved outcomes is comparative only, and even then, based on emphasising the possibility for improved outcomes when set against the assumed immutability of the current welfare-based perspective. Legal form may matter, but the form itself may matter less than its relationship to the local legal culture.[11]

Substantive aspects

If we always reached the best outcome for children regardless of the framework or conceptual tools employed within that framework, would there be any argument over which approach we adopted? Consideration of the suggested expressive and process-oriented benefits of thinking of children in terms of rights and children's rights reveals that much of the argument as to why it is important to think of children in those terms is contingent on improved outcomes for children in practice. This argument is also put more directly.

---

[11] McNamara (2007) concludes from his comparative study of approaches to the legal recognition of human rights in various jurisdictions that legal form matters in two ways: first, that legal form matters, but as part of the local legal culture; second, that the legal form itself is also a source of normative authority.

Choudhry and Herring (2010), for example, contend that a rights-based approach 'produces better results' (p. 108):

> ... [A] major benefit of the HRA approach is that it avoids a conclusion that it is appropriate to make an order which causes significant harm to adults because to do so will produce a tiny amount of welfare for the child (p. 110).

As their focus on adults' interests reveals, this is not an argument that recommends that thinking of children in terms of rights will necessarily lead to better outcomes for children from a child-centred perspective. Further, it assumes that the 'significant harm' suffered by the adults concerned will not impact on the child. In a typical residence and contact dispute, the various parties' interests are usually intertwined with parents' well-being impacting on the child, so that the posited scenario is more theoretical than likely to arise in practice.

Whilst this is a sound child-centred critique of this particular outcome-oriented argument, there remains the possibility of truly child-centred improved outcomes for children. However, in order to argue that it is important to children to think in terms of rights or children's rights, we need clear evidence of improved child-centred outcomes in situations where the child's status as the rights-holder is critical. This is particularly important given that the 'welfare principle' itself does not dictate any specific outcome: why should the application of rights or children's rights necessarily be better for children than regulating them through the notions of duties owed to them, or through the 'welfare principle' and concomitant 'best interests' assessment? As I have argued that the expressive and process-oriented arguments in favour of thinking of children in terms of children's rights turn on outcomes for children, the need to demonstrate the likelihood of such improved outcomes becomes the lynchpin of the debate.

4. Child-centred difficulties with interpreting and applying particular children's rights

In this and the next section, I argue that there are real difficulties created by the theoretical accounts of children's rights and rights frameworks within which children's rights operate, which mean that thinking of children in terms of children's rights does not of itself make it more likely that better outcomes will be secured.

Delineating the debates over content and framework

If we simply asked which approach was better, rights or welfare, a standard reply would be that, '... in the vast majority of situations there would be no difference in result whether a rights-based approach or a welfare-based approach was taken' (Herring, 2011: 446). More concretely, in *Re H (Children) (Contact Order) (No 2)* (2002), Wall J similarly reasoned that '... a proper application of the checklist in s. 1(3) of the 1989 Act is equivalent to the balancing exercise required in the application of art 8 [ECHR],...' ([59]).[12] Whilst empirically correct, this type of response risks overlooking an important issue of complexity in terms of how we understand a 'rights-based approach' for the purpose of this comparison.

When thinking about the potential to lead to better outcomes for children, it might be important to examine separately the potential impact of individual children's rights compared to the adoption of a rights-based framework for analysis. Individual children's rights could operate within a rights-based or welfare-based framework under the current law, most obviously within either an ECHR or s. 1, Children Act 1989 framework. Similarly, a rights-based framework, such as that under the ECHR, could encompass both individual children's rights and other competing rights or welfare considerations.

Much of the evidence for evaluating the potential of a rights-based approach is based on comparing a s. 1, Children Act 1989 approach, within which individual children's rights operate alongside welfare considerations, against an ECHR approach, within which rights and welfare also both operate. This means that the idea that we can draw much support from recent case law to compare ostensibly pure rights-based and welfare-based approaches may be somewhat misleading and risks obscuring the extent and means in which children's rights can improve outcomes. That is not to say that we might not attempt to construct a pure understanding of a rights-based approach, and ask if that might improve outcomes for children. Whether part of such a pure approach or as individual children's rights within a mixed approach, it is important to consider whether we can say that children have particular children's rights in a way that might improve outcomes for children.

Children as holders of children's rights

There are two conventional theoretical accounts of rights that are relied upon to determine the content of children's rights in a particular dispute, the 'interest theory' and the 'will theory' (also known as the 'choice theory').[13] On the interest theory, a right protects a child's interests; hence, she may be a

---

[12] Similar *dicta* can be found in other leading judgments. See, for example, *Re KD (A Minor: Termination of Access)* (1988), Lord Templeman: 812, Lord Oliver: 825; *Re B (A Child) (Adoption by One Natural Parent)* (2001), Lord Nicholls: [30-31]; *Glass v. UK* (2004) (ECtHR): [75] (importance to be attached to *dictum* limited by factual context).

[13] For an introduction to these theories, see Archard (2002).

rights-holder even though a third party exercises the right on her behalf in protection of her interests.[14] On the will theory, a right protects a child's choice; she has a right only if she has sufficient capacity to be able to exercise that right herself.[15] In what follows, I explain why neither theory, even in 'modified' form, enables us properly to see children as rights-holders, hence adequately advance their independent position.

Will theory

The will theory fails because of the necessity for a rights-holder to possess capacity.[16] This leads to two related difficulties for children's rights. First, young children will almost certainly lack the capacity required and even adolescents may not be adjudged capable, depending on the decision-making context. As a result of this exclusion of young children from holding children's rights,[17] it is not possible to claim that children as a class are rights-holders under the will theory.

What if we sub-divided 'children' into categories? Could we then say that all adolescents, or merely just all 17 year-olds for example, had children's rights under the will theory? Arguably not, because the requisite capacity necessarily varies according to decision-making context. To the extent that any older child might be recognised as having a right to decide, the fact-specific approach means that seeing the child as rights-holder states the conclusion rather than operating as the beneficial basis for argumentation outlined in the previous section.

Secondly, and relatedly, even if we are able to conclude that any particular child has sufficient capacity to be seen as a rights-holder, there are real difficulties with the version of 'capacity' used to determine that. As currently formulated, the test is technically cognitive only,[18] but in specific cases courts have also taken into account psycho-social development under the guise of the cognitive test as a means of heightening the standard to which the child is held.[19]

---

[14] Representative of an interest theory approach is MacCormick (1984).

[15] For an account and modified version of the will theory, see Eekelaar (1998).

[16] Griffin (2002) goes further and argues that, for this reason, infants do not have human rights (pp. 27-28).

[17] Before proceeding to endorse the interest theory, Fortin (2009) describes this conclusion as having '... an unattractive logic' (p. 12).

[18] As set out by Lord Scarman in *Gillick v. West Norfolk & Wisbech AHA* (1986). Lord Fraser (p. 127) also adopted a cognitive approach to capacity, but very clearly set it within the context of a 'best interests' framework, in relation to which a series of five factors needed to be considered by the doctor before he or she could determine that treatment without parental consent was justified.

[19] For example, in *Re E (A Minor) (Wardship: Medical Treatment)* (1992), a 15-year-old boy suffering from leukemia sought to refuse blood transfusions needed to save his life. In purely

Even if the test were reformulated in terms of a more expansive understanding of capacity, as in the recent Canadian Supreme Court decision in *AC v. Manitoba* (*Director of Child and Family Services*) (2009), it still necessarily remains a discretionary test, hence a conclusion to reasoning only. So does a child possess any real rights if she must rely on others in this way to determine when she can make rights claims? Eekelaar (2007) quite rightly argues that

> ... it is clear that not to allow a child who meets the constraints on competence to make such a decision is to withhold from the child a right he or she is claiming, for if the right claimed is not socially recognised, the child does not have it (p. 158).

However, the inherent difficulties in determining whether the child does 'meet[.] the constraints on competence' remain.

Interest theory

The critical failing of the interest theory lies in its attempted solution to the central difficulty with the will theory – the possession of capacity. As a result, there are three aspects in relation to which the interest theory is insufficiently child-centred, hence unable to increase the likelihood that better outcomes would be secured for children: first, the determination of who gives content to the claimed interests; second, the consequences of that determination for the empowerment of children; and third, the attempted accommodation of choice within the interest theory. Of these difficulties, the first is arguably the most significant.

Recognising that not all children are capable decision makers, hence capable of asserting rights on their own behalf, the interest theory installs an adult as the capable exerciser of rights. Yet, this has the unfortunate consequence that a child is a rights-holder in a situation in which the third party exercising

---

cognitive terms alone, Ward J considered the boy was capable. However, after adding other non-cognitive considerations to the capacity test, Ward J concluded that the boy lacked the capacity to refuse:

> I find that A is a boy of sufficient intelligence to be able to take decisions about his own well-being, but I also find that there is a range of decisions of which some are outside his ability fully to grasp their implications. Impressed though I was by his obvious intelligence, by his calm discussion of the implications, by his assertion even that he would refuse well knowing that he may die as a result, in my judgment A does not have a full understanding of the whole implication of what the refusal of that treatment involves (p. 224).

In particular, Ward J included the following psycho-social matters within the cognitive capacity test: the ability to understand the impact of the full process of dying, particularly seeing his family's distress (p. 224) and the particular details of the pain and fear that he would suffer as he died – the frightening struggle for breath, of which neither the treating physician nor Ward J had informed him (p. 224).

the child's right has asserted claims with which the child disagrees. So the child that seeks to refuse medical treatment, or desires residence and contact arrangements other than those the favoured by their guardian *ad litem* or parents, can end up having a 'right' to an outcome she does not want. Thus, in *Re W (Contact Proceedings: Joinder of Child)* (2001), Butler-Sloss P reasoned that '[t]he child has a right to a relationship with his father even if he does not want it. The child's welfare demands that efforts should be made to make it possible that it can be' ([16]). Reasoning such as this may be inevitable if we cannot develop a child-centred approach since, as Mnookin remarks, '[d]eciding what is best for a child poses a question no less ultimate than the purposes and values of life itself' (in Guggenheim, 2005: 40).

Can we constrain the decision-maker in a child-centred way to underpin an interest theory approach? There are at least a couple of options.[20] We could try to construct a hypothetical instantaneously-mature version of the child, and consider how that hypothetical mature-child would want their interests protected. As that child is fictional, of course, there is no realistic way to achieve this so that we would have a person to ask what outcome she might prefer. Perhaps instead we could imagine the child has become an adult, and ask that adult-child looking back how they would have wanted their interests protected. Given that the adult-child has been shaped by their experiences as a child, however, she is not the same person as the child, hence this child-centred attempt also falls apart as we again have no one to ask what outcome they would prefer.

Without clear means for bringing the actual child within the decision-maker's identity, the decision-maker remains truly external to the child and it is not clear whether it is accurate to describe the child as a rights-holder. Dwyer (2006) is pragmatic about this conclusion, reasoning that although

---

[20] This is much like the attempt to make the 'best interests' exercise truly child-centred; see Archard (2006) for more detailed discussion of this point. Although the literature tends to distinguish consideration of the notion of 'best interests' from children's rights theories, I suggest that this notion is intimately connected to the interest theory of children's rights. To the extent that the child does not herself determine either whether to make a claim, or the nature of her claim made under a 'best interests' approach, the third party exercising that right on behalf of the child (usually her parents) must apply her own conception of 'best interests' in deciding these matters. In theory, the point of distinction ought to be that, as the child has status as a rights-holder, an interest theory of children's rights is necessarily child-centred, whereas a 'best interests' approach may be seeking to achieve what a third party considers 'best' for the child without necessarily being truly child-centred. If we fail to develop a satisfactory child-centred account of the child as rights-holder under the interest theory, however, then the two approaches appear to collapse into each other.

As discussed below, a similar issue regarding proxies also arises if we attempt to modify the constraints of the 'will theory' by use of proxy decision-makers for younger children.

... such proxy decision-making is for various reasons imperfect ... [that] does not mean that it is not the best, most utility-maximizing strategy for making decisions about children's lives, all things considered and in light of the available alternatives (p. 131).

There is a sense in which it would be odd if a child's status as a rights-holder reached by such use of proxy decision-making led to better outcomes for children. The need to resort to pragmatic proxy-based solutions means that there is necessarily nothing within this conception of children's rights itself that entails improved outcomes for children from a truly child-centred perspective.

The second difficulty in constructing an interest theory account of children's rights relates to the first. As discussed above,[21] one of the arguments for regulating children in terms of children's rights is that rights are empowering. Yet, if we accept a proxy approach to the exercise of decision-making, we may actually be disempowering children. As Federle (2009) argues,

While the interest theory does have the advantage of permitting us to speak about the rights of children without reference to the child's actual ability to obligate others, it ultimately remains an impoverished account because it disadvantages children. Premised on a conception of neediness and vulnerability, interest theory reinforces the dependence of children in ways that underscores their powerlessness while promoting their incompetencies. This, in turn, permits adults to claim they are protecting children when the choices made may better serve adult interests and agendas (p. 324).

The final difficulty faced by an interest theory of children's rights lies in its accommodation of choice. Fortin (2009) suggests that under the interest theory children '... have an interest *in* choice, as they develop an ability to reach choices' (emphasis in original, p. 14; cf. p. 20). This is also evident in practice, as the presence of the child's wishes on the s. 1(3), Children Act 1989 checklist demonstrates. Based on this role for choice, Fortin disagrees (p. 14) with Federle's (1994: 353) argument that the interest theory disadvantages children by emphasising their vulnerability or 'incapacities' (p. 353). Both arguments have some force and are not incompatible, so the expressive aspect of thinking of children in terms of interests may emphasise their dependency whilst, in fact, much of what protecting those interests entails involves the child's choices.

Yet, accommodating choice as an interest may not be as straightforward as Fortin (2009) suggests. Choice may not be an interest like all others taken into account. When choices are protected, they are valued not just for contributing to the best outcome for the child, objectively understood, but also subjectively. Choice plays a different role in the decision-making exercise.[22]

---

[21] See note 10, above, and corresponding main text.
[22] Brennan (2002: 63-67) discusses this issue as it relates to MacCormick's defence of an interest theory of children's rights and as part of her 'gradualist account'.

Modified and reconciling theories

At least in part because of the failings of the two basic approaches to theories of children's rights, there have been various arguments presented for theories that seek to modify either the will or interest theory, or reconcile the two theories to combine the better elements of each. Eekelaar's 'working principle' is a widely-embraced example of the former.[23]

Eekelaar (1992: 230-31; cf. 2007: 155-62) proposes three categories of interest that are protected by children's rights: basic, developmental, and autonomy. The first of these is 'preeminent' (p. 231) in status, and the other two 'can reasonably be compromised' (p. 231) if giving effect to them would prevent the child from reaching adulthood without 'the maximum opportunities to form and pursue life-goals which reflect as closely as possible an autonomous choice' (1994: 53). Yet, children may be able to learn from their own minor mistakes as that is part of learning to make decisions well. Children's competent decisions may be overridden, but Eekelaar is careful in expressing caution about the circumstances in which that may occur (1994: 57; 1998: 206). He argues that however we determine a child's competence, if we override a competent child's claimed right, she does not have that right (2007: 158, discussed above).

If the autonomy interest could be overridden on the basis of *any* detriment to the child's basic and/or developmental interests that would mean that the overall account represented the worst of both the interest theory and the will theory – we would not be able to determine the younger child's interests in a truly child-centred way and we would not know with any certainty at what point the child became sufficiently autonomous that this harm assessment was no longer applicable.

One might still argue that Eekelaar's approach nevertheless falls foul of the critical weaknesses of both the interest theory and the will theory. Whilst a child is able to learn from her more minor mistakes in decision-making, we still need to determine at what point the child becomes sufficiently capable that they should be entitled to decide as well as how a younger child's interests can be understood in a sufficiently child-centred manner. In respect of the latter concern, Eekelaar (2007: 159) draws on a larger approach to capacity based

---

[23] Though often critiqued as if it were, Eekelaar (1998) is quite clear that the 'working principle' is not a theory of rights, but rather simply an account of what we mean when we say children have rights. In other words, he is seeking to explain the current law, not offer a normative basis for it:

> ... [T]his is not an argument about what rights people, and children in particular, should have, nor even an argument that they should have *any* rights at all. It is merely an attempt to identify an essential element of decisions which recognize that people have rights (emphasis in original, p. 203).

in his modification of a will theory approach; he argues that if the child is not presently capable, we should consider whether we might wait for the child to develop capacity, and then revisit the decision to be made.

Eekelaar (2007) supports his argument by revisiting the decision in *Re M* (*Child's Upbringing*) (1996), a controversial residence dispute case involving a Zulu child, who was sent back to his parents in South Africa after several years in the UK, but then had to be returned to the U.K. after six months. He suggests that a better outcome would have been for the child to remain in England with contact with his parents, so that he could decide where he wanted to live after he reached capacity. On the facts, this would likely have been a much better outcome for the child. The difficulty lies in seeing this as a better outcome brought about through children's rights. Whilst the child's status as a 'potential' rights-holder led Eekelaar (2007: 158) to conclude that the child should remain in England, this was achieved through valuing the maximisation of the future range of options open to the child above other rights and interests. Elsewhere (Eekelaar, 1998), he has argued that:

> In a rights-oriented world, adults are entrusted with developing its new members in such a way that they can exercise their autonomy as fully as possible when competent. This demands, of course, health and intellectual development. It also demands maximising opportunities for self-determination in establishing relationships and self-identity. These may be said to be manifestations of the interests of children... But, within a rights framework, they are not just *any* interests which the adult world *happens to determine*, at any one time, as being good for children. They are linked to a vision of a society of autonomy-enhancing individuals (emphasis in original; p. 205).

Yet, I would argue that this maximisation is a consequence of valuing autonomy as the overriding outcome, rather than an inherent feature of a child's incipient status. Whilst maximising long-term potential for autonomy may be an important – perhaps even the most important goal – the decision to treat it as the desired outcome is external to the child. This does not enable us to set out in child-centred terms how we should determine the content of *individual* (basic and/or developmental) rights at stake. As a result, it is not clear that, as critical as it is to value the developing autonomy of children, we can rely on the 'working principle' to explain how children can be seen as rights-holders in respect of the individual children's rights asserted by and for them.

5. Child-centred difficulties with frameworks for decision-making

If the content of individual children's rights is unable to be determined in a properly child-centred manner, it might still be useful to think in terms of children having children's rights if the framework in which those rights are weighed is more likely to lead to better outcomes. This framework could be rights- or welfare-based. As explained at the start of the preceding section, discussion as to whether it is better to think of children as having children's rights tends not to distinguish carefully between children's rights operating within a rights-based framework and children's rights operating within a welfare-based approach. In order for us accurately to determine whether it is better to see children as holders of children's rights, these various possibilities need to be kept distinct. When thinking about whether either framework enables better outcomes, we also need to consider the potential impact of differentiating between situations where the only party before the court is the child and situations in which the child's interests potentially clash with those of other parties.

Welfare-based framework

Children's rights can be taken into account alongside welfare concerns within a welfare-based framework. The leading decision of *Gillick v. West Norfolk & Wisbech AHA* (1986), for example, is just such a case. When considering who might give valid consent for the provision of contraceptive advice and treatment to children under 16, the majority concluded that, if the girl concerned had capacity, her consent was sufficient. Lord Scarman reasoned that '... parental rights yield to the child's right to make his own decisions when he reaches a sufficient understanding and intelligence to be capable of making up his own mind on the matter requiring decision...' (p. 186). Lord Fraser, however, approached the issue with a stronger focus on the welfare framework, and made clear that '[t]he solution depends upon a judgment of what is best for the welfare of the particular child' (p. 173). Whilst Lord Scarman's remarks suggest a strong notion of children's rights within a welfare framework, it is Lord Fraser's narrower perspective that has come to underpin subsequent cases.[24]

In the previous section, I argued that there is no truly child-centred way to give content to a particular children's right. Thus, employing children's rights within a welfare-based framework cannot *of itself* lead to improved outcomes for children. Better results would follow only if *both* a welfare-based framework were employed in a way that offered only a partial perspective on what was best for the child *and* the non-child-centred understanding of children's

---

[24] See *Re R (A Minor) (Wardship: Consent to Treatment)* (1991); *Re W (A Minor) (Medical Treatment: Court's Jurisdiction)* (1992); *Re E (A Minor) (Wardship: Medical Treatment)* (1992), as discussed in note 19, above. Gilmore and Herring (2009) argue in favour of the narrower approach in *Re R* and *Re W*. The decision in *R (on the application of Axon) v. Sec of St for Health* (2006) went no further than *Gillick*, but further cemented both its application in the context of advice on sexual issues and the 'best interests' framework within which the capable under-16-year-old's decision operates.

rights enlarged or re-emphasised the considerations taken into account within the welfare exercise. There is some evidence of this in practice.

In *Mabon v. Mabon* (2005), the English Court of Appeal had to decide whether to grant three teenage boys independent representation[25] in a residence dispute between their parents. Allowing the appeal in favour of granting representation, Thorpe LJ reasoned that '[t]he right of freedom of expression and participation outweigh[ed] the paternalistic judgment of welfare' ([28]). But he left room for welfare to underpin a decision that the child was insufficiently capable to be granted such representation if it posed an obvious risk that they could not understand ([29]). In this way, the rights of the child operated to enlarge the welfare exercise, to ensure that the boys' autonomy was sufficiently respected, but larger welfarist concerns also imposed outer limits on that respect.

To the extent that the welfare framework would not have been employed in this way, thinking of these children in terms of rights led to a better outcome from their perspective. Yet, this possibility for improved outcomes is not because of children's rights directly, but because of the perception of children's rights. A welfare framework, properly employed (particularly in terms of placing appropriate weight on s. 1(3)(a)), might equally be capable of achieving the same beneficial results for children.

In *Re R* (*A Child*) (2009), for example, the English Court of Appeal had to determine whether the lower court had taken sufficient account of a nine-year-old's views in making a residence order in favour of the father, when the child wished to live with his mother. The majority concluded that the lower court had not, with Rix LJ reasoning that the court had '... erred in not giving any real effect to the child's wishes' (*Re R* (2009): [58]). He considered the child to be '... a mature and thoughtful child close to the age of 10, who expressed his wishes rationally and ... with considerable emotional understanding' (*Re R*: [58]). The outcome in *Re R* (2009) demonstrates that a fuller understanding of welfare-based reasoning within a welfare framework may achieve the same beneficial outcomes from a child's perspective as the use of rights-based reasoning did in *Mabon*.

Rights-based framework

Children's rights can be taken into account in two ways in a rights-based framework. If the child is the only party before the court, children's rights can form the entire content of the rights exercise. If the child is one of several parties

---

[25] Under Rule 9.2A of the Family Proceedings Rules 1991, the court shall grant leave for independent representation '... if it considers that the minor has sufficient understanding to participate as a party...'.

with rights at stake, children's rights will need to be balanced against those other parties' rights.

To the extent that there is no coherent child-centred way to give content to individual children's rights, any improvement in outcomes for children where the child is the only party before the court would not be inherent in the use of children's rights in reasoning. Rather, such improvement in outcomes would follow from either the perception of the requirements imposed by particular children's rights, or from the nature of the rights-based framework itself.

If it is the former, one might argue that, as noted above in discussion of *Mabon* (2005) and *Re R* (2009), a welfare-based approach could achieve the same improvement. Whilst correct, the possibility of improved outcomes via the perception of the changes required by rights-based thinking could be argued to be sufficient to underpin reform arguments. As our overriding concern is that children benefit from better outcomes in disputes affecting them, correlation between framework and outcomes is as significant as causative connection. But this argument for a rights-based framework would fall away, if clarification of the potential of the current welfare-based approach would be easier to implement and more coherent as a matter of theory.

Alternatively, improved outcomes might stem from the nature of the framework. If a rights-based framework changes or differently balances the considerations taken into account within that framework, regardless whether those individual considerations are framed in terms of rights or welfare, there might be good reason to adopt that framework if it produces better outcomes. To the extent that there is no child-centred way to ascribe content to an individual children's right, it seems unlikely that the mere fact that the framework is rights-based leads to more favourable outcomes for the child. Yet, that is not to say that particular conceptions of a rights-based framework might not do so.

Eekelaar's 'working principle' (discussed above), for example, proposes one possible framework, which balances competing rights and privileges the outcome in favour of the child's developing autonomy unless that would cause significant detriment to the child. If we consider this framework to provide better outcomes than the current approach, that might provide good reason for moving to that particular rights-based framework. Yet, even if we did prefer it, it is arguably not a children's rights framework; the basis for the weighting in favour of autonomy in the process of evaluation does not flow from the fact that the child is a rights-holder, but from an external determination of the desirability of enabling children to develop their autonomy. Further, as the improved outcomes result from a particular conception of a rights-framework, not the idea of a rights-framework itself, we might consider whether the same autonomy-enhancing perspective might not be equally achieved using a welfare framework.

What if the child is one of several parties whose interests are at stake? Would a rights-based framework either provide or be more likely to provide better outcomes for the child? The idea of a rights-based framework itself necessitates no particular outcomes. As a result, much turns on the specific rights framework adopted. If the framework does not prioritise children's interests, there is nothing within the rights framework itself that suggests the possibility of better outcomes for children through adopting this approach.

The unsatisfactory nature of this conclusion had led to the development of particular conceptions of the appropriate rights framework in practice. More particularly, in order to improve outcomes for children, the European Court of Human Rights emphasised the place of welfare considerations within the rights exercise. In *Johansen v. Norway* (1996), the Court emphasised the child's 'best interests' as part of the Art 8(2) justification for infringing upon parents' Art 8(1) rights:

> In this regard, a fair balance has to be struck between the interests of the child in remaining in public care and those of the parent in being reunited with the child... In carrying out this balancing exercise, the Court will attach particular importance to the best interests of the child, which, depending on their nature and seriousness, may override those of the parent ([78]).[26]

In its subsequent decision in *Yousef v. Netherlands* (2002), the ECtHR expressed this weighting of children's interests in stronger terms, and reasoned that

> ... in judicial decisions where the rights under art 8 of parents and those of a child are at stake, the child's rights must be the paramount consideration. If any balancing of interests is necessary, the interests of the child must prevail (p. 590).

That approach has not been widely endorsed in subsequent case law.[27] Instead, the ECtHR has generally followed the *Johansen* line of jurisprudence, describing children's interests as 'particularly important'.[28]

---

26) Bonner, Fenwick, and Harris-Short (2003: especially 579-80) suggest that this approach may place less weight on children's interests than our domestic 'welfare' principle. They conclude as follows:

> The exercise demanded of the judge under Article 8 ECHR, when compared with that under section 1 of the Children Act 1989, is thus, at a fundamental level, quite different and may result in a very different substantive conclusion (p. 580).

27) But there are also instances of the ECtHR adopting the *Yousef* language of paramountcy: see, for example, *Marie v. Portugal* [2004] 2 FLR 653: [77]; *Kearns v France* [2008] 1 FLR 888: [79].

28) See, for example, *Haase v. Germany* (2004): [93]; *Chepelev v. Russia* (2007): [27].

The Court's use of welfare considerations to privilege children's interests makes clear that it is not the framework itself that leads to or makes more likely better outcomes, but rather the content ascribed to that framework, whether expressed as rights, children's rights, or welfare concerns. Further, better outcomes may not even require the privileging of children's interests, as Eekelaar's (2002) conflict-focused argument for the reconstruction of the welfare principle makes clear. In taking into account the interests of others, however, Eekelaar does suggest that '... there should be a degree of detriment to which a child should never be subjected if avoidable' ('Qualifications – privilege and appropriateness' section, [3]).

6. Different conceptual approaches to the same content

The preceding discussion makes plain that children's rights are not entirely discrete (Fortin, 2006: 311)[29] from children's welfare or duties owed to children. All three concepts concern the same content, serving as different lenses on the legal regulation of children's lives. We have reason to prefer one approach to another only if it either makes it more likely that better outcomes will be reached for children or if there are other, non-outcome-oriented reasons in favour of adopting that conceptual framework. In section 3, above, I suggested that both the expressive and process-oriented arguments raised in support of thinking that children have children's rights are in fact contingent upon the potential for improved outcomes for children through children's rights. In sections 4 and 5, I demonstrated that neither individual children's rights nor the adoption of a rights-based framework could necessarily improve or make more likely improved outcomes for children. As a result, I contend that we have no reason to think that regulating children in terms of children's rights is necessarily better than alternative approaches.

There is a sense in which this conclusion need not cause concern. The Supreme Court of Canada's recent decision in *AC v. Manitoba* (*Director of Child and Family Services*) (2009) illustrates this well. The Court was asked to determine as a matter of principle whether a legislative provision, which applied a 'best interests' test to under-16-year-old children could be applied in a way that sufficiently respected her decision-making capacity. A majority of six to one held that it could be, and therefore was constitutional.

Giving the lead judgment, Justice Abella reasoned that the 'best interests' standard operates as '... a sliding scale of scrutiny, with the adolescent's views

---

[29] Fortin discusses the assumption of discreteness in the debate as to whether it is better to legally regulate children from a rights- or welfare-based perspective.

becoming increasingly determinative depending on his or her ability to exercise mature, independent judgment' ([22]). Whilst not explicitly stating that the child will become the sole decision-maker once she has attained a certain level of capacity, the logic of this reasoning suggests that ought to be the approach adopted on an appropriate set of facts. This logic is reinforced by Abella J's subsequent reference to the child's wishes becoming 'the controlling factor' ([87]) when the court is '... so convinced of a child's maturity' ([87]).

AC thus offers much stronger protection to the capable child's decisions than the approach in *Gillick* and its subsequent confinement.[30] Whereas in *Gillick*, the child is called upon to consent only after a medical practitioner has already decided that treatment would be in the child's 'best interests', in *AC* the child's views are made central to the initial assessment of whether treatment would be in the child's 'best interests'. Further, that assessment extends to both refusal and consent, whilst English jurisprudence has made clear that *Gillick* extends only to consent.

Yet, the potential for improved outcomes for children in *AC* does not support an argument in favour of thinking of children in terms of children's rights. Whilst the analysis in *Gillick* was framed in rights-based terms, the critical reasoning in *AC* is expressed in terms of autonomy, but not explicitly rights. The basis for this omission becomes clear from Abella J's subsequent reasoning:

> ... [T]he distinction between principles of welfare and autonomy narrows considerably – and often collapses altogether – when one appreciates the extent to which respecting a demonstrably mature adolescent's capacity for autonomous judgment is 'by definition in his or her best interests' ([84]).

Thus, the concept employed – children's rights or 'best interests' – becomes irrelevant where the content dictates a particular outcome. The suggestion from the majority's reasoning in *AC* is that this applies where the necessary outcome is that of respecting the child's capable decision.

The interwoven rights and welfare-based reasoning in *Re A (Children) (Conjoined Twins: Surgical Separation)* (2001) suggests that this conclusion might also hold true in respect of younger children, whose rights and interests may be in conflict. The English Court of Appeal was unanimous that the conjoined twins should be separated, knowing that this would lead to the certain death of one of the children, but make the survival of the other a possibility, when leaving them conjoined would result in both dying.

Lord Justice Ward adopted a 'best interests' framework (p. 180 et seq.); he accommodated both children's right to life within that framework but, as he

---

30) Discussed above at notes 18-19, 24, and corresponding main text.

determined that that right added nothing to the balancing exercise (p. 196), the 'best interests' of each of the twins were weighed against each other to reach the decision to separate (pp. 182-90, 196-97). Lord Justice Brooke agreed with this 'best interests' balancing, which preferred the interests of the stronger twin to those of the weaker (p. 205), but also reasoned – in his discussion of the criminal law issues at stake – that separation would respect the bodily integrity of both of the twins (p. 240).

Lord Justice Walker took a significantly different approach. He noted that the 'best interests' exercise usually required balancing one sibling's interests against the other's (pp. 242-43), but he did not consider that approach appropriate here because of the implications for sanctity of life arguments (p. 243). Instead, Walker LJ reasoned that it would respect the right to life (p. 254) and the 'best interests' of both – to which he ascribed the right to life and dignity as key content considerations – to be separated (p. 258). The different balance of rights- and welfare-based reasoning in each of the three judgments in *Re A* (*Conjoined Twins*) thus highlights the extent to which the outcome can dictate the content ascribed to both types of consideration.

Whilst Abella J's comments in *AC* explicitly highlight the potential for such convergence (above, [84]), other aspects of her reasoning and Binnie J's dissent cast doubt on the extent to which we should rely on the logic of convergence of children's rights and 'best interests' where the better outcome is not in doubt. Whilst arguing that the child's views become 'increasingly determinative', she also contends that the child's argument that

> ... the mature minor doctrine means that mature children are, at common law, entitled to make *all* decisions related to their medical care, including the decision to refuse life-saving medical treatment, ... miscasts [the doctrine's] actual development and application, both in Canada and abroad ... [and] also seriously misrepresents the limits on the ability to accurately assess the maturity in any given child (emphasis in original, [47]).

Given this reasoning, we might yet wonder to what extent we can or should rely on future courts sufficiently to value children's views if they are not cast in terms of children's rights. This concern reinforces Binnie J's dissent:

> Under [the majority's] interpretation of the [statute], even if a minor under 16 demonstrates his or her capacity, he or she is still not treated in the same manner as a minor who is 16 and over. His or her demonstrated capacity remains one consideration among others (however much its weight increases in correspondence with the maturity level and the nature of the treatment decision to be made), and is in no way determinative ([194]).

Whilst it is not obvious that a mere correlative connection between the concept used and the outcome reached should be sufficient justification for adopting a rights-based framework and children's rights reasoning, it is also not clear that we can dismiss it. If legal actors believe that thinking of children in terms of children's rights changes the approach that should be taken then, even if they are mistaken, that may lead to improved outcomes for children; the improved consequences of acting under that mistaken belief may also constitute a reason why, despite the theoretical incoherency, it might be important to move more fully to legally regulate children in terms of children's rights. In other words, even if the logic of non-discreteness of conceptual approaches is sound, Binnie J's caution may be much more important in practice.

7. Concluding thoughts: possible responses to the quandary

Let me conclude by making plain my claim in this article. I am not arguing that children do not have rights; understood in the sense of fundamental human rights, children are plainly rights-holders. I am also not arguing that they do not have children's rights; they may well do so even though the theoretical basis upon which they possess rights currently evades us. I am arguing that it neither adequately protects children nor necessarily enhances their status in society to use rights-based reasoning in legal disputes involving or affecting children.

I have based this argument on three related contentions: firstly, that the expressive and procedural reasons for thinking it is important to see children as having children's rights are contingent upon improved outcomes; secondly, that we do not currently have a child-centred theory of children's rights that improves, or increases the likelihood of improved outcomes in legal practice; thirdly, in the absence of such a theory, we currently have no good evidence that it benefits children to think of them in terms of legal children's rights. Whilst each of these points is contentious, the idea of a necessary connection between the theory and practice of children's rights may require the greatest substantiation. Representative of the standard perspective, Archard (2004) suggests that:

> Perhaps it is a fundamental mistake legally to give children that to which they are not morally entitled. Nevertheless, giving children legal rights will make a huge difference to how we think about them (p. 56).

If we could demonstrate a causative connection between thinking of children in terms of children's rights and improved outcomes for children, it would make sense to think of them in terms of children's rights despite the theoretical incoherency. The difficulty is that the relationship between improved outcomes and children's rights reasoning is necessarily correlative only because we have no conception of children's rights that ensures better outcomes from a child's perspective. And yet, if courts, such as the Court of Appeal in *Mabon*

(2005), and other legal actors believe that the language of children's rights and a rights-based process leads to better outcomes, it might be a mistake to overlook that potential for correlation.

We are thus left with at least three options. Firstly, we could focus our efforts on reinvigorating the potential of the 'best interests' framework and reasoning, so that we do not need to rely on rights-based reasoning to bring out the latent potential of a 'best interests' approach.

Secondly, as an alternative, we could embrace the public perception that children have children's rights and that it matters that children have children's rights.[31] This would require acknowledgment that this approach would be most beneficial for children if we could transform the unreliable correlative relationship between approach and outcomes into a causative approach. Thus, we could work to develop a truly child-centred understanding of what it means to say that children have children's rights, so that thinking of children in terms of children's rights would necessarily lead to better outcomes for children.

Thirdly, if the theoretical quandary sought to be addressed through the second option remained unresolved, we might yet revisit the potential of thinking of children in terms of duties owed to them. Whilst not purporting to be child-centred in the way of children's rights, the inherent requirement to more explicitly consider and weigh individual duties might yet achieve better outcomes than the more discretionary 'best interests' approach under the current law. Whether a duty-based perspective would be readily accepted as compatible with the approach adopted under the ECHR is another matter.

If the overarching concern is best outcomes for children as assessed from children's perspectives and the purposes for which we want to believe that children have rights might be better achieved than presently, this larger debate is certainly one worth having.

Acknowledgements

I began thinking about the ideas in this paper following discussion at the International Society for Family Law North American Regional Conference, Vancouver, 18-20

---

[31] In discussing the perceived difficulties of the will theory of rights in explaining how children are rights-holders, Dwyer (2006) notes that

[t]he view that children and incompetent adults cannot and do not have any 'rights' would strike the vast majority of people as preposterous...

... Will Theorists who insist that rights exist only where a claim-holder also holds a power of enforcement are urging that the legal system adopt an understanding of rights and a usage of the term *right* that is patently inconsistent with established usage and settled expectations in a large and important area of the law (emphasis in original, p. 301).

June 2007. I am grateful to participants, especially co-panelists Barbara Ann Atwood and James G. Dwyer, for their thoughtful comments.

References

Archard, D.W., *Children, Family and the State* (Aldershot: Ashgate, 2003).

Archard, D.W., *Children: Rights and Childhood*, 2nd ed. (New York: Routledge, 2004).

Archard, D.W., 'Children's rights'. In *The Stanford Encyclopedia of Philosophy*, Winter 2002 ed., E.N. Zalta, ed., online: <plato.stanford.edu/archives/win2002/entries/rights-children/> (21 March 2006).

Arneil, B., 'Becoming versus being: A critical analysis of the child in liberal theory'. In *The Moral and Political Status of Children*. eds. D. Archard & C.M. Macleod (New York: OUP, 2002) 70–94.

Bainham, A., 'Can we protect children and protect their rights?', *Family Law* 32 (2002): 279–289.

Bonner, D., Fenwick, H. & Harris-Short, B., 'Judicial approaches to the human rights act', *International Comparative Law Quarterly* 52 (2003): 549–285.

Brennan, S., 'Children's choices or children's interests: Which do their rights protect?'. In *The Moral and Political Status of Children*. eds. D. Archard & C.M. Macleod (New York: Oxford University Press, 2002) 53–69.

Brighouse, H., 'What rights (if any) do children have?'. In *The Moral and Political Status of Children*. eds. D. Archard & C.M. Macleod (New York: Oxford University Press, 2002) 31–52.

Choudhry, S. & Fenwick, H., 'Taking the rights of parents and children seriously: Confronting the welfare principle under the human rights act', *Oxford Journal of Legal Studies* 25 (2005): 453–492.

Choudhry, S. & Herring, J., *European Human Rights and Family Law* (Oxford: Hart Publishing, 2010).

Dwyer, J.G., *The Relationship Rights of Children* (New York: Cambridge University Press, 2006).

Eekelaar, J., 'The importance of thinking that children have rights', *International Journal of Law, Policy and the Family* 6 (1992): 221–235.

Eekelaar, J., 'The interests of the child and the child's wishes: The role of dynamic self-determinism', *International Journal of Law, Policy and the Family* 8 (1994): 42–61.

Eekelaar, J., 'Children's rights: From battle cry to working principle'. In *Liber Amicorum Marie-Thérèse Meulders-Klein: Droit Comparé Des Personnes Et De La Famille*. ed. J. Pousson-Petit (Brussels: Bruylant, 1998) 197–215.

Eekelaar, J., 'Beyond the welfare principle', *Child and Family Law Quarterly* 14 (2002): 237–250.

Eekelaar, J., *Family Law and Personal Life* (Oxford: Oxford University Press, 2007).

Federle, K.H., 'Rights flow downhill', *International Journal of Children's Rights* 2 (1994): 343–368.

Federle, K.H., 'Looking ahead: An empowerment perspective on the rights of children', *Temple Law Review* 68 (1995): 1585–1605.

Federle, K.H., 'Review essay: Rights, not wrongs', *International Journal of Children's Rights* 17 (2009): 321–329.

Feinberg, J., 'The nature and value of rights'. In *Rights, Justice, and the Bounds of Liberty: Essays in Social Philosophy* (Princeton: Princeton University Press, 1992) 143–58.

Fortin, J., 'Accommodating children's rights in a post Human Rights Act era', *Modern Law Review* 69 (2006): 299–326.

Fortin, J., *Children's Rights: The Developing Law*, 3rd ed. (Cambridge: Cambridge University Press, 2009).

Freeman, M.D.A., *The Rights and Wrongs of Children* (London: Pinter, 1983).

Freeman, M.D.A., 'Review essay: What's right with rights for children', *International Journal of Law in Context* 2 (2006): 89–98.

Freeman, M.D.A., 'Why it remains important to take children's rights seriously', *International Journal of Children's Rights* 15 (2007): 5–23.

Freeman, M.D.A., 'Children's rights as human rights: Reading the UNCRC'. In *The Palgrave Handbook of Childhood Studies*. eds. J. Qvortrup, W.A. Corsaro & M.-S. Honig (London: Palgrave-Macmillan, 2009) 377–393.

Gardner, J., '"Simply in virtue of being human": The whos and whys of human rights', *Journal of Ethics and Social Philosophy* 2 (2008): 1–22.

Gilmore, S. & Herring, J., '"No" is the hardest word: Consent and children's autonomy', *Child & Family Law Quarterly* 23 (2011): 3–25.

Griffin, J., 'Do children have rights?'. In *The Moral and Political Status of Children*. eds. D. Archard & C.M. Macleod (New York: Oxford University Press, 2002) 19–30.

Guggenheim, M., *What's Wrong with Children's Rights* (London: Harvard University Press, 2005).

Herring, J., *Family Law*, 5th ed (Harlow: Longman, 2011).

MacCormick, N., 'Children's rights: A test case for theories of rights'. In *Legal Right and Social Democracy: Essays in Legal and Political Philosophy* (Oxford: Oxford University Press, 1984).

McNamara, L., *Human Rights Controversies: The Impact of Legal Form* (London: Routledge-Cavendish, 2007).

O'Neill, O., 'Children's rights and children's lives', *Ethics* 98 (1988): 445–463.

Sunstein, C.R., 'On the expressive function of law', *University of Pennsylvania Law Review* 144 (1995–1996): 2021–2053.

Cases Cited

UK

A v. UK (Human Rights: Punishment of a Child) [1998] 2 FLR 959.
A (Children) (Conjoined Twins: Surgical Separation), Re [2001] Fam 147 (EWCA).
B (A Child) (Adoption by One Natural Parent), Re [2001] UKHL 70.
E (A Minor) (Wardship: Medical Treatment) [1992] 2 FCR 219.
Gillick v. West Norfolk & Wisbech AHA [1986] AC 112.
Glass v. UK [2004] 1 FCR 553 (ECtHR).
H (Children) (Contact Order) (No 2), Re [2002] 1 FLR 22 (Fam Div).
KD (A Minor: Termination of Access), Re [1988] AC 806.
M (Child's Upbringing), Re [1996] EWCA Civ 1320.
Mabon v Mabon [2005] EWCA Civ 634.
R (A Child), Re [2009] EWCA Civ 445.
R (A Minor) (Wardship: Consent to Treatment), Re [1991] 4 All ER 177 (EWCA).
R (on the application of Axon) v Sec of St for Health [2006] EWHC 37.
W (A Minor) (Medical Treatment: Court's Jurisdiction), Re [1992] 2 FCR 785 (EWCA).
W (Contact Proceedings: Joinder of Child), Re [2001] EWCA Civ 1830.

ECtHR

Chepelev v. Russia [2007] 2 FCR 649.
Haase v. Germany [2004] 2 FCR 1.
Johansen v. Norway (1996) 23 EHRR 33.
Kearns v. France [2008] 1 FLR 888.
Marie v. Portugal [2004] 2 FLR 653.
Yousef v. Netherlands [2002] 3 FCR 577.

Canada

AC v. Manitoba (Director of Child and Family Services) 2009 SCC 30.

Legislation and international instruments cited

Children Act 1989.
Children Act 2004.
Family Law Reform Act 1969.
United Nations Convention on the Rights of the Child, 20 November 1989, 1577 U.N.T.S. 3.

The Long Awaited: Past Futures of Children's Rights

Anne McGillivray
Professor of Law, University of Manitoba
Email: Anne.McGillivray@ad.umanitoba.ca

> If you can look into the seeds of time,
> And say which grain will grow and which will not,
> Speak then to me, who neither beg nor fear
> Your favours nor your hate.
> *Macbeth* (ca. 1600-08, Act I Scene III)

> ... for childhood is the greatest of all mysteries, being full of the unknown future, and containing the germ of all that will, or alas! will not, develop itself in us ...
> Ernest Legouvé, 1881 (1:81)

Chimeras

A sleeping boy cradles the huge head of a chimera. Elderly, female and nude, it resembles a dugong genetically crossed with a human. It smiles in its sleep, or perhaps that is just the shape of its enormous mouth. The boy's cheek is pillowed on the creased and flabby flesh of its shoulder, his hand curled into its thin grey hair. Titled 'The Long Awaited', the scene is a life-size installation by Patricia Piccinini (2008). It is troubling. Who would allow a child near such a creature? But it is apparent that he loves it or her and she, or it, loves him. The title, too, is troubling. Who has waited long, for whom? Was she made for him, an experiment gone right or wrong, or was he made for her, the desired child of her strange infirmity? What joins them in their deep content? Were they at first afraid, the monster and the child? In what world could such difference so lovingly co-exist? It is a future world, a science-fiction world, in which genetics craft chimeras and the familiar embraces the strange. It is a world informed in central ways by rights.

If the relationship between Piccinini's enigmatic figures evokes rights, then it challenges classic liberal thinking in which the rights-holder is envisaged as an able-bodied and autonomous adult male. The relationship reflects a very different way of understanding rights and the subject of rights. Born of injustice, impelled by the horrors of human wrongs and visions of better worlds, rights diminish fear of the other by acknowledging shared humanity and celebrating difference (McGillivray, 1994, 2012c). As markers of relationships of equality, rights are about love. As nodes in webs of interdependence, rights allow autonomy to flourish. This is not the absurd autonomy of John Wayne fictions and extreme liberty claims. It is the yearning for autonomy inscribed on the child's heart (McGillivray, 2012b) and limned in the gestalt of the chimera, 'a vessel to be filled with possibility, with a plurality of autonomous yearnings' (Williams, 1991:16). Rights are embedded in being. Their codification is short-hand for what it means to be human or, to take another metaphor, the skeletal support structure of the shared enterprise of becoming human. Rights are embodied in children. They are written in children's nascent neurology, its development so intricate and delicate that wrong touch and hateful words bring illness and mental disorder, reduce intelligence and affect future generations of children. Rights are essential to childhood.

The sculpture's title – 'The Long-Awaited' – is evocative of the present state of children's rights. With the advent of the Convention on the Rights of the Child, we stand on the threshold of possibility. Imagining the future of children's rights means imagining new relationships and new ways of being human. Futures are imagined in the present but it is only when the future has melted imperceptibly into the past do we know what our choices will have made of childhood. Will it be the eden we sometimes imagine it anyway to be, or the dystopia of ignorance and exploitation it is for millions now, whose childhood is relegated to corporations or parents or closed communities that abuse children's bodies or credulity and indoctrinate hate and fear? Wordsworth's (1802) Child may endlessly father the Man but making rights-respecting futures takes conscious, deliberated action. As Susan Marks (2011:75) observes, 'history is a social product, not given but made. And if it has been made, it can be remade differently.' History frames possibilities and 'change unfolds within a context that includes systematic constraints and pressures' but there is nothing necessary about the future. To imagine futures is to imagine the societies – utopic, dystopic, edenic – that we fear or desire.

To imagine futures is to scrutinise the past for the cause-and-effect that lets us make the futures we want. The course of human rights for the most part has been a reaction to random events (Marks, 2011). Punishment builds children's character, so criminal assault is legally justified. Parents own children's belief, so the law must defer to parents' religious rights. There is no place for the state in relationships of intimacy, so raising a child is a purely private matter. We believed all this once. Many still do. The relationship between ideology and social reform is tricky. Failure of the imagination –the failure to think beyond the ideological and the practicable to the child's subjectivity and autonomy – may twist the good intended into hell for its recipients. Reforming childhood may mark a people for generations into the future, as did the 'civilizing' regimes that severed indigenous children from community and ethos (McGillivray, 1997b). Presuming parental and tutorial benevolence and protecting religious and parental justifications for the violation of children's bodies and rights, as we have done for well over a thousand years in Western law, hurt children in ways we refuse to consider or fail to imagine. Adult freedom of religion was at stake in the polygamous community of Bountiful, British Columbia, but the harm done to children – sexual abuse, physical abuse, exploitation of labour, denial of education rights – justified the criminal law's prohibition of polygamy (Polygamy Reference Case, 2011; McGillivray, 2013).

This paper is an invitation to improve our imagination of the future of children's rights by thinking about social, cultural, environmental and biological contingents and contexts. Utopias and science fictions and the trajectories of history are invoked in these imaginings. From every event flows streams of possibility. Rights-thinking means locating those streams in which children rights will best flourish or are at greatest risk. It means, imagining how they may be followed, blocked or redirected, and acting accordingly. Utopian thinking has played a dangerous role in thinking about children's rights.[1]

The Utopian Imagination

Imagining utopias – 'new and better ways of organizing human life and society, different civilizations, without the flaws and limitations of the one the writer happens to live in, and more pleasing to its citizens' as John Crowley (2006:37) puts it – has a long tradition. Thomas More invented the word in 1516 to name his 'best state of public weal'. It is both Utopia ('no place') and Eutopia ('good place'): 'Wherfore not Utopie, but rather rightely my name is Eutopie, a place of felicitie'. For Peter van de Kamp (2012:253), 'The search for a better world is fairly inherent in the human condition, but so is the sobering, and sometimes reassuring, realization that such a world does not exist. This antithesis is encapsulated in our use of the word 'utopia', topologizing in one collocation the Greek prefix for 'not' (oÛ) and for 'good' (eÜ).' However felicitous they appear, utopias are rarely places in which any but their makers would wish to live.

A century after More published his tale of discovery of his imagined isle, Comenius (1663) began inventing his utopic Pansophia, a reform of everything

---

[1] I am grateful to John Crowley for setting me straight on the distinction between the utopic and the edenic, and for his comments on this paper.

through knowledge of all held by all, in which science, philosophy, politics and religion from a harmonious luminous whole uniting children, women and men in omniscience and compassion. It would bring world peace. For Utopians, 'pearls and other gems [are] the badges of slavery, the marks of infamy, or the playthings of children' (More, 1516: Bk. II). For Pansophists, children are 'dearer to parents ... than pearls and gems' (Comenius, 1633:61). Utopia's children serve adults, learn trades and are exchangeable, with excess ones given to families with too few. Pansophia's children are educated in a surprisingly modern way according to their stage of intellectual and physical development, learning building on learning (Piaget, 1993). They are never hit. As Comenius explains, 'Indeed, by any application of force we are far more likely to produce a distaste for letters than love for them ... we should try to remove its indisposition by gentle remedies, but should on no account employ violent ones' (Piaget, 1993:7). His *Orbis Pictis* (1658), the first children's picture-book, was used as a text in Europe and North America for over two centuries.

When a big idea strikes – feminism, equality, new sciences, democracy – it inspires new worlds, 'a wholly other civilization arising out of the husk of the abandoned and collapsed old civilization' (Crowley, 2006:42). Comenius set his paradise at the heart of the labyrinth of his decaying war-torn world. So, too, the 1939 New York World's Fair featured the utopia of Democracity when the Depression's labyrinth of poverty, child mortality, and social injustice was barely ending (Crowley, 2006:45). Rational and geometric, a place of satellite suburbs, elevated highways, television and robots, streamlining, autogyro landing fields and nuclear energy, it was peopled by cheerful folk discussing the hard work and co-operation needed to make a decent world for children. Democracity embodied the 'longing for cleanliness, health and safety and a little ease in a world that did not express them generously'. The past is swept away. But of course it was not. A world war driven by the potent, dark, and irrational utopias of Nazism and Fascism was to begin mere months after Democracity's unveiling.

If the world is chaotic and unforgiving, another one is – or has to be – possible. A thought experiment can create in a mind's eye-blink a new biology or social architecture, new sciences, new worlds. 'More than social criticism, more than proposals for change or philosophies of human happiness, the great utopian projects are enormous and highly original fictions', their makers 'engaged in something which writers of literary fiction have only dared to do in the modernist twentieth century: refashioning the world into fiction, replacing it with imagined worlds of their own' (Crowley, 2006:48). This endless fashioning of fictional future worlds is science, or speculative, fiction.

Science fiction offers worlds of robed and ancient contemplatives who gave up children eons ago or give birth once a millennium, peaceful crafting women's worlds of single-story houses and few children besieged by unrecon-structed men (or free of them), worlds of intelligent frog-creatures voraciously cleansing their gene pools of unfit hatchling, post-apocalyptic quasi-dystopic worlds in which every community is its own thought-experiment and every childhood different, worlds of orphaned children who invent cargo-cults and await the hero's coming, and worlds of gene-bending bio-engineers birthing made-to-order children on domed asteroids or terra-sculpted moonlets. Children born without conscience deploy strange powers to overthrow adult rule. Children are chosen from poorly-performing schools to be consumed as recreational drugs by slavering aliens, or raised in perfect schools to ensure the quality of their harvested organs, or launched aboard spaceships as robot-raised embryos to breed the generations needed to colonise Goldilocks plan-ets light-years away, or disappear altogether and inexplicably from the world. Imagined worlds are rooted in the present. Where children appear, they reflect contemporary fears about childhood. Children are, after all, infinite mirrors of ourselves.

Who imagines these futures? Children do, for one. In a 1993 Australian study, children imagined violent 'depersonalised and uncaring' worlds split between 'haves and have-nots', oppressive technological worlds, environ-mentally-destroyed worlds, and 'politically corrupt and deceitful' worlds (Hutchinson, 1999:s. 4.3). Some children, mostly boys, preferred 'technocratic dreaming' futures of 'techno-fix solutions' while girls more often preferred demilitarised worlds and the greening of science and technology. Children imagined inter-generational equity, an imperative of responsibility to future generations, and 'making peace with people and planet' through new ethics and new ways of living. They want their schools to let them imagine futures and to give them the ecological literacy and conflict-resolution skills that let them make the future they want. A 1995 UK study found that younger chil-dren and boys generally are less pessimistic about the future but all children fear war, violence, and a degraded environment. Girls are 'less likely to embrace uncritically technocratic dreaming or 'glamorous high-tech solu-tions" (Hutchinson, 1999:s. 5). Schools, children thought, should help them make hope practical.

Herbert George Wells does, for another. A prolific writer of almost every sort of book, Wells is best remembered for his 'science romances' introducing many of the familiar tropes of science fiction. In *The Time Machine* (1895), the child-like Eloi are exploited as foodstuff by the technologic troglodytic Morlocks. Sentient chimeras created by dark science on *The Island of Dr. Moreau* (1896) are taught The Law but assert their liberty and defy their maker. *The War of the Worlds* (1897) is won by blood-borne bacteria that kill the blood-feeding Martians. Children grown to 40 feet high on *Food of the Gods* (1904) claim the right to be different from their parents. New technologies – aerial warfare, biological warfare, lasers, atomic weapons, radio-active ruin, parallel universes – make their first appearance in Wells's stories. His *World Brain* (1937), 'an efficient index to all human knowledge, ideas and achievements' and 'a complete planetary memory for all mankind', is endowed with a sort of sentience – 'the concentration of a craniate animal and the diffused vitality of an amoeba'. In its potential for the 'intellectual unification of our race', the World Brain recalls Comenius's unification of all by knowledge held by all. Consisting of modern technologies – microfilm distributed by airplanes, free throughout the world – it is a cognate of the Internet and a basis for Wells' World State.

Like Utopia, the World State was inspired by Plato's Republic but it would lack Utopia's flaws, most notably its intolerance. It would be a *Modern Utopia* (1905). 'Now what sort of question would first occur to two men descending upon the planet of a Modern Utopia? Probably grave solicitude about their personal freedom. Towards the Stranger ... the Utopias of the past displayed their least amiable aspect. Would this new sort of Utopian State, spread to the dimensions of a world, be any less forbidding?' As 'universal Toleration is certainly a modern idea, and it is upon modern ideas that this World State rests', toleration would be a central principle. 'But even suppose we are tolerated and admitted to this unavoidable citizenship, there will still remain a wide range of possibility.' If 'the question [is] one of 'Man versus the State', then Wells chooses 'the compromise of Liberty'. For Wells, 'the age of a world of fragmented, separate, and competing states was at an end' (Whelan, 2012:44). His 'revolution of conspiracy' – the education of all for collective world citizenship, combined with the 'completest freedom of speech, criticism and publication' – would result in a 'new and complete' World State. More pragmatic than the Fabians with whom he had been closely associated (Lodge, 2011), Wells saw no conflict between human rights and top-down planned communities: 'The more highly things are collectivised the more necessary is a legal system embodying the Rights of Man' (quoted, Partington, 2007: n.p.).

The World State would be based not on Pansophia's static perfection or Fabian snail's-paced piecemeal reform, but on a scientific socialism. Its legal system would be founded on a 'fuller, more jealously conceived restatement of the personal Rights of Man' to be 'fully defined in a code of fundamental human rights' (quoted, Whelan, 2012:46). The first step to world peace and the World State, then, was a universal declaration of human rights (Partington, 2007: n.p.). Wells's discussions with President and Eleanor Roosevelt inspired Roosevelt's Four Freedoms — freedom of speech and belief, freedom from want and fear — which express the essence of Wells's wordy document. (Burger, 1992: 470). In the early months of the Second World War, Wells wrote a pamphlet titled, 'The Rights of Man. What are we fighting for?'. Translated into multiple languages, discussed in newspapers across Europe and dropped behind enemy lines, it was to put a quick end to the war, turning 'good Germans' against Hitler by showing them a rights-based future (Burger, 1992:467; Walz, 2002:437). The plan's 'rather utopian' naivety was made plain in the disaster of Dunkirk and the bombing of London shortly after (Whelan, 2012:47). In *The Rights of Man* (1940a: Preamble), Wells reiterates 'the imperative need for a declaration'. Drafts were submitted to United Nations Declaration Drafting Committee chaired by Eleanor Roosevelt (Roosevelt, 1945-1962: Part 2). 'It is evident that other human rights advocates at the time recalled Wells's Declaration' and some of his language is reflected therein (Burger, 1992; Whelan, 2012: 47).

In a 1942 letter to the *Tribune*, Wells predicted that until a declaration of rights becomes 'the fundamental law of a federated world', 'this earth will be ruled entirely by pampered old lags' (Partington, 2003:129). Without rights embedded in law, the World State will collapse into totalitarianism. 'The populations under their sway, after a phase of servile discipline, are plainly doomed to relapse into disorder and violence. Everywhere war and monstrous economic exploitation break out, so that those very same increments of power and opportunity which have brought mankind within sight of an age of limitless plenty, seem likely to be lost again, it may be lost for ever, in an ultimate social collapse' (quoted, Partington, 2003:128). The rhetoric echoes that of *The War of the Worlds* (1895: Book 1 ch. 1): 'Yet across the gulf of space, minds that are to our minds as ours are to those of the beasts that perish, intellects vast and cool and unsympathetic, regarded this earth with envious eyes, and slowly and surely drew their plans against us. And early in the twentieth century came the great disillusionment.'

And so it was for Wells. His Rights of Man influenced the genesis and content of the Universal Declaration of Human Rights (1948) and the ensuing International Covenant on Civil and Political Rights (1966) and the UN Convention on the Rights of the Child. His World State, premised like Pansophia on universal knowledge and equality and, like Pansophia, lovingly reworked across a lifetime, came to nothing.

For Crowley (2006:51), the 'utopian impulse is not social criticism but the furthest reach of the impulse to construct fictions'. Fiction as thought experiment, as a means of exploring futures flowing from contemporary events from every possible angle by deploying multiple agonists with differing experience and points of view, is another matter. In contemplating the futures of children's rights, speculative fiction may be precisely what is needed. In these imaginings, the past is not swept away. It is the source of futures, as much for what ought not happen as for what should be. Whatever the future of children's rights, it will not erase the past. The past is key to what (not) to do in making the future of children's rights.

Past Futures

Is childhood universal? Is childhood biological? Anthropologists John Whiting and Irvin Child (1953:63) write, 'Child training everywhere seems to be in considerable part concerned with problems which arise from universal characteristics of the human infant and from universal characteristics of adult culture which are incompatible with the continuation of infantile behaviour.' In every culture, children are guided through profound changes to body and brain, socially-undesirable behaviours are trained away, and children's sexual expression is delayed. Little else, anthropologically speaking, is universal about childhood. Whether childhood is a *sentiment* or *conception* as Philippe Ariès (1962; McGillivray, 1997a) posits, or the child 'nothing but an imaginary species' as Hélène Cixous (1982:234) claims, or merely unimaginable 'except in relation to a conception of the adult' as Chris Jenks (1996:3) concludes, or a site of emotional projection by adults upon children as Jacqueline Rose (1984) writes of Peter Pan, or a tribe apart as Patricia Hersch (1999) terms adolescents, we do not understand either childhood or children very well. The study of childhood is itself compromised. Ludmilla Jordanova (1990:79) observes that historians 'are the products of societies that currently hold complex, deeply contradictory, and largely unarticulated views about children. Our capacity to sentimentalise, identify with, project onto, and reify children is almost infinite.'

Biological explanations of childhood have not been much better. Confusing biology with class, gender, ethnicity or culture is most obvious (to us) in other cultural and historic contexts – in the 'other' children of Victorian Britain, for example, or the slave children in the Americas – and least obvious (to us) in our own. Why look at what you have already seen? But that which is closest to us is hardest to see. So Jacob Weill (1882:10) could conclude that individuality or personality ('completely independent life') emerges at two, before which the infant is 'vegetative' and 'parasitic' and William James (1890:462) that infant perception is 'one great blooming, buzzing confusion'. We now see infants interacting with others from birth, using expression, gaze, mimicry, crying, touch, and 'cuteness' (large eyes and forehead, facial foreshortening) to maintain caregiver proximity (Wenegrat, 1984:51 et seq.) and expressing the full range of human emotion – love, anger, sorrow, pleasure, pain. Traditional cultures did not practise child corporal punishment (McGillivray, 1997b, 1999; Diamond, 2012: ch. 5). Comparing the skill level and maturity of a five-year-old Amazonian child with a same-age North American child demonstrates the role of culture in perceptions of children and of perception on children's capability (cf. Kolbert, 2012; Diamond, 2012: ch. 5). In the past two decades, we have learned more about children's neurological development than we imagined there was to be known, including the dramatic re-organisation of the adolescent brain (Jetha and Segalowitz, 2012). We know we cannot push children into being other than themselves (Gopnik, 2000). We know that emotional abuse (Hibbard *et al.* 2012), physical assault (Durrant and Ensom, 2012), sexual exploitation, environmental toxins and the teratogenic effects of alcohol on the fetus (Committee, 2000) damage cognition and development. Poverty affects children's test scores, drop-out rates, drug use, violence and the likelihood of protective apprehension and criminal arrest. But what of the harm done by keeping children ignorant and exploiting their credulity? What we do to children affects them deeply. It builds or shreds the psyche. Acts and omissions trivial to an adult may damage children deep at the neurological level. Where children are silenced, their bodies speak. That children's rights are about children's bodies suggests that rights-based futures are not utopian, but deeply practical.

If rights are not (just) products of covenants and courts but are rooted in respect and relationship, then children's rights are visible before history began. They may be traced in the social practices of other species, ethics innate in human infants, prehistoric art and burial practices, folk tales with cross-cultural resonance, and tales and mythologies with deep cultural resonance. The trajectory of rights across history is a slowly widening arc embracing more children, encompassing more circumstances, conferring more rights and becoming more deeply embedded in law, policy, and the polity. History discloses some very bad thinking about what is the future-oriented good for children.[2]

Before History Happened

Primates show cooperation, empathy, reciprocity, and altruism, behaviours at the basis of rights (Wade, 2007). Capacity for moral choice is innate. Infants of six months react negatively to a 'bad' shape that causes another to fall downhill, choosing instead the 'good' shape that helps it climb (Khamsi, 2007). Children may be instinct with law (Guttentag, 2009). A Neolithic marble figure (ca.5000-3500 BCE) shows a child leaning trustingly into the back of a seated adult, its hand seeming to stroke the adult's hair. The death of children may have spurred evolution – those infants most successful in attracting adult resources are most likely to live to pass that set of survival traits to their offspring (Atkinson and Volk, 2008). How Neolithic children are

---

[2] The five sections here following are based on my 2012 curriculum for Children and the Law which in turn was inspired by a course developed for McGill University by Desmond Manderson and his colleagues. I am grateful to Professor Manderson for his comments on the course.

buried shows how they were valued by their communities (Waterman and Thomas, 2011).

Ancient tales collected in the Bible tell of rage-driven mass murders of children – Elijah calling out the she-bears to maul the teasing children (2 Kings 2:23), Herod's slaughter of the innocents (Matthew 2:16-18) – and twelve Proverbs urge their vigorous beating. Lot offers his young daughters to the mob to spare his angelic guests the Sodomites' lust (Genesis 19) and Abraham is ready to kill his only son (Genesis 22:1-13). The ash-child Cinderella and her kin play out the drama of step-parent conflict in cultures throughout the world (Daly and Wilson, 1998), demonstrating girls' ingenuity (Windling, n.d.) and rights (Covell, 2010). Modern classics like Maurice Sendak's *Where the Wild Things Are* (1963) evoke the deep agenda – love and hunger, punishment and desire, banishment and reconciliation – embedded in the mythology of law and in the law that informs literature for children (Manderson, 2003).

From the Romans to the Moderns

The influence of Roman law on English law is most evident in that body of law governing marriage, family and childhood, for centuries under the jurisdiction of the Roman-based ecclesiastical courts. With the re-emergence of Justinian's Digest in 1070, Roman precepts concerning such common law questions as the liability of children were adopted by English jurists. The place of children under Roman law depended on status – owned or abandoned, slave or free, male or female, *infantia* or capable of legal speech. The power of the Roman father over every aspect of the child's life (and death) and the legal treatment of unowned and slave children have no modern equivalent. The new-born infant of whom Statius wrote, 'he demanded the novel air with trembling wails' while tenderly cradled in the poet's arms, was *verna*, house-reared, and Statius's property to be sold on or trained up to minister to his owner's sexual desires (Thoneman, 2011). While these modes of childhood would now attract the attention of the police, Roman doctrines of paternal power (McGillivray, 2012c) and *parens patriae* (McGillivray, 2004) are reflected in modern law and human rights codes. They underlie the 'parental rights and duties' referenced in the Convention on the Rights of the Child as well as in the duties of the state set out therein. In the latter days of the Roman empire, there are signs of what we now see as children's rights – the right to life, expressed as the edict terminating the paternal powers to inflict death on any child of the household, the edicts establishing the child's rights to maintenance and emancipation, and the right of children under 14 to the special dispensation of the law.

Mid-sixteenth century children populate Bruegel's 1560 painting 'Children's Games' but a closer look reveals mimicry of adult pursuits. In *Kinder-spel* (1625), Dutch lawyer and popular poet Jacob Cats draws moral lessons from children's play: 'Play, even if it appears without sense, / Contains a whole world therein: / ... You will find there, I know it well, / Your own folly in children's games.' As Ariès (1962) describes it, the pre-modern child was a miniature adult moved swiftly from infancy to adult society and childhood was a blissful state in an undifferentiated world (McGillivray, 1997). From late sixteenth-century regimes for segregated instruction and surveillance of children, childhood began to emerge as a *sentiment*, a bounded social construct explicitly about itself. The artists of Georgian Britain led the way. By featuring the child subject in their works and by promoting change through prints sentimentalising childhood, they extended the New Childhood from the aristocracy to the middle classes (Steward, 1995; Stone, 1982; King, 2007). In 1690, John Locke questioned paternal ownership of children and in 1692 promoted a child-centred education in which praise was to be given in public and shame or remonstrance only in private. Seventy years later, Jean-Jacques Rousseau (1762) inserted play into the education of his fictional *Émile*, although he deposited his own infants at the gates of the local foundling hospital. His depiction of children as pure, as *sauvage*, to be protected from the contamination of society contrasts oddly with the *enfant sauvage* of the New World captivity narrative (McGillivray, 1999). Criminal cases heard at London's Old Bailey during this period remind us of the children untouched by the New Childhood. In this period, we see intimations of emergence of the rights to be heard, to be educated, to play, and to freedom of association and the bestowal of affection.

The spirit of nineteenth-century reform is captured in the 1834 *Report from His Majesty's Commission for Inquiring into the Administration and Practical Operation of the Poor Laws* and the 1837 British House of Commons *Report of the Select Committee on Aborigines*. The Select Committee was concerned with 'Native Inhabitants of Countries where British Settlements are made ... to promote the spread of civilization among them'. The Poor Laws Commission dealt with the outcast closer to home. Overseers or protectors, training aimed at low-level employment, and assimilation were recommended in both reports. Both stressed childhood and the need to civilise the young pauper or Aboriginal through education and Christianity. The nineteenth-century evangelical charity movement campaigned for the salvation of children through better treatment. The modern genre of children's literature has its roots here (cf. *The Youth's Magazine*, 1807). Charles Dickens's children – Twist (1839), Nell (1841), Copperfield (1850), Pip (1861) – illuminate the evils of the New Poor Law, the barrenness of charity, and the 'other childhood' of Victorian England. Charles Kingsley's *The Water-Babies* (1863) inaugurated children's fantasy. The first cleric to endorse Darwin's *Origin of Species*, Kingsley found salvation for Tom the sweep's boy in a weird amalgam of evolutionary theory, Christianity and Celtic myth. A decade later, photographic images of Mary Ellen, an abused

New York child of ten, were deployed to symbolise the shift from a charitable and salvationist model to a scientific legislative model of child protection. Agencies were empowered to remove cruelly-used or neglected children from parental custody to be assigned to the state-licensed foster homes that were swiftly replacing the orphanage. Conditions for children in factories and mines were improved, the use of small children as climbing-boys was abolished, and rights to protection from abuse and exploitation began to emerge.

Empire and Its Others

With the end of the Hudson's Bay Company charter and the opening of the Canadian West to settlement in the late nineteenth century, something had to be done with the Indians (McGillivray, 1997b). Adults were made wards of the state and confined to reserves where lessons in citizenship might be learned. Childhood was made the locus of civilisation. The 1837 British Select Committee on Aborigines concluded, 'True civilization and Christianity are inseparable: the former has never been found, but as a fruit of the latter'. If indigenous adults were infantilised on the path to civilisation, children were literally pressed into its service. From the 1860s to the 1960s, children were forced to attend church-run federal residential schools far from home and the 'degrading influence of the tepees', as the *Calgary Herald* opined in 1893 (McGillivray, 1997b:154). The 1889 Indian Affairs Annual Report explained, 'The boarding school disassociates the Indian child from the deleterious home influences to which he would otherwise be subjected. It reclaims him from the uncivilized state in which he has been brought up. It brings him into contact from day to day with all that tends to effect a change in his views and habits of life. By precept and example he is taught to endeavour to excel in what will be most useful to him.' But as a Presbyterian missionary observed in 1903, the schools were nothing more than an attempt 'to educate & colonize a people against their will'. Culture excised, Indian children would be fit British-Canadian citizens. The legacy of their abuse and the attenuation of cultural and family ties damaged them, their kin and their communities down to the present generation.

England's romance with its Empire – vast wild spaces to be explored, fortunes to be made and natives to be befriended, exploited, studied or shot – is refracted in multiple ways in literature for children. Tales of creation and lessons from the mystical and natural dwellers of the Americas taught indigenous children of origins, wonders, and dangers (Canada's First Nations, n.d.) but it was the contrived wild boy Peter Pan who renewed the myth of childhood in Edwardian London at the opening of the twentieth century (Rose, 1984). Peter Pan first appears as an infant consorting with fairies in *The Little White Bird* (Barrie, 1902), a book for adults. A version of the story featuring an older Pan became a pantomime (Barrie, 1904), followed by *Peter Pan in Kensington Gardens* (Barrie, 1906) excerpted from *The Little White Bird* as a children's book illustrated by Arthur Rackham and, last, the familiar *Peter and Wendy* (Barrie, 1911). For those boys who were to be made into sterner stuff, Lord Baden-Powell recounted fireside yarns of his frontier adventures in *Scouting for Boys* (1908), inaugurating a world-wide movement aimed at building children's character and physique. Rights to protection, education, and information began to emerge.

The Century of the Child

As Ellen Key (1909) predicted, the twentieth century was the century of the child, although perhaps not quite in the way she meant. It rapidly became a century of atrocities revealed – mass murders of children and the fact, ubiquity, forms and harms of child abuse – and of the unequivocal declaration of rights for children. The Victorian child-saving movement morphed into the Progressive Era, in Canada the Age of Hygiene, and was swallowed by two world wars bracketing the Great Depression (McGillivray, 1992). The atrocities of the second, with input from the utopian dreaming of H.G. Wells, inspired the Universal Declaration of Human Rights (UDHR, 1948) which in turn inspired the 1959 Declaration on the Rights of the Child and the 1989 Convention on the Rights of the Child (Convention). Anne Frank, in hiding from 1942 to 1944 during the Nazi occupation of Amsterdam, betrayed at 14 and dead of typhus in Bergen-Belsen at 15, left behind her account of growing up under the Third Reich (Frank, 1952). Over 1.5 million Jewish children died with her. With a forward by Eleanor Roosevelt, Chair of the UDHR drafting committee, her diary was misrepresented as a girlish message of hope. Later performances of her story appropriated the voice of this iconic child, downplayed her Jewish identity and obscured the anti-Semitism of the Holocaust (Ozik, 1992; Chatterly, 2012).

Physical punishment remained a widely-practised parental power. Resulting injuries and deaths were readily explained as childhood misadventures. Radiology technology developed during the Second World War provided a window into children's bodies, disclosing histories of abuse in subdural bruising and half-healed fractures. The 1962 publication of 'The Battered Child Syndrome' (Kempe *et al.* 1962; McGillivray, 1992) showed that torture of children is not confined to the atrocities of war and racism. It is also an atrocity of everyday family life. Physical abuse became near-synonymous with childhood but corporal punishment powers remained virtually untouched. When Freud replaced his Seduction Theory, which described the sexual abuse of girls by fathers and brothers, with his Oedipal Complex, which returned sexual abuse to the imaginary (Wolff, 1995), psychiatry sheltered pedophiles and their victims. With the recovery of women's lives in second-wave feminist consciousness-raising ('the personal is the political'), the ubiquity of child sexual abuse was uncovered. That girls are victims and family males are perpetrators was a tidy fit with theories of patriarchal oppression. By the 1980s, sexual abuse had overtaken physical abuse as 'child abuse', legislation was enacted and revised at an astonishing pace and the law of evidence was reformed (McGillivray, 1990, 1999, 2007). New child pornography laws conflated art and innocence with criminal acts and illegitimate desire (Higgonet, 1998). The later discovery that boys are victims too, and in great numbers, has lent an unfortunate nuance to *Scouting for Boys* (Moore and Mackrael, 2007).

In the annals of children's rights, the Convention is the century's greatest achievement, yet its first substantive article establishes parental powers. Article 5 'asserts that Parties to the Convention should defer to the child's parents or guardians when determining the scope of the child's exercise of rights' (Price Cohen, 2006:196). The Convention mentions parents 36 times, 19 of its 41 substantive articles defer to them; and its language of 'parental rights' suggests a proprietary role for parents rather than a fiduciary one (McGillivray, 2012c). Repairing the Convention's flaws, resolving its compromises and making it function as a declaration of the rights of children, not of parents, religious leaders and ethno-cultural groups (McGillivray, 2013), is the continuing task of the future.

Into the New Millennium

At the opening of the twenty-first century, the orphaned wizard Harry Potter (Rowling, 1997-2007) emerged as the iconic child. Growing from a neglected childhood into a gloomy adolescence under the gaze of millions of children, taught by cruel or incompetent masters, subjected to terrifying tests of moral and magical fortitude, his destiny uncertain despite his great and secret powers, he embodies the yearning and contradictions of contemporary childhood. At the dawn of the new millennium, corporal punishment remains symptomatic of the extreme power imbalance between children and adults (McGillivray, 1998; Freeman, 2010). The Supreme Court of Canada ruled in Canadian Foundation (2004) that 'trivial' corporal punishment violates no right of the child, although the court banned its use by teachers (McGillivray, 2012a). The decision is 'note[d] with regret' by the Committee on the Rights of the Child (2012). Some religions require beating children (Boesveld, 2011; Eckholm, 2011) and US home-schooling is largely fuelled by the need to punish out of sight of the state. The Home School Legal Defense Association (n.d.) advises homeschoolers to secure doors and windows before 'administering corporal discipline' and to obtain written permission before beating the children of others.

The Association has mounted a campaign against US ratification and use of the Convention.

The Phoenix Inquiry into the prolonged torture and murder of a five-year-old Manitoba girl by her mother and stepfather while under state supervision (Lambert, 2013) is just the latest of dozens of investigations into child protection failures in Canada. The poisonous intersections of despair, poverty, addiction, racism and learned violence carry the legacies of child-hating and Indian residential schooling into the future. Canada, one of the world's healthiest economies, has seen child apprehension rates skyrocket due not to severe injury or neglect but to poverty, chaotic conditions and behavioural disabilities, according to Dr. Charles Ferguson (correspondence with the author, 26 July 2012), Director of the Winnipeg Child Protection Centre, expert witness and world pioneer in the examination of children for sexual abuse. Placing children in culturally-familiar homes is compromised by the fact that they often are affected by the same conditions as the original ones. Even so, children refuse to return to their parents. Reported sexual abuse is down, partly a result of the exhausted supply of 'historical' cases. Children rarely testify. The courts have yet to learn how to hear young children and adolescents refuse to take the stand. Intergenerational maltreatment is the norm. 'The irony is that many parents, having suffered dreadfully in their childhood, swear never to repeat but they almost invariably do. They fall in with, or choose, blighted partners of a similar fate, and the cycle repeats itself, often with even more diabolical outcomes.' Most child homicide victims are under three. The average Manitoba sentence for child-killing is three years. Remote communities lack counseling for children suffering drug use, suicidal ideation, violence and lack of intellectual stimulation. Because of remoteness and community degradation, schools are war zones. One school recently cancelled kindergarten because the community's preschoolers were all in care elsewhere.

The rights-respecting schools conceived by Katherine Covell and Brian Howe of Nova Scotia's Cape Breton Children's Rights Centre have taken root in Hampshire County, UK but not in Canada (Covell *et al.* 2008, 2010). They show high levels of student engagement, literacy, self-esteem and scholastic performance, and significant reductions in drop-outs, bullying and teacher burnout. Landon Pearson's Children's Rights Academic Network brings together children from across Canada to discuss rights. Academics respond with written commentary. Folk-singer Raffi Cavoukian's Centre for Child Honouring promotes respect for children and the earth. With few but notable exceptions, children remain in the dark about their rights.

So do the governments of Canada. Marv Bernstein (correspondence with the author, 23 September 2012), Chief Advisor on Advocacy to UNICEF Canada, former Saskatchewan Children's Advocate and former legal counsel to the

Ontario Association of Children's Aid Societies, notes on behalf of UNICEF Canada that we are at a crossroads in translating paper rights into lived ones. Implementing the Convention's guiding principles – the rights to non-discrimination, best interests as a primary consideration, life, survival and development, and participation – would go far in making a rights-respecting future, one that leaves no child out because of being Aboriginal, poor, immigrant or in state care. Canada's constitution poses problems. Education, health and child welfare are under provincial and territorial aegis but Aboriginal peoples, immigration, youth justice and divorce are under federal aegis. Together with weak respect for children's rights, this enables inter-governmental disputes over who owes the child what duty. Courts seldom consider the Convention which, lacking enabling legislation, has no binding force. Raising the profile of childhood in the national psyche requires at the least that ministers ensure departmental consistency with the Convention. Creating the office of National Children's Commissioner would ensure inter-departmental co-ordination, program impact assessment, appropriate budget allocation, public reporting and respect for children's rights but Bill C-420 was defeated in December 2012 (Canada, 2012). As Bernstein observes, children are human beings, not human becomings. They are not interested in being our hope for the future.

Near Futures

Children's rights are embedded in children's bodies. Children's rights are physically linked to children's well-being and to their development into and through adulthood. It is not only children who benefit from children's rights, although that should be reason enough to respect them. Respecting their rights benefits the biosocial environment on which the lives of all depend. Children are not small adults. Blows, words, and toxins trivial to adults cause children profound cognitive and developmental harm, damaging them deep at the neurological level. 'We are conducting a vast toxicological experiment in which the research animals are our children' (Landrigan, 2001). Metaphorically, children are the salamanders signaling the health of our environment – family, community, state, biosphere. If actual rates of depression (Costello *et al.* 2006) or autism spectrum disorder (Autistic, n.d.) have not risen, their sheer prevalence in children suggests that all is not well. Whatever the cause of soaring obesity rates in developed countries, it signals a profound and disturbing change in human health.

What is the impact of the media-driven environment – video games, cell phones, text messaging, computers, television, iPods, MP3 players – in which children are immersed for an average seven hours and 38 minutes a day, or ten hours and 45 minutes of multi-tasked media content, the equivalent of school or a full-time job (Kaiser, 2012)? For the equivalent of every school day, children learn that males are brutal and violent, females are sexy, identity and self-worth is what you own and adults are good only for getting what you want (Bakan, 2011). What is the impact of corporate advertising on the child's sense of self? Children are endangering themselves through over-consumption. Viewing violence causes neurological damage (Warburton and Braunstein, 2012). Children cannot protect themselves from clever corporate messages backed by billions of advertising dollars that cause them to spend billions more. Is the new childhood a corporate childhood in which rights belong to corporations and the child's sole right is to consume for self-pleasure? This is the techno-future side of science fiction.

Buyers of sperm and ova can select traits of future children (Knouse, 2013). Pre-implantation genetic diagnosis is unregulated. Selection against genetic disorders is accepted. Should parents be permitted to select for gender, skin, and eye colour or, perhaps, for some desired disability? Does this bind children to parents' prejudices and raise the spectre of 'a proliferation of blond-haired, blue-eyed, light-skinned, non-disabled males'? Every year, multi-embryo transfer in Canada puts 840 infants in neo-natal and intensive care for 42,000 days, causes brain injuries in 46 babies and kills up to 40 (Kirkey, 2012). Do parents have an unfettered right to make decisions about procreation? This is science fiction as social engineering.

Mysterious ailments have taken children's lives since before history happened. Nodding head disease affects 3,000 Ugandan Acholi children between five and fifteen, causing spasms and helplessly bobbing heads (Muhumuza, 2012). Growth is stunted. Children fall into fires and ponds. Cognition is destroyed. In late stages of the disease, children cannot perform simple tasks or recognise their parents. Three hundred children so far are dead. Researchers studying the disease since 2009 have found no cause or treatment. Villagers say it is the legacy of Joseph Kony, whose Lord's Resistance Army abducted between 66,000 and 104,000 Acholi children to be made into sex slaves and killing machines. After Kony left Uganda in 2006, nodding disease arose in the villages most affected by his depredations. It is a story of an innocence so defiled that innocence itself becomes diseased, an evil so potent that it takes on a life of its own after its instigator is gone. This is the horror side of science fiction.

Killer robots – 'lethal autonomous machines' – are on the near horizon (Anderson and Waxman, 2012). Lethal weapons systems will 'inevitably' be added to the capacities of robotic systems already in the battlefield. Initially, humans will be in robot decision-making loops but with the 'inevitable and incremental evolution' in robot capacity, the human role will diminish. As robots will confer such 'humanitarian advantages' as avoiding civilian death, banning them is 'ethically questionable'. If robots can be programmed for any target, might it be set at, say, bipeds under one metre? Children are already killed as vermin (Williams, 2012). This is apocalyptic science fiction.

Wells feared that his socialist World State would disintegrate without universal rights but it is socialism itself that is fast disappearing from the world. The Singularity is 'a future period during which technological change will be so rapid, its impact so deep, that human life will be irreversibly transformed' (Kirzweil, 2005, Ch. 1). It is, then, a transhumanist future, 'neither dystopic nor utopian'. Extreme transhumanists, known as 'extropians,' add evolutionary theory to technological advances to predict a 'massive technological upgrade in the human condition' that would end death and disease and bring what science fiction writer Ken MacLeod (2012: n.p.) terms 'the nerd's Rapture'. Without socialism or something very like it to anchor rights, MacLeod warns that rights will disintegrate into a dystopic transhumanism. Socialism appeals to humanity's common interests and 'only the great religions have attempted anything like it. No other secular ideology has tried to be a totalising force in the same way.' While the establishment of the United Nations and of universal human rights expresses 'a common sense of universalism and common humanity' and an inspiring 'liberal, global humanism' it lacks socialism's firm footing in material self-interest. If, as MacLeod suggests, 'the end of socialism as a mass ideology is the end of humanity as an imagined community', then the challenge for humanists is 'to replace the socialist project – or to revive it. Without something like it to underpin a sense of common human identity and common human interest, people will divide on the basis of other identities.'

In millennial ideation, the apocalyptic and dystopic have long run in tandem with the utopian. The utopian ideal of progress 'hinges on millenarianism, with its misplaced trust in a kathartic apocalypse and its subsequent new dawn' (van de Kamp, 2010:260). As Crowley (2006:51) observes, some of history's worst excesses are utopian. Among these are the Third Reich 'which if it had not been tried out by force on living people would seem to us among the most ridiculously limited and unreal of all utopias', the Roman Empire newly-baptized as Holy that crushed the Czechoslovakia of Comenius's day, and the Soviet Union that crushed modern Czechoslovakia in the Prague Spring of 1968. Utopias are best left to the imaginary, never to be tried on living flesh.

Utopian constructs of what is good for children are equally doomed. Children are so much the vehicles of adult desire that utopias have consumed them. Children were massacred under Hitler to preserve the racial purity of other children and murdered by their parents to protect the transcendent utopic vision of Jonestown. They are claustrated in communities that foster ignorance and co-opt credulity and imprisoned in factories that produce cheap clothes and playthings for the children of the rich. Utopian movements intended for the salvation of children or the reform of childhood – the nineteenth-century child migration movement to save children from the gutter and spare the public purse while ignoring the fear, alienation and abuse suffered across oceans, or the 1834 Poor Law reforms that would teach children to loathe poverty and hunger by inflicting worse upon them, or the Indian residential schools that would recreate indigenous children as euro-Canadian subjects but instead facilitated their physical, sexual and spiritual abuse, or the eugenic sterilisation of 'unfit' children in Alberta from 1928 to 1972 to preserve the fitness of future children (and incidentally inspired Hitler). Utopian projects for the reconstruction of childhood failed miserably. They failed because they were not really about children and they failed for lack of imagination.

The historic trajectory of children's rights, slow at the start, has picked up considerable speed. Will it continue, stall, or be interrupted by new failures of the imagination? Setting aside the future in which we all become transhuman chimeras, will children's rights end with the end of the vision of humanity as a shared community, by the loss of a shared human identity? This is, after all, the basis of human rights. Science fiction's power as contextualised thought experiment is well-suited to imagining the near and far futures of children's rights. Placing the child at the heart of the future requires that her interests be disentangled from those of the parent, salvationist, state and corporation, and set fully into the bio-social. It requires an understanding of childhood transcending governmental, religious, disciplinary and cultural approaches. It requires consulting children. Children's rights are human rights. Human rights, as dignity, equality, social balance and redress, arose long before formal declarations of rights, out of a fundamental sense of fairness most keenly felt by children. For the most fragile and least understood members of our species, rights are a matter of life or death. It is by how we treat children now that we are judged in whatever future awaits.

References

American Humane Society, 'Mary Ellen (1874)' (n.d.) at http://www.americanhumane.org/about-us/who-we-are/history/mary-ellen-wilson.html.
Anderson, K. & Waxman, M.C., 'Law and ethics for robot soldiers' *Policy Review* (2012, forthcoming); Columbia Public Law Research Paper No. 12-313.
Ariès, P., *Centuries of Childhood: A Social History of Family Life*. tr. Robert Baldick (London: Jonathan Cape, 1962). Orig. pub. 1960, *L'Enfant et la vie familiale sous l'Ancien Régime*.
Atkinson, J. & Volk, T., 'Is child death the crucible of human evolution?' *Journal of Social, Evolutionary, and Cultural Psychology* 2(4) (2008): 247–260.
'Autistic spectrum disorders' (n.d.) at http://www.autism-help.org/autism-incidence-increase.htm.

Baden-Powell, R., *Scouting for Boys: A Handbook for Instruction in Good Citizenship* (London: H. Cox, 1908).

Bakan, J., *Childhood Under Seige: How Big Business Ruthlessly Targets Children* (Toronto: Allen Lane Canada, 2011).

Barrie, J.S., *The Little White Bird or Adventures in Kensington Gardens* (London: Hoddder, 1902).

Barrie, J.S., *Peter Pan in Kensington Gardens* (London: Scribner, 1906) and at http://www.gutenberg.org/files/26998/26998-h/26998-h.htm#chap01.

Barrie, J.S., *Peter and Wendy* (London: Scribner, 1911).

Bible. King James version at http://quod.lib.umich.edu/k/kjv.

Boesveld, S., 'God wants us to hit our children' *National Post* (12 November 2011) at http://news.nationalpost.com/2011/11/12/god-wants-us-to-hit-our-children/.

Boys' Own Annual (London: Religious Tract Society; Lutterworth, 1879–).

Breugel the Elder, 'Children's games'. In *Oil on Panel, 118 cm H 161 cm (46 in H 63 in)*. (Vienna: Kunsthistorisches Museum, 1560) at http://1.bp.blogspot.com/_-51t5EpBWAM/S664pMQozeI/AAAAAAAAAMs/xj917-Ry5HI/s1600/Bruegel-childrensgames.jpg.

Burgers, J.H., 'The road to San Francisco: The revival of the human rights idea in the twentieth century' *Human Rights Quarterly* 14(4) (1992): 447–477.

Canada. House of Commons Debates, '1st Session 41st Parliament Official Report' *Hansard* 146(190) (3 December 2012) at http://publications.gc.ca/collections/collection_2012/parl/X3-411-190-eng.pdf.

'Canada's first nations: Antiquity: Creation myths' (n.d.) at http://www.ucalgary.ca/applied_history/tutor/firstnations/antiquity.html.

Canadian Foundation for Children, Youth and the Law v. *Canada (Attorney General)*, (2004) 1 S.C.R. 76, 2004 SCC 4.

Cats, J., 'Kinder-spel' *Engraving* (1625) at http://lcweb2.loc.gov/diglib/ihas/loc.natlib.miller.0627/enlarge.html?page = 1&section = &size = 1024&from =

Cavoukian, R., 'Centre for child-honouring' (n.d.) at http://www.childhonouring.org/.

Chatterley, C., 'A critique of holocaust universalization in honour of Anne Frank' (25 April 2012) at http://canisa.org/1/post/2012/04/a-critique-of-holocaust-universalization-in-honour-of-anne-frank.html.

'Children's Rights Academic Network' (n.d.) at http://www.landonpearson.ca/cran.html.

Cixous, H., 'Introduction to Lewis Carroll's *through the looking glass* and *the hunting of the snark*' *New Literary History* 13(2) (1982): 234.

Clean Water Action, 'Time to act: Preventing harm to our children' (n.d.) at http://www.healthytomorrow.org/attachments/time2act.pdf.

Comenius, J., (1633). *School of Infancy: An Essay on the Education of Youth During the First Six Years.* ed. W.S. Monroe (Boston: Heath, 1896).

Comenius, J., *Orbis Pictus.* tr. Charles Hoole (Syracuse: W. Bardeen, 1658).

Comenius (1643), *Didactica Magna.* tr., ed. M.W. Keatinge (New York: Russell & Russell, 1967).

Committee on Substance Abuse and Committee on Children With Disabilities (n.d.), 'Fetal alcohol syndrome and alcohol-related neurodevelopmental disorders' *Pediatrics* 106(2) (2000): 358–361 at http://pediatrics.aappublications.org/content/106/2/358.ful.

Costello, E.J., Erkanli, A. & Angold, A., 'Is there an epidemic of child or adolescent depression?' *J. Child Psychology and Psychiatry* 47(12) (2006): 1263–1271.

Covell, K., Howe, R.B. & McNeil, J.K., 'If there's a dead rat, don't leave it. young children's understanding of their citizenship rights and responsibilities' *Cambridge Journal of Education* 38(30) (2008): 321–339.

Covell, K., Howe, R.B. & McNeil, J.K., 'Implementing children's human rights education in schools' *Improving Schools* 13(2) (2010): 1–16.

Crowley, J., 'The labyrinth of the world and the paradise of the heart'. In *In Other Words.* ed. Crowley (Burton, MI: Subterranean Press, 2006).

Daly, M. & Wilson, M., *The truth about Cinderella: a Darwinian view of parental love* (Yale University Press, 1998).

Diamond, J., *The World Until Yesterday: What Can We Learn from Traditional Societies?* (New York: Viking, 2012).

Disney's Cinderella. Prod. Walt Disney. (Disney, 1950).

Durrant, J.E., & Ensom, R., 'Physical punishment of children: Lessons from 20 years of research' *Canadian Medical Association Journal* 184 (2012): 1373–1377.

Durrant, J.E., Ensom, R. & Coalition, *Joint Statement on Physical Punishment of Children and Youth* (Ottawa: Coalition on Physical Punishment of Children and Youth, 2004) at http://www.cheo.on.ca/english/4220.shtml.

Eckholm, E., 'Preaching virtue of spanking, even as deaths fuel debate' *New York Times* (6 November 2011) at http://www.nytimes.com/2011/11/07/us/deaths-put-focus-on-pastors-advocacy-of-spanking.html?pagewanted = all.

Frank, A., *Anne Frank: The Diary of a Young Girl* (New York: Doubleday, 1952).

Freeman, M.D.A., 'Upholding the dignity and best interests of children: international law and the corporal punishment of children' *Law & Contemporary Problems* 73 (2010): 211–251.

Gershoff, E.T., *Report on Physical Punishment in the United States: What Research Tells Us About Its Effects on Children* (Columbus, OH: Center for Effective Discipline, 2008).

Gopnik, A., 'Children need childhood, not vocational training' *New York Times* (24 December 2000) at http://www.nytimes.com/2000/12/24/weekinreview/ideas-trends-children-need-childhood-not-vocational-training.html?pagewanted = all&src = pm.

Guttentag, M.D., 'Is there a law instinct?' *Washington University L.R.* 87 (2010): 269–328.

Hersch, P., *A Tribe Apart: A Journey into the Heart of American Adolescence* (New York: Ballantyne, 1999).

Hibbard, R., et al., 'Psychological maltreatment' *Pediatrics* 130 (2012): 372–378. Orig. pub. online at http://pediatrics.aappublications.org/content/early/2012/07/25/peds.2012-1552.

Higonnet, A., *Pictures of Innocence: The History and Crisis of Ideal Childhood* (New York: Thames and Hudson, 1998).

Home School Legal Defence Association, 'Corporal punishment: Is it a no-no?' (n.d.) at http://www.hslda.org/courtreport/V11N6/V11N6CA.asp.

Hutchinson, F., 'Taking our children and future generations seriously: Some Australian views of education and the future' (University of York Educational Studies Seminar Series, 22 June 1999) at http://www.metafuture.org/articlesbycolleagues/FrancisHutchinson/Taking%20Children%20Seriously.htm.

International NGO Council on Violence against Children, *Violating Children's Rights: Harmful Practices Based on Tradition, Culture, Religion or Superstition* (The Council, 2012).

James, W., *The Principles of Psychology* (Boston: Henry Holt, 1890).

Jenks, C., *Childhood: Critical Concepts in Sociology* (London: Routledge, 1996).

Jetha, M.K. & Segalowitz, S., *Adolescent Brain Development: Implications for Behavior* (Oxford: Academic Press, 2012).

Jordanova, L., 'New worlds for children in the eighteenth century: Problems of historical explanation' *History of the Human Sciences* 3 (1990): 69–83.

Kaiser Family Foundation, 'Daily media use among children and teens up dramatically from 5 years ago' (10 January 2010) at http://www.kff.org/entmedia/entmedia012010nr.cfm.

Kempe, H.c., et al., 'The battered child syndrome' (1962) at www.kempe.org/download/The_Battered_Child_Syndrome_sm.pdf.

Key, E., *The Century of the Child.* tr. Marie Franzos (G.P. Putnam's Sons, 1909).

Khamsi, R., 'Babies can spot the good, the bad, and the ugly' *New Scientist* (22 November 2007) at http://www.newscientist.com/article/dn12948-babies-can-spot-the-good-the-bad-and-the-ugly.html.

King, M.L., 'Concepts of childhood: What we know and where we might go' *Renaissance Quarterly* 60 (2007): 371–407.

Kirkey, S., 'Fertility doctors back efforts to reduce multiple IVF births' *Ottawa Citizen* (4 May 2012) at http://o.canada.com/2012/05/04/fertility-doctors-back-efforts-to-reduce-multiple-ivf-births/.

Knouse, J., 'Reconciling liberty and equality in the debate over preimplantation genetic diagnosis' *Utah Law Review* (2013, forthcoming); University of Toledo Legal Studies Research Paper No. 2012-20.

Kolbert, E., 'Spoiled rotten: Why do kids rule the roost?' *New Yorker* (2 July 2012) at http://www .newyorker.om/arts/critics/books/2012/07/02/120702crbo_books_kolbert?currentPage = all.

Lambert, S., 'Inquiry hears how mother made daughter swear and belittle herself' *Winnipeg Free Press* (9 January 2012) at http://www.winnipegfreepress.com/breakingnews/inquiry -hears-how-mother-made-daughter-swear-and-belittle-herself-186200562.html.

Landrigan, P., 'Trade secrets' (Moyers Report transcript) (27 March 2001) at http://www.pbs .org/tradesecrets/transcript.html.

Legouvé, E., *Our Sons and Daughters, Scenes and Studies from Family Life*. tr. Emily Mills (London: Remington, 1881).

Locke, J., *Second Treatise of Government* (1690) at http://oregonstate.edu/instruct/phl302/ texts/locke/locke2/2nd-contents.html

——, *Some Thoughts Concerning Education* (1692) at http://www.fordham.edu/halsall/ mod/1692locke-education.asp.

Lodge, D., *A Man of Parts* (New York: Viking, 2011).

MacLeod, K., 'The ends of humanity: Socialism is dead, and the transhuman future looms. Is there any way to recover a sense of global purpose?' *Aeon Magazine* (12 November 2012) at http://www.aeonmagazine.com/world-views/ken-macleod-socialism-and-transhumanism/.

Manderson, D., 'From hunger to love: Myths of the source, interpretation, and constitution of law in children's literature' *Cardozo Law School Public Law Research* (2003). Paper No. 64 at http://ssrn.com/abstract = 375260.

Marks, S., 'Human rights and root causes' *Modern Law Review* 74(1) (2011): 57–78.

McGillivray, A., 'Abused children in the courts: Adjusting the scales after Bill C-15' *Manitoba Law Review Annual* (1990): 549–579.

——, 'Reconstructing child abuse: Western definition and non-Western experience'. In *The Ideologies of Children's Rights*. eds. M.D.A. Freeman & P. Veerman (Dordrecht: Martinus Nijhoff, 1992). 213–236.

——, 'Why children do have equal rights: In reply to Laura Purdy' *International Journal of Children's Rights* 2 (1994): 243–258.

——, 'Governing childhood'. In *Governing Childhood*. ed. McGillivray (Aldershot: Dartmouth, 1997). 1–24.

——, 'Therapies of freedom: The colonization of aboriginal childhood'. In *Governing Childhood*. ed. McGillivray (Aldershot: Dartmouth, 1997). 133–196.

——, '"He'll learn it on his body": Disciplining childhood in Canadian law' *International Journal of Children's Rights* 5 (1998): 193–242.

——, 'Capturing childhood: The Indian child in the European imagination'. In *Law and Literature*. eds. M.D.A. Freeman & Andrew Lewis (Oxford University Press, 1999). 555–580.

——, 'Childhood in the shadow of parens patriae'. In *Multiple Lenses, Multiple Images: Perspectives on the Child Across Time, Space and Disciplines*. eds. H.Goelman, et al. (University of Toronto Press, 2004). 38–72.

——, 'Child sexual abuse and exploitation: What progress has Canada made?'. In *A Question of Commitment: Children's Rights in Canada*. eds. R.B. Howe & K. Covell (Wilfred Laurier Press, 2007). 127–152.

——, 'Nowhere to stand: Correction by force in the supreme court of Canada'. In *Children and the Law: Essays in Honour of Professor Nicholas Bala*. ed. S. Anand (Toronto: Irwin Law, 2012a). 57–76.

——, 'A state of imperfect transformation: Law, myth and the feminine in *outside over there, Labyrinth*, and *Pan's Labyrinth*'. In *Law and Childhood Studies*. ed. M.D.A. Freeman (Oxford University Press, 2012). 10–28.

——, 'Children's rights, paternal power and fiduciary duty: From Roman law to the supreme court of Canada' *International Journal of Children's Rights* 18 (2012): 21–54.

——, 'Believing children or, lessons from bountiful: Religion, rights, schools and the bounda- ries of harm (in submission)' (2013).

Moore, O., & Mackrael, K., 'Scouts Canada refers more than 100 sex abuse allegations to police' *The Globe and Mail* (25 June 2012) at http://www.theglobeandmail.com/news/

national/scouts-canada-refers-more-than-100-sex-abuse-allegations-to-police/article 4367804.

More, T., *Utopia: Concerning the best state of a commonwealth, and the new island of Utopia* (1516) at http://theopenutopia.org/full-text/sources/.

Muhumuza, R., 'Mysterious nodding disease afflicting youths' *Winnipeg Free Press* (31 July 2012) at http://www.winnipegfreepress.com/world/mysterious-nodding-disease-afflicting -youths-164387766.html.

Nedelsky, J.J., 'Reconceiving rights as relationship' *Review of Constitutional Studies* 1 (1993): 1–26.

Neolithic figure (ca. 5000-3500 BCE) at http://www.flickr.com/photos/antiquitiesproject /4443606293/sizes/l/in/photostream/.

Old Bailey (n.d.) at http://www.oldbaileyonline.org/index.jsp.

Ozick, C., 'Who owns Anne Frank?'. In *A Scholarly Look at the Diary of Anne Frank*. ed. H. Bloom (Philadelphia: Chelsea House, 1992). 101–120.

Partington, J., *Building Cosmopolis: The Political Thought of H.G Wells*. (Dartmouth: Ashgate, 2003).

——, 'Human rights and public accountability in H. G. Wells' functional world state'. In *Cosmopolitics and the Emergence of a Future*. eds. D. Morgan & G. Banham (Basingstoke, New York: Palgrave Macmillan, 2007). 163–190.

Piaget, J., 'Jan Amos Comenius' *Prospects* (UNESCO, International Bureau of Education) 23(1/2) (1993): 173–196.

Piccinini, P., 'The long awaited' (2008). Silicone, fibreglass, human hair, leather, plywood, clothing. 92 x 152 x 80cm at http://www.patriciapiccinini.net/works/05Sculptures_2008 -2009/.

Polygamy Reference Case, *Reference re: Section 293 of the Criminal Code of Canada*, 1588 11 BCSC 1588 (British Columbia Supreme Court, 2011).

Price Cohen, C. 'The role of the United States in the drafting of the convention on the rights of the child' *Emory International Law Review* 20 (2006): 187–198.

Roosevelt, E., Papers, Part 2: United Nations Human Rights Commission Correspondence and Publications. (1945–1962) at http://cisupa.proquest.com/ksc_assets/catalog/8971_E.R.Papers UNPt2.pdf.

Rose, J., *The Case of Peter Pan, or, the Impossibility of Children's Fiction* (London: McMillan, 1984).

Rousseau, J.-J., (1762). *Émile or, On Education*. tr. B. Foxley (1911); rev. G. Roosevelt, (1998) at http://www.ilt.columbia.edu/publications/emile.html.

Rowling, J.K., *Harry Potter series* (London: Bloomsbury, 1997–2007).

Sendak, M., *Where the Wild Things Are* (New York: Harper-Collins, 1963).

Steward, J.C., *The New Child: British Art and the Origins of Modern Childhood, 1730–1830* (University of Washington Press, 1995).

Stone, L., *The Family, Sex and Marriage in England 1500–1800* (Harmondsworth: Penguin (abridged ed.), 1982).

Thonemann, P., 'Children in the Roman Empire' (review) *Times Literary Supplement* (12 October 2011) at http://www.the-tls.co.uk/tls/public/article796886.ece.

UN Committee on the Rights of the Child, *Concluding Observations: Canada*. (2012). Sixty-first session, 17 September - 5 October 2012, articles 44, 45.

van de Kamp, P., 'Afterword: Utopia –the ghost of Thomas More'. In *The Literary Utopias of Cultural Communities 1790–1910*. eds. M. Corporaal and E. J. van Leeuwen (Amsterdam, New York: Rodopi, 2012). 253–260.

Wade, N., 'Scientist finds the beginnings of morality in primate behavior' *New York Times* (20 March 2007) at http://www.nytimes.com/2007/03/20/science/20moral.html?_r = 1&page wanted = all.

Walz, S., 'Reclaiming and rebuilding the history of the universal declaration of human rights' *Third World Quarterly* 23(3) (2002): 437–448.

Warburton, W. & Braunstein, D., eds., *Growing Up Fast and Furious: Reviewing the Impacts of Violent and Sexualied Media on Children* (Sydney, AU: Federation Press, 2012).

Waterman, A.J. & J.T. Thomas, 'When the bough breaks: Childhood mortality and burial practice in late Neolithic Atlantic Europe' *Oxford Journal of Archaeology* 30(2) (2011): 165–183.

Williams, E., 'Death to undesirables: Brazil's murder capital' *The Independent* (22 September 2012) at http://www.independent.co.uk/news/world/americas/death-to-undesirables-brazils-murder-capital-1685214.html.

Williams, P.J., *The Alchemy of Race and Rights: The Diary of a Law Professor.* (Harvard University Press, 1991).

Weill, J., *Hygiène de la seconde enfance* (Paris, 1882).

Wenegrat, B., *Sociobiology & Mental Disorder: A New View* (Menlo Park, CA: Addison/Wesley, 1984).

Wells, H.G., *The War of the Worlds* (1895) at http://www.online-literature.com/wellshg.

Wells, H.G., *The Island of Dr. Moreau* (1896) at http://www.online-literature.com/wellshg/.

Wells, H.G., *The War of the Worlds* (1897) at http://www.online-literature.com/wellshg/.

——, *Food of the Gods* (1904) at http://www.online-literature.com/wellshg/.

——, *A Modern Utopia* (1905) at http://www.online-literature.com/wellshg/.

——, *The New World Order: Whether it is Attainable, How It can be Attained, and What Sort of World A World at Peace will Have to Be* (London: Secker and Warburg, 1940).

——, *The Rights of Man or, What are We Fighting For?* (Harmondsworth: Penguin, 1940).

Whelan, D.J., *Indivisible Human Rights, A History* (University of Pennsylvania Press, 2012).

Whiting, J.M. & Child, I.L., *Child Training and Personality* (Yale University Press, 1953).

Williams, E., 'Death to undesirables: Brazil's murder capital' *The Independent* (22 September 2012) at http://www.independent.co.uk/news/world/americas/death-to-undesirables-brazils-murder-capital-1685214.html.

Windling, T., 'Cinderella: Ashes, blood, and the slipper of glass' (n.d.) at http://www.endicott-studio.com/rdrm/forashs.html.

Wolff, L., *Child Abuse in Freud's Vienna: Postcards from the End of the World* (New York University Press, 1995).

Wordsworth, W., 'My heart leaps up when I behold'. In *The Oxford Authors: William Wordsworth.* ed. Stephen Gill (Oxford University Press, 1802).

Children's Rights Research Moving into the Future – Challenges on the Way Forward

Ann Quennerstedt
Associate Professor in Education, School of Humanities, Education and Social Sciences
Örebro University, Sweden
E-mail: ann.quennerstedt@oru.se

Since the late 1980s, research into children's rights has expanded in terms of the objects of study and the number of research projects and active research-ers. This growth has constituted children's rights research as an established and legitimate field of study. The research conducted over the past 20 years has widened and deepened our knowledge of what rights for children are about. It has also identified important questions and opened up new areas for examina-tion. Through collaborations between researchers from different countries, our understanding of variations within the field has been advanced. One of the most important contributions of children's rights research is that it has been a driving force for an upgraded status of children in society. By questioning an image of children as appendices of their families, or the future citizens of a state (Reynolds *et al.* 2006), children's rights research has worked to strengthen the claim that children are 'people in their own right' (cf. Lee, 2005).

As the research field is now established, the time is perhaps ripe to reflect on the work undertaken so far and consider how children's rights research might move forward in the coming years. In recent years, self-critical voices have started to surface within the research field and point to possible areas of con-cern. With this paper, my ambition is to contribute to the deliberations within children's rights research about possible ways forward. In what follows I will highlight what seem to be the most important comments made by other authors and develop these in relation to some areas of concern I find to be urgent for the research field. In short, I will suggest that research into chil-dren's rights needs to address three major challenges: advancing critique, increasing theorisation and contextualising research.

To begin with, I believe that a brief look at the rapid growth of children's rights research is of interest as background to the challenges that will later be elaborated on. In almost every social science discipline researchers are

now addressing children's issues in their respective fields from a rights perspective. An article search of the number of peer reviewed papers attending to
children's rights issues published since 1985 shows the indicative graph of
Figure 1.[1]

As can be seen, an increase of publications started in the early 1990s – probably fuelled by the research interest in children's rights issues following the
adoption of the United Nations Convention on the Rights of the Child in 1989.
For the last 20 years the growth in research publications has been steady: from
59 articles published over the five-year period 1990-1994 to 463 articles in the
period 2005-2009. However, as we can see, the curve also indicates that the
rapid rise in publications may now have halted.

From this limited search we can conclude that the research field of children's rights has been expansive with regard to the volume of published works.
However, despite this growth, research in children's rights is broadly speaking
still very limited in size and scope. Size is a relevant aspect in the research field
in that a large number of researchers active in children's rights research and

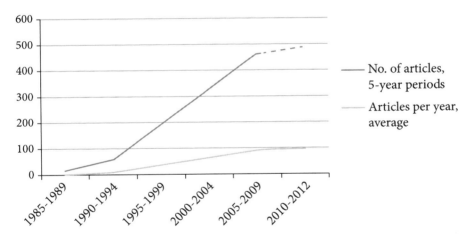

Figure 1. Published children's rights articles 1985-2012.

---

[1] The graph is constructed from a search of the database Ebsco, based on 'children's rights' as
subject term. The search was performed on 11/6/2012. The articles are grouped into five-year
periods, the last period including two and a half years of actual publications and the assumption that the publication rate will remain at the same level for the coming two and a half years
(marked with a dotted line). The 'per year' line is based on actual publications. As the results
are based on only one database, one search word and peer reviewed articles, this search does
not claim to represent a precise picture of research publications in the field of children's rights.
It does however give an indication of the growth of children's rights research over time and
identifies a possible halt in the expansion in recent years.

high publication rates provide a louder and more legitimate voice, which in turn increases the possibility of impacting research and practice. In that sense, the possible decline in researchers' engagement in children's rights research is worrying. When it comes to scope of influence, this is not only related to the volume of research undertaken, but also includes the reception of the research by relevant research addressees. Here, the quality of the research and whether it is perceived to meet the need for knowledge determine how influential it will be.

Central to self-critical reflection is, of course, an investigation into *what* children's rights research has focused on and what has been studied under the banner of children's rights. Such an analysis also needs to include the *character* of children's rights research and to identify and scrutinise dominating themes or approaches. A few review studies have been carried out with the ambition of exploring and analysing research on children's rights.

Reynaert *et al.* (2009) contribute important insights in their critical examination of how understandings of children's rights have been constructed in academic work on the Convention on the Rights of the Child. The authors argue that three recurrent themes can be identified in the academic children's rights discourse. First, there is a clear preoccupation in research with *the competent child and her right to participation*.[2] A rights perspective has here been merged with the work undertaken within sociology of childhood (Qvortrup *et al.* 1994; James *et al.* 1998; James and James, 2004), and the claim that the child should be upgraded to a competent 'being' with full human value in the present. Second, the changing image of childhood that puts children in a new position as rights holders has given rise to discussions about a field of tension between the child and its parents. A possible *children's rights/parents' rights dichotomy* has accordingly attracted considerable research interest.[3] That these two themes are highly visible in children's rights research is confirmed in another review study by Quennerstedt (2011a). Quennerstedt's analysis of how children's rights are constructed in educational research highlights both the participation theme and the child-parent theme.

The third theme in the analysis by Reynaert *et al.* (2009) is, in my view, their most important contribution to reflections on children's rights research. The authors argue that research has engaged in an *international consensus building around children's rights*. The Convention on the Rights of the Child has been

---

[2] Examples of participation research include Lücker-Babel, 1995; Ochaíta and Espinosa, 1997; Matthews *et al.* 1999; Kjørholt, 2002; Cavet and Sloper, 2004; Boylan and Ing, 2005; Grover, 2006; Smith, 2007; Thomas, 2007; Thelander, 2009.
[3] Examples of children's rights/parents' rights research include Bennet, 1996; Thomas and O'Kane, 1998; Westman, 1999; Howe, 2001; Mason and Cohen, 2001; Høstmælingen, 2005; Lundy, 2005; Huntington, 2006; Grover, 2007; Quennerstedt, 2009.

viewed as a standard-setting instrument, and has formed the basis of a vast amount of implementation research. This implementation research has examined how the rights recognised in the Convention have been realised in practice in the various areas of society, and has compared implementation in different regions of the world. Also, the monitoring system and the process for the realisation of the Convention have been objects of study.[4] Although Reynaert *et al.* acknowledge the contributions of the implementation research, they also point to some troublesome consequences. According to the authors, the focus on standard-setting, implementation and monitoring suggests that children's rights are not under discussion and that there is consensus on the meaning of children's rights. In research, argue Reynaert *et al.* (2009, p 528), "[c]hildren's rights are presented as the new norm in policy and practice without questioning or problematizing this new norm." The object addressed in this research is almost always the difference between the provisions of the Convention and reality or practice, and almost never the Convention itself or the meaning of children's rights. The problem, argue the authors, is that children's rights research lacks critique.

In another paper, Reynaert *et al.* (2012) return to the matter of consensus thinking and lack of critique. In their exploration of the polarised debate between 'uncritical proponents' of children's rights and 'uncritical opponents', they argue that proponents of children's rights largely fail to adopt a critical approach. Instead, 'children's rights' are understood in an unambiguous way, and a notion of social consensus constructed. The authors claim that the Convention on the Rights of the Child is perceived as an instruction for policy and practice, and the idea of a 'gap' between the Convention and reality is created – reality does not yet conform to the Convention. The implementation of the Convention thus becomes a matter of following the instruction in order to fill the gap. Research aids this endeavour by explaining the instruction and checking the extent to which changes have occurred in practice. In a way, I would add, the Convention also becomes an instruction for research in that it is seen to point to important matters for researchers to engage with. Reynaert *et al.* (2012) argue that the Convention should instead be a starting point for dialogue and call for critique in children's rights research, by which they mean the questioning of basic assumptions, i.e. not accepting them as truths but as the social construction of children's rights. The authors are looking for 'critical proponents' and hope that the research field of children's rights will become a more contested terrain.

---

4) Examples of implementation research include Cohen *et al.* 1996; Ennew and Miljeteig, 1996; Therborn, 1996; Woll, 2000; Fredriksson, 2001; Lansdown, 2001; Taylor *et al.* 2001; Beeckman, 2004; Quennerstedt, 2011b.

The main problem facing the research field of children's rights is consequently that it is ensnared by consensus. The idea of a true norm, valid in all settings and circumstances, frames the research in a way that incites and supports certain examinations by directing the spotlight in particular directions. The effect is simultaneously that questions lying outside the consensus thinking around children's rights are implicitly discouraged. I would argue that for those of us involved in researching children's rights, a central concern in our way forward would be to deal with the consensus issue. However, in order to do that, we need tools. In the following I suggest three challenges that I believe could serve as tools for positioning children's rights research in a more open and contested space, where new kinds of questions are encouraged, supported, proposed and opposed. These challenges are: a critical approach, a theory driven approach and a contextualised approach.

A Critical Approach

It is fair to say that researchers who work with children's rights issues are supporters of human rights for children. Accordingly, children's rights researchers are neither neutral nor distanced from their object of study, but typically depart from a normative position in which children's human status as rights holders is the norm. This naturally affects the kinds of topics addressed. Some academic work is of course undertaken by those who oppose the idea that children should be seen as human rights subjects, but they would probably not label their work as 'children's rights research'. Further, most children's rights researchers value the Convention on the Rights of the Child highly, and consider it a milestone in the development of rights for children. However, this normative underpinning and valuing of the Convention in children's rights research should not outmanoeuvre critique in the research performed. It is important to distinguish between research and advocacy, which in the words of Reynolds *et al.* (2006) is not always easy: 'Many children's rights researchers have found themselves trapped between the role of the detached observer and the role of the advocate that cannot remain unmoved' (p. 295). The distinction has nevertheless to be upheld, and a key to differentiating between the roles is to adopt a critical approach to the opponents and practices being studied as well as to your own particular points of departure and the 'truths' held in the research field.

The consensus building in research about the meaning of children's rights, as pointed out by Reynaert *et al.* (2009), is a warning that should be taken seriously. An uncritical approach to the Convention as the definition of children's rights is one aspect of consensus building. The Convention on the Rights of the Child (UN, 1989) has been placed in the absolute centre of the research field.

Almost all children's rights research refers to it, often framing and/or motivating research questions with provisions stated in the Convention. Despite the centrality of the Convention, it is rarely itself the object of analysis or discussion (Reynaert *et al.* 2009), but is instead allowed to define rights for children. However, some researchers have begun to question the Convention and its basic assumptions. For example, Veerman (2010) argues that we need to realise that the Convention on the Rights of the Child is ageing, and that it reflects the image of the child and the society of the drafting period. Things have changed since then, including the view of children. Hägglund and Thelander (2011) point to how changing views about children can be related to the sociological theorising which emerged at about the same time as the drafting and adoption of the Convention. The sociology of childhood linked ideas about children's rights with 'constructions of children and childhood, embedded in time-and-place bound discourses, rather than based on a once-and-for-all essential view on rights' (p. 368). Hägglund and Thelander believe that this thinking opens for a research agenda that stretches beyond the Convention as 'a document where 'curriculum-like' norms for what constitutes children's rights are formulated' (p.368). One of the main points these authors make is that the Convention must be seen as a historical and political document, not as children's rights set in stone (cf. Bobbio, 1996).

Another aspect of consensus building is how we talk about children's rights in research. Two researchers who have discussed language use in children's rights research have pointed to problematic consequences of consensus formations in language. Lundy (2007) highlights how 'pupil voice' has become a widespread concept for researchers wishing to investigate children's right to participation in education. She argues that the notion 'voice' is treacherous, and that conceptualising the entitlements recognised to the child in Article 12 of the Convention in the 'cosy' guise of 'voice' may weaken the legal imperative that is the right of the child. Quennerstedt (2010) questions the use of the '3 p's' (rights to provision, protection and participation) for constructing and analysing children's rights; a vocabulary that is extensively used in research (cf. Lundy above). She argues that the increasing use of the '3 p's' to specify children's rights is problematic, first due to the normalising effects of a dominating conceptualisation, second because it separates children's rights from human rights, and third because the '3 p's' model has limited possibilities for adding theoretical depth to analyses. Both these authors are concerned that the emerging consensus about the vocabulary used to discuss children's rights in research is actually becoming an impediment.

To summarise the arguments in this section and clarify some of the suggestions made: the analysis in this paper and by some other authors suggests that children's rights research needs to be more critical. First, research needs to adopt a more critical attitude to the Convention itself and the basic assumptions within it. Regardless of the importance and value of the Convention, it has to be seen as a product of a certain time and context, and is therefore not something to preach, but something to analyse. Second, a critical stance should include suspicion of the tendencies to build consensus in the research field in its various expressions. As Foucault said, '[m]y point is not that everything is bad, but that everything is dangerous, which is not exactly the same as bad. If everything is dangerous, then we always have something to do' (Foucault, 1997, 256). Drawing on Foucault, consensus should thus be regarded as potentially dangerous. In view of this, the research field would do well to encourage a certain amount of disagreement and disparity, since it is the breeding ground for debate, discussion, new thinking and the posing of new questions.

A Theory Driven Approach

A research synthesis of children's rights research in education published 1997-2008 examined how theory had been used in the studied publications (Quennerstedt, 2011). The study showed a relatively low level of theorising: only 9 out of 35 of the examined publications made explicit use of theory to analyse empirical data or pursue an argument. Theoretical underpinning was particularly unusual in publications of an empirical nature. Although this review was limited in that it only covered children's rights research in the field of education, the findings are supported by Reynaert *et al.* (2009) who argue that children's rights research in general is a 'rather undertheorized domain of social science' (p. 529).

How, then, can the presumably low level of theorising in children's rights research be understood and explained? Here, I would like to discuss possible aspects that may be of interest to understand this 'undertheorisation'. As argued above, children's rights researchers typically assume a normative position to their research object, thus making them *proponents* of human rights for children. However, as researchers, they are also *analysts* of children's rights. Such a dual interest in research is not uncommon, e.g. research on the democratic governance of states. However, the dual interest in combination with the strong position of the Convention on the Rights of the Child differentiate children's rights research from other research areas with a normative and analytic interest. The question I would like to raise here is whether the Convention in fact occupies a space that would otherwise be filled with theoretical references. As the Convention is frequently used as (the ultimate) definition of children's rights, and often constitutes the only frame of reference for the research undertaken; it motivates the research questions, is the tool used to analyse data and is the structure against which the results of a study is mirrored. Accordingly, to some extent the Convention can be said to have replaced theory in a lot of the research into children's rights. My suggestion is that the analytic interest has been hindered by the hegemonic status of the Convention, thereby resulting in low levels of theorising and too little distinction between the proponent and analytic aspects of research.

That the Convention outmanoeuvres theory as grounds for discussing rights issues for children can also be seen in other contexts, which are connected to research. For example, Mitchell and McCusker (2008) investigated the teaching and understanding of the Convention on the Rights of the Child in Canadian higher education. They found that courses were largely based on the text and principles of the Convention and that an 'applied approach' was dominant, i.e. how to put the principles into practice. Theoretical underpinning in the work on children's rights was unusual and 'only beginning to emerge' (p. 171). Quennerstedt (2010b) examined how children's rights issues are constructed in Swedish educational policy and found that teachers' knowledge was expressed in policy as decisive for the realisation of children's human rights in Swedish schools. The need to educate teachers was specified as 'bringing the Convention into teacher education' and 'knowledge about the content of the Convention on the Rights of the Child'[5] (p. 128). Higher education and policy are consumers of research, and the Convention as an unquestioned frame of reference is repeated in both those arenas.

Why then, would children's rights research benefit from adopting a more theory driven approach in which the Convention is not allowed to consume the scope for theorising? I would like to suggest three arguments for this. First, it is a matter of how quality and depth can be achieved in research. The Convention was produced in a lengthy exercise of political compromising, where disparate world-views, views of the child and ideas about human rights met and at times collided. Accordingly, it accommodates different agendas and cannot be viewed as a coherent piece of text. Being a political document with inherent tensions, the Convention has limited potential to clarify and explain the complexities within human rights in order to add depth to analyses. Instead, children's rights as an idea, and indeed the Convention itself, need to be approached through philosophy and political science and attention paid to the theorising about rights included in these disciplines. In order to understand the complexities surrounding the realisation of children's human rights in various societies and parts of society, we need to employ social theories such as those found within sociology, anthropology, gender studies etc.

Second, as I see it, two of the most important roles of research are (1) to produce knowledge and in-depth understanding, and (2) departing from such knowledge, to participate in societal discussions. Research is not the sole

---

[5] Quotes translated from Swedish.

producer of knowledge, and certainly not a main debater, but the voice of research is given high status in societal deliberations. This status is related to certain expectations of research-based knowledge, namely that it is derived from systematic and rigorous analysis and undertaken by people who are specifically trained to do such work. This high status position of research also carries a heavy responsibility. The argument touched upon earlier that we need to distinguish between research and advocacy is highly relevant. What the academic study of children's rights should contribute to the wider societal and global discussion about children's and young people's human rights is knowledge and in-depth understanding based on systematic and rigorous analysis. From my point of view, in order to achieve this, theory and theorisation are necessary and important tools.

My third argument for adopting a more theory-driven approach in children's rights research is that the examination of rights issues in various areas of society, e.g. social work, education, health care, law, or from different specific perspectives, e.g. gender, ethnicity, social class, power aspects, needs *particular theorising* from these fields or perspectives. For example, when analysing children's rights in education, educational theorising is vital in order to situate rights issues within the specific context and knowledge interest of education. Similarly, when analysing rights in relation to gender, gender theorising is needed to be able to approach the problems of interest in a qualified way. Accordingly, by employing specific theorising, research into children's rights is brought into the particular area of interest. This contextualisation will be elaborated on in the next section.

Root to the challenge to adopt a more theory driven approach in children's rights research is the concern that the field is generally undertheorised. The relatively low level of theorising can largely be explained by the strong position of the Convention on the Rights of the Child in the research field. The challenge is accordingly to reclaim the space that is too often occupied by the Convention for theory and theorising, and to base research on such a foundation.

A Contextualised Approach

It has been suggested that the academic children's rights discourse is too decontextualised. According to these critics, research, in its preoccupation with a universal conception of rights and how these rights are implemented in practice, often fails to take specific conditions and contexts into account. The consequences of abstract children's rights thinking are that the particular social, economic and historical context of a certain society is overlooked and that the diversity between children as holders of rights is neglected (Reynaert *et al.* 2009; Thelander, 2009). Veerman and Levine (2000) state that it is time to turn the focus away from the global arena – UN bodies and the Convention – towards local policy and institutions where abstract children's rights thinking meets the actual child in his/her specific context. Reynolds *et al.* (2006) and Tarulli and Skott-Myhre (2006) want to move rights research even closer to the children themselves, and argue that children's rights issues need to be investigated in the everyday life-world of children and address how human rights for children impact the life and lived experience of children. Albeit having a somewhat different focus on and conception of what constitutes the interesting context, these authors all believe that contextual factors in the environments in which the rights are to be upheld and acted on are important for understanding children's rights. Research therefore needs to be much more attentive to context.

I would like to suggest that children's rights research would also benefit from another kind of contextualisation. As already touched on in relation to theorisation, I believe that children's rights need to be examined more extensively *within* particular academic domains. When research departs from the Convention, the context in which the rights are studied can easily be perceived as merely an arena for implementation, whether this be health care, law, social work or education. The same questions can then be directed towards all societal areas and institutions. Research questions about children's rights are then not seen as context-specific or discipline-specific, but as universally valid and equally relevant in all settings. I would instead suggest the opposite approach, namely that research into children's rights departs from the particular knowledge interests of a certain academic field. The matter of human rights for children accordingly needs to be incorporated into the core interests of a discipline or a perspective, and research problems about rights need to be formulated from such a merged position. This would mean that questions about children's rights in e.g. law studies are substantially different from those raised in e.g. educational studies, because these disciplines have very different knowledge interests. Reynolds *et al.* (2006) express similar thoughts when they situate children's rights issues within anthropology, and argue that anthropologically oriented investigations of children's rights offer a specific gaze that is different from others.

To give more substance to this argument, I will use my own research field of education to illustrate what such a shift in focus might look like. I will draw on work that in my opinion raises questions about children's rights from a contextualised educational perspective, rather than from an abstracted Convention perspective. A core interest in educational thinking is in *educational processes*, i.e. how the conditions for and the relations and experiences in these processes affect learning. In the following I will give two examples of how this knowledge interest in the field of education has been merged with aspects of children's rights.

McCowan (2010) explores the meaning of the right to education.[6] He sets out from the concern that there is little academic discussion about the nature of the education that is to correspond to the right as expressed in international human rights instruments, and asks 'to what exactly does the right to education actually relate? Does it correspond to access to educational institutions, to a particular form of educational experience or to some educational effect?' (p. 510). With this question, he firmly sets the right within a very central and extensively probed query in the discipline of education; what is education? Rather than accepting the version of education given in human rights documents, he instead turns to his discipline to address the complexity of the matter. In his analysis, McCowan shows how in human rights documents 'education' is largely synonymous with 'schooling', and that specific and prescriptive statements about education in the documents mainly relate to the *institutions* that should provide education and to the *duration* of the education. Little is said in the documents about matters that lie at the heart of educational thinking, i.e. what kind of *processes* education should incorporate. From his educational viewpoint, McCowan argues that the right to education should correspond to the exact reverse, since institution and duration are no guarantee that education has taken place. The answer to the question of what education is thus lies closer to 'participation in educational processes' than 'attending school'.

Education is often assigned a prominent role in order to make children and young people embrace the values inherent in human rights. This is frequently labelled 'children's rights education' or 'human rights education'. In their respective analyses, Todd (2007) and Reynaert *et al.* (2010) clarify how education is often portrayed as instrumental to the purpose of human rights, and that children's rights education is reduced to an implementation strategy for the Convention on the Rights of the Child. The logic is that having knowledge about rights is a prerequisite for practising rights, which in turn leads to a focus on *teaching*, aiming to strengthen respect for children's rights, to socialise children into active and responsible citizens and to prevent violations of children's rights. However, from an educationalist's point of view, education is more than teacher instruction. Todd (2007) maintains that 'knowledge about rights is the bare minimum required and ... the real potential of education lies in its capacities to provoke insights that help youth live well with ambiguity and dilemma' (p. 594). Both these authors argue that the role of education needs to be re-thought in relation to human

---

[6] McCowan focuses his analysis on Article 26 of the Universal Declaration on Human Rights and not on the Convention on the Rights of the Child. I agree with McCowan that although some modifications in the right to education have been made in the CRC compared to the UDHR, the main arguments put forward by McCowan also apply to the CRC.

rights – children's rights education should not be understood as teaching about human rights, but instead should be concerned with learning about rights through *experience in educational processes* (Reynaert *et al.* 2010). Such processes must allow for uncertainty (not fetching the 'correct' answers from a human rights document) and consist of communicative activities where ambiguity and dilemma in relation to rights are given space and attention and are not glossed over (Todd, 2007). Departing from core knowledge interests in the discipline of education, Reynaert et al. and Todd are able to deconstruct and challenge the widespread instrumentally oriented idea of children's rights education. When they ask what children's rights education is they are able to point out that the special potential of education does not lie in instruction, but in educational processes in which complexity, ambiguity and uncertainty are explored and experienced through communication and social relations.

To summarise, the challenge to contextualise the research on children's rights is largely about shifting the perspective. Instead of prioritising the universal and a top-down approach in research, where the urgent research questions spring from universal claims, the opposite position is taken. Priority is given to context, particularity and a bottom-up approach, and consequently that research questions emerge in local settings, with children in their daily lives, or from the knowledge interest in academic disciplines or specific perspectives (e.g. gender). The connection to the universal level is of course relevant and important, but is secondary and not the main point of departure for research.

Concluding Remarks

The aim of this paper has been to make a contribution to the self-critical deliberations taking place within children's rights research. Drawing primarily on the work of Reynaert *et al.* (2009), I have argued that the most urgent concern for the field to address is the widespread consensus on the meaning of children's rights (with the Convention as definition) that leads to the meaning of human rights for children not being critically discussed or problematised. I have thereafter claimed that the three challenges of critique, theorisation and contextualisation may constitute tools with which to deal with this difficulty in the way forward.

It should be emphasised that the three challenges are intertwined, and are not processes or attitudes that are separated from each other. On the contrary, they are facilitators and prerequisites for each other; in order to be critical we need theories that sharpen the gaze; the use of theory is an essential step in the contextualisation of research; departing from context provides a position from which to challenge universal claims. An analytic distinction between them, such as that made in this paper, may however help to clarify how the challenges can be seen as tools and how they might be of support to the researcher.

Research into children's rights has played an important role in precipitating and furthering children's and young people's upgrading as members of society throughout the world. This is a role that research will also need to uphold in the coming years. However, the time is now ripe to scrutinise the grounds for this research and set it on course for the future. It is also of urgent concern that research into children's and young people's human rights opens for questions that have not yet been asked and for aspects that have not yet been discerned. In both these endeavours, I suggest that the three challenges I have outlined in this paper may help to prepare the route for the future of children's rights research.

References

Bae, B., 'Realizing children's right to participation in early childhood settings: Some critical issues in a Norwegian context', *Early Years* 30(3) (2010): 205–218.

Beeckman, K., 'Measuring the implementation of the right to education: Educational versus human rights indicators', *International Journal of Children's Rights* 12(1) (2004): 71–84.

Bennet, J., 'Supporting family responsibility for the rights of the child: An educational viewpoint', *International Journal of Children's Rights* 4(1) (1996): 45–56.

Bobbio, N., *The Age of Rights* (Cambridge: Polity Press, 1996).

Boylan, J. & Ing, P., '"Seen but not heard": Young people's experience of advocacy', *International Journal of Social Welfare* 14(1) (2005): 2–12.

Cavet, J. & Sloper, P., 'The participation of children and young people in decisions about UK service development', *Child Care Health and Development* 30(6) (2004): 613–621.

Cohen, C.P., Hart, S. & Kosloske, S., 'Monitoring the United Nations convention on the rights of the child: The challenge of information management', *Human Rights Quarterly* 18(2) (1996): 439–471.

Ennew, J. & Miljeteig, P., 'Indicators for children's rights: Progress report on a project', *International Jornal of Children's Rights* 4(3) (1996): 213–236.

Foucault, M., *Michel Foucault: Ethics, Subjectivity, and Truth.* ed. P. Rabinow (New York: The New Press, 1997).

Fredriksson, U., 'What can be done to implement international standards concerning children's rights to education worldwide?' In *Children's Rights in Education.* eds. S. Hart et al. (London: Jessica Kingsley Publishers 2001).

Grover, S., 'The right of the child to be heard in education litigation: An analysis of the "intelligent design" Pennsylvania case on the separation of church and state in the public schools', *Education and Law* 18(2–3) (2006): 149–160.

Grover, S., 'Children's right to be educated for tolerance: Minority rights and inclusion', *Education and the Law* 19(1) (2007): 59–70.

Hägglund, S. & Thelander, N., 'Children's rights at 21: Policy, theory, practice. introductory remarks', *Education Inquiry* 2(3) (2011): 365–372.

Høstmælingen, N., 'Mandatory religious education that builds tolerance: Lessons to be learned from Norway?' *International Journal of Children's Rights* 13(4) (2005): 403–412.

Howe, R.B., 'Do parents have fundamental rights?' *Journal of Canadian Studies/Revue d'Etudes Canadiennes* 36(3) (2001): 61–78.

Huntington, C., 'Rights myopia in child welfare', *UCLA Law Review* 53(3) (2006): 637–699.

James, A. & James, A., *Constructing Childhood. Theory, Policy and Social Practice* (Hampshire/New York: Palgrave Macmillan, 2004).

James, A., Jenks, C. & Prout, A., *Theorizing Childhood* (Cambridge: Polity Press, 1998).

Kjørholt, A.T., 'Small is powerful: Discourses on "children and participation" in Norway', *Childhood* 9(1) (2002): 63–82.

Lansdown, G., 'Progress in implementing the rights in the convention: Factors helping and hindering the process'. In *Children's Rights in Education*. eds. S. Hart et al. (London: Jessica Kingsley Publishers, 2001).

Lee, N., *Childhood and Human Value. Development, Separation and Separability* (Maidenhead: Open University Press, 2005).

Lücker-Babel, M.F., 'The right of the child to express views to be heard: An attempt to interpret article 12 of the UN convention on the rights of the child', *International Journal of Children's Rights* 3(3–4) (1995): 391–404.

Lundy, L., 'Family values in the classroom? Reconciling parental wishes and children's rights in state schools', *International Journal of Law, Policy and the Family* 19 (2005): 346–372.

Lundy, L., '"Voice" is not enough: Conceptualizing article 12 of the United Nations convention on the rights of the child', *British Educational Research Journal* 33(6) (2007): 927–942.

Mason, P. & Cohen, C.P., 'Children's rights in education'. In *Children's Rights in Education*. eds. S. Hart et al. (London: Jessica Kingsley Publishers, 2001).

Matthews, H., Limb, M. & Taylor, M., 'Young people's participation and representation in society', *Geoforum* 30(2) (1999): 135–144.

McCowan, T., 'Reframing the universal right to education', *Comparative Education* 46(4) (2010): 509–525.

Mitchell, R. & McCusker, S., 'Theorising the UN convention on the rights of the child within Canadian post-secondary education: A grounded theory approach', *International Journal of Children's Rights* 16(2) (2008): 159–176.

Ochaíta, E. & Espinosa, A.M., 'Children's participation in family and school life: A psychological and developmental approach', *International Journal of Children's Rights* 5(3) (1997): 279–297.

Quennerstedt, A., 'Balancing the rights of the child and the rights of parents in the convention on the rights of the child', *Journal of Human Rights* 8(2) (2009): 162–176.

Quennerstedt, A., 'Children, but not really humans? Critical reflections on the hampering effect of the "3 p's"', *International Journal of Children's Rights* 18(4) (2010a): 619–635.

Quennerstedt, A., 'Den politiska konstruktionen av barnets rättigheter i utbildning [The political construction of children's rights in education]', *Pedagogisk Forskning i Sverige* [*Pedagogic Research in Sweden*] 15(3–4) (2010b): 119–141. In Swedish.

Quennerstedt, A., 'The construction of children's rights in education – A research synthesis', *International Journal of Children's Rights* 19(4) (2011a): 661–678.

Quennerstedt, A., 'The political construction of children's rights in education – A comparative analysis of Sweden and New Zealand', *Education Inquiry* 2(3) (2011b): 453–471.

Qvortrup, J., Bardy, M., Sgritta, B. & Wintersberger, H., eds., *Childhood Matters. Social Theory, Practice and Politics* (Aldershot: Averbury, 1994).

Reynaert, D., Bouverne-de Bie, M. & Vandevelde, S., 'A review of children's rights literature since the adoption of the United Nations convention on the rights of the child', *Childhood* 16(4) (2009): 518–534.

Reynaert, D., Bouverne-de Bie, M. & Vandevelde, S., 'Children's rights education and social work: Contrasting models and understandings', *International Social Work* 53(4) (2010): 443–456.

Reynaert, D., Bouverne-De Bie, M. & Vandevelde, S., 'Between "believers" and "opponents": Critical discussions on children's rights', *International Journal of Children's Rights* 20(1) (2012): 155–168.

Reynolds, P., Niewenhuys, O. & Hanson, K., 'A view from anthropology – Introduction', *Childhood* 13(3) (2006): 291–302.

Smith, A.B., 'Children and young people's participation rights in education', *International Journal of Children's Rights* 15(1) (2007): 147–164.

Tarulli, D. & Skott-Myhre, H., 'The immanent rights of the multitude. An ontological framework for conceptualizing the issue of child and youth rights', *International Journal of Children's Rights* 14 (2006): 187–201.

Taylor, N., Smith, A.B. & Nairn, K., 'Rights important to young people: Secondary students and staff perspectives', *International Journal of Children's Rights* 9(2) (2001): 137–156.

Thelander, N., (2009) *We Are All the Same, But... Kenyan and Swedish School Children's Views on Children's Rights*. PhD Thesis. Karlstad University Studies 36.

Thomas, N., 'Towards a theory of children's participation', *International Journal of Children's Rights* 15(2) (2007): 199–218.

Thomas, N. & O'Kane, C., 'When children's wishes and feelings clash with their best interests', *International Journal of Children's Rights* 6(2) (1998): 137–154.

Todd, S., 'Promoting a just education: Dilemmas of rights, freedom and justice', *Educational Philosophy and Theory* 39(6) (2007): 592–603.

United Nations, *Convention on the Rights of the Child*. General Assembly Resolution 44/25, 20 November 1989. U.N. Doc. A/RES/44/25.

Veerman, P., ' The ageing of the UN convention on the rights of the child', *International Journal of Children's Rights* 18(4) (2010): 585–618.

Veerman, P. & Levine, H., 'Implementing children's rights on a local level: Narrowing the gap between Geneva and the grassroots', *International Journal of Children's Rights* 8(4) (2000): 373–384.

Westman, J.C., 'Children's rights, parents' prerogatives, and society's obligations', *Child Psychiatry and Human Development* 29(4) (1999): 315–328.

Woll, L., 'Reporting to the UN committee on the rights of the child: A catalyst for domestic debate and policy change?' *International Journal of Children's Rights* 8(1) (2000): 71–81.

Economic and Social Rights, Budgets and the Convention on the Rights of the Child

Aoife Nolan
Professor of International Human Rights Law, School of Law
Nottingham University
E-mail: Aoife.Nolan@nottingham.ac.uk

1. Introduction

Recent years have seen an explosion in methodologies for monitoring children's economic and social rights (ESR). Key examples include the development of indicators, benchmarks, child rights-based budget analysis and child rights impact assessments. The Committee on the Right of the Child (ComRC/the Committee) has praised such tools in its work and has actively promoted their usage. Troublingly, however, there are serious shortcomings in the Committee's approach to the ESR standards enshrined in the UN Convention on the Rights of the Child (CRC), which threaten to impact upon the efficacy of such methodologies. This article argues that the Committee has failed to engage with the substantive obligations imposed by Article 4 and many of the specific ESR guaranteed in the CRC in sufficient depth. As a result, that body has not succeeded in outlining a coherent, comprehensive *child rights-specific* ESR framework. Using the example of child rights-based budget analysis, the author claims that this omission constitutes a significant obstacle to those seeking to evaluate the extent to which states have met their ESR-related obligations under the CRC. The article thus brings together and addresses key issues that have so far received only very limited critical academic attention, namely, children's ESR under the CRC, the relationship between budgetary decision-making and the CRC, and child rights-based budget analysis.

---

* The author would like to thank participants at the Economic and Social Rights Academic Network Meeting UK-Ireland (ESRAN-UKI) held at Lancaster University in November 2012 for their valuable comments. Especial thanks go to Jessie Hohmann, Noam Peleg and Evelyne Schmid. All remaining errors are the author's own.

The article opens with a consideration of key issues arising in relation to children as ESR-holders that result from both children's bio-developmental characteristics and their social, political and economic position within society. Next, I address the ESR of children under the CRC and the way in which these rights have been interpreted and applied (or not) by the Committee on the Rights of the Child. In doing so, I pay particular attention to Article 4 of the Convention which provides that,

> States Parties shall undertake all appropriate legislative, administrative, and other measures for the implementation of the rights recognised in the present Convention. *With regard to economic, social and cultural rights, States Parties shall undertake such measures to the maximum extent of their available resources and, where needed, within the framework of international co-operation.*[1]

I then turn to the links that the Committee has made between the attainment of ESR under the CRC and budgetary decision-making, before proceeding to outline the key elements and of child ESR-based budget analysis.

Having highlighted the shortcomings of the ComRC's approach to ESR in terms of both theory and practice, I outline how the Committee might remedy its failure and develop a more convincing approach to children's ESR under the CRC, thereby contributing significantly to the efficacy of child ESR-monitoring methodologies. I conclude with a consideration of the opportunity and challenges afforded by the Optional Protocol to the Convention on the Rights of the Child on a Communications Procedure in terms of the Committee's work on ESR and budgetary issues.

2. Children and ESR: some important observations

The CRC is a child-specific instrument. However, as we will see below, the ESR included within it were strongly influenced by the International Covenant on Economic, Social and Cultural Rights (ICESCR) which accords a wide range of ESR to 'everyone'.[2] Extensive scholarship has now focussed on ESR generally.

---

[1] Italics inserted by author.
[2] The ICESCR makes explicit reference to children in one of its provisions, with Article 10 providing that: 'the States Parties to the present Covenant recognise that: 1. The widest possible protection and assistance should be accorded to the family, which is the natural and fundamental group unit of society, particularly for its establishment and while it is responsible for the care and education of dependent children. Marriage must be entered into with the free consent of the intending spouses. 2. Special protection should be accorded to mothers during a reasonable period before and after childbirth. During such period working mothers should be accorded paid leave or leave with adequate social security benefits.' However, the use of the language 'everyone' elsewhere in ICESCR makes it clear that all of the rights in that instrument apply to children.

Despite this, the specific position of children vis-à-vis such rights has received scant consideration. This relative lack of child-centred analysis with regard to ESR would be unproblematic if there was nothing about children that rendered the content, interpretation and application of their rights different from those of other (specifically, adult) members of society. But, that is not the case.[3]

There are a number of ways in which children are in a significantly different position from adults with regard to their enjoyment of ESR. First, child and adult members of the same family or society are not necessarily accorded the same ESR; under the CRC children are accorded ESR that differ from those of adults under international human rights law.[4]

In addition, children are more vulnerable to violations of their ESR than adults. Wringe has noted two factors that must be borne in mind when considering the position of children with regard to their rights. First, due to their nature and condition, children have a reduced capacity to meet their socio-economic needs either by obtaining or creating sustenance from the resources of their environment.[5] Second, they are less likely to have the skills necessary to gain a stake in the resources of the community by negotiating special rights (i.e. rights which arise from transactions or relationships) for themselves.[6] These factors severely reduce the ability of children to give effect to their own ESR.

Furthermore, children are often affected in an unalike way to adults by violations of a similar nature, both in the short and the longer term. The physical and psychological effects that children suffer as a result of violations of their ESR will generally be greater than those experienced by adults due to their age and lower level of physical and mental development. This is true both in relation to (a) the immediate impact that violations of ESR may have on a child's physical and psychological state, and (b) the long-term detrimental effects on the child's development and future capacity for autonomy resulting from such violations. As the Committee has noted: 'Childhood is a unique period of physical, mental, emotional and spiritual development and violations of children's rights ... may have life-long, irreversible and even trans-generational consequences'.[7]

---

[3] For a more extensive discussion of many of the issues raised in this section, see A. Nolan, *Children's Socio-economic Rights, Democracy and the Courts* (Oxford: Hart Publishing, 2011), Chapter 1.

[4] See, e.g., the right to life, survival and development (Article 6) and the right to the child to rest, leisure, play, recreational activities, cultural life and the arts (Article 31 CRC). Neither of these rights is found in ICESCR.

[5] Wringe, C., *Children's Rights: A Philosophical Study* (London and Boston, Routledge and Kegan Paul, 1981), 135-6.

[6] Ibid.

[7] ComRC General comment No. 16 on State obligations regarding the impact of the business sector on children's rights, UN Doc. CRC/C/GC/16 (2013), para. 4.

Fourth, while the nature of the ESR violations experienced by children and other socio-economically disadvantaged groups may be similar, it is important to bear in mind that children face distinct challenges in terms of the vindication of their ESR compared with many other vulnerable groups. This is due to, amongst other things, their (almost universal) democratic unenfranchisement, their (frequent) legal unenfranchisement,[8] their limited economic power, and their inability to rely on the legal non-discrimination/ equality principles employed by other social minority groups to advance their ESR concerns. It is not that children are necessarily more vulnerable than all other social groups but, rather, that they are *differently* vulnerable.[9]

A fifth crucial point to note is that children who form part of other social minority groups (female, prisoners, people with disabilities) are likely to be more vulnerable to violations of their ESR than children who do not. This is due to their suffering from both the vulnerabilities and disadvantages of the status of childhood and those associated with disability, gender, detention, non-citizenship, status as an indigenous person, mental illness, etc. Indeed, violations of the child's ESR are often the result of deeply-rooted systemic inequality manifested in the experience of multiple discrimination at the individual level. Furthermore, children whose economic and social rights have been violated may become victims of discrimination on that ground also (for instance, due to stigmatic attitudes about street children or persons living with or HIV/AIDS).

Children are a group with evolving needs and capacities – a fact that is clearly reflected in the CRC.[10] Childhood is very clearly not an immutable characteristic; it is notable that not only do the ranks of childhood change continuously due to the new addition of new members and the loss of previous members to adulthood but the ESR-related needs of individual children alter across their childhood. While adults vary in terms of their ESR-related requirements over the course of their lifetime (e.g., as a result of the ageing process or becoming disabled), this is generally to a far lesser degree than over the course of childhood. This needs to be borne in mind when considering how children's ESR should be given effect to – both in the shorter and in the longer term.

Finally, children have a more restricted ability to make and advance rights claims than adults. This is due both to the incapacity of some children (e.g., the very young) to make claims on their own behalf, as well as the socially

---

[8] For examples of the Committee's recognition of these points, see ibid.
[9] For a comparison of the position of children vis-à-vis other vulnerable groups in society, see Nolan above n.4, Chapter 1.
[10] See, e.g., Articles 5 and 14(2), CRC.

constructed exclusion of children from legal and democratic processes which are key to the realisation of ESR.

The observations above can be legitimately criticised as generalised and homogenising. That does not mean that they do not reflect accurately the position and challenges faced by many, if not most, children with regard to ESR enjoyment. In light of this, it is vital that they be taken into account when considering the extent of those rights – and the obligations imposed by such. Indeed, a failure to ignore the reality of children's position vis-à-vis their ESR will impact on the appropriate construal of, and the effectiveness of efforts to satisfy, those rights. This is an important factor to bear in mind when considering the rights/obligations provided for under a deliberately child-specific instrument such as the CRC.

3. ESR under the CRC and the Committee on the Rights of the Child

I now turn to the key framework under consideration in this paper: the CRC. The CRC does not specify which rights are ESR.[11] However, this article proceeds on the basis that the following rights are ESR or have significant ESR elements:[12] the State's duty to ensure to the maximum extent possible the survival and development of the child (Art. 6); the right of disabled children to special care (Art. 23); the right to the enjoyment of the highest attainable standard of health (Art. 24); the right to benefit from social security (Art. 26); the right to a standard of living adequate for the child's physical, mental, spiritual, moral and social development (Art. 27), and the right to education (Arts. 28, 29).[13]

While the CRC imposes ESR obligations on a range of actors including parents,[14] this article will focus on state duties. That is not to ignore the key role that parents play with regard to child ESR satisfaction. However, it is States

---

11) The Committee has noted that 'there is no simple or authoritative division of human rights in general or of Convention rights into two categories' and has emphasised the interdependence and indivisibility of all human rights. (ComESCR General Comment No.5 on General Measures of Implementation of the Convention on the Rights of the Child (Arts. 4, 42 and 44, para. 6), UN Doc CRC/GC/2003/5 (2003), para. 6).
12) This is based on a consideration of those rights (and elements of rights) in the CRC that are reflected in ICESCR.
13) Interestingly, a provision outlining the right to food was submitted to the 1983 session of the open-ended Working Group on the Question of a Convention on the Rights of the Child by Algeria but was ultimately not considered by that body, see UN Doc. E/CN/4/1983/62, Annex II.
14) See, e.g., Articles 18(2), 23(2) and 27(3) CRC. For a consideration of non-state actors in the context of a specific ESR, see ComRC General Comment No.15 on the right of the child to the enjoyment of the highest attainable standard of health (Article 24), UN Doc CRC/C/GC/15 (2003), paras. 79-85.

Parties, not parents, which have the ultimate responsibility under international human rights law for the determination of laws and policies (including budgets) that have key implications for the realisation of children's ESR.[15] Nor will this article address in any depth ESR obligations relating to international cooperation that exist in terms of the CRC.[16] Clearly, international cooperation and the operation of supranational bodies such as international financial institutions have implications for the determination of economic policy and the resources available for disbursement on children's ESR, both internationally and domestically.[17] However, for space reasons, no consideration will be given to the obligation of states to contribute in terms of international cooperation and there will be only passing reference to the obligations of states to take advantage of the resource-related opportunities afforded by international cooperation processes.

ESR under the CRC: Tracing the Parameters

Prior to February 2013, the Committee on the Rights of the Child had not issued a rights-thematic General Comment on any of the ESR under the Covenant. Whilst it had dealt with ESR-related issues in some of its other statements, it had not spelt out the obligations imposed by a particular ESR in detail. The Committee's General Comment on the right of the child to the enjoyment of the highest attainable standard of health (Art. 24)[18] thus constitutes a valuable addition to their work on ESR. That statement does not, however, stand alone and the analysis below reflects the range of statements in which the Committee has addressed Article 4 and the key obligations imposed by ESR under the CRC.

---

[15] While voting parents certainly play a role in terms of determining legislative/executive mandates with regard to law and policy, It cannot be argued convincingly that parents – whether individually or as a group – directly and exclusively set policy or budget priorities.

[16] See, e.g., Articles 4, 23 and 28 of the CRC. For an extensive consideration of these obligations, see W. Vandenhole, 'Economic, Social and Cultural Rights in the CRC: 'Is There a Legal Obligation to Cooperate Internationally for Development?' (2009) 17 *International Journal of Children's Rights* 23; M. Nyongesa Wabwile, *Legal Protection of Social and Economic Rights of Children in Developing Countries: Reassessing International Cooperation and Responsibility* (Antwerp: Intersentia, 2010). For a discussion of international cooperation by the Committee on the Rights of the Child, see General Comment No. 5, paras 60-64; General Comment No.15, paras 86-89; Committee on the Rights of the Child, 'Day of General Discussion – Resources for the Rights of the Child: Responsibility of States', 46th Session (2007) ('Day of General Discussion'), http://www2.ohchr.org/english/bodies/crc/discussion2013.htm, paras. 50-52.

[17] See, e.g., the role of the EU Fiscal Treaty which requires EU member states to constitutionalise a range of budgetary rules that impact upon national budget structure.

[18] For details of the call for submissions and information on the detailed scope and proposed structure of the General Comment, see: http://www2.ohchr.org/english/bodies/crc/callsubmissionsCRC.htm.

The first – and, indeed, the most significant – thing to note when looking at how the Committee on the Rights of the Child has addressed ESR under the CRC is its heavy reliance on the work of the Committee on Economic, Social and Cultural Rights (ComESCR). This latter body is mandated to oversee the progress of State Party adherence to ICESCR.[19] In contrast, the function of the Committee on the Rights of the Child is to examine the progress made by States Parties in achieving the realisation of obligations undertaken in the CRC.[20] While there is clear overlap between the rights set out in the CRC and ICESCR,[21] the Committees are separate bodies with different, instrument-specific mandates.

In its key statement so far on Article 4 CRC, General Comment No.5 on general measures of implementation of the Convention, the Committee on the Rights of the Child highlighted that, 'there are articles similar to art. 4 … such as art. 2 of the International Covenant on Economic, Social and Cultural Rights'.[22] The Committee emphasised that the ComESCR 'has issued General Comments in relation to these provisions which should be seen as complementary to the present general comment', making specific reference to the ComESCR's General Comments Nos. 3 and 9 on the nature of states parties' obligations and the domestic application of the Covenant, respectively.[23]

The Committee went on to state that the second sentence of Article 4 reflects,

> a realistic acceptance that lack of resources – financial and other resources – can hamper the full implementation of economic, social and cultural rights in some States; *this introduces the concept of 'progressive realisation' of such rights*: States need to be able to demonstrate that they have implemented 'to the maximum extent of their available resources' and, where necessary, have sought international cooperation (emphasis added).

It did so despite the fact that there is no reference to the language of progressivity in Article 4.

The Committee noted that the second sentence in Article 4 is 'similar' to the wording under ICESCR and that 'the [ComRC] entirely concurs with the [ComESCR] in asserting that "even where the available resources are demonstrably inadequate, the obligation remains for a State party to strive to ensure

---

[19] See UN Economic and Social Council Resolution 1985/17, 28 May 1985.
[20] Article 43, CRC.
[21] Both instruments include the right to an adequate standard of living (Art. 11, ICESCR), the right to education (Art. 13, ICESCR), the right to the enjoyment of the highest attainable standard of physical and mental health (Art. 12, ICESCR) and the right to social security (Art.9, ICESCR) or to benefit from social security. (For relevant provisions of the CRC, see above.)
[22] General Comment No.5, para. 5.
[23] Ibid, para. 6 and footnote 4.

the widest possible enjoyment of the relevant rights under the prevailing circumstances ...'".[24] Notably, in one of its relatively rare nods to the group-specific focus of the ESR under the CRC, the Committee added that, whatever their economic circumstances, 'States are required to undertake all possible measures towards the realisation of the rights of the child, paying special attention to the most disadvantaged groups'.[25]

In these statements, the Committee deliberately linked its interpretation of the umbrella obligation in terms of ESR under the CRC (Article 4, CRC) with the ComESCR's approach to the umbrella obligation applying to such rights under ICESCR (Article 2(1), ICESCR). This would be unproblematic were it not for the fact that, as will be discussed further below, the wording of Article 2(1) is significantly different to that of Article 4 CRC,[26] providing that:

> Each State Party to the present Covenant undertakes to take steps, individually and through international assistance and co-operation, especially economic and technical, to the maximum of its available resources, with a view to achieving progressively the full realisation of the rights recognised in the present Covenant by all appropriate means, including particularly the adoption of legislative measures.

The Committee did not consider the question(s) of if and how the differences in wording might or should operate. Nor did it address in any meaningful way the implications that the CRC as a child-specific instrument might have for the interpretation and application of Article 4 CRC.

Thus far, General Comment No.5 is the Committee's most extensive 'soft law' statement with regard to the obligations imposed by Article 4. That said, the Committee has fleshed out the framework for ESR under the CRC in greater detail elsewhere, most notably in the recommendations emerging from Day of General Discussion on Resources for the Rights of the Child – Responsibility of States. While these recommendations do not have the status of a General Comment, they constitute a useful indicator of the Committee's thinking with regard to Article 4 and other ESR obligations under the Convention and have formed an increasing part of subsequent, recent General Comments.

The recommendations make clear that 'resources' for the purpose of Article 4 are to be understood in qualitative and quantitative terms; resources are not simply financial in nature but include technological, economic, human and organisational ones.[27] Furthermore, 'available resources' are not just limited

---

[24] Ibid, para. 8.
[25] Ibid, para. 8.
[26] For a discussion of some of the differences between the wording of Article 2(1), ICESCR and Article 4, CRC, see M. Rishmawi, *Commentary on the United Nations Convention on the Rights of the Child: Article 4: The Nature of States Parties' Obligations* (Leiden: Brill, 2006), 3-8.
[27] ComRC Day of General Discussion, para. 24.

to those available in the national context but include those available from the international community through international assistance.[28] Significantly, from a child rights-perspective, the Committee recommended that States 'assess "available resources" beyond financial measures', emphasising the importance of systematically supporting 'parents and families which are among the most important "available resources"' for children.[29]

The Committee proceeded to delineate a framework strongly based on the work of the ComESCR. Echoing that body's General Comment No.3, the ComRC stated that 'progressive realisation' in terms of Article 4 imposes an immediate obligation for States parties to the Convention to undertake targeted measures to move as expeditiously and effectively as possible towards the full realisation of child economic social and cultural rights (ESCR).[30] In addition, the obligation not to take any retrogressive steps that could hamper the enjoyment of ESCR 'is considered to be inherent in the obligation towards progressive realisation of those rights'.[31]

The Committee also adopted the concept of the 'minimum core' of ESR, explicitly citing the ComESCR on this point.[32] While the language employed by the Committee in its description of the minimum core is slightly different from that used by ComESCR,[33] it is clear that it intended to make reference to the latter body's understanding of the minimum core obligation 'to ensure the satisfaction of, at the very least, minimum essential levels of each of the rights' as fleshed out in that body's General Comment No.3.[34] The Committee also emphasised that 'complying with obligations relating to the core of a right should not be dependent on the availability of resources'.[35] In its most recent

---

[28] Ibid.

[29] Ibid, para 25.

[30] For similar language from the ComESCR, see its General Comment No.3 on the nature of States parties' obligations (Art.2 (1)), UN Doc. E/1991/23 (1990), para. 9.

[31] This point has is reflected implicitly in the work of the ComESCR, see ibid.

[32] ComRC Day of General Discussion, paras. 48-49.

[33] The Committee stated that, 'The Committee on Economic, Social and Cultural Rights (CESCR) has systematically underlined this obligation of States, to guarantee at all times, the guarantee at all times, the minimum level of protection (the minimum core content) in the provision of: essential foodstuffs, equal access to primary health care, basic shelter and housing, social security or social assistance coverage, family protection, and basic education' (ibid, para. 48). In fact, the ComESCR stated that: 'a minimum core obligation to ensure the satisfaction of, at the very least, minimum essential levels of each of the rights is incumbent upon every State party. Thus, for example, a State party in which any significant number of individuals is deprived of essential foodstuffs, of essential primary health care, of basic shelter and housing, or of the most basic forms of education is, *prima facie*, failing to discharge its obligations under the Covenant.' (ComESCR GC No.3, para. 10).

[34] ComESCR General Comment No.3, para. 10.

[35] ComRC Day of General Discussion, para. 48. The Committee did, however, appear to confuse the ComESCR's approach to the issues of 'maximum available resources' and 'minimum

statement of the Committee on ESR, General Comment No. 15 on the child's right to the highest attainable standard of health, the Committee highlighted a range of 'core obligations' imposed by that right,[36] echoing the approach of the ComESCR.[37]

The Committee has also followed the ComESCR's lead with regard to delineating other immediate obligations under the CRC. Its reference to the tripartite topology of state obligations, namely that states parties should 'respect protect and fulfil' rights[38] makes it clear that the Committee regards states as being under an immediate duty not to interfere with the enjoyment of ESR and to take steps to prevent third parties from interfering with the enjoyment of such rights.[39] States parties' obligation of non-discrimination is also of immediate effect.[40] With regard to giving effect to this latter obligation, the Committee recognised 'the need for identifying and giving priority to marginalised and disadvantaged groups of children'.[41]

In sum, the Committee's interpretation of Article 4 and hence ESR obligations under the CRC strongly resemble – and indeed almost entirely replicate – that of the ComESCR in relation to ICESR. This is so even where there are clear divergences in language between these two instruments.

The ICESCR and CRC Frameworks: An Ideal Union or an Odd Couple?

To appreciate fully the potential issues surrounding the ComRC's treatment of Article 4 and other ESR provisions under the CRC, it is necessary to turn back

---

core obligations' somewhat, stating in the context of its discussion of the latter that 'where the available resources are demonstrably inadequate, the State concerned is still required to strive to ensure the widest possible enjoyment of the relevant rights under the prevailing circumstances' (ibid).In contrast, the ComESCR made this point about with regard to the enjoyment of ESR generally – not just the 'minimum core' of those rights (ComESCR General Comment No.3, para. 11).

[36] ComRC General Comment No.15, para. 73.

[37] The Committee has adopted this approach in its General Comments since 2000. See ComESCR General Comments 14, 15, 17-19 and 21.

[38] See, e.g., ComRC General Comment No.4 on adolescent health and development in the context of the Convention on the Rights of the Child, UN Doc CRC/GC/2003/4 (2003), para. 3; ComRC, General Comment No.16, paras. 26-31; ComRC General Comment No.17 on the right of the child to rest, leisure, play recreational activities, cultural life and the arts (art.31) (2013), para. 54; ComRC General Comment No.15, paras. 1 and 71-74. The ComRC has not, however, always explicitly used the definitions of these obligations adopted by the ComESCR. See, e.g., General Comment No.15 where the ComRC states that the obligation to fulfill entails 'facilitation' and 'provision' (at para. 71). This is despite the fact that the ComESCR has made it clear that 'promotion' is also a key element of that duty in the context of health. (See ComESCR General Comment No.14, para. 37 and footnote 23.)

[39] For more on these obligations under ICESCR, see I. Koch, 'Dichotomies, Trichotomies or Waves of Duties?' (2005) 5 Human Rights Law Review 81.

[40] See ComRC Day of General Discussion, para. 47; ComESCR General Comment No.3, para. 1.

[41] ComRC Day of General Discussion, para. 40.

to the CRC drafting negotiations.[42] How did this process reflect awareness of the concepts and language set out in ICESCR? What evidence is there of the significance accorded to the differences between the language included in ICESCR and the CRC when considering the appropriateness of the ComRC's interpretation of the CRC?

In considering Articles 4, CRC and 2(1), ICESCR, it is important to note that the Working Group meetings during which the ESR provisions of the CRC were drafted predated the key statements of ComESCR General Comments. General Comment No.3, which was the first detailed attempt at specification of obligations imposed by Article 2(1), was issued in December 1990. As such, the Working Groups did not have access to the detailed delineations of specific provisions in, and issues arising in relation to, ICESCR. That said, it is clear that there was a concern on the part of CRC drafters to render the approach to ESR under the Convention consistent with that of ICESCR.[43]

During the drafting process, reference was made to and/or concern was expressed by delegations with regard to making the draft Convention provisions consistent with those of the ICESCR in a wide range of contexts,[44] including Article 4 on general measures,[45] the rights to education,[46] an adequate standard of living,[47] health,[48] social security[49] and disabled children's rights.[50] Furthermore, during the meeting of the 1983 Working Group, several delegations supported the idea of a heading applying to all of the provisions of the Convention 'concerning social welfare benefits'[51] that would 'incorporate language comparable to Article 2 [ICESCR]'.[52] This approach was not, however, adopted consistently throughout the ESR included in the CRC.

---

[42] The information below on the drafting negotiations is taken from the reports of such included in the United Nations, *Legislative History of the Convention on the Rights of the Child, Vols I and II* (Geneva/New York: United Nations 2007) and S. Detrick, *The United Nations Convention on the Rights of the Child: A Guide to the Travaux Préparatoires.* Given that neither document provides a complete account of all discussions (nor, indeed, do the working group reports), the argumentation below is reflective of a thorough, but not necessarily complete, account of the draft negotiations.

[43] Please note that the article numbers referred to in this section are those ultimately assigned to the respective ESR under the CRC – they do not reflect the Article numbers employed during the draft process.

[44] While there is no express reference to ICESCR in the Travaux Préparatoires with regard to the right to an adequate standard of living in Article 27, that provision bears a very strong resemblance to Article 11, ICESCR.

[45] See, e.g., E/CN.4/1324, para. 1 and E/CN.4/L.1575, para. 43.

[46] See, e.g., E/CN.4/1985/64, paras. 60, 62, 76; E/CN/4/1989/48, paras. 461-463.

[47] E/CN.4/1988/WG.1/NGO/2, para. 3.

[48] See, e.g., E/CN.4/1985/64, para 15.

[49] See, .e.g., E/CN.4/1989/48, paras. 441, 446

[50] See, e.g., E/CN.4/1983/62, para. 60.

[51] See E/CN.4/1983/62, para 60.

[52] Ibid.

There was one element of Article 2(1) ICESCR that was a consistent preoccupation of the CRC drafters: the issue of available resources. Indeed, a concern with resource limitations was reflected frequently in the discussion of all provisions of the CRC and explicitly referred to in the context of particular provisions.[53] Drafter attention to the resource implications of the implementation of Convention rights was not limited to the ESR context, however. The express division in Article 4 between the state obligations imposed by ESCR and CPR under CRC resulted from the response of a number of negotiating states to earlier wording that would have rendered the implementation measures to be taken for *all* Convention rights subject to the availability of resources[54] The USA, Canada, Sweden and New Zealand, Argentina, Portugal and the United Kingdom, 'stated that civil and political rights guaranteed in the International Covenant on Civil and Political Rights[55] were not subjected to the availability of resources and that the Covenant's standards should not be weakened in the child's convention'.[56] With regard to ESCR, they recognised that certain of the rights could be implemented only if sufficient resources' were available.[57]

However, while one aspect of Article 2(1) ICESCR – maximum available resources – is very strongly reflected in the CRC ESR negotiations, the same is not true with regard to the concept of progressive realisation. Whilst there is a mention of progressivity, in the context of the rights to education,[58] an adequate standard of living[59] and social security,[60] as well as the inclusion thereof

---

[53] See, e.g., Working Group discussions of the child's right to an adequate standard of living (inter alia E/CN.4/1985/64, paras 43-52), the right to education (inter alia E/CN.4/1985/64, paras 58-67), Article 4 (inter alia E/CN.4/L.1575, paras 44; E/CN.4/1989/48, paras 172-174), the right to social security (inter alia E/CN.4/1984/71, paras 83, 90), and the right to health (see inter alia E/CN.4/1986/39, Annex IV p.3, in which Bangladesh submitted that that Articles 'such Articles as "health", "standards of living", "compulsory free education" should be made subject to a clause on the economic feasibility in particular countries'). In the context of disabled children's rights, concerns about resources are reflected in the wording of Article 23(2)'s on 'subject to available resources' and Article 23(3)'s inclusion of the language 'whenever possible'. With regard to Article 6, negotiating states considered the inclusion of language on 'within their capacities' and 'available resources' (see E/CN.4/1988/28, paras 14 and 15, respectively) but this was ultimately not included in the final provision.

[54] For examples of such wording, see, e.g., E/CN.4/L.1575, Annex, p.3; E/CN.4/1988/WG.1/WP.1/ Rev.2, p. 7.

[55] This is the sister instrument to ICESR which contains civil and political rights. Together with the Universal of Declaration of Human Rights, these instruments make up the international bill of rights.

[56] See E/CN.4/1989/48, para. 172.

[57] Ibid.

[58] See E/CN.4/1989/48, paras. 460, 463 and 466. See the express reference to progressive achievement of the right to education in Section 28(1).

[59] See, e.g., E/CN.4/1988/WG.1/NGO/2.

[60] See, e.g., ECN.4/1984/71, paras. 86-93. See the implicit incorporation of 'progressivity' in the language of Section 26(1) which refers to the State obligation to 'take the necessary measures to achieve the full realisation of this right'.

in the wording of the right to health provision,[61] it received nothing like the attention that the issue of resources did. Indeed, it is notable that the issue of progressivity does not appear to have been raised in relation to disabled children's rights and – most importantly – Article 4 on general measures.[62] Interestingly, in its technical review, UNICEF argued that 'it is unnecessary to include a resource availability clause in the article defining the nature of States Parties' overall obligations since each of the subsequent provisions of the draft convention dealing with economic or social rights contains a specific phrase effectively limiting the States Parties' obligations in the light of resource availability'.[63] Whilst this recommendation was not acted upon, it is worth noting that no proposal seems was made vis-à-vis the inclusion (or deletion) of an 'umbrella obligation' of progressive realisation or achievement.[64] Rather, the patchy references to progressivity in particular ESR provisions under the CRC seem attributable to the limited attention accorded to that concept by participants in the Working Group discussions.

One might ask what this relative neglect of progressive realisation amounts to and whether it really matters? Does the clear concern with resources reflected in Article 4 effectively 'cover' progressive realisation? Ultimately one must conclude that it does not. Progressive realisation was treated as a discrete element of Article 2(1) by the drafters of ICESCR.[65] The ComESCR has also taken this approach in its practice.[66]

The fact that the rate of progressive realisation is necessarily affected by the extent of resources available to the state does not reduce that concept to simply a restatement of the 'maximum available resources' point. It is thus problematic that the ComRC has failed adequately to acknowledge and address the difference in language (and hence potentially in content) between Article 2(1) ICESCR and Article 4 CRC.

Furthermore, there seems no discernible logic as to why the concept of progressivity is expressly referred to in some ESR provisions (e.g., Articles 24 and

---

[61] See Article 24(2)'s requirement that states 'shall pursue full implementation of the right' and the reference to 'progressive achievement' in Section 24(4). The inclusion of 'progressive' in this latter provision seems to have been a last minute decision – it was literally the last change made to the wording of the Article (E/CN.4/1989/48 para. 431). The documents contained in United Nations and Detrick above, n. 44, include no material that suggests why this wording was included.

[62] There was also no reference to progressivity with regard to Article 6.

[63] See E/CN.4/1989/WG.1/CRP.1.

[64] While the Travaux Préparatoires do not reflect all Working Group discussion/proposals, it would seem highly unlikely that such a significant proposal would not have been recorded.

[65] See P. Alston & G. Quinn, 'The Nature and Scope of States Parties' Obligations under the International Covenant on Economic, Social and Cultural Rights' (1987) 9(2) *Human Rights Quarterly* 156, 172-177 and 228.

[66] See, e.g., ComESCR General Comment No.3, para. 9.

28) but not in others. While this would not matter if Article 4 contained an 'umbrella' reference to progressive realisation in the way that Article 2(1) does, this inconsistency in drafting creates problems for the treatment of progressivity in the context of the CRC generally. Given this, it is hardly surprising that the ComRC should adopt the more coherent, developed framework of ICESCR. It would be better, however, if the ComRC was expressly to justify doing so rather than simply eliding over the notable omission of progressive realisation from Article 4 – an approach that has inevitably proved question-begging. This is arguably particularly necessary given the existence of Article 6 – the right to life, survival and development – which entails both civil and political and economic and social aspects and the drafting negotiations pertaining to which did not include a discussion of progressivity.[67]

The Committee's confused approach to progressive realization – and ESR obligations more generally – is cast into sharp relief in its General Comment No 15. Here, the Committee stated that,

> In accordance with Article 4 of the Convention, States parties shall fulfil the entitlements contained in children's right to health to the maximum extent of their available resources and, where needed, within the framework of international co-operation.[68]

At first glance, this statement seems unproblematic and would appear to reflect the language of Article 4. Indeed, it could be praised for the avoidance of the language of progressivity which is not found in Article 4 (although the irony is that Article 24(4) actually makes explicit reference to 'achieving progressively the full realisation of the right' so a focus on progressive realisation is certainly justifiable in this instance). Here, however, the Committee misapplies the language of fulfil, essentially equating it to 'realisation' or 'implementation'. Aside from the linguistic confusion, this equation of concepts is an issue due to the fact the obligation to fulfill does not directly correspond to the concept of progressive realization, containing as it does both immediate and progressive elements. While the term 'fulfil' need not be employed in the sense of the obligation to fulfil, it seems clear that this was what the Committee intended here.[69] This conceptual confusion is further evidenced in the

---

[67] For an excellent discussion of the drafting processes and Article 6 generally, see N. Peleg, *The Child's Right to Development* (PhD defended at University College London, 28 January 2013).
[68] ComRC General Comment No.15, para. 71.
[69] The statement in question follows this passage: 'States have three types of obligations relating to human rights, including children's right to health: to respect the freedoms and the entitlements, to protect both freedoms and entitlements against third parties or against social or environmental threats, and to fulfil the entitlements through facilitation or direct provision.' (Ibid, para. 72).

Committee's statements that: 'states should demonstrate their commitment to progressive fulfillment of all obligations under Article 24'.[70] It is thus clear that there are serious issues with regard to the Committee's employment of its chosen framework.

Where are We Now?

The discussion so far illustrates that the instrument that the Committee is mandated to monitor is different from ICESCR. As such, the Committee needs to provide a more consistent justification for its whole-hearted adoption of the ESR framework outlined by the ComESCR. I am not suggesting that such a justification does not exist, rather I seek to highlight that it has not yet been provided. It is important to note that the Committee's approach has not received extensive criticism: academics working in the area have frequently adopted the ICESCR framework when discussing children's ESR[71] or have failed to criticise the Committee's approach on this point.[72] As such, it is perhaps not surprising that the Committee has felt untroubled in its approach. Given the Committee's mandate, however, its failure to consider in any depth how 'general' ESR obligations (as interpreted by ICESCR) should be construed or applied in light of children's ESR in the context of the CRC is troubling.

Another problem with the Committee's reliance on the work of the ComESCR is the fact that that model is itself far from perfect. The substantive content of ESR duties such as 'progressive realisation', 'maximum available resources' and the 'minimum core obligation' is complex and subject to contestation.[73] Furthermore, there is an issue of completeness; significant gaps and confusions have been identified in the ICESCR framework as outlined by the ComESCR.[74] However, the ComRC appear oblivious to this in its uncritical

---

[70] Ibid, para. 74.

[71] See, e.g., M. Nyongesa Wabwile, *Legal Protection of Social and Economic Rights of Children in Developing Countries: Reassessing International Cooperation and Responsibility* (Antwerp: Intersentia, 2010), Chapter 2. ; G Van Bueren, 'Combating Child Poverty: Human Rights Approaches' (1999) 21(33) *Human Rights Quarterly* 680, 690

[72] See, e.g., G. van Bueren in M. Langford (ed.), *Social Rights Jurisprudence: Emerging Trends in International and Comparative Law* (New York: CUP, 2008 569, 572.

[73] For more on this point, see QUB Budget Analysis Project, *Budgeting for Economic and Social Rights: A Human Rights Framework* (Belfast, QUB, 2010).

[74] For pieces highlighting confusions and gaps in the ICESCR framework, see, e.g., ibid; K. Young, 'The Minimum Core of Economic and Social Rights: A Concept in Search of Content' (2008) 33 *Yale Journal of International Law* 113; A. Nolan, 'Putting ESR-Based Budget Analysis into Practice: Addressing the Conceptual Challenges' in Nolan, O'Connell & Harvey (eds), *Human Rights & Public Finance* (Oxford: Hart Publishing, forthcoming 2013).

'borrowing' of that body's approach. It thus has failed to realise the problems that it has, probably inadvertently, incorporated into the CRC framework of ESR.

The Committee's failure to engage in a meaningful way with ESR obligations under the CRC is further reflected in its lack of consistent, effective engagement with the language of ESR obligations (e.g., 'progressive achievement' , 'maximum available resources' and 'minimum core') in the context of either its General Comments or Concluding Observations thus far.[75] This gap is perhaps unsurprising: the Committee's report of its Day of General Discussion on Resources states that –

> In the [Foreword of General Comment No.5], the Committee indicated that, given the complexity of the concept of [obligations to develop 'general measures of implementation'] it was 'likely to issue more detailed general comments on individual elements in due course'.

It is notable that this has not yet occurred.

One might be moved to say, 'well, this is all very worrying from a theory perspective, but does it really matter in practice?' The answer is that it does – a lot. When we consider the purpose of the ESR framework outlined by the ComRC – specifically its function in terms of providing guidance to states, advocates, national human rights institutions for children and others with regard to the implementation of the CRC (and in constituting a framework for the evaluation of such) – the inconsistency and gaps identified above are extremely problematic. Nowhere is this more evident than in the highly charged area of budgetary decision-making.

4. The Committee and Budgets

The Committee has made clear that the CRC has implications for state budget decisions, highlighting the link between the attainment of ESR and budgetary decision-making on numerous occasions. In its General Comment No.5, the Committee stated in the context of discussing the obligations imposed by

---

[75] For evidence of this, see C. Price Cohen, *The Jurisprudence on the Rights of the Child, Vol III* (New York: Transnational Publishers, 2005). More recently, none of the Concluding Observations of the Committee from 20 February 2012 to 20 February 2013 included a reference to 'progressive achievement' or 'minimum core'. While there were a small number of references to 'maximum available resources', this was solely in the context of the Committee reiterating the duty rather than evaluating States Parties compliance with such. (See, e.g., Concluding Observations: Madagascar, CRC/C/MDG/CO/3-4, para. 50; Concluding Observations: Cyprus, CRC/C/CYP/CO/3-4, para 16.)

Article 4 CRC, that 'no State can tell whether it is fulfilling children's [ESCR] "to the maximum extent of ... available resources", as it is required to do under Article 4, unless it can identify the proportion of national and other budgets allocated to the social sector and, within that, to children, both directly and indirectly.'[76] Furthermore, states are required to carry out 'a continuous process of child impact assessment (predicting the impact of any proposed law, policy or budgetary allocation which affects children and the enjoyment of their rights) and child impact evaluation (evaluating the actual impact of implementation).'[77] States parties are required to identify ministries and departments dealing with children and to make sure that other ministries are also able to demonstrate how their budget and programmes are consistent with the realisation of children's ESR.[78] According to the Committee, the obligation to 'fulfil' children's economic, social and cultural rights, 'requires States parties to introduce the necessary legislative, administrative, judicial, *budgetary*, promotional and other measures aimed at the full enjoyment of [those rights]' in terms of Article 4.[79]

The Committee's 2010 State Reporting Guidelines ask for information on allocation of resources during the reporting period for social services in relation to total expenditures for social security, health services, education, early childhood development, and child protection measures.[80] States are also requested to provide data on whether the budget allocated for the implementation of the Convention 'is clearly identified and can be monitored as it relates to the comprehensive national strategy and corresponding plan for children'.[81] Reflecting this growing focus on the issue of resources, over the last number of years, the Committee has included a discrete section on 'allocation of resources' in its Concluding Observations.

The Committee has highlighted that it needs to know what steps are taken 'at all levels of Government to ensure that economic and social planning and decision-making and budgetary decisions are made with the best interests of children as a primary consideration'.[82] This budget-conscious approach to Convention interpretation and monitoring is echoed in the Committee's

---

[76] ComRC General Comment No 5, para. 51.
[77] ComRC General Comment No.5, para. 45. The Committee made this observation when discussing the state's duty to ensure both that the best interests of the child are a primary consideration in all actions concerning children in terms of Article 3(1) CRC, and that the Convention is respected in legislation and policy development and delivery at all levels of government.
[78] ComRC Day of General Discussion, para. 30(c).
[79] See, e.g., ComRC, General Comment No.17, para. 54; ComRC General Comment No.16, para. 29,
[80] ComRC 'State Reporting Guidelines', UN Doc. CRC/C/58/Rev.2 (2010), Annex, para 3.
[81] Ibid, para. 19(d).
[82] ComRC General Comment No.5, para. 51.

General Comments,[83] as well as its Guidelines on Periodic State Reports in which it requests State Parties to provide information including 'whether the budget allocated for the implementation of the Convention and its Optional Protocols is clearly identified and can be monitored as it relates to the comprehensive national strategy and corresponding plan for children.'[84] Budgetary data in state reports should 'indicate the resources available and the proportion allocated to children, disaggregated by sectors'.[85] Furthermore, reports should indicate clearly the proportion of allocation and expenditure on children, in relation to other priorities of the government, 'including, but not limited to, military allocation and expenditure.'[86] States parties should 'make children a priority in the budgetary allocations as a means to ensure the highest return of the limited available resources; and make investment in children visible in the State budget through detailed compilation of resources allocated to them'.[87] The Committee has gone so far as to suggest that all states should consider legislating a specific proportion of the public expenditure to be allocated to children[88] – something that is currently only a feature of a very small number of constitutional systems.[89]

The Committee's focus on budgetary issues forms a discrete element of its 2013 General Comment No.15. Here the Committee set out a series of obligations imposed on states with regard to budget allocation and

---

[83] Although the issue of resources is addressed in a considerable number of General Comments, budgets are dealt with in some detail in ComRC General Comment No.9 on the rights of children with disabilities, UN Doc. CRC/C/GC/9 (2007), para 20; ComRC General comment No. 13 on the right of the child to freedom from all forms of violence, UN Doc. CRC/C/GC/13 (2011), paras. 40-42, 71-72 and 74-75; and ComRC General Comment No.17, para. 57(d).

[84] UN Doc, CRC/C/58/Rev.2 (2010), para. 19(d).

[85] ComRC Day of General Discussion, para. 34(c).

[86] ibid.

[87] ibid, para. 30(a).

[88] ibid, para. 23.

[89] For an example of such a measure, the Transitional Provisions of the Ecuadorean Constitution 2008 obliges the state to assign public resources from the General Budget in a progressive manner for the initial basic and secondary education (Dispociones Transitorias, point 18), stipulating an annual increase of at least 0.5 per cent of the GDP until a minimum of 6 per cent is reached (ibid). See also Article 212 of the Brazilian Constitution which requires that: 'the Union shall apply, annually, never less than eighteen percent, and the states, the Federal District, and the municipalities, at least twenty-five percent of the tax revenues, including those resulting from transfers, in the maintenance and development of education.' Article 164 of the Constitution of Taiwan states that 'expenditures of educational programs, scientific studies and cultural service shall be, in respect of the Central Government, not less than 15 per cent of the total national budget; in respect of each province, not less than 25 percent of the total provincial budget; and in respect of each municipality or hsien, less than 35 percent of the total municipal or hsien budget. Educational and cultural foundations established in accordance with law shall, together with their property, be protected'. Admittedly 'education' is not limited to children but children tend to be the main beneficiaries of such.

spending,[90] focussing specifically on law, and policymaking in the health context.[91] States were urged to 'continually assess the impact of macro-economic policy decisions on children's right to health, particularly children in vulnerable situations, prevent any decisions that may compromise children's rights, and to apply the best interests principle when making such decisions'.[92]

A key issue in terms of the current post-financial and economic crises context, is the Committee's statement that states parties are required to demonstrate that 'children, including in particular marginalised and disadvantaged groups of children, are protected from the adverse effects of economic policies or financial downturns'.[93] The Committee has also stated that states commitment to 'progressive fulfilment' of the child's right to health should be prioritised 'even in the context of political or economic crisis or emergency situations'.[94] Furthermore, state emphasis on allocations aimed at economic growth should not be made at the sacrifice of social sector expenditure.[95] Again, this is a crucial point given the 'austerity' measures (including those of a budgetary nature) that have been adopted by a wide range of states parties to the CRC following the crises.[96]

Notably, the Committee has moved beyond simply discussing the importance of budget decision-making vis-à-vis child ESR realisation generally to considering budget analysis methodology specifically. In the recommendations emerging from its Day of General Discussion on Resources in 2007 – at which there was considerable discussion of child rights-based budget analysis methodology – it urged states to 'consider using rights-based budget monitoring and analysis, as well as child impact assessments on how investments in any sector may serve "the best interests of the child"'.[97] It also argued that the 'accurate systematization of [budgetary] data and indicators and an effective analysis of the budget are particularly important requirements for the monitoring of efforts towards the realisation of economic, social and cultural rights

---

90) ComRC General Comment No.15, paras. 104-107.
91) See ibid, para. 106.
92) ibid, para. 105.
93) ComRC General Comment No.5, para. 51.
94) General Comment No.15, para. 74,
95) ComRC Day of General Discussion, para. 31.
96) See, e.g., I. Ortiz, J. Chai & M. Cummins, Austerity Measures Threaten Children and Poor Households: Recent Evidence in Public Expenditures from 128 Developing Countries (New York: UNICEF, 2011)
97) ComRC Day of General Discussion, para 30(b). In its General Comment No.16, the Committee stated that states should adopt child rights-based impact assessments in relation to 'business-related policy, legislation, regulations, *budget*, or other administrative decisions which affect children and the enjoyment of their rights' (para. 78).

for children.[98] Further, the Committee emphasised the importance of transparent and participatory budgeting processes.[99]

Positively, the Committee has progressed beyond simply issuing generic statements directing states to 'increase budget allocations for children' or 'prioritise budgetary allocation for children',[100] to setting out a procedural steps that states should take in order to give effect to children's budgets,[101] and critiquing states failure to do so.[102] However, it has thus far not engaged with evaluating the compliance of specific outcomes of budgetary decisions with ESR obligations under the CRC. This is perhaps unsurprising given that the Committee does not generally adopt a 'violations' approach in its Concluding Observations in the sense of concluding explicitly that a specific act or omission of a State Party constitutes a violation of the Convention.[103] Instead, it prefers to 'express concern' about particular factual situations in which ESR are not being satisfied and to make recommendations.[104] However, although this might explain the Committee's reluctance to evaluate discrete budget decisions in terms of their compliance with ESR, that reluctance is also symptomatic of the Committee's broader failure to make the 'conceptual link' between ESR under the CRC and specific economic/budget decisions in its work. The challenge posed to monitoring methodologies by this omission is demonstrated in the discussion of child ESR-based budget analysis below.

5. Child Rights-Based Budget Analysis

Child rights-based budget analysis is the analysis of budgetary decisions using a framework premised on substantive child rights protections set out in international or national human rights instruments (e.g., in human rights treaties, constitutions or domestic legislation).[105] Ultimately, all

---

[98] ibid, para. 33.

[99] ibid, para. 34(a).

[100] See, e.g., Pakistan, CRC/C/15/Add.2/7 (2003); Nepal, CRC/C/15/ADD/261 (2005).

[101] See, e.g., Bangladesh, CRC/C/BGD/CO/4 (2009). For an example of a 'half-way house' between these approaches on the Committee's part, see Sri Lanka, CRC/C/15/Add/228 (2004).

[102] For some recent examples, see Albania, CRC/C/ALB/CO/2-4 (2012); Canada, CRC/C/CAN/CO/3-4 (2013); and United Kingdom, CRC/C/COK/CO/1 (2012).

[103] For an outline of a 'violations' approach of monitoring ESR, see A. Chapman, 'A "Violations Approach" for Monitoring the International Covenant on Economic, Social and Cultural Rights' (1996) 18(1) *Human Rights Quarterly* 23.

[104] I am grateful to Noam Peleg for his insight on this point. (In conversation, November 2012). For an example of the Committee expressing 'concern' at what it termed 'extensive budget cuts', see Iceland, CRC/C/ISL/CO/3-4 (2012), para. 18-10

[105] For examples of child rights-budget analysis, see International Budget Project's resource page on 'Children and Youths: http://internationalbudget.org/budget-analysis/sectors-issues-demographic/children-youths/. For further examples, see, P. Shastri and E. Ganguly Thukral,

such analysis seeks to determine the impact of budgetary decisions on the implementation and enjoyment of children's rights. Child rights-based budget analysis work has thus far focused predominantly on ESR, rather than their civil and political rights counterparts.[106] This situation is attributable both to the particularly resource-dependent nature of ESR and the fact that the implementation of ESR will frequently entail the allocation and expenditure of additional resources by governments above existing budgetary distributions.

Child ESR-based budget analysis may either be static or dynamic: 'static analysis evaluates a given budget by itself. Dynamic analysis compares the evolution of budgets over time, looking at variations in allocations and spending over different periods'.[107] Dynamic analysis is particularly important when practitioners are seeking to evaluate the extent to which states are giving effect to their obligations to realise progressively children's ESR to the maximum extent of available resources, in terms of Article 4 CRC.

Such work will also vary in terms of the 'budget' being analysed. Budgetary allocations, expenditure, revenue and international and domestic macroeconomic policy all have implications for the enjoyment of children's ESR. Child ESR-based budget analysis may thus focus on a range of different budgetary aspects. Most budget analysis practitioners (including those who focus on children's rights) have focused on the first two budgetary issues, however.[108] This 'bias' in ESR-based budget analysis work is demonstrated by a study carried out by the Queen's University Belfast (QUB) Budget Analysis Project of a range of key case studies and guidance on ESR-based budget

---

Budget for Children Analysis: A Beginner's Guide (Save the Children: Kathmandu, 2010). See also E. Ganguly Thukral (ed), *Every Right for Every Child: Governance and Accountability* (London, Routledge, 2011).

[106] See, e.g., the work of Imali Ye Mwana, IDASA (previously Child Budget Unit) such as S. Cassiem and J. Streak, *Budgeting for Child Socio-economic Rights: Government Obligations and the Child's Right to Social Security and Education* (Cape Town: IDASA, 2001) and J. Streak, *Monitoring Government Budgets to Advance Child Rights* (Cape Town: IDASA, 2003) http://www.idasa.org/our_products/resources/output/monitoring_government_budgets_2/. Other groups, such as the Indian-based HAQ Centre for Child Rights, which produces analyses of the impact of national and state budgets, from a child rights perspective, also address civil and political rights-focussed child rights-based budget analysis in the context of child protection and juvenile justice.

[107] OHCHR, *Report of the High Commissioner for Human Rights on Implementation of Economic, Social and Cultural Rights* (8 June 2009), UN Doc. E/2009/90, 14.

[108] For an example of a recently developed methodology designed to evaluate macroeconomic policies from an ESR perspective (albeit not a child-specific one), see R. Balakrishnan, D. Elson & R. Patel, *Rethinking Macroeconomic Strategies from a Human Rights Perspective* (*Why MES with Human Rights II*) (New York: Marymount Manhattan College/ US Human Rights Network 2009).

analysis.[109] The study's authors found that practitioners examined numerous dimensions of budgets: 'All documents refer to allocation of resources and past expenditure is discussed by 13 out of the 14 documents. Budget outcomes (the impact that the budget has on the enjoyment of ESR) are considered in 12. Budget outputs (the goods and services produced by the budget) are identified in nine reports, while budget revenue streams were cited in eight. Only four papers discuss the macroeconomics of the budget.'[110] There is also variety within child ESR-based budget analysis work in terms of the 'kind' of budget being considered, with actors focusing on national, sub-national or local government level budgets.[111]

While child ESR-based budget analysis efforts will differ in terms of the rights framework used, this chapter will focus on the CRC. That instrument is used widely in budget analysis work; in its review of case studies and guidance, the QUB Budget Analysis Project identified that 9 out of 14 of the leading ESR-based budget analysis documents used the CRC as a point of reference.[112] This is unsurprising given the high levels of ratification of that instrument, the relatively limited number of constitutional frameworks that include detailed child ESR provisions, and the fact that the CRC forms part of the constitutional hierarchy of a number of different countries in which ESR-based budget analysis is practised. Where practitioners employ the CRC as their key analytical framework for the purpose of child ESR-based budget analysis, they make frequent use of the statements of the Committee on the Rights of the Child to support their approach and argumentation.[113]

There are two ways in which the Committee's failure to outline a comprehensive coherent framework for ESR and to link that framework to budgetary decisions impacts on budget analysis. As suggested at the end of the previous section, the first is from a methodological perspective: how can practitioners evaluate budgetary compliance – or indeed monitor compliance of state actions or omissions in any way – with ESR standards, if such standards are unclear and incomplete? This lack of clarity also has implications from an advocacy perspective. If there is doubt about the substantive content of ESR obligations under the CRC, how can advocates convince governments that they are in violation of their ESR obligations and hold them to account for such? Ambiguities and gaps in the CRC ESR framework have contributed to

---

[109] For more on the project, see www.qub.ac.uk/schools/SchoolofLaw/Research/HumanRightsCentre/ResearchProjects/BudgetAnalysis/.

[110] QUB Analysis Project, *Budget Analysis and Economic and Social Rights: A Review of Selected Case Studies and Guidance* (QUB: Belfast, 2010), 6.

[111] See, e.g., the work of IDASA, which has produced 'Budgetbriefs' analysing both national and provincial budgets from a child ESR perspective.

[112] QUB Analysis Project above n. 112, 5.

[113] See, e.g., Shastri & Ganguly above n. 107.

the frequent failure of child rights-based budget analysis practitioners to relate specific budget decisions to particular ESR obligations, as well as a tendency on the part of practitioners to ask 'broad questions' about budget decisions rather than 'hooking' those questions on to CRC language/obligations.[114] Thus, the lack of clarity around ESR obligations under the CRC has resulted in a weakening of the connection between budget analysis work and those legal obligations, thereby weakening the force of the conclusions of budget analysis practitioners.

The focus in this paper is on budget analysis methodology and, indeed, the Committee's historic discomfort with assessing the outcomes of budgetary decision-making through linking them to the language of ESR obligations means that budget analysis practitioners are effectively faced with a 'double whammy' in terms of their work. However, the Committee's inadequate approach to the ESR under the CRC applies to a wide range of methodologies focussing on monitoring children's ESR; specifically, any of those that involve the use of the CRC as an analytical framework. The issue of clarity of standards hampers the ability of the advocates both to use the CRC ESR as standards for monitoring effectively, and to hold government to account for ESR violations. Admittedly, the Committee is certainly not alone in terms of its discomfort with linking budgetary decisions and their impacts with specific ESR obliga-tions; the ComESCR has been criticised on the same grounds.[115] However, the shortcomings on the part of one human rights treaty-monitoring body do not justify that of another – albeit that they may contribute to explaining such.

6. What should the Committee be Doing?

Thus far, the paper has focussed on the shortcomings in the Committee's approach to ESR under the CRC. In this section, I argue that the Committee

---

[114] See, e.g., the Ireland-based Children's Rights Alliance's 'Analysis of Budget 2013 and its Impact on Children' (Dublin: CRA, 2012) which highlights the impact of budgetary decisions on the realization of a range of CRC rights and does mention some ESR obligations but does not engage with these in any depth. See also D. Budlender and P. Proudlock, 'Child-centered Analysis of Government's Budgets 2010-2012' (Cape Town: Children's Institute, University of Cape Town, 2010) which provides an excellent overview of budgetary allocations on children, does not go beyond specifying which constitutional rights are impacted upon by particular budgetary decisions.

[115] See, e.g., A. Nolan, "Budget Analysis and Economic and Social Rights' in E. Riedel et al (eds.), *Contemporary Issues in the Realisation of Economic, Social and Cultural Rights* (Oxford: Oxford University Press, forthcoming). For a discussion of the ComESCR's reluctance to engage with macroeconomic policy issues more generally, see M. Dowell-Jones, *Contextualising The International Covenant On Economic, Social And Cultural Rights: Assessing The Economic Deficit* (Leiden: Martinus Nijhoff, 2004).

needs to interpret the CRC on that instrument's own merits, rather than simply 'copy and pasting' the approach of other supervisory bodies. This is particularly important given my earlier observations with regard to the particular position of children as ESR-holders. As highlighted earlier, the Committee has made an effort to bring a child rights focus to bear with regard to some of the ESR obligations that it has adopted from the ComESCR – albeit inconsistently and only to a limited extent. This has largely taken the form of simply tagging on references to children or child-related issues to the standards set out by the ComESCR,[116] rather than a proper conceptualisation of how exactly these obligations should be construed from a child rights-centric perspective. There are clearly advantages in terms of the Committee making use of that framework; doing so means that it can build on the work of the acknowledged ESR experts in the UN treaty-monitoring ComESCR, thereby strengthening the legitimacy and authoritativeness of its own statements. My argument is not that the Committee should 'reinvent the wheel' unnecessarily. Rather I want to focus on how its current framework could/should be adapted in light of its own mandate.

The Committee has not engaged with a number of key questions that have been raised by commentators or in the context of comparative or regional jurisprudence dealing with children's constitutional ESR. For instance, one might ask whether the Committee on the Rights of the Child should be more assertive in interpreting the CRC as according immediately enforceable entitlements than the ComESCR is with regard to ICESCR. Judicial and quasi-judicial bodies such as the European Committee of Social Rights and national courts have concluded, amongst other things, that children have direct entitlements to the satisfaction of their ESR[117] and that children should be prioritised in the overall realisation of rights.[118] Such decision-makers have also been prepared to find that children's ESR have been violated but those of adults have not, in situations in which both groups have access to the same goods or services.[119] These decisions have been premised (whether expressly or implicitly)

---

[116] See, e.g., the language of ComRC General Comment No.5, para. 8, discussed above in the context of discussions of Article 4.

[117] See, e.g., Constitutional Court of Colombia, Tutela Judgment,*T-200/93* (holding that 'the right to health held by children, as opposed to that of other people was established in the constitution as fundamental' and hence immediately enforceable). See also Constitutional Court of Colombia, Unification Judgment, *SU-225/98* (iterating that the ESR of the child set out in Article 44 of the Colombian Constitution have an essential content of immediate application).

[118] See, e.g. Constitutional Court of Colombia, Tutela Judgment, *T-760/08* (Court ordered the legislatively established contributory and subsidised benefits regimes to be unified. This was to be done in the first case for children and youth, while, with regard to adults, it was to be done progressively taking into account sustainable funding).

[119] See, e.g., European Committee of Social Rights, Complaint No. 14/2003, *International Federation of Human Rights Leagues (FIDH) v. France*, 8 September 2004 (finding that

on the particular position of children in society and in relation to ESR enjoy-ment.[120] Practice has been varied: there is no uniform (or even dominant) 'rule' or approach emerging from the jurisprudence.[121] But what is clear is that bodies are engaging with such questions in the context of dealing with chil-dren's ESR. It is therefore deeply disappointing that the Committee has neither engaged properly with these questions nor in any meaningful way with the implications that children as ESR-holders should have for such.

Another area in which the CRC might be expected to be more expansive than the ComESCR in terms of outlining ESR obligations is with regard to the minimum core obligation. Given children's particular vulnerability to viola-tions of their ESR and the relatively severe impact that such violations may have on them vis-à-vis adults, one might argue that the delineation of a more extensive core obligation than that set out by ComESCR is justified on the basis that children's needs are more acute. This might involve stating that the minimum core of children's rights goes beyond the provision of 'essential foodstuffs, equal access to primary health care, basic shelter and housing, social security or social assistance coverage, family protection, and basic edu-cation'.[122] Of course, if the Committee was to take this approach, they would have to address head-on the ambiguities that exist with regard to the mini-mum core as outlined by the ComESCR.[123] This seems unlikely given the Committee's failure to critically engage with (and sometimes even apply correctly) the ComESCR's approach. With regard to state non-compliance with the minimum core obligation, the ComESCR has stated that 'in order for a State party to be able to attribute its failure to meet at least its minimum core obligations to a lack of available resources it must demonstrate that every effort has been made to use all resources that are at its disposition in an effort to satisfy, as a matter of priority, those minimum obligations'.[124] It is disap-pointing that the ComRC has not sought to suggest that the minimum core of children's rights requires that children should be accorded priority in states efforts to meet the minimum core of the rights of everyone.

---

children's health rights were violated while those of adults were not, even though both groups had similar access to healthcare).

[120] For discussion of these cases from a child ESR perspective, see Nolan above, n. 3 and 'The Child's Right to Health and the Courts' in J. Harrington and M. Stuttaford (eds), *Global Health and Human Rights: Legal and Philosophical Perspectives* (London: Routledge, 2010) 135.

[121] See, e.g., the contrasting approach of the South African and Colombian Constitutional Courts on the question of whether children's constitutional ESR give rise to immediately enforceable entitlements on the part of right-holders.

[122] ComRC Day of General Discussion, para. 48; ComESCR General CommentC No.3, para. 10.

[123] See Young, above, n. 79.

[124] ComESCR General Comment No.3, para. 10.

Following on from the point made above, should the ComRC interpret ESR under CRC as imposing a higher burden of proof on States parties with regard to the extent to which retrogressive measures with regard to child ESR are permissible, than is the case under ICESCR? In his May 2012 Letter to States Parties in relation to the protection of Covenant rights in the context of the economic and financial crisis,[125] the Chairperson of ComESCR outlined the requirements that 'any proposed policy change or adjustment' in response to the crises has to meet. This includes the requirement that the measure must not be discriminatory and must comprise 'all possible measures, including tax measures, to support social transfers and mitigate inequalities that can grow in times of crisis and to ensure that the rights of disadvantaged and marginalised individuals and groups are not disproportionately affected'.[126] It is clear from this and other statements that the ComESCR is concerned about the particular position of vulnerable groups, when it comes to retrogressive measures. Children are clearly contemplated – but only as one of many groups to be taken into account, not as that body's main focus.

In its General Comment No. 17 on the right of the child to rest, leisure, play, recreational activities, cultural life and the arts, the Committee highlighted that: '[n]o regressive measures in relation to the right to play, recreation, rest, leisure or participation in cultural or artistic activities are permitted. If any such deliberate measure was taken, the State would need to prove that it had undertaken careful consideration of all alternatives, including giving due weight to children's expressed views on the issue, and that the decision was justified bearing in mind all other rights in the Convention'.[127] These are the same conditions imposed by the ComESCR in its General Comments,[128]

---

[125] ComESCR 'Letter from CESCR Chairperson to States Parties in the context of the economic and financial crisis', CESCR/48th/SP/MAB/SW, 16 May 2012, http://www2.ohchr.org/english/bodies/cescr/docs/LetterCESCRtoSP16.05.12.pdf.

[126] Ibid.

[127] ComRC General Comment No.17, para. 55. The right to rest, leisure and play is a cultural right and hence subject to the same umbrella obligation as ESR in terms of Article 4. As such, we can extrapolate from the Committee's consideration of the obligations imposed by that right.

[128] In its General Comment No.3, the ComESCR states that 'any deliberately retrogressive measures in that regard would require the most careful consideration and would need to be fully justified by reference to the totality of the rights provided for in the Covenant and in the context of the full use of the maximum available resources'. (ComESCR General Comment No.3, para. 9). This language is echoed in a number of other General Comments (General Comment No.21 on Right of everyone to take part in cultural life, UN Doc. E/C.12/GC/21 (2009), para 65; General Comment No. 19 on the right to social security, UN Doc. E/C.12/GC/19 (2008), para. 42; General Comment No. 18 on the right to work UN Doc., E/C.12/GC/18 (2005), para. 21; General Comment No. 17 on the right of everyone to benefit from the protection of the moral and material interests resulting from any scientific, literary or artistic production of which he or she is the author, UN Doc. E/C.12/GC/17 (2006), para. 27; General Comment No.15 on the right

together with the added requirement that children's expressed views on the issue should be considered. It is positive that there is reference made to children's participation rights here. However, it is striking that there is no reference to children's best interests and the need to ensure their right to life, survival and development despite the fact that these are 'general principles' of the Convention and may be implicated by backward steps in terms of the right in question (and, indeed, all economic, social and cultural rights under the Convention).[129] One could argue that the status of these elements of the CRC as 'general principles' means that they should implicitly be read into the construal of rights in all situations anyway – including in situations of retrogression. However, this is belied by the express reference to only one general principle: Article 12. Given the particularly severe impact on children of violations of their ESR when compared with adults, should there not be a significantly greater burden on states to justify retrogressive measures that affect their rights? In its General Comment No.15, the Committee states that 'Irrespective of resources, States have the obligation to not take any retrogressive steps that could hamper the enjoyment of children's right to health.'[130] One might hope that this signals a new, stricter approach on the part of the Committee in relation to retrogressive measures but it is too early to tell.

There is one final area that one might expect the ComRC to go beyond the ComESCR. This is in the area of age discrimination in the context of ESR. While age discrimination is not expressly prohibited under either the CRC or ICESCR, it could clearly be contemplated under 'other status' in Articles 2(2) and 2 of those instruments respectively. The ComESCR has stated that 'age is a prohibited ground of discrimination in several contexts' including 'in relation to young persons, unequal access by adolescents to sexual and reproductive health information and services amounts to discrimination.'[131] It is clear,

---

to water (Arts. 11 and 12), UN Doc. E/C.12/2002/11 (2003), para. 19; General Comment No.14 on the right to the highest attainable standard of health (Art. 12), UN Doc. E/C.12/2000/4 (2000), para. 32; and General Comment No.13 on the right to education (Art. 13), UN Doc. E/C.12/1999/10 (1999), para. 45.). Some of these statements also set out the requirement to ensure 'there has been the most careful consideration of all alternatives'. (General Comment No. 19, para. 42; General Comment No. 18, para. 21; General Comment No. 17, para. 27; General Comment No.15, para. 19; General Comment No.14, para. 32; and General Comment No.13, para. 45). A number of other General Comments have highlighted that the adoption of any retrogressive measures incompatible with the 'core obligations' under the Covenant would be impermissible. (See ComESCR General Comment No.15, para. 42; ComESCR General Comment No.14, para. 48).

[129] While no mention is made of non-discrimination either, the fact that this is an immediate obligation means that retrogressive measures that are discriminatory would be in violation of the Convention anyway.

[130] ComRC General Comment No.15, para. 72.

[131] ComESCR General Comment No. 20 on non-discrimination in economic, social and cultural rights, UN Doc E/C.12/GC/20 (2009), para. 29.

however, both from this General Comment and other statements of the ComESCR,[132] that the ComESCR is primarily concerned with age discrimination on the basis of 'older age'.[133] Given growing concerns about the disproportionate impact of the global financial and economic crises and the responses thereto on younger people, including children,[134] it is highly desirable that the ComRC should take a strong line on discrimination against children relative to older persons on the basis of age, particularly with regard to access to social benefits, housing, work rights protections and social services. This is especially important given my earlier observations with regard to children's democratic unenfranchisement and their limited ability to exercise indirect influence over democratic decision-making processes that determine laws and policies relating to their ESR and those of other, voting groups. Unfortunately, so far, youth-based discrimination has not been addressed by the Committee, which has focussed primarily on discrimination between specific groups of children in its General Comments[135] – an approach that is unsurprising given the wording of Article 2.

These are some key ways in which the Committee might build on or adapt the ComESCR framework from a child rights-perspective. It is undoubtedly to be welcomed that the Committee has finally issued a General Comment specifically focussed on an ESR – health – in which it has sought to apply the ComESCR framework in the CRC context. However, it still remains for the Committee to engage in a comprehensive child-specific characterisation of the ESR obligations under the CRC.

7. A Final Word: The Challenge and Opportunity Offered by CRC-OP3

This article has bemoaned the shortcomings in the ESR framework outlined by the ComRC from a child rights-perspective. It has highlighted the challenges

---

[132] See, e.g., ComESCR General Comment No.6 on the economic, social and cultural rights of older persons, 13th Session (1995).

[133] Indeed, the ComESCR has gone so far as to say: 'the Committee on Economic, Social and Cultural Rights is of the view that States parties to the Covenant are obligated to pay particular attention to promoting and protecting the economic, social and cultural rights of older persons. The Committee's own role in this regard is rendered all the more important by the fact that, unlike the case of other population groups such as women and children, no comprehensive international convention yet exists in relation to the rights of older persons and no binding supervisory arrangements attach to the various sets of United Nations principles in this area.' (ComESCR General Comment No.6, para. 13).

[134] See, e.g., Report of the Independent Expert on the question of human rights and extreme poverty, Ms. Maria Magdalena Sepúlveda Carmona on the human rights based approach to recovery from the global economic and financial crises, with a focus on those living in poverty, UN Doc. A/HRC/17/34 (2011), para. 23, which states that children have suffered devastating and disproportionate effects of the global economic and financial crises.

[135] See, e.g., ComRC General Comment No.5, para. 12.

that this poses in terms of the Committee furnishing effective guidance both to states in their implementation efforts, and to advocates seeking to hold states to account for non-compliance with such rights. I have argued that this is a particular issue in the budgetary context given the Committee's failure to link the ESR obligations that it has delineated with specific budgetary decisions in a meaningful way. There is, however, both new scope and a potential vehicle for improvement on the part of the Committee.

The coming into force of the Optional Protocol to the Convention on the Rights of the Child on a Communications Procedure provides another opportunity for the Committee to develop its child ESR framework.[136] Crucially, in applying CRC standards to specific concrete situations, the Committee will be required to provide views on whether or not there has been a violation of the Convention.

Given the current global economic context and evidence that children and poor households are amongst those most impacted by austerity measures,[137] complaints with regard to budgetary decisions seem highly likely to be brought before the Committee to consider. If it is to satisfy its mandate in addressing such complaints, the Committee will have to make the 'conceptual link' between ESR under the CRC and specific economic/budget decisions in its work.

Article 10(4) of the Optional Protocol states that when examining violation of economic, social and cultural rights,

> the Committee shall consider the reasonableness of the steps taken by the State party in accordance with Article 4 of the Convention. In doing so, the Committee shall bear in mind that the state party may adopt a range of possible policy measures for the implementation of the economic, social and cultural rights in the Convention.

This provision is based on Article 8(4) of the Optional Protocol to ICESCR providing for a Communications Procedure – a sub-article that was included as a response to efforts on the part of a number of states to introduce a 'margin of appreciation' for states with regard to rights under that Covenant which was met with strong NGO resistance. Debate exists as to whether 'reasonableness' will be interpreted as giving broad 'margin of appreciation' to states with regard to implementing ESCR (or not) or if it simply incorporates a standard of review for rights compliance for South African constitutional jurisprudence

---

[136] As of 6 June 2013, there were 36 signatories and six parties to the Optional Protocol. Ten ratifications are required before the Optional Protocol comes into force.
[137] Ortiz, I., J. Chai an M. Cummins, Austerity Measures Threaten Children and Poor Households: Recent Evidence in Public Expenditures from 128 Developing Countries (New York: UNICEF, 2011), 21.

which would impose a considerably heavier burden on states.[138] Given that the OP-ICESCR came into force in May 2013, the Committee will undoubtedly have somewhere to turn for inspiration by the time it is required to construe Article 10(4).

The fact remains, however, that the Committee will not be able to elide over whether or not the state act or omission complained of is 'reasonable' in terms of Article 10(4) for the purposes of CRC ESR compliance. Nor will it ultimately be able legitimately to avoid engaging with ESR obligations in a meaningful, situation-specific way. As such, the Optional Protocol will present the Committee with an excellent opportunity to address the shortcomings in its current approach to ESR and budgetary issues that impede the work of both those who have responsibility for implementing ESR, and those who seek monitor such implementation.

---

138) For a consideration of the different ways in which Article 8(4) might be interpreted, see C. Mahon, 'Progress at the Front: The Draft Optional Protocol to the International Covenant on Economic, Social and Cultural Rights' (2008) 8 *Human Rights Law Review* 617; B. Porter, 'The Reasonableness of Article 8(4): Adjudicating Claims from the Margins' (2009) 27(1) *Nordic Journal of Human Rights* 39.

Ending the Physical Punishment of Children by Parents in the English-speaking World: The Impact of Language, Tradition and Law

Bernadette J. Saunders
Department of Social Work, Faculty of Medicine, Nursing and Health Sciences
Monash University, Victoria, Australia
bernadette.saunders@monash.edu

Introduction

In an ideal world, children would 'grow up in a family environment, in an atmosphere of happiness, love and understanding' (Preamble, United Nations Convention on the Rights of the Child (CRC), 1989). Yet children throughout the world commonly endure pain and humiliation in the guise of discipline at the hands of family members and others entrusted with their care and protection. Ending the physical punishment of children remains an enormous challenge.

In countries where children's rights to dignity and physical integrity are respected and acknowledged in law, it is more likely that children will be appropriately disciplined without physical punishment. Societal norms, typically endorsed in law, and reflected in attitudes toward children and views about their rightful place in society, affect the manner in which all children in a society may be treated. In societies which tolerate even limited physical punishment as discipline or control, it is a response to children that adults may unthinkingly adopt simply because they can. As an often assumed and unquestioned parental entitlement, physical punishment is arguably the prime manifestation of children's position in a society; it is a clear 'badge of childhood' because children are singled out as 'the only people who can legitimately be hit with impunity' (Freeman, 1996a:100). In societies that condone its use, even children who are not physically punished may witness unquestioned 'disciplinary' violence directed at other children at home and in public. This is a distressing reminder of children's low status and vulnerability. Along with the UN Committee on the Rights of the Child and children's rights advocates around the world, Freeman thus contends that '[t]here is probably no more significant step that could be taken to advance the status and protection of children than to outlaw the practice of physical punishment' (1996a:100).

This paper primarily focuses on the English-speaking, common law countries – Australia, Canada, and the United Kingdom – that have ratified the CRC but have not yet fully outlawed physical punishment. I also briefly reflect on New Zealand, the first English-speaking country to ban physical punishment, and the United States which has neither ratified the CRC nor fully outlawed physical punishment.

A society's language, traditions and laws combine to maintain its status quo. Thus, if we are to fully recognize children's human rights, the language, traditions and laws that promote and perpetuate physical punishment in childhood must be targeted and changed. This paper draws separate attention to language, tradition and law with a view to envisioning a state of affairs where adults and children are accorded equal respect as human beings and any degree of physical violence towards children is regarded as an aberration.

Background

Children's status in society and the laws and policies in place to ensure their optimal development are clearly interrelated. Article 1 of the CRC defines a child as 'below the age of 18 years unless under the law applicable to the child, majority is attained earlier'. In the English-speaking world, children may be criminally liable as young as ten yet, with the exception of both New Zealand where physical punishment is prohibited and Canada where it is limited to between the ages of two and 12, parents may lawfully use 'reasonable' physical force to chastise their children from birth to 18 years old.

Law and societal values

Law is an important symbol – it reflects the values of the society in which it is imposed. Law may also perform an educative or social engineering function, encouraging the development of attitudes and the adoption of behaviours conducive to positive outcomes for the people in consideration of whom it was instigated. It is encouraging for children in English-speaking countries that New Zealand has outlawed physical punishment in all settings (see Crimes (Substituted Section 59) Amendment Act 2007). While reasonable force to protect or restrain a child in specified circumstances remains lawful, clauses in the Act specifically exempt 'the use of force for the purpose of correction', and emphasise already existing police discretion not to prosecute 'where the offence is considered to be so inconsequential that there is no public interest in proceeding with a prosecution' (see Wood *et al.,* 2008). Notably, supporters of the 'loving smack' – 'a classic oxymoron if ever there was one' (Freeman, 1999:138) – have since unsuccessfully attempted via a non-binding citizens' referendum to repeal the new law. Yet research suggests that, as has occurred in other countries that have banned physical punishment, the new law has contributed to changing both the attitudes and the behaviour of New Zealand's parents – increasingly physical punishment is perceived as an unnecessary component of discipline (Children's Commissioner, 2008; Lawrence and Smith, 2009).

Law reform

It is perplexing that in Australia, the UK, Canada and the US similar law reform appears to present insurmountable challenges. On moral as well as incremental legal grounds, intolerance of physical punishment of children in English-speaking countries, even by parents, appears to be gaining momentum (Smith and Durrant, 2011). It is disappointing, however, that moves towards a clear statement in law absolutely rejecting the legitimacy and espousing the immorality of physically punishing children, to any degree in all settings, remain inadequately supported by many and strongly opposed by at least some – 'internal disagreement' is rife (Renteln, 2010:258). Enlightened reform will neither prevent all violent responses to children nor criminalise well-meaning parents. Fear of criminalisation is nevertheless one of several understandable but not well supported factors stunting progress (see Naylor and Saunders, 2011). Among other untenable barriers to outlawing physical punishment in the English-speaking world are long-held beliefs that children are human becomings rather than human beings; that parents own their children; that the home and family matters ought occupy a private sphere largely impervious to societal regulation; that granting rights to children will unduly impose upon the perceived rights of parents; that ill-defined 'normative' physical punishment in childhood 'never did me any harm', was effective, and is a reasonable, necessary and non-violent disciplinary option; and that parents should always be trusted to judge correctly what is in their child's best interests and to act accordingly.

Research questions, debate and laboratory tests

Research and debate in relation to physically punishing children often exclusively focus on physical punishment's effects, effectiveness, and the nature of the punishment from which children should be protected, rather than questioning its appropriateness as a response to children. Minimising or questioning any harmful effects of normative physical punishment, characteristically

defined as 'two open-handed swats on the bottom', and advocating its effectiveness, appear to be the anchor for proponents of 'lawful physical chastisement' (see, for example, Trumbull *et al.*, 2012). Arguments for full abolition are
dismissed on the grounds that it cannot be scientifically proven that so-called
'non-abusive' physical punishment sufficiently affects children to warrant
'spanking injunctions' (Larzelere and Baumrind, 2011). This occurs despite
increasing evidence that, at the very least, physical punishment presents a risk
of harm to children and the adults that they may become (Durrant and Ensom,
2012, discussed further below).

With regard to investigating harmful effects, it is significant that controlled
experiments that set up two groups of children, one group whose parents force
compliance through 'spanking, and another who are disciplined without physical punishment, would now be unethical' (Durrant and Ensom, 2012).
Although such randomized control trials have disturbingly occurred in the
past, with mothers' consent (see, for example, Day and Roberts, 1983), today it
is hard to imagine a research paper on parental discipline, published in a reputable journal and entitled: 'Behaviour Modification and the Brat Syndrome',
discussing 'brat research' in which a mother is instructed to spank her child if
he hits her (Bernal *et al.*, 1968:447). One has to ask what this progressive change
in research ethics says about the act of hitting children. How can it be reasonable and acceptable for parents to punish children physically yet unethical to
set up a controlled experiment to test its effects and effectiveness? Equally
perplexing is some adults' enduring conviction that hitting a child will teach
him or her not to hit others.

Human rights focus

In contrast to arguments that focus on the impact of physical punishment,
arguments that assert children's human rights focus on the child's entitlement
to be treated as respectfully as another person (Newell, 2011). Physical punishment degrades and insults children. As Durrant eloquently contends:

> It should not be necessary, on the issue of fundamental human rights, to demonstrate
> conclusively that violation of those rights leads invariably to harm before ensuring that
> those rights are protected. Nor should the putative 'benefits' of a rights violation be used
> to justify the violation (2011:42).

To children's rights advocates, condemning all forms of prejudicial treatment
of children in all settings, including the home, seems at very least a reasonable
if not a civilised and well overdue step in the 21st century. This is particularly
so given enlightened responses toward other previously disempowered and
victimized members of society, particularly women. As Scutt observes:

...female children and male children, children with a disability and children without – remain the last and final category still in that separate mansion which in the past housed 'Women and Imbeciles, Idiots and Children'. Childhood now exploited by crass commercialism and consumerism remains the last frontier for recognition as 'human' (2009:22).

In the English-speaking world few people would contend that any degree of violence against women or adults with a disability is reasonable or ought to be defensible if, for example, it does not leave a mark or cause harm lasting more than a short period. Such arbitrary, ill-defined and confusing thresholds of acceptability characteristically appear in current 'lawful correction' defences to the assault of children in the guise of discipline (outlined below). Degrees of tolerance of physical punishment promote its adoption, and facilitate volatile environments in which children may be victimised. Why is outlawing the physical punishment of children so objectionable to so many adults in the English-speaking world? It appears that many people simply cannot reconcile the logic and decency of according children, the most vulnerable and impressionable people in society, the same consideration, respect and protection from assault as adults. Indeed, the blind popularity of physical punishment demands a brave, well-informed political challenge that to date is rarely successful in English-speaking countries.

In this context, can children living in the English-speaking world reasonably expect to be better regarded and treated in the future? What needs to occur for children of all ages to anticipate, as a right rather than an optional courtesy, recognition of their human dignity and respect as persons?

The impact of language

Language is used 'not just to name things, but, more importantly to work out how to behave toward other people and the world out there' (Hartley, 1982:1). Language can therefore motivate attitudinal and behavioural change. Ndebele contends that a society's problems will be reflected in its language as it is through language that entrenched attitudes are absorbed and perpetuated (1986, cited in Bailey, 1990). Ngugi wa Thiong'o similarly observes:

> Language is a carrier of a people's culture. Culture is a carrier of a people's values. Values are a carrier of a people's outlook or consciousness and sense of identity...languages [impose] the culture, values and consciousness carried by them (1984: 3–9, cited in Bailey, 1990).

Many adults in English-speaking countries continue to perceive children as 'becomings' – 'less than fully human, unfinished and incomplete' (Jenks, 1996: 9 & 21). This limited understanding of children motivates protective and nurturing responses to them but also discrimination and degradation. Some

English language words and phrases used in reference to children and to actions directed at children reflect and perpetuate their low status, and may facilitate their maltreatment. Critical language awareness is therefore essential to positively changing misguided attitudes and behaviours (see, Cameron, 1985; Saunders and Goddard, 2001, 2010).

Language chosen to refer to children and children's rights

As Freeman observes, '[h]aving a right means having the power to command respect, to make claims and to have them heard' (1997c:10). The perception that children are inferior to or less human than adults appears to have excluded them from the '"everyone" entitled to human rights' (Burdekin, 1994:8). This arguably prompted the need for a Convention on the Rights of the Child which followed two Declarations of Children's Rights, dated 1924 and 1959, that espoused only children's welfare rights. Language has similarly excluded and marginalized women – the word 'he' was historically chosen 'to incorporate "she"' (Lansdown, 1995: 25). It is perhaps not surprising therefore that close examination of the language used in international children's rights documents reveals a significant 'evolution' or 'an adaption [in language] consciously carried out as part of a broader program of social reform' (Bailey, 1990: 87) which sought to boost the status and rights of children.

   In the 1924 Declaration of Children's Rights, 'the child is referred to as "it" ("gender neglected" and objectified)'; in the 1959 declaration, 'the child is identified by the generic "he" (purportedly encompassing "she" but arguably reflecting a male-dominated society and the oppression of females)'; and in the 1989 Convention, the child is referred to as he or she/ him or her acknowledging that 'the child is a person, either male or female, with equal rights and entitlements' (Saunders and Goddard, 2001:448). It is important to recognize that, like adults, children 'have individual identities, an important part of which is a male or female gender' (Saunders and Goddard, 2001:448). Reflecting on the reasoning of those who drafted the Convention, Melton suggests that this advancement in language choice signalled 'an integrated concern with the personhood of children' and the 'protection of dignity' basic to 'all fundamental rights' (1993:24). Importantly, the Convention also finally recognized children's participatory or citizenship rights (discussed below).

   Inappropriate and ill-considered language can reinforce discrimination against people in disadvantaged and disempowered groups. Conversely, language can be empowering (Quennerstedt, 2010) and contribute to the advancement of people's positive recognition and treatment (Saunders and Goddard, 2001, 2010). Language can unmask discrimination and play a role in social reform. It can also 'demean, exclude, stereotype and misrepresent' (Else and Sanford, 1987: 5). In English speaking countries, discriminatory language has played a part in the oppression of women, older people, people with disabilities, people with psychiatric illnesses or social diseases, people whose skin colour is not white, non-English speaking people, homosexuals/lesbians and children. The continued use of language that objectifies children, such as reference to the child as 'it' in media pieces, legal documents and academic writing, may contribute to the perpetuation of degrading and disrespectful responses to children (see Goddard and Saunders, 2000, 2001; Saunders and Goddard, 2001, 2005, 2010). Similarly, words like 'kids', 'adolescent', 'teenager', and 'youth' serve to differentiate children from adults, sometimes in a positive light, but these words are also associated with negative stereotypical images of young people which may perpetuate discrimination, detachment, a lack of empathy and maltreatment. Adults may be derided for child-like behaviour. Expressions such as acting like 'a big kid' or behaving like 'a rebellious teenager' reinforce perceptions of children as less than adults, and cast childhood in a negative light. Language used in reference to children and childhood that is inclusive and complimentary promotes conversation, understanding, tolerance, empathy and respect.

Quennerstedt poses a crucial question: Are children a part of humanity first and foremost as children or as humans? She adds:

> I do not believe that anyone would propose that an adult person...is primarily woman, disabled, indigenous or homosexual, and only thereafter human, and that their rights are based on their group affinity rather than on their human status. Why should it be otherwise for children? (2010: 630-1)

Quennerstedt therefore advocates using all-encompassing human rights terminology, as in civil, political and social rights, when referring to children's rights rather than using the more subtle or 'nice' language of 'provision', 'protection' and 'participation' which refer to the three principles under which the articles of the CRC can be grouped (see, Hammarberg, 1990; Lansdown, 1994). She contends that using human rights terminology that contributes to constructing the child and the child's status as human will promote recognition of the full spectrum of children's rights, though she cautions that children's rights to protection may be undermined (2010:632-3). Quennerstedt's concern highlights the special position of children as 'at once developing beings, in possession of agency, and to varying degrees vulnerable' with 'particular needs for nurturance' (Bluebond-Langner and Korbin, 2007:242). Indeed, Freeman contends that the child's autonomy rights must of necessity be limited in situations where his or her inclination to engage in some behaviours 'could seriously and systematically impair the attainment of full personality and development subsequently...Dichotomies [he observes] should not divert away from the fact that true protection of children does protect their rights' (1992:67, 69).

Definitions of 'physical discipline', and associated language

Phrases such as 'corporal punishment', 'physical punishment', and 'physical discipline' are commonly used interchangeably. They refer to the correction or punishment of a child's behaviour through the deliberate or ill-considered infliction of bodily pain, however minor or intense. Much of the research on physical punishment adopts Straus' (1994) definition which emphasises the adults' intentions and motivations/justifications, and tenuously distinguishes painfully punishing a child from harming him or her – hence the inclusion of the phrase 'but not injury'. He defines physical punishment as:

> ...the use of physical force with the intention of causing a child pain, but not injury, for the purposes of correction or control of the child's behaviour (1994:4-5).

Straus (1996) acknowledges that parents may not be calm and rational when they physically punish a child so the outcome for the child may be more severe than the parent intended. Indeed, injury and other harmful consequences of physical punishment may be 'a matter of chance' (Gonzalez *et al.*, 2008:763). Related to this, children may be unjustifiably punished for normal childhood behaviours when parents' emotional state or challenging circumstances motivate physical responses to children (Silverstein *et al.*, 2009). Bitensky's definition of 'corporal punishment' refers to 'physical force upon a child's body' to cause 'bodily pain so as to correct *or punish* the child's behavior' (2006:xix, emphases added). Both painful punishment and control of children's behaviour may have more to do with selfish power than benevolent pedagogy. Physical restraint to protect a child from harm, however, does not fall within definitions of 'physical punishment'. Significantly, the CRC Committee condemns all 'corporal punishment' and more broadly defines it as 'any punishment in which physical force is used and intended to cause *some degree of discomfort, however light*' (2006:4, emphases added).

Euphemistic language

We know that children in the English-speaking world are physically punished in numerous ways, sometimes in settings such as schools and public places but most often behind closed doors in the child's home. Hitting children is probably the most relied upon form of physical discipline and control. Children are commonly hit with adults' hands but some adults routinely or spontaneously hit children with implements, such as sticks, rulers and belts or any objects within reach. The intensity, repetition and regularity of hitting also vary, and euphemisms, such as 'smacking', 'spanking', 'slapping' and 'tapping' children, are commonly adopted to describe and simultaneously to normalise and minimise the physical punishment that children experience. The variety of methods, and the combination of euphemisms and other minimising words, such as 'just a smack', 'only a little slap', and 'a good hiding', further contribute to an often misleading picture and inherent justification of the child's experience (Saunders and Goddard, 2010). Words that do not camouflage the nature and impact of physical punishment may provoke feelings of uneasiness and regret. Uncompromising words, such as 'violence', 'abuse' and 'assault', to describe 'normalised' physical punishment are not uncommonly dismissed as inappropriate descriptors of 'normalised' physical punishment since they do not normally describe lawful actions (Global Initiative, 2009). More frequent use of these arguably more apt descriptors can thus challenge strongly held beliefs upholding the legitimacy of hitting and hurting children in the context of discipline (see, Bussmann, 2004; Saunders and Goddard, 2010).

Clear, uncompromising language

Encouraging adults to use more precise language to paint a matter-of-fact picture of normalised physical discipline or control may bring about child-focused behavioural change. As Garbarino asserts, adults could more accurately refer to their '"assault against children as punishment"... "assault as discipline"', and he dares adults to 'come right out and say "I favour assaulting children – for their own good of course"' (1996:159). Straus (2000) similarly encourages child protection workers to refer to 'hitting' and 'physically attacking' children so as to discourage physical punishment. Moreover, Bussmann, drawing on Germany's progression toward a ban on physical punishment in 2000, asserts that legal prohibition 'can shift the semantic horizon of parents...to a stricter, more sensitive definition of violence' – use of the word 'violence' in reference to physical punishment effectively challenged its validity (2004:306). 'Clear, uncompromising language' is also integral to 'uncompromising prohibition of all corporal punishment' (Global Initiative, 2009:10).

The impact of tradition

In this section, attention is drawn to the intergenerational transmission of physical punishment and some often unchallenged attitudes towards and views about children that have persisted over generations to support this practice. The known incidence of physical punishment in the English-speaking world and current knowledge about its effects are also briefly noted.

Childhood is a social construction affected by the period of time and the environments in which children live (James and Prout, 1997). However, even within a particular social construction of childhood, individual children experience different childhoods. Some children are fortunate not to be physically punished in their childhood. However, for all children living in societies that condone its use, it remains a possibility, and one which they might reasonably fear for themselves and for other children. Even children who are not physically punished will most likely be aware that for some, perhaps many, children 'disciplinary' pain and humiliation are considered normal and to be expected but only, of course, in childhood.

The intergenerational transmission of physical punishment

Renteln (2010) observes that largely unconsciously acquired cultural norms, affecting both cognition and conduct, are very challenging to discard but within characteristically evolving cultural contexts even popular customary practices may have to cease when they are found to be in violation of basic human rights. The physical punishment of children is a common practice that persists over generations in cultures in which families are largely accorded autonomy; children have traditionally been silenced and disempowered; and children's rights are either not recognised or not fully respected. Even children who are distressed, hurt and angered by parental physical punishment may accept it as their parents' right, and unless it is challenged, children will likely claim the same entitlement when they become parents (Graziano *et al.*, 1996; Saunders and Goddard, 2010). The following 12 year-old children's comments are insightful:

> It's giving the message that it's okay to smack...It's just a big cycle...people are gunna get smacked until someone finally doesn't smack in your family.

> ...you probably won't think...before you act...like your parents have been smacked before as well, and their parents didn't think about it, and so you just do it... (Saunders and Goddard, 2010:199).

This intergenerational denial of children's rights to physical integrity is clearly evidenced in English-speaking countries that have ratified the CRC but fail to act on rebukes from the UN Committee with regard to continuing tolerance of physical punishment (discussed below).

Persistent, demeaning perceptions of children vis-à-vis adults

Scarre argues that persistent thinking about children 'primarily as weak, ignorant, irrational, incompetent, unrestrained and uncivilised' dampens interest in how they are treated, and facilitates an 'unquestioning, complacent acceptance of whatever social, educational and political arrangements have arisen to cope with them' (1989:x). Indeed, as Freeman suggests, '[i]t is surely significant that when we wish to deny rights to those who have chronological adulthood we label them...children' (1997b:86). That adults might also be described as 'becomings' (Hengst, 2003) who engage in questionable behaviours and decision-making is often overlooked. Children are frequently measured against a flawed 'excessively idealized version of adult autonomy, independence and maturity' (Rosen, 2007:299). Indeed, Waksler provocatively suggests that '[j]ust as it turned out that tribal societies are not "child-like", it may be that children themselves are not either. Rather, the idea may be an adult stereotype of children, a stereotype that facilitates adult control and an adult assumption of superiority' (1991:235).

Butler (1975) makes an untoward reference to children and childhood when he explains ageist attitudes to older people as a process of systematically stereotyping and discriminating against them in the same way that racism and sexism denigrates people given their skin colour and gender. Ageism, he argues, permits younger people to differentiate themselves from older people, ceasing 'to identify with their elders as human beings...They are treated like children and insulted by labels referring to old age as "second childhood"' (1975:12). Butler does not concern himself with the insult to children implicit in his explanation – perhaps at the time of writing it did not occur to him but this could be expected as this view of childhood persists.

'Childism'

Young Bruehl (2012) observes Western society's ongoing struggles against racism and sexism and she questions whether existing images, stereotypes and prejudices against children, or 'childism' is even acknowledged. She contends that this '(p)rejudice against children is not the sole or the immediate cause of child maltreatment, but it is the conditio sine qua non' and understanding this discrimination against children is integral to understanding child maltreatment (2012:6). Freeman also maintains that understanding 'violence against children, or child abuse more generally', demands an examination of 'our concept of childhood' and our 'social policies which sustain different levels of rights for children' (2008:7).

Joseph remarked almost 20 years ago that disenfranchisement; financial dependence; an 'essentially 'passive' legal status' as parents' belongings; and the receipt of adult physical discipline, serve to define childhood, and to deny children their human rights (1995:2). Little has changed. As Freeman asserts, '[w]e may no longer subscribe to notions of children as property, but the legacies of such an ideology remain firmly implanted within our consciousness' (2008:7). Archard's depiction of the 'modern' 12 year-old, 'on the threshold of her preparation for adulthood', illustrates the persistent view of the child as less than a person, and childhood as less than adulthood (2004: 35). 'She is at or close to puberty and may more properly be described as a "young person" than a child' (Archard, 2004: 35). Childhood, he continues, is 'an extended stage before and *below* adulthood' and this 'underpins our differential attributions of rights and responsibilities to, respectively, children and adults' (2004:39, emphasis added). While he contends that the liberationists wrongly concluded that every child should possess adults' rights, 'older children are wrongly denied them', and a 'more equal society would help to reduce the 'collective abuse' of children who are victims of poor circumstances and the predisposing social causes of much physical abuse' (2004:218). The persistent misuse of adult power over children must be addressed if, as Freeman foresees, 'the nail' is to be 'stuck in the coffin of corporal punishment' signalling 'the burial of child abuse and much else besides' (2010b:229).

Persistent ambivalence towards children

Rhian Harris, Director of the London Museum of Childhood, emphasises the 'crucial role' of childhood in the development of human beings: 'it deserves to be explored in all its facets: fun, rich, complex and poignant' (2012:7). Amidst the museum's wonderful collection of children's toys, games, dolls, teddy bears, books, clothes and furniture, is a 'tawse, a thick, heavy strap of leather split into sections at the end, with which to hit a child's hands'; sadly, this is one of numerous 'devices' purposefully made to inflict painful punishment at home and at school (2012:39).

Perceptions and responses to children in Western society are bewilderingly inconsistent (Saunders and Goddard, 2001). Concern, care, and affection for children may comfortably coexist with feelings of indifference, aggravation and a willingness to physically hurt and distress them. Countries ratify international treaties and conventions, and proposals to implement children's rights are entertained, yet attitudes regarding children and responses to behaviours typical of children often fall short of the ideals to which these treaties and conventions aspire.

Enduring intolerance and discrimination

Though dated, the following commentary reported in a prominent Australian newspaper highlights a persistent mindset:

> Australians are not a child-centred people. We prefer children to be seen and not heard and sometimes not even seen. We portray children in the media as either victims or offenders, rarely important individuals with rights and needs equal to those of adults (Loane, 1997:43).

In the UK, Madge's research found that 33 per cent of 500 adults agreed with the statement that 'the English love their dogs more than their children' (2006:122). Not surprisingly in this context, a 2006 opinion piece in *The Guardian* newspaper (Bindel (2006) cited in Freeman (2010a:1)) describes school holidays as 'Six Weeks of Suffering' – for adults, of course. Bindel, ironically a co-founder of 'Justice for Women' (a feminist advocacy group in the UK), writes about children whom she describes as 'little monsters', 'undisciplined', 'spoilt', 'hysterical', and 'noisy'. 'Kids', she writes, unreasonably impinge on adults' space and comfort zones, and get 'up our noses'. They invade streets, public transport, museums and restaurants and even turn parks into playgrounds.

Commentary such as Bindel's reflects long-held and persistent perceptions of children as human becomings, incomplete and uncivilised whose proper place is in private settings, such as the home, and institutions, such as kindergartens and schools, specifically set up for their transformation into beings fit for 'civilised' society.

Enduring failure to fully appreciate children

The enduring failure fully to appreciate children's abilities, perspectives, and rights as individuals, often together with indifference towards children's perspectives, stand in stark contrast to the empathetic insights and inspirational appreciation of children apparent in the visionary writings of early advocates for children's rights such as Wiggin, Key and Korczak. Key advocated respecting 'the joys of the child, his tastes, work, and time, just as you would those of an adult' (1909:173) and, as Freeman notes, Korczak worked with children to establish children's parliaments, children's juries, and children's newspapers (2011:3). Wiggin dared to suggest that 'the rod of reason' would have to 'replace the rod of birch' (1892:7), and Key argued that '[c]orporal punishment must be done away with not because it is painful but because it is profoundly immoral and hopelessly unsuitable' (1909:167).

The persistence of physical punishment in the UK, US, Australia, Canada and NZ

Corporal punishment is typically outlawed in all schools before it is banned in the home. To date, it is forbidden in all schools in the UK, Canada, and New Zealand. It is banned in all except two Australian states where it is rarely used in some private schools (Barrett, 2012). In the US it is effectively prohibited in public schools in 31 states and the District of Columbia. It is unlawful in public and private schools in two states but allowed in 19 states (Human Rights Watch, 2008; End All Corporal Punishment of Children, 2012).

Statistics regarding the incidence of violence in the home is likely to be an underestimate but some recent research suggests that in Canada approximately 50 per cent of parents hit their infants and 'toddlers' (MacKenzie *et al.*, 2011). In the US, '94% of toddlers are spanked' (Straus, 2010:29) and 'hitting with an object remains high' (Zolotar *et al.*, 2011:64). Eight-five percent of high school students have been hit; 51 per cent with an implement (Bender *et al.*, 2007). Across the UK physical punishment of children is common with between 48 per cent and 71 per cent of parents admitting its use (Bunting *et al.*, 2010). In Australia, surveys have indicated that 69 per cent of adults across Australia believe 'it is sometimes necessary to smack a naughty child' (Tucci *et al.*, 2006), and 43.4 per cent of parents in the state of Queensland were likely/ very likely to smack children under 12 (Sanders *et al.*, 2007). In New Zealand, where physical punishment was banned in 2007, a recent survey of 500 parents suggests that 50 per cent of parents still rarely or occasionally resort to physical punishment but 44 per cent said they had not hit their children since the ban (Johnston, 2012).

Persistent motivations/rationales

Physical punishment may principally persist because questioning its acceptability can be too unsettling both for the parents who use it and the adults who, as children, experienced it at the hands of parents whom they loved (Bitensky, 2006). Physical punishment is explained in English-speaking countries with reference to pedagogy – teaching children lessons, and religious concepts of sparing the rod and spoiling the child; intergenerational transmission: adopting 'family scripts' (see Byng Hall, 2005) and believing 'it never did me any harm'; catharsis – release of stress, anger, frustration and intolerance; and temperament or the aggressive personality of parents and children (see Gough and Reavey, 1997).

The enduring effects

Gershoff's seminal meta-analysis linked physical punishment with child and adult mental health issues; diminished parent-child relationships and moral internalisation; increases in child and adult aggression, criminal, delinquent and antisocial behaviour; and increased risk of physical abuse and of perpetrating family violence (2002:544). Fearful or in pain, children may immediately comply with a parent's demands but physical punishment is not linked with future behaviour guided by a well developed sense of right and wrong. Subsequent research provides further evidence of links between physical punishment and child/adult aggression (Taylor *et al.*, 2010; Lansford *et al.*, 2012), child/adult mental health issues (Turner and Muller, 2004; Afifi *et al.*, 2012) and resultant injuries and even death (Crandall *et al.*, 2006; Nielssen *et al.*, 2009). Indeed, Durrant and Ensom, in their recent analysis of 20 years of research on physical punishment, conclude that 'physical punishment increases the risk of broad and enduring negative developmental outcomes (2012:1373).

The impact of law

Renteln suggests that it is probably reasonable to conclude that the 'right against corporal punishment is an emerging norm of customary international law' (2010:13). National laws can continue to maintain adults' power over children through physical punishment or they can motivate enlightened changes in society that reflect growing recognition of children as people with social and political rights, and varying needs for adults' protection and guidance. Until children can confidently claim their human rights they will remain vulnerable to abuse and less than optimal development.

The experience or threat of physical punishment may render children compliant and silent, enhancing their vulnerability to multiple forms of abuse by adults upon whom they depend and look up to as role models (see, for example, Mudaly and Goddard, 2009). Arguably,

> ...the roots of child abuse lie not in parental psycho-pathology or in socio-environmental stress (though their influences cannot be discounted) but in a sick culture which denigrates and depersonalizes, which reduces children to property, to sexual objects so that they become the legitimate victims of both adult violence and lust (Freeman, 1997a:76).

International law

To date, 193 countries have ratified the CRC, and following Sweden's example in 1979, 33 countries have enacted law that prohibit corporal punishment. Encouragingly, 25 countries have introduced a ban since 2000, including most recently four African countries – South Sudan, the Republic of Congo, Kenya and Tunisia. In Italy and Nepal, common law decisions to that effect are yet to be codified. As at November 2012, 117 countries have banned corporal punishment in schools, 157 countries have outlawed corporal punishment of children as a sentence for crime, 121 in penal institutions, and 40 in all forms of alternative care (End All Corporal Punishment of Children).

United Nations Human Rights Conventions

Children's rights are internationally recognised under the CRC (1989) (discussed below), and Article 24(1) of the International Covenant on Civil and

Political Rights (ICCPR) which states that: 'Every child shall have, without any discrimination...the right to such measures of protection as are required by his [sic] status as a minor, on the part of his family, society and the State'. This special recognition of children's entitlements to protection does not override children's human rights. Yet the continued recognition of corporal punishment as legitimate discipline in childhood denies children the same protection from assault as adults. It breaches international human rights prohibitions on 'cruel, inhuman or degrading treatment or punishment', including Article 5 of the Universal Declaration of Human Rights, Article 7 of the ICCPR, and Article 16 of the Convention against Torture, and the UN Committee against Torture has advised the adoption and implementation of legislation banning all corporal punishment (see Bitensky, 2006).

The CRC (1989)

Previous declarations on children's rights focused only on welfare entitlements; young children are particularly vulnerable and all children are entitled to be nurtured and protected from harm. However, the CRC importantly acknowledges children's agency and participatory entitlements as citizens. Children are positioned 'as partners in improving their lives', as 'social actors' whose 'status as persons in their own right' entitles them to respect and enables them 'to contribute to their own families and societies' (Durrant, 2011:5).

In relation to the physical punishment of children, Article 19 and 37 of the CRC are particularly significant but Articles 3, 12 and 24(3) can also be raised in arguments condemning its use (see Freeman, 1999:135-136). Article 19 (1) requires that signatories take all 'legislative, administrative, social and educational measures' to protect children from 'all forms of physical or mental violence, injury or abuse[or]maltreatment...while in the care of parent(s), legal guardian(s) or any other person who has the care of the child'. Article 37 states that '[n]o child shall be subjected to torture or other cruel, inhuman or degrading treatment or punishment'. In Article 24(3), cultural traditions which are 'prejudicial to the health of children' are implicitly limited (Renteln, 2010:253). Clearly, this article's relevance to the illegitimacy of physically punishing children increases along with research associating physical punishment with both mental health issues (Gershoff, 2002), and injuries and deaths in childhood (see for example, Nielssen et al., 2009).

It is regrettable that the words 'corporal punishment' are glaringly absent from the Convention (Freeman, 1998). However, the Committee's most recent response to this anomaly, building on previous guidance in its review of States Parties' reports and the respective Concluding Observations, is the adoption of General Comment No. 13 which unequivocally espouses 'the right of the child to protection from corporal punishment' (Committee on the Rights of the

Child, 2011:5). Importantly, as already noted, the Committee includes in its definition of 'corporal punishment' any 'physical force...intended to cause some degree of discomfort, however light' (2006:4). Further, as Renteln (2010) points out, the Committee's General Comment No. 8 ensures that the child's right to dignity and physical integrity trumps the parent's right to justify using corporal punishment given their right to freedom of religious belief provided in Article 18 of the ICCPR. The Committee has stated that: '[f]reedom to practise one's religion or belief may be legitimately limited in order to protect the fundamental rights and freedoms of others'. 'Virtuous violence' (Straus, 2009:1315) or physical punishment motivated by a perceived religious obligation to teach children correct, or acceptable, behaviour as opposed to behaviour that is deviant or inappropriate (Ellison and Bradshaw, 2009) is relevant here as is children's experience of violence motivated by the biblical quotation 'spare the rod and spoil the child' (Proverbs 13:24).

CRC Committee's Concluding Observations (Australia, UK and Canada)

UN Committees on the Rights of the Child have, at every opportunity, criticised governments in Australia (in 1997, 2005, 2011), the UK (in 1995, 2002, 2008) and Canada (in 1995, 2003, 2009, 2012) for failing to prohibit fully corporal punishment. The Committee has particularly frowned upon piecemeal legislative 'reform' that effectively legitimizes specified forms of violence toward children in the guise of discipline, exposing vulnerable children to the risk of injury, and strategically denying them their right to physical integrity (see UN Committee – State Reports).

In its most recent sixty-first session in October 2012, the Committee noted grave concern that Canadian law condones corporal punishment under Section 43 of its Criminal Code. The Committee also expressed 'regret that the 2004 Supreme Court decision, *Canadian Foundation for Children, Youth and the Law* v. *Canada*, while stipulating that corporal punishment is only justified in cases of "minor corrective force of a transitory and trifling nature," upheld the law' (Committee on the Rights of the Child, 2012: para 44). The Committee urged the repeal of Section 43 and an explicit prohibition on 'all forms of violence against all age groups of children, however light', together with strengthened and expanded 'awareness-raising' regarding alternative discipline and the promotion of 'respect for children's rights, with the involvement of children, while raising awareness about the adverse consequences of corporal punishment' (Committee on the Rights of the Child, 2012: para 45).

Article 5 of the CRC acknowledges parents' obligations to direct and guide their children appropriately but as the Committee has made clear this does not include using corporal punishment. It is problematic, however, that some countries have ratified the Convention having interpreted Articles 19(1) and 37 less broadly. Moreover, 'all countries that have ratified the CRC must consider the implications of intervening in the privacy of home, and the political and philosophical implications of criminalising parental behaviours' (Naylor and Saunders, 2012:508). The Committee's 2006 General Comment No.8 is relevant here:

> ...the law does not concern itself with trivial matters...minor assaults between adults only come to court in very exceptional circumstances; the same will be true of minor assaults on children. ...the aim should be to stop parents from using violent or other cruel or degrading punishments through supportive and educational, not punitive, interventions. ...Prosecuting parents is in most cases unlikely to be in their children's best interests.

Outlawing the physical punishment of children in all settings would simply and decisively grant children the same protection from assault that adults assume.

Domestic laws – Australia, Canada, UK and US

In Australia people who unnecessarily impose physical force on another person may be charged with assault. However, Australian law provides a 'lawful excuse' for a parent or guardian who moderately and reasonably assaults their child as a means of 'discipline' or correction. The defence of 'reasonable chastisement' or 'lawful correction' exists in various forms in all Australian states and territories. It stems from Chief Justice Cockburn's decision in 1860 in *R v Hopley* which granted limited permission to parents and schoolmasters to use corporal punishment to correct 'what is evil in the child' (175 ER:1204). In the state of Victoria, Australia, Justice Scholl's decision in 1955 in the case of *R v Terry* (VLR:114, 116) sets the common law defence in the state of Victoria and the Australian Capital Territory:

> ...there are strict limits to the right of a parent to inflict reasonable and moderate corporal punishment on his or her child for the purpose of correcting the child in wrong behaviour. In the first place, the punishment must be moderate and reasonable. In the second place, it must have a proper relation to the age, physique and mentality of the child, and in the third place, it must be carried out with a reasonable means or instrument.

This defence is variously codified in the Northern Territory Criminal Code Act, Section 27; the Queensland Criminal Code Act 1899, Section 280; the South Australia Criminal Law Consolidation Act 1935, Section 20; the Tasmania Criminal Code Act 1924, Section 50; and the Western Australia Criminal Code 1913, Section 257. In the state of New South Wales, specified limits to the defence were codified in 2002. The Crimes Act 1900 (NSW), Section 61AA(2)(b) currently limits the defence of 'lawful correction' to 'reasonable' force applied below the head or neck of the child, and not causing 'harm' to the child 'for more than a short period'. Neither 'harm' nor 'short' is defined.

Significantly, the defence in all Australian states only applies to physical violence 'for the purpose of correct[ion]', or 'to discipline, manage or control' – '[a]s made explicit in *Hopley,* and implicit in *Terry,* there is no defence for actions carried out in anger or frustration or vengeance' (Naylor and Saunders, 2011:510, see also Keating, 2006). Parents who are angry, tired and frustrated unreasonably physically punish their children without forethought, self-control or appropriate disciplinary intent. In these not unusual circumstances, under existing common law or statute, parents' actions may not be defended as lawful chastisement; though judicial comment in cases before them may suggest otherwise (see, for example, Greenwood, 2012; Mayoh, 2010; see also Alexander *et al.,* 2011; Saunders and Cashmore, 2011 re inconsistent legal boundaries, sanctions and decision making).

In Canada, the 2004 Supreme Court decision, noted above, enables parents lawfully to punish children physically but not if it 'risks or causes harm, or is used in anger or frustration or by someone with "an abusive personality" or with a child under two or over 12 years or incapable of learning from physical punishment, or with an object or on the head, or of a degrading, inhumane or harmful nature' (McGillivray and Milne, 2011:104). Durrant and her colleagues note 'confusion and contradiction' as the judiciary is challenged with deciding 'which limitation on reasonable force "trumps" the others' (2008:246), and McGillivray observes that the Supreme Court of Canada in 2004 'lowered the fiduciary bar for parents, upheld the proprietary right of chastisement, and justified a statutory incursion into the autonomy rights of mature children' (2011:22).

In the UK, the Criminal Justice (Scotland) Act (2003) exempts blows to the head, shaking, and the use of implements from corporal punishment that may incredibly be considered 'justifiable assault' of children. The English and Welsh Children Act (2004) and Northern Irish Law Reform (Miscellaneous Provisions) Order (2006) disallow a defence of 'reasonable punishment' in cases of serious assault ('actual bodily harm'), allowing a 'reasonable punishment' defence in common assault cases where no 'grazing, scratches, abrasions, minor bruising, swelling, superficial cuts or a black eye' result (Crown Prosecution Service, 2009:1). 'That children, uniquely, should have *less* protection under the criminal law from assault is', as Hammarberg observes, 'additionally discriminatory and unimaginable, given children's obvious special vulnerability' (2008:2, emphasis in original). In the US, in all states, parents may legally physically punish their children.

It is deplorable that Australian governments remain reluctant to condemn *all* unnecessary violent and degrading treatment of children in light of an Australian Royal Commission's observations over 30 years ago that 'acts to which our ancestors would have been indifferent' now appal us as we increasingly recognise that 'the human rights, dignity and integrity of every man, woman and child should be protected' (1977:159). Similarly appalling in Australia, Canada and the UK are the number of absurd legislative limits which explicitly define rather than reject the legitimacy and inhumanity of violent responses to children – 'instruments' and 'sites of punishment', 'reasons for punishment', 'who can administer punishment', 'degree of force', 'risk of harm' and 'susceptibility to punishment' – a 'shifting geojurispudence of licit and illicit body contacts' (McGillivray, 1997:211). Attempts to distinguish 'ordinary safe smacks and inhuman or degrading punishment' are, as Freeman contends, 'morally bankrupt' – imagine, he taunts, 'legislation which allowed husbands to smack their wives but withheld from them the power to use an implement!' (1999:132). Incremental law reform or 'half measures' stunt necessary attitudinal change in contexts where laws have the power to foster moral behaviour even in relationships involving parents and children – adults must stop 'hitting children because it is wrong…as it is wrong to hit adults' (Freeman, 1999:139).

In countries that have outlawed physical punishment, attitudes and behaviours have changed. Children are aware of their rights and parents know that hitting children is no longer acceptable. The odd 'smack' has not resulted in disrupted families or parental prosecution. Law reform has been part of an educative process that encourages parents to discipline children without violence (see Modig, 2009).

Ending physical punishment in childhood

> Children are our future so they have got to be important…Parents think hitting children is sort of their right…I guess parents have gotta learn to respect children (13yrs) (Saunders and Goddard, 2010:222).

Most of us treasure our children, cherish their endearing attributes, and delight in their company. When children are very young, we enjoy their dependence and their unduly high estimation of us. As children grow we encourage their independence and understand their need to challenge us as they form their own views and make their own decisions. However, some of us perceive children to be an inconvenience, even a burden, as we prioritise our other commitments and agendas. Children may annoy us as they rightly dispute our power over them and question our worldview.

Children's voices on physical punishment

Given long-held perceptions of children's incompetence and their disempowered position in society, it is not surprising that we have traditionally disregarded their views. Indeed, one may wonder how different the CRC might have been had children been consulted (Freeman, 1997c:8), and perhaps a review of the CRC, incorporating children's views, is now timely. Article 12 of the CRC nevertheless recognised children as 'full human being[s], with integrity and personality, and with the ability to participate fully in society' (Freeman, 1996b:3). Only recently, however, have some children been given the opportunity to contribute their perspectives on physical punishment in their childhoods. Research consulting children provides important insights, and demonstrates that even very young children are articulate, insightful, and empathetic; perhaps more empathetic than many adults (Saunders and Goddard, 2010). Indeed, even ardent supporters of physical discipline may be persuaded to see things differently if they hear or read children's descriptions of how physical punishment – experienced or witnessed – adversely impacts on children's sense of self, reinforces their powerlessness and vulnerability, and lowers their perceptions of the adults whom they love and respect.

Children commonly tell us that physical punishment hurts them physically and can escalate in severity; arouses negative emotions, such as resentment, confusion, sadness, hatred, humiliation, and anger; creates fear and impedes learning; is not constructive, children prefer reasoning; and it perpetuates violence as a means of resolving conflict. Children's comments suggest that children are sensitive to inequality and double standards, and children urge us to respect children and to act responsibly (for selected children's views in the English-speaking world see, Willow and Hyder, 1998; Cutting, 2001; Crowley and Vulliamy, 2002; Horgan, 2002; Dobbs *et al.*, 2006; Milne, 2009; Saunders and Goddard, 2008, 2010; Nixon and Halpenny, 2010; Vittrup and Holden, 2010).

Conclusion

Progress towards outlawing physical punishment in childhood is promising but slow and often very challenging. Why is it so hard to concede that the habit of hitting small, vulnerable children and for some parents, hitting young people up to the age of 18, is wrong, unacceptable and unnecessary? We must think about the message that our current laws communicate to children:

> ...if [adults] physical contact with someone, like punching 'em, it's against the law...they could go to jail, they could be charged with assault...And that's exact same for smacking. But...if you're a kid, and it's in the house, it's okay because they're your kids...If you are a kid, it doesn't really matter...because...you barely have any say (9yrs) (Saunders and Goddard, 2010:138).

Our thoughts about children are ingrained in our language, our traditions and our laws. Children are denied the same rights as adults to protection, dignity and respect. Societal tolerance of physical punishment, whether it is justified as discipline, control or the release of emotion, reinforces children's subordination and vulnerability, and impacts their individuality and their potential. In an ideal childhood, discipline is consistent and empathetic; physical punishment is not considered – talking replaces hitting, and tolerance, understanding, gentle persuasion and negotiation, replace violent coercion.

Normalised physical disciplinary practices, passed down from one generation to the next, 'are part of a totality of social relations' and changing 'childhood norms' requires a transformation in 'social conditions' (Pupavac, 2011: 305-6). Santos Pais (2011) has said that '[l]egislation provides an ethical and normative framework to promote values of respect, tolerance and human rights' but law reform alone will not change outdated attitudes and behaviours toward children, symbolized by lawful correction. Full recognition of children's welfare and citizenship rights will require new laws together with changes in our traditional attitudes and responses to children, and our language used in reference to them. Euphemistic language that disguises and minimizes inappropriate discipline should be abandoned; children and adults, and their contributions to society, should be equally valued, and our language should reflect this; and intergenerational responses to, and attitudes toward, children should be questioned and discarded if discriminatory, degrading and disempowering. As Freeman suggests, 'childhood in which children are granted a moral status, in which their rights are taken seriously, will be a better childhood' (1997c:8). However, 'rights without services are meaningless and...services without resources are impossible' (Freeman, 1998:435). Parents and children will require ongoing education and parents will need to be well-supported in their important role as enablers of children's optimal development.

Banning physical punishment is in the best interests of both families and society (Bitensky, 2006). Governments could lead rather than 'slavishly follow' – legislation would educate rather than fruitlessly penalise well-meaning parents, and children's lives could be improved and eventually freed from abuse (Freeman, 2008 :11; see also; Naylor and Saunders, 2011). Most children love and want to please their parents. They also want them to know that they are people with rights, and 'you shouldn't hit people...because there's a better way...than hurting someone (12yrs old child) (Saunders and Goddard, 2010:224). If adults and children are accorded equal respect as human beings, physical punishment of children will become a shameful past practice, remnants of which might continue to stir our emotions in Museums of Childhood.

References

Afifi, T., Mota, N., Dasiewicz, P. et al., 'Physical punishment and mental disorders: Results from a nationally representative sample', *Pediatrics* 130(2) (2012): 1–9.

Alexander, R., Naylor, B. & Saunders, B., *Lawful Correction or Child Abuse: Clarifying the Boundaries, Sanctions and Decision Making Surrounding Physical Discipline of Children*

(CJRC, Monash University, 2011). http://www.cjrc.monash.org/lawfulcorrection/lsb-parental -discipline-final-report.pdf.

Archard, D., *Children, Rights and Childhood* (*2nd ed.*) (London: Routledge, 2004).

Bailey, R.W., 'English at its twilight'. In *The State of the Language*. eds. C. Ricks & L. Michaels (London: Faber and Faber, 1990) 83–94.

Barrett, R., 'States refuse to buckle amid calls to ban cane', *The Australian* (2012). http://www .theaustralian.com.au/national-affairs/education/states-refuse-to-buckle-amid-calls-to -ban-cane/story-fn59nlz9-1226407027267.

Bender, H., Allen, J., McElhaney, P. et al., 'Use of harsh physical discipline and developmental outcomes in adolescence', *Development and Psychopathology* 19 (2007): 227–242.

Bernal, M., Duryee, J., Pruett, H. et al., 'Behavior modification and the brat syndrome', *Journal of Consulting & Clinical Psychology* 32(4) (1968): 447–455.

Bindel, J., 'Six weeks of suffering', *The Guardian* 18 August (2006): 35.

Bitensky, S., *Corporal Punishment of Children: A Human Rights Violation* (Ardsley: Transnational Publishers, Inc, 2006).

Bluebond-Langner, M. & Korbin, J., 'Challenges and opportunities in the anthroplogy of child-hoods: An introduction to children, childhood and childhood studies', *American Anthropologist* 109(2) (2007): 241–246.

Bunting, L., Webb, M. & Healy, J., 'In two minds? – Parental attitudes toward physical punish-ment in the UK', *Children & Society* 24 (2010): 359–370.

Bussmann, K.D., 'Evaluating the subtle impact of a ban on corporal punishment of children in Germany', *Child Abuse Review* 13 (2004): 292–311.

Butler, R., *Why Survive? Being Old in America* (New York: Harper & Row, 1975).

Byng-Hall, J., *Rewriting Family Scripts: Improvisations and Systems Change* (New York: The Guilford Press, 1995).

Cameron, D., *Feminism and Linguistic Theory* (London: Macmillan Press, 1985).

Children's Commissioner, *Omnibus Survey Report: One Year On: Public Attitides and New Zealand's Child Discipline Law* (2008). http://www.repeal43.org/docs/NZChildren'sComm Report.pdf.

Committee on the Rights of the Child, (2006). GENERAL COMMENT No. 8 (2006): The right of the child to protection from corporal punishment and other cruel or degrading forms of punishment (articles 19, 28(2) and 37, inter alia), http://www.ohchr.org/english/bodies/crc/ docs/co/CRC.C.GC.8.pdf.

Committee on the Rights of the Child, *Concluding Observations: Canada. 05/10/2012. CRC/C/ CAN/3-4 Concluding observations/Comments* (2012). http://www2.ohchr.org/english/bodies/ crc/docs/co/CRC-C-CAN-CO-3-4_en.pdf.

Crandall, M., Chin, B. & Sheehan, K., 'Injury in the first year of life: Risk factors and solutions for high risk families', *Journal of Surgical Research* 133 (2006): 7–10.

Crowley, A. & Vulliamy, C., *Listen Up!: Children Talk about Smacking* (Wales: Save the Children, 2002).

Crown Prosecution Service, *Reasonable Chastisement Research Report* (2009). www.cps.gov.uk/ Publications/research/chastisement.html.

Cutting, E., *It Doesn't Sort Anything!* (Scotland: Save the Children, 2001).

Day, D.E. & Roberts, M., 'An analysis of the physical punishment component of a parent train-ing program', *Journal of Abnormal Child Psychology* 11 (1983): 141–152.

Dobbs, T., Smith, A. & Taylor, N., 'No, we don't get a say children just suffer the consequences: Child talk about family discipline', *International Journal of Children's Rights* 14(2006): 137–156.

Durrant, J., 'The empirical rationale for eliminating physical punishment'. In *Global Pathways to Abolishing Physical Punishment*. eds. J. Durrant & A. Smith (New York: Routledge, 2011) 42–63.

Durrant, J. & Ensom, R., 'Physical punishment of children: Lessons from 20 years of research', *Canadian Medical Association Journal* 184(12) (2012).

Durrant, J., Sigvaldason, N. & Bednar, L., 'What did the Canadian public learn from the 2004 supreme court decision on physical punishment?', *International Journal of Children's Rights* 16 (2008): 229–247.

Ellison, C. & Bradshaw, M., 'Religious beliefs, sociopolitical ideology, and attitudes toward corporal punishment', *Journal of Family Issues* 30(2009): 320–340.

End All Corporal Punishment of Children, www.endcorporalpunishment.org.

Freeman, M., 'Taking children's rights more seriously', *International Journal of Law & the Family* 6 (1992): 52–71.

Freeman, M., 'The Convention: An English perspective'. In *Children's Rights: A Comparative Perspective*. ed. M. Freeman (Aldershot: Dartmouth, 1996a) 93–112.

Freeman, M., 'Introduction: Children as persons'. In *Children's Rights: A Comparative Perspective*. ed. M. Freeman (Aldershot: Dartmouth, 1996b) 1–7.

Freeman, M., 'Beyond conventions – towards empowerment'. In *The Moral Status of Children: Essays on the Rights of the Child*. ed. M. Freeman (The Netherlands: Kluwer Law International, 1997a) 63–83.

Freeman, M., 'The limits of children's rights'. In *The Moral Status of Children: Essays on the Rights of the Child* (The Netherlands: Kluwer Law International, 1997b) 83–103.

Freeman, M., 'The moral status of children'. In *The Moral Status of Children: Essays on the Rights of the Child* (The Netherlands: Martinus Nijhoff Publishers, 1997c) 1–19.

Freeman, M., 'The sociology of childhood and children's rights', *International Journal of Children's Rights* 6 (1998): 433–444.

Freeman, M., 'Children are unbeatable', *Children & Society* 13 (1999): 130–141.

Freeman, M., *Can We Conquer Child Abuse If We Don't Outlaw Physical Chastisement of Children?* (2008). Paper presented at the ISPCAN Congress, Hong Kong, 9 September.

Freeman, M., 'The human rights of children', *Current Legal Problems* 63 (2010a): 1–44.

Freeman, M., 'Upholding the dignity and best interests of children: International law and the corporal punishment of children', *Law & Contemporary Problems* 73 (2010b): 211–251.

Freeman, M., 'Introduction'. In *Law and Childhood Studies: Current Legal Issues Volume 24*. ed. M. Freeman (Oxford: Oxford University Press, 2011) 1–9.

General Comment No. 13 'Article 19: The right of the child to freedom from all forms of violence', 56th Session 17 February 2011, http://www.crin.org/docs/CRC.C.GC.13_en_AUV-1.pdf.

Gershoff, E., 'Corporal punishment by parents and associated child behaviors and experience: A meta-analytic and theoretical review', *Psychological Bulletin* 128(4) (2002): 539–579.

Global Initiative to End All Corporal Punishment of Children, *Prohibiting Corporal Punishment of Children: A Guide to Legal Reform and Other Measures* (2009). http://www.endcorporalpunishment.org/pages/pdfs/LegalReformHandbook.pdf.

Goddard, C. & Saunders, B., 'The gender neglect and textual abuse of children in the print media', *Child Abuse Review* 9 (2000): 37–48.

Goddard, C. & Saunders, B., 'Journalists as agents and language as an instrument of social control', *Children Australia* 26(2) (2001): 26–30.

Gonzalez, M., Durrant, J., Chabot, M. et al., 'What predicts injury from physical punishment? A test of the typologies of violence hypothesis', *Child Abuse & Neglect* 32 (2008): 752–765.

Gough, B. & Reavey, P., 'Parental accounts regarding the physical punishment of children: Discourses of dis/empowerment', *Child Abuse & Neglect* 21(5) (1997): 417–430.

Graziano, A., Hamblen, J. & Plante, W., 'Sub-abusive violence in child-rearing in middle-class American families', *Pediatrics* 98(4) (1996): 845–848.

Greenwood, C., 'Mother who was jailed for slapping children is freed after judge says her actions were 'similar to those of many loving parents across the land'', *MailOnline* 1 October, (2012). http://www.dailymail.co.uk/news/article-2211201/Mother-jailed-smacking-children-freed-judge-says-actions-worse-loving-parents.html.

Hammarberg, T., 'The UN convention on the rights of the child - and how to make it work', *Human Rights Quarterly* 12(1) (1990): 97–105.

Hammarberg, T., (2008). Memorandum: UK Corporal Punishment, Council of Europe. http://www.unhcr.org/refworld/topic,4565c22529,4565c25f329,,0,COECHR,,.html.

Harris, R., 'Forward'. In *Museum of Childhood: A Book of Childhood Things*. ed. S. Wood (London: V&A Publishing, 2012) 7.

Hartley, J., *Understanding News* (London: Methuen, 1982).

Hengst, H., 'The role of the media and commercial culture in children's experiencing of collective identities'. In *Children in Generational Perspective*. eds. B. Mayall & H. Zeiher (London: Institute of Education Education, 2003) 111–132.

Horgan, G., *It's a Hit not a Smack* (Northern Ireland: Save the Children, 2002).

Human Rights Watch, *A Violent Education: Corporal Punishment of Children in US Public Schools* (New York: Human Rights Watch, 2008).

James, A. & Prout, A., *Constructing and Reconstructing Childhood: Contemporary Issues in the Sociological Study of Childhood* (London: Falmer Press, 1997).

Jenks, C., *Childhood* (London: Routledge, 1996).

Johnston, M., 'More parents rule out smacking children', *NZ Herald* 2 April. (2012). http://www.nzherald.co.nz/nz/news/article.cfm?c_id=1&objectid=10796068.

Keating, H., 'Protecting or punishing children: Physical punishment, human rights and English law reform', *Legal Studies* 26 (2006): 394–413.

Key, E., *The Century of the Child* (New York: G. P. Putnam's Sons, 1909).

Lansdown, G., 'Children's Rights'. In *Children's Childhoods: Observed and Experienced*. ed. B. Mayall (London: Falmer Press, 1994) 33–44.

Lansdown, G., 'Children's rights to participation and protection: A critique'. In *Participation and Empowerment in Child Protection*. C. Cloke & M. Davies. London: Pitman Publishing, 1995) 19–38.

Lansford, J., Wager, L., Bates, J. et al., 'Forms of spanking and children's externalising behaviors', *Family Relations* 61 (2012): 224–236.

Larzelere, R. & Baumrind, D., 'Are spanking injunctions scientifically supported?', *Law & Contemporary Problems* 73 (2011): 57–87.

Lawrence, J. & Smith, A., *Discipline in Context: Families, Disciplinary Practices for Children Aged under Five* (Wellington: Families Commission Blue Skies Report No 30/09, 2009).

Loane, S., 'UN goes to bat for kids', *The Sydney Morning Herald* 8 October (1997).

MacKenzie, M.J., Nicklas, E. & Brooks-Gunn, J., 'Who spanks infants and toddlers? Evidence form the fragile familes and child well-being study', *Child Youth Services Review* 33 (2011): 1364–1373.

Madge, N., *Children These Days* (Bristol: The Policy Press, 2006).

Mayoh, L., 'Mum jailed for slapping drunk daughter, 16', *The Sunday Telegraph* 9 May, (2010). http://www.news.com.au/national-old/mum-jailed-for-slapping-drunk-daughter-16/story-e6frfkvr-1225864070836.

McGillivray, A., 'He'll learn it on his body': Disciplining childhood in Canadian law', *International Journal of Children's Rights* 5 (1997): 193–242.

McGillivray, A., 'Children's rights, paternal power and fiduciary duty: From Roman law to the Supreme Court of Canada', *International Journal of Children's Rights* 19 (2011): 21–54.

McGillivray, A. & Milne, C., 'Canada: The rocky road'. In *Global Pathways to Abolishing Physical Punishment: Realizing Children's Rights*. eds. J. Durrant & A. Smith (New York: Routledge, 2011) 98–111.

Melton, G., 'Human dignity and the experience of children: The UN Convention as a framework for policy in developed countries'. In *Implementing the UN Convention on the Rights of the Child in Australia*. eds. J. Harvey, U. Dolgopol & S. Castell-McGregor (Adelaide, South Australia: Children's Interest Bureau, 1993) 23–29.

Milne, E., *I Don't Get Sad, Only When My Mum Smacks Me* (London: Children are Unbeatable! Alliance, 2009).

Modig, C., *Never Violence – Thirty Years on from Sweden's Abolition of Corporal Punishment* (Sweden: Save the Children, 2009).

Mudaly, N. & Goddard, C.R., *The Truth is Longer than a Lie: Children's Experiences of Abuse and Professional Interventions* (London: Jessica Kingsley, 2006).

Naylor, B. & Saunders, B., 'Parental discipline, criminal laws and responsive regulation'. In *Law & Childhood Studies*. ed. M. Freeman (Oxford: Oxford University Press, 2011) 506–530.

Newell, P., 'The human rights imperative to eliminate physical punishment'. In *Global Pathways to Abolishing Physical Punishment: Realizing Children's Rights*. eds. J. Durrant & A. Smith (New York: Routledge, 2011) 7–27.

Nielssen, O., Large, M., Westmore, B. et al., 'Child homicide in New South Wales from 1991 to 2005', *Medical Journal of Australia* 190(1) (2009): 7–11.

Nixon, E. & Halpenny, A., *Children's Perspectives on Parenting Styles and Discipline: A Developmental Approach* (Dublin: Office of the Minister for Children and Youth Affairs, 2010).

Pupavac, V., 'Punishing childhoods: Contradictions in children's rights and global governance', *Journal of Intervention and Statebuilding* 5(3) (2011): 285–312.

Quennerstedt, A., 'Children, but not really humans? Critical reflections on the hampering effect of the '3 p's', *International Journal of Children's Rights* 18 (2010): 619–635.

Renteln, A., 'Corporal punishment and the cultural defense', *Law & Contemporary Problems* 73 (2010): 253–279.

Rosen, D., 'Child soldiers, international humanitarian law, and the globalization of childhood', *American Anthropologist* 109(2) (2007): 296–306.

Royal Commission on Human Relationships, *Final Report* (Canberra: Australian Government Publishing Service, 1977).

Sanders, M., Markie-Dadds, C., Rinaldis, M. et al., 'Using household survey data to inform policy decisions regarding the delivery of evidence-based parenting interventions', *Childcare, Health and Development* 33 (2007): 768–783.

Santos Pais, M., *Brazil to Adopt Legal Ban on Corporal Punishment of Children* (2011). http://srsg .violenceagainstchildren.org/story/2011-05-19_334.

Saunders, B. & Cashmore, J., 'Australia: The ongoing debate about ending physical punishment'. In *Global Pathways to Abolishing Physical Punishment*. eds. J. Durrant & A. Smith (New York: Routledge, 2011) 83–97.

Saunders, B.J. & Goddard, C., 'The textual abuse of childhood in the English-speaking world: The contribution of language to the denial of children's rights', *Childhood* 8(4) (2001): 443–462.

Saunders, B.J. & Goddard, C., 'The objectification of the child through 'physical discipline' and language: The debate on children's rights continues'. In *Children Taken Seriously: In Theory, Policy and Practice*. eds. J. Mason & T. Fattore (London: Jessica Kingsley, 2005) 113–122.

Saunders, B.J. & Goddard, C., 'Some Australian children's perceptions of physical punishment in childhood', *Children & Society* 22(6) (2008): 405–417.

Saunders, B.J. & Goddard, C., *Physical Punishment in Childhood: The Rights of the Child* (Chicester: John Wiley & Sons, 2010).

Scarre, G., ed., *Children, Parents and Politics* (Cambridge: Cambridge University Press, 1989).

Scutt, J., 'Sparing parents pain or spoiling the child by the rod: Human rights arguments against corporal punishment', *University of Tasmania Law Review* 28(1) (2009): 1–22.

Silverstein, M., Augustyn, M., Young, R. et al., 'The relationship between maternal depression, in-home violence and use of physical punishment: What is the role of child behaviour?', *Archives of Diseases in Childhood* 94 (2009): 138–143.

Smith, A. & Durrant, J., 'Introduction to the global movement to ban physical punishment of children'. In *Global Pathways to Abolishing Physical Punishment*. eds. J. Durrant & A. Smith (New York: Routledge, 2011) 3–6.

Straus, M., *Beating the Devil Out of Them: Corporal Punishment in American Families* (New York: Lexton Books, 1994).

Straus, M., 'Spanking and the making of a violent society', *Pediatrics* 98 (1996): 837–834.

Straus, M., 'Corporal punishment and primary prevention of physical abuse', *Child Abuse & Neglect* 24 (2000): 1109–1114.

Straus, M., 'The special issue on prevention of violence ignores the primordial violence', *Journal of Interpersonal Violence* 23 (2009): 1314–1320.

Straus, M., 'Prevalence, societal causes, and trends in corporal punishment by parents in world perspective', *Law & Contemporary Problems* 73 (2010): 1–30.

Taylor, C., Mangarella, J., Lee, S. et al., 'Mother's spanking of three-year old children and subsequent risk of children's aggressive behavior', *Pediatrics* 125 (2010): 1057–1065.

Trumbull, D., Larzelere, R. & Nieman, P., 'Harsh physical punishment and appropriate spanking are very different', *Pediatrics eLetter* July 23, (2012). http://pediatrics.aappublications.org/content/early/2012/06/27/peds.2011-2947/reply#content-block.

Tucci, J., Mitchell, J. & Goddard, C., *Crossing the Line: Making the Case for Changing Australian Laws about the Physical Punishment of Children* (Ringwood: Australian Childhood Foundation, 2006).

Turner, H. & Muller, P., 'Long-term effects of corporal punishment on depressive symptoms in young adults:potential moderators and mediators', *Journal of Family Issues* 25 (2004): 761–782.

UN Committee on the Rights of the Child, *State Reports*, http://www2.ohchr.org/english/bodies/crc/crcs61.htm.

United Nations Convention on the Rights of the Child, (1989).

United Nations Committee Against Torture, (2008), http://www2.ohchr.org/english/bodies/cat/docs/followup/40th/AustraliaCOBsExtractsfollowup.pdf.

van Boven, T., *Report of the Special Rapporteur of the Commission on Human Rights on the Question of Torture and Other Cruel, Inhuman or Degrading Treatment or Punishment* (2002). http://www.unhchr.ch/Huridocda/Huridoca.nsf/0/2107741d197b2865c1256c390032be06/$FILE/N0247560.pdf.

Vittrup, B. & Holden, G.W., 'Children's assessments of corporal punishment and other disciplinary practices: The role of age, race, SES, and exposure to spanking', *Journal of Applied Developmental Psychology* 31 (2010): 211–220.

Waksler, F., ed., *Studying the Social Worlds of Children:Sociological Readings* (London: Falmer Press, 1991).

Wiggin, K.D., *Children's Rights: A Book of Nursery Logic* (Boston: Houghton, 1892).

Willow, C. & Hyder, T., *It Hurts You Inside: Children Talking About Smacking* (London: National Children's Bureau, 1998).

Wood, B., Hassall, I. & Hook, G., *Unreasonable Force: New Zealand's Journey towards Banning the Physical Punishment of Children* (Wellington: Save the Children, 2008).

Young-Bruehl, E., *Childism: Confronting Prejudice Against Children* (New Haven: Yale University Press, 2012).

Zolotar, A., Thoedore, A., Runyan, D. et al., 'Corporal punishment and physical abuse: Population-based trends for three-to-11-year-old children in the United States', *Child Abuse Review* 20 (2011): 57–66.

The Third Optional Protocol to the UN Convention on the Rights of the Child? – Challenges Arising Transforming the Rhetoric into Reality

Rhona Smith
Professor of International Human Rights, University of Northumbria UK
rhona.smith@northumbria.ac.uk

Introduction

The Third Optional Protocol to the UN Convention on the Rights of the Child seeks to fill a lacuna in the current raft of core UN international human rights instruments by establishing an individual complaints mechanism for aggrieved children. Complaints can be raised by children against any ratifying State.[1] These will be considered by the UN Committee on the Rights of the Child, a body of independent experts already established which currently receives periodic State reports (submitted in terms of the UN Convention on the Rights of the Child).[2] With the Optional Protocol to the International Covenant on Economic Social and Cultural Rights also open for signature,[3] this now means that each of the core UN treaties has an optional individual complaints mechanism. Many of these individual complaint processes are not especially popular with States, or even individual complainants. By way of comparison, the regional systems receive more communications and are generally accepted by proportionately more of the high contracting parties of each respective

---

[1] By 'ratifying State', it is States which have ratified the third optional protocol as well as the Convention or indeed one or both of the first two protocols (note that the United States of America, for example, has ratified the optional protocols but remains one of the only States not to have ratified the Convention). As of March 2013, there are three ratifications to the third optional protocol (Gabon, Germany and Macedonia) and a total of 35 signatures. With the exception of Germany's instrument of ratification, all signatures/ratifications were in 2012.

[2] Article 44, UN Convention on the Rights of the Child 1989.

[3] The Optional Protocol to the International Covenant on Economic, Social and Cultural Rights, as of March 2013, ten ratifications have been secured and thus the optional protocol entered into force on 5 May 2013 (Article 18).

treaty.[4] The extent to which the State has engendered public awareness of human rights standards and the mechanisms available for monitoring compliance therewith is, of course, a determinative factor.

Children occupy a unique position in international human rights. They obviously enjoy recognised core human rights and can expect these to be enforceable at a national level and even internationally, albeit reality may not match the rhetoric in terms of remedies available to them. In addition, children enjoy those rights and freedoms articulated in the UN Convention on the Rights of the Child though many of these specific children's rights are obviously far from fully realized. A more strategic, child centred approach to children's rights is necessary when it comes to complaints to national and international bodies to ensure the best interests of the child are adequately represented.

This paper will consider three questions which arise in respect of creating a complaints mechanism for children's rights: will children know their rights; will they be able to access the complaints mechanism; and will their rights be accepted and articulated nationally as separate from those of their parents? Each will be considered in turn. It will be argued that strengthening of national human rights mechanisms is vital to ensure the distinct interests of the child are adequately represented, unnecessarily usurped by neither State nor parents.

The Third Optional Protocol to the Convention on the Rights of the Child

The text of the Third Optional Protocol[5] to the UN Convention on the Rights of the Child was adopted by the Human Rights Council in June 2011,[6] then the General Assembly in December 2011,[7] and opened for signature in 2012. As Yanghee Lee, member of the Committee on the Rights of the Child, notes, the desirability of an individual complaints process for children's rights had been mooted since the outset.[8] However, to date children and their representatives

---

[4] For example, the regional Council of Europe's European Court of Human Rights has the most substantial caseload. It receives considerably more complaints than all the other regional and international entities mentioned combined, a situation set to continue despite the entry into force of Protocol 14 – see also the Brighton Declaration 2012 - <http://www.coe.int/en/20120419-brighton-declaration>.

[5] Available http://www2.ohchr.org/english/bodies/hrcouncil/OEWG/index.htm.

[6] UN Human Rights Council resolution 17/18, UN Doc A/HRC/RES/17/18, 13 July 2011.

[7] UN General Assembly resolution 66/138, UN Doc A/RES/66/138, 19 December 2011.

[8] Lee, Y., 'Communications procedure under the Convention on the Rights of the Child: 3rd Optional Protocol', *The International Journal of Children's Rights,* 18(4) (2010): 567.

have had to pursue any infringements of general rights and freedoms before other UN or regional bodies, a beneficial consequence of the overlapping nature of many core treaties. Now the third optional protocol seeks to provide the Committee on the Rights of the Child[9] with competency to receive and consider individual and inter-State complaints[10] concerning the application of the convention. Its preambular paragraphs reaffirm 'the status of the child as a subject of rights and as a human being with dignity and evolving capacities' as well as recognising that 'children's special and dependent status may create real difficulties for them in pursuing remedies for violations of their rights' – issues identified and discussed in this article were evidently in the minds of the drafters of the protocol. Nevertheless this is not the first international treaty specifically aimed at children's communications – the African Charter on the Rights and Welfare of the Child 1990 explicitly permits communications 'from any person, group or [recognized] nongovernmental organization', albeit the author must be named.[11] Irrespective of this, that system is subject to reservations from States parties, is confidential and there is little evidence of widespread usage.[12]

In essence, the Third Optional Protocol to the UN Convention on the Rights of the Child does not deviate from other similar UN mechanisms. It is offered in a separate protocol, a common device chosen to permit ratification of the principal treaty and thus acceptance of its content, without obliging a State to accept individual communications.[13] Protocols also allow for treaty reform (in this instance, adding a different method of monitoring) without changing the core treaty.[14] (Other treaties, such as the Convention on the Elimination of Racial Discrimination, and indeed, the original European Convention on

---

[9] For information on the Committee, see Convention on the Rights of the Child, Articles 43 et seq.

[10] Article 10, Third Optional Protocol to the UN Convention on the Rights of the Child.

[11] Article 44, African Charter on the Rights and Welfare of the Child 1990.

[12] See generally, T. Kaime, *The African Charter on the Rights and Welfare of the Child* (Pretoria, Pretoria University Press, 2009); A. Lloyd, 'A Theoretical Analysis of the Reality of Children's Rights in Africa: An Introduction to the African Charter on the Rights and Welfare of the Child', *African Human Rights Law Journal* 2(1) (2002): 11; D. Chirwa, 'The merits and demerits of the African Charter on the Rights and Welfare of the Child', *International Journal of Children's Rights* 10 (2002): 157.

[13] See also the International Covenant on Civil and Political Rights 1966, first optional protocol; Optional Protocol to the Convention on the Elimination of Discrimination against Women; Optional Protocol to the International Covenant on Economic, Social and Cultural Rights (entry into force 5 May 2013).

[14] On this in respect of the optional protocol to the International Covenant on Economic, Social and Cultural Rights, see M. Scheinin, 'The Proposed Optional Protocol to the International Covenant on Economic, Social and Cultural Rights: A Blueprint for UN Human Rights Treaty Body Reform – Without Amending the Existing Treaties', *Human Rights Law Review* 6(1) (2006): 13.

Human Rights, contain an article within the main treaty facilitating individual communications which a contracting State has explicitly to accept on or after ratification. This was intended to emphasise the centrality of the complaints mechanism.) States electing to ratify the third optional protocol accept a new function of the Committee on the Rights of the Child, viz. that of receiving individual communications. Conforming to normal procedures respecting the sovereignty of States, all complainants must have exhausted available and accessible domestic remedies prior to the matter being brought to the Committee.[15] This entails engaging the relevant judicial and any compulsory quasi-judicial mechanisms, though can also include reference to national human rights mechanisms, as discussed below.

Individual communications under the third optional protocol may be submitted by or on behalf of a single child or a group of complainants claiming to be victims of a violation of the Convention (or its two additional protocols).[16] The Committee may elect to request a State to take interim measures to prevent further deterioration in the circumstances complained about.[17] Communications are subject to familiar admissibility criteria[18] and will be considered in closed sessions, with the State invited to transmit its response for consideration by the Committee; viability of reaching a friendly settlement will also be considered.[19] Should no friendly settlement emerge, the Committee will deliberate, then transmit its views and any recommendations to the parties before it.[20] A follow up procedure is available to ensure that the State takes appropriate action.[21] In a wider context, the role of all UN treaty bodies and the efficacy of their follow-up procedures are under review and undergo regular (small, due to confines of treaty interpretation) reform.[22] Thus although this function is new to the Committee on the Rights of the Child, the treaty bodies as a whole, through the regular Chair meetings, are endeavouring continually to strengthen the effectiveness of the monitoring process to ensure best possible protection and promotion of human rights.

---

[15] This is a common provision in international and regional human rights organisations – see for example, Article 35, European Convention on Human Rights; Article 5(2)(b), first optional protocol to the International Covenant on Civil and Political Rights.

[16] Article 5, Third Optional Protocol to the UN Convention on the Rights of the Child.

[17] Ibid. Article 6.

[18] Ibid. Article 7.

[19] Ibid. Articles 8-10.

[20] Ibid. Article 10.

[21] Ibid. Article 11.

[22] On problems with treaty bodies, and the ongoing reforms, see K. Ban, *Report of the Secretary-General Measures to improve further the effectiveness, harmonization and reform of the treaty body system*, UN Doc A/66/344, 7 September 2011, and for background, see P. Alston and J. Crawford (eds) *The Future of UN Human Rights Treaty Monitoring* (Cambridge, Cambridge University Press, 2000). United Nations High Commissioner for Human Rights, *Report on strengthening the human rights treaty bodies*, UN Doc A/66/860, 26 June 2012.

In sum, the third optional protocol establishes a mechanism by which children, and/or their representatives, may bring complaints before a UN Committee concerning infringements of the UN Convention on the Rights of the Child, or its first two protocols. As with all existing UN treaty body individual complaint mechanisms, any Committee opinion will be binding *inter se* but will have no further legal effect and the emphasis is on securing a friendly settlement. 'Closed door' negotiations will take place with States to seek agreement on discharging the complaint.

There is little doubt that this protocol is a positive step, in keeping with universalising human rights and reflecting the fact that many countries (particularly outwith the UN's Western European and Others Group) are young countries with children and young people the dominant demographic.[23] However, imbuing children with a right of complaint, whilst fair and equal, brings a unique set of challenges. The three questions identified above will now be addressed.

1. Will Children know their Rights?

Perhaps it is axiomatic but if children are unaware of their rights, they will not be able to take any steps to exercise those rights. Two main issues arise from this: the availability and accessibility of information on the Convention and indeed other human rights treaties; and the age and/or capacity of the child. For the former, the Convention itself makes it clear that States are under an obligation to publicise and generate awareness of the rights and freedoms. This also relates to the literature on human rights education. For the second issue, the age and capacity of the child, this will be considered in more depth later and links clearly to the second question, that of whether children can access the Committee on the Rights of the Child's complaints mechanisms or indeed applicable national mechanisms.

In terms of the Convention itself, Article 42 makes it clear that 'States Parties undertake to make the principles and provisions of the Convention widely known, by appropriate and active means, to adults and children alike'. This ties in to other global initiatives. For example, the UN Decade of Human Rights Education 1995-2004 sought to ensure 'training, dissemination and information efforts aimed at the building of a universal culture of human rights through imparting knowledge and skills and the moulding of attitudes'.[24] This

---

[23]   Africa, as a region, has the youngest median age of population, a median age below 20 years for several States.

[24]   *Plan of Action for the United Nations Decade for Human Rights Education 1995-2004: Human Rights Education – lessons for life* UN Doc A/51/506/Add.1, para. 2. The Decade was proclaimed by General Assembly resolution 49/184, UN Doc A/RES/49/184 (1994).

was followed by the World Programme on Human Rights and Training,[25] the first phase of which focussed on promoting human rights education at the primary and secondary levels. Whilst this objective continues unabated, the objectives are being rolled out, *inter alia*, to tertiary level education institutions and providers in the current, second, phase. Further impetus can be drawn from the UN Declaration on Human Rights Education and Training,[26] Article 1 of which states: 'Everyone has the right to know, seek and receive information about all human rights and fundamental freedoms and should have access to human rights educationand training.'. These programmes are not innovative, rather they draw on the longstanding aim of the international organisation to achieve global human rights awareness.[27] On adopting the Universal Declaration of Human Rights in 1948, the General Assembly also exhorted States to publicise the terms of the Declaration throughout their territories 'by every means within their power'.[28]

Human rights education is inevitably linked to, indeed a corollary to, human rights in education.[29] After all, it is necessary that all children everywhere are entitled to learn about their rights, not just a few in particular schools or countries. The '4A' approach to the right to education is thus highly relevant[30] – human rights education, to be effective, must be accessible to all children (this includes financially and geographically), available in a language and style they understand, acceptable in terms of content and culture and adaptable to best fit the needs of, in this instance, the child. Education should develop the child's understanding and 'respect for human rights, fundamental freedoms and the maintenance of peace'.[31] Human rights education is thus critical to education. Children must learn and appreciate their rights and responsibilities in order to develop their personality and dignity in preparation for their full participation in society.[32]

---

[25] Proclaimed by General Assembly resolution 59/113, UN Doc A/RES/59/113 (2004).

[26] Final adoption by General Assembly resolution 66/137, UN Doc A/RES/66/137 (2011).

[27] For a review of models, see *inter alia* M. Bajaj, 'Human Rights Education: Ideology, Location and Approaches' 33(2) Human Rights Quarterly (2011) 481-508.

[28] General Assembly resolution 217 III (D), 10 December 1948, para. 1.

[29] Tomasevski, K., *Human rights in education as prerequisite for human rights education* Right to Education Primer 4 (RWI and SIDA, Lund and Stockholm, 2001), available http://www.right -to-education.org/sites/r2e.gn.apc.org/files/B6h%20Primer.pdf.

[30] See, for example, the UN Special Procedure's Right to Education website - </www.right-to -education.org/node/226>.

[31] Articles 29, UN Convention on the Rights of the Child. See also UN Committee on the Rights of the Child, General Comment 1 (2001) The Aims of Education, UN Doc CRC/GC/2001/1 (2001); M. Nowak, 'The Right to Education' in A. Eide, K. Krause and A. Rosas (eds) *Economic, Social and Cultural Rights* (2nd ed, Dordrecht, Martinus Nijhoff, 2001) at p. 251.

[32] Paraphrasing Universal Declaration of Human Rights 1948, Article 26(2).

Human rights education is, however a work in progress, notwithstanding the international, regional and national efforts to render the Convention on the Rights of the Child accessible to children and publicise its contents. The goals of human rights education have not yet been met. While there is no doubt that children should know their rights, equally there is little doubt that many, if not most, children, do not. Obviously this presents a problem. If this first question is to be answered in the negative, the Third Optional Protocol begins with a marked disadvantage. Indeed it almost renders the next question moot.

2. *Will Children be Able to Access the new Mechanism Provided by the Convention on the Rights of the Child?*

If children are unaware of their rights generally, and of the existence of the Convention on the Rights of the Child particularly, then they are unlikely to know of and thus be able to access the new individual complaint mechanism. However, engaging with the new mechanism is not only a matter of awareness. Children frequently lack capacity to initiate national enforcement opportunities, thereby precluding invocation of the complaints' mechanism.

Age and capacity do not only impact on knowledge of rights, ensuring understanding and even articulation of rights. They are also key limiting factors on enforcing rights. This is something unique to the Convention on the Rights of the Child as the main beneficiaries of the rights and freedoms articulated in the treaty inevitably lack legal capacity to institute judicial and often quasi-judicial proceedings in their own country. They are thus dependent on adults with full capacity to act on their behalf, which leads onto the third question outlined below – that of whether the rights being actioned are truly those of the child or rather of her/his parent. To an extent, this problem may be moot. If previous patterns are repeated then, notwithstanding the popularity overall (amongst States) of the Convention on the Rights of the Child, there are likely to be few ratifications of the Third Optional Protocol. Accordingly, few children may be able to access the complaints mechanism. Of the world's most populous countries, China, India, Indonesia and the United States of America generally do not accept individual communication mechanisms for treaties to which they are party. (African children (many of whom are demographically almost or actually a majority in the State) have the additional protection offered by the African Union's Charter on the Rights and Welfare of the Child.)

Whilst this article focuses on the UN Convention on the Rights of the Child, children enjoy a range of exercisable rights under core human rights treaties,[33]

---

[33] The core UN human rights treaties are the Convention on the Elimination of All Forms of Racial Discrimination; the International Covenant on Civil and Political Rights, the International

and many have opportunities to submit individual complaints to associated committees.[34] Children may also bring complaints and cases before regional human rights bodies: the European Court of Human Rights;[35] the Inter-American Court or Commission for Human Rights;[36] the African Commission on Human and Peoples' Rights[37] and the African Court of Justice and Human Rights.[38] Nevertheless, comparatively few cases are brought by children to these international and regional fora. Reflecting on this and the primary responsibility of States themselves to secure all treaty rights within their jurisdiction, one former member of the UN Committee on the Rights of the Child, Professor Lucy Smith, argues that strengthening national complaints procedures will have more effect than adding a complaints mechanism to the UN Convention on the Rights of the Child.[39] It will certainly create most accessible opportunities for enforcing rights.

As with all other individual complaint mechanisms, children are required first to exhaust domestic remedies. Legal capacity as an issue thus needs to be addressed if children's rights are to become a reality. This was recognized and much-debated during the discussions on the drafting and adoption of the third optional protocol.[40] Children, to an extent, lack legal capacity in all jurisdictions thus initiating complaints (particularly against the state) is problematic, or even impossible. Children require some form of adult representation. Problems may be encountered should parents/guardians not support the child's complaints in those jurisdictions requiring parental consent to initiate a complaint. Of course, in some instances, the child will be too young even to articulate the infringed right her or himself – though note the comments by

Covenant on Economic, Social and Cultural Rights, the Convention against Torture and other Cruel, Inhuman or Degrading Treatment or Punishment, the Convention on the Elimination of All Forms of Discrimination against Women, the Convention on the Rights of Migrant Workers and their Families, the Convention on the Rights of Persons with Disabilities and the Convention on Enforced Disappearances.

[34] If the State so notifies, individual complaints can be made before the Human Rights Committee, the Committee on the Elimination of Racial Discrimination, the Committee on the Elimination of all forms of Discrimination against Women, the Committee on the Rights of Persons with Disabilities etc.

[35] European Convention on Human Rights, Article 34 provides for individual complaints against States. For those brought on children, see the Theseus database of the Council of Europe, accessible via http://www.coe.int/t/dg3/children/caselaw/CaseLawChild_en.asp.

[36] OAS Convention on Human Rights, Article 48 et seq; OAS Charter for those States not ratifying the Convention.

[37] African Charter on Human and Peoples' Rights, Article 55 et seq.

[38] Protocol of the Statute of the African Court of Justice and Human Rights.

[39] Smith, L., 'Monitoring the CRC' In *International Human Rights Monitoring Mechanisms, Essays in Honour of Jakob Th. Moller*. Eds G. Alfredsson, J. Grimheden, B. Ramcharan and A. de Zayas (The Hague, Martinus Nijhoff, 2nd ed, 2009), 115.

[40] See Working group materials <http://www2.ohchr.org/english/bodies/hrcouncil/OEWG/index.htm>.

the UN Committee on the Rights of the Child.[41] As children mature, they can articulate their rights if (a very significant 'if') they are aware of their rights.[42] They may even acquire increments of legal capacity depending on national law, albeit such capacity may not extend to initiating complaints on issues pertinent to the convention.[43] In terms of Article 12 of the Convention on the Rights of the Child, the child enjoys an evolving right to be heard and to have his or her opinion taken into account in matters concerning him or her.[44] Human rights education initiatives are crucial, as noted above. However, very young children are not always able to make known violations or infringements of their rights in a way that is understood or can be transformed into a complaint. Even when able to talk and make themselves understood, children (indeed so too adults) lack familiarity with the language of human rights and indeed national monitoring mechanisms. It is therefore perhaps inevitable that complaints will be brought before the Committee on behalf of children by lawyers, parents, guardians and others. This is normal under other treaties and in national courts.[45] The extent to which each truly represents the interests of

---

[41]   Committee on the Rights of the Child, General Comment 7 (Rev 1) *Implementing Child Rights in early Childhood,* at para. 14, UN Doc CRC/C/GC/7/Rev.1, 20 September 2006, para. 14(a), available http://www2.ohchr.org/english/bodies/crc/docs/AdvanceVersions/General Comment7Rev1.pdf.

[42]   Phase one of the current World Programme of Human Rights Education ran from 2005 to 2009 with the goal of embedding human rights education at the primary and secondary school levels – see Plan of Action UN Doc A/59/525/Rev.1.

[43]   Note that the International Covenant on Civil and Political Rights does not specify an age of majority, leaving it to each State – see Human Rights Committee, General Comment 17, 7 April 1989, available in compilation document UN Doc HRI/GEN/1/Rev.9 (Vol. I) at para. 4.

[44]   For elaboration, see Committee on the Rights of the Child, General Comment 12 (2009) on the rights of the child to be heard, UN Doc CRC/C/GC/12. This provision frequently appears reflected in cases concerning child welfare and protection, medical treatment and those concerning child residency following parental separation and divorce. On the English position, see, for example, J. Fortin, *Children's Rights and the Developing Law* (Cambridge, Cambridge University Press, 3rd ed, 2009); D. Arcgard and M. Skivenes, 'Balancing a Child's Best Interests and a Child's Views' *International Journal of Children's Rights* 17 (2009): 1; J. Munby, 'Making Sure the Child is Heard' *Family Law* (2004): 427; J. Fortin, 'Children's Representation through the Looking Glass', *Family Law* (2007): 500; S. Gilmore and J. Herring, '"No" is the hardest word: consent and children's autonomy', *Child and Family Law Quarterly* 23 (2011): 3; F. Raitt, 'Judicial discretion and Methods of Ascertaining the Views of a Child', *Child and Family Law Quarterly* 16 (2004): 151. For an interesting contrast, a review of children as witnesses in Canada, see N. Bala, A. Evans and E. Bala, 'Hearing the voices of children in Canada's criminal justice system: recognising capacity and facilitating testimony', *Child and Family Law Quarterly* 22 (2010): 21; C. Davies, 'Access to justice for Children: the voice of the child in custody and access', *Canadian Family Law Quarterly* 22 (2004): 153. For the position in Australia, and beyond, see P. Parkinson and J. Cashmore, *The Voice of a Child in Family Law Disputes* (Oxford, Oxford University Press, 2008); P. Parkinson and J. Cashmore, 'Judicial Conversations with Children in Parenting Disputes: The Views of Australian Judges', *International Journal of Law, Policy & the Family* 21 (2007): 160.

[45]   Eg, *De Gallicchio and Vicario v. Argentina* UN Doc CCPR/C/53/D/400/1990, 27 April 1995, the Human Rights Committee considered complaints brought on the subject of a young girl by her

the child, viewed objectively and subjectively, will indubitably be questionable in some instances, although in partial amelioration thereof, the third optional protocol does require the complaint to be brought with the consent of the victim, 'unless the author [of the complaint] can justify acting on their behalf without such consent'.[46] This provision is potentially open to abuse with vexatious complaints not necessarily at the instigation of the child but is necessary as some children, by their very age and/or capability, cannot instigate or consent to complaints.

A number of articles in the Convention itself recognise the limitations of children – Article 8(2), for example, requires a child deprived of elements of her or his identity be provided by the State with appropriate assistance to re-establish that identity. The Committee has identified the need to protect rights in early childhood as a key issue, and encourages States parties 'to take all appropriate measures to ensure that the concept of the child as rights holder with freedom to express views and the right to be consulted in matters that affect him or her is implemented from the earliest stage in ways appropriate to the child's capacities, best interests, and the rights to protection from harmful experiences'.[47] Whilst this article considers children of formal school age, earlier in the same paragraph, the Committee on the Rights of the Child expresses its view that very young children make choices and make their views known 'long before they are able to communicate through the conventions of spoken or written language'.[48] While this may be true, the lack of familiarity with the scope, content and language of rights is clearly problematic.

Arguably an omission in the third optional protocol is the lack of provision for a neutral curator ad litem, guardian, or litigation friend to be appointed to help the child with the communication process. Indeed, it appears the process is predicated on adult involvement or at least mature children capable of acting on their own behalf, if only to initiate the proceedings. Of course, when addressing children's rights it is all too often the silent millions who are most in need. Access to justice is frequently denied them for a myriad of

---

newly discovered grandmother; the intersection of education and religious rights was considered by the European Court of Human Rights in a case brought jointly by a mother and her children, continued with consent after the child reached majority – *Lautsi v. Italy* Application 30814/06 European Court of Human Rights 18 March 2011, see also D. McGoldrick, 'Religion in the European Public Square and in European Public Life – Crucifixes in the Classroom?' *Human Rights Law Review* (2011) 451.

[46] Article 5(2), Third Optional Protocol to the UN Convention on the Rights of the Child.

[47] Committee on the Rights of the Child, General Comment 7 (Rev 1) *Implementing Child Rights in Early Childhood*, UN Doc CRC/C/GC/7/Rev.1, 20 September 2006, para. 14(a), available http://www2.ohchr.org/english/bodies/crc/docs/AdvanceVersions/GeneralComment7Rev1 .pdf.

[48] Ibid, para 14.

reasons. Some countries, at the forefront Norway, have established children's commissioners or children's ombudspersons.[49] These may sit as part of a recognized National Human Rights Institution[50] or separately. Although these bodies perform valuable functions including strong advocacy of children's rights, not all these entities have the capacity to consider individual complaints from children. Unsurprisingly, the third optional protocol preamble encourages States to continue to develop appropriate national measures to allow children to seek redress at the national level. An increase in such bodies may prove to be an indirect consequence of the protocol.[51]

Even with a national mechanism in place, although children's rights may be promoted at the national level, they are not necessarily any more enforceable, in part due to the legal capacity issues outlined. Accordingly the prior exhaustion of domestic remedies (Article 7(1(e))) could be thwarted more regularly than its equivalent provisions in respect of other treaties and, in the absence of a children's commissioner, or equivalent, children may thus have limited or no recourse in law to challenge the actions of the State. Should such a child be unable to persuade parents, guardians, or a relevant NGO to institute proceeding on her or his behalf, then exhausting domestic proceedings will prove impossible and no complaint to the Committee on the Rights of the Child could be initiated. Furthermore social and cultural imperatives may preclude, or at least dissuade, a child from seeking to institute proceedings, even where capacity is recognised. Challenging parental decisions, a school or the State itself, may be an anathema to a respectful child. There are thus obvious barriers to children accessing the new mechanism in the Third Optional Protocol.

---

[49] See further Committee on the Rights of the Child General Comment 2 (2002) UN Doc CRC/C/2002/2 on the role of national human rights institutions in protecting and promoting children's rights and General Comment 5 (2003) UN Doc CRC/C/GC/2003/5 on general measures of implementation of the Convention on the Rights of the Child (Arts. 4, 42, and 44, para. 6). For the position in Norway, see generally the Act 5 (1981) which established the Ombudsman for Children in Norway, materials available in English on the Barneombudet website at http://www.barneombudet.no/english/. See also the European Network of Children's Ombudsmen, information available at http://www.crin.org/enoc/; N. Thomas, B. Gran and K. Hanson 'An independent voice for children's rights in Europe? The role of independent children's rights institutions in the EU' *International Journal of Children's Rights* 19 (2011): 429.

[50] Paris Principles on National Human Rights Institutions, adopted by General Assembly Resolution 48/134, UN Doc A/RES/48/134 of 20 December 1993, <www2.ohchr.org/english/law/parisprinciples.htm>.

[51] See also the comments of L. Smith, 'Monitoring the CRC' in G. Alfredsson, J. Grimheden, B. Ramcharan and A. de Zayas (eds) *International Human Rights Monitoring Mechanisms, Essays in Honour of Jakob Th. Moller* (Martinus Nijhoff, 2nd ed, 2009) at p. 115.

3. Will Children's Rights be Recognised and Articulated Nationally as Separate from those of their Parents?

Capacity and knowledge are not the sole problems. The congruence and convergence of parental and children's rights adds a further dimension. Earlier treaties note the special minor status of children.[52] The Convention on the Rights of the Child itself reflects the tension between children as independent rights holders and children as 'objects of concern' and thus in need of protection. Children are rights holders under the Convention and, in terms of the third protocol can exercise those rights at the international level, yet children are subject to parental control as indeed may be their rights.[53] The Convention itself recognizes that 'parents or, as the case may be, legal guardians, have primary responsibility for the upbringing and development of the child'.[54] There is strong evidence nationally and internationally that parental rights and responsibilities often usurp those of their children.[55] Children can also be subject to control by the State in respect of their rights, education being an obvious example.[56] As Geraldine Van Bueren notes: '[t]raditionally international law ... has not attempted to regulate the quality of the relationships within the family. ...in order to protect the rights of the child, human rights fora are now having to consider issues concerning State responsibility balanced against the privacy of individual family members'.[57] Undoubtedly the Third Optional Protocol will only magnify this. Just as State sovereignty was once viewed as a barrier to international human rights – it was controversial for international organisations to comment on what was perceived as internal affairs of the State, ie how a State treated its citizens – so now piercing the veil of the family is the new barrier confronting advocates of international human rights. For many people, this will be seen as 'a step too far', creating a 'nanny State', robbing parents of their basic national and even natural law right to bring up their own children.

---

[52] Eg, Article 24 International Covenant on Civil and Political Rights 1966.
[53] Eg, religion – Article 14(2) of the Convention on the Rights of the Child.
[54] Ibid, Article 18(1).
[55] See, *inter alia*, the cases below, 'within both the ECtHR and English courts there has been little attention given to the independent rights of children, which are often subsumed within claims to the rights of their parents', p. 241, S. Choudhry and J. Herring, *European Human Rights and Family Law* (Oxford, Hart, 2010); J. Fortin *Children's Rights and the Developing Law* (Cambridge, Cambridge University Press, 3rd ed, 2009); A. Bainham, *Children: The Modern Law* (Bristol, Jordans 3rd ed, 2005); chapter 2, J. Pardeck *Children's Rights – policy and practice* (Basingstoke, Routledge 2nd ed, 2006); P. Jones and S. Welch *Rethinking Children's Rights –attitudes in contemporary society* (New York, Continuum, 2010).
[56] UN Convention on the Rights of the Child, Article 28.
[57] Van Bueren, G., *The International Law on the Rights of the Child* (The Hague, Kluwer, 1998) at p. 72.

The potential clash of rights claimed by parents/guardians, the State and children in education matters highlights this. Laura Lundy notes that '[t]here are few areas where the private and public dimensions of family life converge to such an extent as when a parent sends his or her child to be educated in a state school'.[58] Many complaints arise when parents or guardians object to aspects of their children's education as provided by the State – States are required to ensure a child is educated, and can even detain a child for that purpose without infringing that child's right to liberty. Indeed it is arguable that there is even a duty incumbent on children to avail themselves of basic educational provision in furtherance of the provisions on developing human rights education.[59]

> Traditionally the interrelationship between the right to education and the right to free-
> dom of conscience has been perceived as a balance between the duties on a State and the
> rights of parents. The child, as the beneficiary of education, was perceived by interna-
> tional law as a valuable but silent receptacle of knowledge.[60]

This creates obvious difficulties if a child wishes to challenge aspects of his or her own rights to education.

The relevant provisions on the right to education frequently reference parents' rights to select and/or influence the education of their children. Article 26(3) of the Universal Declaration qualifies the right of everyone to education, free and compulsory at the elementary stages with a caveat that 'Parents have a prior right to choose the kind of education that shall be given to their children'. This is elaborated in Article 13 (3) of the International Covenant on Economic, Social and Cultural Rights, '[t]he States Parties to the present Covenant undertake to have respect for the liberty of parents and, when applicable, legal guardians to choose for their children schools, other than those established by the public authorities, which conform to such minimum educational standards as may be laid down or approved by the State and to ensure the religious and moral education of their children in conformity with their own convictions.'[61] Perhaps tellingly, no similar provision relating to parents' rights appears in the Convention on the Rights of the Child. Corporal

---

[58] Lundy, L., 'Family Values in the Classroom? Reconciling parental wishes and children's rights in State schools', *International Journal of Law, Policy and the Family* 19 (2005): 346; see also D. Monk, 'Parental Responsibility and Education: taking a long view', in *Responsible Parents and Parental Responsibility* eds. R. Probert, S. Gilmore and J. Herring (Oxford, Hart, 2009).

[59] For an analysis of this tension with respect to sex education, see the aptly titled C. Packer, 'Sex Education: Child's Right, Parent's Choice or State's Obligation?' in *Of Innocence and Autonomy: Children, Sex and Human Rights.* Ed. E. Heinze (Farnham, Ashgate, 2000).

[60] G. Van Bueren *The International Law on the Rights of the Child* (the Hague, Kluwer, 1998), 240.

[61] See also, Article 18(4) International Covenant on Civil and Political Rights.

punishment, religious education and sex education in schools provide rich case law on this matter. In some instances, parents have objected to the education practice/ provision,[62] in other instances, the complaints were brought by, or on behalf of, the child/children.[63]

Arguably there is no real reason why children's views on education should thus be secondary to those expressed by their parents, the more so as the child matures.[64] Children do not, however, have totally unfettered rights. Even under that Convention, children are recognised as being under parental control. Article 5 provides that 'States Parties shall respect the responsibilities, rights and duties of parents or, where applicable, the members of the extended family or community as provided for by local custom, legal guardians or other persons legally responsible for the child, to provide, in a manner consistent with the evolving capacities of the child, appropriate direction and guidance in the exercise by the child of the rights recognized in the present Convention'. Such control is not viewed as subjugation, but rather as constructive and supportive, guiding children towards adulthood.[65] In effect, this reflects both the

---

[62] For examples, see *Hartikainen v. Finland* (agnosticism) Application 40/1978, Human Rights Committee, UN Doc CCPR/C/12/D/40/1978; *R v. Secretary of State for Education and Employment (ex parte Williamson)* [2005] UKHL 15 (corporal punishment) (see generally, H Cullen, 'R (Williamson) v. Secretary of State for Education and Employment – accommodation of religion in education' *Child and Family Law Quarterly* 16(2) (2004): 231; J. Eekelaar, 'Corporal punishment, parents' religion and children's rights' *Law Quarterly Review* 119 (2003): 370; J. Gau, 'Corporal punishment – religious justification – Convention rights' *Ecclesiastical Law Journal* 7 (2004): 491).

[63] For examples on religion, see *Lautsi v. Italy*, above; *Multani v. Commission Scolaire Marguerite-Bourgeoys* [2006] 1 SCR 256 (<http://scc.lexum.org/en/2006/2006scc6/2006scc6 .pdf>) (see also A. Crawford, 'Learning Lessons from Multani: Considering Canada's Response to Religious Garb Issues in Public Schools' *Georgia Journal of International and Comparative Law* 36(1) (2007): 159); *Fatimah binti Sihi v. Meor Atiqularahman* [2005] 2 MLJ 25 (Court of Appeal, Putrajayam) (see also L. Thio and J. Ling-Chien, 'Religious Dress in School: The serban controversy in Malaysia' *International and Comparative Law Quarterly* 55 (2006): 671); *R (on the application of Begum (by her litigation friend, Rahman)) (Respondent) v. Headteacher and Governors of Denbigh High School (Appellants)* [2006] UKHL 15 (see, *inter alia*, M. Idriss, 'Dress codes, the right to manifest religion and the Human Rights Act 1998: the defeat of Shabina Begum in the House of Lords' *Coventry Law Journal* (2006): 58). On corporal punishment, see *Canadian Foundation for Children, Youth and the Law v Canada (Attorney General)* [2004] 1 SCR 76 (discussed R. Leckey, 'Embodied Dignity' *Oxford University Commonwealth Law Journal* 5.1 (2005): 63); and OMCT complaints against various European States before the European Social Committee overseeing the implementation of the Council of Europe's European Social Charters.

[64] See *Lautsi v. Italy*, above.

[65] Eg, Article 14(2) on freedom of religion and belief – see also Article 5(2) of the Declaration on the Elimination of All Forms of Intolerance and Discrimination Based on Religion or Belief 1981. On approaches to children's rights, see the overview in J. Herring, 'Parents and Children' in J Herring (ed.) *Family Law: issues, debates, policy* (Willan Publishing, 2001).

Mill[66] approach (education is the primary responsibility of parents) and Rousseau's concept of education being aimed at securing the independence of the child through evolving supportive individual liberalization.[67]

As Lundy notes, '[i]n schools, as elsewhere, decisions must be made as to the situations in which the benefits of uniformity and equality might be set aside in the interests of the sometimes conflicting goals of tolerance and respect for diversity'.[68] This conflict is set to deepen with the opening of the Convention on the Rights of the Child for individual communications. Preempting this development, it was stated that '[i]n particular, a means must be found to accommodate the child's independent views on the issue as well as the wider public interests at stake.'[69] The latter point remains especially problematic – to what extent should the views of the child be considered when determining the curriculum and discipline within the school environment? Van Bueren concludes her review of the Convention on the Rights of the Child's education provision (written shortly after the convention entered into force) by noting, 'it is too early to conclude whether the reconstructing of the right to education as belonging to the child as well as to the parent will create a wider consensus for change'.[70] Unfortunately, as the cases and communications discussed indicate, no paradigm shift has been effected in the intervening decades although there is increased recognition of children as individual rights holders. Moreover, the issues identified are not unique to education, education has been discussed above as it aptly illustrates the potential difficulties which can arise and challenges a child who considers her or his right to be infringed, may encounter, particularly when the parent/guardian and even the State may claim different, opposing, rights.

The Chair of the Committee on the Rights of the Child acknowledged that some States were for, and some vehemently against, children making complaints and noted that the interests of the parents and the child are often contradictory.[71] Article 2 of the third optional protocol provides: '[i]n fulfilling the functions conferred on it by the present Protocol, the Committee shall be guided by the principle of the best interests of the child. It shall also have

---

[66] Mill, J. *On Liberty* (1859 <www.bartleby.com/130/>) Online part V – Applications, see also E. West, 'Liberty and Education: John Stuart Mill's Dilemma' *Philosophy* 40 (1965): 129.

[67] J. Rousseau, *Emile ou l'education Book 2* (1762, available in English <www.ilt.columbia.edu/pedagogies/rousseau/em_eng_bk2.html>).

[68] Lundy, L., 'Family Values in the Classroom? Reconciling parental wishes and children's rights in State schools', *International Journal of Law, Policy and the Family* 19(2005): 346, 365.

[69] Ibid, L. Lundy at p.366; see also E. Craig, 'Accommodation of Diversity in Education – a Human Rights Agenda?' *Child and Family Law Quarterly* 15(3) (2003): 279; B Hale, 'The voice of the child' *International Family Law Journal* (2007): 171.

[70] Van Bueren, G., *The International Law on the Rights of the Child* (The Hague, Kluwer, 1998) p. 256.

[71] Press release <www.ohchr.org/EN/NewsEvents/Pages/ChildrenComplaints.aspx>.

regard for the rights and views of the child, the views of the child being given due weight in accordance with the age and maturity of the child.' Obviously, this echoes the terminology of Articles 3(1) and 12 of the Convention on the Rights of the Child itself. However, it begs the question whether a child could prove a complaint against the express wishes of his/her parents/guardian, especially when the child lacks any legal capacity.[72] For younger children, the problem is more acute.

Conclusions

When the third optional protocol enters into force, it is clear that the mechanism will have the capacity radically to shape contemporary children's rights. Treating children's rights the same as others' rights is undoubtedly attractive from an equality perspective. Certainly, many proponents of children's rights have long argued for stronger enforcement opportunities.[73] There is further support for this position from a rights perspective as it consolidates the position of the Convention and offers children a more 'child-friendly' process than perhaps would be encountered should the comparable provisions of one of the other core treaties be used.

Notwithstanding the view that the protocol is a positive development, the foregoing analysis indicates a number of potential problems which the Committee and child authors of communications may encounter. Like all other optional individual communication procedures, it is unlikely that the protocol will have a high take up rate. Despite the near universal ratification of the Convention, the experience of other core treaties indicates that many States consider individual communications a step 'too far' at present though they may be willing to be bound by a treaty at the international level, and even to establish a national human rights institution.

The creation of national mechanisms may be a 'side effect' of the protocol, irrespective of the number of ratifications it may attract. This will certainly have the potential to enhance children's rights. Such national mechanisms may take a myriad of forms. The generic form is part of a national human rights institution and thus a mechanism established in accordance with the Paris Principles.[74] A more specific model is that of children's commissioners or ombudspersons, the Norwegian model being one of the earlier and most

---

72) On minor children, see K. Scheiwe, 'Between autonomy and dependency: minors' rights to decide on matters of sexuality, reproduction, marriage, and parenthood: Problems and the state of debate – an introduction', *International Journal of Law, Policy and the Family* (2004): 262.
73) Eg, M. Freeman, 'The Future of Children's Rights' *Children and Society* 14 (2000): 277, 290.
74) Paris Principles, above note 50.

successful examples, as noted above. The UN Committee on the Rights of the Child is forthright in its support for such mechanisms.[75] In Europe, the European Network of Ombudspersons for Children[76] monitors and coordinates activity between national mechanisms. Establishing a national children's mechanism should provide a voice for children, advocate their rights, investigate complaints and offer governmental advice which will not only allow for children's views to be fed into the legislative and political process but also represented at government levels. Positive and sustained representation of children's interests from a non-partisan position would ensure the best interests of the child remain at the forefront of national laws and policies. It should also limit the instances in which children's rights are infringed and thus the need to litigate arises. Should legal action be necessary, some form of national mechanism could facilitate access to the courts, through advice, assistance, and even representation. This can ameliorate the capacity issue.

Perhaps the most problematic issue is the individious position of children, especially younger children lacking legal capacity under national law. The position of the child is often not discussed in national judgments, or even represented adequately, although clearly affected by decisions. None of the corporal punishment cases, for example, were brought by a child, although the European Social Committee (OMCT) and Canadian cases were brought on behalf of the child in the manner anticipated under the third optional protocol. When commenting on national human rights institutions, the UN Committee on the Rights of the Child argues that there are 'additional justifications... for ensuring that children's human rights are given special attention. These include the facts that children's developmental state makes them particularly vulnerable to human rights violations; their opinions are still rarely taken into account; most children have no vote and cannot play a meaningful role in the political process that determines Governments' response to human rights; children encounter significant problems in using the judicial system to protect their rights or to seek remedies for violations of their rights; and children's access to organizations that may protect their rights is generally limited'.[77] Such a mechanism could even diffuse any tension between parents and children offering mediation and reconciliation options if required. An independent entity can also ensure that children's views are heard and considered at all levels.

---

[75] See, eg, its General Comment no. 2, The role of independent national human rights institutions in the promotion and protection of the rights of the child, UN Doc CRC/GC/2002/2 (2002) issued to 'encourage States parties to establish an independent institution for the promotion and monitoring of implementation of the Convention' (para. 2). See also para. 7.

[76] See http://crin.org/enoc for more information including a list of full and associate members.

[77] UN Committee on the Rights of the Child, General Comment 2(2002) above, para. 5.

The questions discussed above indicate areas of difficulty realising children's rights as enforceable through individual complaints. These difficulties are not necessarily insurmountable. The Third Optional Protocol aims to provide a mechanism in furtherance of the effective realization of children's rights. As an objective, this has considerable merit. However, many children's rights can already be litigated under other treaties, thus arguably this development is compounding issues of overlapping treaty obligations and simply layering remedies. Should the Committee on the Rights of the Child maintain its traditional strong focus on children's rights, being guided by the best interests of the child at all times, it is feasible that a new and exciting stream of jurisprudence could emerge in which children's rights even in education, are accorded at least equal weight to the interests of the parents/ guardians and the teachers. That would be truly dramatic progress towards ensuring children's rights are adequately and effectively promoted and protected. Establishing viable and effective national mechanisms seems to be a *sine qua non* of progress towards that goal. Yes, there is a cost implication and no one would maintain they are a panacea for the plight of children around the world. However, they can work and they can be agents of change. For the rhetoric of children's rights to become a reality, maybe just maybe, they are worth considering.

A Child's Right to Enjoy Benefits of Scientific Progress and Its Applications

Brian Gran[a], Margaret Waltz[b] and Holly Renzhofer[b]
a) Professor
brian.gran@case.edu
b) Doctoral students
margaret.waltz@case.edu; holly.renzhofer@case.edu

Introduction

Adopted in 1966 as part of the International Bill of Human Rights, Article 15 of the International Covenant on Economic, Social and Cultural Rights (ICESCR) calls for the rights to take part in cultural life, to benefit from one's artistic, scientific, and other kinds of work, and for the focus of this article, to enjoy benefits of scientific progress and scientific applications (REBSPA). While important research has been undertaken on REBSPA, some experts contend its conceptualization is underdeveloped.[1] As a children's right, REBSPA has not received significant attention.

A child's REBSPA raises questions for and opens the door to possible changes in young people's lives. Extra considerations are needed to implement a young person's REBSPA, given their vulnerability and reliance on adults. These concerns may make the human rights objective of equality more challenging to achieve for young people. If implementation of REBSPA is achieved, young people may experience improvements in health, education, and other areas of life science affects.

After presenting Article 15's REBSPA and its background, this article examines studies of this right, particularly its potential impacts for human rights. It then considers REBSPA's possible effects on children's rights, finding they have not received due attention, even though young people stand to

---

[1] See Richard Pierre Claude, Science in the Service of Human Rights (2002); Audrey R. Chapman, *Towards an Understanding of the Right to Enjoy Benefits of Scientific Progress and its Applications*, 8 (1) Journal of Human Rights 1 (2009); Audrey R. Chapman, *A "Violations" Approach for Monitoring International Covenant on Economic, Social, and Cultural Rights*, 18 (1)

benefit greatly from scientific progress and its applications. Finally, this article presents potential indicators of children's REBSPA, acknowledging that more work is needed to comprehend fully what this right may mean to children.

The International Covenant on Economic, Social and Cultural Rights

Although there are limits to international action on human rights, many improvements in human rights have taken place since World War II.[2] The Universal Declaration of Human Rights offers guidance, help, and inspiration to people, including children, all over the world by 'setting forth the human rights and fundamental freedoms to which all men and women, everywhere in the world, are entitled, without any discrimination.'[3] The Universal Declaration of Human Rights and the International Human Rights Covenants, consisting of both the International Covenant on Economic, Social and Cultural Rights and the International Covenant on Civil and Political Rights, comprise the International Bill of Human Rights. ICESCR was adopted in 1966 and entered into force in 1976.

Article 15 of the International Covenant on Economic, Social and Cultural Rights

Article 15 of the ICESCR states:
1. The States Parties to the present Covenant recognize the right of everyone:
   (a) To take part in cultural life;
   (b) To enjoy the benefits of scientific progress and its applications;

Human Rights Quarterly 23 (1996); Olivier De Schutter, *The Right of Everyone to Enjoy the Benefits of Scientific Progress and the Right to Food: From Conflict to Complementarity*, 33 (2) Human Rights Quarterly 304 (2011); Maya Sabatello, *Advancing Transgender Family Rights through Science: A Proposal for an Alternative Framework*, 33 (1) Human Rights Quarterly 43 (2011); Jeffrey H. Toney, Hank Kaplowitz, Rongsun Pu, Feng Qi, and George Chang, *Science and Human Rights: A Bridge towards Benefiting Humanity*, 32 (4) *Human Rights Quarterly* 1008 (2010); Hans Morten Haugen, *Human Rights and Technology—A Conflictual Relationship?*, 7 Journal of Human Rights 224 (2008); Farida Shaheed, Report of the Special Rapporteur in the field of cultural rights, *The right to enjoy benefits of scientific progress and its applications*, UN General Assembly (2012).
[2] Jack Donnelly, *International Human Rights* (2010); Philip Alston, Ryan Goodman and Henry J. Steiner, *International Human Rights in Context: Law, Politics, and Morals* (2007).
[3] U.N. Office of the High Commissioner for Human Rights, Fact Sheet No.2 [Rev. 1] (1996).

(c) To benefit from the protection of the moral and material interests resulting from any scientific, literary or artistic production of which he is the author.

2. The steps to be taken by the States Parties to the present Covenant to achieve the full realization of this right shall include those necessary for the conservation, the development and the diffusion of science and culture.

3. The States Parties to the present Covenant undertake to respect the freedom indispensable for scientific research and creative activity.

4. The States Parties to the present Covenant recognize the benefits to be derived from the encouragement and development of international contacts and co-operation in the scientific and cultural fields.

The primary focus of this article is the right of young people to enjoy the benefits of scientific progress and its applications (1 (b)). Paragraphs 2 and 3 obligate national governments to take steps so that this right can be realized, including development of science and its diffusion, and ensuring respect of freedoms necessary to scientific research. To meet these obligations, a government must create an environment that allows for free scientific research, for which academic freedom is necessary.[4] A national government must develop international communications about science, as well as protect people from misuse of science.[5]

A corollary to the right to benefits of scientific progress is a general principle that human rights are universal.[6] An overarching goal for implementing human rights is to ensure use of human rights does not differ across suspect, discriminatory classes.[7] Consequently, when implementing a human right such as REBSPA, this human right must benefit the 'most disadvantaged and vulnerable', with one objective of removing barriers to 'mainstream standards'.[8] REBSPA raises particular concerns. For instance, Chapman emphasizes that individuals have the right to be protected from harmful effects of science.[9] Donders (2011) contends that states should not only

---

[4] Venice Statement nd: paragraph 8.
[5] Venice Statement nd: paragraph 13.
[6] Jack Donnelly, Universal Human Rights: In Theory and Practice (2005); Bryan S. Turner, Vulnerability and Human Rights (2006). But see Thomas M. Franck, *Are Human Rights Universal?*, 80 (1) Foreign Affairs 1 (2001).
[7] U.N. Office of the High Commissioner for Human Rights, What are Human Rights?
[8] Audrey R. Chapman, *Reintegrating Rights and Responsibilities: Toward a New Human Rights Paradigm*, in Kenneth W. Hunter and Timothy C. Mack (editors), International Rights and Responsibilities for the Future (1996).
[9] Audrey R. Chapman, Towards an Understanding of the Right to Enjoy Benefits of Scientific Progress and its Applications, 8 (1) Journal of Human Rights 1 (2009).

prevent government agencies from harming people through science, they should protect people from harms arising from actions of third parties.[10]

Progressive realization of rights and minimum core expectations

The principle of progressive realization of human rights articulates that governments should act as expediently and efficiently as they can to implement human rights, but recognizes that implementation and enforcement of many human rights demand resources that may be scarce for some jurisdictions.[11] In countries where resources are limited, governments are expected to need more time to meet human rights requirements.[12]

Some rights are less expensive than others.[13] REBSPA will probably require significant resources, both to establish scientific institutions and to provide on-going support necessary to scientific work and education. Some efforts to implement REBSPA, however, require less resources. For instance, the freedom of scientists to undertake their work necessitates protections to do their work. That is, government merely needs to ensure that others, as well as government, do not interfere with or persecute a scientist who is doing scientific research.

The principle of minimum core obligations is that governments are expected to meet minimum treaty commitments, regardless of available resources. According to the U.N. Office of the High Commissioner for Human Rights, a minimum core obligation imposes on a government that it 'ensure the satisfaction of, at the very least, minimum essential levels of each of the rights...'[14] If a national government fails to implement the minimum basic aspect of a right, whether 'essential' health care or education, among other rights, that failure is '*prima facie*', evidence that it is failing to 'discharge its obligations' according to the relevant treaty.[15]

---

[10] Donders, Yvonne. 2011. 'The right to enjoy the benefits of scientific progress: in search of state obligations in relation to health'. 14 (4) Medicine, Health Care, and Philosophy 371-381.
[11] Audrey R. Chapman, *Reintegrating Rights and Responsibilities: Toward a New Human Rights Paradigm*, in Kenneth W. Hunter and Timothy C. Mack (editors), International Rights and Responsibilities for the Future (1996).
[12] International Covenant on Economic, Social, and Cultural Rights, Article 2 (1966).
[13] Stephen Holmes and Cass Sunstein, The Cost of Rights (2000).
[14] U.N. Committee on Economic, Social, and Cultural Rights, *General Comment Number 3, The nature of States parties obligations* (1990).
[15] Id.

Ratification of ICESCR

At this time 160 national governments have ratified or acceded to the ICESCR. A handful of national governments have signed, but not yet ratified, the ICESCR, including Belize, Comoros, Cuba, Palau, Sao Time and Principe, South Africa, and the United States. By signing a treaty, a government indicates its support of the treaty and its intention to ratify (UNICEF 2012), as well as that the national government will refrain from actions in conflict with the specific treaty.[16] Some countries have neither signed nor ratified the ICESCR, including Andorra, Antigua and Barbuda, Bhutan, Botswana, Brunei, Haiti, Malaysia, Mozambique, Myanmar, Nauru, Oman, Qatar, Saint Kitts and Nevis, Saudi Arabia, Singapore, St. Lucia, Tonga, Tuvalu, the UAE, and Vanuatu.

Reservations, understandings, and declarations

A State Party may qualify its ratification of the ICESCR through filing a reservation, understanding, or declaration. A *reservation* is an instance in which a national government indicates ratification of the ICESCR, except for a particular article (or articles). A reservation may be filed if there is an apparent conflict in law with the ICESCR. *Understandings* are 'interpretive statements that clarify or elaborate' meanings of treaty terms. A *declaration* is an opportunity a national government takes to say its practice, for instance, does not coincide with the particular article, but will at a later date.[17]

There are no reservations, understandings, or declarations concerning Article 15 of the ICESCR.

UN Committee on Economic, Social and Cultural Rights

Established in 1985, the Committee on Economic, Social and Cultural Rights (CESCR) is a group of 18 independent experts 'that monitors implementation of the International Covenant on Economic, Social and Cultural Rights by its States parties.'[18] The Committee holds two sessions a year. Member states are

---

[16] United Nations, *Vienna Convention on the Law on Treaties* (1969). UNICEF. 2012. Definition of Key Terms Used in the UN Treaty Collection. Accessed October 22, 2012: *www.unicef.org/crc/files/Definitions.pdf*.

[17] Congressional Research Service, Library of Congress, *Treaties and Other International Agreements: the Role of the U.S. Senate: A Study Prepared for the Committee on Foreign Relations, U.S. Senate* (2001).

[18] U.N. Office of the High Commissioner for Human Rights, Committee on Economic, Social and Cultural Rights, *Monitoring the economic, social, and cultural rights* (2012).

required to report their progress on the implementation of the rights two years after initially agreeing to the Covenant. After the initial report, States Parties are required to submit a report every five years. The Committee then reviews the reports and addresses issues national governments face in implementing the ICESCR.

The Committee publishes General Comments. In various General Comments, the Committee has emphasized the importance of REBSPA to older individuals (General Comment 6), vocational education (General Comment 13), equal access of men and women to scientific participation (General Comment 16), and protection of moral and material interests arising from scientific production (General Comment 17).[19] The Committee has not yet published a General Comment directly dealing with Article 15's right to enjoy the benefits of scientific progress and its applications.

States Members' Reports to the U.N. Committee

Discussions of Article 15 have historically not been included in the State Members' Reports for the U.N. Committee on Economic, Social and Cultural Rights. In more recent years, however, States Parties have begun to discuss how rights articulated in Article 15 are and are not realized in their countries. This shift occurred around 2006 as nine to ten countries reported on Article 15 in 2005 and 2004 respectively, and roughly 20 countries have been reporting on Article 15 each year since 2006. However, the percentage of reporting countries that mention Article 15 in their report to the Committee varies by year, and ranges from 100 per cent (2004 and 2005) to 76 per cent (2008). The percentages of other reporting countries that mention Article 15 are as follows: 95 per cent (2009, 2011, 2012), 94 per cent (2006), 90 per cent (2007) and 85 per cent (2010). Thus, in the past two years, not only has the number of countries reporting been on the higher end of the range of 20 and 21 (2011 and 2012 respectively), but 95 per cent of those countries reporting have also mentioned Article 15 in their report, an improvement compared to previous years.

When discussing Article 15, however, the main focus of the States Parties' reports has tended to be how they are implementing the right to culture, not

---

19) U.N. Committee on Economic, Social, and Cultural Rights, *The economic, social, and cultural rights of older persons* (General Comment 6; 1995); U.N. Committee on Economic, Social, and Cultural Rights, *The right to education* (General Comment 13; 1999); U.N. Committee on Economic, Social, and Cultural Rights, *The equal right of men and women to the enjoyment of all economic, social and cultural rights* (General Comment 16; 2005), and U.N. Committee on Economic, Social, and Cultural Rights, *The right of everyone to benefit from the protection of the moral and material interests resulting from any scientific, literary or artistic production of which he is the author* (General Comment 17; 2005).

REBSPA. For example, during the reporting session that took place in April of 2012, the five reporting countries of Ethiopia, New Zealand, Peru, Slovakia, and Spain discussed in great detail the laws, constitutional amendments, and executive decrees that are in place to protect the right to cultural life.

In the last year, however, the right to benefits of scientific progress has received new attention by governments in their reports to the U.N. Committee. Government reports tend to emphasize new budget allocations to science, administrative improvements, establishment of scientific institutions, advancement of science education, and identification of significant barriers to implementing REBSPA. When governments discuss young people's rights to benefits of scientific progress, their focus is exclusively on education.

When a government reports on REBSPA, most indicate higher budgetary allocations toward science. For the May 2012 session, the Azerbaijan government referred to a national plan on science, which includes increased budget allocations and administrative improvements (paragraphs 595-598). For the same session, the government of Japan reports that it plans to increase budget outlays toward science and aims to promote scientific endeavours (paragraphs 388-389). In November, the government of Ecuador said it would increase its budget expenditures on science (paragraph 466).

Some governments that report on REBSPA to the U.N. Committee highlight improvements in administration. In its May 2012 report, Japan identifies steps it is taking to advance young people's REBSPA, such as helping a local government organization, Science World Gifu Research Information Center, encourage young people's interest in science (paragraph 403). The May 2012 report by the Iran government indicates its Constitution supports scientific and technological inquiry and investigation, which it undertakes through establishment of research centers and encouragement of researchers (paragraph 439). The December 2012 Lithuanian report identifies establishment of new laws that will promote scientific progress (paragraphs 1136-1138). The Kuwaiti government reports establishment of various organizations that have responsibilities of promoting science (paragraphs 160 and 161). As parts of its economic strategy, Lithuania is employing science and technology parks (paragraphs 1161-1163).

The Japanese government identifies means by which it fosters dissemination of science (paragraphs 391-396) and international cooperation (paragraph 408-411). The Ethiopian government notes that it distributes information about science via radio once a week, and distributes materials about science and technology. The governments of Ecuador (paragraph 474) and Kuwait (paragraph 163) support international cooperation.

Rarely does a government refer to young people's rights to benefits of scientific progress and its applications. When a government does, its concern is education. In its December 2012 report, the Lithuanian government points to education as key to improvements in REBSPA (paragraph 1131). The government of Rwanda emphasizes in its December 2012 report the educational efforts it is taking in promoting REBSPA, including more tuition support, ensuring syllabi emphasize science, and improving elementary science and technology courses (paragraph 321), among other efforts. The New Zealand government has set up the Science Learning Hub, a website where educators and students can find information about science. The Peruvian government reported establishment of a new scholarship that permits graduate work in specific areas, including agriculture and genetic research.

National governments point to limitations and challenges they face in realizing the rights included in Article 15. These limitations range from financial struggles, that enforcing Article 15 requires sufficient resources, to how violence can inhibit human rights advancement. The Rwandan government acknowledges economic difficulties (paragraph 326), as do the Mauritanian, Tanzanian, and Bulgarian governments. The Ethiopian government indicates it is trying to distribute technology, but structures are not in place in many economic sectors. The government indicates its desire to improve university education, but notes that qualified researchers and academics are not sufficiently available, as well as the appropriate infrastructures needed to do research and provide education.

Despite this noticeable upswing in attention given to the right to benefits of scientific progress, the reports filed by the governments of Albania, Denmark, Iceland, Jamaica, and Togo in 2012 do not refer to REBSPA.

The Venice Statement

The Venice Statement arises from a 2009 meeting sponsored by UNESCO that focused on elements of REBSPA and steps needed to implement the right in practice.[20] The Venice Statement outlines three duties belonging to State Parties to the ICESCR: to respect, to protect, and to fulfill. According to the Venice Statement, governments should *respect* freedoms necessary to doing science, such as autonomy, freedom of speech, freedom to assemble in professional societies and to collaborate, and to ensure science is not used to interfere with enjoyment of other human rights and freedoms. Along with respect of other human rights, the Venice Statement indicates expectations that governments should *protect* other human rights from infringement through the use of science and technology, including research subjects. The Venice Statement articulates a duty to *fulfil* several components of the right to

---

[20] *Venice Statement on the Right to Enjoy the Benefits of Scientific Progress and its Applications*, adopted in July 2009 by a group of experts.

benefits of scientific progress. These components range from monitoring harms arising from science to offering opportunities 'for public engagement in decision-making about science and technology and their development...' Governments are obligated to ensure access to benefits of scientific progress does not differ according to discriminatory criteria. Another duty to fulfil is to ensure effective science curricula is instituted in all levels of all schools, which the Venice Statement says will lead to development of scientific skills.

The Venice Statement indicates non-government actors have critical roles to play in implementing REBSPA. Scientists are expected to consider this right as they conduct their research. Civil society actors should advocate for this right and protect victims whose rights have not been respected, protected, or fulfilled. For-profit firms are also expected to advance this right. One example the Venice Statement points to is that for-profit firms should 'consider implementing the Guidelines on Pharmaceutical Companies and Human Rights' (note we believe the proper title is 'Human Rights Guidelines for Pharmaceutical Companies in relation to Access to Medicines'[21]).

UN Expert on and Special Rapporteur in the field of cultural rights

Sociologist Farida Shaheed became the UN Expert and Special Rapporteur in the field of cultural rights in 2009. Her functions focus on cultural rights.[22] According to resolution 19/6 of 22 March 2012, Dr. Shaheed's assignment was extended to 2015. Dr. Shaheed has not reported on concerns surrounding REBSPA arising from country visits to Saint Vincent and the Grenadines (November 2012), the Russian Federation (April 2012), Morocco (September 2011), Austria (April 2011), or Brazil (November 2010). She has initiated discussions about the right via other avenues.

On 9 December 2011, Dr. Shaheed held a Public Consultation in Geneva on 'the right to enjoy the benefits of scientific progress and its applications'.[23] Through this Public Consultation, as independent expert, Dr. Shaheed requested U.N. member states to respond to a set of 11 questions.[24] In addition,

---

[21] U.N. Office of the High Commissioner for Human Rights, *Human Rights Guidelines for Pharmaceutical Companies in relation to Access to Medicines* (2007).
[22] U.N. Human Rights Council, Resolution 10/23, *Independent Expert in the field of cultural rights* (2009); U.N. Human Rights Council, *Resolution 19/6, Special Rapporteur in the field of cultural rights* (2012).
[23] Office of the United Nations High Commissioner for Human Rights, *The right to enjoy the benefits of scientific progress and its applications, Consultation organized by the Independent Expert in the field of cultural rights*, Ms. Farida Shaheed (2011).
[24] Independent expert in the field of cultural rights, Ms. Farida Shaheed, *Questionnaire on the right to enjoy benefits of scientific progress and its applications: Member states* (2011).

Dr. Shaheed posed the same questions to civil society organizations.[25] It is important to note that questionnaires distributed to the member states and stakeholders only contained questions about science education when it came to the interests and rights of young people. On 14 May 2012, the U.N. General Assembly published Dr. Shaheed's report on the Public Consultation.[26] Her report was based on 22 U.N. Members States' responses (note that the Report indicates 21 Member States reported: UN 2012: 3) to the questionnaire, one response by a U.N. agency, the World Intellectual Property Organization, and 12 'stakeholders', including two academics.

In her report to the U.N. General Assembly, Dr. Shaheed notes that REBSPA cannot be considered separate from 'the right to participate freely in the cultural life of the community', the other right articulated in ICESCR Article 15.[27] According to Dr. Shaheed, to fulfill REBSPA, state parties to ICESCR should ensure that science is accessible by everyone, without discrimination.[28] Another key component is that everyone should have opportunities to contribute to science and should enjoy opportunities to participate in decisions about science.[29]

As noted, Dr. Shaheed's mandate does not explicitly refer to REBPSA. Her mandate also does not explicitly refer to young people's rights and interests in scientific progress. In her report to the U.N. General Assembly, however, Dr. Shaheed does emphasize that 'positive steps' should be taken to ensure that young people, as a marginalized group, should not experience discrimination in exercising REBSPA.[30] Dr. Shaheed refers to the International Drug Purchase Facility as an example of an initiative that has produced new medicines and enhanced access to health care for young people.[31] She points to efforts undertaken by some member parties in providing access to computer technologies and the internet to young people as scientific improvements. Dr. Shaheed states that young people should possess the right to express opinions on the institutions through which they receive their science educations.[32] While Dr. Shaheed does discuss obligations of third parties, such as companies and nonprofit organizations, her report does not articulate responsibilities of parents and children's caretakers in ensuring young people's REBSPA.[33]

---

[25] Independent expert in the field of cultural rights, Ms. Farida Shaheed, *Questionnaire on the right to enjoy benefits of scientific progress and its applications: Civil society* (2011).
[26] U.N. General Assembly, *Report of the Special Rapporteur in the field of cultural rights, Farida Shaheed, the right to enjoy the benefits of scientific progress and its applications* (2012).
[27] Id. at 3.
[28] Id. at 1, 9.
[29] Id. at 1, 9, 12.
[30] Id. at 10.
[31] Id. at 11.
[32] Id. at 12.
[33] Id at 19.

Other relevant international treaties

Other international treaties offer insights into Article 15. The UDHR (1948) predates the ICESCR and asserts two rights relevant to science.[34] The first is that everyone has the right to share in the benefits of science and technology. The second is that everyone has the right to have his or her intellectual property protected. The Declaration on the Use of Scientific and Technological Progress in the Interests of Peace and for the Benefit of Mankind declares that while scientific developments should be shared internationally, they should not be used to discriminate or limit an individual's freedoms as declared in the UDHR.[35] The Proclamation of Tehran, International Conference on Human Rights makes three assertions: that states should uphold the standards of the ICESCR; that the rights of the family and the child must be protected; and also that the 'aspirations of the younger generation for a better world ... must be given the highest encouragement'.[36] The Universal Declaration on Bioethics and Human Rights states that the benefits of scientific research should be shared 'with society as a whole and within the international community'.[37] The International Declaration on Human Genetic Data asserts that scientific research must ensure 'accuracy, reliability, quality and security'.[38]

These treaties are evidence of international support of the right to benefits of scientific progress. They indicate national governments not only are aware of, but also have stated their obligation to advance the right to benefits of scientific progress. The U.N. Convention on the Rights of the Child, however, does not delineate a young person's REBSPA.[39]

Scholarship on the right to benefits of scientific progress

Scholars have undertaken groundbreaking work on Article 15, offering insights to policy makers and stakeholders. Chapman asserts that everyone has three rights when it comes to the right to benefits of scientific progress.[40] The first right is to access the benefits of scientific progress and technology without being discriminated against, which includes being able to 'freely participate

---

[34]   Universal Declaration of Human Rights (1948).
[35]   Declaration on the Use of Scientific and Technological Progress in the Interests of Peace and for the Benefit of Mankind (1975).
[36]   Proclamation of Tehran, International Conference on Human Rights (1968).
[37]   Universal Declaration on Bioethics and Human Rights (2005).
[38]   International Declaration on Human Genetic Data (2003).
[39]   U.N. Convention on the Rights of the Child (1989).
[40]   Audrey R. Chapman, *Towards an Understanding of the Right to Enjoy the Benefits of Scientific Progress and Its Applications*, 8 (1) Journal of Human Rights 1 (2009).

in the cultural life of the community'.[41] The second right is to be protected from the harmful effects of science and technology. The third is that everyone has the right to have his or her intellectual property protected. To achieve these three rights, states must first allow for academic freedom. Academic freedom will then enable states to create environments that allow for free scientific research. Finally, states must develop international communication within the field of science, as well as protect their citizens from the misuse of science. Chapman also reminds that societal conditions matter to implementing Article 15.[42]

Müller's work focuses on Section III of the Venice Statement, 'Elements of the Normative Content and State Obligations', because it 'concretises the REBSPA [the right of everyone to enjoy the benefits of scientific progress and its applications] in detail for the first time'.[43] Müller discusses 'how the REBSPA is interpreted; the categorisation of the obligations flowing from it; the understanding of "science" and the aims of science that underlie the right; and the potential for the REPSPA [sic] to function as a cross-cutting principle of the ICESCR'.[44] He concludes that the obligations of the right should 'include, above all, an obligation to create an institutional framework and to adopt policies and laws in relation to science and technology that enable individuals to freely conduct scientific research, to access the benefits of scientific progress and to be protected against the harmful effects of science and technologies'.[45] Additionally, Müller calls for the formation of institutions and policies related to science in accordance 'with human rights principles: namely, non-discrimination and equal treatment; the concentration on marginalized and disadvantaged groups; participation; and international cooperation and accountability'.[46] Lastly, Müller argues that states must be in accordance of Article 2 of the ICESCR and work towards the realization of these rights as quickly as their resources will allow.

Schabas maintains that to implement the right to maintain cultural heritage and take part in cultural life, the state must respect freedom of scientists to conduct research, build facilities for research, preserve the right to culture of minorities, and also protect the rights of indigenous peoples.[47] He contends that science by and large has primarily focused on problems afflicting the rich,

---

[41] Id. at 4.
[42] Id. at 22-23.
[43] Amrei Müller, *Remarks on the Venice Statement on the Right to Enjoy the Benefits of Scientific Progress and its Applications (Article 15(1)(b) ICESCR)*, 10 (4) Human Rights Law Review 765 (2010).
[44] Id. at 767.
[45] Id. at 782.
[46] Id.
[47] William Schabas, *Study of the Right to Enjoy the Benefits of Scientific and Technological Progress and its Applications*, in Yvonne Donders & Vladimir Volodin (editors), Human Rights in Education, Science and Culture, Legal Developments and Challenges, 273-308 (2007).

instead of problems affecting people who have low incomes.[48] As he notes, 'Somewhere in the world – mainly in Africa – one child dies every 30 seconds of malaria'.[49] Implied in Schabas' comments is the notion, which is agreed to by other human rights experts, that because human rights should extend to everyone, those least well off may stand to gain the most.

An American Association for the Advancement of Science (AAAS) coalition is undertaking several efforts to study and provide support to REBSPA.[50] Over 30 scientific organizations are members of the coalition. The AAAS coalition pursues five areas: (1) welfare of scientists, (2) science ethics and human rights, (3) service to the scientific community, (4) service to the human rights community, and (5) education and information resources. The fourth area, service to the human rights community, strives to work with scientists in advancing human rights, particularly REBSPA. The fifth area, education and information resources, is developing syllabi and other educational materials, among other steps.

International conferences have focused on REBSPA. A conference was held in Amsterdam in 2007 and in Galway in 2008 to discuss member parties' obligations in implementing REBSPA. UNESCO, the Amsterdam Center for International Law, and the Irish Centre for Human Rights supported both meetings.[51] In February 2010, Lea Shaver organized a conference on the right to science and culture at Yale University's Law School Information Society Project.[52] During this conference, Shaver pointed out that government actors make choices in devoting resources to REBSPA implementation. Donders noted that what REBSPA means is unclear, and reminded participants that human rights are interrelated. Wyndham urged various constituencies to become involved in helping to realize REBSPA, and Gray and Rens directed attention to whose voices are heard in debates over benefits arising from scientific progress and its applications.[53]

Children's rights to enjoy benefits of scientific progress and its applications

Because little research exists on the role of the right to enjoy benefits of scientific progress and its applications for children, questions about and ramifications of the right for young people deserve more attention.

---

[48] Id. at 297.
[49] Id.
[50] American Association for Advancement of Science, Science and Human Rights, shr.aaas.org.
[51] Report of the Experts' Meeting on the Right to Enjoy Benefits of Scientific Progress and its Applications, Amsterdam (2007).
[52] Yale University Law School Information Society Project, yaleisp.org/2010/02/a2k4main.
[53] Id.

A starting point is to consider vulnerability of young people and their reliance on adults. Scholars contend that the right to scientific advancements is being denied to those vulnerable groups who are not 'independent decision-makers', including children.[54] Given the vulnerabilities of young people, and that young people must often rely on adults, extra attention must be given to children's reliance on adults when it comes to this right. Are additional institutions and resources needed to ensure young people enjoy full entitlement to the right to benefits of scientific progress? For instance, should independent children's rights institutions be asked to monitor enforcement of REBSPA for young people? What consequences do young people face if adults do not enjoy full entitlement to this right? Must adults possess REBSPA before young people can? What concerns arise for young people who do not live with and enjoy the support of their parents and families? Do governments need to take extra steps and devote extra resources to children who live in care of government or foster families?

A major objective is ensuring equality to human rights.[55] How can the goal of equality be extended to young people when it comes to REBSPA? The 2007 experts' conference emphasized concerns about gender differences to REBSPA.[56] In terms of progressive realization and minimum core, are young people entitled to similar, less, or greater expectations to REBSPA relative to adults? How can national governments be sure that young people do not experience discrimination when it comes to their rights, a right articulated in Article 2 of the UNCRC?[57] Do differences by gender in who possesses university degrees in scientific disciplines and professions shape boys' and girls' exercise of their right to benefits of scientific progress?

REBSPA will potentially benefit children in many ways. This right may yield better health outcomes and superior educations, for instance, all of which are considered rights under the Convention on the Rights of the Child. Indeed, REBSPA may intersect with several rights articulated in the UNCRC.

The right to benefits of scientific progress will affect a young person's right to health, which can positively influence the right to survive and develop, one way being through science's impacts on standards of living.[58] Scientific

---

[54] Deborah Cook, Anne Moore-Cox, Denis Xavier, François Lauzier, and Ian Roberts, *Randomized Trials in Vulnerable Populations*, 5 Clinical Trials 61.
[55] Universal Declaration of Human Rights (1948).
[56] Report of the Experts' Meeting on the Right to Enjoy Benefits of Scientific Progress and its Applications, 39, Amsterdam (2007).
[57] U.N. Convention on the Rights of the Child (1989).
[58] Yvonne Donders, *Study on the legal framework of the right to take part in cultural life*, in: Y. Donders and V. Volodin (eds.) Human Rights in Education, Science and Culture: Legal Developments and Challenges (2007); U.N. Convention on the Rights of the Child, Articles 24 and 27 (1989).

advancements can provide cleaner environments and drinking water, access to sufficient nutritious foods, and adequate housing.[59]

To take advantage of medical care, such as communicating concerns to providers and giving medical assent or consent, an understanding of scientific principles will encourage young people to ask questions and approach health care with less anxiety.[60] Children will also benefit from the ability to access information that is important to their health and well-being through mass media.[61]

One of the key means by which a young person can exercise the right to benefits of scientific progress is through education.[62] Technological advancements, like the internet, will benefit young people's education. As Donders argues, a young person's internet access can supplement libraries and textbooks.[63]

Another right belonging to young people is the ability to form an opinion and participate in decision making.[64] Young people can participate in debates over deployment of scientific resources and trade-offs in how scientific resources are used and how decisions are made.[65] Employing the right to information and learning how to digest such information will enable young people to express opinions about scientific progress and to use their vote.[66]

Technology may either help young people implement their rights or be used to thwart enforcement of their rights. In terms of helping young people, DNA evidence may enable a young person to enforce the right not to be illicitly transferred or trafficked, as well as to assure the presumption of innocence in a criminal trial (UNCRC Article 40).[67] As Chapman has emphasized, technology can also be used to weaken rights, particularly those rights belonging to vulnerable groups. During armed conflict, technology can also be used to target locations where young people spend significant time, such as schools and homes. Internet technology is used to traffic young people, which violates

---

[59] German Ministry for Economic Cooperation and Development, *Fact sheet: Energy. A Human Rights-Based Approach in the Energy Sector*, Applying Human Rights in Practice: Fact sheets on a human rights-based approach in development cooperation (2008).

[60] Id.

[61] U.N. Convention on the Rights of the Child, Articles 17 and 24 (1989).

[62] Id., Article 28.

[63] Yvonne Donders, *Study on the legal framework of the right to take part in cultural life*, in: Y. Donders and V. Volodin (eds.) Human Rights in Education, Science and Culture: Legal Developments and Challenges (2007).

[64] U.N. Convention on the Rights of the Child, Articles 14, 23, and 31.

[65] Audrey R. Chapman, *Towards an Understanding of the Right to Enjoy the Benefits of Scientific Progress and Its Applications*, 8 (1) Journal of Human Rights 1 (2009).

[66] Leonard Rubenstein and Mona Younis, *Scientists and Human Rights*, 322 (5906) Science 1303 (2008).

[67] U.N. Convention on the Rights of the Child, Articles 11, 35, and 40 (2)(b)(i)) (1989).

Article 3 of the Optional Protocol to the Convention on the Rights of the Child on the sale of children, child prostitution and child pornography.[68] Medical technology is used to harvest and transfer organs illicitly, a violation of Article 3 of the Option Protocol on the sale of children, child prostitution, and child pornography.[69]

In sum, the right to benefits of scientific progress may enable young people to enforce existing rights, including the right to education. Science can also be used to weaken young people's rights and harm their interests and welfare.

Potential indicators of children's REBPSA

An indicator can reveal whether a young person possesses the right to enjoy the benefits of scientific progress and its application. An indicator can help identify what entities and individuals are responsible for implementing Article 15 (1) (b). An indicator can then be used to determine whether that entity or individual has done its job: to what degree has that entity or individual implemented the human rights treaty?[70] Hunt conceptualized indicators according to three types: structural, process, and outcome.[71] After a review of each type of indicator is undertaken, a discussion of potential indicators fitting each type is presented.

Structural indicator

A structural indicator assesses whether or not 'key structures, systems and mechanisms are in place' that indicate whether a right can be implemented.[72] As such, a structural indicator may indicate whether an institution or institutional feature is in place. A structural indicator can be used to determine degrees by which a national government has made the right to benefit from scientific progress part of their legal system. An example of a structural indicator is whether or not a national government has ratified the ICESCR. ICESCR

---

[68] Optional Protocol to the Convention on the Rights of the Child on the sale of children, child prostitution and child pornography (2000).
[69] Id.
[70] Sakiko Fukuda-Parr, *The Metrics of Human Rights: Complementarities of the Human Development and Capabilities Approach*, The Economic Rights Working Paper Series Working Paper 14. The Human Rights Institute, the University of Connecticut (2010); Judith V. Welling, *International Indicators and Economic, Social, and Cultural Rights*, 30 (4) Human Rights Quarterly 933 (2008).
[71] Paul Hunt, *The right of everyone to enjoy the highest attainable standard of physical and mental health*, Report of Special Rapporteur of the Commission on Human Rights to the UN General Assembly (2003).
[72] Id. at 8.

ratification does not require progressive realization given only government ratification or accession is needed. ICESCR ratification is a sign that a national government invests in rights articulated in the treaty, including REBSPA.

Process indicator

A second type of indicator is a process indicator. A process indicator demonstrates whether activities necessary to reach a particular rights-related objective are being met. Hunt says they measure effort, rather than outcome.[73] Trends in International Mathematics and Science Study (TIMSS) data provide information on number of hours taught toward science education.[74] One variable is proportion of science instructional time as a proportion of total instructional time for eighth graders.[75] TIMSS collects data on math and science proficiency every four years. For the year 2007, TIMSS data are available for 36 countries.

A claim to science education does carry a correlative obligation of a duty holder to provide education. Given significant differences in resources, a claim to science education is expected to be progressively realized. The TIMSS indicator is a proportion of instructional time devoted to science relative to total instruction time, which obviates the need to consider necessary resources. The U.N. Committee on Economic, Social and Cultural Rights has identified provision of basic education as meeting a member parties' minimum obligation.[76] The TIMSS data provide insights into the degree to which member parties are providing basic science education.

Outcome indicator

An outcome indicator indicates the results of the right's implementation. For the right to benefits of scientific progress, an outcome indicator would demonstrate whether young people are benefiting from what we think scientific progress should provide. As such, if we anticipate that a right to benefits of scientific progress will result in quality of life improvements, an outcome indicator would demonstrate whether or not those improvements are found.

---

[73] Id. at 9.
[74] Trends in International Mathematics and Science Study (TIMSS), timssandpirls.bc.edu.
[75] TIMSS, 2007 International Science Report. TIMSS & PIRLS International Study Center, Lynch School of Education, Boston College: Boston, Massachusetts (2007).
[76] U.N. Committee on Economic, Social, and Cultural Rights, *The nature of States Parties' Obligations*, General Comment Number 3 (1990).

Chapman discusses that conceptualizing the right to benefits of scientific progress may focus on fruits, investment, or both.[77] By fruits, she seems to have in mind that people experience improvements resulting from rights implementation. Chapman's idea reminds us of the links between possible indicators: structure of laws that prohibit interference with academic freedom, process of scientific research, and access to scientific knowledge. As Hunt notes, many factors shape outcomes, including structures and processes.[78] For example, a better-educated public on science may partially be due to stronger rights to information.[79]

The percentage of 8th grade students who are proficient in scientific education is an outcome indicator of the right to benefit from scientific progress. Scientific knowledge is one outcome of the right to benefit from scientific progress. In turn, scientific knowledge opens the door to further scientific progress. The OECD Programme for International Student Assessment (PISA) collects data every three years about what knowledge and skills students have learned.[80] PISA data are available for the OECD countries as well as an additional 18 countries.[81]

An examination of children's REBSPA

Do young people enjoy REBSPA? Given the recommendation Dr. Shaheed made to the U.N. General Assembly that, 'States promote science education at all levels and integrate human rights components into all science education, including training and continuing education programmes...,' an analysis of indicators of young people's science education is undertaken.[82]

A structural indicator of a young person's right to benefits of scientific progress is if their national government has ratified the ICESCR. A process indicator is how much educational time is devoted to science. An outcome indicator is the percentage of 8th grade students who scored at a proficient

---

[77] Audrey R. Chapman, *Towards an Understanding of the Right to Enjoy the Benefits of Scientific Progress and Its Applications*, 8 (1) Journal of Human Rights 1 (2009).

[78] Paul Hunt, *The right of everyone to enjoy the highest attainable standard of physical and mental health*, Report of Special Rapporteur of the Commission on Human Rights to the UN General Assembly (2003).

[79] United Nations Development Programme, *A Guide to Measuring the Impact of Right to Information Programmes* (2006).

[80] OECD Programme for International Student Assessment, www.pisa.oecd.org.

[81] Sakiko Fukuda-Parr, Terra Lawson-Remer, and Susan Randolph, *An Index of Economic and Social Rights Fulfillment: Concept and Methodology*, 8 Journal of Human Rights 195 (2009).

[82] U.N. General Assembly, *Report of the Special Rapporteur in the field of cultural rights, Farida Shaheed, the right to enjoy the benefits of scientific progress and its applications* (2012).

Table 1. Indicators of Young People's Right to Benefit from Scientific Progress.

Country	Year of ICESCR ratification	8th grade Science Instructional Time as per cent of total Instructional Time (2007)	8th grade Science Proficiency (Level 4+) (2009)	8th grade Science Proficiency (Level 4+): Boys (2009)	8th grade Science Proficiency (Level 4+): Girls (2009)	8th grade Gender Proficiency Ratio
Australia	1975	12	39.1	39.9	38.2	1.05
Colombia	1969	10	2.6	3.4	2.0	1.70
Hong Kong	1976	10	48.9	50	47.6	1.05
Israel	1991	10	16.8	18.1	15.5	1.17
Italy	1978	6	24.4	25.6	23.2	1.10
Japan	1979	10	46.5	45.3	47.6	0.95
Jordan	1975	13	4.6	3.6	5.5	0.66
Korea, Republic of	1990	11	42	42	42	1.00
Norway	1972	10	26.5	26.5	26.4	1.00
Singapore	Not signed or ratified	14	45.6	45.5	45.8	0.99
Taipei (Taiwan)	2009 (deposit rejected by UN)	12	34.6	36.1	33.1	1.09
Thailand	1999	10	5	4.5	5.4	0.83
Tunisia	1969	5	2.4	2.7	2.0	1.35
Turkey	2003	8	10.2	9.7	10.9	0.89
United States	Signed, but not ratified	13	29.3	32.5	25.9	1.26

level in science. Given concerns about discrimination and overarching objectives of equality when it comes to human rights, this article examines a gender ratio of 8th grade science proficiency as an indicator of equality in outcomes. Fourteen countries are selected that span Africa, Asia, the Americas, Europe, the Middle East, and Oceania. These 14 countries are not diverse when considering wealth. All belong to upper middle income or high income economies, according to the World Bank.

This analysis suggests critical differences exist across and within countries in children's REBSPA. Considering structures of whether or not a national government has committed to ensuring its citizens enjoy REBSPA, of the 14 examined countries, 12 national governments have acceded to or ratified ICESCR. Only two have not yet ratified: Singapore and the United States. The Taiwan government attempted to deposit its ratified ICESCR, but the United Nations rejected it. Globally, this structural indicator indicates strong commitments have been made to children's REBSPA.

A process of ensuring young people experience REBSPA is time spent on science education. The U.N. Expert recommends that U.N. member states support science education.[83] Data from TIMSS provide evidence of substantial differences in instructional time devoted to science education, ranging from a low of 5 per cent in Tunisia to a high of 14 per cent in Singapore. It is important to note that for the other country whose national government that has not ratified, the United States, the proportion of instructional time devoted to science is second highest, tied with Jordan, at 13 per cent.

An outcome of a child's REBSPA is whether the child comprehends scientific ideas. An indicator of this outcome is what proportion of students achieves Level Four on the 2009 PISA proficiency scale, which is based on six levels. If a student achieves Level Four proficiency, she can understand science's role in phenomena, including comprehending how scientific explanations are useful to understanding 'life situations'.[84] Students attaining Level Four are capable of communicating decisions using 'scientific knowledge and evidence'. Students attaining Level Four comprehend scientific ideas and applications beyond basic knowledge. Jordan, second highest in devoting instructional time to science, scores third lowest in 8th grade proficiency, with only 4.6 per cent of its 8th grade students achieving Level Four or higher. Colombia devotes 10 per cent of instructional time to science, yet scores second lowest, 2.6 percent of its 8th grade students achieving Level Four or higher proficiency. Italy, which devotes the second lowest proportion of instructional time to science, nevertheless scores almost in the middle when considering the proportion of its 8th grade students achieving Level Four proficiency or higher.

A goal of human rights is equality, particularly when it comes to human rights advances. Considering gender ratios of science proficiency among grade students, across ten of the examined countries, larger percentages of boys experience Level Four proficiency or higher compared to girls, with Colombia having the greatest disparity, 1.7 between male and female students. In four countries, more girls enjoy Level Four proficiency or higher relative to boys, with 5.5 per cent of 8th grade girls living in Jordan testing at Level Four proficiency or higher compared to 3.6 per cent of 8th grade boys. It is important to note that for the two cases at the extremes, Colombia and Jordan, low proportions of 8th grade students achieve Level Four proficiency or higher.

---

[83] Id. at 20.
[84] PISA, PISA 2009 Results: What Students Know and Can Do: Student Performance in Reading, Mathematics, and Science (2010).

Hong Kong is an example of a country whose young people seem to possess strong rights to enjoy benefits of scientific progress and applications. Hong Kong ratified the ICESCR in 1975. Its typical school devotes a high proportion of instructional time to science among compared countries, and it has the largest proportion of 8th grade students achieving Level Four proficiency or higher. On the one hand, ICESCR ratification does not automatically result in extensive REBSPA. Of the examined countries, Tunisia's government was among the first to ratify the ICESCR. Nevertheless, compared to the other countries, in Tunisia the amount of instructional time devoted to science is among the lowest, and typical Tunisian students fare poorly on science proficiency exams. On the other hand, not ratifying ICESCR does not clearly result in less science education and worse science proficiency outcomes for young people. While Singapore has not yet ratified the ICESCR, on average its schools devote the most instructional time to science, and its typical student scores among the highest on proficiency levels.

High proportions of instructional time devoted to science do not necessarily result in scientific proficiency among young people. As noted, considering a young person's education, a typical young person living in Jordan experiences the second highest proportion of educational time devoted to science, yet its average student scores among the lowest science proficiency scores.

These indicators point to the need to undertake research on questions about how legal structures shape human rights processes, and what other factors are necessary to attain strong outcomes for children's rights. They raise questions about the importance of human rights treaties to processes thought positively to impact young people's lives, including whether children enjoy the benefits of scientific progress and its applications.

Conclusion

Efforts are accelerating to clarify the meaning of the right to enjoy the benefits of scientific progress and its applications, and what its implications are for human rights and actors and institutions that will shape implementation of the right. Various actors are taking crucial steps to implement the right, as evidenced by the Vienna conference and the recent work of the U.N. expert.

For young people, the meaning and ramifications of the right to benefits of scientific progress have not received significant attention, yet they may be consequential. This article is a small step forward in deliberating on this right for young people and how it may affect their lives, including important implications for other children's rights.

REBSPA may open the door to significant improvements in young people's lives, and may at the same time produce greater vulnerability and inequality for young people. It is clear that implementation of the right to benefits of scientific progress may lead to improvements in young people's health and well being, to greater participation in their communities, and to stronger legal protections, among other advances. To enjoy this right, however, children will rely on adults, particularly parents and caretakers, and institutions adults control, to understand and benefit from this right. For instance, if a child's parents do not possess strong science backgrounds, their efforts to help and protect their child may be limited. The society in which a child becomes an adult will shape a young person's exercise of this right. If their community, for example, does not support equal education among girls and boys, children and their society will face long-term challenges in benefiting from scientific progress.

This article presents initial analyses of potential indicators of young people's right to benefits of scientific progress. These analyses indicate indicators are available and accessible to begin analyses of children's right to benefits of scientific progress. Inequalities in young people's outcomes arising from the right to enjoy benefits of scientific progress are demonstrated through a science education indicator.

Indicators of young people's REBSPA indicate that whilst ICESCR ratification is widespread, the amount of instructional time devoted to scientific education varies across countries. Indeed, children living in countries whose national governments have not ratified the ICESCR may still receive comparatively high amounts of scientific instructional time, and comparative proportions of young people may score well on science proficiency exams. One indicator, a ratio of science proficiency, presents evidence that girls and boys do not experience similar outcomes from the right to benefits of scientific progress. This evidence suggests further research is needed to explore how and why young people experience the right to enjoy benefits of scientific progress and its applications.

International Human Rights Standards and Child Imprisonment: Potentialities and Limitations

Barry Goldson[a] and Ursula Kilkelly[b]
a) Charles Booth Chair of Social Science, Department of Sociology, Social Policy and
Criminology, School of Law and Social Justice, The University of Liverpool, UK
b.goldson@liv.ac.uk
b) Professor of Law and Dean, Faculty of Law, University College Cork, Ireland
u.kilkelly@ucc.ie

Introduction

It is practically impossible to determine, with any degree of accuracy, the number of child prisoners worldwide. As Harvey and Lloyd have observed:

> different countries have different definitions of [penal] detention, different methods of collection and collation of data and many countries have ineffectual or nonexistent statistical collection. Therefore data is unreliable and difficult to compare.[1]

Notwithstanding the difficulties in retrieving and collating reliable comparative data, however, authoritative sources estimate that, at any given time, approximately one million children are imprisoned worldwide.[2] Despite the shocking nature of this statistic it is almost certainly an under-estimate.[3] For example, more than 600,000 children and young people are imprisoned annually in the USA alone.[4]

What is clear is that wherever we might care to look around the world, child prisoners are typically drawn from the poorest, most disadvantaged, structurally vulnerable and oppressed sections of their respective populations, and children from racial and ethnic minorities are persistently over-represented.[5]

---

[1] R. Harvey & A. Lloyd, *Youth Justice in Action Campaign Report* (London: Children's Legal Centre and YCare International, 2006) 27.

[2] P.S. Pinheiro, *World Report on Violence Against Children* (Geneva: United Nations, 2006) 191.

[3] C. Hamilton et al., *Administrative Detention: A Global Report* (London: UNICEF Child Protection Section, 2011) 1.

[4] Annie E. Casey Foundation, *Kids Count Data Book: Moving Youth from Risk to Opportunity* (Baltimore: Annie E Casey Foundation, 2004) 9.

[5] See P.S. Pinheiro, *World Report on Violence Against Children* (Geneva: United Nations, 2006); A. Piquero, 'Disproportionate minority contact', *Future of Children* 18(2) (Fall 2008): 59–79;

Furthermore, the low level of social value routinely afforded to such children (often deemed 'unsuitable victims' with 'lesser status'), 'renders them particularly prone, by omission or commission, to systematic maltreatment'.[6] In other words, child prisoners are especially susceptible to a wide spectrum of human rights violations including, at the sharp end, multiple expressions of violence.

In February 2003, Paulo Sergio Pinheiro was appointed, at Assistant Secretary-General level, to direct the 'United Nations Secretary-General's Study on Violence Against Children' (the Study).[7] The principal objective of the Study was to investigate all forms of violence against the world's children and to analyse the impact of such phenomena. The Study was undertaken in collaboration with the Office of the High Commissioner for Human Rights, the United Nations Children's Fund and the World Health Organisation. Informed by comprehensive consultations with government departments, international human rights agencies, civil society organisations, research institutions and children and young people themselves, it comprises the most wide-ranging and detailed analysis of its type in history. Throughout the course of the Study, a series of 'thematic consultations' – involving leading international experts – convened in order to provide subject-specific reports. In the 'Violence Against Children in Conflict with the Law' report, the Director of the Study observed that:

> Children in conflict with the law ... are one of the *most vulnerable* groups to the *worst forms of violence* ... Public opinion about the involvement of children in illegal activities and the search for immediate answers have led to the introduction of insane repressive methods ... the *recurrent* and *banalised* use of *institutionalization* is surely problematic.[8]

Furthermore, the NGO Advisory Panel to the Study stated that:

> "tough on crime" policies and negative media and public images of ... socio-economically disadvantaged children'; 'the over-use of detention' and '*impunity* and *lack of accountability*

J. Hayes & G. O'Reilly, *Emotional Intelligence, Mental Health and Juvenile Delinquency* (Cork: Juvenile Mental Health Matters, 2007); B. Goldson, 'Child incarceration: Institutional abuse, the violent state and the politics of impunity', in *The Violence of Incarceration.* eds. P. Scraton & J. McCulloch (London: Routledge, 2009) 86–10. UNICEF, *Justice for Children: Detention as a Last Resort Innovative Initiatives in the East Asia and Pacific Region* (UNICEF, 2011).

[6] B. Goldson, 'Child incarceration: Institutional abuse, the violent state and the politics of impunity', in *The Violence of Incarceration.* eds. P. Scraton & J. McCulloch (London: Routledge, 2009) 89.

[7] P.S. Pinheiro, *World Report on Violence Against Children* (Geneva: United Nations, 2006).

[8] P.S. Pinheiro, 'Opening remarks from Paulo Sergio Pinheiro', in NGO Advisory Panel for the United Nations Secretary-General's Study on Violence Against Children *Violence Against Children in Conflict with the Law: A Thematic Consultation* (Geneva: United Nations, 2005) 17–18.

by law enforcement agents, institutions and staff, [are] some of the key issues that facilitate violence against children in the justice system.[9]

Set against a backdrop of global child imprisonment and the widespread violations of children's human rights, it is somewhat paradoxical that the United Nations Convention on the Rights of the Child (CRC) – the most widely ratified human rights instrument in the world – provides, at Article 37(c), that the arrest, detention or imprisonment[10] of children should only ever be applied as 'a measure of last resort and for the shortest appropriate period of time' and that 'every child deprived of liberty shall be treated with humanity and respect for the inherent dignity of the human person, and in a manner which takes into account the needs of persons of his or her age'. So, whilst the CRC falls short of prohibiting the detention of children altogether, it imposes obligations on States Parties to limit its use and to ensure that, if and when imprisoned, children are treated appropriately. There is manifest tension, therefore, between the practical realities of child imprisonment (globally) on the one hand and the provisions of international human rights standards on the other hand.

Such paradox and tension lies at the heart of this article which aims to examine critically the application of international human rights standards, treaties, rules, conventions and guidelines to the actual practices of child imprisonment. We recognise the vital *potentialities* of the CRC and related human rights standards to pacify the more problematic excesses of child imprisonment. But we also remain cognisant of the practical *limitations* of international human rights law and reserve a sense of scepticism in respect of the legitimacy of – what might be termed – 'human rights approaches' to the penal detention of children.

Applying International Human Rights Standards to Challenge the 'Adultification' of Child Prisoners

Our article has its origins in a collaborative intervention designed to challenge the continued practice of detaining children under 18 years in St Patrick's Institution in Ireland, an adult penal establishment. St Patrick's Institution is a medium security prison and at the time of the intervention it held boys and young men between the ages of 16-21 years. The provisions of the Children Act

---

9) NGO Advisory Panel for the United Nations Secretary-General's Study on Violence Against Children, *Violence Against Children in Conflict with the Law: A Thematic Consultation* (Geneva: United Nations, 2005) 4.

10) Although Article 37 includes all forms of deprivation of liberty, this article is concerned with penal detention only. Accordingly, the terms 'imprisonment', 'penal detention' and 'detention' are used interchangeably throughout the article.

2001, as amended, allow the penal detention of children (aged 16-17 years) – remanded or sentenced – in St Patrick's Institution with adults (aged 18-21 years).[11] The practice of mixing child and adult prisoners in this way has attracted censure from authoritative international human rights bodies including: the United Nations Committee on the Rights of the Child,[12] the Council of Europe Commissioner for Human Rights[13] and, most recently, the European Committee of Social Rights.[14] Furthermore, in 2011, the European Committee for the Prevention of Torture and Inhuman and Degrading Treatment recommended – in respect of the continued detention of children in St Patrick's Institution – that 'the Irish authorities take the necessary steps to ensure that juveniles deprived of their liberty in Ireland are held in appropriate detention centres for their age group'.[15] In addition to the forceful critique and recommendations made by the international human rights bodies, prominent non-governmental organisations including the Irish Penal Reform Trust,[16] together with the independent watchdog, the Ombudsman for Children, have, for many years, campaigned for the removal of children from St Patrick's Institution.[17] More recently, such efforts have finally begun to yield positive effects.

In 2012, the Minister for Children and Youth Affairs announced the first step in a process that will end the detention of children in St Patrick's Institution. From 1 May 2012 all 16-year olds sentenced or remanded to penal detention are sent to a Children Detention School,[18] with the result that, at the time of

---

[11] Under the Children Act 2001, children under 16 years are detained in Children Detention Schools.

[12] United Nations Committee on the Rights of the Child, (2006) *Consideration of Reports submitted by States Parties Under Article 44 of the Convention Concluding Observations: Ireland*, CRC/C/IRL/CO2, paras. 72–73.

[13] Council of Europe, (2008), Report of the Council of Europe Commissioner for Human Rights Thomas Hammarberg on his Visit to Ireland 26-30 November 2007, CommDH (2008), paras. 68–72.

[14] Council of Europe, *European Committee of Social Rights Conclusions 2011 (Ireland), Articles 7, 8, 16, 17, 19 and 27 of the Revised Charter*, p.19.

[15] Council of Europe, *Report to the Government of Ireland on the visit to Ireland carried out by the European Committee for the Prevention of Torture and Inhuman or Degrading Treatment or Punishment (CPT) from 25 January to 5 February 2010*, CPT/Inf (2011) 3, para. 26.

[16] Irish Penal Reform Trust, *Detention of Children: International Standards and Best Practice* (Dublin: IPRT, 2009). See also Irish Penal Reform Trust, *PRT Briefing: Detention of Children in St Patrick's Institution* (Dublin: IPRT, 2011).

[17] Ombudsman for Children (2006) *Advice of the Ombudsman for Children on the Proposed Changes to the Children Act 2001*, pp. 19–21. On the specific circumstances of detention in St Patrick's see Ombudsman for Children, *Young People in St Patrick's Institution A Report by the Ombudsman for Children's Office* (Dublin: OCO, 2011).

[18] 'Minister Fitzgerald to End Detention of 16 and 17 Year Olds in St. Patrick's Institution. New Ministry Secures Capital Funding to End Detention in Adult Prison After 27 Years of Inaction'. 2nd April 2012. See the details of the Press Statement at: http://www.dcya.gov.ie/viewdoc.asp?DocID=1842.

writing (September 2012) only 17 year olds remain in St Patrick's.[19] The provisions of international human rights standards – that prohibit the detention of children with adults and support a 'child-appropriate regime' – and the pressure exerted by national and international organisations were particularly persuasive in achieving this change in practice. As such they are indicative of the *potentialities* of applying such standards in campaigning for, and achieving, progressive penal reform.[20] Paradoxically, however, precisely the same case also exposes the intrinsic *limitations* of such approaches. Indeed, the extent of reform remains circumscribed in two key ways. First, newly remanded and/or sentenced 17-year-old children continue to be sent to St Patrick's Institution pending the development and expansion of the Children Detention School estate.[21] Second, children aged 17 who are currently detained in St Patrick's Institution continue to be imprisoned with adults, in conditions that fall far short of international human rights standards.

Although the 'adultification' of child prisoners has been, and remains, a particular problem in Ireland, it is by no means exceptional (see below). Many other jurisdictions/countries continue to detain children with adults and/or fail to provide a 'child-appropriate regime' for child prisoners.[22] As stated, however, the case pertaining to St Patrick's Institution illuminates the value - notwithstanding the limitations – of strategically mobilising international human rights standards (reinforced by academic research and practice experience) in efforts to drive progressive reform. We turn now towards an elaboration of the core provisions of such standards.

International Human Rights Standards and Child Imprisonment

Three key instruments comprise the foundations of international law in respect of juvenile/youth justice in general and child imprisonment in particular.

First, the *United Nations Standard Minimum Rules for the Administration of Juvenile Justice* (the 'Beijing Rules') were adopted by the United Nations

---

[19] In August 2012, the last 16-year old was released from St Patrick's Institution. See Cormac O'Keefe, 'Call to speed up release of 17-year-old boys from jail', Irish Examiner, 7 August 2012 at http://www.irishexaminer.com/ireland/call-to-speed-up-release-of-17-year-old-boys-from -jail-203294.html.

[20] Ibid.

[21] Although their population has fallen significantly in recent years, and they offer a regime more focused on children's welfare the Children Detention Schools are not, themselves, immune from criticism. See the recent reports of the Health Information and Quality Authority, the independent inspectorate that inspects the Schools at http://www.hiqa.ie.

[22] B. Goldson & J. Muncie, 'Towards a global 'child friendly' juvenile justice?', *International Journal of Law, Crime and Justice* 40(1) (2012): 47–64.

General Assembly in 1985.[23] The Rules provide guidance for the protection of children's human rights in the development of separate and specialist juvenile/youth justice systems. Rule 19.1 states: 'the placement of a juvenile in an institution shall always be a disposition of last resort and for the minimum necessary period' and Rules 17.1(b) and 17.1(d) provide: 'restrictions on the personal liberty of the juvenile shall... be limited to the possible minimum' and 'the well-being of the juvenile shall be the guiding factor in his or her case'.

Second, the *United Nations Guidelines on the Prevention of Delinquency* (the 'Riyadh Guidelines') were adopted by the United Nations General Assembly in 1990.[24] The Guidelines are underpinned by diversionary and non-punitive imperatives: 'the successful prevention of juvenile delinquency requires efforts on the part of the entire society to ensure the harmonious development of adolescents' (para. 2); 'formal agencies of social control should only be utilized as a means of last resort' (para. 5) and 'no child or young person should be subjected to harsh or degrading correction or punishment measures at home, in schools or in any other institutions' (para. 54).

Third, the *United Nations Rules for the Protection of Juveniles Deprived of their Liberty* (the 'Havana Rules') were adopted by the United Nations General Assembly in 1990.[25] The Rules centre a number of core principles including: deprivation of liberty should be a disposition of 'last resort' and used only 'for the minimum necessary period' and, in cases where children are deprived of their liberty, the principles, procedures and safeguards provided by international human rights standards, treaties, rules and conventions must be seen to apply.

The core provisions contained within the 'Beijing Rules', the 'Riyadh Guidelines' and the 'Havana Rules' were bolstered, in 1990, when the CRC came into force. As noted, Article 37 is especially salient in providing that: 'no child shall be subjected to torture or other cruel, inhuman or degrading treatment or punishment' (Article 37a); 'imprisonment of a child shall be... used only as a measure of last resort and for the shortest appropriate period of time (Article 37b) and 'every child deprived of liberty shall be treated with humanity and respect for the inherent dignity of the human person, and in a manner which takes into account the needs of persons of his or her age. In particular, every child deprived of liberty shall be separated from adults unless it is considered in the child's best interest not to do so' (Article 37c).

---

23) United Nations Standard Minimum Rules for the Administration of Juvenile Justice (The Beijing Rules) Adopted by General Assembly resolution 40/33 of 29 November 1985.

24) United Nations Guidelines for the Prevention of Juvenile Delinquency (The Riyadh Guidelines) Adopted and proclaimed by General Assembly resolution 45/112 of 14 December 1990.

25) United Nations Rules for the Protection of Juveniles Deprived of their Liberty. Adopted by General Assembly resolution 45/113 of 14 December 1990.

In order to monitor the implementation of the CRC into law, policy and practice, the CRC provides for the *United Nations Committee on the Rights of the Child* comprising of 18 democratically elected members drawn from the 193 States Parties that have ratified the Convention. The main monitoring mechanism used by the Committee is the reporting process after which the Committee adopts formal Concluding Observations containing its assessment of the extent to which implementation has been achieved in the State Party in question.[26] The Committee also issues 'General Comments' to elaborate the means by which the provisions and requirements of the CRC should be applied within specific subject-domains.[27] The 'General Comment' in respect of juvenile/ youth justice[28] emphasises the principle that jurisdictional systems must seek to safeguard the child's dignity at *every point of the justice process* and stresses that recourse to judicial proceedings (and especially custodial detention) should only ever be operationalised as measures of *last resort*. In short, the 'Comment' provides that the primary aims of human rights-compliant juvenile/youth justice are to meet the child's needs and to protect their best interests.

The United Nations/global human rights instruments are further buttressed, within the European context, by a movement towards 'child friendly justice' driven by the Council of Europe. By extending the human rights principles that inform the 'European Rules for Juvenile Offenders Subject to Sanctions or Measures',[29] the Committee of Ministers has formally adopted specific 'Guidelines for Child Friendly Justice'.[30] The Council of Europe emphasises that the objective of the 'guidelines' is to:

---

[26] The third Optional Protocol to the CRC, adopted by General Assembly Resolution 66/138 of 19 December 2011, makes provision for individual children to communicate complaints to the Committee for consideration. The Protocol has not yet entered into force.

[27] Between 2001-09 the United Nations Committee on the Rights of the Child issued 12 'General Comments': 'The Aims of Education'; 'The Role of Independent Human Rights Institutions'; 'HIV/AIDS and the Rights of the Child'; 'Adolescent Health'; 'General Measures of Implementation for the Convention on the Rights of the Child'; 'Treatment of Unaccompanied and Separated Children Outside Their Country of Origin'; 'Implementing Child Rights in Early Childhood'; 'The Right of the Child to Protection from Corporal Punishment and Other Cruel or Degrading Forms of Punishment'; 'The Rights of Children with Disabilities'; 'Children's Rights in Juvenile Justice'; 'Indigenous Children and Their Rights Under the Convention' and 'The Right of the Child to be Heard'.

[28] United Nations Committee on the Rights of the Child, *General Comment No. 10: Children's Rights in Juvenile Justice*, Forty-fourth session, 15 January-2. February (Geneva: Office of the High Commissioner for Human Rights, 2007).

[29] Council of Europe, *European Rules for Juvenile Offenders Subject to Sanctions or Measures* (Strasbourg: Council of Europe Publishing, 2009).

[30] Council of Europe, *Guidelines of the Committee of Ministers of the Council of Europe on Child Friendly Justice,* (Adopted by the Committee of Ministers on 17 November 2010 at the 1098th meeting of the Ministers' Deputies), (Strasbourg: Council of Europe, 2010).

guarantee the respect and the effective implementation of all children's rights at the high-est attainable level... giving due consideration to the child's level of maturity and under-standing and the circumstances of the case... [Child friendly] justice is accessible, age appropriate, speedy, diligent, adapted to and focused on the needs and rights of the child, respecting the rights of the child.[31]

In short, taken together the United Nations and the Council of Europe human rights standards, treaties, rules, conventions and guidelines provide what is now a well-established 'unifying framework' for modeling juvenile/youth justice statute, formulating policy and developing practice in all nation states to which they apply.[32] Within this general context, four key issues that pertain particularly to the practices of child imprisonment merit further attention: the separation of child and adult prisoners; the provision of 'child appropriate regimes'; the protection of child prisoners' rights and the operation of independent complaints and inspection mechanisms.

The Separation of Child and Adult Prisoners

Since the establishment of discrete juvenile justice systems throughout Europe in the 19th century, the practice of separating children from adults in penal facilities has been driven in part by knowledge of the negative consequences of exposing children to more 'hardened' adult offenders and the associated desire to reduce the risk of 'contamination'. Furthermore, there is a substantial volume of international evidence illuminating the fact that many child/youth prisoners have compelling (unmet) welfare needs and many children and young people import multiple vulnerabilities into penal institutions.[33] There is also widespread knowledge of bullying in youth custody, whereby younger children are particularly prone to intimidation from older youths (and adults). On both counts – reducing the prospect of 'contamination' and offsetting the

---

[31] Council of Europe, *Guidelines of the Committee of Ministers of the Council of Europe on Child Friendly Justice,* (Adopted by the Committee of Ministers on 17 November 2010 at the 1098th meeting of the Ministers' Deputies), (Strasbourg: Council of Europe, 2010): section 11(c).

[32] For a fuller discussion see B. Goldson & G. Hughes, 'Sociological criminology and youth justice: Comparative policy analysis and academic intervention', *Criminology and Criminal Justice* 10(2) (2010): 211–230.

[33] See for example: F. Farrant, *Troubled Inside: Responding to the Mental Health Needs of Children and Young People in Prison* (London: Prison Reform Trust, 2001); B. Goldson, *Vulnerable Inside: Children in Secure and Penal Settings* (London: The Children's Society, 2002); R. Harris & N. Timms, *Secure Accommodation in Child Care: Between Hospital or Prison or Thereabouts?* (London: Routledge, 1993); Her Majesty's Chief Inspector of Prisons, *Young Prisoners: A Thematic Review by HM Chief Inspector of Prisons for England and Wales* (London: Home Office, 1997); D. Lader, N. Singleton & H. Meltzer, *Psychiatric Morbidity among Young Offenders in England and Wales* (London: Office for National Statistics, 2000).

risk of harm – it is imperative to ensure that children are completely separated from adults in penal detention.

With respect to the legal requirements, Article 1 of the CRC defines a child as 'every human being below the age of 18 years unless, under the law applicable to the child, majority is attained earlier'. This means that every child – including children in conflict with the law/young offenders – is entitled to the rights that are protected and promoted by the provisions of the Convention. Equally, as discussed, Article 37(c) of the Convention makes special provision for the rights of children deprived of their liberty and, in particular 'every child deprived of liberty shall be separated from adults unless it is considered in the child's interests not to do so'. Furthermore, according to the United Nations Committee on the Rights of the Child, this means, put simply, that no child deprived of his/her liberty shall be placed in 'an adult prison or other facility for adults'.[34] Underpinning this right, the Committee refers to 'abundant evidence that the placement of children in adult prisons or jails compromises their basic safety, well-being, and their future ability to remain free of crime and to reintegrate'.[35]

Additionally, the imperative to ensure the separation of child and adult prisoners has been reinforced by the European Committee for the Prevention of Torture (CPT), the body established under the Council of Europe's *European Convention for the Prevention of Torture and Inhuman and Degrading Treatment or Punishment*. Indeed, the experience of the CPT – which conducts periodic and *ad hoc* inspections of detention facilities throughout the 47 Council of Europe member states – has led to it recommending a strengthening of the CRC Article 37 standard and the removal of any exception to the rule that child prisoners should be separated from their adult counterparts,[36] noting that 'the risks inherent in juvenile offenders sharing cellular accommodation with adult prisoners are such that this should never occur'.[37]

The Provision of 'Child-Appropriate Regimes'

In the relatively rare cases where a child's behaviour places her/him and/or others at demonstrable serious risk in the community and where there is literally no suitable non-custodial alternative available to the courts, it may be necessary – as a measure of last resort and for the shortest appropriate period of time – to restrict the liberty of the child. International law is clear that in

---

[34] Committee on the Rights of the Child, General Comment No 10, CRC/C/GC/10, para. 85.
[35] Committee on the Rights of the Child, General Comment No 10, para 85.
[36] Committee for the Prevention of Torture and Inhuman or Degrading Punishment, 28th Annual Report 2007-2008.
[37] Portugal – CPT/Inf (2009) 13, para. 42.

such cases where detention is deemed unavoidable, small welfare oriented secure children's homes – that can be managed in ways that are both human rights compliant and practically effective[38] – are most fit for purpose. Conversely, prison detention in general and, more particularly, placing children in *adult* prison detention is singularly inappropriate.

It follows that States Parties should establish 'separate facilities for children deprived of their liberty, which include distinct, child-centred staff, personnel, policies and practices.'[39] More generally, Article 40 of the CRC provides that every child alleged as, accused of, or recognised as having infringed the criminal law has a right to be treated:

> in a manner consistent with the promotion of the child's sense of dignity and worth, which reinforces the child's respect for the rights and freedoms of others and which takes into account the child's age and the desirability of promoting the child's reintegration and the child's assuming a constructive role in society.

This is supported by academic research (extending across a range of disciplines) revealing that children in conflict with the law are a particularly vulnerable group, whose circumstances warrant special treatment.[40] In recent years, neuroscience research on brain development combined with the standard contained in Article 37 of the CRC has persuaded the United States Supreme Court that children are less culpable than adults for their behaviour, causing it to revisit its approach to the sentencing of juveniles (including the question of whether a child should be detained in penal custody).[41]

The Protection of Child Prisoners' Rights

Consistent with the requirement for a 'child appropriate regime' in penal facilities for children, the United Nations Committee on the Rights of the Child[42] has specified a range of additional rights pertaining to child prisoners as follows:

---

[38] See for example: B. Goldson, *A Sense of Security: Curricula for the Induction and Training of Staff in Secure Accommodation* (London: National Children's Bureau, 1997); P. Gabbidon & B. Goldson, *Securing Best Practice* (London: National Children's Bureau, 1997).

[39] Committee on the Rights of the Child, General Comment No 10, para. 85.

[40] See, for example, L. Steinberg & E. Scott, *Rethinking Juvenile Justice* (Harvard University Press, 2008); L. McAra & S. McVie, 'Youth crime and justice: Key messages from the Edinburgh study of youth transitions and crime', *Criminology and Criminal Justice* 10 (2010): 211–230.

[41] *Roper v Simmons 543 US 551 (2005); Graham v Florida 560 US (2010) and JDB v North Carolina 564 US (2011)*. See also *Miller v Alabama*, decided 25 June 2012, which found the imposition on a juvenile of life without parole in non-homocide cases to be contrary to the US Constitution's protection from cruel and unusual punishment.

[42] Committee on the Rights of the Child, General Comment No 10, para. 89.

- Children should be provided with a physical environment and accommodations which are in keeping with the rehabilitative aims of residential placement, and due regard must be given to their needs for privacy, sensory stimuli, opportunities to associate with their peers, and to participate in sports, physical exercise, in arts, and leisure time activities;
- Every child of compulsory school age has the right to education suited to his/her needs and abilities, and designed to prepare him/her for return to society;[43] in addition, every child should, when appropriate, receive vocational training in occupations likely to prepare him/her for future employment;
- Every child has the right to be examined by a physician upon admission to the detention/correctional facility and shall receive adequate medical care throughout his/her stay in the facility, which should be provided, where possible, by health facilities and services of the community;
- The staff of the facility should promote and facilitate frequent contacts of the child with the wider community, including communications with his/her family, friends and other/persons or representatives of reputable outside organizations, and the opportunity to visit his/her home and family;
- Restraint or force can be used only when the child poses an imminent threat of injury to him or herself or others, and only when all other means of control have been exhausted. The use of restraint or force, including physical, mechanical and medical restraints, should be under close and direct control of a medical and/or psychological professional. It must never be used as a means of punishment. Staff of the facility should receive training on the applicable standards and members of the staff who use restraint or force in violation of the rules and standards should be punished appropriately;
- Any disciplinary measure must be consistent with upholding the inherent dignity of the child and the fundamental objectives of institutional care; disciplinary measures in violation of article 37 of CRC must be strictly forbidden, including 'corporal punishment, placement in a dark cell, closed or solitary confinement, or any other punishment that may compromise the physical or mental health or well-being of the child concerned.'[44] On the issue of separation, the CPT has recommended its use 'in extremely rare cases' for security and safety reasons in order to protect highly vulnerable juveniles or to deal with juveniles who pose a threat to others.[45] Clearly the placement of juveniles in isolation for periods longer than a few days does not meet this standard'.

Furthermore, both the *United Nations Rules on the Protection of Juveniles Deprived of their Liberty* (the Havana Rules) and the *European Rules for Juvenile Offenders Subject to Sanctions or Measures*[46] impose extensive specifications for regimes in penal institutions holding child prisoners including the right to protection from harm, to health, to education and leisure and to contact with

---

[43] Research shows that there are difficulties inherent in ensuring that children enjoy their right to education to the maximum extent in detention. See Lanksey, 'Promise or Compromise? Education for young people in secure institutions in England', *Youth Justice* 11(1) (2011): 47–60.

[44] See also Committee on the Rights of the Child, General Comment No 13, *The Right of the Child to Freedom from All Forms of Violence*, CRC/C/GC/13 (2011).

[45] Committee for the Prevention of Torture and Inhuman or Degrading Punishment, 18th Annual Report, p 11.

[46] Recommendation (Rec) 2008 11, adopted by the Committee of Ministers of the Council of Europe on 5 November 2008 .

family and the 'outside world'.[47] Given the particular vulnerabilities of child prisoners to violence – as reported by the United Nations Secretary-General's Study on Violence Against Children (see above) – the Council of Europe Commissioner for Human Rights has also recommended that 'small facilities are likely to provide safe[r] environments for children', and he has proposed the adoption of additional measures – to be set out in national law – to ensure that the rights of all child prisoners are protected.[48]

The Operation of Independent Complaints and Inspection Mechanisms

It is clear that giving legal protection to the rights of child prisoners does not, in itself, guarantee that the same rights will be upheld in practice. Accordingly, international standards provide that efficient and robust complaints procedures and representation systems must be in place to ensure that children in penal detention can access remedies if and when their rights are violated. Equally, monitoring mechanisms must be maintained in order that penal institutions holding children are routinely and rigorously independently inspected.[49] The United Nations Committee on the Rights of the Child[50] states:

- Every child should have the right to make requests or complaints, without censorship as to the substance, to the central administration, the judicial authority or other proper independent authority, and to be informed of the response without delay; children need to know about and have easy access to these mechanisms;
- Independent and qualified inspectors should be empowered to conduct inspections on a regular basis and to undertake unannounced inspections on their own initiative; they should place special emphasis on holding conversations with children in the facilities, in a confidential setting.

Similarly, the Council of Europe *Guidelines on Child-friendly Justice* specify that children must have access to independent complaints mechanisms and be provided with information necessary to enable them to make effective use of such remedies.[51]

---

[47] See also Penal Reform International, *Safeguarding Children in Detention: Independent Monitoring Mechanisms for Children in Detention* (London: Penal Reform International, 2011) 44–57.

[48] Commissioner for Human Rights, *Issues Paper on Juvenile Justice*, at pp 14–15.

[49] For more detailed discussion see Penal Reform International, *Safeguarding Children in Detention: Independent Monitoring Mechanisms for Children in Detention* (London: Penal Reform International, 2011).

[50] Committee on the Rights of the Child, General Comment No 10, para 89. More generally see Committee on the Rights of the Child, General Comment No 5, CRC/GC/2003/5, paras. 24 and 65.

[51] The Guidelines on Child-friendly Justice were adopted by the Council of Europe Committee of Ministers on 17 November 2010.

International Human Rights Standards in Practice

Several commentators have highlighted considerable dissonance between the *rhetoric* of human rights discourse and the *reality* of juvenile/youth justice interventions (especially penal detention) for many children.[52] Indeed, the United Nations Committee on the Rights of the Child has itself observed that:

> ... many States parties still have a long way to go in achieving full compliance with CRC, e.g. in the areas of procedural rights, the development and implementation of measures for dealing with children in conflict with the law without resorting to judicial proceedings, and the use of deprivation of liberty only as a measure of last resort... This may be the result of a lack of a comprehensive policy for the field of juvenile justice. This may also explain why many States parties are providing only very limited statistical data on the treatment of children in conflict with the law.[53]

Such dissonance is apparent from even a schematic review of reports produced by the Committee on the Rights of the Child, the European Committee for the Prevention of Torture (CPT), other human rights agencies and academic researchers with regard to the four key issues considered here.

The Separation of Child and Adult Prisoners

The Equal Justice Initiative in the USA has noted that:

> Juveniles placed in adult prisons are at heightened risk of physical and sexual assault by older, more mature prisoners... Children sentenced to adult prisons typically are victimized because they have 'no prison experience, friends, companions or social support.' Children are five times more likely to be sexually assaulted in adult prisons than in juvenile facilities.[54]

---

52) See for example: B. Abramson, *Juvenile Justice: The 'Unwanted Child' of State Responsibilities. An Analysis of the Concluding Observations of the UN Committee on the Rights of the Child, in Regard to Juvenile Justice from 1993 to 2000* (Brussels: International Network on Juvenile Justice/ Defence for Children International, 2000); Defence for Children International, *From Legislation to Action? Trends in Juvenile Justice Systems Across 15 Countries* (Geneva: Defence for Children International, 2007); B. Goldson & J. Muncie, 'Towards a global 'child friendly' juvenile justice?', *International Journal of Law, Crime and Justice* 40(1) (2012): 47–64; U. Kilkelly, 'Youth justice and children's rights: Measuring compliance with international standards', *Youth Justice: An International Journal* 8(3) (2008): 187–192; J. Muncie, 'The punitive turn in juvenile justice: Cultures of control and rights compliance in western Europe and the USA', *Youth Justice: An International Journal* 8(2) (2008): 107–121.

53) Committee on the Rights of the Child, General Comment No 10, para 1.

54) Equal Justice Initiative, *Cruel and Unusual: Sentencing 13- and 14-Year Old Children to Die in Prison* (Alabama: Equal Justice Initiative, 2008) 14.

Similarly, the *New York Times* has reported that:

> youths under 18... in adult jails or prisons... according to federal statistics... made up only 1 per cent of the inmates in jails and prisons, but 21 percent of the victims of sexual violence. Numerous studies show that placing children in adult prisons leads to more suicide, victimization and recidivism, which is costly in both human and economic terms.[55]

Despite this, James Austin and his colleagues found – in a 'study [that] represents the most thorough examination to date of the issues presented by youth who are incarcerated in adult facilities'[56] – that:

> Approximately 107,000 youth (younger than 18) are incarcerated on any given day; of these, approximately 14,500 are housed in adult facilities. The largest proportion, approximately 9,100 youth, are housed in local jails, and some 5,400 youth are housed in adult prisons. Of the 50 states and the District of Columbia, 44 house juveniles (age 17 and younger) in adult jails and prisons'.[57]

Of course, the United States is the only advanced western democracy not to have ratified the CRC and, as such, it is not bound by its Article 37(c) provision: 'every child deprived of liberty shall be separated from adults'.[58] Not unlike the USA, however, and with the same damaging effects, the practice of detaining children in adult penal institutions continues to apply in many countries that have ratified the CRC. In the Australian state of Queensland, for example, the Commission for Children and Young People and Child Guardian observe: 'there is a compelling child rights-based justification for the removal of 17 year olds from adult prisons' before going on to note:

> The treatment of 17 year olds as adults in the criminal justice system and their incarceration in adult prisons, is contrary to Australia's obligations under the *United Nations Convention on the Rights of the Child* and ignores the recommendations of the Australian Human Rights and Equal Opportunity Commission and the Australian Law Reform Commission.[59]

---

[55] Editorial, *New York Times* 'Children Can Never be Safe in Adult Prisons' (April 8, 2012) Available at: http://www.nytimes.com/2012/04/09/opinion/children-can-never-be-safe-in-adult-prisons.html.

[56] J. Austin, K. Dedel Johnson & M. Gregoriou, *Juveniles in Adult Prisons and Jails: A National Assessment* (Washington DC: United States Department of Justice, 2000) x.

[57] Ibid: x.

[58] However, as noted above, the CRC has been influential in recent Supreme Court jurisprudence around sentencing of those under 18 years.

[59] Commission for Children and Young People and Child Guardian, *Removing 17 year olds from Queensland Adult Prisons and Including Them in the Youth Justice System* (Brisbane: Commission for Children and Young People and Child Guardian, 2010) 10–11.

Equally, the Committee on the Rights of the Child has drawn attention to similar violations of children's human rights in several European jurisdictions. For example:

> Austria, Finland, Ireland, Germany, Portugal, Switzerland and the UK... have each been specifically criticized for failing to separate children from adults in custody and/or for facilitating easier movement between adult and juvenile systems owing to diminishing distinctions between the two.[60]

The Committee has also expressed serious concern about the ill-treatment of children by adult inmates in mixed detention facilities in Hungary.[61]

The CPT has professed similar critique. Following its visit to Ireland in 2010, for example, it concluded that 'St Patrick's Institution does not provide a suitable environment for the detention of juveniles (conditions, regime, staffing)',[62] and recommended that 'the Irish authorities take the necessary steps to ensure that juveniles deprived of their liberty in Ireland are held in appropriate detention centres for their age group.[63] Furthermore, the CPT has highlighted comparable human rights violations following its visits to Germany,[64] Estonia,[65] Croatia,[66] Slovakia[67] and Portugal.[68] Failure to separate children from adults in pre-trial detention and in police custody is also an ongoing concern.[69] In all such cases girls are especially disadvantaged, with Penal Reform International contending that it is particularly important that girls 'are held separately from women, given that girls make up a very small percentage of young offenders and the right of girls to be held separately from women is frequently violated'.[70]

The Provision of 'Child-Appropriate Regimes'

The CPT has claimed that 'the essential components of an appropriate custodial environment for juveniles are: accommodation in small units; a proper

---

[60] B. Goldson & J. Muncie, 'Towards a global 'child friendly' juvenile justice?', *International Journal of Law, Crime and Justice* 40(1) (2012): 52.

[61] Committee on the Rights of the Child, Concluding Observations: Hungary, CRC/C/HUN/CO, para. 61.

[62] Committee for the Prevention of Torture and Inhuman or Degrading Punishment, Report to the Government of Ireland on the Visit to Ireland carried out by the CPT from 25 January to 5 February 2010, para. 26.

[63] Ibid.

[64] Germany - CPT/Inf (2007) 18, p. 44.

[65] Estonia - CPT/Inf (2005) 6, p. 17.

[66] Croatia – CPT/Inf (2008) 30, p. 23.

[67] Slovakia - CPT/Inf (2010) 1, p. 41.

[68] Portugal - CPT/Inf (2009) 13, p. 24.

[69] See for example, Slovenia - CPT/Inf (2008) 7, p. 37.

[70] Penal Reform International, *Safeguarding Children in Detention: Independent Monitoring Mechanisms for Children in Detention* (London: Penal Reform International, 2011) 50.

assessment system to ensure suitable allocation to units; a multi-disciplinary team (preferably of mixed gender) selected and specially trained for work with juveniles.'[71] It has also emphasised that 'juveniles who are deprived of their liberty ought to be held in detention centres specifically designed for persons of this age, offering regimes tailored to their needs and staffed by persons trained in dealing with the young'.[72]

In practice, however, the extent to which such standards apply and children's human rights are respected varies greatly, both *between* and *within* States Parties.[73] In some countries, such variation is contingent upon the legal status of child prisoners (children on remand often receive a much poorer regime relative to those who have been sentenced),[74] while in others the failure to adapt penal regimes to meet the specific needs of girls is a key issue.[75] As the CPT has explained: 'while a lack of purposeful activity is detrimental for any prisoner, it is especially harmful for juveniles, who have a particular need for physical activity and intellectual stimulation'.[76] For this reason, the Committee on the Rights of the Child has been particularly critical of countries that fail to ensure that child prisoners have sufficient opportunity for learning, working or participating in social, educational or arts courses.[77]

In many countries the physical fabric of penal institutions holding children is manifestly unfit for purpose. In England and Wales, for example, the Chief Inspector of Prisons has observed that:

> One of the most important factors in creating a safe environment is size... The Prison Service, however, may hold children in what we regard as unacceptably high numbers and units. Units of 60 disturbed and damaged adolescent boys are unlikely to be safe... There are therefore already significant barriers to the Prison Service being able to provide a safe and positive environment for children; and the question whether it should continue to do so is a live one.[78]

---

[71] Turkey – CPT/Inf (2005) 18, para. 73.

[72] Ireland – CPT/Inf (2011) 3, para. 26.

[73] Austria - CPT/Inf (2010) 5, pp. 37-38.

[74] For example see Finland - CPT/Inf (2009) 5, page 39; Slovakia - CPT/Inf (2010) 1, page 41. For further discussion on this issue see S. Freeman & M. Seymour, '"Just Waiting": The nature and effect of uncertainty on young people in remand custody in Ireland', Youth Justice: An International Journal 10(2) (2010): 126–142.

[75] Greece - CPT/Inf (2010) 33, p. 58. For further general discussion on this issue see: Burman & Batchelor, 'Between two stools? Responding to young women who offend', Youth Justice: An International Journal 9(3) (2009): 270–285; All Party Parliamentary Group on Women in the Criminal Justice System, *Inquiry on Girls: From Courts to Custody* (London: The Howard League for Penal Reform, 2012).

[76] Cyprus - CPT/Inf (2008) 17, p. 31. Committee on the Rights of the Child, Concluding Observations: Latvia, CRC/C/LVA/CO/2, para. 62.

[77] Committee on the Rights of the Child, Concluding Observations: Estonia, CRC/C/15/Add.196, para. 50.

[78] Her Majesty's Chief Inspector of Prisons, *Annual Report of HM Chief Inspector of Prisons for England and Wales, 2001–2002* (London: The Stationery Office, 2002) 36–37.

Specialisation among staff is also thought to be crucial for the purposes of implementing a 'child-appropriate regime' and the CPT has repeatedly emphasised the importance of ensuring that all staff working with child prisoners are: suitably experienced, skilled and qualified; recruited with care; offered specially tailored induction and provided with ongoing training. Moreover, it has recognised, in respect of Ireland for example, that working with children in penal institutions may be challenging and as a result:

> The staff called upon to fulfill that task should be carefully selected for their personal maturity and ability to cope with the challenges of working with – and safeguarding the welfare of – this age group. More particularly, they should be committed to working with young people, and be capable of guiding and motivating the juveniles in their charge. All such staff should receive professional training, both during induction and on an ongoing basis, and benefit from appropriate external support and supervision in the exercise of their duties.[79]

Such imperatives often fail to translate into practice, however. With regard to the Netherlands, for example, the CPT has noted: 'a high rate of staff turnover combined with the difficulty in recruiting new, well-trained staff, obviously has an impact on the quality of care provided',[80] and, in Austria, it found that newly appointed staff working with children in penal institutions receive insufficient specialised training.[81] Whether regimes in penal institutions can ever truly be 'child appropriate' is a matter for debate. More certain is that – despite the international human rights standards – child prisoners across the world are regularly exposed to unsuitable treatment and conditions. In England this prompted Mr Justice Munby, a High Court Judge, to conclude that:

> They ought to be – I hope they are – matters of the very greatest concern to the Prison Service, to the Secretary of State for the Home Department and, indeed, to society at large. For these are things being done to children by the State – by all of us – in circumstances where the State appears to be failing, and in some instances failing very badly, in its duties to vulnerable and damaged children... [these are] matters which, on the face of it, ought to shock the conscience of every citizen.[82]

---

[79]   Ireland - CPT/Inf (2011) 3, p. 25.
[80]   Netherlands - CPT/Inf (2008) 2, p. 38. For a fuller discussion on the general issue see: B. Goldson, *A Sense of Security: Curricula for the Induction and Training of Staff in Secure Accommodation* (London: National Children's Bureau, 1997); P. Gabbidon & B. Goldson, *Securing Best Practice* (London, National Children's Bureau, 1997).
[81]   Austria - CPT/Inf (2010) 5, p. 34.
[82]   Munby, The Honourable Mr Justice, *Judgment Approved by the Court for Handing Down in R (on the application of the Howard League for Penal Reform) v. The Secretary of State for the Home Department*, 29 November, (London, Royal Courts of Justice, 2002): paras. 172 and 175.

The Protection of Child Prisoners' Rights

Despite the range of international standards pertaining to the protection of child prisoners' rights, problems with implementation persist throughout Europe, as elsewhere in the world.[83] At the extremes the CPT has described conditions as appalling[84] but, more routinely, obstructions to maintaining family contact, exposure to harm – from other prisoners, prison and police officers and/or self-induced – and the imposition of segregation and solitary confinement characterise fundamental violations of human rights.

It is not uncommon for child prisoners to be confined in penal institutions at great distance from their families making the maintenance of regular contact extremely difficult. For example, the CPT has questioned whether child prisoners in Latvia have sufficient opportunities to maintain contact with their families and has recommended that the Latvian authorities abolish restrictions on child prisoners' contacts with the outside world.[85] Similarly, in Poland, the Committee on the Rights of the Child has criticised the fact that not all penal detention centres facilitate contact with family or provide adequate living standards for child prisoners.[86] The CPT has also criticised the quality of facilities made available for family visits in the UK and has made a number of recommendations for improvement.[87]

The duty of care and the obligation to protect child prisoners from harm is embedded within the international human rights standards, but both the CPT and the Committee on the Rights of the Child have expressed profound concerns in this regard. The CPT has identified problems of inter-prisoner violence in Ireland[88] and Latvia, [89] for example. Bullying, in all of its forms, is a particular problem. Perhaps the most obvious expression of bullying is physical assault, much of which goes unreported – thus unrecorded – owing to the intense antipathy to the practice of 'grassing' within penal culture and, worse still, the consequences of being labelled a 'grass'. In the UK, 56 per cent of children surveyed by Her Majesty's Chief Inspector of Prisons in one Young Offender Institution reported that they had felt 'unsafe', 'nearly a quarter said they had been hit, kicked or assaulted' and there 'had been 150 proven assaults

---

[83] For an assessment of 'best practice' in this area see Irish Penal Reform Trust, *Detention of Children: International Standards and Best Practice* (Dublin: IPRT, 2009) available at ww.iprt.ie.
[84] Lithuania - CPT/Inf (2009) 22, p. 28 and p. 18 in respect of police detention; Montenegro – CPT/INf(2010) 3, para. 114.
[85] Latvia - CPT/Inf (2009) 35, p. 44.
[86] Committee on the Rights of the Child, Concluding Observations: Poland, CRC/C/15/Add.194, para 50.
[87] United Kingdom – CPT/inf (2009) 30, p. 47.
[88] Ireland –CPT/Inf (2011) 3, para. 32.
[89] Latvia - CPT/Inf (2009) 35, p. 25.

in eight months'.[90] Furthermore, child prisoners are also exposed to other forms of 'bullying' including sexual assault; verbal abuse (including name-calling; threats; racist, sexist and homophobic taunting); extortion and theft; and lending and trading cultures – particularly in relation to tobacco – involving exorbitant rates of interest that accumulate on a daily basis.[91]

In addition to inter-prisoner bullying, child prisoners are also vulnerable to violence from prison and police officers. Following its visit to Latvia, for example, the CPT reported serious allegations of child prisoners being abused by prison staff[92] and when it visited Austria, several allegations were received from children in respect of physical and/or verbal abuse during police questioning.[93] Similar concerns were expressed following the CPT's visits to Denmark,[94] Lithuania[95] Poland[96] and Slovenia.[97] In the latter case, the CPT expressed concern about the fact that such allegations were not taken seriously by the judiciary and others in authority and recommended that 'these allegations [should] be recorded in writing, a forensic medical examination immediately ordered, and the necessary steps taken to ensure that the allegations are properly investigated'.[98]

The use of disciplinary measures and 'restraint' techniques (the application of physical force) are also a common cause for concern. The CPT has made it clear that 'all forms of physical chastisement must be both formally prohibited and avoided in practice... and that inmates who misbehave should be dealt with only in accordance with the prescribed disciplinary procedures'.[99] The Committee has drawn specific attention to the inappropriate use of 'restraint'. In the Netherlands, the Committee expressed concern about the systematic handcuffing of child prisoners and the manner and duration of 'restraints'.[100] In respect of the UK, the CPT asserted that 'only specifically designed non-pain compliant manual restraint techniques, combined with better risk assessment of young people and enhanced staffing skills should be used in juvenile establishments'.[101] Despite this recommendation, however, the use of 'restraint' on

---

[90] Her Majesty's Chief Inspector of Prisons, *Annual Report of HM Chief Inspector of Prisons for England and Wales, 2003–2004* (London: The Stationery Office, 2005) 56.
[91] B. Goldson & D. Coles, *In the Care of the State? Child Deaths in Penal Custody in England and Wales* (London: INQUEST, 2005) 28.
[92] Latvia - CPT/Inf (2009) 35, p. 25.
[93] Austria - CPT/Inf (2010) 5, p. 12.
[94] Denmark - CPT/Inf (2008) 26, p. 14.
[95] Lithuania - CPT/Inf (2009) 22, p. 12.
[96] Poland - CPT/Inf (2006) 11, p. 12.
[97] Slovenia - CPT/Inf (2008) 7, pp. 12-13.
[98] Slovenia - CPT/Inf (2008) 7, p.13.
[99] The Former Yugoslavia Republic of Macedonia - CPT/Inf (2008) 5, para. 117.
[100] Netherlands - CPT/Inf (2008) 2, pp. 41-43.
[101] United Kingdom – CPT/inf (2009) 30, p.50.

child prisoners in England and Wales continues to be both widespread and damaging. The Ministry of Justice and the Youth Justice Board have reported: '6,904 incidents of restraint in 2009/2010, of which 257 resulted in injury'[102] and the Chief Inspector of Prisons has observed that 'in most establishments the use of force remain[s] high'.[103] In one private penal institution for children the Chief Inspector of Prisons explained that 'due to serious concerns about... Oakhill Secure Training Centre, we were asked... to inspect and report... using our expertise in custodial contexts. We found... staggering levels of use of force [which]... had been used 757 times in nine months'.[104] The Chief Inspector reported similarly on a state-managed prison, adding that such practices are also inadequately reviewed and/or monitored:

> At Castington, we found, and surveys showed, that the use of restraint was high; moreover, it had resulted in four confirmed or suspected fractures among children and young people. There had been no external independent review. Only in two of the eight establishments was use of force adequately monitored by the safeguarding committee.[105]

The CPT has also focused on self-harming behaviour amongst child prisoners and has advised that special measures are necessary to ensure children's protection. In respect of Ireland, for example, the CPT recommended a 'proactive approach by the prison health-care services... particularly as regards psychological and psychiatric care' with 'individual assessment(s) of their needs at regular intervals'.[106] Moreover, in respect of the UK the Committee has highlighted the importance of ensuring that 'the health care service offered to juveniles constitute(s) an integrated part of a multidisciplinary (medico-psycho-social) programme of care' including 'close coordination between the work of an establishment's health care team (doctors, nurses, psychologists, etc.) and that of other professionals (including social workers and teachers) who have regular contact with the minors' with a view to ensuring that 'the health care delivered to juveniles deprived of their liberty forms part of a seamless web of support and therapy'.[107] Notwithstanding such recommendations, however, self-harm remains widespread in penal institutions holding

---

102) Ministry of Justice and the Youth Justice Board Youth Justice Statistics 2009/10 England and Wales (London: Ministry of Justice, 2011) 4.

103) HM Chief Inspector of Prisons for England and Wales, *Annual Report 2010–11* (London: HM Inspectorate of Prisons, 2011) 62.

104) HM Chief Inspector of Prisons for England and Wales, *Annual Report 2007–08* (London: HM Inspectorate of Prisons, 2009) 69.

105) HM Chief Inspector of Prisons for England and Wales, *Annual Report 2008–09* (London: HM Inspectorate of Prisons, 2010) 67.

106) Ireland –CPT/Inf (2011) 3, para. 57. On this issue see also Ombudsman for Children, *Young People in St Patrick's Institution A Report by the Ombudsman for Children's Office* (Dublin: OCO, 2011) 34–38.

107) United Kingdom - CPT/Inf (2009) 30, para. 97.

children. In a period of just 11 months, for example, there were 1,324 reported incidents of self-harm by children in Young Offender Institutions in England and Wales alone.[108] Moreover, at the extremes, self-harm can be fatal. Between July 1990 and January 2005, for example, 28 children died in penal custody in England and Wales.[109]

Finally, the vexed question of solitary confinement or segregation. According to the CPT, if children are to be 'held separately from others, it should be for the shortest possible period of time and they should in all cases be guaranteed appropriate human contact.'[110] The Committee has also noted 'any form of isolation of juveniles is a measure that can compromise their physical and/or mental well-being' and has recommended that such a measure be 'highly exceptional' and 'last no longer than is strictly necessary'.[111] Notwithstanding this, the solitary confinement of child prisoners in Austria, the Netherlands, Germany and Spain has been heavily criticised by the CPT[112] and the Committee on the Rights of the Child has raised similar concerns in respect of Denmark.[113] In England and Wales an independent inquiry reported that – over an 18 month period – six penal institutions 'used solitary confinement 2,329 times' and, of the five institutions that provided information about the number of children segregated '519 had been placed in solitary confinement'.[114] Such children, it was found, 'could be held in segregation for days and even weeks at a time'.[115]

The Operation of Independent Complaints and Inspection Mechanisms

Robust inspection and independent monitoring of penal institutions is vital if there is to be any prospect of protecting and promoting the human rights of child prisoners. Complaints and representation mechanisms are also essential and, according to the CPT, child prisoners should:

---

[108] HM Chief Inspector of Prisons for England and Wales, *Annual Report 2004–05* (London: HM Inspectorate of Prisons, 2006) 16.
[109] B. Goldson & D. Coles, *In the Care of the State? Child Deaths in Penal Custody in England and Wales* (London: INQUEST).
[110] Cyprus - CPT/Inf (2008) 17, p. 37.
[111] CPT 18th General Report, p. 11.
[112] Austria - CPT/Inf (2010) 5, page 43; Netherlands - CPT/Inf (2008) 2, page 40; Germany - CPT/Inf (2007) 18, page 48; Spain - CPT/Inf (2011) 11, p. 64.
[113] Committee on the Rights of the Child, Concluding Observations: Denmark, CRC/C/DNK/CO/3, para. 58.
[114] The Lord Carlile of Berriew QC, *An Independent Inquiry into the Use of Physical Restraint, Solitary Confinement and Forcible Strip Searching of Children in Prisons, Secure Training Centres and Local Authority Secure Children's Homes* (London: The Howard League for Penal Reform, 2006) 61.
[115] Ibid: 64.

have avenues of complaint open to them, both within and outside the establishments' administrative system, and be entitled to confidential access to an appropriate independent authority (for example, a visiting committee or a judge) that is competent to receive – and, if necessary, act upon – juveniles' complaints.[116]

In respect of the UK, the CPT has noted that it is 'important that young persons with potential grievances are able to make themselves heard either through the formal complaints system or through being given an opportunity to express themselves directly to staff (in the presence of their caseworker or a manager if they so desire)'.[117] However, the Committee has also noted that, in practice, many child prisoners appear to have little faith or confidence in them.[118] Similarly, following its visit to Malta, the CPT expressed concern that despite the appointment of a Commissioner for Children, visits to penal institutions were relatively rare.[119] In response to criticism that Ireland's Ombudsman for Children was not empowered to receive complaints from child prisoners detained in adult prison, the law has now been changed to enable this to take place.[120] At best, independent complaints and inspection mechanisms provide limited practical safeguards. At worse, such mechanisms are conspicuous only by their absence. The reality, therefore, is that many child prisoners – a profoundly vulnerable group[121] – 'live with a spectre of fear and an enduring feeling of being unsafe'.[122]

So, wherever we might care to look, even a cursory analysis of the practical realities pertaining to the separation of child and adult prisoners, the provision of 'child-appropriate regimes', the protection of child prisoners' rights and the operation of independent complaints and inspection mechanisms, reveals fundamental dissonance between international human rights standards and the everyday experiences of children in penal detention. The illustrations considered above are neither aberrations nor exceptions; rather they represent standard and routine aspects of a wider global phenomenon.

To take England and Wales as a final consolidating example, findings drawn from an aggregated synthesis of reports prepared by Her Majesty's Inspectorate of Prisons is particularly illuminating in respect of the conditions and

---

[116] Cyprus - CPT/Inf (2008) 17, p. 2.
[117] United Kingdom – CPT/inf (2009) 30, para. 110.
[118] See for example, United Kingdom – CPT/inf (2009) 30, p. 51.
[119] Malta - CPT/Inf (2011) 5, p. 53.
[120] See 'Minister Fitzgerald extends Children's Ombudsman's remit to cover St. Patrick's Institution', 23 June 2012 at http://www.merrionstreet.ie/index.php/2012/06/ (the Irish Government News Service).
[121] B. Goldson, *Vulnerable Inside: Children in Secure and Penal Settings* (London: The Children's Society).
[122] B. Goldson & D. Coles, *In the Care of the State? Child Deaths in Penal Custody in England and Wales* (London: INQUEST, 2005) xxii.

treatment endured by child prisoners and amplifies the discussion above: widespread neglect in relation to physical and mental health; endemic bullying, humiliation and ill-treatment (staff-on-child and child-on-child); racism and other forms of discrimination; systemic invasion of privacy; long and uninterrupted periods of cell-based confinement; deprivation of fresh air and exercise; inadequate educational and rehabilitative provision; insufficient opportunities to maintain contact with family; poor diet; ill-fitting clothing in poor state of repair; a shabby physical environment; and, in reality, virtually no opportunity to complain and/or make representations.[123] Notwithstanding the breadth, depth and significance of international human rights standards, therefore, and even by taking full account of geo-political specificities, such negative and neglectful processes define the conditions typically endured by child prisoners in all corners of the world.

The Limitations of Human Rights Standards and Penal Reform 'Talk'

The vital significance of international human rights standards for providing a global 'unifying framework' and a set of underpinning benchmarks for informing progressive law, policy and practice in the juvenile/youth justice sphere – together with a range of common reference points against which progress may be assessed – has been explored by ourselves and others elsewhere.[124] The Irish example – where interventions based on the international standards and supported by national and international watchdogs have led to positive reform in child/youth imprisonment – shows the genuine potential of advocacy, underpinned by human rights standards, for forging progress. But we also

---

[123] Children's Rights Alliance for England, *Rethinking Child Imprisonment: A Report on Young Offender Institutions* (London: Children's Rights Alliance for England, 2002) 49–137.

[124] See for example: B. Goldson & G. Hughes, 'Sociological criminology and youth justice: Comparative policy analysis and academic intervention', *Criminology and Criminal Justice* 10(2) (2010): 211–230; B. Goldson & J. Muncie, 'Rethinking youth justice: Comparative analysis, international human rights and research evidence', *Youth Justice* 6(2) (2006): 91–106; B. Goldson & J. Muncie, eds., *Youth Crime and Juvenile Justice: Children's Rights and State Responsibilities* (London: Sage, 2009); B. Goldson & J. Muncie, 'Towards a global 'child friendly' juvenile justice?', *International Journal of Law, Crime and Justice* 40(1) (2012): 47–64; U. Kilkelly, 'Youth justice and children's rights: Measuring compliance with international standards', *Youth Justice* 8(3) (2008): 187–192; U. Kilkelly, *Youth Justice in Ireland: Tough Lives, Rough Justice* (Dublin: Irish Academic Press, 2006); U. Kilkelly, L. Moore & U. Convery, *In Our Care: Promoting the Rights of Children in Custody* (Belfast: Northern Ireland Human Rights Commission, 2002); U. Kilkelly, R. Kilpatrick, L. Lundy *et al.*, *Children's Rights in Northern Ireland* (Belfast: Northern Ireland Commissioner for Children and Young People, 2006); J. Muncie, 'The punitive turn in juvenile justice: Cultures of control and rights compliance in western Europe and the USA', *Youth Justice* 8(2) (2008): 107–121.

recognise the limitations of international human rights standards in respect of their implementation and practical effect.

In 'reviewing the laws of the Commonwealth States with regards to life imprisonment of children' – including 'life imprisonment without parole', 'life imprisonment with the possibility of parole', 'detention at the pleasure of the executive or the courts' and/or 'indefinite detention sentences' – Ratledge reports that: '45 out of 54 Commonwealth States provide for one or more of the types of life imprisonment'.[125] Moreover, in at least 40 countries of the world – almost all of which have ratified the CRC – children can still be sentenced to whipping, flogging, caning or amputation and, in at least seven States, child offenders can lawfully be sentenced to death by lethal injection, hanging, shooting or stoning'.[126] Between 1990-2011, Amnesty International has documented 87 executions of child offenders in 9 countries and has observed that:

> The use of the death penalty for crimes committed by people younger than 18 is prohibited under international human rights law, yet some countries still execute child offenders. Such executions are few compared to the total number of executions in the world. Their significance goes beyond their number and calls into question the commitment of the executing states to respect international law.[127]

To return to Paulo Sergio Pinheiro who, as noted, was appointed to direct the 'United Nations Secretary-General's Study on Violence Against Children':

> For most of us, it is inconceivable that adults can be implicated actively in such barbarity to children – yet thousands are every day, in governments and parliaments, in courts and in the administration of these punishments. It makes a mockery of the international and regional human rights systems that such gross violations should continue.[128]

If such 'gross violations' make a 'mockery of the international and regional human rights systems' at the extremes, many of the 'standard violations' considered above, expose the more routine limitations of the same systems.

Such limitations raise profound questions concerning the very legitimacy of so-called 'human rights approaches' to the penal detention of children. The fact that human rights law permits the detention of children – in the knowledge that it often imposes serious and harmful effects – and then attempts to

---

[125] L. Ratledge, *Inhuman Sentencing: Life Imprisonment of Children in the Commonwealth* (Child Rights Information Network, 2012). Available at: http://www.crin.org/docs/Inhuman Setencing.pdf.

[126] Child Rights Information Network 'Ending Inhuman Sentencing of Children' (2012). Available at: http://www.crin.org/violence/campaigns/sentencing/.

[127] Amnesty International 'Executions of Juveniles since 1990' (2012). Available at: http://www.amnesty.org/en/death-penalty/executions-of-child-offenders-since-1990.

[128] P. S. Pinheiro cited in Child Rights Information Network 'Ending Inhuman Sentencing of Children' (2012). Available at: http://www.crin.org/violence/campaigns/sentencing/.

limit such effects is arguably, in itself, an anomaly. In many countries of the world 'reform talk' emphasises the efforts that are being made towards developing more 'child-friendly' juvenile/youth justice policies, practices, procedures and more 'humane' penal institutions and operational regimes. On one level such reforms provide reassurance. On another, as Medlicott has observed, 'many so-called policies, after all, exist more at the level of claim and representation on paper than in operational practice'.[129] To put it another way:

> The concept of 'safer custody' or the 'caring prison' is, in essence, an oxymoron. There is little or no evidence to imply that the innumerable policies, practices and procedures designed to provide safe environments for children in penal custody have succeeded.[130]

Or, as Miller has reflected:

> Reformers come and reformers go. State institutions carry on. Nothing in their history suggests that they can sustain reform, no matter what money, staff, and programs are pumped into them. The same crises that have plagued them for 150 years intrude today. Though the casts may change, the players go on producing failure.[131]

Indeed, despite the various policy and procedural reforms – and the determined practical efforts of (some) operational staff to take account of the specific needs of child prisoners – penal custody remains an unsuitable environment for children. Irrespective of reform efforts and no matter how the practices of penal detention are 'dressed up' in human rights and/or penal reform 'talk', therefore, to punish a child by way of imprisonment ultimately amounts to the deliberate imposition of 'organised hurt'.[132]

Conclusion: Towards Penal Reduction and Abolition

As stated, informed global estimates suggest that approximately one million children are detained in penal institutions across the world. Historical and contemporary international evidence reveals that children in institutions *per se*, and particularly those detained in prisons and other penal facilities, are especially vulnerable to human rights violations and myriad forms of

---

[129]   D. Medlicott, *Surviving the Prison Place: Narratives of Suicidal Prisoners* (Aldershot: Ashgate, 2001) 219.
[130]   B. Goldson & D. Coles, *In the Care of the State? Child Deaths in Penal Custody in England and Wales* (London: INQUEST, 2005) 61.
[131]   J. Miller, *Last One Over the Wall: The Massachusetts Experiment in Closing Reform Schools*, second edition (Columbus: Ohio State University Press, 1998) 18.
[132]   H. von Hentig, *Punishment: Its Origins, Purpose and Psychology* (London: Hodge, 1937).

violence and abuse. This is not a phenomenon that 'belongs' exclusively to the majority 'poor world'. Indeed, as discussed throughout this article, it is also present within and across 'advanced' industrialised democracies in the 'rich world'.

Politicians, policy-makers and courts of law are not *obliged* to lock-up children in this way. Rather, they *choose* to do so. Moreover, they exercise such choice in the knowledge that penal detention is not only deleterious to the well-being of child prisoners, but that it is also profoundly irrational and spectacularly counter-productive when measured in terms of crime prevention and community safety. To summarise an enormous body of knowledge, the practices of child imprisonment are:

> *Dangerous*: ... juvenile corrections institutions subject confined youth to intolerable levels of violence, abuse, and other forms of maltreatment.
> *Ineffective*: the outcomes of correctional confinement are poor. Recidivism rates are uniformly high, and incarceration in juvenile facilities depresses youths' future success in education and employment.
> *Unnecessary*: a substantial percentage of youth confined in youth corrections facilities pose minimal risk to public safety.
> *Obsolete*: scholars have identified a number of interventions and treatment strategies in recent years that consistently reduce recidivism among juvenile offenders. None require – and many are inconsistent with – incarceration in large correctional institutions.
> *Wasteful*: most states are spending vast sums of taxpayer money and devoting the bulk of their juvenile justice budgets to correctional institutions and other facility placements when non-residential programming options deliver equal or better results for a fraction of the cost.
> *Inadequate*: Despite their exorbitant daily costs, most juvenile correctional facilities are ill-prepared to address the needs of many confined youth. Often, they fail to provide even the minimum services appropriate for the care and rehabilitation of youth in confinement'.[133]

Accordingly the concept of 'child-friendly' penal detention has no evidential foundation. Nor does an imagined 'human rights approach' to child-imprisonment comprise a legitimate substitute for engaging with a determined and strategically applied policy of penal reduction and, ultimately, abolition. We end with a recommendation, therefore. We recommend, on the basis of a studious analysis of international evidence, that the global juvenile/youth justice policy, practice and research communities should collaborate to develop determined strategies to secure the abolition of child imprisonment. Of course, we appreciate the practical challenges involved in realizing such an objective and are also aware that it requires reform of juvenile justice systems more

---

[133] R. Mendel, *No Place for Kids: The Case for Reducing Juvenile Incarceration* (Baltimore: Annie E. Casey Foundation, 2011) *passim* 5-25. See also B. Goldson, 'Child Imprisonment: A case for abolition', *Youth Justice* 5(2) (2005): 77–90.

broadly. In our view, this provides no reason for shirking such responsibility, however. In the meantime, interventions that serve to restrict liberty 'as a measure of last resort and for the shortest appropriate period of time' – for the small number of children whose behaviour is legitimately deemed to place them and/or others at *demonstrable serious risk* – must be far more rigorously monitored and held to account in accordance with international law as a minimum and non-negotiable standard.

Authors of Their Own Lives? Children, Contracts, their Responsibilities, Rights and Citizenship

Tom Cockburn
University of Bradford
t.d.cockburn@bradford.ac.uk

The issue of 'contracts' has a long and extensive literature in political theory.[1] At least since the 17th century onwards, the 'social contract' has been the cornerstone of citizenship theory in the English-speaking world. Few theorists, and no political programmes, have since explored the formulation of autonomous and independent people coming together to formulate a social contract amidst economic inequality and with the complete writing out of children from this agreement.[2] Children are not alone in this exclusion as women, prisoners and 'foreigners' were also written out as 'incompetent', incomplete, unduly under the influence of other people or as 'undeserving'. Thus, within a supposed society of free and equal individuals showed, some were portrayed as in some ways less, or incomplete, human and thus lacking the capacity of writing contracts. Even today, while we may be tempted to congratulate ourselves on the better ways we recognise and protect the rights of children, a cursory look at the statistics on domestic violence and child abuse dents such optimism.

This article revisits contract theory and suggests that a focus on contracts provides a deeper understanding of what it is to be human and the concomitant rights that spring from this. Thus despite children being a 'special case' and having higher levels of protection and intervention than adults, this always remains a gift that does not have the clarity or effectiveness that contracts provide, thereby, accounting for some of the vulnerabilities children have from their full human rights. Secondly, a focus on children's 'ability' to write

---

[1] For an interesting analysis of 'social contract' theory from a feminist perspective, see Carole Pateman's (1988) *The Sexual Contract*. John Rawls (1972, 1993) is perhaps the most eloquent and influential liberal development of the term.

[2] With the exception of John O'Neill (1994).

contracts illustrates in a clear way the evolving capacities of the child and the graduated way in which children are expected to gain responsibilities (Lansdown, 2005). For instance, there is no real bar to children making the contract to purchase a glass of milk (assuming the child can afford it); however, there are restrictions to a child purchasing alcohol, an 'offensive weapon' or exchanging a contract of marriage. This more complex and contested formulation of rights tends to be embedded in specific case laws at a local level, in direct contrast to the more abstract forms of rights that tend to present children as vulnerable and lacking. Thirdly, viewing children as authors of contracts, rather than passive recipients, a different approach to issues such as consumerism and wider social inequalities can be illustrated. Finally, attention to children's right to make contracts illustrates ways in which children's rights are curtailed and to identify actions to support them from those adults and organisations concerned with children's rights. In short, and given the paucity of direct attention, a focus on children's contracts may provide an agenda for further research or for social action.

Social Contracts, Citizenship and Children

So what is a 'contract'? In most countries that adhere to commercial law a contract is basically an agreement between two parties, where one party supplies a service and the other pays for it. It needs to be noted that the discussion below focuses on practice used in English law. Although, divergent approaches to interpretations will be adopted world wide, there is still some form of legal recognition to the various ways that legally binding contracts can be drawn up (McKendrick, 2011). The most common way of making a contract is for both parties to sit down and draft a contract in writing, with all the terms and conditions laid out. Regardless of whether this contract is set down in writing, or given orally, it is still a binding contract under law. Thus under the eyes of the law oral contracts are just as legally binding as written contracts (albeit less easy to enforce). These must include an offer, acceptance and an intention to create a legally binding contract. There are a variety of ways in which this can be achieved in different media, such as e-mails, faxes, telephone calls, etc are all considered binding legal contracts. What is important is the degree of acceptance of the contract made or implied and any breach can legally be disputed. Contracts are thus legally binding and the terms and conditions set out in a contract are of paramount importance. However, most courts recognise that contracts can be limited or deemed unfair if the contract was inequitable, or there was a lack of good faith between the parties, or there was an imbalance in the terms towards one of the parties' rights and obligations.

Discussion of contracts amongst political philosophers begins by looking at the work of John Locke. Locke's *Two Treatises of Government*, was published in 1690 in order to justify the 'English Revolution'[3] of 1688 and we find that personal liberty is the overriding ideal, of which, political society exists entirely to protect that personal liberty. Locke uses the word 'property' to include human life and refers to 'that which belongs to each person and encompasses each person's life, liberty and possessions'. Property, for Locke, is an important term referring to the thing a person needs to be free; the sole purpose of political society is the protection of each person's property from invasion or appropriation from others, whether this is other private individuals or governments. The invasion or appropriation of a person's property is a violation of their rightful freedom. For Locke, the only kind of political arrangement that protects people's rightful amount of personal liberty is the one to which they owe obedience. In order to justify political society Locke instigates a hypothetical pre-social 'state of nature'. In the state of nature all persons are equal: by this Locke means that nobody is entitled to exercise absolute power over another. Nobody is born a slave and everyone is equal in the eyes of God and in the eyes of reason, therefore, all individuals have an equal right to be free. However, participants come together in a form of contract with one another and a sovereign to create the peace and provide a force capable of ensuring the proficient exchange of contracts.

However, in Locke's work, and in general liberal political theory, there is a fundamental tension in social relationships under this social contract. On the one hand, people are moral equals and possess equal rights to their own preservation and the respect to have the equal recognition to author their own contracts with government and other private citizens. But on the other hand, they are fundamentally unequal in relation to material possessions, as there is a right to 'free exchange' and to transmit their property to others. This material inequality distorts the moral equality of the original position in the 'state of nature'. Locke went on to justify slavery, 'domestic rule' and 'ordinary discipline' of men over women, children, 'servants' and waged employees, because of their material or social dependence. In effect, these people traded in their fundamental freedoms for financial and social support. This rule of independence (or lack of dependence), under the social contract, realistically made men of property as the only full holders of political and civil rights, and thus the only full members of society. However, Locke's ideas were advances on existing patriarchal theories; Locke questioned the extent of women's passivity, contested the literal ownership of children and queried the structuring

---

[3] This was not necessarily a 'revolution' as was to be later used to describe the French, American and industrial revolutions. It was more a takeover of the Catholic Stuart throne by the protestant William of Orange.

society according to kinship. In contrast to previous political philosophers, Locke argued that 'parenthood', although an important institution, nevertheless required specific rights and limits. Parental authority was only a temporal one and was restricted to the period of a child's life that preceded the 'age of reason'. Locke states:

> Children … are not born in this full state of equality, though they are born to it. Their parents have a sort of rule and jurisdiction over them when they come into the world, and for some time after, but it is a temporary one. The bonds of subjection are like the swaddling clothes they are wrapt up in and supported by the weakness of their infancy. Age and reason as they grow up loosen them, till at length they drop quite off, and leave a man at his own free disposal (Locke, 1986, p. 142-143).

In *Some Thoughts Concerning Education*, published in 1693, Locke introduced a 'developmental' understanding of a child's nature. The purpose of education was to produce a rational man by controlling and structuring the child's environment where learning would be like writing on the blank slate of a child's mind. Central to Locke's psychology of children was the distinction between the child without reason and the (educated) adult in possession of reason. Children thus do not, and cannot, hold property and thus have no executive rights to offer in any government of consent and can only have their natural rights protected by either parents or government. He thus retained children in a subordinate position at a societal level since they could not 'reasonably' engage in the consenting to a social contract and were instead dependent upon others.

Cunningham (1995) notes that although Locke says children 'should be treated as rational creatures' and thus their curiosity encouraged, nevertheless, this incipient child-centredness 'was continually blunted by his stress on the overall purpose which was to produce an adult who conformed to the role of someone in her or his rank' (Cunningham, 1995, p.64). Thus, there was a focus on education that was to produce citizens not in the here and now but as a 'complete' adult citizen who would materialise in the future.

Contract theory developed and was refined in the 18th and 19th century by thinkers such as Jean-Jacques Rousseau, Adam Smith, John Stuart Mill, amongst others, into a system of natural rights that served to exclude women and children, as well as the economically impoverished. Even the children of the property-owning classes were considered 'pre-moral', unable to comprehend or act appropriately in the contract-making public sphere, free from dependence upon others. In the 19th century, with the industrial revolution, new ideas came to prominence that challenged the exclusivity of natural rights and citizenship. New, large scale and more powerful women's and working class movements challenged many of the assumptions of natural law to lay claims for extending citizenship. The extension of these groups and the development of the new 'social contract' by Beveridge in the 1940s consolidated adult civil and political rights and added new social rights to health care and income security (Marshall, 1950). Although these movements arguably bene-fited children's material lives, this was to the detriment of children's moral natural rights to one increasingly shaped by the bourgeois image of 'inno-cence', 'incompetence' and 'vulnerability'. Thus, there is very little discussion of extending political rights to children, with the exception perhaps of a mod-est lowering of the voting age.

Contemporary Contracts and Children

The Lockean assumption of contracts and reason can be seen in English con-tract law as a case in hand. A 'minor' is any individual under 18 years of age. This is, of course, historically constructed and variable: it had been 21 until the Family Law Reform Act of 1969 defined the age of majority at 18. Prior to this throughout history the age of majority, if defined, varied (Holdsworth, 1936). Today, English law presumes that children under the age of seven years do not have the power to make contracts, along with those adults deemed mentally ill, or those who are very drunk or drugged. If a minor under seven does enter into a contract the law always assumes that he or she cannot understand the implications. Children lack the 'real capacity' to enter into a contract with them, although the adult party to whom the child contracts is bound by their contract. Thus, the 'general rule' of English (and most modern legal systems) is that contracts have a caveat where a minor will remain protected even to the disadvantage of the other party. The minor is able to cancel any contract at any time prior to reaching the age of majority and for a reasonable period after that time.

However, minors do need to be able to create binding agreements, and are legally bound to their contract, when acquiring essential items for living. These 'necessaries' include goods and services, which are considered necessary for ordinary living or are beneficial to them. These are mostly to do with contracts for service, apprenticeships, education or employment that tend to affect minors at the older teenager age range, although not exclusively so. The ration-ale behind this exception is to give organisations certainty when entering into a contract with a child that enables that child to earn his living or to start to do so. This is fairly evident in the cases of education and apprenticeships. It also includes obvious purchases, such as food and clothing. Contracts with minors span a wide range of situations and include expensive and far-reaching purchases. Minors may contract for the purchase or lease of land, or for a ser-vice which carries with it ongoing obligations (such as marriage settlements, or the purchase of shares); such a contract will be binding upon the minor upon reaching the age of majority, should they not choose to repudiate it within a reasonable amount of time. The 'reasonableness' of the amount of time varies. Financial obligations, which fall before repudiation, are binding on minors and a minor in an agreement to rent a flat may be sued for non-payment of rent.

Minors have the capacity to enter into contracts for employment, and these are binding when the terms are of benefit to the minor. Thus minors are bound to employment contracts providing the employer provides a safe and generally is to the advantage of the minor.

Although it is clear that contracts for necessaries can legally bind minors, the terms of such a contract may defeat it. Where a contract contains particularly burdensome or unfair terms, the courts may decide that a minor does not have the capacity to be bound by them. For instance, if a minor hires a car and through no fault of their own they are involved in an accident, the hire company cannot place the risk of the hire entirely at the minor's jeopardy.

Under English law the necessities of one minor will not necessarily reflect those of another. The particular circumstances, such as age and immediate needs, may lead to differing outcomes. This is seemingly unproblematic if one accepts all children to have a similar degree of equality; however, this cannot be assumed in England, given the large levels of economic and social inequality. Indeed, looking not just at purchases but at educational contracts, are the benefits of going to a poorly run school to a child's benefit? Yet many children of poorer parents are obliged to do just that.

Contracts and Evolving Capacities

Although social contract theory can be seen to operate more clearly in those countries which owe most to the liberal tradition, such as the United Kingdom or North America, inequalities and the influence of liberal and neo-liberal ideas can be seen in other European corporatist, Catholic and social democratic 'welfare regimes' (Esping-Andersen, 1990). The liberal assumption of the incompetent, vulnerable, innocent, 'blank slate' that characterises children in political theory, is only partially accepted in the everyday world. The complexities in which children's competencies are engaged in are recognised, even by legislators. Thus in England there are specific laws which define the ages in which people can buy aerosol paint (16), firearms (17 with a firearms certificate), knives and fireworks (both 18). Interestingly, there are no limitations on what age children can have body piercing.

There are no limitations as to when a child in England can open a bank or building society account, other than those defined by the individual banks or building societies. Credit or overdrafts can also be obtained, although this is usually subject to a guarantor, as we saw in the previous section, under-18s are not responsible for debts. This freedom from responsibility, while an important and necessary element of protection for children, comes at the price of financial independence. Furthermore, legislation actively denies children under a certain age of the ability to engage in the contract of exchanging their labour, so fundamental in establishing citizen identity. At a wider level the limits to children's ability to contract for credit prevents children and young people from setting up their own organisations, since it is necessary in English law for a treasurer to be named to set up a recognised civil society organization (Cockburn and Cleaver, 2009).

Thus, children have been compelled to be dependent upon adults. The lions' share of the responsibility for children falls to a child's biological parents. Indeed, in official documents 'adults with children' claiming benefits are referred overtly as 'adults with *dependents*'. In the 20th century the 'welfare state', especially after World War II, had part responsibility for children. The post-War state had responsibilities to provide income, education, health and housing for all citizens at the point of need to all, including children. However, in recent years parents are becoming more responsible for their children with a shrinking away of the state's responsibilities. Such and Walker (2005) have noted that the problem of rights and responsibilities being framed through dependency leaves parents as alone responsible for ensuring the rights of children are met.

Children's ability to contract or negotiate a contract with the state has never been taken into consideration. The move towards a more contractual welfare state around ideas of 'consumerism' and 'choice' has, at least nominally, provided contractual space for adult agency in the negotiation of choices. However, in legislation on parental choice in education, for instance, there is no room for reciprocity, interactivity and negotiations of rights and responsibilities between parents and children. As incompetent 'adults in waiting', children are excluded from the responsibilities of the adult world.

Children under 16years of age are reliant on parental approval to engage in the significant contracts that affect their lives in the fields of education, housing, income and so on. There is the interesting exception of children between 16 and 18 years of age where a gradual increase in contractual competence is assumed. Although, there is little logic to how the age increments are put in place. Children at 16 can live alone, have children and write employment contracts, yet cannot begin to apply for a car driver's licence until they are 17.

These specific legal stages in this sense seem absolute. However, when this is transferred into the real lived lives of children the complexities of the issues surrounding 'evolving capacities' can be discerned. The European Convention on Human Rights (ECHR) – enacted in the UK by the Human Rights Act 1998 – argues that self-determination for those with relevant competence is no different, whether they are an adult or a child. Indeed, the ECHR and the United Nations Convention on the Rights of the Child (UNCRC) advances the notion of generic children's rights. In English law, as noted above however, the more 'abstract' principles of legislation are interpreted and re-interpreted though 'case law'. It is the large body of case law that has been evolved and shaped through the national political culture of politicians, media and the general public.

The relationship between children's and parents' rights has been referred to above. During the 1980s debates in the UK added another dimension to children's 'competence' by engaging with medical knowledge. At first sight, the *Gillick* principle and the Children Act 1989 empowered children under 16 to receive contraceptive advice without parental knowledge to protect children fearful of their involvement (Clayton, 2000). A child could give consent – thus the ability to write a contract – to medical surgery without a parent's consent. A child's 'competence', Lord Scarman described as a 'significant understanding and intelligence to enable [him or her] to understand fully what was proposed' (quoted in Perera, 2008, p.413). Furthermore, there is no necessary lower age limit for this competence in English law and the Lords felt that there could be children as young as 12 that could give consent. There is no necessary scientific grounds on why this cannot be lower than 12; however, this frequently does not fall below 14 in real cases.

This was a considerable move forward in children's rights and debates soon formed on the very difficult area of what is actually the level of understanding required for a child to gain competence? Fundudis (2003) argues, in the medical context, that this requires a patient to specifically understand and weigh up information to arrive at a decision. This in other words is the *capacity* to understand, interpret and evaluate information and this is extremely difficult to prove and places the burden of proof on a doctor. The child's entitlement to veto conflicting parental wishes is usually qualified by the necessity of support from another adult, in particular doctors' opinions that can counter parental views. Thus, the measures of a child's competence and capacity to be right are only correct when other adults agree that it is correct. Thus the rights of competent children under 16 are not set clearly in statute but are only given this through case law and the effectiveness of the Human Rights Act 1998 and other diets of human rights are yet to be fully understood.

Children and Consumption

It is very hard for discussions of children's role as consumers to move away from the image of children as a 'victim': a victim of advertisers, adult sexual themes or as being at the receiving end of inequalities of income and consumption. It is certainly unarguable that children in advanced capitalist societies are the targets of multi-billion dollar enterprises from the high streets, media and commercial spaces. Indeed, commercialism is increasing in terms of its market valuation and entrenching itself, with the new media, into more and more spaces where children live. Thus, consumption is seen as something which children are socialised into, moving from incompetent consumers as children to competent consumers as adults. Children and consumption is often placed ambiguously as either empowered or exploited. Most academic and popular contributions have fed into the 'child as exploited' model. Thus Neil Postman's (1982) *The Disappearance of Childhood* characterizes children and childhood as becoming 'lost' as the media's 'total disclosure' of information that forces children to 'grow up quickly'.

The exception to this has been from the Childhood Studies and sociological perspectives (see Martens *et al.* 2004) that have attempted to bring in children's own experiences and understandings of consumption (Pilcher, 2011). While this increasing and valuable body of literature is welcome, Daniel Cook (2009), however, notes that businesses and enterprises seeking to provide goods and services for children have long engaged with children's wants, desires, viewpoints and choices. It is the other world of adults around policy makers, parental fears and a branch of media happy enough to pander to these fears that have presented children as only victims and exploited beings blank and passive enough not to be able to resist the actions of marketers.

The passive image of a child consumer thrown about, manipulated and buffeted by marketers and hard-hitting sales people does not reflect the reality of children's relationships with consumerism. Nairn (2011) has shown how children, while coveting certain brands and technologies, did not regard them as central to their well-being. Instead, material objects and consumer goods were wanted to fulfil certain symbolic and social functions in their lives. Thus, goods and services were wanted because of the social utility, rather than the individual utility.

Cook (2009) also acknowledges that it is through the vehicle of consumption and media activities that children form relationships with their parents and other adults, thereby dispelling some of the fears of a 'disappearance of childhood', or a separation of the worlds of adults and children. As Peterson (2005) has pointed out, it is through global brands and media entertainments that has enabled an intermixing of childhoods across continents, cultures and classes.

There are still, nevertheless, problems with consumerism. Notably, those children from low-income families who find themselves outside of a great deal of valued culture. According to Wilkinson and Pickett (2009), increased economic inequality influences the well-being of children and might easily lead to social exclusion. The lack of financial resources may develop into social marginalization because resources are needed in order to be a participative member in society. As noted above in contemporary society, consumption is central in people's everyday lives and the construction of their identities. Therefore, consumption – the purchasing and possession of goods and services from the market – has become an important dimension of social inclusion, especially among children and young people. Put the other way, lack of financial resources can exclude children from social activities and networks (Pugh, 2004).

Redmond (2009) nevertheless notes that children experiencing poverty are active in creating models and strategies to influence the consequences of poverty and moderate their effects. On the other hand it is necessary to remain cautious about giving children unrealistic capacities; Cook (2005: 156) notes the 'empowered child is superheroic. As an active, knowing being who makes her or his own meaning out of every morsel of culture, the empowered child offers hope, rather than fear, about the ultimate locus of power in the world.' Children, like adults, are both individual and dependent social agents and the one should not exclude the other. Thus, as Cook (2009) concludes: 'children's place in consumer culture must be engaged in ways that recognize the hand of corporate power in the hyper-commercialization of childhoods while also acknowledging children's stake in commercial life as something other than exploitation' (Cook, 2009, p.343).

The most useful ways of understanding children as consumers is recognising that although they may be on the receiving end of consumer exploitation, they are also empowered by the practices of writing contracts around consumption. A recognition of the multi-layered nature of children's consumption practices serves to go beyond the straightforward and taken for granted assumptions about contracts, children and childhood.

Contracts and Social Provision

If the act of consumption is rarely entirely an individual action and social by nature, the writing of contracts are also social in character and thus it is necessary to move away from seeing them as an individual act. Some writers have argued that the increasing shift towards privatised consumption has transformed social relations, moving the power away from those who control the delivery of goods and services to those who use it (Saunders, 1986). Therefore, the argument goes, individuals will have more control over the state and public sector classes. There has been a shift away from state or collectively provided to privately funded services. For instance, in 2007 nearly 17 per cent of British children attended independent school (DCSF, 2007). There has been an ever-increasing move towards 'markets' within public provision, thus the 'social contract' envisaged by Beveridge in the 1940s between the state and people can be seen as a series of Lockean contracts with service providers across both the public and private sectors.

The more contractual nature of the individual and state relationship does not lead to positive outcomes for all. It is necessary to distance ourselves from the merits of the move towards a more 'consumerist' provision, the critiques of which stretch beyond the purposes of this article. Very quickly, there is growing evidence of this 'consumerism' leading to greater inequalities, a restriction in the relationships between service provider and receiver, and so on (Vandenbroucke and Vleminckx, 2011). However, it is necessary to note that children may be presented with some opportunities to participate as consumers, as well as a danger of being further left out of these decisions. Rather than the state entering into a contract with children themselves they are more directly contracting with parents and carers as those *responsible* for children.

It is hoped that parents would engage with children with major decisions, such as school choice, where to live, decisions on medical treatment, and so on. There is some evidence too that families are increasingly doing this (Mayall, 2009). However, it is necessary to point out that there is no compulsion (and little encouragement) for children to participate in parental decisions over these matters (Jones and Welch, 2010). Indeed, the direct provision of services by the state has been seen by some commentators as a subverting of parental power (Holland *et al.* 2005). Thus some children may become removed from the greater 'choices' offered within a marketised system of state and social provisions. Indeed, evidence exists that discrimination takes place in some families because of gender, birth order and sexuality where even emotional security and affective support are lacking, let alone equitable participation in social rights (Engle, 2006).

Conclusion

So why should there be attention paid to children as contracting citizens? There are many reasons why encouraging children as authors of their own contracts could lead to distinct problems. First, it could fragment children as a social category into a series of individuals isolated from common causes. There is, of course, an obvious view that sees contracts as a potentially divisive construct that may contribute to maintaining social inequalities. Additionally, identities of consumption are arguably shallow and trivial. Furthermore, as environmentalists have argued, socio-cultural patterns of over-consumption, within the neo-liberal economies of developed societies, present an impending ecological threat to individual, social and global well-being. Finally, issues around contract cover goods and services provided by the state, collective or private markets. These do not cover arguably the most important aspects of children's lives: the care and love they receive. These are provided in the context of domestic production and given by siblings, mothers, fathers and other carers. Thus it is essential to maintain a critical distance to what an attention to contracts may offer.

However, contracts have real, tangible and enforceable obligations on all parties and allow children to be real partners in issues. These issues can affect their lives in important areas, such as decisions on housing, education and health. These should not be refused lightly.

The process of drawing up and agreeing contracts presents an image of an agentic person who is active, important and has access to some form of power. This is in marked contrast to the constructions of passivity, vulnerability, risk and endangerment that has characterised the history of childhood: one only has to look at images of the 'schooled' child, or the 'sick' child, 'poor' child, the 'child in danger', on which the state and others have 'intervened' with such ambiguous results. Those in receipt of state welfare are presented as passive and dependent whether there are contracts or not. A focus on contracts may offer some ways of progressing beyond negative stereo-typing to a more complex and social child.

References

Clayton, M., 'Consent in children: Legal and ethical issues', *Journal of Child Health Care* 4(2) (2000): 78–81.

Cockburn, T. & Cleaver, F., *How Children and Young People Win Friends and Influence Others: Children and Young People's Association, their Opportunities, Strategies and Obstacles.* A report to inform the inquiry into the Future of Civil Society in the UK and Ireland. Summer 2009. (London: Carnegie UK Trust, 2009).

Cook, D., 'The dichotomous child in and of commercial culture', *Childhood* 12(2) (2005): 155–159.

Cook, D., 'Children as consumers'. In *The Palgrave Handbook of Childhood Studies.* eds. J. Qvortrup, W. Corsaro & M. Hönig (Basingstoke: Palgrave Macmillan, 2009).

Cunningham, H., *Children and Childhood in Western Society Since 1500* (London: Longman, 1995).

DCSF, *The Composition of Schools in England* (London: Department of Children, Schools and Families, 2007).

Engle, P., *Comparative Policy Implications of Children's Rights in United Nations Committee on the Rights of Child, United Nations' Children's Fund and 'Implementing Child Rights in Early Childhood': A Guide to General Comment 7. Implementing Child Rights in Early Childhood* (The Hague: Bernard van leer Foundation, 2006).

Esping-Andersen, G., *The Three Worlds of Welfare Capitalism* (Cambridge: Polity, 1990).

Fundudis, T., 'Consent issues in Medico-Legal procedures', *Child and Adolescent Mental Health* 8(1) (2003): 18–22.

Holdsworth, W., *History of English Law* (London: Sweet and Maxwell, 1938).

Holland, S. et al., 'Democratising the family and the state? The case of family group conferences in child welfare', *Journal of Social Policy* 34(1) (2005): 59–77.

Jones, P. & Welch, S., *Rethinking Children's Rights* (London: Continuum, 2010).

Lansdown, G., *The Evolving Capacities of the Child* (Geneva: UNICEF, Innocenti Research Centre, 2005).

Locke, J., *Two Treatises of Government* (London: Everyman, 1690/1986).

Martens, L., Southerton, D. & Scott, S., 'Bringing children into the sociology of consumption', *Journal of Consumer Culture* 4(2) (2004): 155–182.

Marshall, T.H., *Citizenship and Social Class* (London: Pluto, 1950/1992).

Mayall, B., 'Generational relations at family level'. In *The Palgrave Handbook of Childhood Studies*. eds. J. Qvortrup, W. Corsaro & M. Hönig (Basingstoke: Palgrave Macmillan, 2009) 175–187.

McKendrick, E., *Contract Law* (Basingstoke: Palgrave Macmillan, 2011).

Nairn, A., *Child Well-being in the UK, Spain and Sweden: The Role of Inequality and Materialism* (York: UNICEF/IPSOS MORI, 2011).

O'Neill, J., *The Missing Child in Liberal Theory: Towards a Covenant Theory of Family, Community, Welfare and the Civic State* (Toronto: University of Toronto Press, 1994).

Pateman, C., *The Sexual Contract* (Cambridge: Polity, 1988).

Perera, A., 'Can i decide please? The state of children's consent in the UK', *European Journal of Health Law* 15 (2008): 411–420.

Peterson, M., 'The *Jinn* and the computer: Consumption and identity in Arabic Children's Magazines', *Childhood* 12(2) (2005): 177–200.

Pilcher, J., 'No logo? Children's consumption and fashion', *Childhood* 18(1) (2011): 128–141.

Postman, N., *The Disappearance of Childhood* (New York: Laurel, 1982).

Rawls, J., *A Theory of Justice* (Oxford: Clarendon Press, 1972).

Rawls, J., *Political Liberalism* (New York: Columbia University Press, 1993).

Redmond, G., 'Children as actors: How does the child perspectives literature treat agency in the context of poverty? *Social Policy and Society* 8(4) (2009): 541–550.

Saunders, P., 'Consumption sector cleavages', *Society and Space* 4(2) (1986): 155–163.

Such, E. & Walker, R., *Journal of Social Policy* 34(1) (2005): 39–57.

Wilkinson, R. & Pickett, K., *The Spirit Level: Why More Equal Societies Almost Always Do Better* (London: Allen Lane, 2009).

Vandenbroucke, F. & Vleminckx, K., 'Disappointing poverty trends: Is the social investment state to blame?', *Journal of European Social Policy* 21(5) (2011): 450–471.

Justifying Children's Rights

John Tobin
Associate Professor, Melbourne Law School, University of Melbourne, Australia
j.tobin@unimelb.edu.au

Introduction

Can the idea of human rights for children be justified? Does an answer to this question really matter? Children's rights are, after all, already recognised in international law, most notably the Convention on the Rights of the Child. They are increasingly included in national constitutions (Tobin, 2005) and considered by judicial bodies at the international, regional and domestic levels (Tobin, 2009; Sloth Nielsen, 2008). They are also increasingly used as a policy framework by governments (Lundy, 2012; Stalford, 2011), a research paradigm by scholars (Reynaert, 2009) and as an advocacy tool by civil society worldwide (Fernando, 2001; Tobin, 2011).

Despite this widespread engagement with the discourse of children's rights some still believe that the idea of children's rights has 'failed to secure a coherent ... intellectual foundation' (Minow, 1995; Guggenheim, 2005, *ix*) and 'remains largely under-theorised' (Dixon and Nussbaum, 2012). This is not to suggest that the conceptual foundations of children's rights have been entirely neglected. This may have been the case 25 years ago, when Michael Freeman lamented the absence of a 'reasoned normative thesis' to explain the moral grounds for children's rights. (Freeman, 1987, 300). In the intervening years, scholars, including Freeman himself, have increasingly sought to answer his question, 'what is the moral justification for giving rights to children?' (Freeman, 1987, 304). The literature tends to fall into three broad camps – those who support the idea of rights for children because of its role in securing their dignity (Freeman, 1992, 2007, 2010; Archard, 2004; Eekelaar, 2008); those who

* Special thanks to Philip Alston, John Eekelaar, Laura Lundy, Michael Freeman, Doris Schroeder, Jason Pobjoy, Chris Dent and Elliot Luke for their helpful comments on earlier drafts of this article. All errors remain the author's own. Thanks also to Elliot Luke for his excellent research assistance. Research funding for this paper was provided by the Australian Research Council Discovery Grant, DP12014 'Children's Rights: From Theory to Practice'.

oppose the idea of rights for children because of their lack of capacity (Purdy, 1994; Griffin, 2009); and those who oppose the idea because of concerns such as the impact of rights on the family structure (Goldstein *et al.* 1998; Guggenheim, 2005; Seymour, 2005), the Western origins of human rights, or a preference for alternative discourses such as obligations (O'Neill, 1988, 2002) or an ethic of care (King, 1997; Arneil, 2002).

This paper aims to interrogate some of the central questions posed by these competing theories and assess whether the idea of human rights for children can be justified. It consists of three parts. Part I considers the preliminary question of whether such an inquiry is necessary. It concludes that an examination of the conceptual foundations of children's rights serves two critical functions – one practical the other philosophical. From a practical perspective, it has the capacity to assist in resolving broader dilemmas with respect to the meaning of these rights and encourage more reflective practice by proponents of children's rights (Reynaert, 2012, 156). It also has the potential to dampen opponents' scepticism about the idea of children's rights by establishing a 'secure intellectual standing' that can address its 'conceptual doubts.' (Sen, 2004, 317.)

Part II explores whether the idea of human rights for children under the CRC can be justified. A focus on the CRC has been adopted because, although this instrument has been described as 'the unavoidable contemporary context for thinking about the status of children' (Archard, 2004, 218), its conceptual foundations have escaped the close attention of commentators. It will be argued that there is an overlapping consensus as to the conceptual foundations of children's rights under the CRC. This consensus is facilitated by a *conception* of dignity in which all human beings, including children, have unique value and a *conception* of children as being vulnerable relative to adults yet possessing an evolving capacity for agency and autonomy. It is this *conception* of children, which is empirically grounded and socially constructed, that provides the foundation for the 'special' human rights that are granted to children under international law.

Moreover, this conception of human rights for children is grounded in an *interest* theory rather than the rival *will* theory of rights. Children may sometimes lack the capacity to exercise their rights but it is their *interests*, not their *capacity*, which found their rights. With respect to the determination of which *interests* justify elevation to the status of a human right, a *social interest* theory is preferred to other explanations, such as an 'urgent' (Beitz, 2005, 109-10) or 'basic' interest theory (Buchanan and Hessler, 2009, 213). This social interest theory consists of both *descriptive* and *substantive* dimensions. The former refers to the deliberative process by which interests are elevated to the status of rights, whereas the latter demands that this process should *include* both rights-holders and duty-bearers. However, this requirement creates a serious dilemma when seeking to justify the CRC conception of rights, because the drafting process was dominated by Western states and completely excluded children. Part III therefore uses the social interest theory of right to assess whether the conception of rights under the CRC can be justified. It concludes that this is the case and that this instrument is capable of producing a culturally sensitive, dynamic, inclusive and relational conception of rights that remedies many of the deficiencies associated with the traditional conception of human rights as being Western, adult-centric, individualistic trumps.

1. The need to establish the conceptual foundations of children's rights

During the drafting of the CRC, there was no discussion about the moral rights of children. The explanation for this is ostensibly pragmatic. According to Geraldine Van Bueren, '[i]n the context of the silent emergency of childhood deaths from malnutrition and disease, philosophical dialogue can appear too much like a game' (Van Bueren, 1995, 6). Philosophers would rightly take umbrage at this suggestion whose interest in the conceptual foundations of human rights is motivated by a desire to enhance the legitimacy of this concept. However, given the urgent need to address the tragic experiences of so many of the world's children, the extent to which there is a need to establish the conceptual foundations of children's rights is debatable when the concept is already recognised in international, regional and domestic legal systems, and is increasingly drawn upon by advocates seeking to address the needs of children.

The view taken here is that to evade this question 'demonstrates a lack of intellectual responsibility' (Freeman, 1994, 493) by neglecting a fundamental element of the human rights idea, thereby jeopardizing its legitimacy. This argument rests on the proposition that the human rights of children consist of three interconnected dimensions—*legal, political, and moral* (Frost, 2010, 711). The justification of the *legal* dimension rests on the premise that they are recognised as legitimate standards within legal systems, the most significant of which is the CRC (Griffin, 2009, 203). The *political* dimension relates to advocates' use of this idea as a tool to assess the legitimacy of measures that have an impact on the experiences of children within and between states (Archard, 2004, 218; King, 2004, 275). The justification for this approach draws on the claim that the idea of human rights for children is a global enterprise that provides the 'settled norms of political discourse' (Beitz 8; Frost, 1996; Moyn, 2010, 222) whereby states voluntarily accept relevant treaty obligations as the standards by which the legitimacy of their efforts to secure children's interests will be assessed.

But relying solely upon legal and political justifications risks overlooking the reality that, despite states' apparent acceptance of this idea, (signified by treaty ratification), there remains widespread disagreement as to the *moral* status of human rights generally and children's rights, specifically. As such, there is a need to address the perceived 'softness' of human rights [for children] and its 'conceptual doubts', if 'the idea of human rights [for children] is to command reasoned loyalty and establish a secure intellectual foundation' (Sen, 2004, 317). In this light, the supposed 'self-evident' nature of human rights (Henkin, 1990, 2) is problematic. Indeed, in the absence of a secure conceptual foundation, children's rights risk becoming invisible to, or rejected by, those for whom they are not self-evident. They also become vulnerable to conscious or unconscious manipulation by those who wish to use them as a rhetorical device by which to advance a subjective vision of what children's rights should mean (Kennedy, 2002). A right for which there is no recognised conceptual foundation quickly risks becoming an empty rhetorical vessel into which subjective preferences or political agendas may be poured.

In such circumstances, there is a pressing need for a firm conceptual foundation and moral justification for the idea of human rights for children. The resultant inquiry seeks to advance their status by offering an 'intellectually compelling' case to justify their inclusion within the lexicon of international human rights (Sen 317; Griffin 204; Archard and MacLeod, 2002, 15; Fortin, 2009, 3). Thus, the need to justify the idea of human rights for children serves two critical and complementary functions – one philosophical and one practical. It seeks to address the concerns of those who are sceptical of the conceptual foundations of this idea. At the same time, it also serves to ground and constrain the enthusiasm of those for whom this idea and the meaning of such rights are already self-evident (Reynaert, 2012, 155), *and* those who would manipulate the meaning of children's right to align with their own political agendas.

2. The conceptual foundations of the CRC

A. *Looking for foundations in incompletely theorized agreements*

How then can the idea of rights for children under the CRC be justified? The first problem raised by this question is that the CRC, like all international legal instruments, is an example of an 'incompletely theorized' agreement. This term, coined by Cass Sunstein, describes the process by which a common agreement is reached by consensus in circumstances where there is disagreement as to the reasons or principles underlying the agreement (Sunstein, 1995). The concept of incompletely theorized agreements aptly reflects the nature of international human rights instruments, which are generated by processes that must accommodate 'a moral universe that is diverse and pluralistic', and allow for agreement between states without the need for adherence to a particular theory of general principles (Sunstein, 1995, 1748).

In practice this means that states were able to agree on the inclusion of children's rights within the CRC without formal agreement on the *specific* principles or moral theory justifying this approach. This reflects what Sunstein would describe as mid-level, principled, agreement (Sunstein, 1739). Although states may have had differing theories with respect to why children's rights are justified or why a specific right may be justified, they put aside these differences for the sake of achieving consensus on the need to recognise *the idea* of children's rights. The incompletely theorized nature of the CRC does not mean, however, that it is devoid of *any* moral content. This invites a question as to which conception of children's rights is reflected in the agreement of states parties to the CRC.

B. The concept and conceptions of childhood under international law

It is customary to hear the contention that childhood is a social construct. Moreover, in the opinion of commentators such as Ariés , the concept of childhood is a relatively recent development (Ariés, 1962). However, as Archard has explained, the idea of childhood has been known to all societies throughout history (Archard, 2004, 19-24). Where societies have differed is in their *conception* of childhood; that is, where the distinction between childhood and adulthood lies and the social and legal consequences that attach to being a child (Archard, 2004, 27-36).

International law is no different. The first ILO Conventions adopted in 1919 and 1920, sought to regulate the night work of young persons, generally defined as someone under the age of 18, and stipulated 14 as a minimum age for work at sea and agriculture.[1] In contrast, the more recent ILO Conventions 138 and

---

[1] See the ILO Convention concerning the Night Work of Young Persons Employed in Industry, 1919; ILO Convention Fixing the Minimum Age for Admission of Children to Employment at Sea, 1920; ILO Convention concerning the Age for Admission of Children to Employment in Agriculture, 1921; and ILO Convention concerning the Compulsory Medical Examination of Children and Young Persons Employed at Sea, 1921.

182, insist on 18 as the age at which childhood ends.[2] Additional Protocols I and II to the Geneva Conventions maintain 15 years of age as the point below which states and armed groups cannot recruit or use children in armed conflict.[3] Both the 1924 and 1959 Declarations on the Rights of the Child provide specific rights for children but fail to define the child. Moreover, the Universal Declaration of Human Rights ('UDHR') and the International Covenants for Civil and Political Rights ('ICCPR') and Economic Social and Cultural Rights (ICESCR'), which each provide specific protection for children, also fail to define the child.[4] Thus the concept of childhood is a constant feature of the international legal landscape but its conception differs.

With respect to the CRC, Article 1 defines a child as any person under the age of 18 years, unless the age of majority is defined earlier under domestic law. This is a classic illustration of the incompletely theorized nature of the CRC. States agreed on the *concept* of childhood but were unable to agree on its *boundaries*, that is, the point in time at which childhood began and ended. Unsurprisingly, deep philosophical differences as to when life begins between Catholic states and the Holy See on the one hand and Western states on the other, almost derailed the drafting process. It was consequently left to individual states to determine when childhood should begin (Alston, 1990).

Deep cultural differences between states also made agreement on the end of childhood elusive and the best that could be achieved was to create a rebuttable presumption in conceptualisation of 18 years as the upper threshold (Legislative History 301-12). Given this lack of certainty with respect to when childhood begins and ends, a question arises as to whether this particular conception of childhood under the CRC can be justified. It is certainly incompletely theorized but this does not mean that it is necessarily incoherent or arbitrary. This is because the CRC creates a process by which a state can determine the beginning and end of childhood within its own jurisdiction.

However, a further issue exists as to whether the concept of childhood can actually be justified. The point to stress here is that although the outer boundaries of the concept remain socially constructed and flexible under international law, there remains agreement among states as to the concept of childhood. As will be argued below, the deliberative process by which this agreement was achieved provides a good, albeit imperfect, moral justification

---

[2] See ILO Convention concerning Minimum Age for Admission to Employment, 1973, Arts. 3 and 9; ILO Convention concerning the Prohibition and Immediate Action for the Elimination of the Worst Forms of Child Labour, 1999, Art. 2.

[3] See Protocol Additional to the Geneva Conventions of 12 August 1949, and relating to the Protection of Victims of International Armed Conflicts, Art. 77; and Protocol Additional to the Geneva Conventions of 12 August 1949, and relating to the Protection of Victims of Non-International Armed Conflicts, Art. 3.

[4] UDHR, Art. 25(2); ICCPR, Art. 24 and ICESCR, Arts. 10 and 12(2).

for the idea of childhood. Importantly, this social agreement has also an empirical foundation.[5] Although children have greater cognitive capacity than was previously believed, their *evolving* cognitive and physical development means that they will often remain dependent on others for their care and protection. This empirical reality justifies the idea expressed in the preamble of the CRC that childhood is a period of 'special vulnerability [relative to older persons] during which children are in need of special protection.'

However, this conception of children as being vulnerable yet evolving in their autonomy raises two further considerations. First is the need for special protection consistent with a conception of childhood that is presumed to end at 18 years. Can this particular conception of childhood be justified? Does a child of 15, 16 or 17 years really need special protection relative to adults, or are their physical and mental capacities sufficiently aligned with the capacities of persons over 18 of age? Although this issue is addressed in detail in Part III, it is sufficient to note here that the presumptive nature of the definition of a child under the CRC is sufficiently flexible to accommodate the evolving nature of children's capacities and as such can be justified.

The second consideration is whether granting human rights to persons who may lack the capacity to exercise them is justified. Competency is more complex and fluid concept than is often assumed and children's competency in all areas of life has historically been undervalued (Freeman, 2007, 12-13). At the same time, young children do not enjoy the same competencies (in terms of reasoning and understanding) as adults are assumed to possess. This raises the question of whether the idea of human rights for children has a *moral* justification.

C. *The idea of human rights for children – does capacity matter?*

There are competing theories with respect to the question of who is entitled to rights. The most common theory used to deny rights for children is the *will* or *choice* theory, under which the capacity to exercise rights is a prerequisite to entitlement. It reflects a traditional Western liberal understanding of rights and is deeply embedded in the ideas of reason and autonomy. For proponents of this model, such as Harry Brighouse, '[t]he further an agent departs from the liberal model of the competent rational person, the less appropriate it seems to

---

[5] Research concerning children's development is extensive. It is acknowledged that this literature remains problematic and commentators have warned of the dangers associated with developmental theory: (Mayall 2000; Cordero 2012). However, the position taken here is that children's cognitive and physical development cannot be reduced to a *mere* social construction. It is also a biomedical fact – children's cognitive and physical development evolves over time. The real issue is how we interpret this difference and the consequences for understanding the relationship between adults and children.

attribute rights' (Brighouse, 2002, 31). For Brighouse, given that children depart from this model they should not be entitled to fundamental *agency* rights (Brighouse, 2002, 31-32). Thus, under a will theory of rights, as Onora O'Neill famously declared, a child's 'main remedy is to grow up' (O'Neill, 1988, 463).

Similarly, James Griffin denies human rights to *infants* on the basis that they are 'not normative agents' (Griffin, 2009, 83). For Griffin, infants lack personhood because they lack consciousness and must therefore be seen as *potential* agents rather than actual agents (Griffin, 2009, 84). As such they are not entitled to human rights. Moreover, for Griffin, children's vulnerability does not provide a justification for their rights. He concedes that their vulnerability 'imposes substantial obligations on us not imposed by those able to look after themselves. But one must not 'run together a justification of an obligation and a justification of a right' (Griffin, 2009, 85). This last point may be convincing – not all moral obligations should be human rights – but his reliance on agency to justify human rights is problematic for three reasons.

First, it denies human rights for the least powerful members of society. Infants may not have the capacity to claim rights, but Griffin's approach would deny infants the right to have others assist them to claim their entitlements on their behalf. He would force infants to rely on other sources of obligation to motivate others to address their needs and satisfy their interests, such as charity, ethics, or equity. Although it is important to recognise moral obligations arising from alternative conceptions of justice, even Griffin himself has recognised that '[i]f one can claim a right, one is not dependent upon the grace or kindness or charity of others' (Griffin, 2009, 92). Moreover, if it is accepted that the idea of rights is motivated by a desire to create systems of accountability that regulate the exercise of power by constraining the powerful and empowering the disempowered (Federle, 2011, 449; Cordero 2012, 367), then Griffin's approach is problematic. If rights are contingent on capacity or competency, they become 'exclusive and exclusionary' and children, who are 'unable to define themselves as competent beings', are effectively denied access to the discourse of rights and its capacity for empowerment and accountability (Federle, 2011, 448).

Second, Griffin's motivation for excluding infants from human rights is ultimately more strategic than philosophical. He aims to restrict the 'ballooning of the discourse', and to develop 'criteria for correct and incorrect use of the term' and 'end the damaging indeterminateness of sense of the term "human right"' (Griffin, 2009, 92-93). But his insistence on the idea of a 'correct use' only makes rights more exclusionary, and excluding infants from the benefits of human rights will not counteract the indeterminacy of rights. If indeterminacy is his real concern, then he needs to focus more on the process by which agreement is arrived at with respect to the *meaning of a right*, as opposed to excluding an entire cohort of persons from an entitlement to rights (Tobin, 2010).

The third problem with Griffin's model is that it represents a foundational-ist or essentialist understanding of human rights, in which rights are grounded in *his* understanding of the values *he* considers essential to personhood: autonomy, liberty and minimum provision (Griffin, 2009, 51). Scholars have increasingly challenged naturalist or foundationalist theories in favour of allowing for a multiplicity of justifications (Beitz, 2009; Mitchell, 2010; Eekelaar, 2011; Chase, 2012) – a position that is consistent with the idea of the CRC as an incompletely theorized agreement. John Eekelaar makes this point well in his critique of Griffin's thesis in light of the reality that the CRC provides rights for all children:

> If children without agency are given the same protections in the same circumstances by the same bodies and in the same documents as children with agency, what is gained by insisting that only the protections of children with agency are grounded in human rights while those lacking it have right of a different kind, differently grounded in an independent obligation? (Eekelaar, 2011, 234)

Thus, for Eekelaar, it is more prudent to conclude that states' acceptance of the idea of human rights for children, 'may rest on a number of grounds, of which personhood is but one' (Eekelaar, 2011, 234).

A further problem with Griffin's model is that his understanding of person-hood, which emphasises normative agency, reflects a will or agency theory of human rights. Although autonomy is a central feature of the literature on the foundations of human rights, a will theory and the idea that capacity is a pre-requisite to entitlement, is not the only basis upon which to ground rights. The main alternative is the interest theory (Brennan, 2002), under which 'it does not matter that rights-holders are not in a position to assert rights… what it is to be a right-holder… is merely to be a direct intended beneficiary of someone else's duty bound performance' to recognise the interests of the right holder (Goodin and Gibson, 1997, 188). Significantly, not only do many scholars endorse this model (MacCormick, 1976; Raz, 1984; Kramer, 1998; Freeman, 2010), it is also the preferred theory of rights reflected in international instru-ments, including the CRC. The only prerequisite for an entitlement to human rights *under international law* is that a claimant is a human being. International law recognises children as human *beings* and not merely *becomings* and they are therefore entitled to human rights, irrespective of their capacity to exer-cise them. Children may lack capacity to exercise their rights but they do not lack interests, and it is their *interests*, not their *capacity*, which form the foun-dation of rights under an interest theory.

However, offering a theory which provides a moral justification for *granting* human rights to children (and indeed to any persons who lack capacity) does not resolve deeper questions about whether the actual *idea of human rights* itself can be justified and if so, which *interests* of children should be recognised as rights. It is to these questions that I now turn.

D. Grounding human rights – the persistence of natural rights

Historically, human rights were founded upon notions of natural law and the inherent dignity of Man (sic). Traces of this approach can be detected in the text of the international human rights instruments. For example, the preambles to the UDHR, ICESCR, ICCPR and CRC each refer to the *'inalienable rights of all members of the human family'* (emphasis added). Since Bentham's attack on the idea of natural rights as being nonsense upon stilts, the legitimacy of these metaphysical foundations has been repeatedly challenged (Beitz 49-59; Sen 316; Stammers, 1999; Eekelaar, 2011; Chase, 2012). At the same time, persistent references to this origin cannot be ignored.

There are two potential responses to this dilemma. First, such references might be considered to reflect the personal values and preferences of the drafters. John Humphrey, who headed the UN body tasked with drafting the UDHR, has recounted his concern at the inclusion of philosophical concepts in the UDHR at the behest of French drafter, René Cassin. With respect to Article 1 of the UDHR, Humphrey reflected that, '[a]part from the fact that at least part of this statement is of questionable truth, it is purely hortatory and adds nothing to the authority of the Universal Declaration of Human Rights' (Humphrey, 1984, 44). Thus, given the diverse moral and cultural perspectives of the states drafting the UDHR, it is possible that many representatives may have assumed that such references were to have no substantive impact on the nature of obligations under the UDHR.

A second way to view these references is to focus on their strategic purpose rather than to treat them as an exposition of the theoretical foundations of human rights (Rosenblum, 2002, 305). Under this approach, it is the political attraction of the idea of inalienable human rights for all members of the human family, including children, that is significant. The famous international law scholar, Hersch Lauterpacht, was committed to grounding rights in natural law (Lauterpacht, 1950, 74). But in his 1950 commentary, *International Law and Human Rights,* he described the 'renaissance of the law of nature' at the beginning of the 20th century as an 'unmistakable result of the urge to find a spiritual counterpart to the growing power of the nation state' (Lauterpacht, 1950, 112). For Lauterpacht, the subsequent rise of the German state meant that 'the law of nature became once more a vital element in the affirmation of the sanctity of the individual and in the craving to find a basis of the law more enduring than the enforceable will of the sovereign' (Lauterpacht, 1950, 112).

This insight reveals the political and strategic role of the idea of natural or inalienable rights. It also suggests that following World War II, overtures to inalienable rights could be interpreted as a moral and political strategy to constrain the power of the nation state and to elevate the status of human rights. Moreover, as this strategy had sufficient appeal among those drafting the UDHR, it was not met with any substantive resistance. In subsequent years, given the absence of any reason to abandon this strategy, this commitment to the idea of inalienable rights in the UDHR became acculturated as a permanent feature of all subsequent instruments, including the CRC.

However, this only provides a possible explanation for the persistence of natural and inalienable rights within the lexicon of international human rights law. It does not provide a sufficient moral justification for the idea of human rights. This is not to dismiss the significance of the idea of natural law because, as Lauterpacht's comments indicate, its inclusion is intimately connected with ideas about the need to regulate the power of the state and elevate the status of the individual. However, if we are seeking a secure conceptual foundation for the idea of human rights generally, including children's rights, then we must look elsewhere. In this respect, the concept of dignity has become something of a default position.

E. The concept of dignity as both coterminous and foundational

The idea of inherent dignity occupies a revered place within human rights law, but its role remains conflicted and problematic. In the case of the UDHR, ICCPR and CRC, human rights and dignity are stated to be coterminous (UDHR: 'Whereas recognition of the inherent dignity *and* of the equal and inalienable rights . . .' (emphasis added); ICCPR and CRC: 'recognition of the inherent dignity *and* of the equal and inalienable rights of all members of the human family' (emphasis added)). In contrast, inherent dignity is treated as the foundation of human rights in the preamble to the ICESCR ('Recognizing that these rights *derive* from the inherent dignity of the human person . . .' (emphasis added)). It is hard to conceive of a more striking example of incomplete theorization; rights being simultaneously – both coterminous with and derived from dignity.

Moreover, the idea of *inherent* dignity within human rights instruments is also incomplete. It is generally taken to reflect the Kantian notion of dignity, which posits that dignity is the inviolable property of all human beings (Schroeder, 2010), but this is problematic for three reasons. First, it is unaccompanied by a moral justification (Schroeder, 2010). Second, if dignity is inalienable, it can never be lost. For Killmister, this presents the risk that human rights will offer 'little in the way of guidelines for action' because 'there is nothing to fear from those acts which are sometimes said to threaten us'. Third, and especially relevant to the idea of children's rights, is what Schroeder refers to as the Kantian cul de sac. By this she means that under Kant's theory, dignity belonged to human beings 'because of their reasoning faculties which give them the freedom and ability to distinguish moral from immoral actions' (Schroeder, 2012, 329). According to this account of dignity, children, at least younger children, who are not 'morally self legislative', would be denied rights (Schroeder, 2012, 330). Thus, dignity, at least in the Kantian sense, may only offer a 'thin' philosophical justification for children's rights (Schroeder, 2010, 124). Indeed, Schroeder has suggested that it may be more advisable to 'achieve contractual agreement on specific human rights and dispense with a reference to dignity in constitutions' altogether (Schroeder, 2010, 116). It is a confronting argument given the special status of inherent dignity within human rights discourse.

A dilemma therefore exists with respect to the role of dignity in justifying the idea of children's rights. Should we embrace the view expressed by scholars such as Habermas that human dignity provides 'the moral source from which all rights derive their meaning' (Habermas, 2010, 466) or is Schroeder's plea to 'separate the conjoined twins' more convincing? Habermas' suggestion that '[h]uman dignity is one and the same everywhere and for everyone' and thus 'grounds the indivisibility of all human rights' is difficult, if not impossible, to reconcile with the reality of a world characterized by difference (Habermas, 2010, 468). At the same time, Schroeder's approach may be excessive given the special place of dignity human rights discourse.

One possible means of addressing this dilemma is to adopt an intermediary position which neither embraces dignity as the foundation of all human rights nor banishes it entirely from discussion. This approach could involve the acknowledgement that, just as the notion of inherent rights played an important political role in transcending philosophical differences during the drafting of the UDHR, so too did the idea of *inherent* dignity. Habermas himself has acknowledged that 'the concept of human dignity undoubtedly made it easier to reach an overlapping consensus ... during the founding of the United Nations and more generally when negotiating human rights agreements' (Habermas, 2010, 467). Indeed, the widespread use of this concept in national constitutions, philosophical writings, religious beliefs and contemporary social movements has turned it into a 'rallying cry' for the international human rights movement (McCrudden, 2008, 677-78). Thus, the appeal to dignity arose because of its capacity to be 'used as a linguistic-symbol' that could represent 'different outlooks thereby justifying a concrete political agreement on a seemingly shared ground'. But as McCrudden has explained, '[u]nlike in linguistics ... where a placeholder carries no semantic information, dignity carried an *enormous amount of content, but different content for different people*' (McCrudden, 2008, 678). Thus, while commentators have labeled dignity a 'useless' (Macklin, 2003, 1419) and a 'deeply obscure' concept (Griffin, 2009, 203), McCrudden has distilled an overlapping consensus consisting of three broad elements: first, that 'every human being possesses an intrinsic worth merely by being human'; second that this 'worth should be recognised and respected by others' and third, that 'the State should be seen to exist for the sake of the individual human being and not vice versa' (McCrudden, 2008, 679).

When viewed within this framework, the fact that dignity is stated to be both coterminous and foundational is largely irrelevant. Its inconsistent treatment merely reflects the incompletely theorized nature of international human rights instruments. What matters is that an overlapping consensus exists with respect to the values that underlie its inclusion – a moral commitment to the 'unique' worth (Habermas, 2010, 474) of the individual child; the need to respect this worth (Archard, 2004, 218; Habermas, 2010, 469); and the role of the state in securing this conception of children. Moreover, given the inclusion of provisions such as Articles 5 and 12 of the CRC, children are also 'acknowledged as having agency and as having a voice that must be listened to' (Archard, 2004, 58). Their voice may be not be determinative and their capacity remains evolving, but given the historical invisibility and silencing of children, this consensus is, as Archard observes, 'no mean achievement' (Archard, 2004, 58).

This overlapping consensus is also consistent with the interest theory of rights adopted under international standards. If all human beings have worth purely by virtue of being human, and rights are the means by which this worth is realised, then an entitlement to rights need not depend on the capacity to exercise them. But while this discussion provides some insight into the role played by dignity in justifying the idea of human rights, it says very little about the justification of those *interests* that are elevated to the status of human rights. In the following sections I therefore examine the basis upon which to determine which interests ought to be recognised as human rights.

F. Grounding rights in interests

Commentators offer a variety of tests to determine the basis upon which interests can be justified as rights. Joseph Raz, for example, argues that only those interests that are of 'ultimate value' to the wellbeing of an individual are sufficient to form a right (Raz, 1988, 176-83). James Griffin contends that an interest is only sufficient to be recognised as a right if it can be established as a component of normative agency (Griffin, 2009, 179-87). Allen Buchanan and Kristen Hessler understand human rights as 'moral claims grounded in basic human interests' (Buchanan and Hessler 213), while Charles Beitz argues that only 'urgent individual interests' against certain predictable dangers qualify (Beitz 109-110).

The concept of childhood and the varying conceptions of childhood leads commentators to identify differing interests that are seen as being peculiar to children relative to adults, yet still suitable for recognition as human rights. John Eekelaar, for example, suggests that there are three types of interest – basic, developmental, and autonomy – which justify children's rights (Eekelaar, 1986, 161), while Neil MacCormick argues that children have an 'uncontestable interest in being cared for, nurtured and loved' which is worthy of protection (MacCormick 305). Ruth Adler identifies a set of basic and intrinsic interests for children that are deserving of the status of rights (Adler, 1985, 458). Whilst Goodin and Gibson identify shelter, education, basic health care, and care by a loving adult as interests that can be attributed to all children (Goodin and Gibson 38).

Despite such variance, the theme that unites these theorists is that they all offer a vision of rights that is linked to those interests considered as essential for achieving their vision of what it means to be a human being and entitled to a *life of dignity* and *self-worth*, and the *role of rights* in securing that vision. This is not the place to undertake a critical analysis of the various interest theories advanced by commentators to justify the particular interests which they consider deserving of the status of human rights. Rather, the focus of this inquiry is to determine whether a persuasive account can be offered to justify the inclusion of the various interests of children under the CRC as being suitable for recognition as human rights. In addressing this question, the first point to make is that given the incompletely theorized nature of the CRC, and the contested nature of those theories that seek to offer comprehensive accounts as to the proper nature and content of human rights, there is a need to ensure that the search for the perfect does not become the enemy of the good.

With this in mind, in order to justify using various interests of children to ground human rights, it is not necessary to identify a comprehensive moral theory (the 'perfect' justification which in any event is incapable of implementation given the inevitability of incompletely theorized agreements in international law). It is recognised that this approach is at odds with that adopted by someone like Griffin, who is concerned that there is *no* agreement under international law on the criteria by which rights are derived from the idea of what it means to be human (Griffin, 2009, 16). Thus, he is anxious to provide human rights, and by implication the special rights accorded to children, with a substantive conceptual foundation. But there is a *prima facie* question as to whether the underlying assumption upon which he bases his endeavour is sound. Is there really *no agreement* as to the foundations of the rights granted to children under the CRC?

G. Using a 'social' interest theory to justify children's rights

The argument made here is that, although incompletely theorized, a level of moral agreement underlies the CRC as reflected in the deliberative process which leads to the recognition of particular interests for children as human rights. The theoretical basis for this agreement may remain incomplete, but this should not preclude it from possessing a *good* justification. Given the incompletely theorized nature of the CRC, the interests that ground and justify children's rights can never be considered inherent or capable of determination by reference to a single test or moral theory. Instead, the identification of these interests will always be contested, negotiated, historically contingent, and produced by particular social processes. Hence, the idea of a *social* interest theory of rights to capture the social and deliberative process by which rights are created and recognised.

This social interest theory of rights carries three considerations for the conceptual foundations of human rights for children. First, there is a need to consider not simply the interests that ground a right but also the obligations of the duty bearer responsible for the fulfilment of those interests; second, an explicit recognition of the struggle to regulate power in the production of rights; and third, an awareness of the need for reflective practice when examining the foundations of human rights for children in a world characterised by diversity.

The need to justify both interests and obligations
In its most basic form, a right is as an entitlement of X that gives rise to duties or obligations that can be claimed against Y (Raz 166). Under an interest theory, a human right is a species of the genus *rights* that is granted to, or recognised for a person by virtue of being a human where, in the case of international law, the duty bearer is the state. Characterised thus, it is not simply the interest that must be justified, but also the *actual* obligation or duty with respect to the realisation of the interest that has been elevated to the status of a right. This requirement ought to provide comfort to scholars like Griffin who are concerned at the 'ballooning' of human rights (Griffin, 2009, 12) because under a social interest theory, a mere claim that an interest should be elevated to the status of a human right is insufficient because the duty bearer must also accept an obligation with respect to the claim before a human right can be justified.

Recognising the role of power
Second, in focusing on a theory to explain the moral foundations of human rights, there has been a tendency to overlook the organic role that rights have assumed in the regulation of power *and* the deliberative nature of how human rights are produced (Stammers 981). As Habermas explains, 'human rights have always been the product of resistance to despotism, oppression and

humiliation' (Habermas, 2010, 466). It has been the desire to respond to human suffering and the experiences of perceived injustice within states that has contributed to both the *idea of* and the *claim to* human rights (Lauren, 2003; Hunt, 2007, 15-34; Tobin, 2012, 14-43). A social interest theory of rights recognises this organic and political process.

Importantly, children's rights, like all human rights, also emerged as a tool to regulate the relationship between the powerful and the powerless, between the governed and the governing – to respond to the perceived failings and excesses of particular approaches to governance and power distribution within society, whether in public or private setting (Stammers 980; Guggenheim, 5; Farson, 1974; Holt, 1974; Eekelaar, 1986). Of course, this view is contrary to a trend within some of the contemporary critical literature on children's rights, which perceives this idea as a tool for the regulation of childhood (Grahn-Farley, 2003; Nakata, 2012; Barnes, 2013). This literature certainly raises some interesting questions about how the discourse of children's rights can be (mis)understood, but it is entirely decontextualised in the sense that it overlooks the historical motivations for the emergence and development of the idea of children's rights.

Although this is a complex story, historically children were seen simply as the property of their fathers – a legacy of the Roman doctrine of *patria potestas* – with little role for the state unless children were abandoned. It was not until the late 19th and early 20th centuries that this proprietary model was challenged when evidence of the harm suffered by children in both private and public settings led to a welfare model committed to the best interests principle. To be fair, this principle was 'very beneficial for children' because it demanded a reorientation away from an exclusive focus on parental and adult interests to a consideration of children's interests (Eekelaar, 2008, 159). It also legitimised state intervention in the private sphere, where this was necessary to secure a child's best interests.

However, the welfare principle also had its 'dark side' (Eekelaar, 2008, 159) and regularly operated as a 'code' or 'proxy' (van Krieken 39) for the interests of others, in circumstances where children's voices were largely absent from any assessment of their best interests. As a new sociology of childhood emerged in the 1970s and 1980s in which children were viewed as *beings* and not merely *becomings,* the claim of human rights for children became stronger (Freeman, 2010, 9-19). Children were no longer passive objects in need of assistance but rather, subjects with evolving agency and an entitlement to participate in matters affecting them. When viewed within this historical context, rather than seeking to regulate childhood, the idea of children's rights emerged as an explicit challenge to the systems and processes that had previously been used to govern, regulate, subordinate and silence children. A social interest theory of rights locates discussion of the foundations of children's rights within this

historical context and recognises the social process that led to the development of the idea of human rights of children.

The need for reflective practice

In a pluralistic world in which values, preferences and experiences vary widely,
it is dangerous to insist upon the idea that the list of interests justifying rights
must be derived from a comprehensive and internally coherent theory (Young,
2010, 14). Reflective practice requires awareness that as individuals we are
restricted in our conception of which interests matter for all human beings,
including children. A social interest theory of rights recognises the need to
mitigate the impact of individual values and preferences in the identification
of those interests that are deemed worthy of being rights.

It therefore requires a much more deliberative and inclusionary process by
which interests, and the attendant duties imposed on states, are identified as
suitable for designation as rights. This deliberative process provides a 'means
of collective problem solving which derives its legitimacy from the wisdom,
ideas and criticisms reflected in the diverse opinions of those who participate
in such a practice' (Young, 2010, 6). Importantly, this model is also consistent
with an inclusionary vision of human rights, as opposed to alternative models
that restrict rights on the basis on capacity, or restrict those interests deemed
suitable for recognition as rights based on a particular theory reflecting
individual sensibilities and preferences. But in this sense, a social interest
theory consists of two dimensions – a descriptive dimension and a substantive dimension – both of which have consequences for the justification of the
conception of children's rights under the CRC.

H. The substantive dimension of a social interest theory

The *descriptive* dimension of a social interest theory refers to the deliberative
process by which agreement is achieved on those interests that are elevated to
the status of a right. It recognises that such agreement, although incompletely
theorized, reflects a level of moral consensus amongst participants in the
drafting process. But a social interest theory of rights also has a *substantive*
dimension that demands that the identification of the interests deemed suitable for recognition as rights and the attendant duties imposed on states,
should each occur via a collaborative and deliberative process that *includes*
both rights-holders (or their representatives) and duty-bearers (or their representatives). This is consistent with Iris Marion Young's theory of deliberative
decision-making to the extent that a 'decision is normatively legitimate only if
all those *affected* by it are included in the process of discussion and decision-
making' (Young, 2010, 23). Moreover, by focusing on the identity of the parties
involved in identifying the interests suitable for recognition as rights, the

substantive dimension of the social interest theory also addresses Eekelaar's concern that proponents of 'interests formulations of rights are notably reticent in stating how the "rights holders" interests are constructed and by whom' (Eekelaar, 2008, 136).

At this point, a major obstacle to the justification of the rights for children under the CRC arises. The deliberative process that led to the adoption of this instrument after ten years of negotiations did not include children. According to Freeman, '[t]he Convention thus encodes a set of rights and takes an image of childhood from the perspective of the adult world looking in almost as an external observer on the world(s) of children' (Freeman, 1998, 439). On reflection, this may be overstating the impact of the exclusion of children's voices from the drafting process. Ultimately, the experience of childhood also belongs to all adults, and with age comes wisdom (hopefully) and an understanding of life that most of us would concede would have been of benefit in our younger years. At the same time, the nostalgic perspectives of adults provide at best a partial insight into the interests of children. Moreover, even if we rely on the collective perspective of adults to identify children's interests, this presumes that children as a cohort, and indeed individual children themselves, necessarily lack capacity, insight and expertise with respect to their interests, when evidence tells us that this is not the case.

However, this does not mean that the idea of children's rights under the CRC has *no* conceptual foundation. The deliberative process that led to the adoption of the CRC still produced an agreement, albeit an incompletely theorized one, on the fundamental idea that children are entitled to human rights. However, the exclusion of children's views produces a dilemma under the substantive dimension of a social interest theory. Thus, in the final section of this paper I will draw on the social interest theory to examine not only the implications of this deficiency but also those other concerns that are routinely raised to challenge the conceptual foundations of the CRC and its conception of children's rights.

3. Using a social interest theory to critique the conception of children's rights under the CRC

When examining the CRC through the lens of a social interest theory, the exclusion of children's voices – what I have termed the adult construction dilemma – is not the only source of concern. Western dominance during drafting also challenges the inclusiveness of the process. Thus, the present discussion analyses both the adult construction dilemma and the relativist challenge in order to determine the extent to which the conception of children's rights is compromised under the terms of a social interest theory. It reveals that the significance of each of these critiques is overstated and that the malleability of the text of the CRC allows for both the views of children and diverse cultural perspectives to inform the understanding and implementation of children's rights.

The remainder of part III uses the social interest theory to examine the legitimacy of those concerns and objections that are routinely raised to challenge the conception of children's rights under the CRC. These concerns are described as the anti-family concern and the liberationist and protectionist objections. The conclusion drawn is that much of the conceptual opposition to children's rights is associated with a preference for a *will theory* of rights; a failure to read the actual text of the CRC; or insistence on a particular interpretation of the CRC that overlooks the potential for an alternative and persuasive interpretation that would to address the cause for concern.

A. The adult construction dilemma

The history of *rights* discourse reveals a vision of an adult (and more specifically a male adult) as the subject of rights. Irrespective of whether the origins of this discourse are traced to religious texts or the Enlightenment, capacity for reason and autonomy have historically been linked with an entitlement to rights. As children have been assumed to lack this capacity, they have been denied rights. But as discussed above, this capacity or will theory has been increasingly challenged by an interest theory of rights in which the only prerequisite for rights is the status of being a human being. Moreover, the interest theory is the model conceptualisationed under the international human rights instruments that have been negotiated and agreed upon by states.

The granting of human rights to children, however, has not been accompanied by their involvement in the identification of those interests that should be elevated to the status of rights. This process has been undertaken entirely by adults, which is contrary to the terms of the social interest theory. This does not mean that international human rights law is blind to the particular interests of children. This criticism might be leveled at the early human rights instruments, such as the UDHR, ICCPR and ICESCR, which largely reflect an adult catalogue of interests. However, the CRC and its optional protocols were specifically drafted to accommodate the lived experiences of children. Thus, it cannot be said that the discourse of human rights has been constructed with only the *adult* human in mind (*cf* Cordero, 2012, 365).

Moreover, the interests identified as suitable for recognition as human rights for children are invariably informed by the lived experiences of children, albeit as interpreted and understood by adults. For example, working children were and continue to be subject to exploitation (ILO, 2010), thus Article 32 of the CRC prohibits *exploitative* child labour; and children were and continue to be subject to violence, neglect and abuse within the home (World Report on Violence Against Children, 2006) thus Article 19 demands protection against violence. Moreover, developments in the psychological and sociological litera- ture concerning conceptions of childhood during the latter part of the 20th century have also challenged assumptions about children's capacity and pro- vide support for recognition of their evolving capacities and their right to have their views heard under Articles 5 and 12, respectively.

Thus, the interests recognised as rights in the CRC do not simply reflect adult interests, but reflect an understanding or conception of children's inter- ests, which is interpreted and construed by adults. But this is still problematic under the *substantive* dimension of a social interest theory, which requires that the identification of those interests deemed suitable for recognition as rights involves a deliberative process drawing on the perspectives of both the beneficiaries of those rights and of the duty bearers. A question therefore exists as to whether this deficiency can be addressed. In response to this dilemma four points are made.

(a) *A rebuttable presumption*
First, the presumption in favour of the inclusion of rights beneficiaries in draft- ing is rebuttable. As Upendra Baxi has warned, the 'ritualistic invocation of the mantra of "participation" simply bypasses some further hard problems' (Baxi, 2010, 12). This warning is particularly apt with respect to children and espe- cially very young children who will often lack the interest and/or physical and intellectual capacity to participate, either directly or indirectly through repre- sentatives, in the deliberative process. The CRC is sensitive to this reality and requires, under Article 12(1), that states' obligation to assure to children the right to express their views in all matters affecting them is only applicable to those who are 'capable' of forming a view. But even in the case of older chil- dren who will be capable of forming views on many matters that affect them, there are still logistical and conceptual challenges to the facilitation of their effective and representative involvement. Participation requires time and resourcing. Issues also arise with respect to the extent to which the views of a child or a group of children can be taken as representative of the views of all children (of course, the same challenges also exist with respect to the partici- pation of adults).

In such circumstances, Eekelaar has argued that the rights recognised for such persons, whether adults or children, can still be justified if these rights 'refer to protection of interests, which we can *safely say they would recognise as theirs*' (emphasis added) (Eekelaar, 2008, 137). This seems reasonable but it does not address concerns associated with an adult-centric deliberative process. As a minimum, those who do take part in the deliberative process, whether adults or children, and who purport to represent children's interests, must ensure that they do not simply substitute their own interests. In this respect, Article 3 of the CRC, which demands that children's best interests be a primary consideration in all matters concerning them, is critical. But something more is required if the identification of children's best interests is to accommodate what children actually believe to be in their interests.

(b) *The role of participatory research in mitigating the risk of proxy interests*
It is suggested that the risk that children's representatives might substitute their own interests for those of children can be mitigated when the identification of children's interests is empirically founded. Such evidence draws on the lived experiences of children rather than assumptions and speculation about their interests to justify their rights. Thus, if there was evidence that demonstrated that children 'consciously repudiated an alleged interest, its protection could not be said to be in furtherance of their rights' (Eekelaar, 2008, 137). But caution must still be exercised here because research with children cannot be seen as a panacea to the child participation deficit in the CRC. As Cordero has warned, 'we cannot speak of merely making children's rights dependent on the sociology, psychology or anthropology of childhood ... when these are *disciplines also exclusively driven by adults*' (emphasis added) (Cordero 2012, 367). Faced with this dilemma, for Cordero the solution is to 'make the rights of children *dependent on children's voices*' (Cordero 2012, 367).[6] But such an approach risks swinging the pendulum too far and is incompatible with a social interest theory of rights.

The rights of any group cannot be entirely dependent on the voices of that group. Apart from the reality that children do not speak with one voice, under the substantive dimension of a social interest theory, rights are produced (and understood) as a result of a deliberative process involving all interested parties, beneficiaries and duty-bearers. To make rights for children dependent *solely* on the voices of children is to ignore the collaborative nature of the rights exercise. Thus, adults who play a role in the realisation of children's rights, whether as parents, state officials, professionals working with children, cultural or religious representatives, must be involved (either directly or through representatives) in this process. Children too have a critical role to play and their views must be given due weight in accordance with their age and maturity (more on this later).

Equally importantly, research concerning children, which allows for the identification of their interests *and* the measures required for their realisation, must also be performed in a manner that perceives children as active collaborators rather than passive objects of inquiry. If adults are to understand the

---

[6] *Id.*

lived experiences and interests of children fully, there is a need for research projects and participatory research methodologies that allow adults to understand children's interests and what it means to be a child, '*as lived by and understood by children themselves*' (Cordero 2012, 368). This approach, which is increasingly referred to as a rights-based approach (Lundy and McEvoy, 2012), seeks to re-conceptualise the relationship between researcher and subject such that research is undertaken *with* rather than *on* children. It is not without its own methodological, conceptual and logistical challenges. However, for present purposes, it is sufficient to note that participatory research methodologies with children have the capacity to reveal diverse conceptions of childhood, promote respect for children, empower children and offer a rich empirical basis for policy and action which recognises children's lived experiences and the interests which children themselves prioritise (Beazley, 2011, 159). As such, this research has the capacity to address many of the deficiencies arising from the exclusion of children's views during the drafting of the CRC.

(c) *Reading the CRC as an illustrative list of children's interests*
The third point to be made in relation to the adult construction of the CRC is that the list of interests recognised as rights should be read as *illustrative* rather than exhaustive. Commentators often criticise the CRC for the marginalisation of certain childhoods and omission of rights that may have been included had children been involved in drafting, such as the rights to work or be loved (Ennew, 1995, 202; Freeman, 2000; Nieuwenhuys, 2009). But such a criticism overlooks the potential of Article 3 to provide a mechanism by which children themselves can agitate for additional interests beyond those already listed.

There has been a tendency to interpret Article 3 simply as restating the welfare principle; that is, that children's best *interests* must be a primary consideration in all matters concerning them. Historically, adults have been the sole arbiters of what constitutes a child's *interest*. But such an approach is inconsistent with the Article 3 requirement that children themselves be entitled to play a role in the identification of those *interests* (Eekelaar, 2006, 160-62). This is because Article 12 of the CRC, which provides children with a right to express their views in all matters affecting them, demands that an understanding of children's best interests must be informed by children themselves where they have the capacity to make such a contribution. Children are therefore entitled to demand that those interests, which they prioritise, but which may not be listed as rights in the CRC, must nonetheless remain a primary consideration in all actions concerning them. The interpretation of Article 3 must not play 'into a savior vision of human rights' in which children's interests 'are determined exclusively by those with power to provide to those less privileged' (Chase, 2012, 515). On the contrary, children's rights, and by implication their interests, represent 'objects of struggle that can be seized from below and in that process redefined' (Chase, 2012, 515). Under a social interest theory of rights, children must be part of this process and Article 3 of the CRC provides a normative foundation to demand such an approach.

(d) *The role of children's views in the interpretation and implementation of their rights*

The final point to make with respect to the adult construction of the CRC is that the meaning of many of the rights enumerated in this instrument and the measures required for their *implementation* are anything but settled. Elsewhere I have outlined a model for what I describe as a constructive approach to treaty interpretation (Tobin, 2010), a core element of which is the idea that the relevant interpretative community has an interest in and must contribute to the accepted understanding of a particular right and the measures required for its implementation. Children must be considered a part of this interpretative community with respect to both the interpretation and the measures required for the implementation of their rights under the CRC.

To take one example, Article 19 protects children against all forms of violence, abuse and neglect but provides no definition of these terms. Thus there is a risk that adult conceptions of violence and abuse will be used exclusively to inform the understanding of this obligation when children themselves may have different conceptions of what amounts to violence (Saunders and Goddard, 2008; Morris and Hegarty 2012). It is within this context that the CRC Committee has explained that, 'in conceptualizing violence ... the critical starting point and frame of reference must be the experience of children themselves' (CRC/C/111 para 704). The reality is that many children, especially young children, will often be unaware that they have been the victims of conduct that violates Article 19. Moreover, as the CRC Committee has recognised, socio-cultural barriers often impede children from expressing their experiences or seeking assistance and states must therefore take measures to alleviate these barriers (CRC Committee, 2011 paras 12 & 63).

However, Article 12 still creates a normative expectation with respect to children's role in the interpretation and implementation of their rights. It requires that states assure children who are capable of forming views with the right to express those views in *all matters affecting* them. This provision remains clouded by ambiguity, but a persuasive argument can be made that the interpretation of the rights under the CRC is, itself, a matter '*affecting*' children. This is because the interpretation of a human right granted to children will inform the measures adopted to implement it, which in turn will *affect* children.

Importantly, Article 12 imposes a positive duty on states to take reasonable measures to create mechanisms that will enable children with appropriate capacity to play a constructive role in the determination of those measures necessary to secure the implementation of their rights (CRC Committee, 2009, paras. 48-49). It does, however, qualify the relevance of a child's views which need only be given due weight in accordance with the child's age and maturity. Commentators have interpreted this as rendering the evaluation of a child's view subject to 'the particular theory of development' held by the adult interpreter (Smith, 2002, 75). It is conceded that there is always the risk that Article 12 could be interpreted to allow 'adults to retain authority over children' (Archard, 2004, 66) or to allow the CRC to operate as an 'instrument for the denial of children's citizenship' (Milne, 2005, 41). But there is also the prospect that a persuasive and alternative interpretation of Article 12 could be offered to demand that adults cede their authority over children *and* actively facilitate their citizenship. I will address this point in further detail below but first I wish to turn my attention to the relativist challenge.

B. *The relativist challenge*

Unlike children, who were never invited to take part in drafting, all states were invited to participate in the Working Group that drafted the CRC. In reality, however, drafting was dominated by Western states (Legislative History 933-937). States from Africa, the Asia-Pacific, the Middle East and Latin America were present but 'extremely poorly represented' (Harris-Short, 2001, 304; Le Blanc, 1995, 27-37). Moreover, many of the non-Western states lacked the resources and support services to match those enjoyed by Western states. Thus, from the perspective of a social interest theory of rights, this lack of *effective* participation by many states remains problematic and undermines the legitimacy of this instrument.

This concern is generally understood as the relativist challenge and represents a constant obstacle to efforts to justify all international human rights, including children's rights. The preamble to the Universal Declaration of Human Rights may proclaim 'a common standard of achievement for all peoples' but for many, international human rights simply reflect Western values and preferences. It is within this context that the *concept* of human rights for children is said to be alien to non-Western cultures and the CRC is said to reflect a Western *conception* of childhood (Burman, 1992; Ennew, 2002; Harris-Short, 2003; Appell, 2009; Pupavac, 2011). The general universal/relativist debate has been canvassed in detail elsewhere and need not be repeated here. Instead it is sufficient to make six observations in the context of children's rights from a social interest theory perspective.

(a) *A normative commitment to culture*
Despite Western dominance during the drafting of the CRC, as observed by Sonia Harris-Short, 'the determined and constructive participation throughout the drafting process of states such as Algeria, Argentina, Senegal and Venezuela,

ensured that the CROC reflected at least to some extent, a diversity of cultural traditions' (Harris-Short, 2001, 322). Indeed, a close examination of the text of the CRC reveals a stronger commitment to cultural diversity than is generally assumed. Article 1 provides states with flexibility in relation to when childhood begins and ends; Article 5 requires states to respect the rights, responsibilities and duties of parents, members of the extended family or community, as provided for by local custom; Article 17 requires states to disseminate material of cultural benefit to the child with respect to children's linguistic needs; Article 29 requires that education be directed not only to respect for a child's parents, but also respect for his or her 'own cultural identity, language and values' and the national values of the country in which the child is living; Article 30 recognises a child's right to enjoy his or her own culture and language; and Article 31 respects the child's right to participate fully in cultural life.

Thus the CRC should not be interpreted as advocating an atomistic, Western, liberal conception of childhood that severs children from the associated cultural values and practices into which they are born (cf Mayall 245). On the contrary, the CRC conception of childhood and understanding of how children's rights are to be understood and realised is culturally sensitive. There are, however, limits to the level of cultural deference permissible under the CRC. For example, Article 5 only tolerates the exercise of parental rights and practices accepted under local custom to the extent that this discretion is exercised subject to a child's evolving capacity and designed to provide appropriate *direction and guidance* in a child's exercise of his or her rights.

This conception of childhood clearly conflicts with alternative conceptions under which children are deemed either to lack capacity or to remain subject to the exclusive control of their parents. However, these alternative conceptions will be held not just *within* non-Western states, but also Western states. Indeed, it is worth recalling that the USA is one of only three states, along with Somalia and South Sudan, not to have ratified the CRC. Moreover, an Australian inquiry into the CRC revealed that 51 per cent of submissions opposed it (Australian Senate Inquiry, 1998). Thus, it is an oversimplification to suggest that the CRC reflects a Western conception of childhood. A more accurate assessment is that it reflects a normative commitment to a conception of childhood in which the rights of children are understood and mediated by reference to the cultural practices in they live.

(b) *The incompletely theorized concept of culture*
Despite this explicit deference to culture, the concept of culture itself is not defined in the CRC. This is yet further evidence of the incompletely theorised nature of this instrument. In practice, much of the relativist debate within the human rights space refers to either an 'essentialized' conception of culture or a conception of culture as 'national identity' (Merry, 2006, 6-16). The former

views culture in negative and backward terms and uses it as a basis for intervention to address harmful cultural practices. Within this context, the universal standards of the CRC are interpreted in light of dominant Western values as a civilising discourse, which is used to critique children's treatment in non-Western states. In contrast, the idea of culture as national identity is used to resist attempts to enforce CRC standards on the assumption that this instrument reflects values that have no place within the culture of non-Western states.

A further understanding of culture, which is preferred by anthropologists such as Sally Merry, understands culture to be contentious and fluid (Merry, 2006, 14-16). It will always be contested as social practices within a community shift over time in response to changing power dynamics. This view rejects the essentialised and national identity conceptions of culture, but accepts that there will always be dominant social practices within a society, which are embedded in systems of power (Merry, 2006, 14-16).

This conception aligns with the ideas unpinning a social interest theory of rights. It demands that when speaking about the relativist challenge, there will always be a need first to enquire as to the status and identity of both those who advocate *and* resist calls for the implementation of children's rights. It makes no assumptions about the legitimacy or otherwise of dominant cultural practices but, as with a social interest theory, requires an inquiry into the social process by which these practices have been adopted and agreed upon. Moreover, the legitimacy of such practices, and the extent of deference to them, must be assessed in light of the extent to which those affected are included in the process leading to adoption.

(c) *The fallacy of a Western and non-Western conception of childhood*
An examination of the relativist debate by reference to the idea that culture is contentious also reveals that it is misleading to talk about a Western and a non-Western *conception* of childhood. A more accurate approach, and one that is consistent with a social interest theory of rights, is to acknowledge that there are various *conceptions* of childhood *within* both Western and non-Western states which will always remain contentious, dynamic and historically contingent. At times certain conceptions are more dominant and have a greater impact on social practices and regulatory policies relating to children.

Within the context of the relativist challenge to international human rights law, there is a tendency to assume that the *dominant* Western conception of childhood is 'based on the idea that children should be protected from the adult world'; that 'childhood is a time of play and training for adulthood' and that children are entitled to rights without the burden of responsibilities' (Pupavac, 1998). In contrast, under the dominant non-Western counterpart, children are said to have duties to family and the broader community, while

the realities of poverty often mean that they must work and engage in activities that are demonised in Western states (Pupavac, 1998). Regardless of
whether these conceptions actually reflect the dominant Western and non-
Western notions of childhood, a question arises as to whether the CRC promotes this alleged Western conception of childhood to the exclusion of a non
Western conception.

The preamble and text of the CRC certainly view children as being in need
of special protection because of their vulnerability relative to adults. The
nature of this protection, and whether it can be justified, is discussed in further
detail below. At this point it is sufficient to note that this conception of childhood is also the foundation for the *African Charter on the Rights and Welfare of
the Child*.[7] It is therefore misleading to suggest that this conception is peculiar
to Western states. Moreover, the text of the CRC does not necessarily seek to
exclude children from the adult world but rather to protect them from *exploitation* upon entry into it. For example, Article 32 does not protect children
from work *per se*, but from *economic exploitation*, Article 34 does not protect
children from prostitution or pornography but from their *exploitative use* in
these activities and Article 36 protects them from all forms of exploitation
prejudicial to their welfare. Thus, the CRC seeks to protect children from
exploitation in the adult world, but it does not necessarily seek to exclude them
from that world.

The perception that the CRC reflects an individualistic conception of childhood which excludes a non-Western understanding of children having broader
family and community responsibilities is also unsupported by the drafting history and text of the CRC. During drafting, Senegal recommended the inclusion
of an Article to the effect that the 'child has the duty to respect his parents and
give them assistance in case of need' (Legislative History 363). Significantly,
the values underlying this proposal received wide support among members of
the working group (Legislative History 363). However, resistance to its inclusion arose due to a concern that this was a moral obligation that could not be
given legal substance because it would be impossible to enforce in practice
(Legislative History 353). The resultant compromise was to include the 'development of respect for a child's parents' as one of the aims of education under
Article 29 (Legislative History 363). Importantly, this demands that states take
active measures to realise this aim in the development of their education
systems (CRC Committee, 2001 para 22).

---

[7] The fourth preambular paragraph of the African Charter provides that 'the situation of most
African children remains critical due to the unique factors of their socio-economic, cultural,
traditional and developmental circumstances, natural disasters, armed conflicts, exploitation
and hunger, and on account of the child's physical and mental immaturity he/she needs *special
safeguards and care*' (emphasis added).

(d) *The role of culture in interpreting children's rights*

The final point to make with respect to the relativist challenge is that a social interest theory of rights anticipates that the ambiguity in the text of the CRC provides scope for cultural practices and values to be considered for interpretive purposes *and* in the context of measures for implementation. There will always remain a risk that children's rights might be used and interpreted in a hegemonic way to displace, devalue or colonise competing agendas, including non-dominant cultural values (Kennedy, 2002, 108-09). Indeed, there is evidence to suggest that the CRC Committee has tended to interpret the CRC in a way that is not sufficiently accommodating of cultural differences. For example, its identification of traditional practices that are harmful to children (under Article 24(3)) tends to focus almost exclusively on non-Western practices such as female genital cutting, forced marriages and traditional adoption practices (Harris Short, 2001, 332-349; Tobin, 2009, 378-86). But it has failed to classify practices, which are common in the West, such as corporal punishment (Tobin, 2009, 381) and the sexualisation of young girls (Rush and La Nause, 2006), as being harmful traditional practices. The result is that the traditions and culture of non-Western states 'are constantly presented as a "problem", while those of Western states remain unproblematised (Harris-Short, 2001, 350).

An alternative interpretation is to adopt an approach that is more collaborative and less dismissive of non-Western conceptions of childhood. The lens through which the CRC is interpreted need not, and indeed should not, focus on dominant Western values and experiences. Moreover, cultural diversity has a legitimate and critical role to play in identifying the measures required for the implementation of a right. I have discussed this requirement elsewhere as the principle of 'local context sensitivity' (Tobin, 2010, 40-43), which disapproves of the automatic transfer of Western expectations and understandings with respect not only to the meaning of a right but also to the measures for its implementation. It accepts that these measures will not be universal and require sensitivity to the social, cultural and political practices, thereby allowing a degree of discretion for states.

At the same time, this does not allow for cultural or traditional practices to be invoked as in defence of alleged violations of a child's rights. As Philip Alston has explained, '[j]ust as culture is not a factor which must be excluded from the human rights equation so too must it not be accorded the status of a metanorm which trumps human rights' (Alston, 1994, 20). Accordingly, Article 24(3) demands that '[s]tates parties shall take all effective and appropriate measures with a view to abolishing traditional practices prejudicial to the health of children'. The measures required for the elimination of such practices, however, are not to be imposed or defined exclusively by reference to Western values or expectations. On the contrary, a context-sensitive approach favours local collaboration and consultation rather than the imposition of hegemonic visions of the content and scope of children's rights (Tobin, 2009).

The preceding discussion demonstrates that when viewed through the prism of a social interest theory, much of the anxiety arising from the view that the CRC is Western-dominated and adult-centric is exaggerated. This instrument may remain incompletely theorized, but it still has a clear commitment to accommodating cultural diversity and the views of children. Addressing the challenges presented to the idea of children's rights by the adult construction dilemma and the relativist challenge, however, still leaves this idea vulnerable to critique from other perspectives. It is to these that I now turn.

C. The anti-family concern

A strong source of objection to the concept of children's rights generally *and* the CRC conception of rights is the perception that they undermine the family unit by promoting a conception of childhood that is severed from, and potentially antithetical, to the idea of the family. An examination of this critique reveals two central deficiencies. First, it is unsupported by the actual text of the CRC. Second, it is informed by a *will theory* of rights, which is inconsistent with the *interest theory* of rights adopted under the CRC.

A normative commitment to the family and parents

Under the CRC, children and the realisation of their rights are very much situated within the context of the family (Tobin, 2005). The family is identified in the preamble to the CRC as being 'the fundamental group of society and the natural environment for the growth and wellbeing of all its members and particularly children'. As such, the family is to be 'afforded the necessary protection and assistance so that it can fully assume its responsibilities within the community'. The preamble also states that children 'should grow up in a family environment, in an atmosphere of happiness, love and understanding.'

Moreover, the text of the CRC provides that states must respect the rights, duties and responsibilities of parents with respect to their children (Art. 5); education is to be directed to respect for a child's parents (Art. 29); parents have primary responsibility for the care of their children (Arts. 18 and 27); states must assist parents in the performance of this responsibility; (Arts. 18 and 27); and children must not be removed from their parents unless necessary to secure a child's best interests (Art. 9). In light of these provisions, there is no textual foundation for the argument that the CRC undermines the family unit. Indeed, it offers a conception of rights, which is deeply relational when compared with the individualist conception traditionally associated with rights discourse (Federle 460-62; Minow, 1986).

A relational conception of rights

Children's rights under the CRC are not claims to be asserted against the state to be enjoyed in isolation from parents and family. On the contrary, there is an expectation that the realisation of children's rights will be deeply connected and interdependent with the exercise of parental rights, responsibilities and local customary practices. As such, the family, and indeed the community and culture in which a child lives, will be the context in which their rights will be understood, mediated and enjoyed. Moreover, this relational conception of rights is consistent with children's own conception of their relationship with adults. As sociologist Berry Mayall has observed, '[c]hildren recognise the central importance of child-family relationships... They emphasise interdependence and reciprocity, rather than lonely autonomy as central values' (Mayall, 2000, 254). Thus, whereas 'Western liberal thinkers have regarded the autonomous independent moral agent as the highest form of life, children regard relationships as the cornerstone of their lives' (Mayall, 2000, 256). Significantly, the CRC recognises the special relationship between children and parents and indeed the culture in which they live. It therefore challenges an individualistic and masculinist orthodoxy by offering a conception in which the young person's autonomy is both evolving and relational.

It is important to acknowledge that for some commentators, the CRC's deference to adults is still considered unwarranted and reflects an overly protective and paternalistic conception of children's rights. Since the legitimacy of this particular critique will be examined in the next section, it is sufficient to note here that the contention that the CRC is anti-family has no basis.

The conception of family under the CRC – due deference with limits

A more accurate assessment of the CRC is that it reflects a particular conception of the family *and* the parent-child relationship, which is hostile to alternative conceptions of these ideas. Tension arises in at least five areas. First, although the CRC allows for deference to parental rights and responsibilities, this remains subject to the child's evolving capacities and is only permissible where parental powers are exercised so as to *guide and assist* the realisation of children's rights. This approach is inconsistent with a conception of the family in which parents maintain exclusive *power and control* over a child and are not required to respect their evolving capacities.

Second, the CRC tolerates no violence, abuse or neglect towards a child in the care of a parent or guardian (CRC Committee, 2011). This conception contrasts sharply with those in which a reasonable level of violence (and more specifically, corporal punishment) is accepted as a legitimate disciplinary technique for children (cf *Plonit v. Attorney General,* 2000; *Canadian Foundation for Children and Youth and the Law v. Canada,* 2004; CRC Committee,

2007). Third, Article 1(1) of the CRC demands that parents share common responsibilities for a child's upbringing and development. This conception contrasts with those who embrace gendered responsibility for child rearing. Fourth, the CRC offers no definition of 'family' or 'parents' – a further example of its incompletely theorized nature. Thus, the possibility remains that these terms may be interpreted to challenge dominant and traditional understandings of the 'family' and 'parents'. For its part, the CRC Committee has observed that '[w]hen considering the family environment the Convention reflects different family structures arising from the various cultural patterns and emerging familial relationships' and 'it would seem hard to argue for a single notion of the family' (CRC Committee, 1994, 2.1). It is within this context that I have also argued elsewhere that an interpretation of the terms 'parent' and 'family' that is informed by and consistent with the best interests of a child, demands recognition of the possibility and legitimacy of single or same-sex parented families, and the possibility that a child may have multiple parents (Tobin, 2004, 11-12). The CRC therefore offers a conception of the family and the idea of parents that will conflict with alternative conceptions.

Fifth, the CRC offers what could be termed a *collaborative* or *cooperative* conception of the relationship between state and family as regards children's upbringing. This sits somewhere between the liberal *individualist* conception of the family, in which the state must not interfere with a family unless a child is at risk, and the *collectivist* conception, in which child-rearing is under direct control of the community (Archard, 2004, 167-191). Under a collaborative/cooperative model, parents have primary responsibility for children's upbringing but the state (and by implication the broader community from which the state will draw its resources) plays a critical role in assisting parents. Thus, Article 18(2) provides that states 'shall render appropriate assistance to parents ... in the performance of their child rearing responsibilities' and Article 27(3) requires states to take appropriate measures, in accordance with national conditions and within their means, to assist parents and others who are responsible for a child's development, including through the provision of 'material assistance and support programmes particularly with regard to nutrition, clothing and housing.' As such, the CRC advocates a model that enables parents to make claims upon the state and by implication the broader community to take reasonable measures to provide them with necessary assistance to satisfy their parental responsibilities.

In light of such provisions, any suggestion that children's rights under the CRC threaten the integrity and communal fabric of effective family functioning is without foundation. Instead of pitting the rights of parents against those of children, the CRC actually offers a relational rather than individualistic conception of rights. It recognises that as children's autonomy evolves, the role of parents in assisting in the realisation of children's rights, will diminish. But an understanding as to the meaning of children's rights cannot be separated from their family and indeed the culture in which they live.

D. The liberationist and protectionist objections

The CRC is routinely challenged on the grounds that it offers a conception of childhood in which children are either abandoned to their autonomy (Hafen and Hafen, 1996) *or* subject to an excessively protectionist regulatory agenda that is controlled by adults (Cordero 2012, 68; Barnes, 2013; Federle 82). Neither of these claims withstands scrutiny. The liberationist objection, like its anti-family counterpart, is underpinned by the assumption that the CRC reflects a will theory of rights (and thus grants children full autonomy) when in fact it reflects an interest theory (that recognises their evolving and relational autonomy). For its part, the protectionist objection displays no understanding of the idea that protection rights, and not simply autonomy rights, are an underlying feature of *all* international human rights and not just children's rights.

The contemporary liberationist objection traces its origins to the early childhood liberationist agenda of the 1970s in which commentators such Holt (1974) and Farson (1974) advocated a radical conception of childhood in which children were to enjoy the same rights as adults. But this idea has never gained traction among political and philosophical commentators (Purdy, 1992; Archard, 2004, 70-77). Nor does the CRC support this vision. On the contrary, as discussed above, a central part of the moral justification for the CRC is the special vulnerability of children relative to adults and the need to protect them. This protective justification actually consists of two parts – a position that has not been recognised in the literature. First, the idea that children must be protected against potential harm (both physical and non-physical) from others – the *risk of exogenous harm* – and second, the idea that children must be protected against potential harm from themselves – the *risk of endogenous harm.*

Exogenous harm

The risk of exogenous harm is actually a fundamental feature of *all* human rights instruments and is not peculiar to the CRC. Examples of these general protective rights include the right to life, the prohibition against torture, cruel inhuman and degrading treatment, the right to humane detention conditions and the prohibition of discrimination. The justification for such rights arises because of an acceptance that all individuals, whether adults or children, can find themselves in relationships in which a power differential renders them vulnerable to harm. The interest in avoiding such harm founds recognition of such rights, which oblige states to take reasonable measures to protect individuals. It is thus incorrect to suggest that '[a]dults are not protected against exploitation, abuse, neglect or negligent mistreatment' (Archard, 2004, 60) and that *protection rights* are peculiar to children's rights. Human rights law seeks to protect *all human beings*, adults and children, from harm and abuse.

The CRC acknowledges a greater range of scenarios in which children are considered in need of special protection against exogenous harm. As such, there is an issue as to whether the inclusion of these scenarios can be justified. For example, do children need the development of appropriate media guidelines to guard against information and material that is injurious to their wellbeing (Art. 17)? Do children need states to take measures to protect them against all forms of violence and abuse while in the care of parents (Art. 19)? Do children deprived of their family environment, refugee children and children with disabilities require special protective measures (Arts. 20, 22 and 23)? Do working children need to be protected against exploitation (Art 32)? It is not necessary to examine the justification for each of these rights here and it is sufficient to note that the lived experiences of children provide an empirical basis for requiring states to take special measures to protect children in these circumstances. The tragic reality is that children's physical vulnerability and cognitive ability relative to adults exposes them to abuse, violence, harm and exploitation which is not restrained by cultural or temporal boundaries.

However, the fact that the CRC demands protection against exogenous harm does not *necessarily* infantilise children or construct them as mere objects for regulation, intervention and control by adults. It is important to recall that human rights law also requires protective measures for adults when they are in vulnerable situations. The real issue arises with respect to the *identification* and *implementation* of the protective measures and the extent to which the views of the intended beneficiaries, whether adults or children, are taken into account. Are they perceived simply as victims in need of salvation or are they seen as exploited individuals who possess agency but have been forced to make choices in conditions not of their choosing? (Phoenix, 2002, 362).

In addressing this dilemma, the CRC actually offers more guidance than other human rights instruments. This is because Article 12 requires the views of children to be taken into account in all matters affecting them. The scope of this provision must extend to the measures adopted by adults for children's protection because such measures will, to borrow the words of Iris Marion Young, 'significantly condition' a child's 'options for action' (Young, 2010, 145). As such, the CRC promotes a more inclusive and consultative model of decision-making with respect to matters affecting children than other treaties, which are silent as to the process by which states must determine appropriate measures to secure human rights. Thus, the CRC rejects a conception of children that renders them objects or victims in need of protection, in favour of a one in which their evolving agency and capacity must be taken into account. At the same time, it is important to acknowledge that for many, the alleged autonomy offered by Article 12 remains deeply problematic. I address their concerns below. However at this point I turn to the issue of endogenous harm.

Endogenous harm

The CRC does not actually explicitly demand that adults ensure that children do not harm themselves. However, this is implied in the text of Article 5, which provides that states must respect the rights and responsibilities of parents and guardians to provide *direction and assistance* to children in the exercise of their rights. The CRC therefore concedes that children do not always have the same capacity as adults and that adults will often have to exercise a child's right on his or her behalf. Thus, whilst adults are presumed to know what is in their own best interests, no such presumption exists for children. A question arises as to whether this distinction is justified.

In short, the answer is, yes. Intuition tells us what the evidence confirms. Children do not always act consistently with their best interests. A young child may only see the ball on the road whereas an older person will (hopefully) see the oncoming car; a young child may see the gratification that comes from eating candy whereas an older person will (hopefully) see the health consequences; an adolescent may see the peer acceptance that comes with taking drugs or drinking alcohol but an older person will (hopefully) see the health and lifestyle consequences. Of course, adults routinely and repeatedly indulge in activities that are self-harming – however human rights law makes no attempt to prevent them from undertaking such activities. This is because adults are *presumed* to have the capacity to understand the consequences of their actions and are thus free to consent to involvement in activities even when they present a risk to their own interests.

This presumption does not apply to children, whose capacities are presumed to evolve with age, an idea that Eekelaar refers to as 'dynamic self-determinism' (Eekelaar, 1994, 54). Thus Articles 3, 5 and 18 of the CRC presume that there will be occasions when parents and adults must act to secure children's best interests. However, this presumption is rebuttable and does not provide adults with absolute power to regulate every aspect of a child's life until they turn 18. On the contrary, this power remains subject to a child's, evolving capacities, which anticipates occasions when the views of a child with sufficient understanding must be respected, even though they conflict with the views of a parent. In other words, the conception of childhood under the CRC entertains that, for children who demonstrate competency with respect to a particular issue, there will be a point where the assessment of the child's best interests is aligned with and determined by reference to the child's *own* views. This flexibility allows for the CRC to address the concern raised above as to the justification for the conception of children being all persons under the age of 18. This is because the CRC does not treat children as a homogenous group and the powers that are granted to adults to regulate their lives must accommodate children's evolving capacities (Archard, 2004, 65).

Radical or regressive – the conception of children's autonomy under Article 12
The obligation to assure that children's views are heard in the decision-making process *and* to ensure that these are weighed according to age and maturity presents a radical departure from previously held conceptions of childhood. For example, under the doctrine of *patria potestas*, children were literally the property of their father and were neither seen nor heard, whereas under the welfare model, children may have been seen but there was no expectation that they be heard. In contrast, the conception of childhood under the CRC demands that children are both seen and heard.

However, as noted above, many commentators doubt the extent to which the CRC, and in particular Article 12, recognises children's evolving autonomy. For them, children's participatory rights are ultimately subordinated to the interests of adults who have the power to determine how children express their views, the matters upon which children express their views and the weight to be accorded to them. As such, adults remain the sole arbiters of children's best interests and far from being a tool of empowerment, the CRC is seen as an instrument for the continued subjugation for children. This fear may well be aligned with the reality that many contemporary practices that seek to promote children's participation and autonomy in decision-making, remain tokenistic. But such an outcome is neither necessary nor compatible with a contextual interpretation of Article 12 of the CRC and this is so for five reasons.

The role of evidence
First, the weight to be given to a child's views under Article 12 is not to be determined subjectively. Where the evidence supports a finding that a child is competent or has the capacity to understand an issue, as is often the case with respect to issues like medical treatment, there is no longer a moral justification to treat the child differently to an adult. The special vulnerability that provided the justification for special protection ceases to exist.

The broad scope of Article 12
Second, the scope of children's participatory rights under Article 12 extends not just to matters that directly concern them, but to *all matters affecting* them. Thus, there is the potential for the rights of other persons, whether adults or other children, to be involved in measures taken by a state which may also affect a child, such as planning laws, social security laws and sentencing laws.

In such circumstances, the views of an individual child will not necessarily be determinative since Article 3 provides only that children's best interests are a primary consideration. But Article 12 demands that a decision maker must still take a child's views into account in the decision-making process – an expectation that most of us would have with respect to the views of any adults who may also be affected, but which is not generally recognised explicitly in human rights treaties. In this sense, Article 12 demands a transformation of the decision-making process to be more inclusive and deliberative – an approach that is consistent with the substantive dimension of a social interest theory of rights and represents an advance on general human rights treaties which do not impose such a specific demand upon states (CRC Committee, 2009; Young, 2010, 53).

Reconceptualising participation

Third, the obligation to *assure* to children an opportunity to express their views demands that states must take positive measures to enable children to express their views appropriately for their age and level of maturity. Traditional adult-centric methods to facilitate participation in decision-making will not always be accessible or appropriate for children. To adapt the words of Iris Marion Young, the 'terms of the discourse' may make 'assumptions' that children do not share, and the interactions may privilege adult styles of expression to the exclusion of children's modes of expression (Young, 2010, 53). Thus, Article 12 demands new conceptions of participation that have the capacity to transform the decision-making process and make it more *inclusive* by bringing into play views that would otherwise go unheard (Thomas, 2007).

The nexus between development rights and autonomy rights

Fourth, critiques of Article 12 and the other participatory rights under the CRC tend to overlook the impact of developmental rights on children's ability to participate in deliberative decision-making. For example, ensuring that children are healthy, housed and have access to a high quality education empowers children, who are better equipped to assert their claims for rights, including their right to participate in decision-making about matters that affect them (Eekelaar, 2006, 156; Young, 2010, 31). Thus, to read the CRC as simply an instrument that entrenches adult power is to overlook the cumulative impact of the rights provided for in this instrument on a child's development and capacity for effective participation. It is also to forget that the human rights enterprise is concerned with empowering the disempowered and regulating the exercise of power over vulnerable persons, whether they are adults or children. As such, Article 12 must be interpreted to affirm, rather than undermine, these objectives by demanding an inclusive form of deliberative decision-making.

In support of children's citizenship

Finally, to interpret the CRC as a 'substantial and thorough instrument for the denial of children's citizenship' (Milne, 41) is to arrive at an interpretation that remains entirely detached from the text of the CRC. Article 12 demands positive measures to facilitate and encourage children to *express their views* in line with their evolving capacity – hardly a vision that is inconsistent with active citizenship. Moreover, to subordinate such views automatically to the interests and perceived 'expertise' of adults is inconsistent with the right to development under Article 6, which extends beyond physical and mental development to a child's social development. As Eekelaar has argued, the 'duty of a child's carers is to establish the most propitious environment for the child [and] further to develop the personality growing within him or her' (Eekelaar, 2008, 156-57). The infantilisation of children and dismissal of their views cannot be reconciled with a child's social development when research demonstrates that devolving responsibility and listening to children actually enhances their self-esteem and understanding of citizenship (Hart 1992, 4; Flekkøy and Kaufman, 1997, 55; Lansdown 2001, 6; Chawla, 2002, 14; UNICEF, 2003, 4).

Moreover, Article 29 provides that a child's education shall be directed to the development of respect for human rights and preparation for a *responsible life* in society in the spirit of understanding, peace and tolerance. An approach to decision-making that dismisses a person's competency and insights based simply on their age promotes a conception of citizenship that is difficult, if not impossible, to reconcile with the aims of a child's education under the CRC. If the idea that children have *value* simply by being human is accepted, it becomes incongruous to *devalue* their views, insights and opinions simply because they are children. To value children because they are human beings demands that their views, when expressed, must also be respected and not simply dismissed because of assumptions about their lack of expertise and understanding (Mayall, 2000, 245 & 257).

A radical reconceptualisation of the adult/child relationship

Thus, Article 12 presents a radical re-conceptualisation of the adult-child decision-making relationship (Lansdown 2001, 1). Indeed, it has the capacity to satisfy Iris Marion Young's assertion that 'the normative legitimacy of a democratic decision depends on the degree to which those affected by it have been included in the decision-making processes *and* have had the opportunity to influence the outcomes' (Young, 2010, 5-6). Although it places a burden on adults to act in children's best interests, it also demands that adults must not be considered the sole arbiters of a child's best interests. It also requires that adults work with children to create inclusive communication systems and processes that allow for children's views to be heard in all matters affecting them; that the views of children must be taken into account and treated seriously in decision-making processes; and that decision-makers must explain to children why certain decisions have been made. It accepts that there will be occasions when adults must take sole responsibility for making decisions that are in children's best interests, but there will be others when adults and children must undertake the decision-making process collaboratively and even more controversially when adults must devolve the decision-making process to children themselves (Hart 1992; Treseder, 1997; Shier, 2001; Thomas, 2007; Hinton, 2008).

Thus, to suggest that under the CRC, adults 'retain final authority over children' (Archard, 2004, 66) is neither a necessary nor persuasive interpretation of this instrument. Contrary to Archard's suggestion, there is no 'may' in the text of Article 12 to qualify the obligation to give a child's views due weight (Archard, 2004, 66). It simply refers to 'the views of the *child being given* due weight'. Thus Article 12 is capable of being interpreted to offer more than simply a 'right to have an *opportunity to influence* the person who will otherwise choose for the child' (emphasis added) (Archard, 2004, 66). It can also be interpreted to require that a child's views *must* be given due weight, in which case the CRC anticipates that the views of a child of sufficient maturity and understanding will be determinative of his or her best interests. Importantly, such an interpretation is not only consistent with the text of Article 12, but also consistent with the conceptual foundations of children's rights. If a child demonstrates competence equivalent to that of an adult with respect to a particular issue, then the justification for special measures to protect the child against endogenous harm no longer exists.[8]

4. Conclusion – more than the offer of a chocolate frog

In a recent child protection case in Victoria Australia, an issue arose regarding the capacity of two girls aged 9 and 11 to provide instructions to their lawyer.[9] The case involved allegations of domestic violence and drug abuse by their mother. The girls provided instructions to the effect that they did not wish to live with their mother and wanted to remain with their aunt and uncle. The

---

[8] This does not mean that bright line age restrictions are unjustifiable with respect to the regulation of children's behaviour *as a class*. As Eekelaar has explained, in such circumstances 'general age restrictions can be placed on the attainment of legal competence because it would be unreasonable to expect individual assessments of actual competence in each case' (Eekelaar 2008, 157). For a fuller discussion of children's evolving capacities and the issue of age based restrictions see: Lansdown, Gerison, *Innocenti Insight: The Evolving Capacities of the Child* (2005).

[9] *A B v. Children's Court of Victoria* [2012] VSC 598 (Austl.).

mother subsequently raised an allegation of sexual abuse against the uncle. The girls indicated that they wished to see their uncle but were unable to provide any instructions on the sexual abuse claims. The Magistrate was far from satisfied with this approach and declared:

> I may as well ask them, 'Do you want a chocolate frog in your morning tea tomorrow?' It is not going to assist me that they get on well with [the uncle] or they get on badly with him ... The fact remains these children can't participate in one of the two key issues in terms of instructing. They are not mature enough.[10]

The Magistrate then proceeded to appoint an independent children's lawyer for the children who was not required to act on their instructions. However, the matter was appealed to Supreme Court of Victoria, where the judge overturned the Magistrate's ruling and declared that '[i]t is sufficient that the child be mature enough to give instructions on one of more the issues that arise or may arise in the hearing or proceeding.'[11] The children's views were not necessarily determinative of the legal issues at hand but they had a right for their views to be heard and treated seriously by the judge.

You may ask, what is the relevance of this case to the issue of whether the idea of human rights for children can be justified? The answer is that it reflects differences in the treatment of children that arise when autonomy is conceived of in absolute terms, rather than being conceived of as evolving. Children's lack of capacity (both real and perceived) has and continues to provide the bedrock upon which many commentators would deny human rights for children. Moreover, this denial of rights infantilises children and reduces them to mere objects in need of protection. The offer by the Magistrate to provide a chocolate frog in the children's morning tea indicates not only a lack of respect for these children but also implies suspicion with respect to the value of their views regarding those matters on which they could provide instructions. In contrast, the decision of the appeal court demonstrates a commitment to respect the rights of children, including their right to be heard within the context of their evolving capacities.

But this paper has sought to demonstrate more than the idea that autonomy need not be conceived of in absolute terms. It has advanced the idea of a social interest theory of rights to offer a good, albeit imperfect justification for the idea of human rights for children, as expressed under the CRC. Ultimately, this theory of rights reflects Sally Merry's idea that human rights is primarily a cultural system – fluid and contentious (Merry, 2006, 16) – that produces and constructs rather than discovers some metaphysical vision of the rights to

---

[10] *Id.*, ¶¶ 20-21.
[11] *Id.*, ¶ 106 (also noting that in many proceedings an adult may also be able to give instructions with respect to a limited number of issues: ¶107).

which children are entitled. Thus, the preamble to the CRC may assert the inherent dignity and inalienable rights of every child, but this instrument cannot be taken to reflect a comprehensive theory of human dignity for children or 'the existence of a universal human nature' (Rorty, 1993,116). Rather, it reflects a historically contingent and contested understanding of the rights to which states have agreed, albeit under an incompletely theorized agreement, that will shift and change over time. This dynamism does not, however, produce an arbitrary theory of human rights for children, but one that is contingent on the 'anthropological realities' and 'contemporary political conditions' that characterise the environment in which the CRC was negotiated (Freeman, 1994, 513-14).

For commentators like Griffin, who are eager to fix the parameters of human rights, the malleability of the CRC is problematic. But in many respects this malleability is its greatest strength. Indeed without it, the legitimacy of the CRC would be seriously compromised under the substantive dimension of a social interest theory because of its adult, Western-centric origins. Provisions such as Articles 3 and Article 12 allow for children to play a constitutive role in shaping the meaning of their rights under the CRC and express their views on which additional interests are deserving of protection. Thus, far from being a settled catalogue of rights and interests, the CRC offers the potential for a dynamic and inclusive evolution of children's rights in which children must play an active role, consistent with their evolving capacities.

This potential will not be realised, however, if contemporary social systems fail to recognise children's right to be both seen and heard. As John Eekelaar explains, '[n]o society will have begun to perceive its children as rights holders until adults' attitudes and social structures are seriously adjusted towards making it possible for children to express views and towards addressing them with respect' (Eekelaar, 1992, 228). This is the practical challenge that threatens the effective implementation of the vision for children offered in the CRC; a vision in which they are no longer conceived of in purely instrumental terms or as objects in need of protection, but as human beings in possession of rights and unique and equal value, just like their adult counterparts. It is a vision that demands more than simply the offer of a chocolate frog.

References

1 Journal Articles

Alderson, P., 'Young children's human rights: A sociological analysis', *International Journal of Children's Rights* 20(2) (2012): 177–198.

Alston, P., 'The unborn child and abortion under the draft convention on the rights of the child', *Human Rights Quarterly* 12(1) (1990): 156–178.

Appell, A., 'Child-Centred jurisprudence and feminist jurisprudence: Exploring the connections and tension', *Houston Law Review* 46(3) (2009): 703–759.

Buchanan, A., 'The egalitarianism of human rights', *Ethics* 120(4) (2010): 679–710.

Burman, E., 'Local, global or globalised? Child development and international child rights legislation', *Childhood* 3(1) (1992): 45–66.

Chase, A., 'Legitimizing human rights: Beyond mythical foundations into everyday resonances', *Journal of Human Rights* 11(4) (2012): 505–525.

Chawla, L., 'Insight, creativity and thoughts on the environment: Integrating children and youth into human settlement development', *Environment and Urbanisation* 14(2) (2002): 11–21.

Coady, M., 'The continuing importance of thinking that children have rights', *Australian Journal of Professional and Applied Ethics* 7(1) (2005): 47–235.

Cordero Arce, M., 'Towards an emancipatory discourse of children's rights', *International Journal of Children's Rights* 20(3) (2012) 365-421.

Dixon, R., & Nussbaum, M., 'Children's rights and a capabilities approach: The question of special priority', *Cornell Law Review* 97(3) (2012): 549–593.

Eekelaar, J., 'The emergence of children's rights', *Oxford Journal of Legal Studies* 6(2) (1986): 161–182.

Eekelaar, J., 'The importance of thinking that children have rights', *International Journal of Family Law* 6(1) (1992): 221–235.

Eekelaar, J., 'Naturalism or pragmatism? Towards an expansive view of human rights', *Journal of Human Rights* 10(2) (2011): 230–242.

Evans, T., 'International human rights law as power/knowledge', *Human Rights Quarterly* 27(3) (2005): 1046–1068.

Ferguson, L., 'Not merely rights for children but children's rights: The theory gap and the assumption of the importance of children's rights', *International Journal of Children's Rights* 21(2) (2013) 177–208.

Fernando, J., 'Children's rights: Beyond the impasse', *Annals of the American Academy of Political and Social Science* 575 (2010): 8–24.

Fortin, J., 'Children's rights: Are the courts now taking them more seriously?', *King's Law Journal* 15(2) (2004): 253–272.

Franks, M., 'Pockets of participation: Revisiting child centred participation research', *Children and Society* 25(1) (2011): 15–25.

Freeman, M., 'Taking children's rights seriously', *Children and Society* 1(4) (1987): 299–319.

Freeman, M., 'Taking children's rights more seriously', *International Journal of Law and the Family* 6(1) (1992): 55–71.

Freeman, M., 'The philosophical foundations of human rights', *Human Rights Quarterly* 16(2) (1994) 491-514.

Freeman, M., 'The future of children's rights', *Children and Society* 14(4) (2000): 277–293.

Freeman, M., 'Why it remains important to take children's rights seriously', *International Journal of Children's Rights* 15(1) (2007): 5–23.

Freeman, M., 'The human rights of children', *Current Legal Problems* 63(1) (2010): 1–44.

Frost, R., 'The justification of human rights and the basic right to justification: A reflexive approach', *Ethics* 120(4) (2010): 711–740.

Goodin, R., & Gibson, D., 'Rights, young and old', *Oxford Journal of Legal Studies* 17(2) (1997): 185–203.

Grahn-Farley, M., 'Beyond right and reason: Pieree schlag, the critique of normativity and the enchantment of reason: A theory of child rights', *University of Miami Law Review* 57(3) (2003): 867–398.

Habermas, J., 'The concept of human dignity and the realistic utopia of human rights', *Metaphilosophy* 41(4) (2010): 465–480.

Hafen, B., & Hafen, J., 'Abandoning children to their autonomy: The united nations convention on the rights of the child', *Harvard International Law Journal* 37(2) (1996): 449–491.

Harris-Short, S., 'Listening to the other? The convention on the rights of the child', *Melbourne Journal of International Law* 2(2) (2001): 304–350.

Harris-Short, S., 'International human rights law: Imperialist, inept and ineffective? Cultural relativism and the UN convention on the rights of the child', *Human Rights QuArterly* 25(1) (2003): 130–181.

Hinton, R., 'Children's participation and good governance: Limitations of the theoretical literature', *International Journal of Children's Rights* 16(3) (2008): 281–285.

Kennedy, D., 'The international human rights movement: Part of the problem?', *Harvard Human Rights Journal* 15 (2002): 101–125.

King, M., 'The Child, childhood and children's rights within sociology', *King's Law Journal* 15(2) (2004): 273–300.

Lundy, L., & McEvoy, L., 'Children's rights and research processes: assisting children to (in) formed views', *Childhood* 19(1) (2011): 129–144.

Lundy, L., McEvoy, L., & Bronagh, B., 'Working with young children as co-researchers: An approach informed by the united nations convention on the rights of the child', *Early Education and Development* 22(5) (2011): 714–736.

Macklin, R., 'Dignity is a useless concept', *British Medical Journal* 327 (2003): 1419–1420.

Mayall, B., 'The sociology of childhood in relation to children's rights', *International Journal of Children's Rights* 8(3) (2000): 243–158.

McCrudden, C., 'Human dignity and the judicial interpretation of human rights', *European Journal of International Law* 19(4) (2008): 655–724.

Milne, B, 'Is participation as it is described by the united nations convention on the rights of the child the key to children's citizenship?', *Journal of Social Science* 9 (2005): 31–42.

Minow, M., 'Rights for the next generation: A feminist approach to children's rights', *Harvard Women's Law Journal* 9 (1986): 1–24.

Minow, M., 'Whatever happened to children's rights?', *Minnesota Law Review* 80(2) (1995): 267–298.

Mitchell, M., 'Justifying human rights: Perry, kohen and the overlapping consensus', *Journal of Human Rights* 9(3) (2010): 363–372.

Morris, A., Hegarty, K. and Humphreys, C., 'Ethical and safe: Research with children about domestic violence', *Research Ethics* 8(2) (2012): 125–139.

O'Neill, O., 'Children's rights and children's lives', *Ethics* 98(3) (1988): 445–463.

Phoenix, J., 'In the name of protection: Youth prostitution reforms in england and wales', *Critical Social Policy* 22(2) (2002): 353–375.

Pupavac, V., 'The infantilisation of the south and the UN convention on the rights of the child', *Human Rights Law Review* 3(2) (1998): 1–6.

Pupavac, V., 'Misanthropy without borders: The international children's rights regime', *Disasters* 25(2) (2011): 95–112.

Purdy, L., 'Why children shouldn't have equal rights', *International Journal of Children's Rights* 2(3) (1994): 223–241.

Reynaert, D. et al., 'Between "believers" and "opponents": Critical discussions on children's rights', *International Journal of Children's Rights* 20(1) (2012): 155–168.

Rosenblum, P., 'Teaching human rights: Ambivalent activism, multiple discourses and lingering dilemmas', *Harvard Human Rights Journal* 15(1) (2002): 301–316.

Schroeder, D., 'Dignity: One, two, three, four, five, still counting', *Cambridge Quarterly Healthcare Ethics* 19(1) (2010): 118–125.

Schroeder, D., 'Human rights and human dignity: An appeal to separate the conjoined twins', *Ethical Theory and Moral Practice* 15(3) (2012): 323–335.

Sen, A., 'Elements of a theory of human rights', *Philosophy and Public Affairs* 32(4) (2004): 315–356.

Seymour, J., 'Parental rights and the protection of children: A presumption against state intervention?', *Australian Journal of Professional and Applied Ethics* 7(2) (2005): 16–30.

Shier, H., 'Pathways to participation: Openings opportunities and obligations', *Children and Society* 15(2) (2001): 107–117.

Smith, A. B., 'Interpreting and supporting participation rights: Contributions from sociological theory', *International Journal of Children's Rights* 10(1) (2002) 73-88.

Stammers, N, 'Social movements and the social construction of human rights', *Human Rights Quarterly* 21(4) (1999) 980-1008.

Sunstein, C., 'Incompletely theorized agreements', *Harvard Law Review* 108(7) (1995): 1733–1772.

Thomas, N., 'Towards a theory of children's participation', *International Journal of Children's Rights* 15(2) (2007): 199–218.

Tisdall, K., 'The challenge and challenging of childhood studies? Learning from disability studies and research with disabled children', *Children and Society* 26(3) (2012): 181–191.

Tobin, J., 'Increasingly seen and heard: The constitutional recognition of children's rights', *South African Journal of Human Rights* 21(1) (2005): 86–126.

Tobin, J., 'Parents and children's rights under the convention on the rights of the child: Finding reconciliation in misunderstood relationship', *Australian Journal of Professional and Applied Ethics* 7(2) (2005): 31–46.

Tobin, J., 'Judging the judges: Are they adopting the rights approach in matters involving children', *Melbourne University Law Review* 33(2) (2009): 579–625.

Tobin, J., 'The international obligation to abolish traditional practices harmful to children's health: What does it mean and require of states?', *Human Rights Law Review* 9(3) (2009): 373–396.

Tobin, J., 'Seeking to persuade: A constructive approach to human rights treaty interpretation', *Harvard Human Rights Journal* 23(1) (2010): 1–50.

Tobin, J., & McNair, R., 'Public international law and the regulation of private spaces: Does the convention on the rights of the child impose an obligation on states to allow gay and lesbian couples to adopt?', *International Journal of Law, Policy and Family* 23(1) (2009): 110–131.

van Krieken, Robert, 'The best interests of the child and parental separation: On the civilizing of parents', *Modern Law Review* 68(1) (2005): 25–48.

2   Books

Adler, R., *Taking Juvenile Justice Seriously* (Edinburgh: Scottish Academic Press, 1985).

Alderson, P., *Young Children's Rights: Exploring Beliefs, Principles and Practice* (London: Jessica Kingsley, 2008).

Alston, P., & Gilmour-Walsh, B., *The Best Interests of the Child: Towards a Synthesis of Children's Rights and Cultural Values* (Florence: UNICEF, 1996).

Alston, P., *The Best Interests of The Child: Reconciling Culture and Human Rights* (Oxford: Oxford University Press, 1994).

Archard, D., *Children: Rights and Childhood* (London: Routledge, 2004).

Ariès, P., *Centuries of Childhood: A Social History of Family Life* (London: Vintage Books, 1965).

Beitz, C., *The Idea of Human Rights* (Oxford: Oxford University Press, 2009).

Eekelaar, J., *Family Law and Personal Life* (Oxford: Oxford University Press, 2006).

Farson, R., *Birthrights* (New York: Macmillan, 1974).

Flekkøy, M., & Kaufman, N., *The Participation Rights of the Child: Rights and Responsibilities in Family and Society* (London: Jessica Kingsley, 1997).

Fortin, J., *Children's Rights: The Developing Law* (Cambridge: Cambridge University Press, 2009).

Frost, M., *Ethics in International Relations: A Constitutive Theory* (Cambridge: Cambridge University Press, 1996).

Gilligan, C., *In a Different Voice: Psychological Theory and Women's Development* (Boston: Harvard University Press, 1982).

Goldstein, J. et al., *Beyond the Best Interests of the Child* (New York: The Free Press, 1973).

Goldstein, J. et al., *Before the Best Interests of the Child* (New York: The Free Press, 1980).

Goldstein, J. et al., *The Best Interests of the Child* (New York: The Free Press, 1998).

Griffin, J., *On Human Rights* (Oxford: Oxford University Press, 2009).

Guggenheim, M., *What's Wrong with Children's Rights* (Boston: Harvard University Press, 2005).

Guzman, I., *Parent Police: The UN wants your Children* (Lafayette: Huntington House, 1991).

Hart, J. et al., *Children Changing their World: Understanding and Evaluating Children's Participation in Development* (London: Plan UK, 2004).

Hart, R., *Children's Participation: From Tokenism to Citizenship* (Florence: UNICEF, 1992).

Henkin, L., *The Age of Rights* (New York: Columbia University Press, 1990).

Hobbes, T., *The Elements of Law, Natural and Politic* (Oxford: Oxford University Press, 1994).

Holt, J., *Escape from Childhood: The Needs and Rights of Children* (Dutton: Boston, 1974).

Humphrey, J., *Human Rights and the United Nations: A Great Adventure* (Dobbs Ferry, NY: Transnational, 1984).

Hunt, L., *Inventing Human Rights: A History* (New York: W.W. Norton & Company, 2007).

King, M., *A Better World for Children?* (London: Routledge, 1997).

Kleninig, J., *Philosophical Issues in Education* (London: Croom Helm, 1982).

Lansdown, G., *Promoting Children's Participation in Democratic Decision-Making* (Florence: UNICEF, 2001).

Lansdown, G., *Innocenti Insight: The Evolving Capacities of the Child* (Florence: UNICEF, 2005).

Lauterpacht, H., *International Law and Human Rights* (London: Stevens & Sons, 1950).

Le Blanc, L., *The Convention on the Rights of the Child: United Nations Law Making on Human Rights* (Lincoln, NE: University of Nebraska Press, 1995).

Lundy, L. et al., *The United Nations Convention on the Rights of the Child: A Study of the Legal Implementation in 12 Countries* (London: UNICEF, 2012).

Macnaughton, G., Hughes, P., & Smith, K., *Young Children as Active Citizens: Principles, Policies and Pedagogies* (Newcastle: Cambridge Scholars, 2008).

Merry, S., *Human Rights and Gender Violence: Translating International Law into Local Justice* (Chicago: University of Chicago Press, 2006).

Moyn, S., *The Last Utopia* (Boston: Harvard University Press, 2010).

Purdy, L., *In Their Best Interest? The Case Against Equal Rights for Children* (Ithaca, NY: Cornell University Press, 1992).

Raz, J., *The Morality of Freedom* (Oxford: Oxford University Press, 1986).

Rosemond, J., *A Family of Value* (Kansas City, MO: Andrews & McMeel, 1995).

Tobin, J., *The Right to Health in International Law* (Oxford: Oxford University Press, 2012).

Treseder, P., *Empowering Children and Young People Training Manual: Promoting Involvement in Decision-Making* (Dunfermline: Carnegie UK Trust, 1997).

Van Bueren, G., *The International Law on the Rights of the Child* (Leiden: Martinus Nijhoff, 1995).

Young, I., *Inclusion and Democracy* (Oxford: Oxford University Press, 2010).

3 Edited Books

Alston, P., 'The best interests principle: Towards a reconciliation of culture and human rights'. In *The Best Interests of the Child: Reconciling Culture and Human Rights*. ed. P. Alston (Oxford: Oxford University Press, 1994) 1.

Arneil, B., 'Becoming versus being: A critical analysis of the child in liberal theory'. In *The Moral and Political Status of Children*. eds. D. Archard & C. Macleod (Oxford University Press: Oxford, 2002) 70.

Baxi, U., 'The place of the human right to health and contemporary approaches to global justice'. In *Global Health And Human Rights: Legal And Philosophical Perspectives*. eds. J. Harrington & M. Stutterford (New York: Routledge, 2010) 1.

Beazley, H. et al., 'How are the human rights of children related to research methodology?' In *The Human Rights of Children: From Visions to Implementation*. eds. A. Invernizzi & J. Williams (Ashgate: Farnham, 211) 159.

Brennan, S., 'Children's choices or children's interests: Which do their rights protect?'. In *The Moral and Political Status of Children*. eds. D. Archard & C. Macleod (Oxford University Press: Oxford, 2002) 53.

Brighouse, H., 'What rights (if any) do children have?'. In *The Moral and Political Status of Children*. eds. D. Archard and C. Macleod (Oxford University Press: Oxford, 2002) 31.

Buchanan, A., & Hessler, K., 'Specifying the content of the human right to health care'. In *Justice and Health Care: Selected Essays*. eds. A. Buchanan & K. Hessler 213 (Oxford: Oxford University Press, 2009) 203.

Chrstensen, P., and James, A., *Research With Children: Perspectives and Practices* (Routledge: New York, 2008).

Eekelaar, J., 'The interests of the child and the child's wishes: The role of dynamic self-determinism'. In *The Best Interests of The Child: Reconciling Culture and Human Rights*. ed. P. Alston (Oxford: Oxford University Press, 1994) 54.

Ennew, J., 'Outside childhood: Street children's rights'. In *The Handbook of Children's Rights: Comparative Practice*. ed. B. Franklin (New York: Routledge, 2001) 202.

Freeman, M., & Veerman, P., eds., *The Ideologies of Children's Rights* (Leiden: MArtinus Nijhoff, 1992).

Federle, K., 'Rights flow downhill'. In *Children's Rights: Progress and Perspectives*. ed. M. Freeman (Leiden: Martinus Nijhoff, 2011) 447.

Gross, B., & Gross, R., eds., *The Children's Rights Movement: Overcoming The Oppression of Young People* (Garden City, NY: Anchor Books, 1977).

Kramer, M, 'Rights without trimmings'. In *A Debate over Rights: Philosophical Enquiries*. eds. M. Krmaer, N. H. Simmonds, & H. Steiner (Oxford: Oxford University Press, 2000) 7.

Lundy, L., & McEvoy, L., 'Childhood, the united nations convention on the rights of the child and research: What constitutes a rights-based approach?'. In *Law and Childhood Studies*. Vol. 14. ed. M. Freeman (Oxford: Oxford University Press, 2012) 75.

MacNaughton, G., & Smith, K., 'Children's rights in early childhood'. In *An Introduction to Childhood Studies*. ed. M. J. Kehily (Maidenhead: McGraw International, 2009) 161.

Mason, J., & Falloon, J., 'Some sydney children define abuse: Some implications for agency and childhood'. In *Conceptualising Child-Adult Relations*. eds. L. Alanen & B. Mayall (New York: Routledge, 2001) 99.

Rorty, R., 'Human rights, rationality and sentimentality'. In *On Human Rights*. eds. S. Shute & S. Hurley (New York: Basic Books, 1993) 111.

Saballa, M., MacNaughton, G., & Smith, K., 'Working with children to create policy: The case of the australian capital territory's children's plan'. In *Young Children as Active Citizens: Principles, Policies and Pedagogies*. eds. G. MacNaughton, P. Hughes, & K. Smith (Cambridge: Cambridge Scholars Publishing, 2008) 62.

Stalford, H., & Drywood, E., 'Using the CRC to inform EU law and policy making'. In *The Human Rights of Children: From Visions to Implementation*. eds. A. Invernizzi & J. Williams (Farnham: Ashgate, 211) 179.

4   Reports

Australian Senate Inquiry, *United Nations Convention on the Rights of the Child* (Parliament of Australia, Joint Standing Committee on Treaties Australia 17th Report Commonwealth of Australia 1998).

Committee on The Rights of The Child, *Discussion Day on the Role of The Family in The Promotion of The Rights of the Child* (1994).

International Labour Organization, *Accelerating Action Against Child Labour: Global Report Under the Follow-Up to the ILO Declaration* on *Fundamental Principles and Rights at Work 2010* (2010).

Tobin, John, *The Convention on the Rights of The Child: The Rights and Best Interests of Children Conceived Through Assisted Reproduction* (Victorian Law Reform Commission Occasional Paper 2004).

UNICEF, *World Report* on *Violence Against Children* (2006).

5 Theses

Barnes, A., *The Legal Construction of the Child in the United Nations Convention* on *the Rights of the Child*, PhD Thesis, College of Law, Australian National University, Canberra.
Nakata, S., *Governing Childhood: The Politics of Becoming Adult*, PhD Thesis, School of Social and Political Sciences, University of Melbourne, Melbourne.

6 Cases

A B v. Children's Court of Victoria [2012] VSC 598 (Australia).
Canadian Foundation for Children, Youth and the Law v. Canada (Attorney General) [2004] 1 SCR 76 (Canada).
Plonit v. Attorney General [2000] 54(1) IsrSC 145 (Israel).

7 International Treaties

Geneva Convention Relative to the Protection of Civilian Persons in Time of War of August 12, 1949, opened for signature 12 August 1949, 75 U.N.T.S. 287.
International Covenant on Civil and Political Rights, opened for signature 16 December 1966, 999 U.N.T.S. 171.
International Covenant on Economic, Social and Cultural Rights, opened for signature 16 December 1966, 993 U.N.T.S 3.
International Labour Organization Convention Concerning Minimum Age for Admission to Employment, adopted at the 58th ILC Session, 26 June 1973.
International Labour Organization Convention Concerning the Age for Admission of Children to Employment in Agriculture, adopted at the 3rd ILC Session, 16 November 1921.
International Labour Organization Convention Concerning the Compulsory Medical Examination of Children and Young Persons Employed at Sea, adopted at the 3rd ILC Session, 11 November 1921.
International Labour Organization Convention Concerning the Night Work of Young Persons Employed in Industry, adopted at the 1st ILC Session, 28 November 1919.
International Labour Organization Convention Concerning the Prohibition and Immediate Action for the Elimination of the Worst Forms of Child Labour, adopted at the 87th ILC Session, 17 June 1999.
International Labour Organization Convention Fixing the Minimum Age for Admission of Children to Employment at Sea, adopted at the 2nd ILC Session, 9 July 1920.
Protocol Additional to the Geneva Conventions of 12 August 1949, and Relating to the Protection of Victims of International Armed Conflicts, opened for signature 8 June 1977, 1125 U.N.T.S. 3.
Protocol Additional to the Geneva Conventions of 12 August 1949, and Relating to the Protection of Victims of Non-International Armed Conflicts, opened for signature 8 June 1977, 1125 U.N.T.S. 609.
Universal Declaration of Human Rights, G.A. Res. 217A (III), UN GAOR, 3rd sess, 183rd plen mtg, U.N. Doc. A/RES/217A (III) (10 December 1948).
Vienna Convention on the Law of Treaties, opened for signature 23 May 1969, 1155 U.N.T.S. 331.

8 Treaty Body Materials

Committee on the Rights of the Child General, *General Comment No 8: The Right of the Child to Be Protected Against Corporal Punishment and Any Other Cruel or Degrading Forms of Punishment,* CRC/C/GC/8 (2007).

Committee on the Rights of the Child, *General Comment No 12: The Right of the Child to Be Heard*, CRC/C/GC/12 (2009).

Committee on the Rights of the Child, *General Comment No 13: The Right of the Child to Freedom from All Forms of Violence*, CRC/C/GC/13 (2011).

9 *Other*

Rush, E., & La Nauze, A., *Corporate Paedophilia* (Australia Institute Discussion Paper No 90, 2006).

Incorporation of the United Nations Convention on the Rights of the Child in Law: A Comparative Review

Laura Lundy[a], Ursula Kilkelly[b], Bronagh Byrne[c]
a) Professor of Education Law and Children's Rights
Director, Centre for Children's Rights, Queen's University, Belfast
L.Lundy@qub.ac.uk
b) Faculty of Law, University College Cork
c) School of Sociology, Social Policy and Social Work,
Queen's University, Belfast

Introduction

'The fate of human rights – their implementation, abridgement, protection, violation, enforcement, denial, or enjoyment – is largely a matter of national, not international, action'[1]

The fate of children's rights as a bespoke subset of human rights is, of course, the same: the translation of the promises of human rights law into reality for children is dependent not just simply or even mainly on international monitoring and review, but rather on the national actions of the governments who have ratified them. This was recognised from the outset in Article 4 of the United Nations Convention on the Rights of the Child ('CRC' or 'the Convention') which requires States Parties to:

> undertake all appropriate legislative, administrative, and other measures for the implementation of the rights recognized in the present Convention. With regard to economic, social and cultural rights, States Parties shall undertake such measures to the maximum extent of their available resources...

---

* The authors would like to acknowledge the support and valuable input of the UNICEF-UK staff throughout the course of the study, in particular Dragan Nastic, Lisa Payne and Sam Whyte. Gratitude is also due to the UNICEF Nat.Coms and John Tobin, School of Law, University of Melbourne who provided us with contacts for the field visits. We are grateful to all those who commented on drafts and agreed to be interviewed. We would also like to acknowledge the research assistance provided by Jason Kang, a law student at the University of Emory, Atlanta who was an intern at Queen's University, Belfast during the project.
[1] Donnelly, J. *Universal Human Rights in Theory and Practice* (2nd edition) London and Ithaca: Cornell University Press, p. 171.

International human rights treaties do not, in general, specify how States Parties are to give effect to their obligations at the domestic level, but require them to take 'all appropriate measures'.[2] It is up to states to determine how best to implement their international treaty obligations, subject to the satisfaction of those obligations in practice.[3] This article considers the ways in which a variety of countries have chosen to incorporate the CRC, drawing on a study conducted by the authors for UNICEF-UK.[4] The purpose of the study was to identify the most effective and practical ways of giving effect to the Convention in law, drawing on experience in 12 purposively selected countries. The article begins with a review of the methods employed, followed by an examination of the various ways in which incorporation has occurred. These have been categorised into examples of direct incorporation (where the CRC forms part of domestic law) and indirect incorporation (where there are legal obligations which encourage its incorporation); and full incorporation (where the CRC has been wholly incorporated in law) and partial incorporation (where elements of the CRC have been incorporated). This is followed by an analysis of the impact of incorporation on the implementation of the CRC, drawing on evidence and interviews conducted on field visits in six of the countries under review. The article concludes with a discussion of the other non-legal measures of implementation which emerged as key underpinnings for the success of legal measures of incorporation, followed by some reflections about what can be done to further support and facilitate a culture of respect for children's rights.

The UNICEF-UK study

The research team was commissioned by UNICEF UK to carry out a study of the legal implementation of the CRC in 12 countries. The overall purpose of the project was to research examples of incorporation of the Convention in countries beyond the UK in order to compile evidence of the most effective, practical and impactful ways of embedding children's rights into domestic law. The investigation was framed from a children's rights perspective and comprised of three key stages. First, a literature review was carried out with respect to

---

[2] See, for example, Human Rights Committee (1981) *General Comment 3, Implementation at the National level* at para. 1. Geneva: UN.
[3] Committee on Economic, Social and Cultural Rights (1990) *General Comment 3: The nature of states parties obligations*, Geneva: UN, at para. 4. See also Tobin, J. (2005) 'Increasingly seen and heard: the constitutional recognition of children's rights', *S.Afr J on Human Rights*, 21, p. 89.
[4] Lundy, L., Kilkelly, U., Byrne, B. and Kang, J. (2012), *The United Nations Convention on the Rights of the Child: A study of legal implementation in 12 countries*, London: UNICEF-UK.

the legal and non-legal implementation of human rights treaties generally, and the CRC specifically. The second stage of the project consisted of desk research on 12 countries identified by UNICEF-UK in conjunction with the research team and the Project and Advisory Boards. The countries were chosen to reflect a suitable mix of countries with: common and civil law structures, national and federated states, strengths in different aspects of the general measures of implementation, and varied child rights legislative models. The choice of countries was also influenced by their perceived degree of relevance to and relative influence on the UK. The 12 countries chosen for inclusion in the study were: Australia, Belgium, Canada, Denmark, Germany, Iceland, Ireland, New Zealand, Norway, South Africa, Spain, and Sweden.

To guide the development of each country report, the research team developed an analytical framework, allowing for the identification of: (i) the types of legislative measures adopted across jurisdictions; (ii) the characteristics of these measures; and (iii) the enablers and challenges in their development. Each country study drew on: States Party reports submitted by the identified countries to the Committee on the Rights of the Child; the Concluding Observations issued to these jurisdictions by the Committee; and relevant legislative and policy documentation pertaining to each country. While these documents provide a rich source of documentary evidence, we were aware of their limitations and in particular that the States Party reports and Concluding Observations provide a particular and partial representation of the position in each country at a specific point in time.[5] To supplement these and to ensure that the most relevant and up to date information was captured in each country, draft versions of each country report were disseminated to international partners and contacts with UNICEF national committee offices, academics, government and NGO sector colleagues for feedback which was integrated into the country reports. This input was crucial to ensuring that the project team had a more accurate and nuanced understanding of the current reality in the state party under investigation.

Based on the data gathered, the research team selected a number of countries for in-depth analysis and review for the final stage of the project. Selection criteria were based on: (i) efficacy, that is, the apparent effectiveness and efficiency of the legislative model with respect to children's rights; and (ii) feasibility, that is, the appropriateness of the legislative model and implementation measures for the UK context. On the basis of these criteria, five countries were selected for field visits: Belgium, Germany, Ireland, Norway and Spain; and Australia for remote study. In total, 58 interviews were carried out through the course of the study with representatives from: the relevant government

---

[5] Prior, L. (2003) Using documents as social research, London: Sage.

department or agency with responsibility for children's rights; the Children's Commissioner/Ombudsperson, where established; leading academics and researchers; lawyers; children's sector organisations; service providers and practitioners; and those directly involved in the development and out-workings of the legislative model as appropriate. An additional objective of the interviews was to ascertain the impact, if any, of legal incorporation. While research was conducted into available childhood data sets (including international indices such as UNICEF scorecards, the PISA survey and WHO statistics), it was apparent from the outset that it was impossible to track chains of causation between legal implementation of the CRC and improved children's outcomes. However, it was possible in the interviews to investigate the perceived impacts of legal incorporation from the point of view of key stakeholders and to explore more generally whether and how these developments were instrumental in terms of building a culture of respect for children's rights.

Approaches to incorporation

Implementation is the process whereby States Parties take action to ensure the realisation of rights in the CRC for all children in a jurisdiction.[6] Although implementation of the CRC is mandatory following ratification, the measures used to implement the Convention fall within each state's discretion.[7] Incorporation – giving legal effect to the treaty in domestic law – is one means of implementing the CRC and although research indicates that those states in which the Convention has been incorporated – directly or indirectly, systematically or sectorally – are associated with a greater degree of implementation, the legal process of incorporation cannot be isolated from the range of measures that are necessary to implement the CRC successfully. Moreover, the way in which the CRC is given legal effect is highly contingent upon the constitutional and legal systems of individual countries. For example, in some countries (monist states), once the CRC is ratified, the Convention automatically becomes part of national law, whereas in others (dualist states), an act of parliament is required to transpose the Convention into the domestic legal order. Where the CRC is not automatically incorporated, only those provisions of the CRC that are expressly incorporated into national law will have legal effect.

---

[6] Committee on the Rights of the Child, (2003), *General Comment No. 5 (2003) Implementation* UN/CRC/GC/2003/1, Geneva: United Nations.
[7] See Human Rights Committee, General Comment 3, Implementation at the National Level (1981) at para. 1. See also Committee on Economic, Social and Cultural Rights (1990) General Comment 3: The Nature of States Parties Obligations, at para. 4. See also Tobin, J. (2005) 'Increasingly seen and heard: the constitutional recognition of children's rights', *S.Afr J on Human Rights*, 21, p. 89.

Other factors will determine the legal status of the Convention in national law after it has been incorporated, in particular where it sits in the hierarchy of the legal system. For example, in some jurisdictions, the CRC is equivalent to national statute law, whereas in others it will have constitutional status, superior to legislation. Separate again is the question of whether the Convention is justiciable and whether it can be used as a binding authority in the courts.

A study carried out by the UNICEF Innocenti Research Centre in 2007 noted that, at that time, the CRC had been directly incorporated into national law in two thirds of the 52 countries covered by the study. CRC provisions had been incorporated into the constitutional order of one third of the countries studied.[8] Our study, carried out in 2012, found that full and direct incorporation of the Convention had taken place in just three countries of the 12 examined (Belgium, Norway and Spain), although a further four states had already or were in the process of incorporating some of the Convention's provisions into their constitutions in some form (Ireland, Iceland, South Africa and Sweden). However, we found it more common for states to incorporate specific Convention provisions into relevant legislation, rather than transposing the entire treaty into the national legal system. Those provisions most frequently incorporated on a sectoral basis were the best interests principle in Article 3 and the right to be heard in Article 12. The following section considers the different approaches adopted by the 12 states in our study towards incorporation of the CRC. It first considers examples of direct incorporation where the CRC in full or in part has been incorporated into the constitution or legislation. It then considers indirect incorporation (where other approaches are used to give the CRC legal effect in the domestic legal order).

Direct incorporation

Direct incorporation is when the Convention, either in full or in part, is incorporated directly into the domestic legal system. This can happen either at constitutional level or at the level of statute, parliamentary instrument or act.

Constitutional Incorporation – in full or in part
Given that it is the most important instrument in the domestic legal order, incorporation of the Convention or specific CRC provisions into the national constitution must be seen as evidence of a commitment to recognition if not implementation of children's rights at the highest level. Tobin notes that greater attention has been accorded to the rights of children within

---

8) UNICEF Innocenti Research Centre, (2007) *Law Reform and Implementation of the CRC*, Florence: UNICEF.

constitutions adopted post CRC[9] and recent years have seen an increasing trend towards enshrining children's rights in national constitutions. Of the 12 countries studied for UNICEF, six had taken or were taking steps to incorporate provisions of the CRC into their constitutions. Only Spain could be said to have incorporated the Convention into its constitution in its entirety, notwithstanding that this constitutional provision predates the CRC itself. In particular, Article 39(4) of the 1978 Constitution establishes that '[c]hildren shall enjoy the protection provided for in the international agreements safeguarding their rights'. As a result, CRC provisions can be argued before the Constitutional and Supreme Courts.[10] Although beyond this its effect is less clear, interviewees suggested that the constitutional commitment to children's rights created a symbolic 'red line' that could not be crossed. It also prompted full incorporation of the CRC into domestic law via the Organic Law on the Legal Protection of Children and Young People, adopted in 1996.[11] It is also worth noting that, although the CRC is not fully incorporated into the Constitution in Belgium, its status – the CRC was automatically incorporated on ratification – is considered superior to both statute and the Constitution.[12]

A much more common approach among the countries studied was to incorporate select provisions of the CRC into their constitutions. This was identified in four additional countries – Belgium, Ireland, South Africa and Sweden – with active consideration being given to this at the time of the study in Iceland[13] and in Norway also.[14] There was some consistency in the provisions selected for constitutional incorporation with the most common practice being to incorporate the best interest principle (under Article 3) and the right of the child to be heard (under Article 12). For instance, in 2000, these provisions were given explicit expression in Article 22bis of the Belgium Constitution

---

9) Tobin, J. *supra* note 3.
10) Spain's third and fourth state party report to the Committee details case law considered by these courts on constitutional matters affecting children's rights. See CRC/C/ESP/3-4, 12 June 2010, para. 78 with summary details of the judgments provided in Lundy, Kilkelly, Byrne and Kang, p. 67.
11) *Organic Law on Minors' Criminal Responsibility*, 5/2000, available at http://noticias.juridicas .com/base_datos/Penal/lo5-2000.html, accessed 8 April 2013.
12) Belgium's Initial State Party report to the Committee on the Rights of the Child, CRC/C/11/ Add.4, 6 September 1994, para. 2.
13) Iceland subsequently voted to adopt a new constitution, including provision for children's rights, on 20 October 2012, See http://reut.rs/WB695x and http://bit.ly/XK5men, accessed 8 April 2013. The Convention on the Rights of the Child was incorporated into Icelandic law on 20 February 2013.
14) In Norway, the Storting's Human Rights Commission recommended the inclusion of children's rights into the Norwegian constitution in 2011. See Human Rights Commission, Report to the Presidium of the Storting by the Human Rights Commission concerning human rights in the Constitution, 2011, p. 3, available at http://bit.ly/Xw2Rkp, accessed on 8 April 2013.

along with Article 2 (non-discrimination principle) and protection for the moral, physical, psychological and sexual integrity of children.[15] They are referenced in the recent change to the Irish Constitution also.[16] Section 28(2) of the South African Bill of Rights stipulates that a child's best interests are of 'paramount importance in every matter concerning the child'. Explicit recognition is given to the child's right to a name and nationality from birth, family or alternative care, basic nutrition, shelter and health care and social services. It also recognises the right of the child to protection from maltreatment, neglect, abuse or degradation, from exploitative labour practices and recognises children's rights relating to detention and work. A further provision; Section 29, deals with the right to education.[17] The South African Constitutional Court has handed down a number of significant judgments that have directly or indirectly affirmed children's rights. However, the Constitutional Court has yet to recognise Section 28 as giving rise to a directly enforceable immediate obligation against the state in any previous case.[18] Sweden has also given constitutional expression to specific CRC provisions. In particular, Chapter 2 (Fundamental rights) of the Instrument of Government which forms part of the Constitution, contains two provisions which address the rights of children specifically: Article 7 contains a provision with respect to the determination of a child's nationality, and Article 18 stipulates that all children covered by compulsory schooling shall be entitled to a free basic education at a public school. In addition, as of January 2003, Article 2 of Chapter 1 (Basic principles of the form of Government), requires public institutions to combat discrimination on a number of grounds, including age.[19] More importantly, perhaps, the Swedish Constitution was amended in 2010 and in particular, Article 2, Chapter 1 of the Instrument of Government now stipulates that 'public institutions shall promote the opportunity for all to attain participation and equality in society *and for the rights of the child to be safeguarded.*' (emphasis added).[20]

---

[15] Committee on the Rights of the Child, Concluding Observations: Belgium, CRC/C/15/Add.178, para. 3.

[16] The full text of the wording can be found in the Thirty-First Amendment of the Constitution (Children) Bill 2012 http://bit.ly/10LPklK, accessed on 8 April 2013.

[17] See Committee on the Rights of the Child, Concluding Observations: South Africa, *CRC/C/15/Add.*122, para. 3. For the full text of the Charter see http://www.info.gov.za/documents/constitution, accessed 8 April 2013.

[18] See for example Constitutional Court of South Africa *Minister for Welfare and Population Development v. Fitzpatrick and Others*, BCLR 713 CC, 2000, para. 17.376; Constitutional Court of South Africa, *Government of the Republic of South Africa v. Grootboom*, BCLR 1169 (CC), 2001; Constitutional Court of South Africa, *Minister of Health and Others v. Treatment Action Campaign and Others*, BCLR 1033 (CC), 2002.

[19] See Sweden's third State Party report, CRC/C/125/Add.1, paras. 249, 250, 251.

[20] See the details at http://www.sweden.se, accessed 8 April 2013. Proposition 2009/10:80 entered into force on 1 January 2011.

Ireland, whose 1937 Constitution already contained certain references to children within the context of the family (which enjoys very strong protection[21]), was amended to insert a new provision dealing with children's rights – Article 42A – into the Constitution in 2012. The first section of Article 42A contains an explicit statement that '[t]he State recognises and affirms the natural and imprescriptible rights of all children and shall, as far as practicable, by its laws protect and vindicate those rights.'[22] However, most of the remaining provision is limited to placing a duty on the parliament to enact legislation on children's rights (especially the best interests principle and the right to be heard), rather than giving these principles direct constitutional expression. This approach, of making legislative incorporation mandatory under the Constitution, has some hallmarks of the indirect model of incorporation (in that it stops short of incorporating substantive provisions into the Constitution).

Statutory incorporation – in full or in part
All of the countries studied had, in one way or another, taken steps to incorporate the CRC either in full or in part into domestic legislation. Three states – Belgium, Norway and Spain – have incorporated the Convention in its entirety into national law. In Belgium, this happened automatically by virtue of its ratification of the CRC. In Norway, this was a decision of the parliament taken in 2003, four years after the enactment of the Human Rights Act of 1999 which incorporated the International Covenant on Economic, Social and Cultural Rights (ICESCR), the International Covenant on Civil and Political Rights (ICCPR) and the European Convention of Human Rights (ECHR) into Norwegian law. It came following a recommendation of the CRC Committee.[23] The CRC has formed part of Spain's domestic law since its ratification of the treaty in 1990.[24] In both Australia (2011) and Denmark (2001), incorporation of the CRC was considered, but ultimately rejected.[25]

---

[21] This is similar to the provision contained in the German constitution. See Lundy, Kilkelly, Byrne and Kang, p. 43. On the Irish Constitution, see further Kilkelly, U. and O'Mahony, C. (2007), 'The Proposed Children's Rights Amendment: Running to Stand Still?' *Irish Journal of Family Law*, vol. 2, p. 19.

[22] See the Thirty-First Amendment of the Constitution (Children) Bill 2012 http://bit .ly/10LPklK, accessed on 8 April 2013.

[23] See the Norwegian NGO Coalition on the CRC, Supplementary report to the UN Committee on the Rights of the Child, 1999; UN Committee on the Rights of the Child, Concluding Observations: Norway, CRC/C/15/Add.126, 2000a.

[24] Spain. Second State Party report to the Committee on the Rights of the Child, CRC/C/70/ Add.9, 12 November 2001, paras. 170-171.

[25] See Denmark, Third State Party report to the UN Committee on the Rights of the Child, CRC/C/129/Add.3, 2005, para. 16. In relation to Australia, see the details of the review and the action plan that resulted at http://bit.ly/16HbCdL, last accessed 8 April 2013.

Almost all of the states examined in the UNICEF study could be found to have incorporated some of the CRC provisions into their sectoral laws on children's matters. Incorporation of the Article 3 best interest principle was found to be widespread. In all countries, it was found to be a fundamental principle in family law,[26] and in some other countries it has been extended into areas like youth justice (e.g. Spain and Ireland[27]) and immigration and refugee law (e.g. Norway and Sweden).[28] Many countries have also incorporated into statute the right of the child to be heard and/or to be represented.[29] For example, this principle has strong protection in German law, with respect to children's participation in court proceedings,[30] in Norwegian law, where children have strong participation rights in alternative care proceedings[31] and in South Africa and Ireland, where it has underpinned the establishment of student councils in schools.[32] To date, what is clear is that countries appear to have focused mainly on incorporating two main principles – Articles 3 and 12 – into their sectoral laws on children's matters, with some extension into other areas. There is little evidence of other CRC provisions being given statutory expression and Spain stands out as the only country, short of full incorporation, which has incorporated other substantive rights into a children's statute. In particular, the Spanish Organic Law from 1996 enshrines a number of civil rights for children including the right to freedom of thought, conscience and religion, the right to information, the right to freedom of assembly, the right to freedom of expression and the right to be heard within the family and in administrative and judicial proceedings. In addition, the Law addresses the rights of children at risk or in need of protection, and regulates adoption procedures. Furthermore, Spain's Organic

---

[26] For example, see the Commonwealth Family Law Act 1975 (Australia); the Children's Act 2005 (Norway); the Act on Parental Responsibility, 2007 (Denmark); the Care of Children Act 2004 (New Zealand) and the Children Act 1989 (England and Wales).

[27] See the Children Act 2001, as amended (Ireland); and Organic Law No. 5/2000, Organic Law on Minors' Criminal Responsibility (Spain). See also the ACT *Children and Young People Act 2008* (Australia).

[28] See the Immigration Act 2008 (Norway) and the Aliens Act 2005 (Sweden). See also the Borders, Citizenship and Immigration Act 2009 (United Kingdom) and case-law of the Canadian Supreme Court in *Baker v. Canada (Minister of Citizenship and Immigration)*, 2 SCR 817, 1999 (Canada).

[29] See, for example, the Children's Act 2005 and the Kindergarten Act, 2005 (Norway); the Organic Law on the Legal Protection of Children and Young People, 1996 (Spain) and the Adoption Act 2010 (Ireland).

[30] See the *Act on Proceedings in Family Cases and in Matters of Non-contentious Litigation* (Germany).

[31] On implementation of the 2005 Act see Skjørten, K., *Samlivsbrudd og barnefordeling*, Gyldendal Akademisk, Oslo, 2005; cited in Skjørten, K. And Barlindhaug, R., 'The involvement of children in decisions about shared residence', *International Journal of Law, Policy and the Family*, vol. 21, 2007, pp. 373–385. See also the Victoria Children, *Youth and Families Act 2005* (Australia).

[32] See the Education Act 1998 (Ireland) and the South African Schools Act 84 of 1996 (South Africa).

Law on Minors' Criminal Responsibility from 2000 outlines Spain's juvenile justice procedures and regulations and gives primacy to the best interests principle.

Indirect incorporation

In addition to those states which have taken measures to incorporate CRC provisions directly into either national laws at the level of either statute or constitution, some states have taken measures which can be described as indirect incorporation. In effect, these measures are aimed to give the CRC some effect in national law but they stop short of making substantive rights part of the domestic legal order. The most significant of these measures can be found in Wales, which in March 2011 adopted the Rights of Children and Young Persons (Wales) Measure. The Measure requires Ministers of the Wales Assembly to have due regard to the requirements of the CRC and its Optional Protocols when making decisions about a provision to be included in an enactment, the formulation of a new policy and/or legislation, or a review of or change to an existing policy and/or legislation.[33] The result of the Measure is not to incorporate the CRC directly into national law therefore but rather to require decision-making to take account of the requirements of the CRC. Scotland is also in the process of introducing similar legislation. The Children and Young People Bill (Scotland) was introduced to Parliament on 17 April 2013 and will place a duty on Scottish Ministers keep under consideration whether there are any steps which they could take which would or might secure better or further effect in Scotland of the CRC requirements, and to take identified steps if deemed appropriate.[34] It is accompanied by a duty to raise awareness and understanding of the rights of children and young people. This measure builds on the measures introduced in some countries designed to require law making to take account of children's rights obligations. For instance, in the Flanders Region of Belgium, every draft decree that impacts on the interest of young people under 25 years must be accompanied by an impact assessment. Although an evaluation has questioned the efficacy of the measure (known as its acronym 'Joker'),[35] it is likely to be introduced in the French speaking

---

[33] See Rights of Children and Young Persons (Wales) Measure (2011), available at http://www.legislation.gov.uk/mwa/2011/2/contents, last accessed 3 May 2013. See further Williams, J. 'General legislative measures of implementation: individual claims, 'public officer's law' and a case study on the UNCRC in Wales', *International Journal of Children's Rights*, vol. 20, 2012, pp. 224–240, p. 226; Williams, J. (2013) *The United Nations Convention on the Rights of the Child in Wales*, University of Wales Press: Cardiff.

[34] Children and Young People (Scotland) Bill, available at http://www.scottish.parliament.uk/parliamentarybusiness/Bills/62233.aspx, last accessed 3 May 2013.

[35] See Desmet, E., Op de Beeck, H. and Vandenhole, W., *Evaluation of the Child and Youth Impact Assessment (JoKER)*, Kenniscentrum Kinderrechten, Gent, 2012.

Region in the near future.[36] Australia has also taken such a route, with the enactment in 2011 of the Human Rights (Parliamentary Scrutiny) Act. This introduces a requirement for statements of compatibility to accompany all new bills, which must contain an assessment of whether the bill or legislative instrument is compatible with the seven core international human rights treaties that Australia has ratified, including the CRC. The procedure is new and there is as yet no published example of change occurring as a result of a perceived incompatibility with the CRC.[37]

In summary then, there is considerable evidence of the incorporation of the CRC into the national law of the countries studied. Incorporation of the two main CRC principles – best interests and the right to be heard – is now widespread in family law and some countries have extended the principles to other laws affecting children. Several countries have taken steps to give constitutional expression to children's rights and others are considering or have considered this step. The result is that all countries studied here can be said to have incorporated the CRC directly in full or in part into national law whether at statutory or constitutional level. Finally, a number of countries have adopted measures designed to ensure that the CRC is taken into account in law and policy making. The impact of these approaches is considered below.

The impact of incorporation

The review of comparative practice in relation to the implementation of the CRC in the 12 countries included in this study indicates that: each of the countries in the study is taking the implementation of the CRC seriously, albeit in various ways and with varying degrees of commitment. The legal and policy responses to implementation by necessity vary on a country by country basis and are determined to a large extent by its legal and administrative structures as well as political and public attitudes to international human rights law in general and children's rights in particular. While recognising that these are often the determining factors, there were some overarching messages which can be drawn from across the country studies about the impact of systematic approaches to incorporation.

In the countries where there had been specific, high-level incorporation of the CRC, interviewees were more likely to say that children were perceived as rights-holders and that there was a culture of respect for children's rights. It

---

[36] Belgium, Third and fourth State Party reports to the UN Committee on the Rights of the Child, CRC/C/BEL/3–4, 2010.
[37] However, interviewees commented on its potential for positive effect. See Lundy, Kilkelly, Byrne and Kang, pp. 30-31.

remains unclear whether this enhanced respect for children's rights explains why there had been more systematic incorporation to begin with or was in fact a by-product of it. In some countries, interviewees reported a general culture of respect for rights (Norway, Belgium), while others suggested that one had developed in the wake of conflict and significant reconstruction (Spain, South Africa). In others, human and child rights were not considered to be the normal discourse with values such as child-centredness or equity having more purchase (Australia). In several countries, child protection or 'the child as victim' were reported as being more common public attitudes (e.g. Ireland, Germany) and, in several instances, the tension between parents' rights and children's rights appeared to be part of the ongoing discussion, with adverse impact for the acceptance of children's rights (Australia, Germany, Ireland). While it was suggested that a deliberate decision to incorporate (as in Norway) might have more impact than instances where the CRC has automatically become part of domestic law upon ratification (Belgium, Spain), this is difficult to determine. Nonetheless, the process of discussion and consultation around incorporation was recognised as having a positive role in advancing understanding and engaging with key stakeholders (e.g. with young people in Iceland), even where the outcome of that did not result in incorporation (as in Australia). Where it had taken place, incorporation clearly provided the springboard or basis from which a range of other measures and initiatives to implement the Convention were either launched or flowed naturally as a consequence.

One of the reported consequences of incorporation at a high level (for instance, in the constitution or through an act of general implementation) was that CRC principles appeared to be more likely to be translated into domestic law. It was reported variously that it gave politicians, public officials and NGOs who wanted to advance the cause of children's rights a 'hook' or 'leverage' which was particularly influential when it came to ensuring integration of the principles in domestic law and policy. So, for example, the adoption of the CRC in the Spanish Constitution paved the way for the two key Organic Laws covering a comprehensive range of CRC rights, including civil and political rights.[38] Likewise, in Norway (and Sweden), there appears to be a more systematic approach to incorporation of CRC articles, whereas in other countries (such as Australia, Germany and indeed the UK), sectoral incorporation was the norm and was more likely to be confined to the area of family law and to Articles 3 and 12 in particular. While the latter is important, it falls somewhat short of full implementation of the CRC as required by Article 4.

While incorporation provided opportunities for the CRC to be used in litigation, it was equally clear that incorporation had not opened a floodgate of

---

[38]   Lundy, L., Kilkelly, U., Byrne, B. and Kang, J. (2012), supra n.4, p. 65.

strategic litigation involving children, thus dispelling an ongoing fear for those governments considering legal incorporation. There were examples of high profile public interest litigation in all of the countries studied, with some successes notable in countries where it has been incorporated in such a way as to allow for direct enforcement.[39] However, the main impact of incorporation on legal action was that key principles of the CRC were more likely to be cited in routine cases involving children. For example, a Norwegian study of high court decisions on residence for children found that the wishes of children aged over 12 are considered important in the decisions. Half of the children between seven and eleven years expressed their wishes in the judicial decisions.[40] Consideration of the child's best interests and efforts to ensure that their views were taken seriously in legal actions involving them was also reported to be routine in cases in Belgium.[41] Thus, children's rights-based approaches were guiding and infusing judicial decision-making on the everyday cases affecting children's lives.

In all countries in the study, the most vulnerable groups of children (separated children, asylum seekers, indigenous children and children in conflict with the law) continued to fare less well compared to their peers, irrespective of the steps taken to incorporate the CRC. Throughout the interviews this was linked to higher levels of poverty and social exclusion. In several countries (including Spain and Germany), interviewees suggested that separated children and asylum seekers were not seen as rights holders in the same way as other children and this was linked, to an extent, to the weakness of the CRC in these areas. For this reason perhaps, some of the most effective forms of redress were perceived to lie in constitutional or domestic equality protections rather than specific child rights arguments although it is clear that a variety of strategies were important in addressing these intractable issues. Interviewees also highlighted their concerns about the impact of the recession on children's rights, albeit that some suggested that a benefit of incorporation of the CRC was that it provided a line over which government could not step in relation to the introduction of austerity measures.

A final recurring theme in relation to the impact of incorporation in law was the fact that the measures adopted were not consistent across different regions within one States Party, even where there had been significant steps taken to

---

[39] See, for example, Spain. Lundy, L., Kilkelly, U., Byrne, B. and Kang, J. (2012), supra n.4, p. 67.
[40] Skjørten and Barlindhaug (2007) The involvement of children in decisions about shared residence *International Journal of Law, Policy and the Family* 21, 373–385. However, in only 17 out of a total of 129 cases were the child's wishes the main reason, or one of a number of reasons, for the outcome. In cases where the child's wishes were the main reason for the decision, the child was nine years old or older.
[41] Lundy, L., Kilkelly, U., Byrne, B. and Kang, J. (2012), supra n.4, pp. 37-38.

incorporate the CRC at a high level. In many of the case study countries, the state party ratified the CRC but key responsibility for ensuring its implementation in law, policy and practice rested with devolved or federated regions which had significant responsibility for areas such as education, health and social care (Australia, Belgium, Germany, Spain). Decentralisation of power, through devolution and delegation of government, does not reduce the direct responsibility of the State Party's Government to fulfil its obligations to all children within its jurisdiction, regardless of the State structure.[42] However, it was clear that some of the responsibility on the State Party to ensure implementation of the CRC was diluted in the transfer of responsibility, with the central government limiting its role sometimes to monitoring and compiling the periodic report. Many interviewees suggested that central government should explicitly retain overall responsibility for implementation of the CRC and take a more active role in ensuring that local regions/ states are actively and consistently implementing the Convention. It was suggested that this would work best through national mechanisms to co-ordinate activity which would develop national agreements on key issues which cross regional boundaries (e.g. Australia has a system of co-operative agreements, known as 'Co-Ags' which have enabled government departments to collaborate to produce national level agreements on issues such as child care standards). Others suggested that greater consistency could be encouraged further by targeted national funding for particular policies and by having greater consistency in data collection.

Non-legal measures of implementation in support of incorporation

The Committee on the Rights of the Child has made clear throughout its General Comments, and General Comment 5 in particular, that effective implementation of the CRC is not achieved by legislative measures alone. It has identified a range of non-legal measures that are needed for effective implementation, including the development of particular structures, training and awareness and other activities.[43] The research looked at all of these in the contexts of the countries studied. It was clear that a range of approaches was being adopted to support implementation of the CRC, including the development of national plans for children, data collection across children's lives, child participation in decision-making processes at governmental and/or local

---

[42] Supra n. 6. The Committee has reiterated that in any process of devolution, States parties have to make sure that the devolved authorities have the necessary 'financial, human and other resources effectively to discharge responsibilities for the implementation of the Convention'.
[43] Supra n.6.

authority levels, and child budgeting.[44] However, for the purposes of this paper, four in particular emerged as core to the success of any legal strategy to implement the CRC: training and awareness, the role of independent human rights institutions, data and national action plans.

Training and awareness

The State has a duty under the CRC to develop training and capacity-building for all those involved in the process of implementing Convention rights and for all those working with and for children.[45] This should be systematic, ongoing, and integrated into all professional training codes and educational curricula.[46] The significance of awareness-raising is grounded in Article 42 of the CRC which obliges States Parties to make its principles and provisions widely known. In spite of the emphasis in the CRC on children being informed about their rights, research has highlighted the continuing lack of accurate knowledge and awareness of children's rights.[47] The need for training and awareness on the CRC itself was reiterated time and time again by interviewees in the study who recognised that, at every level, from legislation to case law and policy development to service provision for children, effective implementation was contingent upon awareness of children's rights. This was not just about knowledge of the articles of the Convention or about children's issues like child protection, but an understanding of children as the subject of rights – entitled to be treated with dignity and respect and to exert influence on their own lives. For example, while the best interest principle has been widely incorporated in legislation, awareness of the CRC was perceived to be crucial to ensuring it was applied in a way that was rights compliant. In spite of this, and the Committee's recommendation that States develop a comprehensive strategy for disseminating knowledge of the CRC,[48] there were few examples of systematic training for duty bearers. Examples of good practice include legal training for the legal profession and judiciary in Norway and Belgium which has led to an increased number of cases where the CRC is cited,[49] while in Australia, human rights education targeted at schools, communities, public

---

[44] See Lundy, Kilkelly, Byrne and Kang, n.4 (2012).
[45] United Nations (2003) General Comment No.5. supra n.6 at para. 48.
[46] United Nations (2003) General Comment No.5, supra . 6 at para. 53.
[47] See, for example, Alderson, P. (1999) Civil rights in schools: The implications for youth policy. *Youth and Policy* 64: 56-72; Covell, K. & Howe, B. (1999). The impact of children's rights education: A Canadian Study. *International Journal of Children's Rights* 7(2):171–183; Howe, R. B., & Covell, K. (2005). *Empowering Children: Children's Rights Education as a Pathway to Citizenship.* Toronto: University of Toronto Press.
[48] United Nations (2003) General Comment No.5 supra n. 6 at para. 33.
[49] Lundy, Kilkelly, Byrne and Kang (2012), pp.39 and 61.

servants and those working with children, is one of the core principles of its recent *Human Rights Framework*.[50]

While there was widespread recognition in the study of the need to educate adults working with children and to increase sensitivity among the public, few interviewees, with Norway being an exception, identified education for children about the UNCRC as important in the implementation strategy: it was seen as something that the CRC requires as a substantive right rather than as a means of implementation. There was very little focus on the ideas of building children's capacity to claim their rights now. However, some interviewees recognised that children's rights education would change culture over generations as children become future duty bearers. Most countries had included aspects of human rights and child rights in the general curriculum, although these were rarely extensive and often optional elements. There were, however, interesting examples of child rights education in most jurisdictions. In Nova Scotia, Canada, for example, child rights education has been integrated into schools as part of the health and social studies curriculum from kindergarten up to Grade 6,[51] while in Denmark, the CRC forms part of human rights education more generally.[52] Whilst the need to include education about the Convention in national curricula has been emphasised by the Committee on the Rights of the Child,[53] in practice this was not evident in the countries studied, with much of this work being undertaken by NGOs.

Independent national human rights institutions

Independent national human rights institutions (NHRIs) have been identified as an important mechanism to promote and ensure the implementation of the CRC and the Committee has welcomed the establishment of children's ombudspersons/children's commissioners to this end.[54] In order to ensure their independence and effective functioning, the Committee has highlighted that children's commissioners must have adequate infrastructure, funding (including specifically for children's rights, within broad-based institutions), staff, premises, and freedom from forms of financial control that might affect their independence. They must have the power to consider individual complaints

---

[50] Human Rights Branch (2010) *Australia's Human Rights Framework*, Attorney-General's Department: Commonwealth of Australia.
[51] Canada's Second State Party Report to the United Nations Committee on the Rights of the Child (2003), CRC/C/83/Add.6, para. 1338.
[52] Denmark Fourth State Party Report to the United Nations Committee on the Rights of the Child (2010), CRC/C/DNK/4, para. 31.
[53] United Nations (2003) General Comment No.5, supra n.6 at para. 18.
[54] United Nations (2002) General Comment No.2: *The role of independent national human rights institutions in the promotion and protection of the rights of the child*, Geneva: UN, CRC/GC/2002/2 at para. 1.

and petitions and carry out investigations, including those submitted on behalf of or directly by children,[55] and to support children taking cases to court.[56] Not all national children's rights institutions are obliged to monitor the CRC and much will depend upon the establishing legislation. Most of the countries in the study had a children's commissioner or ombudsman. Australia was a late exception, having only recently decided to appoint a national children's commissioner,[57] although there were children's commissioner offices in each of the states.[58] The absence of a Commissioner or Ombudsperson at federal level was also the case in Canada; however a number of Provinces had established Child and Youth Advocates in addition to the Youth Services Section of the Nova Scotia Office of the Ombudsman and the Québec Commission des droits de la personne et des droits de la jeunesse. Not all countries had independent monitoring mechanisms; in Germany for example, the Children's Commission at federal level is a subcommittee of the parliamentary Committee for Family Affairs, Senior Citizens, Women and Youth.[59]

A 2011 study by Save the Children of the general measures of implementation across five countries in Europe found that mandates and roles differed between children's commissioners/ombudspersons.[60] Similarly, the bodies examined in this study had very different powers and resources, often not as extensive as those invested in the four UK children's commissioners. However, where an Ombudsman approach had been adopted, as in Spain and Ireland, it was considered that the ability for children to make complaints directly to the office for investigation played an important role in the enforcement of the CRC. The Commissioners/Ombudsman offices were perceived to be core to monitoring implementation across time, to holding government to account and to ensuring consistency in the implementation of the CRC at times of political change. They also have a key awareness raising role. The extent to which the commissioners or ombudsman's offices were able to fully realise their mandate was often hampered by the limited resources available. Practice and resourcing also varied considerably across States within federal jurisdictions.[61]

---

[55] United Nations (2002) General Comment No.2 supra n. 54 at para. 6.

[56] United Nations (2002) General Comment No.2, supra n. 54 at para. 25.

[57] The first National Children's Commissioner for Australia took up post on 25 March 2013.

[58] For a summary of the remit and powers of state-based children's commissioners, see Australian Institute of Family Studies, 'Children's commissioners and guardians', 2011, http://www.aifs.gov.au/nch/pubs/sheets/rs15/ last accessed 27 March 2013.

[59] Germany's Second State Party Report to the United Nations Committee on the Rights of the Child (2003),CRC/C/83/Add.7, at para. 15.

[60] Save the Children (2011) *Governance Fit for Children: To what extent have the general measures of implementation of the UNCRC been realised in five European Countries?* Stockholm: Save the Children.

[61] Interviewees indicated that these offices were under threat due to cuts in public sector spending.

National plans for children

Almost all of the countries in the study had a national plan for children.[62] The effective protection of children's rights through a unifying, comprehensive and rights based national strategy rooted in the Convention has been strongly emphasised by the Committee.[63] Where such plans have been in place, these have taken different forms and varied in their content, goals and implementation structures. In some instances plans have not always been renewed at the end of their timespan; Germany's National Action Plan for a Child Friendly Germany, for example, ended in 2010 while Spain's National Strategic Plan for Children and Adolescents finished in 2009 with its successor still under discussion. Interviewees suggested that for these to be most effective, there needed to be concrete action plans supported by measurable targets and indicators, and appropriate resourcing – core factors which have been reiterated by the Committee in its General Comment.[64] In rare instances national plans were linked to CRC implementation as in the Flemish Community in Belgium[65] and in Canada.[66] Yet, even where this was not the case, it is clear that an ambitious national strategy can drive implementation of the Convention in particular areas. Ireland's National Children's Strategy 2000-2010 is a key example of a plan where the inclusion of participation as a key policy goal has led to a whole range of innovative and ambitious participation initiatives, including the development of structures for children to feed into local decision-making. Where national plans are used to establish infrastructure and to embed children's rights into administrative decision-making, they can have a clear impact on children's rights awareness and implementation.

Comprehensive data on children

Sufficient and reliable data collection on children, disaggregated to enable identification of discrimination and disparities in the realisation of rights is an essential part of implementation of the Convention.[67] An annual comprehensive

---

[62] Australia's National Human Rights Action Plan considers the CRC along with the other six core treaties but is not specific to children. The Australian Research Alliance for Children and Youth are in the process of developing a national plan for children's well-being. See http://www.thenestproject.org.au/ last accessed 27 March 2013. However, this is not a government initiative.
[63] United Nations (2003) General Comment 5, supra n.6 at para. 28
[64] United Nations (2003) General Comment 5, supra n. 6 at para. 32.
[65] Flemish Action Plan for the Rights of the Child, 2004. This was subsequently incorporated into the Belgian National Action Plan for Children (2005-2012).
[66] A Canada Fit for Children (2004).
[67] United Nations (2003) General Comment 5, supra n.6 at para. 48.

report on the state of children's rights in the jurisdiction is recommended by the Committee on the Rights of the Child.[68] The collection of good quality data on children's lives is particularly important in facilitating an examination of the disparity between 'the de jure protection and de facto realization of human rights'[69] and helping to identify and explain the causes and variation in the failure to implement children's rights.[70] There was general agreement among interviewees that children's rights implementation is underpinned by comprehensive data; that this needed to be collected systematically in a way that identifies the most vulnerable categories of children; and that change needed to be tracked over time. Several countries, such as Spain[71] and Germany,[72] publish official annual state of children's rights reports and these were identified as useful. Some have invested quite considerably in data collection; Ireland for example has developed a national longitudinal study called *Growing up in Ireland*[73] which is producing a wealth of qualitative and quantitative information about children's lives and a clear evidence base for policymakers. Elsewhere, the *Australian Early Development Index*[74] will track children across time and includes specific data collection for vulnerable groups, including indigenous children. However, in most instances, the focus was on key child development and well-being indicators rather than the full range of children's rights. Attempts to develop and employ child rights indicators remain rare.[75] Across the studies, interviewees highlighted that without comprehensive, consistent, up-to-date, disaggregated data it was very difficult to understand or track the impact of government policy on children. Interviewees also referred to the need for effective ways of evaluating whether government policy on children's issues was having its desired effects.

---

[68] United Nations (2003) General Comment 5, supra n. 6 at para. 29.

[69] Landman, T. (2005) *Protecting Human Rights: A Compara.tive Study*, Washington D.C: Georgetown University Press, p.5.

[70] Carvalho, E. (2008) *Measuring Children's Rights: An Alternative Approach*, International Journal of Children's Rights, 16, pp. 545-563, p. 545.

[71] Government of Spain (2011) *Childhood in Figures 2009*, Universidad Complutense Madrid, Madrid, http://bit.ly/UEltsy, last accessed 27 March 2013.

[72] Book VII of the Social Code (Child and Youth Services) (Section 8(1)) (1990) places an obligation on the Federal Government, the Bundestag and the Bundescrat to report on the situation of, and developments relating to, children during each legislative period.

[73] Growing up in Ireland National Longitudinal Study of Children, see http://www.growingup.ie/ last accessed 27 March 2013.

[74] Australian Early Development Index, see http://ww2.rch.org.au/aedi/index.cfm?doc_id=13051 last accessed 27 March 2013.

[75] South African Human Rights Commission/UNICEF South Africa (2011) South Africa's Children – A Review of Equity and Child Rights, http://bit.ly/MmB1MR last accessed 27 March 2013. See generally, Lundy, L. (2013 forthcoming), *The United Nations Convention on the Rights of the Child an Child Well-Being*, Chapter 94 in BenArieh, A., Casas, F., Frones, I., and Korbin, J., The *International Handbook of Child Well-Being*, Springer.

Conclusion

The UNICEF-UK study provides a wealth of information on the various measures, legal and non-legal, taken by the countries studied to advance implementation of the CRC into domestic law, policy and practice. It identifies many of the factors that serve to promote children's rights at national level and highlights those strategies that have been proven to be most effective in both implementing the CRC in law and policy and in persuading decision-makers and duty bearers about the importance and value of implementing the CRC at national level. Where possible, the effectiveness of those approaches was clarified although it remains difficult to establish in any definitive or scientific way the actual impact on children's lives of the approaches and measures taken. Nevertheless, what emerges from the research is an understanding that children's rights are better protected – at least in law if not also in practice – in countries which have given legal status to the CRC in a systematic way and which have followed this up by establishing the necessary systems to effectively support, monitor and enforce the implementation of CRC rights. Equally, it is clear that each country must find its own path towards full implementation: there is no single route to be taken, no one right way to proceed. While the aim of the research was to identify some of the most effective approaches adopted, what also emerged were some interesting findings, primarily drawn from the stakeholder interviews, on the people, processes and contexts which made these legal changes possible.

Across the country studies, there was evidence of significant advocacy work by NGOs, who were often targeting legal and constitutional reform and regularly took the lead in the shadow/alternative reporting process to the UN Committee on the Rights of the Child. While it is impossible to identify all of the NGOs active in this area, impressive advocacy work was being carried out by, inter alia, the UNICEF NatComs and a number of high profile co-ordinating bodies. This appeared to be most effective when it employed a combination of strategies such as the engagement of the public and media on the issue, the pursuit of a strategic legal approach and persistent lobbying, based on the CRC, of Government and decision-making bodies. In terms of the latter, it was seen to be important to have key advocates or supporters in Government or in public office. In many countries, the most significant changes in relation to legal implementation of the CRC can be traced to their support by a particular champion – a politician, a key government official, an experienced law professor or an NGO leader – with influence. Interviewees identified a number of such champions working in different areas, including constitutional change, policy reform and participatory practices (e.g. Belgium, Germany, Norway, Ireland). NGOs were conscious of the need to identify and support such champions as part of their advocacy and lobbying strategies. However, while change often stems from a particular political champion, there was a recognised danger that reliance on such individuals meant that support for the CRC could ebb and flow. This is especially the case when the individual is in a political party which has lost power as the issue can be seen as being identified with that party. On the other hand, when the champion is a public official, there can be continuity and an opportunity to build support and ensure consistency over time. Reliance on key individuals to drive implementation also makes it difficult to sustain progress if the culture and the infrastructure to support it have not been sufficiently established.

An additional driver towards implementation was the effect of peer pressure effect from pioneering developments within individual regions in the jurisdiction. Thus, while there is ongoing concern about inconsistency in approaches across regions discussed above, one of the advantages of devolved power in federated systems was that it often enabled one region or jurisdiction to lead, prompting others to follow, unconstrained by limitations existing at federal or national level. In each country, certain areas or regions were identified as being at the forefront of the implementation of the CRC (such as Victoria in Australia, Catalonia in Spain, Berlin in Germany and, in different respects, the Flemish and French Communities in Belgium) and it was suggested that these regions played an important role in encouraging good practice elsewhere. The finding is of particular interest in the UK as the devolved administrations of Wales and Scotland adopt novel approaches to CRC incorporation. Goodman and Jinks suggest that recalcitrant actors can be encouraged to implement human rights obligations through one or more of three processes – coercion, persuasion and/or acculturation.[76] Thus, when one region steps forward in terms of legal incorporation, much may be achieved in terms of convincing others (persuasion) or at least prompting the feeling that their peers ought to be doing or be seen to be doing more than they are (acculturation).

Finally, the CRC reporting process was also identified as an important element of building a culture of respect for rights and an opportunity to advocate for increased incorporation of the CRC in law. Many of the interviewees had been involved in reporting to the Committee either as a government representative or as part of the alternative reporting process. It was clear that constructive engagement in the reporting process can be a driver to greater implementation, with several government interviewees reporting a greater level of awareness and personal commitment to the CRC in the wake of their experience and others pointing to the potential of the reporting process to

---

[76] Goodman R. & Jinks, D. (2004) How to influence states: socialisation and international human rights law, Duke Law Journal 54(3) 621-702.

engage the public and the media on children's rights issues. It was suggested that the reporting process opened discussion around the legal incorporation of children's rights within the states party and encouraged dialogue and discussion between duty-bearers and key stake-holders.

In summary, it is clear that in many countries the systematic incorporation of the CRC into domestic law provided a platform from which other legal and non-legal measures developed. Although it is possible to argue that incorporation was not indispensable to the measures that followed (i.e. that measures short of incorporation might achieve the same results), the research shows that it is an important goal in itself to give the CRC the force of national law. In particular, both the process of incorporation – which raises awareness and can be accompanied by systematic training of decision-makers – and the result – where the CRC becomes internalised in the national level system – have significant value in 'bringing rights home' to children and to duty-bearers. As the research shows, positive consequences flow from this– in the form of how children's rights are perceived and implemented in practice – that would be difficult to achieve through other means. Related to this is the impact that systematic incorporation can have on the content of domestic law and policy and, as those who are governed by the national law and policy framework – state officials and decision-makers – work with the national law, the CRC starts to infuse the decisions they make and how they are made. Of course, all of this must be underpinned by systematic children's rights training and a robust infrastructure designed to monitor, support and enforce implementation, if its potential is to be fully realised. Here several stakeholders – UNICEF, national human rights institutions, NGOs, academics and the media for example – have key roles. The work that they undertake – as watchdogs observing and documenting progress, auditing compliance, holding government to account, lobbying for change and engaging and raising the awareness of the public – is essential in ensuring that progress towards full implementation is sustained.

Children with Disabilities: A Critical Appraisal

Maya Sabatello
Center for Global Affairs, NYU, USA
msabatello@nyu.edu

The rights of children with disabilities have long been neglected in international human rights law. Certainly, the adoption of the Convention on the Rights of the Child in 1989 was intended to be a turning point. The CRC is a milestone instrument to advance children's rights and it explicitly includes children with disabilities within its scope. In practice, very little attention has been given to the rights of children with disabilities. Studies show that discrimination against children with disabilities is rampant in all societal settings, that children with disabilities are consistently excluded from participation in social, cultural and other events, and that also in comparison to their non-disabled peers, their voice is all too often silenced.

The Convention on the Rights of Persons with Disabilities (CRPD), adopted by the United Nations General Assembly in 2006, strove to remedy this neglect. The CRPD's expressed purpose is 'to promote, protect and ensure the full and equal enjoyment of all human rights and fundamental freedoms by all persons with disabilities, and to promote respect for their inherent dignity' (Article 1). Following much advocacy work of persons with disabilities and their representative organisations, it also includes an array of provisions needed to implement this goal with respect to children with disabilities. As such, the CRPD provides an important step in the advancement of the rights of children with disabilities. Yet, given the multifaceted aspects of the issue and its reliance on political processes, the CRPD's implementation needs to overcome some significant challenges.

This essay contemplates the future of the rights of children with disabilities in light of the CRPD. The next Part provides the background to the CRPD and gives a snapshot of the situation of children with disabilities around the world. Part II considers the limitations of the CRC in advancing the rights of children with disabilities. Focusing on children, Part III looks at the CRPD's central provisions and explains the remedial measures that have been adopted in this regard. The next part considers the issue of assistive technologies. The argument advanced is that, especially when children's perspectives are taken into account, assistive technologies are at the heart of national and international efforts to implement and advance the rights of children with disabilities, most importantly, a right to inclusion. Accordingly, I overview the CRPD's provisions referencing to assistive technologies and consider the issue from a child-centred perspective. In Part V, I discuss the challenges that arise in the CRPD's implementation, and the final Part draws conclusions.

Children with Disabilities: A Snapshot

It is estimated that out of the close to a billion people worldwide who live with a disability, 150-200 million of them are children under the age of 18.[1] Whilst this estimate includes a range of physical, mental, intellectual and sensory impairments (as well as combinations thereof), it is further estimated that 90 million children aged 0-14 experience 'moderate or severe disability', and 13 million children in this age group experience severe difficulties (World Report on Disability, 2011). Additionally, as with other persons with disabilities, it is estimated that 80 per cent of children with disabilities reside in developing countries.

In terms of rights, since children with disabilities fall within the scope of the CRC, they have the same rights as other children. This includes negative and positive rights, the right to welfare and to autonomy and participation as relevant to the entire scope of civil, political, economic, social, cultural and humanitarian rights. The CRC further explicitly references children with disabilities. It is the first human rights treaty to include disability within its stipulated prohibited grounds of discrimination (Article 2), as well as to dedicate an entire article to children with disabilities. Article 23 calls upon states to 'recognize that a mentally or physically disabled child should enjoy a full and decent life, in conditions which ensure dignity, promote self-reliance and facilitate the child's active participation in the community.' It also requires states to recognise the right of a child with disability to have effective access to special care and assistance, emphasising in particular education, training, health care services, rehabilitation services, preparation for employment and recreation opportunities 'in a manner conducive to the child's achieving the fullest possible social integration and individual development, including his or her cultural and spiritual development' (Article 23(2), (3)). Given the needs of developing countries, Sub-paragraph 4 calls upon states to 'promote, in the spirit of international cooperation, the exchange of appropriate information

---

[1] A child in this paper means, as defined in the CRC, Article 1: every human being below the age of eighteen years unless under the law applicable to the child, majority is attained earlier.

in the field of preventive health care and of medical, psychological and functional treatment of disabled children,' including methods of rehabilitation, education and vocational services.

In reality, children with disabilities in both developing and developed countries fare worse than their non-disabled peers with respect to every stipulated right. Studies show that, children with disabilities are more vulnerable to infanticide and to premature death in residential and other institutions than other children (UNICEF, 2012). This clearly contravenes one of the CRC cornerstone provisions stipulating the child's inherent right to life, survival and development (Article 6). The child's right to live with his/her parents and family, and rights to be free from torture, inhuman and degrading treatment or punishment as well as from arbitrary deprivation of liberty (Articles 9 and 37 of the CRC) are regularly violated. Numerous children with disabilities all around the world are commonly removed from their homes and families and placed in institutions, where they are exposed to harsh physical restrictions and violence, while many others are hidden away at home and out of public view (Sullivan,2009; UNICEF, 2012). Conversely, in (developed) countries where the governments have taken steps towards de-institutionalisation and reduced residential services for persons with disabilities, other community support has not been improved (Boezaart, 2012). As a result, the social, emotional, and, significantly, also economic strain on families of children with disabilities has increased, creating less favourable environments for the child's development.

In stark contrast to Articles 19 and 34 of the CRC, children with disabilities worldwide are 4-10 times more likely to incur and be impacted by violence than their non-disabled peers in ostensibly all private and public social settings: from war and ethnic conflicts, to custodial and institutional settings, to families, to school, and in travel to school (Sullivan, 2009; de Silva de Alwis, 2009; HRW 2010). The rates of sexual, emotional and verbal abuse and neglect are also especially high, with girls with disabilities being at greater risk of violence, injury, abuse, neglect or negligent treatment, maltreatment and exploitation, also when compared with boys with disabilities (de Silva de Alwis, 2009; UNICEF, 2011; UNICEF, 2012). Furthermore, in many countries, including France, the US, Australia, the UK and India, girls with disabilities are at risk of being denied reproductive and sexual rights through forced sterilisation at the request of their guardians (HRW, 2010). Also, appropriate measures for, *inter alia*, identification, reporting, and investigation of abuse, as well as access to the judicial system in such instances and to physical and psychological recovery services as required in Articles 19 and 39 of the CRC, are commonly unavailable.

Studies show further that, contrary to the right to health (Article 24, CRC), children with disabilities are at least twice as much likely to be denied access to nutrition, healthcare and rehabilitation services than their non-disabled peers (Sullivan, 2009). As the same time, children with disabilities, especially children with developmental disabilities including autism, attention deficit disorder and attention deficit hyperactivity disorder, were found to be at a significantly higher risk of injury from falls, burn-related injuries, and motor vehicles and bicycles crashes (World Report on Disability, 2011). Additionally, the right to education often is not materialised for children with disabilities. Surveys in developing countries in Africa, Latin America and Southeast Asia show that children with disabilities 6-17 years old have lower rates of school enrollment and attendance (Mitra, S. *et al.* 2011). 'Lower rates' in this context is significant: according to data collected by UNESCO, 90 per cent of children with disabilities in developing countries do not attend school, representing more than one-third of the 67 million children who are out of school world-wide (UNESCO, 2003). The educational situation of children with disabilities is grim also elsewhere. According to recent studies, roughly 1.1 million of children with disabilities of primary-school age in Central and Eastern Europe and the Commonwealth of Independent States region are unac-counted for and likely, out-of-school, and in any case, the educational oppor-tunities available to them outside institutions or special schools are limited (UNICEF, 2007; UNICEF, 2012). Here too there is a gender aspect: girls with disabilities are less likely to attend school than boys with disabilities (UNESCO, 2003).

The implications of this exclusion are staggering and persist as the children become adults. The literacy rate among persons with disabilities is estimated at three per cent and only one per cent among women with disabilities (UNESCO, 2003). The lack of access to education often prevents children and youth with disabilities from entering the labour market, resulting in signifi-cantly higher rates of poverty later on. This adds to the costs associated with raising a child with disabilities – already recognised as significantly straining on families of children with disabilities – leading to a cycle of poverty among children and adults with disabilities. Indeed, the World Bank has estimated that one in five of the world's poorest people is a person with disabilities (Braithwaite and Mont, 2008) – a fact that remains true also in more devel-oped countries. For instance, four in 10 children and young people with disa-bilities in England are living in poverty (Ramesh, 2011), and 28 percent of children with disabilities in the US live below the federal poverty line, account-ing for almost twice as children without disabilities (Parish *et al.* 2008). Children who grow up in poverty in both developing and developed countries are also at greater risk than others of acquiring cognitive, motor and social-emotional disabilities due to conditions that are mostly preventable such as malnutrition, poor health and unstimulating environments (UNESCO, 2010; World Report on Disability, 2011). And whilst it has been argued that poverty is both a cause and a consequence of disability, it is also heartbreaking that children have very little say about either of these aspects in their everyday lives.

What Happened to the Rights of Children with Disabilities?

That the CRC failed to improve the rights of children with disabilities may be no surprise. As Michael Freeman eloquently observed more than a decade ago, the rights of children all around the world are continuously violated – most likely more rather than less since the adoption of the CRC, the mere difference being that now, these violations receive public attention (Freeman, 2000). What is especially troubling with respect to children with disabilities, however, is not only the magnitude of their human rights violations, but that, until recently – and in fact, still today – these violations have passed unnoticed. Indeed, children with disabilities are invisible in rights talk compared to both their non-disabled peers and other persons with disabilities.

A few philosophical and practical reasons account for this invisibility. First, the historical perception of persons with disabilities as objects of charity and as passive recipients of welfare rather than as bearers of rights applied even more so to children with disabilities. Paradoxically, Article 23 of the CRC reflects this approach as well. Notwithstanding the provision's requirement that states 'facilitate the child's active participation in the community,' it is mostly focused on the welfare needs of children with disabilities and not on their rights (Jones and Marks, 1997, 184). This is problematic on two levels. Welfare rights are commonly viewed as expensive and unreasonably burdensome for states to implement. Indeed, Article 23 itself allows for this conclusion since it explicitly conditions the provision of services to children with disabilities 'on available resources'. Thus, despite studies showing that the benefits of an inclusive society –both monetarily as well as personal and social gains – surpass the costs (Stergious-Kita *et al.* 2010), states can easily deny disability claims for assistance and accommodation on the basis of lack of resources. Further, because Article 23 is dedicated to children with disabilities, its focus on welfare rights may have given the (wrong) impression that a needs-based approach is the only – or at least the paramount – aspect that ought to be addressed. This may also explain why the shift that has occurred since the adoption of the CRC with respect to the recognition of children as active agents and bearers of rights (as meager as it may be) has seemingly misses children with disabilities.

Second, the stigma associated with disabilities has had significant implications on their rights. As many parents refuse to acknowledge their child's impairment, children with disabilities often do not have access to the services he/she is entitled to under Article 23 of the CRC which are contingent on proving the child's 'eligibility.' Moreover, in various developing countries, the birth of children born with disabilities is not registered and they are at higher risk of abandonment or of being locked in the house (de Silva de Alwis, 2009; UNICEF, 2012). Practically, then, children with disabilities remain invisible as citizens and are denied the opportunity to exercise any of their rights.

These factors have further been translated into lack of appropriate and comprehensive states' policies that address the rights of children with disabilities under the CRC. Notwithstanding national legislations and policies such as the Americans with Disabilities Act of 1990 and the (current) Equality Act of 2010 in the UK that focus on persons with disabilities, children included, as of 2006, less than a third of the countries in the world have had disability non-discrimination laws in place. Further, as an analysis of the governmental reports and the concluding observations of the Committee under the CRC between 2000 and 2003 found, except where expressly mentioned in the CRC, in areas of education, training, healthcare services and rehabilitation services, the rights of children with disabilities were disregarded. Similarly, states commonly do not provide child-protection services and prevention health-related programmes that are accessible to children with disabilities (UN General Secretary's Study on Violence against Children, 2005). Despite continuous efforts of the Committee monitoring the CRC's implementation, especially after the publication of this analysis, to raise awareness among states to their obligations in respect to children with disabilities (General Day of discussion; CRC, General Comment No. 9; and Concluding Observations summarised in Quinn and Degener, 2002), not much progress has been made.

Finally, the CRC's model of disability may account for the exclusion of such children from 'rights talk': it is based on the principle of non-discrimination which is insufficient to advance the rights of children with disabilities (Jones and Marks, 1997, 182-3). The principle of non-discrimination under international human rights law allows for different treatment if the distinction is made on the basis of reasonable and objective criteria, and if it is to achieve a legislative purpose. With regard to children with disabilities, because they may appear or behave differently, this criterion is commonly used, thus in practice, permitting and legitimising discrimination and segregation. Two glaring examples are the common practice of separate education for children with disabilities, which is not viewed as discrimination, and the sterilisation of girls with disabilities. The latter medical procedure is usually performed at the request of the guardians in order to enable them to better care for the girl or arguably to protect the girl child from sexual abuse, although no other children are subject to such invasive medical procedures for the convenience of their parents or care-takers, and the 'protection argument' has repeatedly proven wrong (Jones and Marks, 1997, 188; Freeman, 2000). An accompanying principle of inclusion is thus essential – yet it was not incorporated in the CRC despite proposals to do so.

The CRPD and Children's Rights

The CRPD aimed at addressing the appalling situation of children with disabilities and at responding to the failures of the CRC to improve their rights. It was adopted after three decades of disability activism, and just over three years of intensive negotiations at the United Nations. The drafting process was characterised by high involvement of persons with disabilities and their representative organisations, creating an instrument that intends to reach all persons with disabilities, children included.[2] Save the Children took a step forward: in an effort to increase the visibility of children with disabilities as bearers of rights, it organised for a group of young people with disabilities to attend one session at the UN and to 'make the case for themselves' at the plenary session of the Ah-Hoc Committee that was authorised to draft the CRPD (Lansdown, 2013).

The CRPD takes a social, inter-relational approach to disability, calling attention to the interaction between one's impairment, society, and context, rather than focusing, as traditionally was the case, merely on the medical deficit one may have. It stipulates as its purpose 'to promote, protect and ensure the full and equal enjoyment of all human rights and fundamental freedoms by all persons with disabilities, and to promote respect for their inherent dignity' (Article 1). In addition to the core requirements of equality, non-discrimination and equality of opportunity (Articles 3 (b), (e), (g) and 5), and *in lieu* of the criticism raised about the CRC, the concept of inclusion occupies a prominent place. Among the General Principles governing the treaty are 'Respect for inherent dignity, individual autonomy including the freedom to make one's own choices, and independence of persons'; 'full and effective participation and inclusion in society'; and, uniquely, 'Respect for difference and acceptance of persons with disabilities as part of human diversity and humanity' (Article 3 (a), (c) and (d)). Accessibility, another stipulated General Principle of the CRPD that is critical for inclusion, is further elaborated on in a separate article (Articles 3(f) and 9), as is the requirement of awareness-raising 'throughout society' regarding the dignity of persons with disabilities and their

---

[2] Due to disagreements among the drafters, the CRPD does not include a definition of disabilities or person with disabilities. However, Article 1 of the CRPD denotes that 'Persons with disabilities include those who have long-term physical, mental, intellectual or sensory impairments which in interaction with various barriers may hinder their full and effective participation in society on an equal basis with others.'

capacities and contribution to society (Article 8). Further, the CRPD requires the adoption of an array of measures – legislative, administrative and others – to abolish negative stereotypes and to remove the various physical, environmental, institutional and informational barriers that prevent persons with disabilities, children included, from being full participants in society. Indeed, the notion of discrimination on the basis of disability itself is now tied with inclusion. It is defined to mean 'any distinction, exclusion or restriction on the basis of disability which has the purpose or effect of impairing or nullifying the recognition, enjoyment or exercise of all human rights and fundamental freedoms,' and, importantly, including the denial of reasonable accommodation (Article 2).

Although the Convention applies to all persons with disabilities, the rights and needs of children with disabilities occupy an important place throughout it. First, to ensure consistency in international human rights law, the CRPD references to the CRC and reaffirms the latter's fundamental principles of the child's best interests as a primary consideration and the child's right to participate and to be heard (Articles 3, 12, and 5, CRC (respectively); Article 7, CRPD). Further, the CRPD stipulates the principle of 'evolving capacities' among the treaty's General Principles that guide the treaty's implementation (Article 3), and responding to criticism raised about this principle in the CRC (Freeman, 2000), without the tie with the parents and family. Additionally, the principle of participation is re-instated in the CRPD's provision on General Obligations and elaborated on to require that children with disabilities are 'closely consulted with and actively involved' in the development and implementation of legislation and policies to implement the CRPD (Article 4(3)).

Second, aware that the rights of children with disabilities under the CRC were lost when not explicitly stipulated, the drafters of the CRPD opted for the so-called 'twin track approach' to hone in on the rights and protections of children with disabilities. That is, the CRPD frames the rights of children with disabilities in dedicated articles while, at the same time, references to the rights of children with disabilities were mainstreamed and incorporated throughout the Convention. Accordingly, Article 7 of the CRPD focuses in its entirety on children with disabilities, requiring that states take 'all necessary measures' to ensure that children with disabilities fully enjoy all human rights and fundamental freedoms as other children, including civil, political, economic, social and cultural rights. Article 6 of the CRPD focuses on women with disabilities and explicitly includes also girls with disabilities. This article recognises the multiple layers of discrimination experienced by woman and girls with disabilities. It contains a similar requirement to Article 7, and for this purpose, it also obligates states to take 'all appropriate measures to ensure the full development, advancement and empowerment of women.' In doing so, the CRPD aimed to address the gender dimension of disability-discrimination.

The CRPD contains references to the rights of children with disabilities throughout the treaty. The substantive articles of the CRPD reiterate civil, political, economic, social and cultural rights as exist in other human rights treaties, including the CRC – from the right to be heard, to the right to be registered, to have a name and to nationality, to family and privacy, to protection from abuse, neglect and torture, to health, to education, and to standard of living. Importantly, the rights are tailored to the needs, protections and rights of children with disabilities.

Accordingly, with regard to the child's right to be heard, the CRPD requires that children with disabilities are 'provided with disability and age-appropriate assistance to realize that right' (Article 7(2), (3)) and, alarmed by the incidents of violence against children with disabilities, it requires that states adopt 'child-focused legislation and policies' to ensure appropriate legal redress of instances of exploitation, violence and abuse against persons with disabilities (Article 16(5)). Given the lack of registration, Article 18 of CRPD explicitly requires that states ensure that persons with disabilities are not deprived, on the basis of disability, of their ability to obtain, possess and utilise documentation of their nationality or other documentation of identification, and reinstate the CRC's requirement with regard to children with disabilities that registration shall be 'immediately after birth' and include the rights to a name, to acquire nationality and, as far as possible, to know and be cared for by their parents.

Article 23 tailors the 'equal rights with respect to family life' to children with disabilities. It requires that states eliminate discrimination in family matters and stipulates an unequivocal right of persons with disabilities, including an explicit mentioning of children, to retain one's fertility. The article also requires that states undertake positive measures to 'prevent concealment, abandonment, neglect and segregation of children with disabilities' and that for the implementation of this right, states 'shall undertake to provide early and comprehensive information, services and support to children with disabilities and their families' (Article 23(3)). Sub-paragraph 4 further stipulates that 'a child shall not be separated from his or her parents against their will' and that such separation shall take place only when it 'is necessary for the best interests of the child,' clearly stating that, 'In no case shall a child be separated from parents on the basis of a disability of either the child or one or both of the parents.' Furthermore, the article requires that when the immediate family is unable to care for a child with disabilities, 'every effort' should be undertaken to provide 'alternative care within the wider family, and failing that, within the community in a family setting' (Article 23(5)).

In the context of education, the CRPD requires states to establish an inclusive education system and that 'Effective individualised support measures are provided in environments that maximise academic and social development, consistent with the goal of full inclusion' (Article 24). Accordingly, the provision explicitly obligates states to ensure that children with disabilities are not 'excluded from free and compulsory primary education,' that reasonable accommodation as well as other relevant support are provided within the general education system to facilitate their effective education, and that education of children who are blind, deaf or deafblind is delivered 'in the most appropriate languages and modes and means of communication.' States are also required to eliminate discrimination with respect to the right to health, and to provide health services that are needed specifically because of one's disabilities, including early identification and intervention as appropriate, as well as services designed to minimise and prevent further disabilities among children (Article 25). Aware of the rates of poverty among persons and children with disabilities, specific reference is additionally made to states' obligations to ensure access by persons with disabilities to social protection programmes and poverty reduction programmes, highlighting in particular girls with disabilities (Article 28(b)).

Finally, although the CRPD was not intended to create new rights, the drafters stipulated rights that may otherwise seem obvious yet that with regard to persons and children with disabilities, have been consistently denied. Of particular relevance are: access to justice, the right to live independently and being included in the community, habilitation and rehabilitation, and the right to participate in cultural life, play, recreation and leisure, and sporting activities (Articles 9, 13, 19, 26, 30, respectively).

Whereas the importance of these rights is clear with regard to all persons with disabilities, the latter right to participate in play, recreation and sports are uniquely critical to children with disabilities. Studies consistently show that although the importance of physical activities to one's wellbeing and to the prevention of secondary impairments is well established, children with disabilities have only limited access to such activities. The prime reasons are environmental barriers, such as inaccessible space or specialised equipment, economic costs when appropriate facilities are unavailable in one's community, lack of skilled trainers who are aware of the needs of children with disabilities, and the misconceptions and negative attitudes about children with disabilities in play and sports activities by coaches, schools, communities, and families (Taub and Greer, 2000; Devas, 2003; Poulsen and Ziviani, 2004). Consequently, children with disabilities often have lower levels of cardio-respiratory fitness, lower levels of muscular endurance and higher rates of obesity (Murphy, Carbone, and the Council on Children with Disabilities, 2008). In this sense, the CRPD's explicit reference to sporting activities for children with disabilities takes seriously the CRC enshrined requirement of 'healthy development' (see especially, Articles 6, 24, 27, 29 and 32, CRC), unseen in other core human rights treaties: sporting activities are viewed as a *right*.

The transformation of sporting activities into a right is especially important given the history of sports in the disability context. Until recently, participation in sporting activities and exercise for children with disabilities were seen merely through medical and rehabilitation lenses, as part of the child's therapy (Taub and Greer, 2000). Contrary to this approach, it is increasingly evident that play and sporting activities are important for the social inclusion of children with disabilities. Such activities provide the child with opportunities to socialise with other children, including non-disabled peers, to develop friendships, skills and competencies, express creativity, and positively to affect the self-esteem and identity construction of the child (Murphy *et al.* 2008; Fay and Wolff, 2009).

There is only limited literature on the perspectives of children with disabilities on sports activities, but the studies that exist reinforce the above-mentioned findings. For instance, in a study of children with disabilities ages 10-17 in the US, the children expressed not only the physical benefits of their participation in play and sporting activities in schools but also the equalising factor: showing physical abilities, legitimating of a social identity, increased feelings of self-enhancement or self-worth, emotional benefits, increased social integration, sociability and social alliances (Taub and Greer, 2000). Importantly, these finding were supported also by the children's peers. As the researchers found, 'classmates and friends also tend to think they [the children with disabilities] possess legitimacy as children because of their physical activity.' (Taub and Greer, 2000, 410). In another study in Canada, children with disabilities aged 5 to 16 indicated that they would be more involved in activities that are 'fun' and that increased their sense of success, in addition to 'doing and being with others' (Heah *et al.* 2007, 42). Although concerns were raised that competitive play and sporting activities may reduce the 'fun' as the children grow older and find it harder to keep up with their non-disabled peers (Heah *et al.* 2007), arguably, assistive technologies may at least partially overcome this barrier as well. Indeed, assistive technologies are critical for inclusion to take place.

I thus now turn to consider the issue of assistive technologies and children under the CRPD.

Assistive Technologies and Children's Rights

The inextricable connection between scientific developments and human development and rights cannot be overstated. Not only have historically the two evolved simultaneously with mutual influence on the development of one another, but, more importantly, there is no doubt that today, scientific developments cut across many other social values and civil, political, economic, social and cultural rights (CESCR, General Comment No. 17). This includes not only the right to health, but also other rights such as to education, information, and, increasingly, also to socio-cultural identity.

Indeed, it is for this reason that one's right to enjoy scientific developments was stipulated early on within the human rights corpus and reiterated in subsequent international and regional instruments – most importantly are the references made in Article 27 of the Universal Declaration of Human Rights and in Article 15 of the International Covenant on Economic, Social and Cultural Rights (UDHR; ICESCR; for other regional instruments see, Report of Special Rapporteur in the field of Cultural Rights, 2012).

But the CRPD has taken this right to a new level. An array of articles in the CRPD evidently ties between the development and provision of new technologies and persons with disabilities' exercise of their human rights. Further, although the CRPD does not define assistive technologies, it uses assistive technologies in plural, referring to 'any product, instrument, equipment or technology adapted or especially designed for improving the functioning of a person with disability,' including assistive devices, mobility aids, Braille, and augmentative and alternative modes, means and formats of communication (Borg *et al.* 2011; see also Article 2). Among the General Principles of the treaty is states' obligation 'To undertake or promote research and development of, and to promote the availability and use of new technologies, including information and communications technologies, mobility aids, devices and assistive technologies, suitable for persons with disabilities,' as well as the provision of accessible information about such mobility aids, devices and assistive technologies (Article 4). The provision on accessibility includes 'information and communications technologies and systems, including the internet' and the requirement that states promote 'the design, development, production and distribution of accessible information and communications technologies and systems at an early stage' (Article 9). In both articles, which are considered found often provisions of the treaty, special attention is given also to the development and availability of affordable technologies (Articles 4(g), 9(h)).

Additionally, Article 20 on personal mobility requires that states facilitate access by persons with disabilities to quality mobility aids, devices, and assistive technologies, and encourage entities that produce such technologies 'to take into account all aspects of mobility for persons with disabilities.' References to states' obligation to promote access of persons with disabilities to assistive devices and technologies exist also with regard to habilitation and rehabilitation (Article 26) and participation and political and public life (Article 29), whereas the provision on education (Article 24) requires states to facilitate the learning of Braille, alternative script, augmentative and alternative modes, means and formats of communication and orientation and mobility skills. Finally, for the first time in a human rights treaty, the CRPD stipulates states' recognition of the importance of international cooperation and its promotion, requiring them, *inter alia*, to facilitate cooperation in research and access to scientific and technical knowledge and to provide 'technical and economic assistance, including by facilitating access to and sharing of accessible and assistive technologies, and through the transfer of technologies' (Article 32). Indeed, the CRPD's references to the variety of such technologies both in the treaty's guiding provisions as well as substantive ones has arguably established an entitlement of persons with disabilities with rights to assistive technologies so to ensure full and equal enjoyment of all human rights (Borg *et al.* 2011). As such, assistive technologies are also inherently at the heart of national and international efforts to implement and advance the rights of children with disabilities, most importantly, a right to inclusion.

The case of children with disabilities is most illustrative in this regard. From prosthesis to limbs, from mobility devices to hearing aids, and from information and communication technologies to nanotechnology, there is no doubt that without access to such assistive technologies, children with disabilities face a barrier that significantly impedes their participation in social, cultural, and educational settings, and later on, also economic and employment opportunities. Conversely, access to assistive technologies is instrumental in enabling the social inclusion and participation of children with disabilities. For instance, in a study with children with cerebral palsy aged 8 to 15 in Taiwan, most of the children who had or used assistive technologies since childhood tended to value their devices positively (Borg *et al.* 2009). The researchers found that the children tended to describe their devices as important and helpful not only in overcoming their physical limitations, but also in enabling them to perform better in the school setting, increase their confidence in their relationship and participation in play and school activities with their peers, and overall, develop a sense of belonging. Another study focused on children aged 8 and 19 years old in the UK who needed the continuing support of medical technologies such as mechanical ventilation, tracheostomy, and oxygen therapy (Kirk, 2010). Although some of the children expressed ambivalence toward the technologies, recognising them both as socially enabling and disabling in their lives, the merits of these technologies are stressed. Certainly, more studies are needed to shed light on the perspectives of children with disabilities on the benefits and shortcomings of *various* assistive technologies, as well as to learn how gender, age, cultural background, social environment, and impairments intersect in this regard. But the findings of existing studies should not be overlooked. As the researchers point out, not only do the children manage the technologies on their own as 'everyday life activity' and as a way of living 'normal life', but for most of them the technology is also conceived as part of them physically and plays a role in their process of social and personal identity formation. Importantly, then, access to assistive technologies is inherent and integral to the experience of children with disabilities as *being*.

The Rights of Children with Disabilities: A Reality?

As impressive as the CRPD's list of rights may appear, a cardinal question is whether the treaty would be implemented. Having a dead-law treaty would do no good to the rights of children with disabilities –as well as to other persons with disabilities and to the corpus of international human rights law as a whole.

Certainly, there is room for optimism. The CRPD's relatively quick negotiation process, its rapid entry into force and the high number of states that signed and ratified it are a sign of the political support the treaty has gained (although, of course, this was seemingly the case also with the CRC). Further, as the CRPD essentially complements existing treaties, especially relevant for our discussion are the Convention on the Elimination of All Forms of Discrimination against Women (CEDAW) and the CRC (de Silva de Alwis, 2009), its implementation does not require 'starting from scratch' as the previous human rights treaties. Significantly, the CRPD's focus group also differs from previous human rights treaties: it is truly universal. No one is immune from obtaining a disability at one stage or another, and most people have a person with a disability in his/her close circle of family and friends. There is therefore a hope that in the conventional gap between states' showing political support in a treaty and their political will in actually implementing it, the CRPD will present a different case.

Indeed, since the adoption of the CRPD, the number of programmes and organisations aimed at the advancement of rights of children with disabilities has mushroomed. The seeds planted in 2002 to strengthen international cooperation to accelerate the integration of disability issues into mainstream social and economic development efforts matured in 2008, following an agreement between the World Bank and the Burton Blatt Institute at Syracuse University (BBI). Subsequently, the Global Partnership for Disability and Development (GPDD) was established to reduce the extreme poverty and exclusion of, *inter alia*, children with disabilities residing in poor countries, including in the context of disaster management (http://www.gpdd-online.org/). The World Bank has joined forces with the WHO to issue the World Report on Disability in 2011, which includes the most comprehensive-to-date discussion on children with disabilities, and it stated its commitment to children with disabilities especially in issues such as child health, communicable diseases, and education for all (Guernsey *et al.* 2007; World Report on Disability, 2011). UNESCO has formally mainstreamed the theme of children with disabilities into its work in 2006. Moving beyond its previous focus on inclusive educa-tion, the organisation now works to address the neglect and abuse of the rights of children with disabilities on an international scale. Following a year of consultation, in September 2012 it established The Global Partnership on Children with Disabilities (GPcwd), a network of more than 100 organisations, including international NGOs, national/local NGOs, Disabled People's Organisations (DPOs), governments, academia and the private sector, to pro-vide a platform for advocacy and collective action to advance the rights of children with disabilities at the global, regional and country levels (www .unicef.org). Other international non-governmental organisations are taking on board they need to address disability discrimination (e.g., HRW), and Save the Children too has expanded its work to include children with disabilities in a more meaningful way.

Internet communication has played a prominent role in these develop-ments – as it had during the negotiations of the CRPD (Sabatello, 2013). Online discussions are taking place routinely among actors all around the world, and children with disabilities can participate (as long as they have access to internet). Instances of violations of the rights of children with disabilities are regularly posted, thematic issues are explored, and calls for actions are made. These on-line discussions are further valuable when issues pertaining to chil-dren with disabilities are considered during the annual Conference of States Parties – a forum to discuss the implementation of disability rights, uniquely established under the CRPD (Article 40) – consolidating the international disability rights community. They can also be helpful when the Committee under the CRPD considers states' reports or individual communications – an option that, unlike the CRC, exists as an Optional Protocol of the CRPD.

Efforts to create an inclusive society for children with disabilities take place also on the national level of both developed and developing countries. Community-based rehabilitation programmes are promoted by international and national initiatives as the way forward (see, e.g., WHO, *CBR Guidelines*, 2010). Such programmes take a multi-sectoral strategy that empowers persons with disabilities to access and benefit from education, employment, health and social services, and they are implemented through the efforts of all stakeholders. Whether through governmental policies, the work of non-governmental organisations, persons with disabilities and their families or, increasingly, the collaboration between such entities, many strive to improve the conditions and rights of children with disabilities.

Some of these initiatives have been successful. For instance, a community-rehabilitation programme in a disadvantaged community near Allahabad, India, has enabled children with disabilities to attend school for the first time, has increased the overall participation of persons with disabilities in the com-munity, and led to more people bringing their children with disabilities for vaccination and rehabilitation (Dalal, 2006). The concept of inclusive education gains traction. It has been adopted in most developed countries such as the US, Italy, New Zealand, and the OECD countries (with some exceptions, such as the UK, Belgium and Germany), and in developing countries, educational reforms are increasingly taking place on the national level or as pilot projects (World Report, 2011; Read *et al.* 2012). Other policy changes in mainly developed countries such the US, the UK, and Australia focus on alleviating the socio-economic status of children living in poverty, as well as on de-institutionalization of children with disabilities (e.g., AusAID; WHO/EU, 2010; Read *et al.* 2012). In 2010, the Committee of Ministers of the Council of Europe issued its recommendation to the member states to replace institutional provision with community-based services within a reasonable timeframe, and Romania, for example, has prided itself on closing 70 per cent of its institutions for children between 2001 and 2007 (Recommendation CM/Rec(2010)2; World Report, 2011).

Yet, from these initiatives it is difficult to learn the potential and drawbacks of the CRPD in advancing the rights of children with disabilities worldwide. Successful initiatives are generally on small scale, and it is unclear if they can be replicated elsewhere. The success (or failure) of a programme is also tied to other factors. In Ghana, Guyana and Nepal, for instance, a community-based rehabilitation project showed only limited impact because of the lack of provision of physical rehabilitation, assistive devices and other services within the national healthcare system (World Report on Disability, 2011). The extent of involvement of children with disabilities in the development and execution of such programmes is also uncertain. The small number of child-led organisations, especially those of children with disabilities, may account for this silence (Tisdall, 2012), as well as the lack of accessible internet and communication technologies.

From a global perspective, it is hard not to be somewhat pessimistic about the feasibility of the CRPD to improve the rights of children with disabilities, most certainly if one expects such improvements in the near future. As past experiences with other human rights treaties have shown, especially when the treaty's implementation depends on transforming deeply-held social and cultural beliefs as well as stigma, changes are slow to occur. This is especially so with regard to the CRPD as the conceptual transformation that is required is far reaching and transcends multiple ingrained dichotomies. These include not only the blurring of traditional divides such as public/private, state/individual, individual/community, and domestic/international (Megret, 2008), but significantly, also of *who* are the subjects deserving rights. Previous core human rights treaties – especially, the International Covenant on Civil and Political Rights, the International Covenant of Economic, Social, and Cultural Rights, as well as CEDAW – have focused on adults who are autonomous and rational decision-makers. The CRC, while extending rights to non-adults, is nonetheless focused on children who are *in the process* of obtaining these characteristics of autonomy and rational decision-making. The expectation is that for children to bear rights, they have to be sufficiently communicative to do so; the underlying assumption being that ultimately, childhood is a stage that everyone will (or should) grow out of (Sabatello, 2009; Tisdall, 2012).

The CRPD breaks ground in this regard as in addition to the relatively traditional social construction of gender and age, it requires re-conceptualisation of autonomy versus dependency, capacity versus incapacity, and also of the medical versus the social, and the recognition of various forms of communication – including non-verbal, behavioural, and non-communication altogether. Thus, although the CRPD's effort to put aside conventional dichotomies is laudable –indeed, it provides a far more humane perception of the individual members of society –promoting the rights of children with disabilities will not be easy. This is exacerbated by the barrier of paternalism, which is often higher for children with disabilities than it is for other children, and which requires a sweeping shift to allow the voice of children with disabilities and their need in support – rather than substitutive decision-making – to be heard (Mortier *et al.* 2011). But it also goes deeper: children with disabilities have to cross the barrier of being recognised and accepted as subjects rather than objects, and as individuals whose lives have meaning.

Given the critical role of assistive technologies, one also needs to wonder about the practicality of it, especially considering the prevalence of disability in developing countries. Because of prohibitive patent laws, assistive technologies are often too costly for purchase and are beyond reach for many in poorer countries (Report of Special Rapporteur in the field of Cultural Rights, 2012). Also when the technologies are available, the lack of appropriate expertise in assessing and fitting the devices as well as the lack of other relevant services, including the provision of information about the technologies and the awareness of negative stigma towards such technologies, prevent a wide use (Borg *et al.* 2009; Huang *et al.* 2009; Borg *et al.* 2012).

It follows that, it is not surprising that there is a large gap between the need and provision of assistive technologies. For example, studies in Malawi, Mozambique, Namibia, Zambia and Zimbabwe show that only 17-37 per cent of people received the assistive devices they needed (WHO, 2011). And more generally, the WHO estimates that in low and middle income countries only 5-15 per cent of people requiring assistive technologies have access to it, that less than 3 per cent of those who need hearing aids have access to it, and that most of the 0.5 per cent who need prosthetic and orthopedic devices as well as most of the 1 per cent who need wheelchairs do not have such devices at all (World Report on Disability, 2011; WHO, 2011). Similarly, only 10 per cent of children who are blind in such countries have access to tools for writing Braille (Connell, 2004). Studies further show that gender and young age create another set-back: women and children are less likely to have access to such technologies (Borg *et al.* 2012). In Nigeria, for instance, one of the stipulated reasons for the lack of hearing aids for children less than five years old is that 'children are often considered too young to be fitted with these devices' (Olusanya *et al.* 2005).

The magnitude of this want becomes all the more worrying when one realises, first, in many of these countries the healthcare services, including proper screening and diagnosis for various conditions is lacking; second, assistive technologies cannot remedy on their own the lack of pavements, appropriate community programmes that offer activities for children with disabilities and universally designed outdoor public play spaces – which are recurring themes in disability studies worldwide (Heah *et al.* 2007; Woolley, 2012); and third, the lack of access to assistive technologies in developing countries can refer also to some of the most low-tech, basic and widely used technologies in the West. As a study in Brazil for example found, many children drop out of school for the simple fact that they lack reading glasses (World Report on Disability, 2011). Notwithstanding the CRPD's requirement of international cooperation and the fact that some initiatives in this regard are under way, for the treaty to be implemented the political will must come as a clear triumph over international politics.

The concern about lack of access to needed assistive technologies is relevant also in developed countries. First, the CRPD's assumption that assistive technologies are essential for the advancement of the rights of persons with disabilities may turn foul as, practically, innovative technologies could include also medically-oriented devices such as genetic engineering, brain-chips, and other neuro-scientific devices that are inserted to 'normalise' one's body, hence seemingly contradicting the CRPD's spirit. Although the CRPD requires a shift to a social approach of disability and, as the CRC, also that the child's voice is heard, dilemmas arise. Which technologies are in line with the social model (and acceptable) and which are not? And especially with regard to children, who is to decide? As with other children, adults' perspective may be different from the views of the child, and parents or caregivers who are the natural proxies may not accurately represent the experiences and wishes of the child (Tisdall, 2012). Considering that such devices are often used from an early age, and before the child can express his/ her opinion, the decision is ultimately in the hands of adults – be it parents, physicians or others – creating an inherent tension (and a possible clash) between parental (and societal) desires to 'fix' the child and the CRPD's explicit requirements of 'respect for difference' and 'respect for the right of children with disabilities to preserve their identities' (Article 3(d), (h)).

Another challenge with assistive technologies arises in light of the debate about enhancement. Historically, scientific developments merely aimed at restoring or mimicking the 'normal' functioning of the body. Current initiatives in contrast often aim at maximising the functions beyond it. The example of Oscar Pistorius, a double-amputee sprinter, reflects the ensuing dilemma: his use of prosthesis was viewed as bestowing him unfair advantage, meriting his initial exclusion from the Olympic competition. Although the controversy around Oscar Pistorius arose only when he was an adult, the implications of this decision are equally relevant for children with disabilities. First, this decision implies that resorting to medical devices may furnish a new justification for exclusion, thus, in practice, undermining the CRPD's goals. Second, it suggests that medical devices provided as reasonable accommodation should be limited to those that allow for average performance but not above it, hence practically re-establishing a hierarchy between children with disabilities and their 'able-bodied' peers. This is especially concerning as, despite the CRPD, decisions about eligibility criteria are often made by non-disabled people.

Still another challenge revolves around the question of which assistive technologies do states have an international obligation to provide under the scope of reasonable accommodation for its disabled-population. In 2003, the European Court of Human Rights found inadmissible a parental request that the Netherland's health insurance provides their child, who had Duchenne Muscular Dystrophy, with a robotic arm. Despite evidence showing that it would give him more autonomy in handling objects and greatly improve his quality of life, the Court declined to intervene due to the cost of such a device (*Sentges v. The Netherlands*, 2003). Moving fast forward, to the post-CRPD era, was the Court wrong in its decision? Would its refusal to intervene in a national decision about allocation of resources stand, given the CRPD's shift to the realm of positive obligations? The answer is not clear. Certainly, the financial consideration is likely to remain – indeed, despite efforts of the disability rights movement during the negotiation process, the CRPD's requirement for reasonable accommodation ultimately includes the condition of 'not imposing a disproportionate or undue burden' (whatever that means) (Article 2; see also NUH, 2007). Although in the past few years the ECHR has increasingly adopted decisions that support disability-rights, requiring *inter alia* that states uphold the right of persons with disabilities to vote and to political participation, as well as to de-institutionalisation and to be free from harassment (*K.A. v. Hungary*; *Glor v. Switzerland*; *Stanev v. Bulgaria; Glass v. the UK; Ðorđević v. Croatia*; see also, MDAC, 2007), so far it has not been requested to revisit its approach to assistive technologies and children with disabilities. Further, the ECHR has long been reluctant – as have other courts around the world – to interfere in governmental budgetary or allocation of resources decisions (O'Cinneide, 2009). Thus, even though the CRPD stipulates positive obligations on states – indeed, without appropriate resources, the disability revolution is not likely to succeed – it is yet to see how the ECHR and other courts would rule if a case similar to *Sentges* reaches their door.

Because the CRPD is the result of a political process – however inclusive of persons with disabilities it may have been – and the fact that the CRPD was not aimed at creating new rights, it is important to acknowledge that some of the criticism raised with respect to the scope of the CRC remained (Freeman, 2000; Veerman, 2010). Of particular relevance is the lack of references to some of the most marginalized groups of children with disabilities: street children and gay children, children with disabilities and HIV/ AIDS, and children belonging to indigenous communities who, in contrast to the CRC, are now merely mentioned in the CRPD's Preamble. Although the CRPD is intended to include such groups – as all other groups of children with disabilities – the experience of children with disabilities under the CRC shows that, unless they are explicitly mentioned, they are more likely to remain invisible. This is a concern that disability rights activists should bear in mind as they forge ahead with implementation efforts.

Finally, the issue of genetic selection is also worth mentioning. The practice of genetic selection raised fervent controversy in the past few years, especially regarding the selection for boys, but also, increasingly so, given the rise of pre-natal screening for disabilities with the expectation that if a child is diagnosed with a disability, it will be aborted (Asch *et al.* 2003). In the context of the CRPD, this issue was debated during the negotiations on the right to life (Article 10; UN Enable, Archives). However, the discussion became politicized because of its entanglement with the question of the woman's right to abortion and given that no agreement could be reached on the issue also among the organizations of persons with disabilities that participated in the negotiations, the CRC's compromise of leaving this issue beyond the treaty was upheld (Alston, 1990). It is nonetheless likely to be revisited, not least because of the cases arriving to the dock of the ECHR. Indeed, in a recent decision against Italy, the ECHR seemingly grants a *de facto* human right to access to pre-implantation genetic diagnosis in cases where there is a probability of genetic disorder (*Costa and Pavan v. Italy*; see also, *K. v. Latvia* concerning the lack of screening of a child with Down's Syndrome (undecided)). Although naturally, the decision revolves around parental rights, it may have implications for the rights of existing and future children with disabilities.

Conclusions

The adoption of the CRPD provides a good opportunity to consider the future of the rights of children with disabilities. In comparison to previous international human rights treaties, the CRPD is innovative in its approach to human rights. It takes a far more relational approach to promote human rights, which is essential if we are serious about children's rights (Sabatello, 2009), and indeed, about the rights of all other human beings. It stipulates at its core a right to inclusion, which transcends all other political, civil, economic, social, cultural, as well as development rights; it collapses traditional dichotomies that create black-and-white constructions of individuals that do not reflect human nature; and it is to be implemented through the concurrent right to assistive technologies.

As groundbreaking as the CRPD is, the treaty's implementation is not likely to be an easy or fast-track process. It would require significant political will on both national and international levels, and any changes that would occur in the understanding and especially the implementation of rights of children with disabilities are likely to be small and incremental. Additional studies of the perspectives of children with disabilities about their rights, how they want them to be implemented, and what are the barriers they experience are crucial to develop a child-centred approach to the implementation of the CRPD.

Further, there are a few lessons that can be learned from the experience of the CRC. First is that disability rights activists should try avoiding the situation whereby raising awareness to the rights of children with disabilities ultimately turns to mean merely greater visibility of the abuses of rights rather than actually acting upon such violations. Another lesson is that advocates should ensure that 'no child with disabilities is left behind.' Just as the exclusion of children with disabilities from the rights-discourse cannot be tolerated, so is the lack of attention to children with disabilities belonging to minority groups and other communities that are not explicitly mentioned. There is also a real need for creating opportunities for children with disabilities to be actively involved – and heard – in decisions that impact their lives, yet as the experience of the CRC has shown, this is a daunting task. As discussed, there are some encouraging international and national efforts in this direction, as well as greater 'teeth' of the Committee established under the CRPD given the possibility of individual communication and the discussion during the annual Conference of States Parties. It would be instrumental for disability rights activists, including children, to seize such opportunities and to utilise them for the mobilisation of greater international and national support.

References

Alston, P., 'The unborn child and abortion under the draft convention of the rights of the child', *Human Rights Quarterly* 12 (1990): 156–178.

AusAID, *Development for All: Towards a disability-inclusive Australian aid program* (2009–2014). http://www.ausaid.gov.au/Publications/Pages/8131_1629_9578_8310_297.aspx.

Boezaart, T., 'Protecting the reproductive rights of children and young adults with disabilities: The roles and responsibilities of the family, the state, and judicial decision-making', *Emory International Law Review* 26 (2012): 69–85.

Borg, J., Larsson, S. & Ostergren, P.-O, 'The right to assistive technology: For whom, for what, and by whom?' *Disability & Society* 26(2) (2011a): 151–167.

Borg, J., Lindstrom, A. & Larsson, S., 'Assistive technologies in developing countries: National and international responsibilities to implement the convention on the rights of persons with disabilities', *Lancet* 374 (2009): 1963–1965.

Borg, J., Lindstrom, A. & Larsson, S., 'Assistive technologies in developing countries: A review from the perspective of the convention on the rights of persons with disabilities', *Prosthetic and Orthotics International* 35(1) (2011b): 20–29.

Braithwaite, J. & Mont, D., *Disability and Poverty: A Survey of World Bank Poverty Assessments and Implications* (World Bank, 2008).

CESCR, General Comment 17, the right of everyone to benefit from the protection of the moral and material interests resulting from any scientific, literary or artistic production of which he or she is the author (Article 15, para 1 (c), of the Covenant), U.N. Doc. E/C.12/GC/17 (2006).

Committee on the Rights of the Child, *General Comment No. 9, The Rights of Children with Disabilities* (Forty-third session, 2007), U.N. Doc. CRC/C/GC/9 (2007).

Connell, T., 'The challenge of assistive technology and braille literacy', http://www.afb.org/afbpress/pub.asp?docid=aw090107.

Costa and Pavan v. Italy, Application no. 54270/10, ECHR, 28 August 2012.

CRC, *General Day of Discussion, Children with Disabilities* (1997). http://www.ohchr.org/EN/HRBodies/CRC/Documents/Recommandations/disabled.pdf.

Dalal A.K., 'Social interventions to moderate discriminatory attitudes: the case of the physically challenged in India', *Psychology, Health & Medicine* 11 (2006): 374–382.

De Silva de Alwis, R., 'Mining the intersections: Advancing the rights of women and children with disabilities within an interrelated web of human rights', *Pacific Rim Law & Policy Journal* 18 (2009): 293–322.

Devas, M., 'Support and access in sports and leisure provision', *Disability and Society* 18(2) (2003): 231–245.

Đorđević v. Croatia, ECHR, Application no. 41526/10, judgment of 24 July 2012.

Fay, T. & Wolff, E., 'Disability in sport in the twenty-first century: Creating a new sport opportunity spectrum', *Boston University International Law Journal* 27 (2009): 231–248.

Freeman, M., 'The future of children's rights', *Children & Society* 14 (2000): 277–293.

Glass v. the UK, ECHR, Application No. 61827/00, judgment of 9 March 2004.

Glor v. Switzerland, ECHR, Application No. 13444/04, judgment 30 April 2009.

Guernsey, K., Nicoli, M. & Ninio, A., *Convention on the Rights of Persons with Disabilities: Its Implementation and Relevance for the World Bank* (World Bank, 2007).

Heah, T., 'Successful participation: The lived experience among children with disabilities', *Canadian Journal of Occupational Therapy* 74(1) (2007): 38–47.

HRW, *Human Rights for Women and Children with Disabilities* (2010).

Huang, I.-C, Sugden, D. & Beveridge, S., 'Assistive devices and cerebral palsy: The use of assistive devices at school by children with cerebral palsy', *Child: Care, Health and Development* 35(5) (2009): 698–708.

Jones, M. & Marks, L.A.B., 'Beyond the convention on the rights of the child: The rights of children with disabilities in international law', *International Journal of Children's Rights* 5 (1997): 177–192.

K. v. Latvia, ECHR, Application 33011/08 (undecided).

K.A. v. Hungary, ECHR, Application no. 38832/06, judgment of 20 May 2010.

Kirk, S., 'How children and young people construct and negotiate living with medical technology', *Social Science & Medicine* 71 (2010): 1796–1803.

Lansdown, G., 'Children with disabilities', In *Human Rights and Disability Advocacy*. eds. M. Sabatello & M. Schulze (forthcoming, Penn. Univ. Press, 2013).

Megret, F., 'The disabilities convention: Towards a holistic conception of rights', *International Journal of Human Rights* 12(261) (2008): 266–269.

Mitra, S., et al., *Disability and Poverty in Developing Countries: A Snapshot from the World Health Survey* (World Bank, 2011).

Mortier, K., et al., '"I want support, not comments": Children's perspectives on supports in their life', *Disability and Society* 26(2) (2011): 207–221.

Murphy, N.A., Carbone, P.S. & the Council on Children with Disabilities, 'Promoting the participation of children with disabilities in sports, recreation, and physical activities', *Pediatrics* 121(5) (2008): 1057–1061.

NUH, *Provision of Assistive Technology in the Nordic Countries* (2007), http://hmi.dk/media/provisionassistivetechnology.pdf.

O'Cinneide, C., 'Extracting protection for the rights of persons with disabilities from human rights frameworks: Established limits and new possibilities'. In *The UN Convention on the Rights of Persons with Disabilities: European and Scandinavian Perspectives*. eds. O.M. Arnardottir & G. Quinn (Martinus Nijhoff, 2009) 163–200.

Olusanya, B.O., Luxon, L.M. & Wirz, S.L., 'Screening for early childhood hearing loss in Nigeria', *Journal of Medical Screening* 12(3) (2005): 115–118.

Parish, S.L., et al, 'Material hardship in U.S. families raising children with disabilities', *Council for Exceptional Children* 75(1) (2008): 71–92.

Poulsen, A. & Ziviani, J.M., 'Can I play too? Physical activity engagement of children with developmental coordination disorders', *The Canadian Journal of Occupational Therapy* 71(2) (2004): 100–107.

Quinn Gerard/Theresia Degener, *Human Rights and Disability*. http://www.ohchr.org/Documents/Publications/HRDisabilityen.pdf.

Ramesh, R., 'Four in 10 disabled young living in poverty, report says', *The Guardian* (6 October 2011).

Read, J., Blackburn, C. & Spencer, N., 'Disabled children and their families: A decade of policy change', *Children & Society* 26 (2012): 223–233.

Recommendation CM/Rec (2010) 2 of the Committee of Ministers to member states on Deinstitutionalisation and community living of Children with Disabilities (Council of Europe, 10 February 2010). http://www.crin.org/Law/instrument.asp?InstID=1444.

Report of the Special Rapporteur in the field of cultural rights, Farida Shaheed, The right to enjoy the benefits of scientific progress and its applications (UN A/HRC/20/26, NY, May 2012).

Sabatello, M., *Children's Bioethics: The International Bio-political Discourse on Harmful Traditional Practices and the Right of the Child to Cultural Identity* (Martinus Nijhoff/Brill publishing, 2009).

Sabatello, M., 'The new diplomacy'. In *Human Rights and Disability Advocacy*. eds. M. Sabatello & M. Schulze (forthcoming, Penn. Univ. Press, 2013).

Sentges v. The Netherlands, ECHR, Application no.27677/02, judgment of 8 July 2003.

Stanev v. Bulgaria, ECHR (Grand Chamber), Application no. 36760/06, judgment of 17 January 2012.

Stergious-Kita, M., Yantzi, A. & Jeffrey, W., 'The personal and workplace factors relevant to work readiness evaluation following acquired brain injury: Occupational therapists' perceptions', *Brain Injury* 24(7–8) (2010): 948–958.

Sullivan, P.M., 'Violence exposure among children with disabilities', *Clinical Child Family Psychological Review* 12 (2009): 196–216.

Taub, D.E. & Greer, K.R., 'Physical cctivity as normalizing experience for school-age children with physical disabilities: Implications for legitimation of social identity and enhancement of social ties', *Journal of Sport & Social Issues* 24 (2000): 395–414.

Tisdall, E.K.M., 'The challenge and challenging of childhood studies? Learning from disability studies and research with disabled children', *Children & Society* 26 (2012): 181–191.

UN Enable, http://www.un.org/disabilities/default.asp?id=1423.

UN General Secretary's Study on Violence against Children, *Summary Report of the Thematic Meeting on Violence against Children with Disabilities* (UN, NY, 2005).

UNESCO, 'Gendered outcomes in education: Why girls still held back'. In *Education for All Global Monitoring Report 2003/4* (2003). http://www.unesco.org/pv_obj_cache/pv_obj_id _5AE8EE78E881D08503D5D42C7049E295EB340500/filename/chapter3.pdf.

UNESCO, *EFA Global Monitoring Report 2010, Reaching the Marginalized* (Oxford, 2010).

UNICEF, *Education for Some More than Others?* (Geneva: UNICEF Regional Office for Central and Eastern Europe and the Commonwealth of Independent States, 2007).

UNICEF, *Calls for Children with Disabilities to Be Included in All Development* (3 December 2011). http://www.unicef.org/media/media_60790.html.

UNICEF, *The Right of Children with Disabilities to Education: A Rights-Based Approach to Inclusive Education in the CEECIS Region* (2012).

Veerman, P., 'The ageing of the UN convention on the rights of the child', *International Journal of Children's Rights* 2010 (18): 585–618.

WHO, *Community-Based Rehabilitation: CBR Guidelines* (2010).

WHO, *Joint Position Paper on the Provision of Mobility Devices in Less Resources Settings* (2011).

WHO/EU, *Better Health, Better Lives: Children and Young People with Intellectual Disabilities and Their Families* (WHO, 2010).

Woolley, H., 'Now being social: The barrier of designing outdoor play spaces for disabled children', *Children & Society* (2012).

WHO & World Bank, *World Report on Disability* (WHO, 2011).

Building the 'Big Society': Exploring Representations of Young People and Citizenship in the National Citizen Service

Kate Bacon[a], Sam Frankel[b], Keith Faulks[c]
a) University of Central Lancashire, Preston, UK
KVBacon@uclan.ac.uk
b) Writer and Consultant, Director of Act 4 and The Centre of
Excellence for Social Learning
sam@samfrankel.co.uk
c) University of Central Lancashire, Preston, UK
SFaulks@uclan.ac.uk

Introduction

The United Nations Convention on the Rights of the Child was ratified by the UK in 1991. As such, the UK committed itself to implementing the principles contained within it in UK law. Although concerns have been raised over the tensions, contradictions and cultural biases contained within it (Archard, 2004; Roche, 2004; Wyness, 2006), arguably, it offers a starting point for recognising the child as a participating member of society. Articles 12-15 demand that, with some qualifications and restrictions, children and young people should have the right to express their views and be listened to, they should have rights to freedom of expression, freedom of thought, conscience and religion.[1] Although the Convention stops short of saying that children and young people should be given the right to *make* decisions and does not refer to them as 'citizens', implied within these 'participation rights' is the recognition of the child as meaning-maker. A positive reading of the UNCRC then, suggests that we can identify children and young people (albeit maybe, especially 'young people' or 'older children') as citizens: 'members of society too, with a legitimate and valuable voice and perspective' (Roche, 1999: 479).

The implementation of the UNCRC in the UK has received criticism. For instance, James (2008) has reflected on the gap between the rhetoric and

---

[1] Of particular importance here is the notion that children's views should be given 'due weight' in accordance with their age and maturity.

reality of listening to children and taking their views seriously in the practice of child welfare, Family Court Advisors (FCAs). The Children's Rights Alliance for England (CRAE) has continually drawn attention to the Government's shortcomings in meeting the demands of the UNCRC and the recommendations made by the UN Committee, for instance, in relation to its refusal to raise the age of criminal responsibility and prohibit parents and carers from smacking their children. Similarly, although the Committee recommended in 2008 that all professionals working with children and young people should receive adequate training on the Convention, CRAE concluded that 'no overall strategy [was] in place for disseminating or raising awareness of the UNCRC within civil society, nor is training on the UNCRC a compulsory element of professional training programmes' (CRAE, 2012: 14). This has to be set against the backdrop of a Curriculum Review in England which seems to be set on making citizenship education part of the basic curriculum, where teachers can decide the content of provision, rather than a foundation subject which has to be structured through a published programme of study. This raises questions about the form and content of citizenship education provision and the extent to which it will effectively address issues relating to rights, participation and social learning in the future.

In seeming contradiction to this, the Coalition government have emphasised the importance of providing young people with opportunities to explore 'active citizenship' through their 'flagship' National Citizen Service programme (NCS). NCS is a programme of activities aimed at 16 year olds (although the programme may admit 15 year olds and children older than 16 if they have disabilities) (Cabinet Office, 2011). Young people spend two weeks away from home undertaking a range of tasks and activities and then spend 30 hours working in their local communities. As part of the programme, they design and implement a community-based social action project. The programme has been piloted in 2011 and 2012 and aims to offer 90,000 places by 2014 (Woodhouse, 2012). Ultimately, the government aims to offer this opportunity to all young people in Britain. Before turning to explore representations of citizenship in NCS, we first outline the political context for NCS by describing the 'Big Society' agenda that underpins it.

Building a big society: the vision

Following the General Election of 2010, a Coalition government, consisting of the Conservative Party (led by David Cameron) and the Liberal Democrats (led by Nick Clegg), was established. Upon taking up his post as Prime Minister, David Cameron said that he would 'work hard for the common good and the national interest' (Cameron, 2010c). From his point of view, the common good could be served by building a 'Big Society' where politicians are the people's servants rather than masters and an ethic of social responsibility rather than state control helps to solve problems (Wells, 2011). The central aim, then, is to give power to the 'people', to develop a 'more self reliant participative society' (Lord Wei, 2010). The Government hopes to achieve this in at least five ways: by giving communities more powers (e.g. in local planning, taking over state-run services); by devolving some power from central to local government; by encouraging people to take an active role in their communities (for instance through the National Citizen Service, charitable donations); by supporting co-operatives, mutuals, charities and social enterprises and finally by publishing government-kept data (on government spending, how public services do their jobs, facilitating transparency and accountability) (Coalition Government, 2010).

These ideas all hinge around three central policy areas: social action; public service reform; and community empowerment. NCS is part of the 'social action' policy agenda. For the government, social action means a 'new culture of voluntarism, philanthropy and social action' (Cameron, 2010a). In this respect, citizens are 'drivers' rather than 'passengers' (Cameron, 2010b) and as such:

> citizenship isn't a transaction in which you put your taxes in and get your services out. It's a relationship – you're part of something bigger than you, and it matters what you think and feel and do (Cameron, 2010b).

In contrast to the 'big government' which, according to Cameron, variously does it for you, tells you how to do it or makes sure you do it their way, the Big Society is characterised by a can-do, should-do attitude which will in turn help to create a 'strong society' (Cameron, 2009).

For Cameron, public service reform marks a 'decisive end to the old-fashioned, top-down, take-what-you-are-given model of public services' (HM Government, 2011: 6) and instead means 'opening up' public services by increasing choice, decentralising power to the lowest possible level, enabling charities, social enterprises, private companies and co-operatives to compete to provide services, and through ensuing accountability (HM Government, 2011). As this implies, the Big Society, is also underpinned by an ethos of community empowerment where communities and local councils are given more power to make decisions and shape their neighbourhoods (HM Government, 2010: 3). The role of the central state is thus reduced to the role of guarantor of standards (HM Government, 2011: 11).

In *Big Society Not Big Government* (2010) the Conservative Party set down the values they associate with being a citizen of the Big Society: accountability, engagement, personal responsibility, mutuality, obligation, commitment, creativity and empowerment. In his speech to the Conservative Party in October 2010, Cameron added respect, reason, being 'green', dynamism, activism, taking the initiative, working together and employing give and take. These citizens are 'doers and go-getters' (Cameron, 2010b). Similarly, in his Hugo Young lecture, Cameron emphasised the importance of duty and co-operation (Cameron, 2009).

Of course, these ideas are not new. They can be traced back to academic ideas relating to social capital, the co-operative movement and to the religious ideas of Christianity (see Morrow, 2008; House of Commons Public Administration Select Committee, 2011). Politically, they have continuities with Blair's New Labour as well as the Thatcherite governments of Thatcher and Major, not least through their views on 'active citizenship'.

Thatcherite policies centred around rolling back the state, an emphasis on individual responsibility and voluntary activity (Grace and Whiteman, 2010). This picture of citizenship envisaged 'a dynamic individual who was self-reliant, responsible for his or her own actions and yet possessed a sense of civic virtue and a pride in both country and local community' (Faulks, 1998: 128). In short, these active citizens were cast as effective citizens rather than apathetic citizens (Faulks, 1998). New Labour's 'Third Way' was a blending of ideas from the 'right' and 'left' which incorporated personal responsibility and equal opportunity whilst also being critical of the traditional 'top down' approach of public ownership (Evans, 2002). For New Labour, 'active citizenship' meant that rights came with responsibilities. These citizens, then, had duties towards others.

Macmillan (2011) and Mycock and Tonge (2011) argue that the Big Society could be seen to be a continuation of 'Third Way' politics which in incorporating the values of responsibility, conditionality and contribution, asserts that 'what you might "get" depends on what you are prepared to give' (Macmillan, 2011: 111). In Cameron's words: 'Fairness means giving people what they deserve – and what people deserve can depend on how they behave' (Cameron, 2010b). To return to an earlier point, for Cameron, 'it matters what you think and feel and do' (Cameron, 2010b). This draws attention to the importance of studying representations of young people and citizenship in NCS: just what kinds of behaviour and values does this initiative associate with citizenship and to what extent does it recognise young people's agency in making their own decisions about what constitutes the good society and the good citizen?

Methodology

In order to analyse some official government representations of citizenship and young people through NCS, we conducted a qualitative content analysis (Berg, 2007) of text and audio-visual material available through the Cabinet

Office Website http://www.cabinetoffice.gov.uk/ and also on the official NCS website https://nationalcitizenservice.direct.gov.uk/. Government policies and initiatives such as this are important to study because they are part of the 'cultural politics of childhood': the cultural and political processes through which childhood is constructed. Broadly speaking this involves social, economic, legal and political systems (James and James, 2004).

Using the search term 'National Citizen Service' we located 42 different documents on the Cabinet Office website (see Figure 1). We conducted the search on 1 May 2012. Following our initial analysis of the Cabinet Office documents, we analysed the content of the official NCS website on 23 October 2012.

Our analysis incorporated a number of different stages. First, we independently read through and listened to all the resources and made a list of codes which could be used to describe what we had read/heard. At this stage, we kept these codes as broad as possible so that we could see what kinds of data they would capture. In stage two, we looked within codes to identify more detailed trends and some codes were sub-divided. We then started to group these codes underneath, broader themes. Our central and dominant theme was 'NCS as a rite of passage'. Contained within this were themes relating to 'joining', 'doing' and 'leaving' NCS. Below, we present our findings relating to these main themes and use these to discuss the images of young people and citizenship contained within NCS.

NCS as a rite of passage

NCS is repeatedly and explicitly identified as a rite of passage: a movement from one social status to another. Predominantly, it is identified as a transition to adulthood. This terminology of 'rite of passage' and/or 'transition' is consistently used when describing the nature and aims of the programme and the government's vision for future expansion:

> NCS is not just about volunteering, it's about personal development, mixing, community engagement, transition to adulthood and rites of passage (14).

> National Citizen Service is designed to promote: ... a more responsible society by supporting the transition into adulthood for young people (1:20).

> Participation in the programme is voluntary, but the long-term aim is for NCS to become a rite of passage for all 16-year-olds (3:3).

Adulthood is thus set apart as a different kind of social status to childhood and one which, through completing NCS, participants are moving towards.

This 'journey' towards adulthood is divided up into six distinct 'phases'. Phase 1 is the introductory phase where 'expectations are set and relationships

Table 1: The documents

No.[2]	Title of document	Document type
1	Cabinet Office (2011) Equality Impact Assessment: National Citizen Service Pilots	Government report
2	NCS providers by local authority	Database
3	Cabinet office (2012) National Citizen Service Prospectus	Prospectus for potential NCS providers/organisations
4	Applications invited for new funding to run 2012 National Citizen Service pilots	Webpage
5	Expanding NCS: pre-procurement market engagement	Webpage
6	Communities to feel the force of 700,000 hours of youth power this summer	Webpage
7	National Citizen Service pilots announced	Webpage
8	Copy of NCS-evaluation-pre-qualification-questionnaire-sift-guidance	Table outlining guidance notes and score system for organisations applying to deliver NCS
9	Minister meets South Yorkshire teenagers taking part in National Citizen Service pilot	Webpage
10	Young people are part of the solution not the problem	Webpage
11	National Citizen Service 2012 providers announced	Webpage
12	National Citizen Service – commissioning process for evaluation opens	Webpage
13	Government to open up a multi-million pound market to deliver National Citizen Service	Webpage
14	Major expansion of National Citizen Service for 16-year-olds	Webpage
15	Minister meets Bolton teenagers on the first National Citizen Service	Webpage
16	Orange RockCorps and National Citizen Service Join Forces for Graduation Party	Webpage
17	Pioneering teenagers to help build the Big Society: National Citizen Service now recruiting	Webpage
18	PM launches National Citizen Service pilots	Webpage
19	Prime Minister to launch National Citizen Service pilots for young people	Webpage

---

[2] These numbers correspond to the numbers used to reference the extracts cited in this paper. Where page numbers are specified, the reference '(1:1)' means document 1, page 1.

No.[2]	Title of document	Document type
20	National Citizen Service	Webpage
21	Cabinet Office Prequalification questionnaire for evaluation of national citizen service	Questionnaire
22	Evaluation of NCS: Description of requirements/ Evaluation of National Citizen Service: 2011 and 2012 pilots	Linked Word Document
23	Ten additional NCS 2012 delivery partners announced	Webpage
24	Big Society – overview	Webpage
25	Our response to public comments on social action	Webpage
26	Making Government work better: Francis Maude's visit highlights Manchester's role in spearheading ambitious reforms	Webpage
27	Minister for Civil Society - Private Office	Webpage
28	Francis Maude speech - The Big Society and the City	Webpage
29	Lord Wei stands down	Webpage
30	Francis Maude speech on Big Society and Localism	Webpage
31	Cabinet Office Spending Review settlement	Webpage
32	Big Society - Frequently Asked Questions (FAQs)	Webpage
33	Find out how to make a difference at the European Year of Volunteering 2011 free event in London	Webpage
34	Cabinet Office announces Spending Review settlement	Webpage
35	Giving White Paper – making it easier to take part in a bigger, stronger society	Webpage
36	Department for Education	Webpage
37	Cabinet Office	Webpage
38	Government puts Big Society at heart of public sector reform	Webpage
39	Baroness Warsi: Speech to the Blackburn Diocese Board for Social Responsibility	Webpage
40	PM and Deputy PM's speeches at Big Society launch	Webpage
41	Building a new culture of social responsibility	Webpage
42	Business Compact Case Studies – detailed	Webpage

built between participants and staff'. During Phase 2 participants embark on a one week residential, away from home, where they get involved in out-door, team building activities. Phase 3 is the 'community residential': a 'Full-time residential programme based in participants' home community, with a focus on developing new skills and serving groups in the local neighbourhood (one week)'. (1:53). Phases 4 and 5 are non-residential. During phase 4, participants design a community-based social action project and during phase 5 they deliver 30 hours of social action which includes the implementation of their project in their own community. Phases 4 and 5 are consistently referred to as a 'return home' (see 9, 10, 15, 17).

> They will then return home and spend a further five weeks working in teams to develop a project that will help to change something they don't like about their communities (17).

Phase 6 is identified as an 'on-going' 'graduate programme' (3) which includes training sessions, reunion events and future opportunities for work experience.

Essentially then, NCS involves separation, transition, and reintegration. This journey is depicted as a progressive one. For instance, in one diagram, contained in the NCS prospectus, the six phases are depicted in six parallel columns with a red arrow stretching across the top of them pointing forwards past the 'on-going' stage. Transition to adulthood or 'growing up' is thus constructed as a positive development.

Joining NCS

16 years old: a key point of transition

NCS is aimed at all 16 year olds. According to the government: 'Focusing on one key age group is part of offering a common experience at a common point in young people's personal and social development' (1:44) or 'common stage in their lives' (1:44). The implication is that those similar in age are at a similar stage and will experience NCS in a similar way. This is crystallised on the official NCS website which encourages young people to sign up if they 'want to have the same experience as the thousands of 16 and 17 year olds who took part in the NCS this summer'.

Reflecting a developmentalist 'ages and stages' model of childhood (Wyness, 2006), this implies a rather static conceptualisation of age which unites 16 year-olds as a homogenous group and downplays the significance of other social divisions – like gender, class and ethnicity – for shaping their experiences. This suggests that all entrants will have a common experience, at least in part, because of their similar age.

Although no firm and explicit statements are made about why the age of 16 years has been chosen, it is clear that it is recognised as being a significant point of 'transition':

> The NCS model was developed to focus on young people during a key point of transition in their lives (1:44).

Clues about the participants' 'school leaver' status and the links often made between NCS, further education, higher education and paid work suggest that it is the movement from school to either work or more education that makes this transition so significant:

> 'The pilots are expected to provide about 10,000 places for school-leavers ...' (18)

> We hope [NCS] will create positive influences and greater chances for networking and social mobility when participants are at a transition point in their lives and considering career paths and future directions' (1:25)

> NCS is an opportunity...to make a real difference to your local community... not just fun... boost your CV by learning skills and taking on challenges that employers and universities love (NCS Website)

NCS is therefore partly in the business of preparing young people for work: '[NCS] has the power to create a generation of "work ready", well rounded young people with raised aspirations and greater opportunities in their future' (6). Work is thus strongly associated with adulthood: these 16 year olds are said to be both on the 'cusp of adulthood' (3:2) and on the cusp of paid work. Reflecting their close propensity to adulthood, NCS participants were rarely identified as 'children' but rather as 'teenagers', '16 year olds' or 'young people'. To avoid confusion then, we also refer to the participants as young people in this paper.

Doing NCS

The aims: Building the Big Society

Embarking on NCS means taking part in the building project of the Big Society:

> National Citizen Service is designed to promote: a more cohesive society by mixing participants of different backgrounds; a more responsible society by supporting the transition into adulthood for young people; a more engaged society by enabling young people to work together to create social action projects in their local communities (1:20).

Commonly, the government talk of either 'promoting' or 'building' a more cohesive, responsible and engaged society. NCS is therefore presented as a programme for social change, something which has transformative power in at least three ways. First, social mixing builds cohesion by generating an understanding and respect of difference: 'Participants will broaden their horizons and learn more about respecting difference by spending an intensive period of time working closely with people who may have distinctly different backgrounds, beliefs and abilities from them' (1:23); NCS will 'build cohesion and a better understanding of others' (19).

Second, NCS builds responsibility by 'supporting the transition into adulthood'. Although the means of achieving this aim are more vague, the residential phases are strongly implicated in this:

> A minimum of ten days and nights should be spent on a residential basis away from participants' homes to give the participants the opportunity to develop life skills and resilience, such as managing a budget and cooking meals (20).

Fully-developed 'responsibility' is clearly identified with 'adulthood', the training for which can be undertaken during NCS. This second aim does not stand in isolation from the other aims. For instance, social mixing is part of creating 'well-rounded' future adults: 'Preparing young people for life in a diverse society will be an important contribution to their transition to adulthood' (1:26). Similarly, it is by enabling participation via NCS, that the government aims to generate future active citizens and with them, the Big Society of tomorrow:

> NCS will act as a gateway to the Big Society for many young people, by supporting them to develop the skills and attitudes they need to get more engaged with their communities and become active and responsible citizens (20).

As we can see, NCS reflects Cameron's vision of a broader 'culture change' towards voluntarism, philanthropy and social action. NCS is thus represented as a force for change at both the level of the individual (for example, by generating personal and social development) and at the level of society (generating the Big Society). Importantly, it is seen to be an important access point for *many* young people: most, it is implied, need it in order to get more engaged and become active and responsible.

The challenge

NCS is depicted as 'challenging'. Interested parties are encouraged to 'rise to the challenge' of NCS (20). The first two residential weeks are said to involve 'tough physical activities that will boost their confidence and build their teamwork and leadership skills' (17). In line with this, the outdoor tasks are described as 'personally challenging, and focused on personal and social development'

(20). Often the activities themselves are literally described as 'challenges': for instance, 'team-based challenges' (9) and the 'outdoor challenge' (19). Not surprisingly, then, NCS is represented as an experience that will, to paraphrase one participant, allow young people to 'get out of their comfort zones' (20). This imagery suggests that the process of transition, which these activities represent, is a difficult one.

The process of change

Both NCS (the institution) and participants have roles to play in this transitional process. Whilst NCS 'teaches', 'helps', 'gives', 'prepares' and 'supports', participants 'develop' and 'learn'. NCS *teaches* participants about various dimensions of citizenship: it 'Introduce[s] young people to the concept of civic responsibility as they make the transition into adulthood' (19) and, in line with this, it 'teaches them what it means to be responsible and serve their communities' (3:4). This implies that young people need teaching about social responsibility and that they lack any understanding of this in the first place. As well as imparting knowledge, this teaching is represented as the basis for strengthening self-belief and empowering young people to participate. Thus, NCS also 'teaches them about the power they have as citizens to build the society they want to live in' (17). Although this emphasises the role that the individual can have in shaping society, the implication is that this so called 'power' is rooted in certain behaviours and skills – all of which are pre-specified and built into the design of NCS. Young people's passivity in this process of self-development and NCS design is sometimes also implied by the language of 'giving': NCS will 'give them the skills and confidence to make a difference in their communities' (7). Here NCS is a provider, again implying that young people lack these skills and confidence.

NCS is also depicted as a 'helper': a *contributing* initiative aimed at building positive expectations and community spirit. Thus, we hear that NCS helps to 'give young people the skills, values and confidence they will need as they move into adulthood' (6). NCS will 'help build community spirit and cohesion' (9) and it will 'help people to change their own expectations and others' 'perceptions of what they can achieve' (1:9). Linked to this, *NCS also prepares* young people for life in a diverse society and is important in 'arming them with essential life skills' (30). It supports young people in their 'transition to adulthood' and more specifically to 'develop the skills and attitudes they need to engage with their communities and become active and responsible citizens' (12). Here, NCS is represented as a form of apprenticeship for the future: providing 'support' and 'help' to young people.

In return, participants develop and learn. Through the programme, participants *develop* 'as individuals', they develop their 'attitudes' and 'skills', they develop 'new skills', 'life skills', 'leadership', 'resilience' and 'confidence'. Mirroring the earlier points about 'teaching', participants are said to 'learn more about mixing with others from different backgrounds' (1:5) and 'learn more about respecting difference' (1:10). They also 'learn about how they can make a difference in their communities' (1:5), learn 'new skills that will stretch and challenge them' (3:2) and 'teamwork' (3:4) and importantly, they learn to 'understand the concept of civic responsibility' (18). Participants therefore gain either new or *more* knowledge and skills through NCS.

Importantly, the extent of adult control over the design and direction of the activities seems to change as the programme develops: on the whole, the process of change is depicted as being *more* young-person led towards the end of the programme. In the early residential phases young people spend 'two weeks away from home' where they are 'guided by a dedicated, trained adult team leader' (3:4). This adult-direction seems to continue during phase 3 where they encounter a set of 'structured tasks to develop personal skills; visiting and helping groups in the local neighbourhood' (14). The implication is that these tasks are designed by adults *for* young people. This contrasts with phase 4 which is depicted as offering the opportunity to 'put something back' into society (6) through helping their communities (17) and/or changing 'something they don't like' about their communities (17). This part of the programme tends to be depicted as being led by the young people and only facilitated by adults. Commonly we hear that these projects are 'self-designed' (11,16, 23) or involve young people making significant decisions about the focus of their projects. For instance, we are told that young people choose to 'work on community projects that they feel most strongly about' (9, 10, 15) or 'that matter most to them' (6) or 'that will help to change something they don't like about their communities' (17).

Notwithstanding these points, there are events and images which disrupt this rather linear progression towards increased autonomy. For instance, during the induction phase, codes of conduct may be designed to help stop bullying and disrespectful behaviour and promote respect for difference/equal opportunities. Sometimes it seems that providers compose these *with* the YP: 'many [providers] have proposed to draw up the codes together with participants as part of phase 1 induction activities' (1:30). At other times it seems more like these are adult-designed and imposed *on* the young people: 'Providers will draw up codes of conduct/acceptable behaviour and experiment with the best ways to encourage participants to respect them' (1:14). Reflecting this tension, occasionally this distinction is left unresolved: Pilot providers will [...] develop codes of conduct for/with participants (1:10).

Secondly, throughout the duration of NCS there are 'guided reflection sessions with trained youth workers' which will apparently 'provide a good opportunity for participants to discuss their observations and experiences of diversity' (1:26). These might provide some opportunities to discuss the values of the 'good' society. However, the presence of adult 'guidance' suggests that some parameters are pre-set, possibly not least the assumption that we all 'want' the kind of 'Big society' on offer:

> I want every 16-year-old in our country to be given this opportunity, making them feel more part of our country and helping to build the bigger, stronger society we all want (6).

The lack of agency accorded to young people is also reflected through images of 'service'. Sometimes the programme is literally described as 'a kind of non-military national service' (18). Such terminology is significant. A military process is built on a defined hierarchy that works together to achieve tasks set by political masters. As such it offers little scope for the 'soldier' to question, challenge or input, rather their role is simply to 'do'.

Leaving NCS

The NCS style citizen

Through a process of change marked by developing, learning, teaching, giving, preparing and supporting, an enlightened, aspiring and work-ready person is brought into being: one that has a mixture of skills, attitudes, values and knowledge (see Figure 2).

The NCS graduate is dedicated and enthusiastic about making a difference to society. They are tenacious and hard working and have lots of energy. Rather than being disaffected, they are socially engaged and socially responsible: full of community spirit.

> Having visited National Citizen Service schemes this summer, I have been extremely impressed by the fantastic community spirit being created and the dedication, hard work and tenacity not only of the NCS participants, but also their youth workers and leaders (23).

Because NCS is simultaneously represented as 'supporting the transition into adulthood' (1) and 'supporting [young people] to develop the skills and attitudes they need to ... become active and responsible citizens' (20), it is these qualities which are associated with being an 'adult' and a 'good' citizen.

The changed status of NCS participants (and their success at meeting the 'challenge' of NCS) is marked out through graduation and the ritual of certificate giving:

> At the end of the programme you will be presented with a certificate signed by the Prime Minister to recognise the contribution you will have made to your community and your country (Website)

Table 2: The NCS Graduate

Skills	Life skills
	Leadership
	Communication/ Socialising
	with a mixture of different people
	Teamwork
Attitudes + values	Resilience
	Confidence
	Autonomy
	Responsibility
	Respecting difference
	Respecting equal opportunities
Knowledge	How to make a difference to their communities
	Understand civic responsibility
	How to create a society that they want to live in
	What it means to be socially responsible

In addition, their graduate status can also be indicated on a CV, which, according to Francis Maude, can be interpreted as a sign of 'work-readiness':

> we hope business will work with us on incentives and reward schemes for successful NCS graduates [...] NCS graduation should eventually be a passport to the next stage of a young person's life. An essential mark on anyone's CV - that employers look for. (28)

Hence NCS is represented as marking out candidates from which an employer might choose. In this sense, the message seems to reflect earlier discourses about 'fairness' and people getting what they 'deserve': the state rewards those that are seen to be 'deserving', in this case an NCS graduate who displays a range of socially acceptable behaviours.

The impact

NCS is therefore represented as having an impact on individuals and society. The force of this impact is emphasised through accounts of its 'life-changing' character, the contrasting descriptions of NCS participants delivering social action projects and other young people in society and through images of the 'powerfulness' of NCS.

Depictions of the life-changing nature of NCS emerge through the NCS website where viewers can watch a range of videos featuring the experiences of different young people. A common narrative is of the challenging, transforming and fun activities they have undertook, including meeting new people and trying new things. For many of these young people, this genuine enthusiasm and enjoyment for the social aspect of the scheme sat alongside a growing realisation of the contribution they could make to their communities. Within the documents also, we consistently hear about NCS being a 'life changing experience' (for instance, 1:5; 3:2), how participants had a 'life-changing summer' (3:3) or how it can/or did help 'transform the lives of young people' (3:2; 3:8). In addition to gaining new experiences and changing society, NCS is depicted as being able to alter young people's attitudes and aspirations:

> Nick Hurd, Minister for Civil Society, said: I 've met so many young people who completely changed their outlook on life during this year's National Citizen Service. (14)

This discourse of change is re-told through descriptions of 'young people today'. For example, sometimes, the government spoke of a section of young people who would benefit from NCS. Commonly, these were isolated and alienated people, who had potential to achieve and participate in society, but who lacked self-belief. These young people required motivating and inspiring to make a difference.

> Right now too many young people feel isolated from society. We want to create a new rite of passage, National Citizen Service, which will bring 16-year-olds together from all different backgrounds to give them the skills and confidence to make a difference in their communities (7).
>
> There is a tragic waste of potential in this country today. The young people of this country are as passionate and idealistic as any generation before - perhaps more passionate. But too many teenagers appear lost and feel their lives lack shape and direction (19).

NCS is therefore part of the government's drive to realise this potential in young people:

> The government is committed to introducing the National Citizen Service to give young people an opportunity to develop the skills needed to be active and responsible citizens, mix with people from different backgrounds, and start getting involved in their communities (25)

After participating in NCS, young people 'will undoubtedly reap the rewards of their hard work … and go on inspired to achieve great things' (23).

The force of the impact is also emphasised through images of 'empowerment': NCS is part of the Big Society agenda to give 'power to the people'; it is described as a form of 'youth power' (6), an initiative which demonstrates the 'power of positive youth action' (6). NCS is said to have a 'powerful impact on young people' (16). It has the 'power to create' work-ready individuals (6) and 'empowers young people' to make a difference to their communities (30). In this sense then, 'Young people are part of the solution not the problem' (10). The NCS graduate can be used as a force for change at the societal level: they can build the 'Big Society' of tomorrow: 'The next generation will be ready to use the massive devolution of power to communities that underpins the Big Society' (7). Hence, by having a 'powerful' impact *on* young people, NCS skills-up ('empowers') young people to make a difference to their communities. Ironically, then, this empowerment seems to be largely built on the notion that young people absorb the values, skills, knowledge and attitudes promoted through NCS.

Discussion

Young people as citizens now?

Cast as a rite of passage, NCS is represented as the 'gateway' to 'active and responsible' citizenship and adulthood. Indeed, it reflects the schema set out by Van Gennep in his *Rites of Passage.* According to him a

> complete scheme of rites of passage theoretically includes preliminal rites (rites of separation), liminal rites (rites of transition), and postliminal (rites of incorporation), in specific instances these three types are not always equally important or equally elaborated (1960: 11).

Thus within NCS, the novice is ritually detached from their former status by being physically separated from their home community. As they move through the transitional period, 'The novices are at once put outside and inside the circle of the previously known' (Turner, 1982: 42) by completing tasks and activities in a residential setting within their local communities. Finally, they are reincorporated back into their home communities when they carry out their social action projects and graduate.

It would be wrong to deny the positive experiences that have already been realised through young people's participation in NCS. As one evaluation of the pilots showed (NatCen, 2012), NCS can have a significant impact on young people's communication, teamwork and leadership skills and can build their confidence in sharing ideas. However, there is an important discussion to be had about the extent to which the images that have emerged above reflect a progressive attitude towards children and young people's status as citizens or whether their scope for engagement and participation is ambiguous.

The transformative 'power' of the NCS rite of passage immediately construct discourses of 'lack' around new participants: either the new recruits completely lacked the skills, attitudes/values associated with citizenship which is why the whole process is ultimately so powerful or they partly lacked them which is why it helps to *develop* them. If the transition is so 'life-changing' and 'challenging' then by implication the skills, values and knowledge they have achieved must be significantly different to those they had before entering NCS, even if this is building on a latent citizenship which, with the right teaching and support, can be activated by NCS. At entry point then, the novices are either not citizens at all, or have the seeds of citizenship which can come to fruition through the NCS experience. The personal discovery of NCS, takes the individual from relative social inconsequence to consequence. As such, citizenship is heavily identified with the future (post-NCS), and is certainly something which epitomises full adult status.

These discourses of lack are problematic for at least four reasons. First, they do not show enough respect for the competencies and skills that children and young people do have or the responsible roles that they carry out in their everyday lives. Examples are in abundance. From children and young people actively engaging themselves in their own health care (Mayall, 1996) to caring for other members of their family (Balldwin and Hurst, 2002); from protecting their parents from the impact that family poverty is having on their lives (Ridge, 2002) to protesting against the Iraq war (Cunningham and Lavalette, 2004), or saving their local bus stop from being knocked down (Weller, 2007). Such evidence lends favour to identifying children and young people as citizens *now*. As Bren Neale notes, seeing children as 'young citizens' involves respecting them as people, accepting that they have strengths and competencies (Neale, 2004). Indeed, children and young people, like adults, are human subjects acting within the world and all persons, regardless of age, have different competencies. Respecting them as citizens *now* does not mean we have to see their citizenship status as 'complete' or fixed', but it does mean that we have to recognise their status as social agents who can and do, to varying degrees, intervene in shaping society (Bacon, 2010; Frankel, 2012; Bacon and Frankel, 2013).

Second, these representations of lack play down the role that the structural marginalisation of children and young people can play in explaining their levels of alienation and participation. Whilst they may find ways to demonstrate their responsibility, skills and competencies, there are significant constraints on them doing so, not least adults' control and regulation of community and school life. Whilst there is research which demonstrates examples of effective participation in schools and involving children and young people in local decision making through a range of creative methods (see Willow, 2004; Maitles and Deuchar, 2007), 'in general, research has found that children's participation is limited' (Morrow, 2008: 122). This sits uncomfortably with the need to listen to and take account of children and young people's views as underlined by the United Nations Convention on the Rights of the Child.

Of course, this is not to discount the opportunities that some young people have to participate in public life (for instance, through the UK Youth Parliament and various youth forums) or the enthusiasm that practitioners have for facilitating young people's participation, including those working within NCS. But it does raise important questions about the extent to which young people have the 'resources of power' (Faulks, 1999) – such as access to information, technology, money, space – to exercise their will. Cost-cutting within the public sector has, for instance, restricted the amount of free leisure activities that young people can get involved in, further limiting the places they can go to meet others (Hine *et al.* 2004; Morrow, 2008). Alongside this, dominant discourses of children's incompetence and adult's responsibility and rationality can help to justify their relative exclusion from social life. Indeed, if young people do feel 'isolated' as Cameron has noted, then we have to ask if they ever felt connected and how far they can be held accountable for their social 'detachment'.

Third, these discourses of lack suggest that NCS graduates are more deserving of the title 'citizen' than other young people because in their case, this 'lack' has been addressed and added to. NCS is represented as a moment of moral awakening, a 'common experience' that can take '16 year olds' on a journey of personal discovery and social participation. If this is so and NCS gradate status is a social signifier of 'work-readiness' and 'civic responsibility', then which young people are most likely to have access to this 'privileged' status? Writers have highlighted the additional challenges that face those from low income families in engaging with community action and volunteering: 'poor communities, usually need community development support and other resources to be able to take part on equal terms' (Low, 2011: 11). Indeed, early analysis of NCS has raised questions over the extent to which it is better able to benefit young people from affluent backgrounds, who are already involved in their communities (Mycock and Tonge, 2011). The Strathclyde University report which evaluated the impact of 'The Challenge' (NCS) pilots found that young people from poorer backgrounds were less likely than their middle class counterparts to believe they could make a positive contribution to their communities on completion of NCS. Similarly, the research indicated that young people from more affluent backgrounds were most likely to take on responsibility and leadership roles during the programme (Innovative Routes to Learning and the Applied Educaitonal Research Centre, 2010).

Finally, these discourses of lack imply that citizenship education is failing in its aim to develop young people's social and moral responsibility and community involvement (Advisory Group on Citizenship, 1998). It forces us to ask, what value does education and citizenship education more specifically have? This is worrying within the context of a Coalition-led 'curriculum review' in

England which aims to 'slim down' the curriculum. Certainly citizenship education has been criticised for utilising a future-orientated curriculum which teaches young people about things they see as having little relevance to their present lives as young people (Weller, 2003). However, this need not discount the potential that education has for providing space for young people to activate and display their citizenship status.

> Experiences within schools ... have great potential to shape teenagers' understandings and experiences of democracy, participation, belonging and inclusion (Weller, 2003: 157).

Citizenship education and NCS alike could be spaces for young people to experience democracy, debate the meaning of citizenship and reflect on the roles they carry out in society. This demands that adults develop respectful, inclusive, multi-directional conversations with young people where their views are taken seriously (Roche, 2004).

Young people's participation in defining citizenship

NCS defines citizenship in relation to three core themes: social responsibility, active engagement in society (including voluntary service and paid work) and social cohesion. One criticism, is that it is 'devoid of emphasis on political engagement and other contentious issues, instead focusing on issues of adulthood and social responsibility' (Mycock and Tonge, 2011: 63). As a result, the programme does not sufficiently engage with formal politics and democracy. Whilst such criticisms may be valid, they also rely on adult-centred notions of citizenship which are future-orientated and largely voting-related. Indeed, young people may have quite different definitions of citizenship. For instance, Weller (2007) argues that young people tend to identify with 'postmodern' approaches to citizenship which connect them with people and places far beyond their own local communities (see Faulks, 2000).

The materials we have considered suggest that there are only limited opportunities for young people to engage in debates about the meaning of citizenship whilst participating in NCS. This generates a contradiction: whilst citizenship is defined as actively participating in society, this participation does not seem to extend to shaping the values that characterise the meaning of citizenship. As Mayall has noted, (Mayall, 2002: 87), children and young people 'occupy a moral space where adults do not always respect their moral agency but nevertheless expect them to take on responsibility'. In largely setting the agenda for NCS, adults utilise 'communicative power': 'the control of ideas and the capacity to shape beliefs' (Faulks, 1999: 17). This in turn suggests that the 'participation' experience that NCS provides is predominantly one that is afforded *to* young people *by* adults or as Kellett (2011: 171) puts it, a 'gift of adults, an *allowing* of children's voice' (emphasis in the original). In limiting young people's voices a status quo is maintained in which definitions of citizenship are invariably shaped by those in power as they 'reflect the needs and interests of political and economic elites' (Faulks, 1998: 100). Thus, whilst the government clearly want young people to participate in society, this is largely on the government's terms: linked to creating educated, 'work-ready' people who can provide meaningful and effective voluntary service and facilitate the devolution of power from the state to the 'people'. Specifically in relation to the Big Society, Dinham notes the danger of allowing only the most powerful voices to shape the civic agenda. He warns that this may become a big society for big, well-funded organisations, like large charities, NGOs and the Church of England.

> The Big Society is in danger of reflecting the interests of the most powerful at precisely the time the State is withdrawing from a role in the redistribution of wealth, capacity and power. How can active citizenship in the Big Society ensure fairness? (Dinham, 2010).

Without engaging with the voices of all in society, the nature and meaning of participation will remain limited and the opportunities to further a shared community will be fundamentally flawed.

Conclusion: A big society for 'big' people?

From this analysis it appears that NCS rests on notions of citizenship and the 'good society', which are defined by adult voices and largely associated with adulthood too. As a rite of passage, NCS is depicted as something that young people pass through as they move towards adulthood and paid work and take on their role in the 'Big' society more widely. There are some opportunities for young people to contribute their views, but the value-agenda seems largely prescribed and centred around responsibility, autonomy, independence and community engagement – all of which match up with the Coalition's Big Society agenda. Discourses of lack serve to position new recruits as needing more help in becoming citizens and therefore either completely deny or at the very least play down young people's status as citizens now. Whilst the transformative power of NCS is supposed to create the active and engaged citizens of tomorrow, concern over the lack of social inclusiveness of NCS raises further issues about which social groups can obtain this 'passport' to adulthood and signifier of work-readiness. At both the inter- and intra-generational levels then, NCS seems to reflect a society which is about some, and not yet about all.

References

Advisory Group on Citizenship, *Education for Citizenship and the Teaching of Democracy in Schools* (London: QCA, 1998).

Archard, D., *Children: Rights and Childhood*, 2nd Edn. (London: Routledge, 2004).

Bacon, K. *Twins in Society: Parents, Bodies, Space and Talk* (Basingstoke: Palgrave Macmillan, 2010).

Bacon, K. & Frankel, S., 'Rethinking children's citizenship: negotiating structure, shaping meanings', *International Journal of Children's Rights* (2013).

Balldwin, S. & Hurst, M., 'Children as carers', In *The Well-Being of Children in the UK*. ed. J. Bradshaw (London: Save the Children/ University of York, 2002).

Berg, B.V. *Qualitative Research Methods for the Social Sciences* 6th Edn. (London: Pearson, 2007).

Cabinet Office, 'Equality impact assessment: national citizen service pilots', (2011): available at: *http://www.cabinetoffice.gov.uk.*

Cameron, D., 'The big society hugo young lecture', (2009): available at: *http://www.conservatives.com/news/speeches/2009/11/david_cameron_the_big_society.aspx.*

Cameron, D., 'Big society speech', (2010a): available at: http://www.number10.gov.uk/news/big-society-speech/.

Cameron, D., 'David Cameron's speech to the Tory conference: in full', (2010b): available at: *http://www.guardian.co.uk/politics/2010/oct/06/david-cameron-speech-tory-conference.*

Cameron, D., 'Our big society agenda', (2010c) available at: http://www.conservatives.com/News/Speeches/2010/07/David_Cameron_Our_Big_Society_Agenda.aspx.

Coalition Government, 'Building the big society', (2010): available at: *http://www.networkforeurope.eu/files/files/building-big-society.pdf.*

Conservatives, *Big Society Not Big Government* (2010): available at: http://www.conservatives.com/~/media/Files/Downloadable%20Files/Building-a-Big-Society.ashx.

CRAE, *State of Children's Rights in England* (London: Children's Rights Alliance for England, 2012).

Cunningham, S. & Lavalette, M. '"Active citizens" or "irresponsible truants"? School student strikes against the war', *Critical Social Policy* 24(2) (2004): 255–269.

Dinham, A., 'Active citizenship and the big society', (London: Faiths & Civil Society Unit, Goldsmiths, University of London, 2010).

Evans, B., 'The third way', In *Contemporary Political Concepts*. eds. G. Blakeley & V. Bryson (London: Pluto, 2002).

Faulks, K., *Citizenship in Modern Britain* (Edinburgh: Edinburgh University Press, 1998).

Faulks, K., *Political Sociology* (Edinburgh: Edinburgh University Press, 1999).

Faulks, K., *Citizenship* (London: Routledge, 2000).

Frankel, S., *Children, Morality and Society* (Baingstoke: PalgraveMacmillan 2012).

Grace, C. & Whiteman, R., 'Public service futures'. In *The 'Big Society': Next Practice and Public Service Futures*. ed. R. Tuddenham (London: Solace Foundation Imprint 2010).

Hine, J., Lemetti, F. & Trikha, S., *Citizenship: Young People's Perspectives* (London: Home Office, 2004).

HM Government, 'Building a stronger civil society' (2010) available at: *http://www.cpa.org.uk/cpa_documents/building_stronger_civil_society.pdf.*

HM Government, 'Open public services white paper' (2011) available at: *http://files.openpublicservices.cabinetoffice.gov.uk/OpenPublicServices-WhitePaper.pdf.*

House of Commons Public Administration Select Committee, 'The big society' (2011) available at: *http://www.publications.parliament.uk/pa/cm201012/cmselect/cmpubadm/902/902.pdf.*

Innovative Routes to Learning and the Applied Educaitonal Research Centre, *Final Report on the Evaluation of The Challenge Programme 2009* (Glasgow: University of Strathclyde, 2010).

James, A. & James, A. L., *Constructing Childhood* (Basingstoke: Palgrave Macmillan, 2004).

James, A. L., 'Children, the UNCRC and family law in England and Wales', *Family Court Review* 46(1) (2008): 53–64.

Kellett, M., *Children's Perspectives on Integrated Services* (Basingstoke: PalgraveMacmillan, 2011).

Lord Wei, 'Building the big society', (2010): available at: *http://www.instituteforgovernment.org .uk/sites/default/files/Building_the_big_society_lord_wei.pdf.*

Low, J., 'Build the big society on what we know works', *Adults Learning* 22(7) (2011): 10–11.

Macmillan, R., 'The big society and participation failure', *Poeple, Place 7 Policy Online* 5(2) (2011): 107–114.

Maitles, H. & Deuchar, R., 'Why do they never listen to us! participation and democratic practice in schools'. In *Citizenship Education in Society.* ed. A. Ross (London: CiCe, 2007).

Mayall, B., *Children, Health and the Social Order* (Buckingham: Open University Press, 1996).

Mayall, B., *Towards a Sociology for Childhood* (Buckingham: Open University Press, 2002).

Morrow, V., 'Dilemmas in children's participation in England'. In *Children and Citizenship.* eds. A. Invernizzi & J. Williams (London: Sage, 2008).

Mycock, A. & Tonge, J., 'A big idea for the big society? The advent of national citizen service', *The Political Quarterly* 82(1) (2011): 56–66.

NatCen, *Evaluation of National Citiizen Service Pilots: Interim Report* (London: NatCen Social Research, 2012).

Neale, B. 'Introduction: young children's citizenship'. In *Young Children's Citizenship: Ideas into Practice.* ed. B. Neale (York: Joseph Rowntree Foundation, 2004).

Ridge, T., *Childhood Poverty and Social Exclusion: From a Child's Perspective* (Bristol: Polity Press, 2002).

Roche, J., 'Children: rights, participation and citizenship', *Childhood* 6(4) (1999): 475–493.

Roche, J., 'Children's rights; participation and dialogue'. In *Youth in Society*, 2nd Edn. eds. J. Roche, S. Tucker, R. Thomson & R. Flynn (London: Sage in associaiton with the Open University, 2004).

Turner, V., *From Ritual to Theatre: The Human Seriousness of Play* (New York: PAJ Publications, 1982).

Van Gennep, A., *The Rites of Passage* (Chicago: University of Chicago Press 1960).

Weller, S., '"Teach us something useful": Contested spaces of teenagers' citizenship', *Space and Polity* 7(2) (2003): 153–171.

Weller, S., *Teenagers' Citizenship* (London: Routledge, 2007).

Wells, P., 'Prospects for a big society? Special issue of people place and policy online', *People, Place & Policy Online* 5(2) (2011): 50–54.

Willow, C., 'Consulting with under 12s: A mapping exercise'. In *Young Children's Citizenship.* eds. C. Willow, R. Marchant, P. Kirby and B. Neale (York: Joseph Rowntree Foundation, 2004).

Woodhouse, J., 'National citizen service' (2012): available at: *www.parliament.uk/briefing-papers/ SN06364.pdf.*

Wyness, M., *Childhood and Society* (Basingstoke: PalgraveMacmillan, 2006).

Reflections on the UNCRC's Future from a Transdisciplinary Bricoleur

Richard C. Mitchell
Brock University, Canada
Email: rmitchell@brocku.ca

Introduction

The paper opens with the assumption that the *what* and *so what* phases of implementing the UN Convention on the Rights of the Child have been amply explored for decades now in academic and civil society publications throughout 'world society' (Luhmann, 1982: 131), and particularly in this one. The plethora of recommendations contained within the UN Committee's burgeoning database of 'Concluding Observations' on domestic children's rights reports provides additional evidence that the early implementation stages of the treaty have been accomplished. For those still interested in a fuller implementation and practice of children's rights in any location anywhere in the world, it's always a half-full, and in the same moment, a half-empty glass. It's always the best of times and the worst of times for children in many regions throughout the world, but the future of children's human rights has yet to be fully determined.

As Prout (2001: 19) suggested over a decade ago, the future of childhood is now, though '[w]e live with the knowledge that modernity's project of rational control has limits....The mood is more cautious and reflexive about the status of our understanding, more aware of the complexity of nature and society, more alert to the unintended consequences of our social actions and less sure of our social institutions'. Indeed, such complexities have wrought many new atrocities being committed in every region of the world to be flashed and seared immediately into one's consciousness through various social and traditional media. The uncertainty unleashed by the flood of such images continues as the grim reminder that millions of young people are being dispossessed of even the most basic human rights simply to live and enjoy some form of healthy development. As one of many examples, portions of Syria and its population seethe and burn as I write (*Botswana Gazette*, 2012). In apparent support of a greater appreciation of the human right to healthy child development articulated in Articles 6 and 24 of the CRC, American environmental philosopher J. Baird Callicott made the following observations during a UNESCO conference in Paris (United Nations Educational, Scientific and Cultural Organization, 2012a):

> We humans are intimately connected – with every breath we take, every sip of liquid we drink, and every morsel of food we eat – to the surrounding bio-chemical-physical world. We are as vortices in a flux of energy and materials, distinguishable only as ephemeral structures in that flux. We cannot – that is, we should not – conceive of ourselves as in any way independent of the natural environment. Rather we are continuous with it. The protection of human health and well-being is indistinguishable from the protection of environmental health and well-being.

In line with Callicott's analysis, in a brief chapter entitled *Can We Save Our Civilization?,* a second US-based environmentalist, Lester R. Brown, offers ten areas of grave planetary concern along with ten trends he argues are also cause for great optimism. These concerns and trends are listed below to illuminate and illustrate the similar dichotomous fault lines present in the children's rights discourse.

The perennial dichotomy

Glass half-empty

1. Soil erosion and continent-sized dust storms visible from outer space.
2. Falling water tables from massive over-pumping of aquifers throughout the world.
3. Population growth and unprecedented, ensuing destruction of natural habitats.
4. Melting ice sheets with catastrophic flooding anticipated in low-lying areas particularly such as Vietnam and Bangladesh.
5. Shrinking mountain glaciers and the largest threat to food security in history.
6. Destruction of forests everywhere which are shrinking worldwide by 17 million acres per year.
7. Environmental and climate refugees by the advance of deserts.
8. Disappearing species resulting in the 6th largest period of extinction in geological time due to habitat destruction, climate change and pollution.
9. Spreading hunger due to rising food prices spiking to one billion in 2009 with population growth, grain used to fuel cars, and shortages in irrigation water.
10. Failing states – Brown lists North Korea, Sudan and Somalia heading a growing list and asks readers, how many can we tolerate before a failing civilization?

Glass Half-full

1. Wind power emerges as centrepiece of the new energy economy due to low-costs, abundance and endless capacity especially when compared to oil, gas and coal.
2. Solar power, due to increased production in the US, Japan, Germany – now China, Taiwan, the Philippines, and South Korea – doubles world-wide every two years.
3. Intensifying solar power which is one of the fastest growing sources of new energy due to its use of mirrors to concentrate sunlight – particularly in Northern African nations.
4. Energy from the earth through geothermal resources.
5. Lighting revolution through LEDs which could save enough energy to close 700 of the world's 2700 coal-fired power plants.
6. Electrifying transportation as the 21st century world shifts to highbrids, all-electric and high-speed intercity rail.
7. Bicycles are back climbing from 94 million units in 2002 to 130 million in 2007
8. Fish farming takes off (and while not without multiple detractors) one example is China's aquacultural output at 31 million tonnes annually – double that of poultry.
9. India leads the world in milk production increasing five-fold since the 1970s.
10. Localisation of food production driven by desires for fresh, safe and the smaller carbon footprint of local sources (cited in Crone, 2013: 14-20).

Upon deeper reflection, Brown's list of 'half-empty' realities also appears counter-balanced by mounting empirical evidence of unprecedented decreases in child deaths worldwide in the past half-century (Rosling, 2006). It is quite clear now that diverse transdisciplinary theorists and empiricists are drawing upon ever longer historical trajectories to explain how human societies have become less violent, less brutal and physically and emotionally healthier. Harvard University's Steven Pinker (2011: 378-481) is one such controversial thinker who argues critically and convincingly that the 'rights revolutions' in the latter portion of the 20th century have played a pivotal role in this transformation. In a massively supported counterintuitive thesis, this professor of evolutionary psychology concludes that violence throughout the regions of the world is declining dramatically – much of it due to the promotion and recognition of woman's human rights. He attempts to reconcile this through historical and psychological evidence that identify 'exogenous forces that favour our peaceable motives and that have driven the multiple declines' in interpersonal and societal violence across myriad cultures. A key plank in his platform is how 'efforts to stigmatize, and in many cases criminalize, temptations to violence have been advanced in a cascade of campaigns for "rights" – civil rights, women's rights, children's rights, gay rights, and animal rights' (*ibid.*: 380).

   In response to this perennial 'half-empty half-full' dichotomy, the paper emerges from reflections on two decades as a children's practitioner in British Columbia across the range of 'service provision systems' typical in industrialised states (Moss and Petrie, 2002: 2). I have now added an additional decade as a university-based researcher, educator, and author – all of it framed by the CRC's principles and provisions. From both sides of the perennial debate, I offer a relatively innovative theoretical analysis as a means of creating new momentum. These come not from any kind of modernist or proscriptive notion of that concept, but from the sense that various slaughters, manifold indignities, and execrable discriminatory practices aimed at children, particularly against many girls, and visited daily upon millions, could still be shifted, perhaps are shifting, as we speak. So very often it is difficult to step back from one's own historical, political and cultural location to evaluate whether the UNCRC has made a lasting difference, and perhaps more importantly, to consider if there are additional contributions to healthy human development yet to be made by knowing and implementing this treaty. As noted global thinker Jeffrey Sachs (2008) has observed, 'the old models of statecraft have ceased to work' (in Crone, 2013: 45), and this basic assertion is as good an entry point for re-thinking and re-applying the UN Convention on the Rights of the Child as any I have lately heard.

   As an effort to gain such perspective, I present and argue two main points. First, I'm convinced there remain vast untapped potentials for implementing the human rights of children within present and coming generations, and secondly, a critical transdisciplinary understanding of the treaty can better exploit these opportunities. I further assume that the *now what* phase of the UNCRC is still largely unwritten. The following sections argue for the continued re-theorising of the Treaty along with a more effective holistic application or through its constituent, interdependent sections, in the lived experiences of children. It closes with a case study from the Niagara grape and wine region of Canada that has applied and illustrates these contentions.

Transdisciplinarity, the *Bricoleur* and the UNCRC

While developmental psychologist Jean Piaget is widely credited with coining the term in 1970, the definition underpinning this section builds primarily upon Basarab Nicolescu's elucidation within his *Manifesto of Transdisciplinarity* (2002: 1). He observes that the term 'retains a certain pristine charm, mostly because it has not yet been corrupted by time', but that time may be drawing nigh. Perhaps unsurprisingly, the institutionalisation of transdisciplinarity within universities also has UN antecedents beginning in 1987 through the creation of the International Centre of Transdisciplinary Research and Studies. In 1995, Romanian quantum physicist Basarab Nicolescu co-founded the Reflection Group on Transdisciplinarity with UNESCO – a project initially involving 16 scientific and cultural personalities in the implementation of transdisciplinary methodologies in various fields of international research. One of its main aims is the implementation of these principles in education, and slowly but decisively, transdisciplinarity has gained an international impact, especially in superior educational settings, as universities from all over the world have opened themselves to experimenting with transdisciplinary curricula, research activities, and conferences (Dincă, 2011).

We can readily observe how various discourses of childhood have also attempted to explain the international trajectory of the UNCRC, and while not without contention, these have allowed historical notions of the 'rights of children' to lay a genuine claim to maturity in recent decades. British educators Moss and Petrie (2002: 81) remind us that such 'policy texts are sites of power', and are aiding in establishing new narrative conventions and repertoires of interpretation for argumentation and communication. These sites confer power on preferred modes of speaking and judging along with certain ways of expressing moral and political subjectivity (citing Dutch feminist Selma Sevenhuijsen, 1999). Nevertheless, a pervasive type of disciplinary myopia may be observed enveloping service delivery systems in both minority and majority world settings (Moore and Mitchell, 2008, 2009), and this silo-thinking frequently results in ineffective, even lethal outcomes for children (see Report of the Gove Inquiry into Child Protection, 1995). The challenge for those attempting to apply the treaty as a vehicle to extinguish odious forms of discrimination, or to leverage greater freedom from physical and sexual abuse of children, is to think and operate beyond traditional disciplines like education, law or juvenile justice, psychology, sociology, health, child welfare, or politics. In this way, innovative ways of using treaty principles as methodological tools for interrogating new areas of concern may take one well beyond these socially and politically constructed boundaries.

Freeman (2007) notes the liberation of women and children, soldiers and prisoners from the violence of physical punishment and abusive discipline throughout the 20th century, is still underway in most corners of the world. It is now a cliché to observe how epochal shifts continue to re-position 21st century children, particularly in terms of their global rights to health and wellbeing. It is also abundantly clear that multi- and even interdisciplinary approaches to understanding the UNCRC are inadequate to conceptualise the proliferation of new childhood knowledges exploding across geo-political and pedagogical structures. While such processes play a role in the gradual transformation of human societies and remain a key focus for those promoting the treaty since early days, the child rights 'movement' clearly has much unfinished business.

The most critical problems humanity faces today are complex problems, observe Apgar, Argumedo, and Allen (2009: 255), and similar to Prout's analysis (2001), they contend these times are 'characterized by high levels of uncertainty, multiple perspectives and multiple interlinked processes from local to global scales'. As highlighted in previous work (Moore and Mitchell, 2008, 2011; Mitchell and Moore, 2012), these epistemological and methodological shifts can be aimed at resolving such dilemmas, and are increasingly being mirrored in academic literature of the social sciences, humanities, healthcare, and scientific journals under the rubric of 'transdisciplinarity' (see Russell, 2000; Koizumi, 2001; Nicolescu, 2002; Giroux and Searls Giroux, 2004; Holmes and Gastaldo, 2004; Robinson, 2008; Mitchell, 2010). In an exhaustive review of the range of this discourse, two Canadian health scientists note this definition:

> Transdisciplinarity integrates the natural, social and health sciences in a humanities context, and transcends their traditional boundaries. The objectives of multiple disciplinary approaches are to resolve real world or complex problems, to provide different perspectives on problems, to create comprehensive research questions, to develop consensus clinical definitions and guidelines, and to provide comprehensive health services. Multiple disciplinary teamwork has both benefits and drawbacks. (Choi and Pak, 2006: 351)

These authors further note its holistic typologies and refer to three terms as involving any application of multiple disciplines to varying degrees on the same continuum. The common words for multidisciplinary, interdisciplinary and transdisciplinary are additive, interactive, and holistic, they observe respectively. This type of transdisciplinarity is inherently critical, and is being argued contemporaneously within many traditional discourses. I am suggesting here that appreciating the UNCRC in such a fashion could open up new ways from the entrenched 'tower of babble' where young people's human rights are so often absorbed (Moore and Mitchell, 2009: 30). Arguing in a similar vein, Freirean critical pedagogues Giroux and Searls-Giroux (2004: 102) observe:

> [T]he cultural studies emphasis on transdisciplinary work provides a rationale for challenging how knowledge has been historically produced, hierarchically ordered, and used within disciplines to sanction particular forms of authority and exclusion. Transdisciplinary work often operates at the frontiers of knowledge, and prompts teachers and students to raise new questions and develop models of analysis outside the officially sanctioned boundaries of knowledge and the established disciplines that control them.

Such approaches, they argue, stress both historical relations and broader social formations 'while remaining attentive to new linkages, meanings, and possibilities'. While educators may be forced to work within academic silos, 'they can develop transdisciplinary tools to challenge the limits of established fields and context the broader economic, political, and cultural conditions that reproduce unequal relations of power', they contend (*ibid.*). Taking this fresh approach to re-considering the UNCRC offers just such a set of tools. Without essentialising here, I consider that anyone in any sector interested in greater application of the UNCRC's core principles who re-theorises the treaty in this way could continue the gradual transformation towards survival and more civilized behaviours towards children noted by Rosling (2006), Pinker (2010), and others. Notwithstanding the tentativeness of postmodern child-hoods, the human rights glass then appears 'half-full'.

While attempting to apply treaty principles in numerous social science investigations with young people, I have also found the epistemological and methodological descriptions of the *bricoleur* articulated by US critical peda-gogue Joe Kincheloe to be valuable in stretching across and outside of discipli-nary boundaries. In his text on *Knowledge and Critical Pedagogy*, Kincheloe emphasises that 'we live in an era of disinformation – self-interested data distributed by those with the most power and resources' (2010: vii). 'Critical pedagogy', he emphasises, (ibid.: 8-9) 'is a complex notion that asks much of educators and students who embrace it ... critical knowledge seeks to connect with the corporeal and the emotional in a way that understands at multiple levels and seeks to assuage human suffering'. He contends '[c]ritical educa-tional knowledge emerges neither from subjects nor from objects but from a dialectical relationship between the knower (subject) and the known (object)' (*ibid.*: 29). Similar to Albrecht, Freeman and Higginbotham (1999), Kincheloe and McLaren (2005: 316) note that in efforts to 'expose the various structures that covertly shape our own and other scholars' research narratives, the brico-lage highlights the relationship between a researcher's ways of seeing and the social location of his or her personal history'. This allows for the development of new epistemological and political tools, and new ways of seeing how to apply older ones.

> In this context, bricoleurs move into the domain of complexity. The bricolage exists out of respect for the complexity of the lived world and the complication of power. Indeed, it is grounded on an epistemology of complexity. One dimension of this complexity can be illustrated by the relationship between research and the domain of social theory. (Kincheloe and McLaren, 2005: 317)

They further maintain when one appreciates 'research as a power-driven act, the critical researcher-as-bricoleur abandons the quest for some naïve con-cept of realism, focusing instead on the clarification of his or her position in the web of reality...' (*ibid.*: 316).

In her review of Kincheloe's analysis of this concept, qualitative researcher and internationally renowned scholar Yvonna Lincoln contends:

> [The] bricoleur is far more skilled than merely a handyman [as its definition implies]. This bricoleur looks for not yet imagined tools, fashioning them with not yet imagined connections. This handyman is searching for the nexuses, the linkages, the interconnections, the fragile bonds between disciplines, between nodes of knowledge, between knowing and understanding....it is 'boundary-work' taken beyond the extreme, boundary-work beyond race, ethnicity, sexual orientation, class. (Lincoln, et al., 2001: 693-94)

In the same review, critical theorist (and frequent co-author of the now deceased Kincheloe), Peter McLaren argues that 'Joe's quest for transdisciplinary rigor in the spirit of his ongoing concern with working class struggle, social transformation, and social injustice in contemporary capitalist society' might preclude the inherent danger 'of the bricoleur in the thrall of deep interdisciplinarity lapsing into a form of epistemological relativism' (Lincoln, et al., 2001: 710).

In a sustained effort to avoid a similar fate, I offer the following case study recounting the early stages of a post-secondary scholarship offered to the children of migrant agricultural workers in the prosperous Niagara wine and grape region of Canada wherein I played a pivotal role. While no longer a project for children since the recipient turned eighteen years of age before the award was made, the initiative drew upon the theoretical and methodological resources outlined in the previous sections. Its success also opens up new possibilities for future children from a marginalised and globally shifting community to draw a return on the investment of labour by their absentee parents.

Praxis and the Niagara Migrant Children's Educational Award

Praxis is the Greek term commonly adopted by critical pedagogues, and is defined as an activity that combines theorising with practice, thought with action, for emancipatory purposes. I adopted this stance in 2010 after being approached by an advocacy group for agricultural workers: Dignidad Obrera Agriculturale Migrante (Dignity for Migrant Agricultural Workers). This group is composed of members from the growing labour force of over 5,000 that visit the fertile Niagara Region greenhouse, fruit growing, and wine producing industries each year in south-western Ontario, Canada. They had numerous requests that would be characterised under the academic rubric 'greater social inclusion', one of which was to assist them in developing a scholarship for members of their families. Many of these men (mostly) and women (increasingly) return to the region year after year for eight to ten months under Canada's Seasonal Agricultural Worker Program (or SAWP, 2012) which is run by the federal government with help from authorities in Mexico, Venezuela, the Philippines, and Jamaica among others, mainly in rural areas faced with extreme levels of poverty and chronically high unemployment. During absences, their children are billeted with relatives or cared for by older siblings while their fathers and mothers labour long, arduous hours for what would be subsistence wages in this country, and thus, for which no labour force can be mobilised. To many of these workers, their remuneration is at reasonable enough rates that mean the difference between a family falling apart due to poverty, hunger, stress – or not. For many, the exploitation, uncertainty and conditions of employment are found to be egregious (for example Justice for Migrant Workers, 2012). In the brief but powerful edited text *15 Disturbing Things We Need to Know*, US-based sociologist James A. Crone includes a chapter describing the growing phenomena of nannies, maids, and sex workers being imported into industrialised economies of the world as 'Global Woman' (2013: 21). 'Women from poor, developing countries are migrating to developed nations to work as maids and nannies to raise other people's children but are not able to raise their own children back in their own countries', report Ehrenreich and Russell Hochschild (*ibid.*). To their list, I would add women employed as migrant agricultural workers who also travel throughout world society to labour in the planting, tending and harvesting of the human food chain.

As one familiar with many of the children living in poverty in a wealthy industrialised nation such as Canada I took up the role of a transdisciplinary bricoleur in response to this Niagara advocacy group. Initially, a faculty colleague and I met with our local mayor and requested his partnership which quickly grew to include officials from a regional college and a philanthropic foundation both interested in supporting the initiative. This small network approached senior administrative colleagues at my own university each of whom offered substantial in-kind support by waiving tuition and some additional fees for award recipients. Part-time employment was offered by the university's student union representatives (Brock News, 2012a). The next challenge was to locate a young person from amongst the children of the seasonal community of labourers as an appropriate first candidate. A young woman whose father had been stricken with a health crisis came to our attention (*This Magazine*, 2006). Fast-forward to the summer of 2012, and the story gained national coverage in Canada's largest newspaper (D'Alesio, 2012). A university press release next recounted how Ms. Sayuri Gutierrez, her father an agricultural worker from Mexico employed in the region, was hard-pressed to figure out how she or her family could ever afford a university education. She accepted the Migrant Children's Educational Award (2012), the only university-based stipend of its kind in Canada, as its first recipient. Gutierrez is also the first in her family from either side to attend post-secondary education.

'I feel proud because I'm the daughter of a migrant worker,' she stated. 'The son or daughter of a migrant worker studying in Canada, it sounds impossible when you're in your home country' (Brock News, 2012b).

The award also offered a type of reciprocity for the University community to put into practice the theoretical principles of sustainability (Mitchell, May, Purdy and Vella, 2011; Brock News, 2012a) by applying the widely referenced definition from the 1987 Bruntland Commission for this ambiguous term (UN Economic Commission for Europe, 2012). Simply stated, present generations are compelled to leave enough of the earth's resources for the use of all future generations. Since the campus is one of a small cadre of Canadian universities located in a UNESCO World Biosphere Reserve (UNESCO, 2012b), their framework provided the University a compelling opportunity to practise sustainability through intersecting lenses of science, education and culture. Perhaps unsurprisingly, such approaches were also in line with the University's strategic plans for transdisciplinary initiatives. I was quoted in one press release as follows:

> But it's not just the physical environment that needs to be protected and cared for', Mitchell notes. 'To try and understand sustainability without looking at the people who are working on the land doesn't work,' he says when explaining the award's creation. 'It's these kinds of intersections between and amongst education, science, and culture that brought me to notice the migrant agricultural workers in the Niagara Region. They bring so much prosperity for all of us and yet their experiences are often that of social exclusion, marginalization and even discrimination. (Brock News, 2012b)

Ms. Gutierrez ably attests to these circumstances since she and her family were on the verge of being deported from Canada, but were granted residency on compassionate grounds quite possibly due to the national newspaper coverage on the award (D'Alesio, 2012). Her father also suffers from kidney disease and would be unable to afford life-saving treatment in Mexico (see Auld's analysis of migrant health issues, 2011). 'My family had gone through so many things,' she says. 'I saw how a psychologist was working with my brother when he had his traumas. My mother was going into depression. One day, I thought being in psychology would be a good idea to help people that have family issues or children who go through hard times.' Ms. Gutierrez said receiving the scholarship was like 'winning the lottery,' ensuring her and her family's future (Brock News, 2012b).

Conclusions

The perennial dichotomy for the children's rights 'movement' still remains and the Canadian case study above from Niagara's grape and wine region illustrates how drawing upon new theoretical and methodological tools creates new opportunities to take UNCRC principles and provisions forward. Globalisation continues unabated in much the same kind of dichotomous relationship across nations and cultures, but the paper has argued there are innumerable ways remaining to tap into treaty potentials in order to benefit real people's lives at the same time as breathing life into its texts. The transdisciplinary bricoleur argued for by Giroux and Searls-Giroux (2004), Kincheloe (2010), and Kincheloe and McLaren (2005) among others, allows a contemporary theoretical analysis of the treaty to be taken into academic, governmental and non-governmental sites. While it will always appear the best of times and the worst of times for children in all corners of the world, the future of the UNCRC will always be now.

References

Albrecht, G., Freeman, S. & Higginbotham, N., 'Complexity and human health: The case for a transdisciplinary paradigm', *Culture, Medicine and Psychiatry* 22(1) (1998): 55–92.

Alderson, P., 'Children's health care rights and consent'. In *New Handbook of Children's Rights*. ed. R. Franklin (London: Routledge, 2002) 155–167.

Apgar, J.M., Argumedo, A. & Allen, W., 'Building transdisciplinarity for managing complexity: Lessons from indigenous practice', *International Journal of Interdisciplinary Social Sciences* 4(5) (2009): 225–270.

Auld, A., 'Migrant workers lack health care,' *Globe and Mail*, (19 April 2011): A8.

Botswana Gazette, 'UN chief leads world outcry over Syria "massacre"', (28 August 2012).

Brock Environmental Sustainability Research Centre. (2012) Retrieved September 6, 2012, from http://www.brocku.ca/environmental-sustainability-research-centre.

Brock News, 'News around campus – ESRC Researchers lead efforts for the migrant children's education award,' 28 August 2012. Retrieved 6 September 2012, from http://www.brocku.ca/news/20061.

Brown, L.R., 'Can We Save Our Civilization?'. In *15 Disturbing Things We Need to Know*. ed. J.A. Crone (Los Angeles, London, New Delhi: Sage Publications, 2013) 13–20.

Brown, V.A., Harris, J.A. & Russell, J.A., eds. *Tackling Wicked Problems Through the Transdisciplinary Imagination* (London and Washington: Earthscan Publications, 2010).

Choi, B. and Pak, A., 'Multidisciplinarity, interdisciplinarity and transdisciplinarity in health research, services, education and policy: 1. Definitions, objectives, and evidence of effectiveness', *Clinical Investigation & Medicine* 29(6) (2006): 351-364.

Crone, J.A., ed. *15 Disturbing Things We Need to Know* (Los Angeles, London, New Delhi: Sage Publications, 2013).

D'Aliesio, R., 'Mexican girl's college dream in danger of being undermined', *Globe and Mail* (10 May 2012): A7. Retrieved 6 September 2012, from http://www.theglobeandmail.com/news/national/mexican-girls-college-dream-in-danger-of-being-undermined/article4105835/.

Dincă, I., 'Stages in the configuration of Bararab Nicolescu's transdisciplinary project'. In *Transdisciplinary Studies – Science, Spirituality, Society No. 2* (Bucharest: Curtea Veche Publishing, 2011) 119–136.

Ehrenreich B. & Hochschild, A.R., 'Global women: Nannies, maids and sex workers in the new economy'. In *15 Disturbing Things We Need to Know*. ed. J.A. Crone (Los Angeles, London, New Delhi: Sage Publications, 2013) 21–33.

Freeman, M., 'Why it remains important to take children's rights seriously', *The International Journal of Children's Rights* 15(1) (2007): 5–23.

Holmes, D. & Gastaldo, D., 'Rhizomatic thought in nursing: An alternative path for the development of the discipline', *Nursing Philosophy* 5(3) (2004): 258–267.

Giroux, H.A. & Searls Giroux, S., *Take Back Higher Education: Race, Youth and the Crisis of Democracy in the Post-Civil Rights Era* (New York: Palgrave Macmillan, 2004).

Justice for Migrant Workers. (2012). Retrieved 6 September 2012, from http://www.justicia4 migrantworkers.org/.

Kincheloe, J.L., *Knowledge and Critical Pedagogy – An Introduction* (New York: Springer, 2010).

Kincheloe, J.L. & McLaren, P., 'Rethinking critical theory and qualitative research'. In *The Sage Handbook of Qualitative Research* (3rd ed.) ed. N.K. Denzin & Y.S. Lincoln (Thousand Oaks, London and New Delhi: Sage Publications, 2005) 303–342.

Koizumi, H., 'Trans-disciplinarity', *Neuroendocrinology Letters* 22(4) (2001): 219–221.

Lincoln, Y.S., Pinar, W.F. & McLaren, P., 'Responses – An emerging new bricoleur: Promises and possibilities – A reaction to Joe Kincheloe's "describing the bricoleur"', *Qualitative Inquiry* 7(6) (2001): 693–705.

Luhmann, N., 'The world society as a social system', *International Journal of General Systems* 8(2) (1982): 131–138.

Migrant Children's Education Award. (2012). Retrieved 6 September 2012, from http://studyinniagara.ca/migrantaward/index.html.

Mitchell, R.C., 'Who's afraid now? Reconstructing Canadian citizenship education through transdisciplinarity', *The Review of Education, Pedagogy, and Cultural Studies* 32(1) (2010): 37–65.

———, 'Sustaining change on a Canadian campus: Preparing brock university for a sustainability audit', *International Journal of Sustainability in Higher Education* 12(1) (2011): 7–21.

Mitchell, R.C., May, B., Purdy, S. & Vella, C., 'UNESCO biosphere reserves: Towards common conceptual ground'. In *The Biosphere*, ed. Dr. N. Ishwaran (InTech Open Access, 2012) 285–302. ISBN: 978-953-51-0292-2. Retrieved 6 September 2012, from http://www.intechopen.com/books/the-biosphere/unesco-biosphere-reserves-towards-common-intellectual-ground.

Mitchell, R.C. & Moore, S.A., eds. *Politics, Participation & Power Relations: Transdisciplinary Approaches to Critical Citizenship in the Classroom and Community* (Rotterdam, Boston and Taipei: Sense Publishers, 2012).

Moore, S.A. & Mitchell, R.C., eds. *Power, Pedagogy and Praxis: Social Justice in the Globalized Classroom* (Rotterdam and Taipei: Sense Publishers, 2008).

———. 'Rights-based restorative justice: Evaluating compliance with international standards', *Youth Justice* 9(1) (2009): 27–43.

———. 'Theorising rights-based restorative justice: The Canadian context', *The International Journal of Children's Rights* 19(1) (2011): 81–105.

Moss, P. & Petrie, P., *From Children's Services to Children's Spaces – Public Policy, Children and Childhood* (London: Routledge/Falmer, 2002).

Nicolescu, B., *Manifesto of Transdisciplinarity* (New York: State University of New York Press, 2002).

Pinker, S., *The Better Angels of Our Nature – Why Violence Has Declined* (New York: Viking Press, 2011).

Prout, A., 'The Future of Childhood'. In *First Annual Lecture of The Children's Research Centre* (Dublin: Trinity College, 2001).

Report of the Gove Inquiry into Child Protection in British Columbia. Volume Two: Matthew's Legacy (Victoria: Government of British Columbia, 1995).

Rosling, H., 'Hans Rosling shows the best stats you've ever seen'. *TED Talks* (2006). Retrieved 6 September 2012, from http://ed.ted.com/lessons/hans-rosling-shows-the-best-stats-you-ve-ever-seen.

Russell, W., 'Forging new paths: Transdisciplinarity in universities', *Wisenet Journal – Australia's Women in Science Inquiry Network* 53 (2000): 1–4. Retrieved 6 September 2012, from http://www.wisenet-australia.org/issue53/transdis.htm.

Sachs, J.D., 'A user's guide to the century'. In *15 Disturbing Things We Need to Know*. ed. J.A. Crone (Los Angeles, London, New Delhi: Sage Publications, 2013) 45–53.

Seasonal Agricultural Worker Program of Canada. (2012). Retrieved 6 September 2012, from http://www.hrsdc.gc.ca/eng/workplaceskills/foreign_workers/ei_tfw/sawp_tfw.shtml.

Sevenhuijsen, S., *Citizenship and the Ethics of Care: Feminist Considerations on Justice, Morality and Politics* (London: Norton, 1999).

This Magazine. 'Canada continues to fail guest worker', (5 September 2006). Retrieved 6 September 2012 from http://this.org/blog/2006/09/05/canada-continues-to-fail-guest-worker/.

United Nations Educational, Scientific and Cultural Organization (UNESCO), Social and Human Sciences Sector, Interview with Pr. J. Baird Callicott. Retrieved 6 September 2012, from http://www.unesco.org/new/en/media-services/single-view/news/the_road_to_harmony_between_humans_and_nature_lies_in_a_philosophical_revolution_interview_with_pr_j_baird_callicott/.

——, *World Biosphere Reserves Program* (New York: United Nations, 2012). Retrieved 6 September 2012, from http://www.unesco.org/new/en/natural-sciences/environment/ecological-sciences/biosphere-reserves/.

United Nations Economic Commission for Europe, *Sustainable Development - Concept and Action.* (2012). Retrieved 6 September 2012, from http://www.unece.org/oes/nutshell/2004-2005/focus_sustainable_development.html.

Visser, J., 'Overcoming the underdevelopment of learning: A transdisciplinary view'. Paper presented at the *Symposium on Overcoming the Underdevelopment of Learning* held at the annual meeting of the American Educational Research Association (Montreal, Canada, 19–23 April 1999).

Reconceptualising the Child's Right to Development: Children and the Capability Approach

Noam Peleg
University College London, UK
n.peleg@ucl.ac.uk

Introduction

The UN Convention on the Rights of the Child provides broad protection for children's development. Five articles (Articles 18, 23, 27, 29 and 32) protect eight domains of development (physical, mental, moral, social, cultural, spiritual, personality and talent), and a sixth, Article 6, protects the child's right to life, right to survival and right to development. Nonetheless, it is not clear enough what are the theoretical or practical implications of providing children with the legal right to development. This article suggests that the first stage in interpreting this unique right of children is to establish the meaning or meanings of the terms 'children's development' and childhood. Only then will it be possible to discuss what it means for children to have a *right* to development.

The term 'children's development' is usually perceived in psycho-social terms, focusing on the process of transformation from childhood to adulthood. Such conceptualising of 'children's development' resonates with the conception of children as 'human becomings',[1] and leads to a narrow interpretation of the child's legal right to development, primarily as the child's right to become an adult. This approach subjugates the right to development to support the

---

* The author would like to thank Michael Freeman and Aoife Nolan for their helpful comments. An earlier version of this article was presented at the ESRAN-UKI seminar held in University College Dublin in May 2013. The author would like to thank the participants of this seminar for their feedback. Special thanks to Lana Tatour. Any errors are his.
[1] James, A. *et al, Theorizing Childhood* (Cambridge: Polity, 1998); James, A. and A. James, *Constructing Childhood* (Basingstoke: Palgrave Macmillan, 2004); Lee, N., *Childhood and Society* (Gosport: Open University Press, 2001); James, A. and A. Prout, 'Re-presenting Childhood: Time and Transition in the Study of Childhood' in *Constructing and Reconstructing Childhood*. James, A. and A. Prout, eds. (2nd edition, London: Routledge, 1997) 230-250; Freeman, M.,'The Human Rights of Children' *Current Legal Problems* 63 (2010): 1-44.

child's future, thus overlooking other meanings of childhood and ignores children's agency. As the jurisprudence of the UN Committee on the Rights of the Child demonstrates,[2] this approach also lacks coherency and creates serious difficulties in implementation. The core argument of this article is that changing the definition of 'children's development' can result in reconceptualising the child's right to development as well.

The article suggests that adopting the Capability Approach as an alternative normative framework can remedy these shortcomings in the current understanding of the child's right to development. Adopting the perception of human development as 'freedom'[3] can redefine the meaning of 'children's development' in a way that includes not only the child's developmental psychology, but also the child's entitlement to define the course of her life; to respect the child's life in the present; to respect the child's agency and voice; and to lay the foundations for concrete measures of implementation.

Thus far, the discussions concerning the Capability Approach have largely ignored children,[4] which left it 'under-theorized in relation to children',[5] and children's rights. It was only recently that Martha Nussbaum and Rosalind Dixon have addressed the relationship between children and the Capability Approach, arguing that the Capability Approach can be used as a theoretical justification for prioritising children's welfare rights.[6] Their paper will be discussed in detail later, but it is important to note at this stage that their argument does not address broader questions relating to children's rights, including the child's right to development.

It is beyond the scope of this article to exhaust all the questions that the relationship between the Capability Approach and children's rights raises. Rather, the article will focus on two main questions: whether the Capability Approach's conception of development should be used in analysing the child's right to development, and if the answer is in the affirmative, how it should be done.

The article has four parts. The first introduces briefly the Convention's conception of 'children's development' and right to development, as was interpreted by the UN Committee on the Rights of the Child. It claims that the Committee adopts a 'human becomings' conception of childhood, and

---

[2] Peleg, N., 'Time to Grow Up: The UN Committee on the Rights of the Child's Jurisprudence of the Right to Development' in *Law and Childhood Studies*. Freeman, M., ed. (Oxford: Oxford University Press, 2012) 371-391.

[3] Sen, A., *Development as Freedom* (Oxford: Oxford University Press, 1999).

[4] Comim, F. *et al*, 'Introduction – Theoretical Foundations and the Book's Roadmap' in *Children and the Capability Approach*. Mario Biggeri *et al*, eds. (Basingstoke: Palgrave, 2011) 3-21, 6.

[5] Basu, K., 'Prologue' in *Children and the Capability Approach, ibid*, x.

[6] Dixon, R. and M. Nussbaum, 'Children's Rights and a Capability Approach: The Question of Special Priority' *Cornell Law Review* 97 (2011-2012): 549-593.

therefore its interpretation focuses on the child's life as an adult, thus failing to respect children's agency and voice. Such an interpretation for a core right is somewhat problematic, since it neither provides coherent meaning, nor a concrete means of implementation. The second part introduces the Capability Approach's conception of human development and suggests that it can, and should, be used in interpreting children's development. The third part explores the possibilities of using the Capability Approach when interpreting human rights law, and discusses the potential limitations and advantages of this approach. The fourth and last part delineates three main contributions of the suggested approached: redefining the term 'children's development'; enhancing respect for children's agency and voice; and developing concrete benchmarks to realise the right to development according to the UNCRC's framework.

The current approach to the child's right to development

As noted earlier, the UNCRC provides comprehensive protection for eight different segments of children's development, which join the recognition of children's rights to development in Article 6(2). The importance that the Convention sees in protecting children's development was further empha-sised by the UN Committee on the Rights of the Child in General Comment Number 5, which defines the rights to life, survival and development as one of the Convention's four guiding principles, together with the child's right to non-discrimination (Article 2), the child's right to participation (Article 12) and the principle of the best interests of the child (Article 3).[7] Furthermore, in its guidelines for reporting, the Committee asks States Parties to report on measures taken to ensure children's right to development.[8] Nonetheless, the Committee's jurisprudence demonstrates how difficult it is to interpret the right when your point of departure is the 'human becomings' conception of childhood.[9]

The 'human becomings' conception of childhood perceives children as passive actors, lacking agency, weak, vulnerable, and in need of protection.[10]

---

[7] UNCRC, *General Comment number 5*, CRC/GC/2003/5.
[8] UNCRC, *Treaty-specific guidelines regarding the form and content of periodic reports to be submitted by States parties under article 44, paragraph 1 (b), of the Convention on the Rights of the Child*, CRC/C/58/Rev.2.
[9] Peleg, *supra* n. 2. See also Martin Woodhead's claim that only young children are entitled to this right. M. Woodhead, 'Early Childhood Development: A Question of Rights', *International Journal of Early Childhood* 37 (2005): 79-98.
[10] For non-Western perspectives see, for example, Stafford, C., *The Roads of Chinese Childhood* (Cambridge: Cambridge University Press, 1995); Ito, T., 'New Education For Underprivileged

Childhood and children are positioned against adulthood and adults, and childhood is described as 'the absence of adult qualities'.[11] Children are seen as 'unfinished products',[12] and as human beings in the making. Childhood is therefore a 'journey toward a destination',[13] or as James and Prout articulate it, childhood is 'a highly complex and engineered trajectory towards adulthood'.[14] In a similar vein, children's development has been cared for according to mainstream developmental psychology theories. Using developmental psychology perpetuates the image of the child as a person that ought to 'successfully' or 'normally' climb up the ladder of development, and eventually completes the transition and becomes a fully competent adult. However, developmental psychology, as Erica Burman notes, is neither a homogeneous body of knowledge, nor a neutral one. It creates a specific image of childhood that ultimately enables adults to colonise children and control their lives.[15]

Therefore, when the 'human becomings' conception of childhood is used in conjunction with developmental psychology, it is almost impossible to interpret the right to development in any way other than as a right of the child to become an adult. While circumventing from defining the right to development itself, the Committee prioritises the protection of children's development in one of two ways: it either defines it as a violation of one right of the child, for example the right to education (Articles 28-29) as a violation of the right to development as well, or it determines that a protection of another and different right, for example the right to non-discrimination (Article 2), is a precondition for the realisation of the child's development (and rarely also the right to development).[16] This approach fails to respect children's agency in the context of development, and thus perpetuates the image of the child as an adult in making. It also does not provide a distinct or a coherent meaning to the right to development, which makes it difficult to implement.

In contrast to the 'human becomings' conception, the 'human beings' conception[17] embraces diverse and more complex notions of childhood.[18] According to this approach, children are perceived as active persons and not as

---

Children: The Condition of Children's Rights in Japanese Law', *Paedagogica Historica* 48 (2012): 153-167. See also LeVine, R.A. and R. S. New, *Anthropology and Child Development* (Oxford: Blackwell Publishing, 2008).

[11] Archard, D., *Children: Rights and Childhood* (London: Routledge, 1993) 36.

[12] Smart, C. *et al*, *The Changing Experience of Childhood* (Cambridge: Polity, 2001) 1.

[13] Lee, *supra* n. 1, 8.

[14] James and Prout, *supra* n. 1, 226.

[15] Burman, E., *Deconstructing Development Psychology* (2nd edition, Palgrave: London, 2008).

[16] Peleg, *supra* n. 2.

[17] Wells, K., *Childhood in a Global Perspective* (Cambridge: Polity Press, 2009) 1-24.

[18] Prout, A., *The Future Of Childhood* (London: Routledge, 2005) 7-34; Prout and James, 'A New Paradigm for the Sociology of Childhood? Provenance, Promise and Problems' in James and Prout, *supra* n. 1, 7-33.

'projects',[19] and childhood is being studied independently, and not by comparing children to adults.[20] As human 'beings', children are considered as human rights holders,[21] which means that they 'can exercise agency... as agents, rights bearers can participate. They can make their own lives, rather than having their lives made for them.'[22] As social agents,[23] children can now be seen as part of the social structure and social fabric, and subsequently their active role in it is respected.[24] This respect includes having their opinions heard and taken into consideration. Article 12 of the Convention reflects this perception in acknowledging the child's right to participation.[25]

When one listens to children, one realises just how much children know about their lives and about their world. Children make sense of their own experience of poverty (and what qualifies as 'well-being'),[26] of living on the street,[27] of their health or from the fact that there are dying.[28] Children are also able to articulate what human rights means,[29] and how the UNCRC can be interpreted.[30] If listened to, children can express their own point of view about

---

[19] Smart *et al*, *supra* n. 12, 13.

[20] James and Prout, *supra* n. 1, 8. See also Mayall, B., *Towards a Sociology of Childhood: Thinking From Children's Lives* (Gosport: Open University Press, 2002) 33.

[21] Freeman, M., *The Moral Status of Children* (The Hague: Martinus Nijhoff, 1997). But see Annette Ruth Appell's claim that even so, children's rights are still being measured against their dependency. Ruth Appell, A., 'The Pre-Political Child of Child-Centered Jurisprudence' *Houston Law Review* 46 (2009-2010): 703-757, 721.

[22] Freeman, M., 'Why It Remains Important to Take Children's Rights Seriously', *International Journal of Children's Rights* 15 (2007): 5-23, 8.

[23] James, Allison, 'Agency', in *Palgrave Handbook of Childhood Studies*. Qvortrup, J. et al, eds. (Basingstoke: Palgrave 2009, 2011) 45-54.

[24] *Ibid*, 38-40.

[25] For an analysis of Article 12, see L. Lundy, '"Voice" is Not Enough: Conceptualising Article 12 of the UN Convention on the Rights of the Child', *British Educational Research Journal* (2007) 33: 927-942.

[26] Camfield, L. *et al*, 'What's the Use of "Well-Being" in Contexts of Child Poverty? Approaches to Research, Monitoring and Children's Participation' *International Journal of Children's Rights* (2009) 17: 65-109; Goswami, H., 'Social Relationships and Children's Subjective Well-Being' *Social Indicator Research*, (2011) Online First 26.5.2011; Z. Pavlovic and T. R. Leban, 'Children's Rights International Study Project (CRISP) – A Shift from the Focus on Children's Rights to a Quality of Life Assessment Instrument' *Child Indicators Research* 2 (2009): 265.

[27] Mandel Butler, U., 'Freedom, Revolt and "Citizenship"', *Childhood* 16 (2009): 11-29; See also Raffaelli, M., 'How Do Brazilian Street Youth Experience "the Street"?', *Childhood* 8 (2001) 396-415.

[28] Bluebond-Langner, M., *The Private Worlds of Dying Children* (Princeton: Princeton University Press, 1978) 5.

[29] Ruck, M. D. *et al*, 'Children's and Adolescents' Understanding of Rights: Balancing Nurturance and Self-Determination', *Child Development* 64 (1988): 404; Ruck, M. D. *et al*, 'Adolescents' and Children's Knowledge About Their Rights: Some Evidence For How Young People View Rights In Their Own Lives' *Journal of Adolescence* 21 (1998): 275-289.

[30] Heesterman, W.,'An Assessment of the Impact of Youth Submission on the United Nations Committee on the Rights of the Child', *International Journal of Children's Rights* 13 (2005): 351-378.

their own development. Research shows that children are able to distinguish between the progression of development and the aims it should achieve. They associate 'development' with having a sense of direction in life, and what they see as the natural process of maturation. When perceiving 'development' as a natural process, according to Helga Kelle, the notion of getting older 'can hardly be seen as a personal achievement'.[31] As Priscilla Alderson *et al* have shown,[32] children's ability to express their views and preferences is not necessarily a matter of age, but of space and willingness of adults to listen to them as well. Needless to say, it is not always easy to facilitate children's participation (and decision-making),[33] but problems in implementation should not undermine the foundations of the principle and its pursuit. If we respect children's agency and autonomy, we also need to respect their values and priorities.[34]

Such an approach towards childhood and children's development is radically different from the one that is used today. The alleged paradigm shift in childhood studies has skipped the discussion concerning 'children's development' and right to development. The image of the developing child still dominates and dictates the discussion about this right. For this reason, for example, the right to development is usually overlooked in the literature, even when discussing the connection between law and child development,[35] or international development and children.[36]

In the next section I argue that using the Capability Approach as a theoretical framework can lead to a reconceptualisation of 'children's development', and subsequently the child's right to development, in a way that can offer a remedy to these shortcomings.

---

[31] Kelle, H., 'The Discourse of "Development" – How 9 to 12-Year-Old Children Construct "Childish" and "Future Development" Identified Within Their Peer Culture', *Childhood* 8 (2001): 95-111, 109; In a different context see Maclure, R., 'The Dynamics of Youth Participation: Insights from Research Fieldwork with Female Youth in Senegal', in *Children's Rights and International Development*. Denov, M. *et al*, eds. (New York, Palgrave, 2011) 155-174.

[32] Alderson, P. *et al*, 'The Participation Rights of Premature Babies', *International Journal of Children's Rights* 13 (2005): 31-50.

[33] Holland, S. *et al*, 'Power, Agency and Participatory Agenda: A Critical Exploration of Young's People's Engagement in Participative Qualitative Research', *Childhood* 17 (2010): 360-375.

[34] Ballet, J. *et al*, 'Children Agency and the Capability Approach – A Conceptual Framework' in *Children and the Capability Approach*. M. Biggeri *et al*, eds. (Basingstoke: Palgrave Macmillan 2011) 22-46, 22.

[35] See, for example, Buss, E. and M. Maclean, *The Law and Child Development* (Falmer: Ashgate, 2011), and Freeman, F., 'Emily Buss and Mavis Maclean – The Law and Child Development', *International Journal of Children's Rights* 19 (2011): 705-707, 707.

[36] Hanson, O. and O. Nieuwenhuys, *Reconceptualizing Children's Development in International Development* (Cambridge: Cambridge University Press, 2013).

The capability approach's concept of 'human development'

The Capability Approach (or 'approaches')[37] is a moral theory that focuses on human development, suggesting that 'development' should be conceptualised as 'freedom'.[38] The Capability Approach is a response to the traditional approach, which linked human development to economic growth as a means of eliminating poverty and satisfying people's 'basic needs'.[39] Amartya Sen and Martha Nussbaum, who pioneered this theory, claimed that the traditional conception of human development reflects a narrow understanding of human life and poverty, and is blind to social exclusion. Ignoring those at the margins, Sen and Nussbaum argue, is being disrespectful of people's human dignity. They therefore suggested conceptualising 'development' as a process that facilitates people's ability to live lives worth living,[40] by expanding their capability and increasing their real opportunities. Taking the view that people should not be bound by choices determined by others,[41] they claim that people should have a stake in shaping their own lives in a way that respects their agency.[42]

Arguably, the best way to realise those personal preferences is by respecting people agency and participation in making choices. Participation should not be seen only as a methodological tool, but also as a substantial element of development. Participation guarantees people's freedoms and 'enhances the ability of people to help themselves and also to influence the world... the concern here relates to what we may call the "agency aspect" of the individual'.[43] According to Nussbaum, denying people the ability to choose not only denies their agency but also 'makes life not worthy of human dignity'.[44] According to Sen, freedom to choose is 'both the primary end' and 'the principal means of development'.[45] I therefore argue that utilising this approach

---

[37] It has also been suggested that it should be called 'the capability creation'. Gasper, D., 'What Is the Capability Approach? Its Core, Rationale, Partners and Dangers', *Journal of Socio-Economics* 36 (2007): 335-359, 346.
[38] Sen, *supra* n. 3.
[39] Esteva, G., 'Development' in *The Development Dictionary*. W. Sachs, ed. (London: Zed Books, 1992) 6-25; Streeten, P. and S. Javed Burki, 'Basic Needs: Some Issues' *World Development* 6 (1978): 411-421; On women's basic needs see I. Palmer, 'Rural Women and the Basic Needs Approach to Development', *International Labour Review* 115 (1977): 97-107.
[40] Moore, A. and R. Crisp, 'Welfarism in Moral Theory', *Australian Journal of Philosophy* 74 (1996): 598-613; L. Hamilton, 'A Theory of True Interests in the Work of Amartya Sen', *Government and Opposition* 34 (1999): 516.
[41] Sen, A., *Inequality Re-examined* (Cambridge: Harvard University Press, 1992) 39.
[42] Dixon and Nussbaum, *supra* n. 6, 557.
[43] *Ibid.*
[44] Nussbaum, M. C., *Creating Capabilities – The Human Development Approach* (Cambridge: Harvard University Press, 2011) 31.
[45] *Ibid*, 16.

to human development in the context of children's rights in general, and of the right to development in particular, can radically change the way this right is addressed, and gives it a new necessary meaning.

If development is freedom, then 'unfreedom' is a deprivation of capabilities. For example, unfreedom can be a situation of famine or being under nourished, or having limited access to social services such as health care or functional education. In more abstract terms, Sen suggests that 'unfreedom' should be defined as an inequality 'between women and men [and] denial of political liberty and basic civil rights'.[46] Social, political, economic and cultural power structures constitute the core causes of unfreedoms, since they prevent the marginalised from benefiting from economic prosperity. Arguably, children are structurally positioned in most societies in a chronic condition of 'unfreedon' due to political, social and cultural structures and social attitudes towards children.

Another assertion is that people should not be seen as homogenous or as having equal opportunities. Gender, disability, age, ethnicity or illness have great influence on levels of income and accessibility to social services, which are necessary to maintain similar standards of living. For example, a person with a disability needs to spend a larger percentage of her income on buying medications and treatments (and also needs more access to health care services) than what a person without a disability and a same level of income spends on her health. Therefore, in order to maintain a similar standard of living, these two peoples need different resources. I argue that this analogy applies to children as well. Children should not be seen as a homogenous group, and their unique requirements for living dignified lives ought to be met.[47] A similar conclusion should be reached when taking the approach the agency of every child should be respected. In the context of their right to development, contextualising children's lives based on social attitudes toward their individual characteristics (gender, disability etc.) or their group affiliation (social class, religious etc.) will enable to diversify the meaning of children's development accordingly.

Another significant dimension of the Capability Approach is the idea of 'functions'. According to Sen, functions are 'the various things a person may value being and doing'.[48] This includes, for example, having a job or being healthy, as well as more abstract concepts such as happiness. Sen argues that every person should define his or her own functions, and therefore he does not suggest one definitive set of functions.[49] Nonetheless, a precondition to be

---

[46] *Ibid*, 15.
[47] Cf to Dixon and Nussbaum, *supra* n. 6, 556-563.
[48] Sen, *Development as Freedom, supra* n. 3, 75.
[49] Sen, A., 'Human Rights and Capabilities' *Journal of Human Development* 6 (2005): 151, 157-160.

able to define a set of personal functions and being able to live accordingly, is having necessary capabilities. Sen uses the availability of food as an example to illustrate his point about the connection between functions and capabilities. According to this example, a person might not eat for one of two reasons: either he does not have food, or he has decided to fast or go on a diet.[50] While the latter is a matter of choice (function), the former is a matter of lack of capabilities. Capabilities can therefore be understood as 'the range of options a person has in deciding what kind of life to lead',[51] which 'represent the various combinations of functioning (being and doing) that the person can achieve',[52] and as such constitutes one's freedom. Nussbaum defines capabilities in slightly different terms, claiming that capabilities are those entities that enable people to execute their human functions.[53] Capabilities should therefore be understood as 'what people are actually able to do and to be'.[54] According to Nussbaum, all human beings ought to have the freedom to choose whether they exercise these capabilities and in which ways they do so.[55] Despite the tendency to overlook children in that regard, children too should be seen as entitled to exercise their agency and capabilities. While doing so, it is up to the duty bearers – in the context of the UNCRC they are the child's parents (or other legal guardians), the state and the international community[56] – to enable them to do so. This position is similar, but not identical, to the positions of John Holt and Richard Farson,[57] not least because it is not a call for neglecting children to their rights.[58] Instead it argues for change in the theoretical approach towards children's development and their a bility – and rights – to exercise agency and participate in shaping their own lives.

Distinguishing between internal capabilities and substantial freedoms helps to realise the differences between 'freedom' and 'capabilities'. Internal capabilities are a person's intellectual and emotional capacities, fitness and health, level of learning skills etc. Substantial freedom is the ability to make a choice. This ability depends on personal capacities as well as the political,

---

50) Sen, *Inequality Re-examined, supra* n. 41.
51) Drèze, J. and A. Sen, *India: Economic Development and Social Opportunity* (Oxford: Oxford University Press, 1995) 10.
52) Sen, *Inequality Re-examined, supra* n. 41, 4.
53) M. Nussbaum, M., 'Women's Capabilities and Social Justice', *Journal of Human Development* 1 (2000): 219-247, 242.
54) *Ibid*, 222-223.
55) *Ibid*, 235.
56) Article 4 of the UNCRC.
57) Holt, J., *Escape From Childhood* (Middlesex: Penguin Books, 1974); Farson, R. E., *Birthrights* (Michigan: University of Michigan Press, 1974).
58) Cf to Hafen, B. C. and J. O. Hafen, 'Abandoning Children to Their Autonomy: The United Nations Convention on the Rights of the Child', *Harvard International Law Journal* (1996) 37: 449-492.

social and economic environments as combined capabilities. Based on this distinction, Nussbaum argues that if a given society seeks to promote human capabilities, it ought to support the development of internal capabilities 'through education resources to enhance physical and emotional health, support for family care and love, a system of education and much more'.[59] This distinction clarifies how society can enable the production of internal capabilities, while reducing or eliminating the options of people to function in accordance with those capabilities. For example, people can be given access to education in order to develop their capability to express themselves. But if soon after they are denied the right to freedom of expression, for example, their combined capability is denied as well.[60] Society, therefore, cannot provide and produce combined capabilities 'without producing internal capabilities'.[61] This distinction, and call for holistic and continuing securing capabilities,[62] is vital for children and important for the reconceptualisation of the child's right to development, as the next section elaborates.

The capability approach and the child's right to development

This section develops the argument that children should be seen as entitled to develop, according to the Capability Approach's conception of human development. I suggest that to reconceptualise the meaning of 'children's development' according to the Capability Approach can change the interpretation of the child's right to development. More specifically, it can enhance further respect for children's agency and voice, and it will make it possible to concretise the meaning of the child's right to development. But first, there is a need to address the preliminary questions concerning the ability to adapt the Capability Approach to interpret children's human rights. After answering this question in the affirmative, I will discuss the nexus between the Capability Approach and children.

As has been mentioned earlier, until recently the applicability of the Capability Approach to children has rarely been addressed, and only recently have these questions begun to attract some attention.[63] One of the main reasons for this lack of discussion is rooted, I believe, in Sen upholding the 'human becomings' model of childhood, suggesting that children will enjoy

---

[59] Nussbaum, *Creating Capabilities – The Human Development Approach, supra* n. 44, 21.
[60] *Ibid*, 23.
[61] *Ibid.*
[62] Wolff, J. and A. De-Shalit, *Disadvantage* (Oxford: Oxford University Press, 2007).
[63] See, for example, the collection of articles by Biggeri *et al, supra n.* 4. See also Hanson and Nieuwenhuys, *supra* n. 36.

their freedoms when they become competent adults.[64] Competency is therefore a key difficulty that Sen sees in linking children and the Capability Approach. Madoka Saito expresses a similar concern, when he asks, 'how can we apply the Capability Approach to children, since children are not mature enough to make decision by themselves?'[65] Likewise, Biggeri *et al* assert that the 'Capability Approach obviously implies the individual's capacity for self-determination, which may not apply to children'.[66]

The question of children's competence and capacity to choose is not unique to this context. The question, or the tension, about the relationship between capability and capacities is being asked about almost every aspect of the child's life and rights, including, for example, consent to medical treatment,[67] the age of criminal responsibility[68] and the right of children to vote in a country's general election.[69] These debates are relevant in our context as they demonstrate the dominance of conceptions about children's capacities, thus demonstrating that this is a normative debate rather than a question of having 'empirical' capacities to choose. In other words, it is not children's ability to choose that is debated, but rather the space that society, adults and the law gives children in order to make a choice, and the tolerance for what adults consider to be a mistake.

The issue here is not empirical but normative: whether society and adults, who dominate children's lives, respect children's right to choose and to develop, and if so – to what extent. I therefore suggest that the Capability Approach should be acknowledged as relevant to children for all the reasons that it is considered to be relevant to all human beings, including the elderly and those with disabilities (while acknowledging the fundamental differences between children and these two groups).[70] Claiming that the Capability Approach is not relevant to children because children lack the capacity to choose undermines the core principle of the Capability Approach itself.

---

[64] Saito, M., 'Amartya Sen's Capability Approach to Education: A Critical Exploration', *Journal of Philosophy of Education* 37 (2003): 17, 25.

[65] Saito, *Supra* n. 64.

[66] Biggeri, M. *et al*, 'Children's Agency and the Capability Approach: A Conceptual Framework', *supra* n. 4, 22-45, 24.

[67] A leading case is *Gillick v. West Norfolk and Wisbech Area Health Authority* [1986] AC 112. See Freeman, M., 'Rethinking Gillick', *International Journal of Children's Rights* 13 (2005): 201-217.

[68] Different countries subscribe to different age of criminal responsibility, ranging from the age of 7 to the age of 18. See Melchiorre, A. and E. Atkins, *At What Age Are School-Children Employed, Married and Taken to Court?* (Right to Education Project, London 2011) 30-32.

[69] Jans, M., 'Children as Citizens', *Childhood* 11 (2004): 27-44; Wall, J., 'Can Democracy Represent Children? Towards a Politics of Difference', *Childhood* 19 (2012): 86-100; Roche, J., 'Children: Rights, Participation and Citizenship', *Childhood* 6 (1999): 475-493; Nolan, A., *Children's Socio-Economic Rights, Democracy and the Courts* (Oxford: Hart, 2011) 43-92.

[70] Cf to Dixon and Nussbaum, *supra* n. 6.

One cannot advocate in favour of respecting the human dignity and agency of all people, especially those who formerly were at the margins of their societies (and were perceived to lack certain capacities), while denying the same universal principles from children, by arguing that they lack capacities. Furthermore, the proposition that children lack required capacity is a self-fulfilling prophecy, leading to a situation where children are being denied the opportunity to challenge this presumption, thus perpetuating the denial of their agency.[71] This approach creates a vicious circle that excludes children from the ability to develop, according to the Capability Approach's conception of development as freedom.

Following Nussbaum's discussion about internal and combined capabilities, it can be further argued that once children are given the opportunity to develop their internal capabilities, primarily through education, they will no longer be denied the opportunity or entitlement to develop. This statement can be formulated in human rights terms, thus suggesting that children can develop their internal capabilities when their human right to education is being realised, and their agency is respected. At this point it becomes evident that respecting children's agency and rights is an issue that keeps reappearing in considering any aspect of the child's right to development. Therefore, I will now discuss the applicability of utilising the Capability Approach to analyse human rights law.

Human rights law and the capability approach

Sen distinguished between the ethics of human rights and human rights law, claiming that the moral strength of the former does not require the existence of the latter. At a practical level, Sen claims that human rights law is a good rhetorical tool for creating and imposing obligations on states to provide the capabilities necessary for human development.[72] Referring to the structure of international human rights law, Séverine Deneulim asserts that the Capability Approach enables us to 'look at the institutional framework that allows that right to be fulfilled'.[73] In other words, the Capability Approach can be seen as 'an evaluative framework for assessing states of affairs'.[74] According to this

---

[71] On this see Federle, K. H.,'Rights Flow Downhill', *International Journal of Children's Rights* 2 (1994): 343-368.
[72] Sen, A.,'Capabilities and Well-Being' in *Quality of Life*. Nussbaum, M. and A. Sen, eds. (Oxford: Oxford University Press, 1993) 30-53.
[73] Deneulim, S., 'Ideas Related to Human Development' in *An Introduction to the Human Development and Capabilities Approach*. Deneulim, S. and L. Shahani, eds. (London: Earthscan, 2009) 49-70, 60.
[74] *Ibid.*

approach, human rights analysis defines social structures according to the Capability Approach, but should not follow it in interpreting specific rights. Unlike Sen, Nussbaum is much more in favour of connecting the Capability Approach and human rights, including children's rights.[75]

A different question is concerned with equality and discrimination. While the recognition of diversity among people and the impacts that disadvantages have on people's development is central to the Capability Approach, Deneulim claims that 'the human rights approach does not necessarily take such differences into account',[76] and therefore will not fulfil the Capability Approach's goals. The problem with this liberal argument is that it ignores substantial equality and affirmative action policies. It is against this approach that Dixon and Nussbaum claim that the Capability Approach can be used in order to justify prioritising children's welfare rights,[77] especially those rights that are sensitive 'both to children's welfare needs and to children's agency'.[78] However, in their discussions, Dixon and Nussbaum compare children's competence, agency and rights to the rights of people with intellectual disabilities, claiming that recognition of children's rights is based on a similar 'moral claim of all human beings to be afforded full human dignity, regardless of their capacity for rational or reasoned participation in public or civil life'.[79] Therefore, children's 'vulnerability'[80] justifies affirmative action policies, which aim to provide children with the necessary capabilities to be free.

Such a comparison is highly problematic for a number of reasons. First, it measures children against adult-tailored standards of competency, perpetuating the notion that a competent adult is the standard that children must meet in order to be entitled to develop. Second, it refutes the respect we have for children for what they will become ('human becomings') or for who they are now ('human beings'). Third, it contradicts the perceptions of children as 'human becomings' and as persons in a mode of change and developing their capacities. While children are 'developing' and are capable of change, adults with intellectual disabilities are in a static mode. They do not develop and their capacities, by and large, do not evolve. Fourth, this comparison implies that childhood is some sort of disability. While there may be some similarities between the current cognitive functions of children and adults with mental

---

[75] Nussbaum, M., 'Human Capabilities, Female Human Beings' in *Women, Culture and Development: A Study on Human Capabilities*. M. Nussbaum and J. Glover, eds. (Oxford: Oxford University Press, 1995) 61-104; Nussbaum, M., 'Capabilities as Fundamental Entitlements: Sen and Global Justice', *Feminist Economics* 9 (2003): 33-59.
[76] *Ibid*, 61.
[77] Dixon and Nussbaum, *supra* n. 6.
[78] *Ibid*, 553.
[79] *Ibid*.
[80] *Ibid*, 573-578. The second justification is 'cost effective analysis'; see pp. 578-584.

capabilities, placing them in the same category not only undermines respect for children's human dignity in general, but also raises the question of how children with mental capabilities should be conceptualised, and how they should be treated in light of this view.

I see less significance in using the Capability Approach in order to validate the respect to children's rights, and rather suggest utilising it in a more narrow way, focusing on the implications of using the Capability Approach in the context of the child's right to development. Biggeri *et al* take a similar, more practical, approach, suggesting that 'human rights can be used as the main argument for defending a list of relevant capabilities for children',[81] and that the Capability Approach 'can become a framework for normative evaluation and policy implementation. Therefore, it seems that the libertarian-inspired human rights approach and the Capability Approach can dialogue and complement each other quite well.'[82] Taking this idea forward, they suggest a concrete mode of operation:

> in the case of children, on the one hand human rights can be used as the main argument for defending a list of relevant capabilities for children, and on the other the Capability Approach can become a framework for normative evaluation and policy implementation.[83]

I will return to this point in detail in the next section. First, I will discuss how the Capability Approach can reconceptualise children's development, in the context of the child's right to development.

Reconceptualising 'Children's Development'

Applying the Capability Approach's conception of human development when interpreting the child's legal right to development can lead to three necessary changes: expanding the meaning of children's development beyond its current psycho-social meaning; enabling the development of a practical and concrete means of implementation; enhance the respect for children's agency and their right to participation.

The first contribution of the Capability Approach to the analysis of children's development and the child's right to development is to expand the meaning of the term 'children's development' beyond its current

---

[81] Biggeri, M. *et al*, 'Children's Agency and the Capability Approach: A Conceptual Framework', in Biggeri, M. *et al* (eds) *Children and the Capability Approach, supra* n. 4, 22-45, 39-40.
[82] *Ibid.*
[83] *Ibid.*

interpretation. It enables to diversify the meaning of this term and to stop seeing developmental psychology, which is the current dominant framework, as
the only conceptual framework that should inform the interpretation of this
term. Diversifying the meaning of children's development will inevitably lead
to the rethinking of the concept of childhood. The reason is that the theoretical coherence of the current 'human becomings' will be undermined if 'children's development' does not only mean growing up.

The second contribution derives from the above-suggested change. I suggest using the terminology of capabilities to concretise 'children's development'. While Sen does not define the types of capabilities a person needs in
order to be free, Polly Vizard claims that despite this reservation, international
human rights law can help to generate 'a minimal list of central and basic
capabilities with universal coverage'.[84] According to Biggeri and Mehrotra, the
Capability Approach is a 'framework for normative evaluation and policy
implementation',[85] and it provides normative and positive grounds for promoting these capabilities in children. Similarly, Nussbaum suggests a list of ten
capabilities that she qualifies as concrete, universal, inseparable and essential
to the realisation of human development. The ten capabilities are: life, bodily
health, bodily integrity, sense, imagination and thought, emotions, practical
reason, affiliation, other species and play and control over one's environment.[86] Although Nussbaum considers these as the minimum universal capabilities that are necessary for us to be free, she admits that this list is slightly
ambiguous, so individual societies can elaborate and interpret it differently,
according to their own traditions and histories.[87] According to Vizard, these
ten capabilities can be seen as grounds for a 'human rights based capability
framework',[88] mainly because they resemble the basic universal rights that
are protected by the Universal Declaration of Human Rights and the 1966
Covenants as universal human rights.[89]

This list of capabilities can be seen as relevant for children for two reasons.
First, it meets children's needs and arguably cannot be challenged on the basis
of a pre-requirement for capacities. Second, following Vizard's observation,

---

[84] Vizard, P., 'Specifying and Justifying a Basic Capability Set: Should the International Human
Rights Framework be Given a More Direct Role?', *Oxford Development Studies* 35 (2007):
225-250, 235.
[85] Biggeri, B., *et al*, 'Children's Agency and the Capability Approach: A Conceptual Framework',
in *Children and the Capability Approach, supra* n. 4, 39-40.
[86] Nussbaum, *Creating Capabilities – The Human Development Approach, supra* n. 44, 33-34.
[87] Nussbaum, *Ibid*, 40. See Robeyns' claim that such a list should be rejected since it narrows
down Sen's approach: I. Robeyns, 'An Unworkable Idea or a Promising Alternative? Sen's
Capability Approach Re-examined' (1993) Center of Economic Discussion on Paper 00.30.
University of Leuven, Mimeo.
[88] Vizard, *supra* n. 84, 234-235.
[89] *Ibid*.

many of these capabilities are defined as children's rights by the Convention (which protects the child's right to life, health, bodily integrity, affiliations and play in Articles 6, 24, 19, 7, 8, 9, 11 and 31, respectively), so these rights, or children's entitlement to these capabilities, have universal acceptance (if only due to the near-universal ratification of the Convention). Therefore, taking the Capability Approach's perspective, these rights can be understood as necessary to the realisation of the child's right to development. Moreover, this list of capabilities also resembles the UNCRC's approach to the support of children's development.[90] However, in the context of the Capability Approach, these capabilities – and the rights they resemble – serve a different purpose. These capabilities and corresponding rights support the child's freedom, whilst the Committee takes these rights as means to enable the child to become an adult.

A key problem with this list is that, like the Capability Approach in general, it was not created with children in mind. Biggeri and Mehrotra therefore suggest a different list, which they claim has more relevance to children. Their list includes 14 capabilities: life and physical health; love and care; mental well-being; bodily integrity and safety; social relations; participation; education; freedom from economic and non-economic exploitation; shelter and environment; leisure activities; respect; religion and identity; time autonomy; and mobility.[91] Similar to Nussbaum's list, nine of the capabilities in this list can be named as children's rights under the Convention (Articles 6, 24, 12, 28, 29, 32, 27, 31, 14, 30, 7 and 8, respectively). The remaining capabilities, such as love and care, social relations and respect, are not considered human rights.[92]

By employing the Capability Approach's terminology, it can be argued that realising these rights provides the necessary capabilities for the child to be free. In practice, protecting these rights of children will serve dual purposes: protecting these rights themselves, and protecting all these rights simultaneously and constantly so every child has an equal opportunity to be free. For the children who live in any of the 193 states that signed and ratified the Convention, there is a source of obligation in international human rights law that obliges the different duty bearers to promote their capabilities and thus promote their human development. More specifically, the commitment of states parties is to promote these capabilities to 'the maximum extent possible'.[93]

---

[90] Peleg, *supra* n. 2.
[91] Biggeri, M. and S. Mehrotra, 'Child Poverty as Capability Deprivation: How to Choose Domains of Child Well-being and Poverty', in *Children and the Capability Approach, supra* n. 4, 51.
[92] Though it was suggested that children do have the right to be loved, and the right to 'time autonomy'. See Korczak, J., 'How to Love a Child' in *Selected works of Janusz Korczak*. Wolins, M., ed. (Washington D.C: National Science Foundation, 1967) 355-356.
[93] Article 6(2) of the UNCRC.

The third contribution of the Capability Approach is enhanced respect for the agency of individual children and children as a collective, and for children's right to participation. The Capability Approach's framework enables to emphasise the particular attention that should be given to the child's right to participate in shaping her own future. If children articulate their views concerning their own freedom, it will ease the tension between the two distinct conceptions of childhood – 'human becomings' and 'human beings'. Children should participate in the creation of a new interpretation of the right to development, and contribute their own opinions on the subject. They should also be part of the process of realising the right to development in practice, including in the process of developing implementation tools and practices (for example, development policies and programmes, and drafting new legislation on the subject). Flavio Comim claims that in the context of the Capability Approach, children usually 'are not consulted in the meaning of an active actor in society',[94] though this sort of treatment ignores the fact that 'children would probably define the meaning of being an active actor or citizen differently'.[95] While Comim flags up this latter point as a potential argument against realising children's participation, this argument is in fact an excellent reason why children should participate. Their unique point of view about their own development is the reason for giving them a voice, rather than a reason to continue silencing them. Adopting the view that children, even toddlers,[96] can and should express their preferences enables us to overcome one of the main barriers for implementing the Capability Approach in analysing the child's right to development. Children should play an active role in realising their self-determination, and express their preference about their own future. It seems that Saito is alarmed by this sort of suggestion, and therefore warns us that,

> giving temporary freedom to a child does not always mean that the child will have freedom in future, and similarly, restricting the temporary freedom of a child may well expend the freedom that the child will have in the future. We, therefore, have to consider the freedom for a child in a lifelong perspective.[97]

This concern for the child's future is well placed. However, one should not easily dismiss or undermine the value of the child's life in the present, and its manifestation in the right to participation. This strong preference for safeguarding the child's future undermines the recognition of children as rights

---

94) Comim *et al, supra* n. 4, 7.
95) *Ibid.*
96) See Alderson, *supra* n. 32.
97) Saito, *Supra* n. 64, 26.

holders, depriving them of agency and voice. This preference is based on an assumption that sacrificing children's freedom now will lead to a greater freedom in the future, once the child becomes an adult. Dixon and Nussbaum make a similar claim as they argue that 'we ought to support capabilities that will best promote a long-term future of full capabilities'.[98] But ensuring freedoms in the future should not justify denying all freedoms in the present; rather, the contrary is true. Arguably, ensuring freedoms in the present will enable children to fulfil their potential and pursue lives worth living in the future. For this reason, children's voices and opinions should not be silenced or dismissed, but rather amplified.

I do not argue that care for the child's future should be overlooked when caring for children's development or for children's right to development. However, ensuring that the child will become an adult should also not be the only prism through which children's lives and development are perceived. We should care for children's life at the present time, and realise that children's futures include not only their adulthood, but also their childhood and their future while still being children. The 'future' of a one-month-old baby includes more than 17 years of life before she becomes an adult.[99] Maybe even more importantly, in the 17 years during which this one-month-old child is living, she is experiencing the world and exercising agency, and should have all of her human rights protected, including her right to development.

Conclusion

The article suggests using the Capability Approach as a normative framework to analyse the child's right to development. Children, like adults, should be able to live lives worth living during their entire life span, including their time as children. The point of departure when interpreting the right to development of children should be conceptualising children as active agents in shaping their own life, and respecting that they value different functions and have different capabilities from adults. Incorporating the Capability Approach's understanding of development in the context of the child's right to development can help expand the meanings of 'development' beyond its current psycho-social conception, and the child's right to development beyond its current understanding as the child's right to become an adult. The Capability Approach also suggests how the idea of 'human development' could be realised in practice, delineating what the necessary capabilities are. Children's agency deserves more respect than it currently gets, and such a change will

---

98) Dixon and Nussbaum, *supra* n. 6, 555.
99) According to Article 1 of the Convention, unless an earlier age of majority applies.

shift the attention from questions of competence and welfare to those of human rights. It will enable to articulate the child's right to development as a distinct and concrete human right – the child will be seen to be entitled to grow, not only as in need of growing.

Another implication of respecting children's agency will be to respect children's right to participation, which symbolises children's ability – and right – to make sense of the world around them.[100] Such a connection between children's development and their right to participation has yet to be made. Ignoring children's views in the context of their development perpetuates the image of children as passive subjects, whose sole purpose in life is to sit still and grow up. Children's participation also reflects, and promotes, the understanding of 'development' as an emancipatory process, which is the contribution of the Capability Approach to our analysis. The manifestation of the right to development as an emancipatory right and giving children a voice in this process requires a social and cultural transformation.[101] Such a change includes the creation of a 'political space in which children are empowered to express their own distinctive and submerged point of view'.[102] It will enable children, as a marginalised group, to express their own perspectives[103] about their own development. Nonetheless, respecting children's right to participation does not mean that children will dictate the course of their childhood and future adulthood, not least because no one, child and adult alike, has a free standing in society. Children's participation does not mandate that children should be the only decision makers.

The article examined two lists of capabilities, with only one of them formulated explicitly with the intention to meet children's needs. These lists show that 'children's development' can be translated into human rights terms. However, a more contextualised list should be further developed in order to meet the needs and rights of different children in different circumstances. The suggested capabilities can later be articulated in human rights terms, using the universal acceptance of the Convention as a positive source.

---

[100] Lansdown, G., 'International Developments in Children's Participation: Lessons and Challenges' in *Children, Young People and Social Inclusion*. Tisdall, K. *et al*, eds. (Bristol: The Policy Press, 2006) 139-155.

[101] Lund, R.,'At the Interface of Development Studies and Child Research: Rethinking Participating Child', *Children's Geographies* 5 (2007): 131-148.

[102] Wall, *supra* n. 69, 92.

[103] Thomas, N., 'Towards a Theory of Children's Participation', *International Journal of Children's Rights* 15 (2007): 199-218, 210.

Implementing the Convention on the Rights of the Child for 'Youth': Who and How?

Ellen Desmet

Children's Rights Knowledge Centre, Belgium;
Institute for Foreigners' Law and Anthropology of Law, University of Leuven, Belgium
ellen.desmet@keki.be

I. Introduction

This contribution aims to explore the interactions between children's rights policies and youth policies, and to reflect on whether and how (further) linking these policies could enhance the realization of the rights of children and young people. First, some recent evolutions are identified, which illustrate the pressing issues revolving around (the rights of) young persons/youth. From various angles, there appears to be an ambiguous relationship between the United Nations Convention on the Rights of the Child (CRC) and young persons. Also, the target groups of youth policies and children's rights policies partially overlap. The convergence of these observations leads to the central questions of this article: what are current linkages between children's rights policies and youth policies? And how should/could these interrelations be strengthened, in light of an enhanced implementation of the CRC? The inquiry is carried out at two levels: at the European and international level, on the one hand, and with respect to Flanders (Belgium), on the other. In order to be able to answer the aforementioned questions, the (theoretical) range of overlap between the concepts of 'children' and 'youth' is identified for each institutional level. The article closes with some concluding reflections.

II. Observations leading to the research focus

a. The CRC and young persons: an ambiguous relationship

In recent times, the relationship between the CRC and young persons is increasingly being perceived as somewhat problematical, from different angles. First, it has been noted that, in *implementing* the CRC, the realization of the rights of older children has not received adequate attention, or at least less attention than the implementation of the rights of young children. Second, the relevance of the *text* of the CRC for young people today is being questioned. It is felt that the provisions of the CRC are not responsive enough to the realities of young people's lives in the twenty-first century. Finally, the *personal field of application* of the CRC, i.e. the upper age limit of the concept of 'children', is (again) subject to debate. Hereinafter, these three observations are briefly explained and illustrated. The primary objective of this section is not to discuss substantially these tendencies or evaluate their merits. The observations mainly serve as indicators of the ambivalent relationship between the CRC and young persons, and of the need to pay greater attention to the rights of young persons and the (possible) links between children's rights policies and youth policies. Nevertheless, in order to avoid confusion on the author's stance, a short appreciation will be added, where relevant.

The first observation is that, in efforts to implement the CRC, the rights and concerns of older children, also referred to as 'adolescents', have not received equal consideration as those of young children. It has repeatedly been argued that greater efforts should be directed towards the former age group. As such, the Committee on the Rights of the Child "[has noted] with concern that in implementing their obligations under the Convention, States parties have not given sufficient attention to the specific concerns of adolescents as rights holders and to promoting their health and development".[1] This induced the Committee to adopt General Comment No. 4 (2003) on 'Adolescent health and development in the context of the Convention on the Rights of the Child'. Adolescence is described as "a period characterized by rapid physical, cognitive and social changes, including sexual and reproductive maturation; the gradual building up of the capacity to assume adult behaviours and roles involving new responsibilities requiring new knowledge and skills".[2] The General Comment aims to "raise awareness and provide States parties with guidance and support in their efforts to guarantee the respect for, protection and fulfilment of the rights of adolescents, including through the formulation of specific strategies and policies".[3] Also, in its 2011 edition of the report 'The State of the World's Children', UNICEF shifted its attention from young children (0-9 years) towards adolescents (10-19 years). In recent years, the life circumstances of young children considerably improved in many countries, because of investments in, among others, health care, basic education and nutrition. The new focus on adolescents was explained by arguing that "lasting

---

[1] UN Doc. CRC/GC/2003/4, § 3.
[2] Ibid., § 2.
[3] Ibid., § 3.

change in the lives of children and young people ... can only be achieved and sustained by complementing investment in the first decade of life with greater attention and resources applied to the second" (UNICEF, 2011, p. 2). Within the group of adolescents, there appears to be a tendency to focus concern on the older adolescents, to the detriment of the age group of 10-14 years. Nevertheless, these young adolescents are in a crucial phase of rapid biological and psychological changes, in which they need adequate support from their environment (UNAIDS, 2004).

A second observation concerns the assertion that the text itself of the CRC does not fit well with the current needs and expectations of young people. According to Veerman (2010), more than twenty years after its adoption, the Convention on the Rights of the Child appears outdated with regard to various aspects, such as HIV/AIDS, globalization, alcohol and drug (ab)use, information and communication technologies (ICT)... issues that today stand central in the lives of young persons. He proposes to revise the text of the CRC, in order to be able to better address these challenges young people are currently facing. Another movement that can be linked to this observation, is the one pleading for a greater recognition of 'youth rights', as distinct from children's rights and general human rights (European Youth Forum, 2010; Mahidi, 2010). It is argued that young persons should be recognized as a separate legal category, since they face a range of challenges that are different from those of children and adults with respect to, among others, participation, education, employment and housing. The Convention on the Rights of the Child can be used to cover some aspects of youth rights, but it does not appear as appropriate to tackle the majority of the challenges young people are confronted with today (Mahidi, 2010, p. 62). It is asserted that some provisions may be seen as 'patronising' when applied to young persons (for instance, Article 5 CRC on the rights and duties of parents) (Ibid., p. 61), and that the CRC as a whole is too much focused on 'protection': "[T]he CRC's main concern being to "shield" children from certain social risks, it is highly protective in nature. A Convention on the Rights of Young People should endorse a more proactive approach; it should be a legal document recognising both rights and responsibilities, aiming at fulfilling autonomy for young people, and enabling them to actively participate in society" (European Youth Forum, 2010, p. 9). A proposed way to suitably address young persons' needs and rights in Europe would thus entail drafting a 'European Convention on Youth Rights'. Inspiration could be drawn from similar instruments that have been developed in other regions, such as the African Youth Charter and the Iberoamerican Convention on the Rights of Youth.

As mentioned, the arguments above are referred to here because they point to a tense relationship between the CRC and (the rights of) young persons. It is not the objective of this contribution to substantially address these appeals.

Nevertheless, the author would like to express some reservations, without being exhaustive, which should be taken into account when evaluating the proposals of revising the CRC and drafting a new convention on youth rights. To start, such an endeavour would require the allocation of a substantial amount of financial and human resources, to be invested in meetings and negotiation processes. In times of economic restraint, the question arises whether the resources available should not be devoted to securing the effective implementation of existing human rights provisions. Also, there is the risk that, at the end of the negotiation processes between the different national states, the revised or new text may be more restrictive in recognizing the rights and concerns of young persons, than anticipated now by the proponents of these processes. Moreover, human rights treaties, such as the CRC, contain general principles, which are subject to a progressive and evolutionary interpretation. Openness to a progressive interpretation has been observed with both the European Court of Human Rights (see, for instance, its jurisprudence on the right to respect for private and family life) and the Inter-American Court of Human Rights (see, for instance, its interpretation of the right to property as including the collective property rights of indigenous peoples). It should be carefully examined whether the rights of young people cannot be appropriately realized on the basis of a progressive and contextual interpretation of existing human rights provisions.

A third illustration of the ambiguous relationship between young persons and the CRC concerns the upper age limit of the concept of children. Not only the substantive provisions of the CRC are thus called in question (*supra*), also the personal field of application of the Convention is subject to debate.[4] Article 1 of the CRC defines 'a child' as "every human being below the age of eighteen years unless under the law applicable to the child, majority is attained earlier". The reference to the domestic legal framework allows for flexibility in the application of the CRC, by leaving the possibility of using a lower age limit when majority is reached earlier under national law.

In the last decade, neuroimaging research has demonstrated that the brain is not fully matured by puberty, but continues to develop until the age of about 25 (Johnson *et al.* 2009). This finding has triggered questions about the relationship between neuromaturation and real-life behaviour: does the fact that the brain of adolescents is not fully matured yet, have an impact on the maturity of their judgments? According to many neuroscientists, "empirical support for a causal relationship between neuromaturational processes and real-world behavior is currently lacking" (Ibid., p. 216). Notwithstanding this scientific uncertainty, the fact of adolescent brain immaturity has been

---

[4] Not only the end, but also the beginning of childhood and the application of children's rights to the unborn, have been the topic of discussion (Cornock & Montgomery, 2011).

invoked as an argument to extend the protection of young people, especially in criminal law. For instance, the United States Supreme Court has decided that it is unconstitutional to impose capital punishment on persons who were under the age of 18 when they committed their crimes (*Roper v. Simmons*, 543 U.S. 551 (2005)). One of the arguments in support of this decision was that adolescents do not have the same maturity and sense of responsibility as adults, so they cannot be considered culpable for their crimes in the same way. The finding of adolescent brain immaturity has also led to appeals not to subject young people from 16 to 23 years to adult criminal law (Doreleijers, 2009) and, more generally, to extend the protection of children's rights and youth law to young persons until the age of 25 (Veerman, 2010). As mentioned, a cautious stance is warranted when using neuroscience research in policy making, given that no causal link between neuromaturation and real-life behaviour has been established (yet).

Also during the drafting process of the CRC, the age limit of 18 years to define the end of childhood was contested. Pleadings were mostly held, however, to support an adaptation of the definition in the other direction. At the second session of the open-ended Working Group on the Question of a Convention on the Rights of the Child in 1980, various arguments were advanced in favour of a lower age limit: the UN General Assembly had set an age limit of 15 in relation to the International Year of the Child; the age of 14 implied in many countries the end of compulsory education and/or was the legal marriage age; and setting the age limit at 14 would establish a clear distinction between the concepts of 'minor' and 'child'.[5] Other delegates did not agree with the proposal to lower the age limit, stating that their legal frameworks contained protective measures for children older than 14, and that "they believed that the draft Convention should apply to as large an age group as possible".[6] The 1980 Working Group endorsed the latter position and upheld the proposed age limit of 18 years. In 1989, the year of the Convention's adoption, the representative of Nepal supported an upper age limit of 16 for the definition of a child "as to take into account the concerns of poorer States who may not be able to shoulder the burdens imposed by this convention for children up to 18 years of age".[7]

More generally, the relativity and inherent arbitrariness of legal categories based on the number of years since a person's birth ('chronological age') have been emphasized, and alternative conceptions of age have been advanced. As such, the concept of 'social age' has been proposed as a complementary perspective to chronological age, where social age indicates "the socially

---

[5] UN Doc. E/CN.4/L.1542, § 32.
[6] Ibid., § 33.
[7] UN Doc. E/CN.4/1989/48, § 82.

constructed meanings applied to physical development and roles attributed to infants, children, young people, adults and elders, as well as their intra- and inter-generational relationships" (Clark-Kazak, 2009, p. 1310). Another example constitutes the discourse analytical approach of Aapola (2002), who distinguishes between four main discourses of ages: the discourse of chronological age, the discourse of physical age, the discourse of experiential age, and the discourse of symbolic age, with each discourse having one or more subdiscourses.

In conclusion, these three clusters of observations characterize the relationship between the CRC and young persons as multidimensional, ambiguous, and increasingly at the centre of attention of research and policy.

b. Overlap of the target group of children's rights policies and youth policies

During the last decennia, policies were developed at various governmental and institutional levels towards 'youth', on the one hand, and to support the implementation of 'children's rights', on the other. Although the range of the overlap differs dependent on the governance level (*infra*), at least some 'children' also belong to the target group of 'youth' policies. There is thus a (partial or total) convergence of the target groups of children's rights policies and youth policies.

Combining the aforementioned ambiguous relationship between the CRC and young persons with the overlap in the personal field of application of children's rights policies and youth policies, leads to the question to what extent youth policies (could) contribute to the realization of the rights of the older children (adolescents) covered by the CRC. Are there today linkages between youth policies and children's rights policies? Could these interrelations be strengthened, in view of an enhanced implementation of the CRC? These questions are first addressed at the European and international level. Then, a brief comparison with the Flemish policy on children's rights and youth is carried out.

III. At the international and European level

The present analysis concerns the institutional levels of the United Nations, the Council of Europe and the European Union. Focus is placed on those policy agendas, which are explicitly and primarily oriented to children, youth and children's rights. Within the constraints of this article, other governance levels and sectorial policies (such as education or migration) are not considered. Also, the study is confined to those policies to be taken into account by

European Union Member States internally, excluding EU external policy from its scope.

With respect to both children's rights and youth, the principal policy agendas of the United Nations, the Council of Europe and the European Union were thus identified.[8] As regards children's rights, at the level of the United Nations, the document 'A World Fit for Children' was adopted at the special session of the General Assembly on children in 2002.[9] Until now, there has been no successor to this document. Within the Council of Europe, the programme 'Building a Europe for and with children', launched in 2006, was concretized for its second policy cycle (2009-2011) in what became known as the 'Stockholm Strategy', adopted by the Committee of Ministers in 2008. The Council of Europe is currently finalizing a new 'Strategy on the Rights of the Child' (2012-2015). At European Union level, the European Commission adopted in 2011 the communication 'An EU Agenda for the Rights of the Child'.[10] This communication followed on the Commission's prior (and first) communication on children's rights of 2006, 'Towards an EU Strategy on the Rights of the Child'.[11] Given the recent adoption of the former instrument, both communications are included in the analysis, and particular attention is paid to differences between the two. As concerns youth, the United Nations General Assembly adopted in 1995 'the World Programme of Action for Youth to the Year 2000 and beyond'.[12] In 2008, the Committee of Ministers of the Council of Europe issued 'Resolution CM/Res(2008)23 on the youth policy of the Council of Europe'. Finally, in November 2009, the EU Council of Youth Ministers adopted a resolution 'on a renewed framework for European cooperation in the youth field (2010-2018)'. This resolution was based on the Commission's communication of April 2009 'An EU Strategy for Youth – Investing and Empowering. A renewed open method of coordination to address youth challenges and opportunities'.[13]

a. The range of the age overlap

In order to identify the range of the overlap between the target groups of the policies on children's rights and youth, the definitions of 'children' and

---

[8] For more information on the history and content of these policy agendas, see 'The European and International Policy Agendas on Children, Youth and Children's Rights. A Belgian EU Presidency-Youth Note' of 2010, prepared by this author. The Belgian EU Presidency provided this information to the Council of the European Union in October 2010 (Doc. 14855/10). See also (Desmet, 2010).

[9] UN Doc. A/RES/S-27/2, Annex.

[10] COM(2011) 60 final.

[11] COM(2006) 367 final.

[12] UN Doc. A/RES/50/81.

[13] COM (2009) 200 final.

'youth' used within each organization must be reviewed. With respect to the concept of 'child', the CRC definition is adhered to not only by the United Nations, but also by the Council of Europe[14] and the European Union.[15] The upper age limit of 18 years for children is thus uniformly used by the three organizations. This stands in contrast with the lack of an internationally agreed definition of 'youth'. In its 2009 communication 'An EU Strategy for Youth – Investing and Empowering', the European Commission described the term 'youth' as "[m]eaning broadly speaking teenagers and young adults from 13 to 30 years old".[16] In the Commission's White Paper 'A New Impetus of Youth' of 2001, however, youth was regarded as the period from 15 to 25 years of age.[17] The youth policy of the Council of Europe is oriented to children and young people from the age of 10/12 until 30 years. At the level of the United Nations, young people are generally defined as "the age-cohort 15-24", but it is acknowledged that the meaning of the concept of youth varies across different societies and cultures.[18] Despite these diverse interpretations of the concept of youth, some commonalities may be identified. Within the three organizations, the upper age limit for 'youth' is placed between 24 and 30 years. The lower age limit fluctuates between 10 and 15 years. Children from the age of – depending on the source – 10 to 15 until 18 years old thus fall under the definition of both children and youth, and belong to the target groups of both policy agendas.

b. Current links between children's rights policies and youth policies

Given the partial overlap between the target groups of children's rights policies and youth policies of the United Nations, the Council of Europe and the European Union, the question arises whether links between these policies have been established. This section explores the current cross-references between children's rights policies and youth policies in the main policy documents of these three organizations, as identified above. The limits of such a textual analysis must be stressed. Writing down an intention of cooperation does not guarantee effective implementation. On the other hand, interaction or cooperation may develop spontaneously, without a written basis. Nevertheless, the inclusion (or not) in an organization's main policy documents of references to the 'other' policy field of children's rights respectively

---

[14)] Stockholm Strategy 2009-2011, note 1.
[15)] COM(2006) 367 final, 2.
[16)] COM (2009) 200 final, note 1.
[17)] COM(2001) 681 final, note 1.
[18)] UN Doc. A/RES/50/81, §§ 9-10.

youth, may serve as an indicator of the organization's openness and willingness to interact.

The current policy agendas of the United Nations on children's rights and youth contain no references to the other policy field. A possible explanation is that these policy documents are considerably older than those at European level: the World Programme of Action for Youth was adopted in 1995; the document 'A World Fit for Children' dates from 2002. In contrast, the policy agendas of the European Union and the Council of Europe on children's rights and youth are from 2008 at the earliest. Some of these policy documents include references to the other policy area, and express an interest to exchange and cooperate. The linkages made at the Council of Europe level are the most sophisticated.

The Stockholm Strategy of the Council of Europe Programme 'Building a Europe for and with Children' refers twice to the youth sector. First, under the strategic objective of 'Participation of children and their influence in society', it is stated that the Council of Europe should "reinforce co-operation between children's rights programme [sic] and the youth sector, building upon the youth sector's expertise in the field of participation and making use of the platform offered by the European Youth Forum". Furthermore, the final chapter on 'Partners' mentions that the Council of Europe will develop and consolidate partnerships with, among others, professional networks, in particular in the fields of education, justice, social services, health and youth. Similarly, the Resolution of the Committee of Ministers on the youth policy of the Council of Europe of 2008 includes various references to children's (rights) policies. In the preamble, the Committee of Ministers expresses its conviction that a dynamic youth policy is needed, "which includes children as well as young people", and stresses the importance of following up the programme 'Building a Europe for and with Children'. In the text of the resolution, the Committee of Ministers resolves that "co-ordination between child- and youth-related activities should be further enhanced".

At European Union level, the communications of the European Commission on children's rights of 2006 and 2011 do not include references to the youth field. In lower level documents concerning EU policy on children's rights, links to EU youth policy have been included. As such, in the working document accompanying the 2006 Communication 'Towards an EU Strategy on the Rights of the Child', which offered a preliminary inventory of EU actions affecting children's rights, the key elements of EU youth policy were referred to in the section on child participation, as an interesting observation ("It is interesting to note that...").[19] The precise relationship between these initiatives in the

---

[19] SEC(2006) 889, 11.

field of youth and the upcoming communication on children's rights was not further clarified. Also, in a 'state of play' of the implementation of the 2006 Communication, issued by the European Commission in November 2009, the youth policy documents and programmes were mentioned. It can be deduced from these documents that EU youth policy is, at least implicitly, considered to contribute to the implementation of (EU policies on) children's rights. Therefore, it seems a missed opportunity that the two key communications on children's rights of the European Commission do not establish a connection with EU youth policy.[20]

In contrast, turning to EU youth policy, one of the general initiatives suggested for all fields of action in Annex I of the Council Resolution on a renewed framework for European cooperation in the youth field is "[i]ncluding, where appropriate, a children's policy dimension, having regard to their rights and protection taking into account that the life and future prospects of young people are significantly determined by the opportunities, support and protection received during childhood". The preparatory document for this resolution, the Communication 'An EU Strategy for Youth – Investing and Empowering', states under the field of action of 'social inclusion' that "child, family and youth policies are closely linked and this Communication is complementary to the Commission Communication 'Towards an EU Strategy on the Rights of the Child'". Adopting a cross-sectoral approach, it is noted that youth policies can contribute to delivering results in areas such as "child and family policy, education, gender equality, employment, housing and healthcare".[21] In addition, in Council Conclusions of 19 November 2010 on the European and International Policy Agendas on Children, Youth and Children's Rights, the EU Youth Council underlined "the crucial importance of work undertaken in the area of children, youth and children's rights" and encouraged Member States to take an active role in the ongoing intergovernmental activity in this field.[22] Within the European Union, there thus appears to be a greater openness from the youth sector towards children's rights, than the other way around.

---

[20] The proposal of the Belgian Presidency to include in the 2011 Communication a reference to the renewed framework for European cooperation in the youth field (2010-2018) was thus not followed. The Presidency contribution also referred to the outcome of an expert conference of 'Europe de l'Enfance' in September 2010, where "the need for learning from and cooperating with the youth sector was stressed. Reference was made to the structured dialogue in the field of youth, the renewed open method of coordination, the partnership between the European Union and the Council of Europe in the field of youth, the co-management system in the field of youth of the Council of Europe". (Belgian presidency of the permanent intergovernmental group "Europe de l'Enfance", 2010).

[21] COM (2009) 200 final.

[22] 2010/C 326/01.

c. Possible links between children's rights policies and youth policies

The question arises whether, in addition to and beyond the general cross-references mentioned above, there is further potential for coordination and cooperation between the policies on children's rights and youth of the European Union, the Council of Europe and the United Nations. This potential will be investigated with regard to three aspects: the general objectives of the policies on children's rights and youth, their thematic priorities, and the means of implementation proposed.

A first issue is that the general objectives of the policy agendas on children's rights and youth seem to differ. The general objectives of the policy agendas on children are formulated in terms of *rights* (the promotion and protection of children's rights), whereas the policy agendas on youth take the provision of (equal) *opportunities* as entry point. The policy agendas on children clearly adopt a rights-based approach. There are particularly strong resemblances between the objectives of the European Commission's Communication 'Towards an EU Strategy of the Rights of the Child' of 2006, on the one hand, and the Stockholm Strategy 2009-2011 of the Council of Europe, on the other. A first shared objective is to integrate a child rights perspective in the actions of the organization itself. A second common objective is to support Member States in their efforts to promote and protect children's rights. The Commission's Communication 'An EU Agenda on the Rights of the Child' of 2011 also emphasizes the first objective of including a child rights perspective in EU actions, in its general principle 'Making the rights of the child an integral part of the EU's fundamental rights policy'. The new communication pays less attention, however, to the (second) objective of supporting the Member States in their efforts to implement children's rights. In contrast, youth policies focus more on strengthening the capacities and skills of young people, with the aim of providing them equal opportunities so that they can fully participate in society. The general objectives of the United Nations and Council of Europe youth policies are broadly formulated as the provision of opportunities for full, effective and constructive participation of young people in society. At the level of the European Union, the aim of creating more and equal opportunities is concentrated on education and the labour market. A second overall objective of EU youth policy is "to promote the active citizenship, social inclusion and solidarity of all young people".

This different language in the formulation of the objectives of children's rights policies and youth policies may point to a difference in approach. For, in the latter case policy makers decide they want to create opportunities for a certain group (youth) because this seems interesting, relevant, useful or appropriate. It is another thing to start from the premise that a certain group (children) has rights and that these rights have to be realized. The realization of those rights may then create or increase opportunities. It seems worth considering the potential added value of youth policies adopting a stronger (children's and human) rights-based approach in the formulation of their general objectives. This is not to say that at present, children's and human rights are totally absent from youth policies at European and international level. On the contrary, the Council resolution on a renewed framework for European cooperation in the youth field underlines that "European Youth Policy cooperation should be firmly anchored in the international system of human rights". Within the Council of Europe, 'human rights and democracy' is one of the three priorities of youth policy and action for the next years.[23] Human rights and fundamental freedoms also occupy an important place in the World Programme of Action for Youth. Nevertheless, through the more explicit incorporation of a rights-based approach in the formulation of the general objectives of youth policies, these policies could contribute (and could be seen as contributing) more explicitly and directly to the realization of the rights of young persons, as laid down in the CRC and other human rights conventions.

A comparison of the thematic priorities reveals that 'participation' and 'poverty and social exclusion' are the only two priorities that are common to the policy agendas of both children's rights and youth of the three organizations. The goal of increasing participation of children and youth is running like a red thread through the different policy agendas: the participation of children and youth is to be promoted in democratic processes and structures, on the one hand, and in all aspects of everyday life, on the other. The other shared thematic priority concerns combating poverty and discrimination, and enhancing social inclusion.

Looking at the thematic priorities shared by the agendas of one policy field, but not occurring in the documents of the other policy area, tells us something about the image of children and young people that seems to underlie these policies. There are various themes that are addressed in all three youth policy agendas, but that are not taken up as such in any of the main policy documents on children's rights. These include voluntary activities, creativity, culture and cultural diversity, environment, leisure-time activities, girls and young women, and intergenerational issues. The issue of violence and the focus on vulnerable groups are very prominent in the policy agendas on children's rights, and not in those on youth. The latter two thematic priorities evoke the image of a child as vulnerable and in need of protection. In contrast, young people must be stimulated and supported in, for instance, the development of their creativity, but not so much protected. Both these images should be nuanced.

---

[23] The other two priorities are 'living together in diverse societies' and 'social inclusion of young people'.

The thematic priorities of the youth agendas are also relevant for, especially older, children, whereas young people may also be in need of protection. In this regard, both policy fields could learn from each other, in order to obtain a more balanced approach towards children and young people, which can be related to the balance between the three Ps of protection, provision and participation. Especially with respect to the topics on which the CRC has been considered 'outdated' or 'ageing' (*supra*), the implementation of the youth policy agendas could make an important contribution to the effective realization of the rights of young people.

Not only with respect to thematic priorities, but also as concerns methods of implementation, there is potential for the policy agendas on children's rights and youth to join forces. One approach included in all the policy documents reviewed (on children's rights and youth, at the three levels) is 'cooperation and coordination' with other actors. It would be an interesting exercise to map the actual level of cooperation and coordination in practice. Until recently, a second measure of implementation clearly shared by all policy agendas concerned the allocation of human and financial resources for the implementation of the policies on children's rights and youth. With regard to the European Union's policy on children's rights, however, intentions in this respect have recently become more clouded. The 2006 communication 'Towards an EU Strategy on the Rights of the Child' stated that "[t]he Commission is committed to allocating the necessary human and financial resources to implement this strategy". It was added that "efforts will be made to secure the financial resources necessary to fund the actions proposed in this communication and the future strategy". The new communication 'An EU Agenda on the Rights of the Child' of 2011 makes no mention of (financial or human) resources. It is stated more weakly that the Commission "is ready to offer its support and cooperation" to the policy actions affecting children that are undertaken by Member States, and "will continue to play its part in joint efforts to achieve well-being and safety of all children". These provisions do not live up to the Commission's commitment in the 2006 Communication. Nevertheless, the financial responsibility of the Commission with respect to the new communication could be derived from the text of the 2006 document, where it was included that efforts would be made to secure the financial resources necessary to implement "this communication *and the future strategy*",[24] even though the announced 'strategy' on the rights of the child was renamed (and reduced?) to an 'agenda'.

It also is interesting to see which means of implementation are shared by the policy agendas of one field, but are not mentioned in the documents of the

---

[24] Emphasis added.

other policy area. All three children's rights policy agendas attach particular importance to 'monitoring and evaluation' and to 'communication on children's rights', whereas the youth policy agendas do not include these focuses. Faced with the lack of basic data to guide decision making on children's rights, the 2011 Communication includes a clear choice for evidence-based policy making. Here, inspiration seems to have been drawn from the youth sector, which has a long tradition of (emphasis on) evidence-based policy making. Indeed, one of the two means of implementation shared by all three youth policy documents and – until 2011 – absent from the children's rights policy agendas, concerns precisely knowledge building and evidence-based policy. The second measure of implementation shared exclusively by the three youth policy documents is to enhance the participation of young people in the formulation and implementation of youth policy. In the youth policy agendas, participation is thus not only a thematic priority (*supra*), but also a way of implementing youth policy. The system of co-management employed by the Council of Europe is the most far-reaching in this respect.

d. Conclusion

Within the United Nations, the Council of Europe and the European Union, the policy fields of 'children's rights' and 'youth' are characterized by their own histories and dynamics. They developed in parallel to one another; traditionally there has been little interaction. In more recent policy documents, some openness towards 'the other' is noticeable. The most, although still limited, interconnections between the fields of children's rights and youth are found at the level of the Council of Europe. Although the formulation of the general objectives of children's rights policies and youth policies differs, based on 'rights' and 'opportunities' respectively, a comparison of the thematic priorities and means of implementation of both policy fields reveals that there is substantial potential for increased interaction, mutual learning and cooperation.

IV. At the level of Flanders (Belgium)

In the Flemish Community, a different picture emerges with regard to both the definition of 'youth' and the policy approach.[25] The main documents considered here are the Flemish Youth Policy Plans and the Decree of 18 July 2008 on

---

[25] In Belgium, the competencies on 'youth' and 'children's rights' have been transferred from the federal government to the three communities (the Flemish, the French and the German-speaking Community).

conducting a Flemish policy on youth and children's rights (2008 Decree), which provided an 'integration' of children's rights policy and youth policy. On 28 October 2011, the Flemish Government gave its assent to the draft decree on a 'renewed' youth and children's rights policy (2011 Draft Decree). The draft decree was then submitted to the Flemish Parliament. The 2011 Draft Decree, which will replace the 2008 Decree, aims to continue and strengthen the integration of youth policy and children's rights policy, by refining certain provisions and filling some gaps. This contribution only focuses on the changes (or no changes) between the two decrees that are relevant in the light of the present analysis.

a. Definition of 'youth'

With respect to the definition of 'youth', there is no difference between the 2008 Decree and the 2011 Draft Decree. Both texts define 'youth' as "persons up to and including thirty years, or a part of this population group".[26] In contrast to the European and United Nations definitions, all children, also younger ones, thus fall under this broad definition of 'youth'. On the other hand, the definition leaves open the possibility that only a part of the population group is covered by the concept of 'youth'. As such, both the current and the upcoming decree restrict the concept of youth in certain instances to a segment of this age group. Youth work, for instance, is carried out for or by young persons "from three up to and including thirty years".[27] For the child and youth impact report (*infra*), the upper age limit is set at 25 years.[28] Also, the explanatory memoranda of the 2008 Decree and the 2011 Draft Decree make clear that, as regards children's rights policy, the age group of 0 to 18 years is concerned.

b. The integration of children's rights policy and youth policy

Similar to the European and international level, children's rights policy and youth policy in Flanders are coloured by different origins and developments. From a historical perspective, children's rights policy has its roots in youth care policy, whereas (broader) youth policy has developed out of youth work policy (Reynaert, 2011). In recent times, however, children's rights policy and youth policy have been converging, with respect to both governmental organization and policy approach. In 1997, a minister of the Flemish government was

---

[26] 2008 Decree, art. 2, 1°; 2011 Draft Decree, art. 2, 5°.
[27] 2008 Decree, art. 2, 4°; 2011 Draft Decree, art. 2, 8°.
[28] 2008 Decree, art. 6; 2011 Draft Decree, art. 4.

for the first time appointed as 'coordinating minister for children's rights'.[29] Since 1999, a Flemish minister explicitly carries the competency of 'youth' in its title. In 2006, the two competencies of 'coordination of the policy on children's rights' and 'youth' accrued for the first time to the same minister.[30]

The first Youth Policy Plan (JBP) of 2002 stated that "children's rights are the railway on which a train with several carriages is riding" (JBP, 2002, p. 24). However, the remainder of the plan contained few explicit references to children's rights (Coussée, 2006, p. 39). According to the second Flemish Youth Policy Plan (VJBP) 2006-2009, children's rights offer "not only a legal, but also an ethical framework for Flemish youth policy" (VJBP, 2006, p. 14). A first objective of the plan was to establish by decree a basic structure for "the integration of the Flemish youth policy and the Flemish children's rights policy" (Ibid., p. 23). It was added that "a distinction [is made] between children's rights as legal and ethical framework, on the one hand, and the concrete integration of the instruments of the children's rights and youth policy, as well as the integration of various objectives and actions which can be taken in youth policy and/or children's rights policy, on the other" (Ibid., p. 24). The Decree of 18 July 2008 on conducting a Flemish policy on youth and children's rights gave effect to this double integration movement. The decree merged and adapted the two prior legal bases of children's rights policy and youth policy in Flanders, namely the 1997 Decree on the Child Impact Report and the 2002 Decree on Flemish Youth Policy. During the drafting process of the 2008 Decree, a children's rights actor expressed its concern that the integration of children's rights policy and youth policy would lead to a diminished attention for minors.[31]

(i) *Children's rights as ethical and legal framework for youth policy*
The 2008 Decree defined 'youth and children's rights policy' as

> the integral and integrated vision and the systematic and methodical governmental measures based thereupon that aim at an explicit impact on the youth, with special attention for the International Convention on the Rights of the Child, adopted in New York on 20 November 1989 and approved by decree of 15 May 1991, as ethical and legal framework[32]

---

[29] Until 2004, this was the Minister of Welfare, Health and Equal Opportunities. In 2004, the competency on children's rights policy was transferred from the policy domain of Family and Societal Welfare to the policy domain of Culture, Youth, Sports and Media (Reynaert, 2005, p. 113).
[30] In 2006, this was the Minister of Culture, Youth, Sports and Brussels. Since 2009, the Minister of Education, Youth, Equal Opportunities and Brussels is the coordinating minister for children's rights.
[31] Flemish Parliament, Parliamentary Document 2007-2008, no. 1698/3, p. 7.
[32] 2008 Decree, art. 2, 2°.

The original draft of the 2008 Decree included the text "with special attention for the rights of the child". This was amended to the more narrow formulation "with special attention for the International Convention on the Rights of the Child ... as ethical and legal framework", as cited above.[33] Although the latter formulation puts emphasis on the CRC as the key legal text on children's rights, it leaves out of sight children's rights provisions in other human rights treaties (Vandenhole, 2008). The 2011 Draft Decree positively includes the broader formulation, as it describes 'youth and children's rights policy' as

> the integral and integrated vision and the systematic and methodical governmental measures based thereupon that aim at a noticeable impact on the youth, with special attention for the rights of the child, as ethical and legal framework[34]

However, looking at the definition of 'rights of the child' reveals that a similar narrow approach is taken. The 2011 Draft Decree defines 'rights of the child' as "the rights of the child, mentioned in the provisions and principles of the Convention on the Rights of the Child, adopted in New York on 20 November 1989, and in the accompanying Optional Protocols".[35] Although the definition is positively extended to the Protocols to the CRC, it still does not include children's rights in other legal texts. Another difference between the two definitions is that, pursuant to the 2008 Decree, an *explicit* impact on the youth is aimed at, whereas the 2011 Draft Decree requires a *noticeable* impact. The explanatory memorandum does not comment on this change in wording. During the drafting process of the 2008 Decree, the Children's Rights Commissioner had proposed a more radical amendment, namely to define 'children's rights and youth policy' as "the integral and integrated vision, *based on children's and human rights*, and the systematic and methodical governmental measures based thereupon that aim at an explicit impact on the youth" (Kinderrechtencommissariaat, 2008, p. 6).[36] This proposal clarifies and emphasizes that children's rights are part of the broader human rights framework. Also, the wording 'based on' is stronger than 'with special attention to'. This difference in language is more appreciated by children's rights actors than by the youth sector. During the discussion of the draft text of the 2008 Decree in a Commission of the Flemish Parliament, a representative of the youth sector noted: "Whether it is a youth policy based on children's rights or a youth policy with special attention to children's rights, is not an essential discussion for us."[37] The 2011 Draft Decree does not take up this stronger formulation.

---

[33] Flemish Parliament, Parliamentary Document 2007-2008, no. 1698/2, p. 2 (amendment no. 1).
[34] 2011 Draft Decree, art. 2, 6°.
[35] 2011 Draft Decree, art. 2, 11°.
[36] Emphasis added.
[37] Flemish Parliament, Parliamentary Document 2007-2008, no. 1698/3, p. 9.

The explicitation in the youth policy plans and the legal texts that children's rights should function as a framework for youth policy can difficultly be disputed and is to be supported. However, there may be some unforeseen consequences of this approach. First, it is argued that children's rights should function as a framework, not only for youth policy, but for all policies having an impact on children (for instance, education, housing etc.). Connecting children's rights – at least implicitly – exclusively to youth policy, and in this way 'enclosing' children's rights within youth policy, might entail that less attention is paid to children's rights in the development of policies in other fields. Approaching youth policy as a categorical policy may/should counter this 'danger'. A categorical policy concerns all policy measures that are directed to a category or group (here 'youth'), which shares a certain characteristic (being young), and is to be distinguished from sectorial policies such as culture, sports, education and welfare (Redig, 2011). A second challenge is that by mentioning children's rights as the general framework that underlies and permeates youth policy, less attention is paid to a children's rights perspective in the actual objectives and actions of the policy plan. In his advice on the third Flemish Youth Policy Plan (VJBP) 2010-2014, the Children's Rights Commissioner made a similar observation: "In the VJBP, the importance of the Children's Rights Convention may be made more explicit. The rights of children may be formulated more explicitly as point of departure for the integral vision or as motivation for the actions" (Kinderrechtencommissariaat, 2011, p. 3).

(ii) *Integration of policy instruments on children's rights and youth*
The 2008 Decree provides an integration of the instruments of children's rights policy and youth policy. For instance, the 'contact points' within each administration and governmental institution for 'children's rights' and 'youth policy' were merged into contact points on youth and children's rights policy. Also, the child impact report (KER) was extended towards a youth and child impact report (JoKER), which implied an extension of the personal field of application up to persons younger than 25 years (instead of 18 years before). Reynaert has warned that the integration of the policy instruments on children's rights and youth does not guarantee the development of "an integrated children's rights and youth policy, ... with attention for the interests of children and young persons in all Flemish policy domains" (Reynaert, 2005, p. 114). The 2011 Draft Decree continues this process of integration of policy instruments. The 'Flemish Youth Policy Plan' will be broadened into a 'Flemish Youth and Children's Rights Policy Plan'.[38] The challenge of writing an integrated policy

---

[38] 2011 Draft Decree, art. 3, § 1.

plan on youth and children's rights still lies ahead. For the current term of government, two separate policy plans were still adopted: the third Flemish Youth Policy Plan 2010-2014, and the second Flemish Children's Rights Action Plan (VAK) 2011-2014. The latter plan clarifies the actions envisaged by the Flemish Government during its term of government to bring its policy into agreement with the concluding observations of the Committee on the Rights of the Child with respect to Belgium of June 2010. Given that the third Flemish Youth Policy Plan was already in an advanced stage of drafting when the concluding observations were issued, it was decided to adopt a separate children's rights action plan.

V. Concluding reflections

Comparing the European and United Nations policy approach with the policy of Flanders brings to light some remarkable and substantial differences. Different roads have been taken to implement the Convention on the Rights of the Child for those young persons who still fall under the Convention's definition of children, but who also belong to the target group of youth policies. A first conclusion is that there is consensus on the definition of 'children' as human beings below the age of 18, but that the concept of 'youth' is defined differently by different actors and institutions. Although the specific age limits differ, some or all children also fall under 'youth policies'. As a minimum, this 'overlapping group' concerns the youngsters from 10/15 to 18 years old; this is the case at the international and European level. In Flanders, all children are in principle subject to youth policies, although this may be restricted. Secondly, at the European and international level, children's rights policies and youth policies continue to develop separately, with in recent times some cross-references prudently paving the way for enhanced cooperation and coordination between the two policy domains. Within the Flemish Community, the choice was made to 'integrate' the policies on children's rights and youth, (i) by clearly establishing that children's rights (or at least the Convention on the Rights of the Child and its two Optional Protocols) form the ethical and legal framework for youth policy; and (ii) by integrating the policy instruments on children's rights and youth. Each choice has its advantages and disadvantages: within the European organizations and the United Nations, more cooperation between the policies on children's rights and youth could lead to an enhanced implementation of the CRC for older children. On the other hand, a complete integration of children's rights policy and youth policy, as in Flanders, entails the risk that children's rights become enclosed within youth policy, and that a children's rights perspective is less strongly present in the concretization of the policy plans and objectives. The prospects and potentials of a middle ground should be explored, in which there is extensive interaction and cooperation between children's rights policies and youth policies, without both policies being necessarily completely integrated, as the latter entails the risk of one policy becoming to a greater or lesser extent absorbed by the other.

References

Aapola, S., 'Exploring Dimensions of Age in Young People's Lives. A discourse analytical approach', *Time & Society* 11(2/3) (2002) 295–314.

Belgian presidency of the permanent intergovernmental group "Europe de l'Enfance", 'Contribution of the Belgian presidency of the permanent intergovernmental group "Europe de l'Enfance" to the European Commission regarding the development of a new communication– Towards an EU Strategy on the Rights of the Child', (2010), <ec.europa.eu/justice/policies/children/forum/doc/5th/benoit_parmentier_en.pdf>.

Clark-Kazak, C.R., 'Towards a Working Definition and Application of Social Age in International Development Studies', *Journal of Development Studies* 45(8) (2009) 1307–1324.

Cornock, M. & Montgomery, H., 'Children's rights in and out of the womb', *International Journal of Children's Rights* 19(1) (2011) 3–19.

Coussée, F., 'Kinderrechten, een "natuurlijk" referentiekader voor jeugdwerk?', *Tijdschrift voor Jeugdrecht en Kinderrechten* 7(1) (2006) 38–45.

Desmet, E., *European and International Policy Agendas on Children, Youth and Children's Rights: Comparison and Possible Synergies* (Gent: Kenniscentrum Kinderrechten, 2010), <www.keki.be/documents/comparison.pdf>.

Detrick, S., 'Compilation of the Travaux préparatoires'. In *The United Nations Convention on the Rights of the Child: A Guide to the "Travaux Préparatoires"*. ed. S. Detrick (Dordrecht: Martinus Nijhoff Publishers, 1992) 31–631.

Doreleijers, T.A.H., 'Te oud voor het servet, te jong voor het tafellaken', *Tijdschrift voor Familie- en Jeugdrecht* (7/8) (2009) 181–185.

European Youth Forum, *The State of Youth Rights in Europe* (Brussels: European Youth Forum, 2010).

Johnson, S.B., Blum, R.W. & Giedd, J.N., 'Adolescent Maturity and the Brain: The Promise and Pitfalls of Neuroscience Research in Adolescent Health Policy', *Journal of Adolescent Health* (45) (2009) 216–221.

Kinderrechtencommissariaat, 'Voorstel van decreet Vlaams jeugd- en kinderrechtenbeleid', (2008), Advice no. 2007-2008/4.

Kinderrechtencommissariaat, 'Vlaams Jeugdbeleidsplan III', (2011), Advice no. 2010-2011/5.

Mahidi, M., *The Young and The Rightless? The Protection of Youth Rights in Europe* (Brussels: European Youth Forum, 2010).

Redig, G. & Dierckx, D., 'Categoriaal beleid. Verkenning en denkoefening voor een integrale en interactieve beleidsbenadering', (2011).

Reynaert, D., 'Integratie van de beleidsinstrumenten kinderrechten en jeugd: naar een volwaardige integratie van het kinderrechten- en jeugdbeleid?', *Tijdschrift voor Jeugdrecht en Kinderrechten* 6(3) (2005) 112–114.

Reynaert, D., 'Over kinderrechten als referentiekader voor een jeugdbeleid', (2011) (forthcoming).

UNAIDS (Joint United Nations Programme on HIV/AIDS), *Seen But Not Heard... Very Young Adolescents Aged 10–14 Years* (Geneva: UNAIDS, 2004).

UNICEF (United Nations Children's Fund), *The State of the World's Children 2011: Adolescence. An Age of Opportunity* (New York: UNICEF, 2011).

Vandenhole, W., 'Kinderrechten in Universele en Europese Mensenrechtenverdragen'. In *Kinderrechten in België*. ed. Vandenhole, W. (Antwerp: Intersentia, 2008) 3–15.

Veerman, P.E., 'The Ageing of the UN Convention on the Rights of the Child', *International Journal of Children's Rights* 18(4) (2010) 585–618.

X., *The European and International Policy Agendas on Children, Youth and Children's Rights. A Belgian EU Presidency-Youth Note*, (2010), <www.keki.be/documents/presidencynote.pdf>.

Index